ROUTLEDGE HANDBOOK
OF ETHICS AND WAR

This new Handbook offers a comprehensive overview of contemporary extensions and alternatives to the just war tradition in the field of the ethics of war.

The modern history of just war has typically assumed the primacy of four particular elements: *jus ad bellum*, *jus in bello*, the state actor, and the soldier. This book will put these four elements under close scrutiny, and will explore how they fare given the following challenges:

- What role do the traditional elements of *jus ad bellum* and *jus in bello*—and the constituent principles that follow from this distinction—play in modern warfare? Do they adequately account for a normative theory of war?
- What is the role of the state in warfare? Is it or should it be the primary actor in just war theory?
- Can a just war be understood simply as a response to territorial aggression between state actors, or should other actions be accommodated under legitimate recourse to armed conflict?
- Is the idea of combatant *qua* state-employed soldier a valid ethical characterization of actors in modern warfare?
- What role does the technological backdrop of modern warfare play in understanding and realizing just war theories?

Over the course of three key parts, the contributors examine these challenges to the just war tradition in a way that invigorates existing discussions and generates new debate on topical and prospective issues in just war theory.

This book will be of great interest to students of just war theory, applied ethics, peace and conflict studies, and security studies.

Fritz Allhoff is Associate Professor of Philosophy at Western Michigan University and a Senior Research Fellow in the Centre for Applied Philosophy and Public Ethics at Charles Sturt University, Canberra.

Nicholas G. Evans is a doctoral candidate at the Australian National University and an Adjunct Research Associate at Charles Sturt University, Canberra.

Adam Henschke is a researcher in the Centre for Applied Philosophy and Public Ethics at Charles Sturt University, Canberra.

ROUTLEDGE HANDBOOK OF ETHICS AND WAR

Just war theory in the twenty-first century

*Edited by Fritz Allhoff, Nicholas G. Evans
and Adam Henschke*

Routledge
Taylor & Francis Group

NEW YORK AND LONDON

First published 2013
by Routledge
2 Park Square, Milton Park, Abingdon, Oxfordshire OX14 4RN

Simultaneously published in the USA and Canada
by Routledge
711 Third Avenue, New York, NY 10017

First issued in paperback 2015

Routledge is an imprint of the Taylor & Francis Group, an informa business

British Library Cataloguing in Publication Data

A catalogue record for this book is available from the British Library

Library of Congress Cataloging in Publication Data

Routledge handbook of ethics and war : just war theory in the 21st century / edited by Fritz Allhoff, Nicholas G. Evans and Adam Henschke.
pages cm
Includes bibliographical references and index.
1. Just war doctrine--Handbooks, manuals, etc. 2. Military ethics--Handbooks, manuals, etc. 3. War--Moral and ethical aspects--Handbooks, manuals, etc. I. Allhoff, Fritz. II. Evans, Nicholas G., 1985- III. Henschke, Adam, 1976-
U22.R68 2013
172'.422--dc23
2012049756

ISBN 13: 978-1-138-95304-8 (pbk)
ISBN 13: 978-0-415-53934-0 (hbk)

Typeset in Bembo
by GreenGate Publishing Services, Tonbridge, Kent

CONTENTS

CONTRIBUTORS

Keith Abney, M.A., is a senior lecturer and Research Fellow of the Ethics + Emerging Sciences Group at California Polytechnic State University, San Luis Obispo. His areas of expertise include technology ethics and bioethics, especially related to human enhancements, robotics, and military technologies. He is a co-editor of Robot Ethics (MIT Press) and a contributor to other books, journal papers, and funded reports.

Braden Allenby, Ph.D., is Lincoln Professor of Engineering and Ethics; President's Professor of Civil, Environmental, and Sustainable Engineering; Professor of Law; founding director of the Center for Earth Systems Engineering and Management; founding chair of the Consortium for Emerging Technologies, Military Operations, and National Security; and associate director of the Lincoln Center for Applied Ethics, at Arizona State University. His latest books are *The Techno-Human Condition* (with Dan Sarewitz, 2011), *Industrial Ecology and Sustainable Engineering* (with Tom Graedel, 2011), *The Theory and Practice of Sustainable Engineering* (2012), and *The Growing Gap Between Emerging Technologies and Legal-Ethical Oversight* (with Gary Marchant and Joe Herkert, 2012).

Fritz Allhoff, Ph.D., is Associate Professor in the Department of Philosophy at Western Michigan University, Senior Research Fellow at the Centre for Applied Philosophy and Public Ethics (Australia), and Visiting Scholar at the University of Notre Dame's Centre for Science, Technology, and Values. He is a founding member of the International Intelligence Ethics Association, serves on the editorial board of the International Committee of Military Medicine, and is active in the Consortium for Emerging Technologies, Military Operations, and National Security. He is the author or editor of over twenty books; his latest, *Terrorism, Ticking Time-Bombs, and Torture*, was published by the University of Chicago Press (2012).

Jennifer Mei Sze Ang, Ph.D., is a Lecturer at the Singapore Institute of Management University. She received her Doctorate from the University of Queensland, Australia and is the author of *Sartre and the Moral Limits of War and Terrorism* (New York: Routledge, 2010). Jennifer has published in areas concerning ethics and politics related to works from Jean-Paul Sartre, Hegel, Arendt and Kant, and her main research interests are in the philosophy of Sartre, existentialism and phenomenology, and ethics and politics in contemporary issues.

Tor Arne Berntsen is a chaplain and head of the Ethics Department at the Norwegian Defence University College, Oslo, Norway. He is also a doctoral student at the School of Mission and Theology, Stavanger, Norway, currently working on a dissertation on the peace and reconciliation process in northern Uganda. His published work includes "Negotiated identities: The discourse on the role of child soldiers in the peace process in Northern Uganda," in B. Mæland (ed.), *Culture, religion, and the reintegration of female ex-child soldiers in Northern Uganda* (Peter Lang, 2010); and "Den uskyldige fiende: Militæretiske perspektiver på bekjempelse av barnesoldater" (Norw. "The innocent enemy: Military-ethical perspectives on fighting child soldiers"), in K. Firin, K. Hellemsvik, and J. Haarberg (eds) *Kryssild: militært lederskap i en ny tid* (Tapir, 2007).

Jason P. Blahuta, Ph.D., is an Associate Professor of Philosophy at Lakehead University. His primary research interests are the philosophy of Machiavelli, Asian philosophy, socio-political philosophy and applied ethics. He has published in *Dialogue: Canadian Philosophical Review, Iyyun: The Jerusalem Philosophical Quarterly*, and *Maritain Studies*.

Todd A. Burkhardt is a Lieutenant Colonel in the U.S. Army. Over the last 21 years he has served in variety of positions as an infantry officer to include teaching just war theory at the United States Military Academy, West Point, New York. Upon completion of his dissertation, "Just War and Human Rights: Fighting with Right Intention," at the University of Tennessee in May 2013, he will return to the United States Military Academy as an Assistant Professor in Philosophy where he will once again teach just war theory to future Army officers. His research interests include both political and just war theory.

Malcolm Dando is Professor of International Security at the University of Bradford. A biologist by original training, his main research interest is in the preservation of the prohibitions embodied in the Chemical Weapons Convention and the Biological Weapons Convention at a time of rapid scientific and technological change in the life sciences. His recent publications include *Deadly Cultures: Biological Weapons Since 1945* (Harvard University Press, 2006), which he edited with Mark Wheelis and Lajos Rozsa.

Ned Dobos, Ph.D., is Lecturer in Ethics at the University of New South Wales, Canberra, and an Adjunct Fellow at the Centre for Applied Philosophy and Public Ethics, CSU. His research is focussed on the philosophy of war, military ethics, and business ethics. Ned is the author of *Insurrection and Intervention: The Two Faces of Sovereignty* (Cambridge University Press 2012), and co-editor of *Global Financial Crisis: The Ethical Issues* (Palgrave MacMillan 2011).

Christian Enemark, Ph.D., is an Associate Professor in the National Security College, Australian National University. He has previously held academic positions at the University of New South Wales (Australian Defence Force Academy campus) and the University of Sydney. Christian's primary areas of research are the security implications of infectious disease threats (including biological weapons), the ethics of armed conflict, and theories of security. His latest book, *Armed Drones and the Ethics of War: Military Virtue in a Post-Heroic Age* is forthcoming in August 2013 from Routledge.

Nicholas G. Evans submitted his Ph.D dissertation in December 2012 at the Australian National University, and is an Adjunct Research Associate and Research Assistant at the Centre for Applied Philosophy and Public Ethics, Charles Sturt University, Canberra. His dissertation focussed on the dual-use dilemma, which arises when scientific research, materials or technologies can be used to both benefit and harm humanity. Nicholas is the author of a number of articles in military ethics, the philosophy of science, and ethics, and has taught philosophy, military ethics, and physics at universities around Australia. His research interests include emerging military technologies, public health ethics, concepts of responsibility and autonomy, and friendship.

S. Brandt Ford, M.A., is a Ph.D candidate with the Centre for Applied Philosophy and Public Ethics and a Lecturer with the Australian Graduate School of Policing and Security, both at Charles Sturt University. Brandt has taught at the Australian National University, the Australian Defence Force Academy (University of New South Wales), and the National Security College. Before starting a full-time academic career, he spent ten years in the Department of Defence as a Strategist and Intelligence Analyst. His research interests include: police, military and intelligence ethics; the morality of leadership and power; and the philosophy of weapons technology, and coercion and force.

Michael L. Gross, Ph.D., is Professor of Political Science at The University of Haifa, Israel. His books include *Ethics and Activism* (Cambridge 1997), *Bioethics and Armed Conflict* (MIT 2006), *Moral Dilemmas of Modern War* (Cambridge 2010), and an edited volume, *Military Medical Ethics for the 21st Century* (Ashgate, 2013). Currently he is writing *Ethics and Insurgency: The Moral Bounds of Contemporary Guerrilla Warfare*. Gross has led workshops on battlefield ethics and military medical ethics for the Dutch Ministry of Defence, The US Army Medical Department, The US Naval Academy, and the Medical Corps and National Security College of the Israel Defense Forces.

Adam Henschke has completed a bachelor's degree in Applied Biology/Biotechnology (RMIT, Melbourne Australia), a Diploma in the Biotechnologies of Life (Monash University, Melbourne Australia), a Masters in Bioethics (Monash University, Melbourne Australia), and a Masters in Applied Ethics (NTNU, Trondheim, Norway and Linkoping University, Linkoping, Sweden). He submitted his Ph.D dissertation at the end of 2012, and is currently working as a researcher at the Centre for Applied Philosophy and Public Ethics (CAPPE) for Charles Sturt University in Canberra, Australia. He has taught ethics at Monash University, the Australian National University, and Charles Sturt University. In addition to his interests in military ethics, his most recent research efforts are broadly in fields of bioethics, ethics of technology and philosophy of information and his dissertation focussed on the ethical importance of relations between identity and personal information.

Leonard Kahn, Ph.D., is an Associate Professor in the Department of Philosophy at the United States Air Force Academy. He works primarily in ethical theory and applied ethics. He is the editor of *Mill on Justice* (Palgrave, 2012), and most recently his work has been published in *Ethical Theory & Moral Practice*, *Ethics, Policy, & Environment*, *The Journal of Moral Philosophy*, and *Philosophical Studies*.

Shawn Kaplan, Ph.D., is an Assistant Professor in the Department of Philosophy at Adelphi University. His chief areas of research are international ethics, just war theory, political theory, and Kantian ethics. In addition to articles on Kantian ethics and just war theory, his publications include a series of articles on the nature of terrorism and its potential justifications. He is currently working on a book-length manuscript on this topic.

Daniel H. Levine, Ph.D., is an Assistant Professor in the School of Public Policy and an Assistant Research Scholar in the Institute for Philosophy and Public Policy, specializing in moral and philosophical issues surrounding international law, civil conflict, and peacekeeping operations. Dr Levine also works with the Education Program of the US Institute of Peace, where he oversees work with the Iraqi higher education community. He holds a Ph.D. in Philosophy from Georgetown University, where he taught courses on the philosophy of law, and a Master's of Public Policy from the University of Maryland, College Park. He has also been an activist with Amnesty International and the Save Darfur Coalition.

George R. Lucas Jr, Ph.D., is Class of 1984 Distinguished Chair in Ethics in the Vice Admiral James B. Stockdale Center for Ethical Leadership at the United States Naval Academy (Annapolis), and Professor of Ethics and Public Policy at the Graduate School of Public Policy at the Naval Postgraduate School (Monterey, CA). He is also a Senior Fellow at the Lincoln Center for Applied Ethics at Arizona State University, and Co-director of the Consortium on Emerging Technologies, Military Operations, and National Security (CETMONS). George is the author of five books, more than fifty journal articles, translations, and book reviews, and has also edited eight book-length collections of articles in philosophy and ethics. Among these titles are *New Warriors/New Weapons: Ethics and Emerging Military Technologies* [a special issue of the *Journal of Military Ethics* 9:4 (2010)], *Anthropologists in Arms: the Ethics of Military Anthropology* (AltaMira Press, 2009), *Perspectives on Humanitarian Military Intervention* (University of California Press, 2001), *Lifeboat Ethics: the Moral Dilemmas of World Hunger* (Harper & Row, 1976), and *Poverty, Justice, and the Law: Essays on Needs, Rights, and Obligations* (UPA, 1986).

Bård Mæland, Dr Theol., is a Professor of Systematic Theology at the School of Mission and Theology, Stavanger, Norway, where he is currently serving as the President. He has previously served in the Norwegian Armed Forces as chaplain and researcher. Since 2007 he has chaired a research programme on cultural and religious perspectives on the reintegration of formerly abducted females in the Lord Resistance Army, Northern Uganda. Mæland has co-authored *Enduring Military Boredom: From 1750 to the Present* (Palgrave Macmillan, 2009).

Chris Mayer, Ph.D., is an Assistant Professor of Philosophy in the Department of English and Philosophy at the United States Military Academy and a Lieutenant Colonel in the United States Army. He currently directs the Academy's introduction to philosophy course, a course which all students are required to complete. He also serves as a Teagle Assessment Scholar at the Center of Inquiry in the Liberal Arts at Wabash College. His research interests include ethical theory, just war theory, political philosophy, and assessment of student learning.

Jeff McMahan, Ph.D., is Professor of Philosophy at Rutgers University. He is the author of *The Ethics of Killing: Problems at the Margins of Life* (Oxford, 2002) and *Killing in War* (Oxford, 2009). He has several other books forthcoming from Oxford University Press, including *The Right Way to Fight* and a collection of essays called *The Values of Lives*.

Seumas Miller, Ph.D., is a professorial research fellow at the Centre for Applied Philosophy and Public Ethics (an Australian Research Council Special Research Centre), Charles Sturt University (Canberra), and the 3TU Centre for Ethics and Technology, Delft University of Technology (The Hague). He is the author of numerous academic articles on social action and institutions, and in various areas of professional and applied ethics, including police ethics and terrorism and war. His recent books include *The Moral Foundations of Social Institutions: A Philosophical Study* (Cambridge University Press, 2010), *Terrorism and Counter-terrorism: Ethics and Liberal Democracy* (Blackwell, 2009), and *Ethical Issues in Policing* (with John Blackler) (Ashgate 2005).

Richard M. O'Meara, Ph.D., is a retired Brigadier General (USA) and trial attorney who teaches human rights, security issues, and international law in the Division of Global Affairs, Rutgers University. He has served as a resident fellow at the Stockdale Center for Ethical Leadership, US Naval Academy and has taught governance and rule of law issues in such diverse locations as Cambodia, Rwanda, Chad, Philippines, Guinea, Sierra Leone, Slovenia, Moldova, Ukraine, Bosnia-Herzegovina, Peru, El Salvador, and Iraq. He served as an EMT for the Red Cross in the weeks following the 9/11 attack at the World Trade Center.

Brian Orend, Ph.D., is the Director of International Studies, and a Professor of Philosophy, at the University of Waterloo in Canada. He has taught at Waterloo, Columbia University in NYC, and the University of Lund in Sweden. His research and speaking efforts concentrate on three areas: the ethics of war and peace (especially post-war reconstruction); human rights; and happiness. He is the author of six books, including *The Morality of War* (Broadview, 2006) and, most recently, *Introduction to International Studies* (OUP, 2012).

Emily Pollard, M.A., is a Ph.D. student and part-time tutor at Durham University. She received a first-class degree in Philosophy from the University of St Andrews in 2008, and a Masters from Durham University in 2009. Her primary research interests are in ethics and moral philosophy, particularly concentrating on ethics of war and just war theory. Her paper "Just War Theory and Defensive War: Is Defence a Just Cause for War?" was published in *Philosophical Writings*, in the *Proceedings of the Thirteenth Durham-Bergen Conference 2010*.

Heather M. Roff, Ph.D., is a Visiting Associate Professor of Security Studies at Josef Korbel School of International Studies at the University of Denver, and a Research Associate at the Eisenhower Center for Space and Defense Studies at the United States Air Force Academy. Heather has held positions at the University of Waterloo and the United States Air Force Academy. She is author of *Global Justice, Kant and the Responsibility to Protect*, and has published various articles in academic journals, such as the *Journal for Military Ethics* and *Global Responsibility to Protect*. She also blogs for the *Huffington Post* on issues of international ethics and politics.

Neil C. Rowe, Ph.D., is Professor of Computer Science at the US Naval Postgraduate School, in Monterey, Caliofornia, where he has been since 1983. His main research interests are the modeling of deception, information security, surveillance systems, image processing, and data mining. Recent work has focused on cyberwarfare, digital forensics, and the problems of large-scale data analysis. He is the author of a book on artificial intelligence and 160 technical papers.

Anne Schwenkenbecher, Ph.D., is a Research Fellow at The Nossal Institute for Global Health at The University of Melbourne, Australia. She has previously held positions at the University of Vienna and at the Centre for Applied Philosophy and Public Ethics at the Australian National University, Canberra. Her main research interests are in the ethics of war and terrorism, the morality of groups, and the ethics of climate change. Her book *Terrorism: A Philosophical Enquiry* was published by Palgrave Macmillan in 2012.

Bradley Jay Strawser, Ph.D., is an Assistant Professor of Philosophy in the Defense Analysis Department at the US Naval Postgraduate School in Monterey, California. He is concurrently a Research Associate with Oxford University's Institute for Ethics, Law, and Armed Conflict. He previously held positions as a Research Fellow at the Stockdale Center for Ethical Leadership and as an instructor in the philosophy department at the US Air Force Academy. His research profile is broad, but he works primarily in applied ethics and ethical theory and various issues relating to the ethics of war and violence. He is presently guest editing a special issue of the *Journal of Military Ethics* on the morality of cyber war and has a book forthcoming from Oxford University Press, *Killing By Remote Control: The Ethics of an Unmanned Military*.

Steve Viner, Ph.D., J.D., is an Assistant Professor of Philosophy at Middlebury College. He works primarily on just war theory, philosophy of law, social and political philosophy and ethics. He is a co-editor of *The Morality of War: Classical and Contemporary Readings* (Pearson

Prentice-Hall, 2006). Prior to his current teaching position, he practiced law in both the private and public sectors. He has published articles in *Criminal Law and Philosophy* and *Philosophy and Law* on issues concerning the punishing of unjust combatants, detentions at Guantánamo Bay, and Lon Fuller's work. At present, he is doing research on immigration and human rights.

Richard Werner, Ph.D., is John Stewart Kennedy Professor of Philosophy at Hamilton College. He believes that the aim of philosophy is to understand how things hang together in the broadest possible sense rather than in the analysis of reifications like concepts or language. His research is in the areas of applied ethics, metaethics, and pragmatism. His work has appeared in such philosophical journals as *Social Theory and Practice*, *Analysis*, *Ethics*, *The Monist*, and *Contemporary Pragmatism* as well as philosophical anthologies.

Jeffrey P. Whitman, Ph.D., is a Professor of Philosophy at Susquehanna University in Selinsgrove, Pennsylvania. He earned his B.S. from United States Military Academy in 1977 and his Ph.D. in Philosophy from Brown University in 1991. A career Army officer, he taught at the United States Military Academy for eight years prior to retiring from active duty and is the author of numerous articles on ethics, public policy, and just war theory, as well as *The Power and Value of Philosophical Skepticism* (Rowman and Littlefield, 1996).

INTRODUCTION

Not just wars: expansions and alternatives to the just war tradition

Fritz Allhoff, Nicholas G. Evans and Adam Henschke

The just war tradition spans centuries; for as long as we have thought about war, we have thought about whether it should be undertaken at all and, if so, how.[1] An important progenitor to just-war thinking, St Thomas Aquinas, queried whether war was always sinful and answered in the negative, espousing three criteria by which the justness of war could be established: sovereign authority, just cause, and rightful intention.[2] More recent theorists tend to add consequentialist features to Aquinas's deontological ones. For example, war must be fought as a last resort, there must be a reasonable chance of success, and there must be proportionality between the expected costs and benefits of the war.[3] Broadly speaking, though, war should only be fought against aggressors, whether in self-defense or through humanitarian intervention.[4]

This discussion helps us understand *when* we are allowed to fight, but it tells us nothing of *how* we are allowed to fight; the distinction between these two strains of thinking is critical to understanding just war theory. The point is made powerfully by Michael Walzer, who is worth quoting at length:

> The moral reality of war is divided into two parts. War is always judged twice, first with reference to the reasons states have for fighting, secondly with reference to the means they adopt. The first kind of judgment is adjectival in character: we say that a particular war is just or unjust. The second is adverbial: we say that the war is being fought justly or unjustly. Medieval writers made the difference a matter of prepositions, distinguishing *jus ad bellum*, the justice of war, from *jus in bello*, justice in war.... *Jus ad bellum* requires us to make judgments about aggression and self-defense; *jus in bello* about the observance or violation of the customary and positive rules of engagement. The two sorts of judgments are logically independent.[5]

Aquinas helps to explicate the requirements of *jus ad bellum*, but *jus in bello* has its own requirements. Proportionality shows up here as well, the difference being that soldiers must not use excessive force, as opposed to states not engaging in disproportionate conflicts. A central feature of *jus in bello* is the principle of discrimination, by which non-combatant immunity must be respected; non-combatants are not liable to attack and cannot be justly targeted. Most generally, though, *jus in bello* requires adherence to international humanitarian law and to the law of armed conflict. Not only do these bodies of law limit who may (or may not) be targeted, but they also speak to prohibited weapons, treatment of detainees, and other privileged categories.

While *jus ad bellum* and *jus in bello* anchor the just war theory landscape, they hardly exhaust all the relevant questions. A relative newcomer on the scene, *jus post bellum* raises questions about what is owed after conflict is ended; neither *jus ad bellum* or *jus in bello* address the issue of whether forces owe post-conflict duties of reconstruction, restitution, and so on. But there are other ways in which just war theory—viewed somewhat monolithically since Walzer's seminal work—has been challenged in recent years. For example, a central assumption had been that of the moral equality of combatants, under which combatants cannot be held responsible for an unjust war in which they participate; this commitment follows straightforwardly from the independence that Walzer postulated between *jus ad bellum* and *jus in bello*. Jeff McMahan has powerfully challenged this claim and, with it, a fundamental premise of Walzer's conception.[6]

A broader issue faced by just war theory is the evolving nature of conflict. Walzer was largely writing in response to the Vietnam War, but many of the examples he invoked came from World War I and World War II.[7] More generally, just war theory has tended to focus on conventional forces, such as would be deployed on traditional battlefields by warring nation states. Does conflict really work that way anymore? Certainly it can, though it would be prudential—which is not to say moral or legal—for the weaker side to avoid such configurations. While a typology of such asymmetric conflict takes us too far afield,[8] consider terrorism as an exemplar: terrorists necessarily target those who are not liable to attack and, therefore, eschew the edicts of *jus in bello*.[9] In trying to prevent terrorism, are we still bound by *jus in bello*? Or do its rules crumble given the stakes?[10]

And a third way in which just war theory can be challenged pertains to emerging military technologies. Whereas Aquinas countenanced opposing foes amassing at the border, we can now deploy lethal drone strikes over Afghanistan from controllers' headquarters in the United States.[11] Or, through cyberwarfare, even the notion of *combatants* becomes attenuated; unfortunately, so does our ability to honor the principle of discrimination against non-combatants.[12] Are there ways in which these technologies call for a revision of the just war paradigm, or can they be accommodated within it?

★★★

This book grapples with these and other questions by exploring the relationship between theory and practice. Our contributors examine the theoretical aspects of the just war tradition, their application to modern conflicts, and the way that this tradition is changing—or ought to be changing—in the face of new social and technological development. They cover this broad terrain from a number of perspectives that bear on the ethics of war: philosophical, political, legal, sociological, and technical. These contributors come from diverse backgrounds, and their contributions represent the widest possible views. Our goal is to engage with a range of disciplines and practices, and so this diversity of topics and contributors is by design. It is a rare privilege to begin a book with a philosopher, to move from professors at military colleges to retired Brigadier Generals, and end with a computer scientist. While the contributions are broad, the common thread of the collection is that the practice of war is changing, shifting from a traditional idea of war as two state-based actors physically confronting each other in the world to include state and non-state actors, professional soldiers and children, people and robots. We feel that the just war tradition cannot only speak to these changes but *needs* to respond. As such, the thread is to ask not only what does the just war tradition say about a given change in practice but, also, what does a given change in practice mean for the just war tradition?

The book comprises three parts: changes in the just war theory, changes in the sorts of actors in war, and changes in technology. Each part is each divided into three sections, to provide a frame for the reader in navigating the book. We start from the broadest point of the debate, the conceptual terrain of just war theory, and the basic distinction between *jus ad bellum* and *jus in bello*. We then, over the course of the book, focus in on more specific problems within the ethics of war. The canonical distinctions appear throughout, returning us to our overview and bringing together the varied set of arguments featured here.

The diversity of the book is such that contributors within each section often do not agree with one another. For example, in the opening section on *jus ad bellum*, Jeff McMahan (Chapter 1) and Richard Werner (Chapter 3) present different approaches to a similar problem, the epistemic conditions under which we wage wars. Both conclude that just war theory cannot account for this epistemic burden, and moreover that this failure constitutes a collapse of the central tenet of the canonical form of just war theory put forward by Michael Walzer, the conceptual distinction between *jus ad bellum* and *jus in bello*. McMahan has updated and developed an argument from his recent and highly influential *Killing in War*, arguing that there is an epistemic burden on combatants to know if the cause of a war that they are fighting in is just.

Jeff Whitman, however, argues that, despite deep problems, just war theory presents a pragmatic and powerful view, the value of which lies in its ability to guide international conduct in war (Chapter 2). Whitman argues that the conceptual separateness of *jus ad bellum* and *jus in bello* serves an important role in establishing political norms and upholding international law. He argues that on these pragmatic grounds, we should uphold the classical conceptual distinction now more than ever, and that changing our theoretical construct to justify current military actions misses the critical and evaluative power of just war theory. In this, Whitman agrees with the spirit of McMahan's position that the just war tradition is worthwhile. Whitman serves as a foil to Werner's position that we need to replace the just war tradition with the principle of innocence.

One might wonder why Whitman's chapter separates McMahan and Werner. The answer lies in how we mean to provide such a range of views. These chapters, by virtue of their novelty and challenge to existing work on the ethics of war, often differ in how they approach the same issue. For example, Steve Viner maintains that revisionists about the moral equality of soldiers serve to promote peace and contain the violence in wars. As such, concerns about soldiers should not be limited merely to questions of self-defense and liability (Chapter 4). This argument is likely to conflict with McMahan and Werner, but have certain synergy with Whitman, albeit focusing on different aspects of the ethics of war.

In contrast, S. Brandt Ford (Chapter 5) and Bradley Jay Strawser (Chapter 6) give theoretical grounding to how we incorporate predominantly revisionist concerns into just war theory. Building from an idea not proposed until the most recent edition of Walzer's *Just and Unjust Wars*,[13] Ford provides a grounding of the use of force-short-of-war, identifying conceptual and moral gaps within modern warfare that often does not fit the classic mold of war as a defensive act against state aggression. This posits a revision to both when a military force should be engaged in use of lethal force, and the fundamental purpose served by a military. Strawser then confronts critics of the revisionist approach, specifically those who claim that holding soldiers liable for the justness of their war is not *in practice* possible. Strawser argues to the contrary, holding soldiers accountable under the revisionist program can be incorporated in modern military practice and can better account for the already diverse ranges of liability in war.

Both are concerned with challenges to traditional just war theory, but they are not grouped with Werner and McMahan with good reason. To wit, it is not our intention to pit one aspect of the current debate against the other in those *positional* terms; we wish to keep mutually reinforcing chapters close, but not clumped so as to present "sides" to the debate. Rather, we have organized this book along *thematic* lines to foster continued debate and to enlighten novice readers as to the depth of the current debate, while still providing researchers or educators with a book they can use as reference and textbook.

We do occasionally deviate from this model where we focus less on disagreement and more on development of particular themes. For example, we finish Part I with three discussions around the end of war. Emily Pollard begins with the proposal that *jus post bellum* can—and indeed should—be considered as part of the traditional account of just war, the *jus ad bellum* and *jus in bello* (Chapter 7). Central to Pollard's reasoning is the idea that the considerations of *jus post bellum* are already contained within *jus ad bellum* and *jus in bello*. Further, adding a wholly new category of *jus post bellum* risks fragmenting just war theory. Richard M. O'Meara's chapter also looks at the location of *jus post bellum* (Chapter 8). Extending his focus from just war theories to include international law and realist schools of thought, he holds that we must take *post bellum* considerations seriously. Todd Burkhardt extends the arguments in favor of taking *post bellum* considerations seriously by showing just how important the post-war situation is to the traditional just war category of reasonable chance of success (Chapter 9). Like Pollard, Burkhardt shows the way that *post bellum* considerations already figure in existing just war theory and like O'Meara, he shows just how important it is for a state to take the post-war situation seriously.

We finish the theoretical concerns with Brian Orend, who brings the *jus post bellum* to bear on the modern reality of war (Chapter 10). Looking at Iraq and Afghanistan, Orend examines the cases of Germany and Japan concerning retribution and rehabilitation. While each war is different, if we are to improve the applicability and moral authority of the just war tradition, the theoretical concerns of just war need to be dynamic and responsive to history. Given the relatively recent emergence of *jus post bellum*, a historical perspective can surely help drive the field in directions that are more positive.

As we move from higher-level conceptual issues to concrete cases, we focus on the range of modern conflicts that occur. Specifically, we focus on individuals whose role—and increasingly, profession—it is to prosecute a rapidly diversifying range of conflicts. Part II, "Faces of war: beyond states and soldiers," acts to compare not only the types of war we might fight but the groups and individual actors who engage within these conflicts. Underpinning this is the recognition that the just war tradition needs to recognize that the character of war has changed: military conflict is no longer just about a state going to war with another state. Non-state actors now play a central role in warfare, and those fighting wars have changed too. Modern warfare can now include terrorist groups, private military contractors, child soldiers and the like. These actors— whether considered as groups or individuals—need to be engaged by the just war tradition.

We arrange themes according to the type of diversity we encounter within war. For example, policy and literature frequently reference so-called "irregular warfare" (Chapters 11, 12, 13 and 14). Yet, the concept itself is complex and ambiguous by virtue of describing a relation between parties without specifying who those parties might—or ought to—be. We group chapters in this section according to their depiction of facets of irregular warfare that are not only worthy of study on their own but are worth understanding as they share an idea central to modern debates about ethics and war.

Our discussions begin with Michael Gross (Chapter 11). His concern is on the moral status of non-traditional war participants such as journalists and diplomats. Soft power, the political tool of persuasion without resort to force, is typically seen as a morally superior response to force. However, what soft power tactics are permissible and necessary? Is a journalist allowed to fabricate stories? Can medicine be used as a propaganda tool? Given the capacity for journalists and broadcasters to impact a war's development, Gross asks whether these people can be considered legitimate military targets. Anne Schwenkenbecher then asks what it is to have legitimate authority in a political landscape in which non-state actors are frequently the targets of state military actions (Chapter 12). She argues that the central consideration that determines legitimacy is the popular support and representation of a people, but that this consideration gives us cause to allow for the possibility of legitimate authorities in the form of non-state groups or even individuals.

Continuing the focus on the non-standard roles in modern warfare, Jennifer Mei Sze Ang considers humanitarian interventions (Chapter 13). Like Gross, Ang is concerned with interrogating the *prima facie* intuition that a humanitarian intervention is naturally a morally better option than traditional war. She assesses the moral status of humanitarian efforts, and argues that in order for a humanitarian intervention to retain its "just" status, its goals and methods must maintain their integrity throughout the intervention.

Daniel H. Levine identifies central concerns facing peacekeepers that the normal soldier is not required to face (Chapter 14). Levine identifies strategies for peacekeepers to align their objectives with the popular support and beliefs of the people whose peace they are purported to protect. Linking these four chapters together is the recognition that the groups engaged in warfare—whether under the guidance of state or non-state actors—extend beyond the traditional idea of war as simply state-on-state conflict.

At times, diversity comes not within a term that covers a wide range of distinct objects, but a single endeavor whose individual mechanisms are contentious. In modern military acts, nowhere is this diversity more evident than terrorism and counterterrorism following the "War on Terror." Fritz Allhoff provides not only a generous overview of the complexities of the subject, but links them thematically as exercises in moral exceptionalism (Chapter 15). Allhoff argues that there is no in principle problem with group-based exceptionalism as part of a response to threats of terrorist activity. An alternative to Allhoff is offered by Seumas Miller who claims that, while just war theory can be justifiably modified to account for counterterrorism, these norms then provide limited justification for certain exceptional activities (Chapter 16). Miller then concentrates on targeted killing of terrorists as an example of how these limits might be resolved in practice.

Shawn Kaplan then looks at three ways in which modern warfare can respond to novel security threats (Chapter 17). Discussing the distinctions between defensive, preventative, and punitive warfare, Kaplan shows just how different responses to antiterrorist campaigns are punitive in nature. Importantly, given the general intuition that punitive warfare is not justified, Kaplan shows that—under a Locke model of authority—a state may sometimes be in a position that allows punitive warfare.

We encounter a similar variety when we consider what is seemingly the most enduring object of study in war—the warfighters themselves. We provide a view of the nature of warfighters from the common (the civilian or noncombatant), to the suspect (the Private Military Contractor or PMC), to the taboo (the child soldier). Jason Blahuta begins our investigation by proposing that—given that a range of circumstances are met—innocent civilians are legitimate military targets (Chapter 18).

Ned Dobos concentrates on another new and often problematic creature on the battlefield, the PMC (Chapter 19). Dobos argues that the status of PMCs as businesses exempts them from certain types of activity we expect soldiers to take, including taking on significant risk in the name of protecting noncombatants. However, this same lack of accountability may also extend to the modern professional soldier. Dobos then discusses in detail how we might navigate this commitment to job safety in violent lines of work.

We conclude the section with a look at another morally challenging military actor, the child soldier. Tor Arne Berntsen and Bård Mæland argue that, contrary to popular intuitions, child actors may possess sufficient autonomy to act knowingly in war (Chapter 20). However, their continued status as children may provide adult warfighters with extra responsibilities to prevent the deaths of child soldiers where possible. Moving from journalists engaged in state propaganda, to terrorists and non-combatants, to finish with child soldiers, the diversity of actors in modern war is great and only likely to continue to expand. Again, uniting these chapters are the dual questions of what can the just war tradition offer us here, and how should the just war tradition respond to these non-traditional faces of modern war.

At times, our commitment to confronting the scope of the ethics of war takes us to strange places. Nowhere is this more evident than in Part III, in which our contributors offer perspectives on the changing ways in which the technology of war informs the ethics of war. As technology continues to advance at an unprecedented pace, maintaining an obvious thematic structure becomes a complex task.

In our first section, "Technology and just war theory," we give a brief sketch of how complex this task is by providing an overview of not only how military technology might advance but also how this advance might signal changes in military development and use of technology, and how this feeds back into civil society. Braden Allenby begins this section with an overview of the historical role that technology has played in warfare (Chapter 21). More generally, he shows that any serious consideration of the future of just war theory must take technology seriously. Offering a set of general considerations, Allenby argues that emerging technologies of nanotechnology, biotechnology, information and cognitive technologies require moral assessment as part of just war theory.

Chris Mayer continues our sketch by offering a view on the development of nonlethal weapons (Chapter 22). Mayer outlines recent developments in nonlethals, and then asks if, consistent with the duty to minimize harm, we have an obligation to use nonlethals in military encounters. Answering this question in the positive, Mayer then asks if states have a positive obligation to develop these weapons in order to further their use.

Taking a related field but drawing a different line of enquiry, Malcolm Dando raises the question of the advances in neurochemistry and their application to biological and chemical weapons (Chapter 23). An area of enquiry now debated vigorously within international diplomacy and certain areas of bioethics, Dando brings to the fore the responsibilities of civilian scientists whose work may enable the use of biological or chemical weapons. Dando focuses in particular on neuropharmaceuticals, due to the unique regulatory problems they pose by sitting uncomfortably between the chemical and biological weapons conventions' prohibitory norms. In Chapters 21, 22 and 23, despite their different foci, we see a common aim: technology plays a major role in war, a role that requires recognition and response.

Having discussed general and particular reasons for technological assessments as part of just war theory, we look at a controversial and challenging set of technologies, uninhabited and autonomous military systems in Chapters 24, 25 and 26. Christian Enemark begins this section with a focus on uninhabited military aircraft, drones, and their recent use by the U.S. government (Chapter 24). A key concern is whether such drones lower the threshold for going to war. Furthermore, Enemark investigates the ways in which drones fit with and challenge the basic conditions of just war. Keith Abney continues this theme by looking at the ways that the current use of drones may drive the future developments of just war theory, particularly how drone use sits with legitimate use of coercion (Chapter 25). Shifting from uninhabited military vehicles to autonomous weapons, Heather M. Roff argues that it is impossible to create a weapon that has *moral* autonomy (Chapter 26). The outcome of this is that the moral responsibility for lethal autonomous robots must lie with the software programmers, politicians, and military commanders.

Our final three authors consider cyberwarfare, a new way of fighting that changes our conception of the battlefield altogether. George R. Lucas Jr introduces cyberwarfare with an overview of recent histories of how cyberattacks have been used in Estonia, Georgia, Iran, and Syria (Chapter 27). His focus is on if and when such cyberattacks can be justified within modified just war considerations. Leonard Kahn attends to the specific concern of just cause in cyberwarfare (Chapter 28). He holds that just cause is essential to cyberwarfare, but that it must be modified and include cyberwarfare as an act that extends beyond kinetic attacks. Our final author, Neil Rowe, concentrates on the specific issue of perfidy in cyberwarfare (Chapter 29). Perfidy—the practice of impersonating civilians in conflict—is of special concern to cyberwarfare: Given that perfidy is impermissible in traditional warfare, is it permissible, and if so when, for a cyberattacker to disguise their attack as civilian software or hardware?

This book comprises an attempt to cover the topical issues of the day, with an eye to future practical and theoretical changes in the practice of warfare. We aim to provide readers with a set of mechanisms to understand how the face of just war theory is changing. We are not pretending to offer something partisan toward one part of the current debate, but rather a coherent way of navigating the presently chaotic and disconnected set of concepts and practices. By tying the seemingly disparate topics together with the dual narrative of relations between the just war tradition and modern warfare in practice, we show that there is a way to order the debates. Further, we hope to show that the just war tradition can, and indeed *should*, respond to the changes in how we fight wars.

A comprehensive view is too large for any one volume; rather, we offer a thematic sketch to guide the reader from war's onset, down to the type of gear that soldiers carry and the experiences they have in battle. Throughout, we present divergent positions to offer up the best opportunity for readers to come to grips with the different arguments we might take up as the field advances. Whether this book presents one of those future canonical views, or serves only as a post to mark the evolution of the field is not a question we can reliably answer. What we hope is that, either way, we represent a complex and engaging picture of the state of the art, and promote more conversation on these important issues. If there is a moral to this story, it is that the realm of theory must engage with practice, for the sake of both good theory and good practice.

★★★

The editors acknowledge the support of the Centre of Applied Philosophy and Public Ethics and of Charles Sturt University. Fritz Allhoff thanks Western Michigan University for sabbatical support, and Adam Henschke thanks the Brocher Foundation for its hospitality. Our contributors were timely and responsive to our excessive queries; we appreciate their professionalism and patience. We thank Routledge for helping bring this project to fruition and our editor, Andrew Humphrys. James Otis was an invaluable asset for formatting and bibliographic assistance. Finally, the editors thank each other; it was a privilege all around to work together, the logistics of collaborating across three continents notwithstanding.

Fritz Allhoff
Whitefish, Montana, USA

Nicholas G. Evans
Canberra, Australia

Adam Henschke
Geneva, Switzerland
November, 2012

References

Allhoff, F., *Terrorism, Ticking Time-Bombs, and Torture,* Chicago: University of Chicago Press, 2012.

Gross, M., *Moral Dilemmas of Modern War: Torture, Assassination, and Blackmail in an Age of Asymmetric Conflict,* Cambridge: Cambridge University Press, 2010.

Hoffman, S. (ed.), *The Ethics and Politics of Humanitarian Intervention*, South Bend, IN: University of Notre Dame Press, 1997.

Laberge, P., "Humanitarian Intervention: Three Ethical Positions", *Ethics & International Affairs* 9: 1995, pp. 15–35.

Lin, P., F. Allhoff, and N. Rowe, "Is It Possible to Wage a Just Cyberwar?", *The Atlantic,* June 5, 2012.

McMahan, J., *Killing in War,* Oxford: Oxford University Press, 2009.

Orend, B., *The Morality of War,* Peterborough: Broadview Press, 2006.

Pogge, T., "An Institutional Approach to Humanitarian Intervention", *Public Affairs Quarterly* 6:1, 1992, pp. 89–103.

Reichberg, G. M., H. Syse, and E. Begby (eds.), *The Ethics of War: Classical and Contemporary Readings,* Malden, MA: Blackwell Publishing, 2006.

Strawser, B.J., (ed.), *Killing by Remote Control: The Ethics of an Unmanned Military,* Oxford: Oxford University Press, 2013.

Walzer, M., *Just and Unjust Wars: A Moral Argument with Historical Illustrations*, 4th edn., New York: Basic Books, 2006.

——"Regime Change and Just War," *Dissent Magazine*, Summer, 2006.

Notes

1 For a good overview, see G. M. Reichberg, H. Syse, and E. Begby (eds.), *The Ethics of War: Classical and Contemporary Readings*, Malden, MA: Blackwell Publishing, 2006.

2 Aquinas, II.II.40.1.

3 B. Orend, *The Morality of War,* Peterborough: Broadview Press, 2006.

4 Largely because of issues with state sovereignty, humanitarian intervention is more hotly debated than self-defense. See S. Hoffman (ed.), *The Ethics and Politics of Humanitarian Intervention*, South Bend, IN: University of Notre Dame Press, 1997. See also P. Laberge, "Humanitarian Intervention: Three Ethical Positions", *Ethics & International Affairs* 9: 1995, pp. 15–35. See also T. Pogge, "An Institutional Approach to Humanitarian Intervention", *Public Affairs Quarterly* 6:1, 1992, pp. 89–103.

5 M. Walzer, *Just and Unjust Wars: A Moral Argument with Historical Illustrations*, 4th edn., New York: Basic Books, 2006, p. 21.

6 J. McMahan, *Killing in War,* Oxford: Oxford University Press, 2009.

7 Importantly, not all did; his work on guerilla warfare—explicitly invoking the Vietnam War—was an important contribution to the literature.

8 For such a discussion, see M. Gross, *Moral Dilemmas of Modern War: Torture, Assassination, and Blackmail in an Age of Asymmetric Conflict*, Cambridge: Cambridge University Press, 2010, pp. 13–20.

9 F. Allhoff, *Terrorism, Ticking Time-Bombs, and Torture*, Chicago: University of Chicago Press, 2012, §1.3.

10 Allhoff, *Terrorism,* §2.2.

11 B.J. Strawser (ed.), *Killing by Remote Control: The Ethics of an Unmanned Military*, Oxford: Oxford University Press, 2013.

12 P. Lin, F. Allhoff, and N. Rowe, "Is It Possible to Wage a Just Cyberwar?", *The Atlantic,* June 5, 2012.

13 M. Walzer, *Just and Unjust Wars* 2006, pp. xiv – xv. See also M. Walzer, "Regime Change and Just War," *Dissent Magazine*, Summer, 2006.

PART I

THEORIES OF WAR

Revisiting the just war tradition

Jus ad bellum

1

CAN SOLDIERS BE EXPECTED TO KNOW WHETHER THEIR WAR IS JUST?[1]

Jeff McMahan

One school of thought about the morality of war holds that it is impermissible to fight in a war that lacks a just cause and that soldiers who fight in such a war cannot evade responsibility for their participation by claiming that the government alone is responsible for determining whether the wars it fights are just. It is, however, commonly argued against this view that it is unreasonable to expect soldiers to be competent to judge whether a war is just or unjust. They typically have limited factual information, believe that theirs is a just society incapable of unjust aggression, trust the claims of their government and superior officers, and so on. Soldiers who fight in wars that are objectively unjust because they lack a just cause ("unjust combatants") therefore tend to have one or the other of two mistaken moral beliefs: either that their war is just or that, although their war may be unjust, their participation in it is nevertheless morally permissible. When this is so, does that mean that these soldiers are morally justified in fighting? If not, does it mean that they are at least morally excused – that is, that even though they act wrongly, they are not blameworthy for doing so?

Suppose that certain unjust combatants fight without knowing that their war is unjust. Their ignorance may take several forms. They may be mistaken about matters of empirical fact that are relevant to the moral evaluation of the war. The moral conclusion they draw from the mistaken empirical beliefs might or might not be the correct conclusion to draw from those beliefs. Either way, given that the factual beliefs are false, the probability that the moral belief based on them is true is bound to be low. Alternatively, their belief that their war is just may be false even though all their nonmoral beliefs that are relevant to the moral evaluation of the war are true. That is, although they know all the relevant nonmoral facts, they draw the wrong moral conclusion. In general, mistakes of this sort – those that are purely moral – are significantly less exculpating than mistakes of nonmoral fact, assuming that in both cases the degree of the person's diligence, or lack of diligence, in the formation of the beliefs is the same. If someone knows all the nonmoral facts relevant to the evaluation of a war and there are no special circumstances that might excuse him for drawing the wrong moral conclusion, we regard him as culpable if he fails to draw the right conclusion. If, for example, a Nazi soldier knows that Poland poses no threat to Germany but believes that it is morally justified to seize Polish land by force for the expansion of the superior German nation, he has little or no excuse for his participation in aggression against Poland. Because such purely moral mistakes seldom constitute a significant excusing condition, the following discussion of erroneous beliefs in war will concentrate on mistakes of nonmoral fact.

It is a commonplace in epistemology that it can sometimes be reasonable for a person to have a belief that is in fact false – that is, that he or she may be epistemically justified in having a belief that is false. This may be true when the relevant evidence available to the person is systematically misleading. If an unjust combatant has beliefs about nonmoral facts that are false but epistemically justified and he draws the moral conclusion that would be appropriate if those beliefs were true, we can say either that what he does on the basis of that conclusion is *subjectively* right or justified, or that it is objectively wrong but nevertheless *excused*, either fully or at least to some degree. I will assume that our concern here is with objective justification, so that action that is objectively unjustified is at best excused.

One reason that action based on epistemically justified nonmoral beliefs might be less than fully excused is that there are *degrees* of epistemic justification. A person may be justified in having a certain belief, but only barely so. What this means is that while he is justified rather than unjustified in having the belief, the degree to which he can be justifiably confident in the truth of the belief is low. Alternatively, one might say that the degree of credence that the belief warrants is low. There are thus various possibilities in the case of the unjust combatant whose relevant nonmoral beliefs are epistemically justified: they may be weakly justified, strongly justified, or justified to some intermediate degree. These possibilities are relevant to the question whether he is morally excused for fighting. For whether and to what extent he has an epistemically-based excuse for fighting depends on whether and to what extent the nonmoral beliefs that underlie his belief that he is acting permissibly are epistemically justified.

Suppose, for example, that his relevant nonmoral beliefs are epistemically unjustified but that he accepts them uncritically because they cohere well with the distorted conception of the world supplied by an ideology he accepts. In that case, he has little or no epistemically-based excuse for participating in his side's unjust war.

Suppose, next, that the false nonmoral beliefs that support his decision to fight are epistemically justified, though only barely. That his beliefs are justified is certainly an excusing condition. Yet given that these beliefs warrant only a low level credence, the excuse is weaker than it would be if they instead warranted a high degree of credence – that is, if he could justifiably have a high degree of confidence that his relevant nonmoral beliefs are true.

There is another factor here that is perhaps even more important than the degree of credence he is warranted in according to his beliefs. This is that the degree to which his justified beliefs excuse his objectively wrongful action depends on how much is at stake, morally, in the choice he must make between fighting and not fighting. Suppose that, if he did not have the false nonmoral beliefs that support the permissibility of fighting, he would refuse to fight. The more that is at stake morally in the decision he makes based on these beliefs, the more important it is that his beliefs be true; and the more important it is that the beliefs be true, the less excuse he has if he is in error and acts on the basis of false beliefs. More specifically, the more that is at stake morally in the choice an agent makes on the basis of some belief, the higher the level of *justified* confidence the agent must have in the truth of the belief in order for the belief to ground an excuse of a fixed degree of strength, if the belief is in fact false.

It may help to clarify that last claim to give a schematic example. Suppose a soldier is commanded to fight in an unjust war. He believes, however, and with a moderately high level of credence, that the war is just and that his participation in it is permissible. Suppose that he is in fact epistemically justified in having that belief and in according it that degree of credence. Next imagine two possible variants of the example. In one, the war is small, victory by his side would not be tragic, and in any case he will be deployed in an area in which there is very unlikely to be any fighting, so that his participation is unlikely to make any significant difference. In these conditions, his belief may provide a strong excuse for his participation. In the other possible variant, victory by his side would be a catastrophe from an impartial point of view and his participation would be likely not only to involve the killing of numerous enemy combatants but also to make a significant contribution to his side's war effort. In these conditions, his belief, although justified, would provide only a much weaker excuse for his participation. This is intuitively plausible. The same false belief, with the same degree of epistemic justification, provides a stronger excuse when what is at stake is of lesser moral significance. When what is at stake is of greater moral significance, his belief must be better grounded to provide an excuse of equal strength if the belief turns out to be false.

"What is at stake morally" is not just a matter of the moral gravity of what a person will do if he acts on the basis of an epistemically justified belief – for example, the moral gravity of killing innocent people, which is what a combatant will do if he fights in a war that he justifiably but falsely believes is just. What is at stake is instead comparative: it is the difference between what may happen if an agent acts one way and what may happen if he acts in another way. In the case of a soldier, what is at stake in whether or not he fights is the *moral* difference between the probable outcomes of both options. In this context, the notion of "what is at stake morally" presupposes uncertainty. Thus there are possible moral costs either way. When a soldier is deliberating about whether to fight in a war, and trying to determine whether participation is permissible, what is at stake morally is the moral difference between the two ways in which he might get it wrong: by fighting in a war that is unjust and by refusing to fight in a war that is just.

What makes the soldier's predicament so difficult morally is that, in a choice between going to war and not going to war, there is usually a very great deal at stake, and the conditions in which he must choose are typically conditions of substantial factual and moral uncertainty, in which the justified level of credence in *any* set of relevant factual beliefs is quite low. What should soldiers do in these circumstances? Should they, for example, act on the basis of the factual and moral beliefs that have the highest justified level of credence?

Here are a few simple observations that seem plausible, and that are specifically focused on the case of unjust combatants. Suppose a soldier who voluntarily enlisted earlier is suddenly commanded to fight in a war that has begun unexpectedly. He has little leisure for reflection and the relevant facts are obscure. His government has asserted various factual claims that, if true, would support its further claim that the war is just. But these factual claims have been disputed or denied by others, including experts among the soldier's own fellow citizens. The level of credence he is justified in having in either of the opposing sets of factual claims is low. It is clear, however, that his own country is not in danger. The war is thousands of miles away in a remote country that he knows almost nothing about. He does know, however, that most of the people he would be fighting against are citizens of the country in which the war is being fought. What ought he to do?

He might reflect on his options in the following way. The war is either just or unjust, but he does not know which. Indeed, the one thing he does know is that he lacks relevant knowledge, both factual and moral. Suppose that as a morally scrupulous person, his primary concern is with the impact of his action on the people in the country in which the war is occurring: that is, the people he would be fighting for and those he would be fighting against. If, on the one hand, he refuses to fight and the war is just, he will fail in his duty as a soldier to protect innocent people. He may even allow innocent people to be killed whom he could have saved. Yet if he refuses to fight, he is likely to be replaced by someone else who will be as effective as he would have been. Perhaps the real victim of his refusal to fight would be the person who would replace him and be exposed to the risks of war in his stead.

If, on the other hand, he decides to fight and the war is unjust, he will fail in his duty not to be an instrument in the service of unjust ends. He may also intentionally kill people who are innocent in the relevant sense as a means to those ends. Yet, he may reflect, if he were not to do these things, someone else would replace him and perhaps be even more efficient in killing innocent people and contributing to the achievement of the war's unjust aims.

In short, if he participates and the war is just, he may save innocent lives and make a small contribution to the achievement of a just cause. If he refuses to participate and the war is just, he will fail to save innocent lives and fail to contribute to the achievement of a just cause. If he participates and the war is unjust, he may kill innocent people and make a small contribution to the achievement of an unjust cause. If he refuses to participate and the war is unjust, he will have avoided killing innocent people and contributing to the achievement of an unjust cause. If he participates, whatever he does would probably have been done by someone else had he not participated, and if he does not participate, what he fails to do will probably be done by someone else instead. So it seems that where consequences are concerned, it makes little difference whether he participates or not.

But consequences are not all that matters morally. The soldier's options involve not just risks of harm to others but risks of his own *wrongdoing*. He faces *moral risks*, such as the risk of intentionally killing people who are in fact innocent, of wronging people and violating their rights.

There are three broad reasons why consideration of the moral risks the soldier faces may favor the refusal to fight. One derives from moral asymmetries between doing and allowing and between intending and merely foreseeing. If the soldier refuses to fight and the war turns out to be just, he may *allow* some innocent people to be killed whom he could have saved – though this would not be intended and these people might be saved by someone who replaces him. If he fights and the war turns out to be unjust, he may *intentionally kill* some people who are innocent – though they might also have been killed by his replacement, or someone else, had he not fought. Most of us believe that in most contexts it is more seriously wrong to kill innocent people intentionally than it is to allow innocent people to be killed as an unintended effect of one's failure to act. Our negative duty not to kill is in general stronger than our positive duty to prevent people from being killed. If, as in this soldier's case, the factual claims that support the view that the war is just seem no more likely to be true than those that support the contrary view, it seems that the moral presumption is against fighting, for fighting risks intentionally killing people who are innocent, while not fighting risks unintentionally allowing people who are innocent to be killed.

The force of this point should not, however, be overstated. The claim that he risks intentionally killing innocent people is ambiguous. It could mean that he risks intentionally killing people he will know to be innocent. This is indeed specially objectionable but it is not what this soldier risks. Rather, he risks intentionally killing people who he will believe are not innocent but who are in fact innocent. This may still be more objectionable than killing such people foreseeably but unintentionally, but it is not so objectionable as intentionally killing people he knows to be innocent.

The second broad reason why the moral risks soldiers face may sometimes favor refusal to fight appeals to considerations that are available to soldiers independently of the facts about the particular war in which they have been commanded to fight. One such consideration is that the purely statistical probability that a war is unjust is higher than the probability that it is just. While it is an exaggeration to say, as Elizabeth Anscombe does, that "human pride, malice and cruelty are so usual that … wars have mostly been mere wickedness on both sides," it is nevertheless possible that a war can be wholly unjust on both sides – for example, when both sides are fighting for the possession of territory to which neither as a right.[2] But it is not possible for a war to be wholly just on both sides. For one side can be acting *justly* in fighting the other only if the other is responsible for a wrong that the first side if fighting to prevent or rectify. It is possible for both sides to have just aims, but that is possible only when both also have unjust aims. But if wars may be just on one side and unjust on the other, just and unjust on both sides, or unjust on both sides, but not just on both sides, it follows that states have more often fought wholly unjustly than they have fought wholly justly, and that this must continue to be true.

The third consideration that supports the view that, in conditions of uncertainty, the moral presumption is against fighting is that most people are strongly disposed to believe that their side in any dispute is in the right. Not only is it true that a war in which a soldier has been commanded to fight is statistically more likely to be unjust than just, but it is also true that he is highly likely to believe that it is just even when it is unjust. These two considerations combine to suggest that soldiers should be skeptical of their own sense that their war is just, especially in cases in which the justification for the war is controversial. They should, however, be disposed to *trust* their judgment when they are inclined to believe that their war is unjust. Independently of the facts of the particular case, their judgment is supported not only by statistical probability but also by its being contrary to the natural bias in favor of believing that one is right. In the case of most soldiers, the evidence for their war's being unjust has to be unusually compelling to overcome this bias, and in general the best explanation of why it is compelling is that the war actually *is* unjust.

That the risk of being wrong is greater when a soldier believes his war is just than when he believes it is unjust is one reason why the moral risks are greater in a decision to fight than in a decision not to fight. When a soldier is uncertain about the morality of a war, the presumption should be that the *morally* safer course is not to fight.

The worry, of course, is that the morally safer course for individual combatants may be disastrous for their society. As the traditional just war theorist Francisco de Vitoria argued, "if subjects fail to obey their prince in war from scruples of doubt, they run the risk of betraying the commonwealth into the hands of the enemy, which is much worse than fighting the enemy, doubts notwithstanding; therefore they had better fight."[3] Yet this risk is not as great as Vitoria supposed, at least in our time, if not in his. For when a contemporary state is being unjustly attacked or invaded, it is extremely unlikely that its soldiers will have significant doubts about whether it is permissible to fight in self-defense, either individual or national. One will therefore be hard pressed to find recorded instances in which a significant proportion of soldiers refused to fight on conscientious but not pacifist grounds in a war that was both wholly defensive and objectively just – and even harder pressed to find an instance of such a war that was lost because too many soldiers refused on conscientious grounds to fight in it. And even if a soldier does believe that the war is unjust and refuses to fight, the chance that he will be setting an example that others will be tempted to follow is remote, principally because just wars of national defense are almost always *obviously* just. It therefore seems that Vitoria's concern is misplaced. It is simply not true that if soldiers believe that there is a presumption against fighting when they have significant doubts about the justice of a war in which they have been commanded to fight, that will imperil the security of their society against unjust foreign attack.

One might argue that Vitoria's concern can be more easily allayed. The reason, it might be claimed, why the insistence that soldiers be mindful of the moral risks of fighting need not put their own society at risk is that skepticism about the justice of purely defensive wars is simply never warranted. Just as wars of defense against an armed attack are always permitted under international law, so they are always morally permissible. A soldier is thus entitled to presume, with a high degree of credence, that a war fought against foreign forces, and fought at least initially and perhaps entirely within the borders of his own country, is a just war, so that fighting in it is morally the safer course.

This is, however, a simplistic understanding of defensive war. It is, for one thing, not always clear what counts as a war of defense. When what is at issue is the right to the possession or habitation of disputed territory, what seems like defensive war to one side will look like aggression to the other, and vice versa. In general, moreover, if it is possible for a genuinely defensive war to be unjust, then at least in cases in which it is possible to know the facts that make the war unjust, it must be possible to fight in it without having an epistemically-based excuse, either full or partial. And it is indeed possible for defensive war to be unjust. A defensive war is unjust when the offensive war to which it is a response is a just war. As Emmerich de Vattel wrote in the eighteenth century, "if the enemy who wages offensive war has justice on his side, we have no right to make forcible opposition; and the defensive war then becomes unjust."[4] Most subsequent moral and legal theorists have agreed.

There are at least two types of offensive or aggressive war that are potentially just: preventive war and humanitarian intervention. These are forms of war that are not in the strict sense defensive: they are not responsive to an actual or imminent attack by another state. They are instead responsive, respectively, to a threat of attack that is not imminent, and to violations of human rights within the state that is attacked.

Consider first a just preventive war. Suppose that one state is engaged in planning and preparing for an unjust war against another, that the government of the state that is the potential victim has discovered the plans and preparations, that nonviolent methods have only a very low probability of being able to avert the war, and that if defensive action is deferred until the attack begins, or is about to begin, it will be less effective and more destructive than it would be if undertaken now, preventively. Suppose that in these conditions the state that is threatened launches a preventive war and assume for the sake of argument that this war is just. Assume further that the state that is preventively attacked could, rather than fighting back, renounce its plans for unjust war and offer adequate guarantees that it will not attack. But instead its government decides to fight a war that, though defensive, is unnecessary and unjust.

What ought its soldiers to do when ordered to fight in this defensive war and how ought we to think of them if they fight? Suppose that their government had carefully concealed its plans for unjust war from both its citizens and its soldiers, and that it now indignantly denies that it has had any such plans, which were discovered by the intended victim only through espionage, so that the evidence of the plan cannot be fully disclosed without revealing and thus compromising the sources of the intelligence. This is the most likely background to such a case, since overt preparations for unjust war forfeit the advantages of surprise and invite defensive preparations or even preventive attack. In these conditions, in which ordinary soldiers have no way of knowing about their government's plans and little reason to believe the allegations made by the state that has invaded their country, and in which their immediate deployment is necessary for successful defense, they may be epistemically justified in having a high degree of credence in the belief that their war is just and may thus have a strong or even full excuse for fighting.

This case seems to confirm the view that soldiers are entitled to presume that a defensive war is just and are therefore wholly or at least partially excused if a defensive war turns out to be unjust. There is, however, a second type of unjust defensive war that challenges this view – namely, defense against justified humanitarian intervention. When external intervention is necessary to stop a government from extensively violating the human rights of some group of its citizens, and when the intervention is proportionate to the gravity of the violations and the intended beneficiaries clearly welcome it, humanitarian intervention can be just. When this is so, military resistance to the intervention is objectively wrong.

In this kind of case, it is doubtful that soldiers can be epistemically justified in believing that participation in defensive war is permissible; it is, therefore, also doubtful that they have an epistemically-based excuse if they do participate. For if the violations of human rights are sufficiently extensive to justify military intervention, and sufficiently notorious actually to provoke it, it is extremely unlikely that soldiers will have been unaware of them, or therefore of the reason for the attack that they have been called upon to repel. They should know that their action shields the government in its violations of the human rights of their fellow citizens.

Matters of this sort are, however, never simple. The justification for humanitarian intervention is seldom uncontroversial and thus it is always possible that soldiers may be aware that their government is guilty of violating the human rights of the members of some domestic group and yet reasonably, though mistakenly, believe that the violations are insufficient to justify military intervention. When that is the case, they may have an epistemically-based excuse for fighting, the strength of which would depend upon the degree to which they are justified in believing that the defensive war is just, despite their government's wrongdoing.

It seems, in short, that the claims I have made about the moral risks involved in fighting in war do not apply, at least not with equal force, in the case of defensive war. But even in the case of apparently defensive war, there can be legitimate doubts about whether the war really is defensive and about whether, even if it is clearly defensive, it is just. So even when the war in which a soldier is commanded to fight seems to be entirely defensive, he cannot take it for granted that it is just. There is scope for epistemic error and if the war turns out to be unjust, he cannot count on being automatically excused for participating in it.

Thus far I have considered the epistemically-based excuses that may be available to unjust combatants largely in the abstract. But we should ask whether there are any defensible generalizations about the excuses that unjust combatants have in practice. Are many, or most, unjust combatants excused on grounds of nonculpable ignorance, and if so to what degree?

The general points I have made about what combatants can know independently of the facts about the particular war in which they have been commanded to fight are certainly relevant. Except in cases in which the war is clearly defensive and clearly not responsive to a justified instance of humanitarian intervention, soldiers can know that on a purely statistical basis their war is more likely to be unjust than just and that they will be strongly inclined to believe that it is just even if it is unjust. Assuming that these background considerations ought to dispose them to skepticism, and given that what is at stake in their decision is of the utmost importance morally, it seems clear that it is morally incumbent upon them to deliberate carefully and to be confident of their ability to rebut the apparent presumption against fighting before they commit themselves to fight. Yet it is highly doubtful that many do take seriously their moral duty to examine the reasons for and against their participation in the war.

Part of the evidence for this claim is empirical. It is found in the memoirs that soldiers write, the anecdotal accounts they give to journalists of why they joined, what their thoughts were when they were sent to fight, and so on. It is hard to find descriptions of prolonged and serious moral deliberation in these accounts. There are some but, to the best of my knowledge, not many.

The other, and better, part of the evidence is the extreme rarity of instances in which a soldier or a group of soldiers refuses on conscientious grounds to participate in a war. There has certainly been no shortage of unjust wars, but cases of active-duty soldiers who have refused to participate in them are not common. There are three possibilities. One is that soldiers think carefully about the morality of the war but in the end conscientiously conclude that the war is just. While this is bound to happen in some cases, it cannot be the correct explanation in most cases. It is simply not credible to suppose that most soldiers who fight in unjust wars do deliberate carefully about the morality of the war but invariably get it wrong. It is hard to believe that virtually everyone is that unconquerably obtuse.

The second possibility is that soldiers do deliberate carefully and succeed in many cases in recognizing that their war is unjust but are then consistently overwhelmed by duress or are too weak-willed or cowardly to refuse to fight. This too is implausible, if only because it makes little sense to suppose that people would bother to engage in the hard work of moral reflection unless they expected to be able to act on their conclusions. If they were motivated to deliberate by the desire to avoid wrongdoing, it could hardly be that this desire would then be wholly ineffectual in guiding their action in virtually all cases.

It seems, therefore, that the third possibility is what actually happens in most cases: soldiers simply do not often engage in scrupulous moral deliberation about whether their country's war is just or about whether they ought to fight in it. Yet after the fact they tend to claim a great variety of epistemically-based excuses. In discussing two notorious and egregious Nazi war criminals, Eichmann and Höss, Primo Levi rehearses the litany of excuses that he notes are claimed by all who are accused of wrongdoing in war.

> In substance, these two defended themselves in the classical manner of the Nazi militia, or, better yet, of all militiamen: we have been educated in absolute obedience, hierarchy, nationalism; we have been imbued with slogans, intoxicated with ceremonies and demonstrations; we have been taught that the only justice was that which was to the advantage of our people and that the only truth was the words of the Leader. What do you want from us? How can you even think to expect from us, after the fact, a behavior different from ours and that of all those who were like us? We were the diligent executors, and for our diligence we were praised and promoted. The decisions were not ours because the regime in which we grew up did not permit autonomous decisions: others have decided for us, and that was the only way it could have happened because our ability to decide had been amputated. Therefore we are not responsible.[5]

Levi recounts these familiar excuses with scorn. Why? Not because they simply cannot apply to officials as highly placed as Eichmann and Höss, for Levi explicitly says that they are claimed by "all militiamen." (It is, however, worth noting that the epistemically-based excuses tend to have lesser application the higher a person is in the chain of command.) Perhaps Levi's sense that there is an element of bad faith in the assertion of these excuses derives from the fact that they can all to some extent be anticipated, predicted in advance. We have all heard these claims before – and so had all those who asserted them, long before they found it necessary to proclaim them on their own behalf. But the more these epistemic excuses are publicly asserted, the less available they become. The more often it is claimed that unjust combatants are excused by their ignorance, the less plausible it becomes for subsequent unjust combatants to plead ignorance as an excuse. If they know that their predecessors have pleaded ignorance as an excuse, they know that there are important issues of knowledge and responsibility in war. This makes it less plausible for them to plead ignorance as an excuse. If they were aware that there were important matters about which they were ignorant, why did they not seek to overcome their epistemic deficiencies before committing themselves to fight?

They say, for example, they believed their war was just; but they knew that the same was true of their enemy, and that it was unlikely that they could both be right. Why did this not give them pause? They say they were indoctrinated and conditioned to obey; but they knew when they joined that they would be, and knew when they set off to fight that they had been.

They say their government deceived them; but they knew in advance that governments routinely deceive their citizens, especially in matters of war. People living under totalitarian or authoritarian rule know that their government censors, manipulates, and in general controls the media. If they know from this that their government does not trust them with the truth, they should expect to be lied to. Thus, when soldiers in a totalitarian or authoritarian state fight in an unjust war, their best excuse is likely to be duress. By contrast, soldiers in a democratic country with a free press may have a better excuse if they have fought in an unjust war on the basis of lies told them by their government. But even they may know that their government has fought wars for reasons that do not bear exposure and thus have lied to furnish an acceptable public justification. The *Pentagon Papers* revealed an assortment of lies told to rally support for the war in Vietnam; Reagan lied about the nature of the *Contras* and the sources of their funding in order to make war against Nicaragua; and members of the George W. Bush administration lied repeatedly about weapons of mass destruction in Iraq in order to justify the invasion and occupation of that country to the UN, the Congress, and the American public. The soldiers who will fight in the US's next war will have had access to these facts.

It matters, of course, what the recent history of a soldier's country is like, and what the character of its culture is. It is, for example, morally less risky for a soldier in Norway to obey an order to fight than it is for a soldier in the US to do so, and the Norwegian soldier will accordingly have a stronger epistemic excuse if the war in which he fights turns out to be unjust. But in general it seems that soldiers are unjustifiably complacent in their assumption that the wars in which they are commanded to fight are just. Indeed, whether they turn out to be just or unjust combatants often involves a significant element of moral luck, in that those who fight for a just cause might, if their circumstances were different, fight for an unjust cause with an equal conviction of being in the right. Given the gravity of what is at stake in a decision to go to war, there seem to be relatively few cases in which a soldier who becomes an unjust combatant can truthfully claim that he actually did all of the epistemic work that could reasonably be expected of him and thus has a full epistemically-based excuse for his participation in an unjust war. Most unjust combatants have been negligent with respect to what are, in the context, their rather stringent epistemic responsibilities and thus their ignorance, and the action based on it, are culpable to varying degrees, which is just to say that although their participation in an unjust war may be excused, the excuse is in general partial rather than full.

My argument that the moral risks involved in participation in war may exceed those of non-participation exerts pressure in the direction of a contingent form of pacifism. But this pressure can be resisted, and successfully overcome, when war is just. It can be overcome by careful attention to the facts and careful moral reasoning. There was little uncertainty, for example, that the Allied war against Nazi Germany, and the war against imperial Japan, were just wars. In principle, there can be cases in which a war is in fact just and yet most soldiers are not epistemically justified in believing that it is just, or are even epistemically justified in believing that it is unjust. The risk of this happening is greatest in countries in which the flow of information is tightly controlled and manipulated by the government. Yet in such countries there is little risk that a just war will in fact go unfought, since governments in these countries tend to supply motivation to their soldiers by duress rather than persuasion.

The prevention of unjust wars is among the most important of moral aims. One significant means to the achievement of this aim is to eliminate, to the greatest extent possible, the epistemic excuses available to unjust combatants or, in other words, to enable soldiers to have both a greatly enhanced understanding of the moral character of the war in which they are commanded to fight, and certain forms of legal support if their improved moral understanding leads them to engage in conscientious refusal to fight. I have elsewhere proposed that the best way to pursue this goal would be to establish an impartial international court whose function would be to interpret and administer a reformed and morally better-informed body of law devoted to matters of *jus ad bellum*.[6] But it would take us too far afield to pursue this suggestion here. The important point for our purposes is that if we could offer soldiers a source of guidance about the morality of war that would be more impartial and more authoritative than their own government, this could provide a basis for holding them accountable for their participation in unjust wars – perhaps accountable in law but certainly accountable to their own consciences. This increased accountability could in turn give them an incentive to take their epistemic duties more seriously than they tend to do at present.

Notes

1 This chapter is a revised version of material from *Killing in War* by Jeff McMahan (2009), extract (6769w) from pp. 137–154, by permission of Oxford University Press
2 G.E.M. Anscombe, "War and Murder," in her *Ethics, Religion, and Politics*, Collected Philosophical Papers, vol. III, Minneapolis: University of Minnesota Press, 1981, p. 52.
3 F. de Vitoria, "On the Law of War," in A. Pagden and J. Lawrence (eds), *Political Writings*, Cambridge: Cambridge University Press, 1991, pp. 311–312.
4 E. de Vattel, *The Law of Nations*, Philadelphia: T. & J.W. Johnson, 1863, p. 304.
5 P. Levi, *The Drowned and the Saved*, New York: Vintage, 1989, pp. 28–29.
6 J. McMahan, "The Prevention of Unjust Wars," in Y. Benbaji and N. Sussman (eds), *Reading Walzer*, London: Routledge, 2013.

References

Anscombe, G.E.M. "War and Murder," in *Ethics, Religion, and Politics*, Collected Philosophical Papers, vol. III, Minneapolis: University of Minnesota Press, 1981.
de Vattel, E. *The Law of Nations*, Philadelphia: T. & J.W. Johnson, 1863.
de Vitoria, F. "On the Law of War," in A. Pagden and J. Lawrence (eds), *Political Writings*, Cambridge: Cambridge University Press, 1991.
Levi, P. *The Drowned and the Saved*, New York: Vintage, 1989.
McMahan, J. "The Prevention of Unjust Wars," in Y. Benbaji and N. Sussman (eds), *Reading Walzer*, London: Routledge, 2012.

2

IS JUST WAR THEORY OBSOLETE?

Jeffrey P. Whitman

1. Introduction

Just war theory, the body of moral and legal prescriptions governing the conduct of war, has often been subject to criticisms that question its very coherence. Those with pacifist views see the whole concept of just war as oxymoronic. Applying moral predicates (like just or unjust) to the inherently evil human activity of war makes no sense to them. Those who embrace what they claim to be a more realist or pragmatic position regard the moral rules and legal restrictions governing war as perhaps laudable, but in no way morally binding. In war there are no rules, only winners and losers. Any rule that gets in the way of winning must be disregarded. One group of critics find just war theory (JWT) a pernicious concept that too easily rationalizes the excesses of war, while the other group of critics see it as an unnecessary impediment to the hard-headed decision-making that war demands.

I believe that just war defenders have successfully addressed many of these criticisms in the past. However, these long standing criticisms have received greater attention since the attacks on the United States in September 2001, and the subsequent wars and conflicts those attacks sparked. Critics from both sides have argued that JWT as it is currently understood may be obsolete and either needs radical revision, or needs to be abandoned altogether.

For example, Michael Gross argues that the limits on warfare embodied in JWT and international law wrongly restrict a nation's ability to effectively wage war against insurgents on the modern battlefield. These restrictions provide too much protection against non-state armed adversaries, such as terrorists. On his view, the "innocent civilians" found on the modern battlefield often are not so innocent. These civilians can and do aid, shelter, and hide terrorists, and thereby, claims Gross, become legitimate military targets of the states fighting those terrorists. His argument is particularly salient for democratic states seeking to protect their citizens against adversaries who use their own civilian populations as cover for their attacks. For Gross, the laws of war require change to meet the needs of states (e.g. the U.S. fighting the Taliban, the Israelis fighting Hamas).[1]

Another critic, Andrew Fiala, argues that few wars, particularly the kinds of asymmetrical wars fought today, can satisfy the criteria of just war theory. As a result he argues that the just war is largely a myth.[2] But to argue that the just war is a myth seems to be a renunciation of JWT in practice (if not theory) and an endorsement of pacifism. This view gains further support from a volume edited by Stephen Rockel and Rick Halpern.[3] The various contributors to this work focus on powerful states' apparent indifference and/or lack of care concerning unintended civilian casualties, especially when those casualties are borne by weaker states. Euphemistically labeled "collateral damage" by Western militaries, these civilian casualties have not necessarily been mitigated by the increased use of precision weapons on the part of modern militaries. Rather, as Marc Herold argues in one of the book's chapters, the use of these weapons has merely increased the confidence of Western militaries that they can safely use these weapons in dense urban neighborhoods, even as the ratio of civilian deaths to tons of ordnance dropped has increased.[4] That the laws of war permit such large numbers of "accidental" casualties among civilians indicates to these critics that the JWT underlying these laws tends to legitimize rather than restrict the violence of war. Therefore, JWT requires major revision in this new era of warfare.

As a defender of JWT, I will argue that these critics are mistaken. Given the types of wars and conflicts currently confronting the world as we begin this second decade of the 21st century, JWT is as relevant and important as it ever has been. Furthermore, JWT possesses the necessary conceptual tools to deal with whatever changes in global politics and war-fighting methods demanded in these allegedly new circumstances. To abandon or radically alter a system of moral and legal norms that has been built up over more than a thousand years, and painstakingly codified into international law over several hundred years, would be extremely shortsighted. We need not embrace pacifism and forgo armed resistance to those nations and groups who would take away our freedom and rights, nor must we follow a path that leads to a Hobbesian-like state of war between nations and people governed solely by self-interest. JWT, properly understood and respected, can at least mitigate, even if it cannot entirely eliminate, such unhappy outcomes.

The argument for my view will contain both theoretical and empirical components. The theory of just war I intend to defend is largely attributable to Michael Walzer in his seminal work, *Just and Unjust Wars*.[5] Drawing upon the events and controversies since the September 2001 attacks on the United States, I will attempt to show how the debate over these issues has been inextricably shaped and informed by JWT, by and large for the better. Finally, I will briefly speculate about the future and why I believe JWT will continue to have an important place in the moral landscape of international affairs well into that future.

2. An outdated theory?

As noted in Walzer's theory of just war, the motivating moral value that underlies contemporary JWT is the protection of rights—both the rights of states and their communal life, and the rights of soldiers and civilians on the battlefield. This motivation continues to deeply inform the application of JWT to current armed conflicts. The rules of *jus in bello*, which establish the rights and obligations of combatants and noncombatants, seem particularly salient here. Certain categories of people—civilians, the wounded, and prisoners of war (collectively classified as noncombatants)—are designated "protected persons" under the Geneva Conventions, and therefore should never be subject to intentional attack. Additionally, the *jus in bello* arm of JWT makes an important presumption concerning the moral equality of soldiers. Also referred to as the independence thesis, the claim here is that regardless of the justice of your cause (the *jus ad bellum* judgment), all soldiers must abide by the *jus in bello* restrictions concerning the intentional targeting of noncombatants.

This independence thesis, a key tenet of Walzer's JWT, has generated the most criticism of late when discussing *jus in bello*. The alleged problem concerns asymmetric warfare, a type of warfare especially prevalent in U.S. conflicts today. Although the label may be new, the notion of asymmetric warfare has been around for a long time. It refers to situations where one side in a conflict is vastly superior to the other, and in order to overcome that asymmetry in power, the weaker side employs non-conventional tactics that often violate the *jus in bello* proscription against intentionally harming noncombatants. Examples of such tactics include terrorist attacks and guerilla warfare, the indiscriminate use of weapons of mass destruction (e.g. chemical, biological, and nuclear weapons), as well as information warfare (e.g. using the internet to attack military and civilian information system networks). What is problematic with such tactics is that they often intentionally target noncombatant lives and property, but given the very weakness of the attacker *vis-à-vis* its more powerful adversary, these may be the only effective tactics available to them.

The criticism here is that JWT and the laws of war codified in the Geneva Conventions tend to favor the powerful over the weak, regardless of the justice of the weaker side. The weaker side, in order to effectively press its claims militarily, must necessarily engage in tactics such as guerilla warfare and terrorism, tactics which blur or even ignore the combatant/noncombatant distinction so central to *jus in bello* judgments. The stronger side can more easily observe these distinctions without significantly undermining its military effort.[6] The end result is an undermining of the presumed moral equality of soldiers, perhaps granting the weaker side in a conflict license to intentionally attack noncombatants while holding the stronger side to strict adherence of *jus in bello*.

While there is some truth to this criticism, that this criticism has any force at all speaks to the success of JWT and its applicability to contemporary asymmetric warfare. The terms of the debate are framed by the presumed moral force of noncombatant immunity. First of all, few critics seriously argue that a strong nation, such as the United States, should ignore the combatant/noncombatant distinction despite the restrictions it can sometimes place on military operations.[7] But neither do critics generally argue that groups like al-Qaeda or the Taliban in Afghanistan have no moral obligation to fight in accordance with the rules of *jus in bello*, despite the military superiority of NATO forces there. The criticisms focus on the alleged unfair disadvantage these moral restrictions place on insurgent and guerrilla-type forces. This criticism is particularly poignant if we imagine the insurgents have just cause (satisfy *jus ad bellum*) in their struggle against the superior force.[8] The solution, some have argued, involves a denial of the independence thesis and its concomitant premise concerning the moral equality of soldiers on the battlefield. Soldiers fighting for a just cause would be granted certain *jus in bello* privileges, while soldiers fighting on the unjust side would be subject to certain moral liabilities.[9] Others, most notably Jeff McMahan, have argued that killing in war is no different than killing outside of war.[10] The combatant/noncombatant distinction is broken and soldiers are always morally responsible for whatever killing they do on the battlefield. There is no hiding behind the state that allows soldiers to abrogate this responsibility in any way. They are ultimately responsible for the justness or unjustness of their cause as well as their actions on the battlefield.

I believe this is a wrongheaded approach for both pragmatic reasons as well as reasons of justice. Pragmatically it is very difficult, if not impossible, for soldiers to determine the true justice or injustice of their cause, and then adjust their actions on the battlefield appropriately. As I argued earlier, too many factors mitigate holding soldiers, particularly line soldiers, responsible for *jus ad bellum* infractions.[11] Given these confounding factors, punishing soldiers *ex-post facto* for actions on the battlefield that *prima facie* conform to the established laws of war merely because their cause is unjust (a determination which sometimes cannot be reliably made until the conflict is over) violates our normal notions of justice.[12]

Furthermore, particularly in asymmetrical warfare, adherence to *jus in bello* restrictions (or at least appearing to adhere to them) is generally the key to prevailing in such wars. In struggles of these types (examples include wars of national liberation, wars of secession, and insurgencies in general) the goal of the struggle is winning the support of the people in the region being contested. To use military parlance, the center of gravity in these wars is not some piece of terrain, but winning the support (or at least avoiding the enmity) of the local population, something both sides in the conflict need to recognize if they are to meet with success. This goal is not generally attainable without carefully discriminating between combatants and noncombatants. The United States somewhat belatedly recognized this truth in Iraq with the adoption of their revised counterinsurgency strategy promulgated in the so-called COIN field manual.[13] This revised strategy emphasizes protecting the civilian populace over destroying enemy fighters. As David Kilcullen puts it in his highly influential handbook, one of two fundamentals in counterinsurgency warfare is "to act with respect for local people, putting the well-being of noncombatant civilians ahead of any other consideration … ahead of killing the enemy."[14]

Weaker opponents recognize this as well, and so will also take some steps, as far as their tactics will permit them, to avoid civilian casualties. A good example of this is Mao Zedong's "Eight Points For Attention" that guided his insurgency in China following World War II. Recognizing the need to win over the Chinese people to his cause, he ordered his Army to treat the people of the countryside not as enemy combatants but as innocent civilians, essentially adhering to the rules of *jus in bello*.[15] On the other hand, the perceived failure of the al-Qaeda terrorist network to be more discriminate in their attacks has cost them support among the Arab population of the Middle East, which I would argue has caused them to lose ground in their struggle against their enemies.[16]

Far from seeing *jus in bello* moral judgments as outdated concepts in need of revision, my examples show that these arguments from JWT are central to the moral landscape of warfare, especially asymmetric warfare. Such judgments have both moral force and pragmatic force. The combatant/noncombatant distinction, the moral obligations of soldiers on the battlefield, and the overall goal of mitigating the horrors of war motivate all these arguments. Considerations of military necessity even motivate these arguments. Victory in asymmetric war seems to require attention to *jus in bello*. Sometimes political and military leaders merely pay lip service to these concepts, but the fact that they feel a need to do so points up the powerful nature of these moral judgments, and often (though perhaps not often enough) will actually dictate their actions and the actions of the people they lead.

3. Is the combatant/noncombatant distinction obsolete?

In my argument so far, I have assumed a fairly straightforward and unproblematic distinction between combatants and noncombatants. However, this distinction can be far from unproblematic and represents another line of argumentation questioning the continuing relevance of the *jus in bello* arm of JWT. In fact, much of Michael Gross's argument questions the relevance of this distinction, particularly in light of the Israeli experience in Gaza.[17] McMahan's arguments are relevant here as well.[18] The United States' war on terrorism has also put pressure on this distinction, especially considering the policies adopted by the George W. Bush administration after the attacks of 9/11. Are terrorists soldiers entitled to the rights of soldiers under the Geneva Conventions (particularly benevolent quarantine once captured) or are they criminals subject to criminal law and some form of due process? Alternatively, do they occupy some third category—illegal combatants—and therefore forfeit all rights, either as soldiers or criminals?

The Bush administration settled on this third category, a kind of mixed war-law approach, treating terrorists as soldiers when it suited their goals and criminals when the law model suited their goals. Even the language they settled on in describing the conflict and the enemy was duplicitous in this way. The war model, captured in the notion of a "Global War on

Terrorism," sanctioned the use of military force in fighting the terrorists. Labeling the enemy they were fighting as illegal combatants relied more on the legal model, but without the attendant legal protections of due process and *habeas corpus* for captured terrorists. The policies of extraordinary rendition, torture, secret CIA prisons, and the Guantanamo Bay prison designed to hold captives indefinitely and without trial, were the result of this policy. As Georgetown Professor of Law David Luban argues:

> By selectively combining elements of the war model and elements of the law model, Washington is able to maximize its own ability to mobilize lethal force against terrorists while eliminating most traditional rights of a military adversary, as well as the rights of innocent bystanders caught in the crossfire.[19]

Luban goes on to argue, that if this "hybrid law-war" approach becomes the norm, the war on terrorism presages "the end of human rights, at least for those near enough to be touched by the fire of battle."[20]

But it is here, I would argue, that *jus in bello* judgments play a crucial role. Just because a group or nation (even one as dominant as the U.S.) works to overturn the normal distinctions made by JWT and replace them with new categories, that does not show these categories are obsolete or in need of revision. The way the world *is* should not determine how it morally *ought to be*. And in fact, JWT provides a much needed corrective to this hybrid approach. A category mistake lies at the heart of the hybrid approach. To label the fight against al-Qaeda and other terrorist groups as the "war against terrorism" confuses the fact that terrorism is a tactic used to avoid engaging in direct warfare. It is more indirect even than the guerilla warfare waged by insurgents. The insurgent hides in and among the population, attacking the enemy when the opportunity presents itself, taking refuge in the general population otherwise. Terrorism is different. As Walzer succinctly notes of terrorism, "its purpose is to destroy the morale of a nation or a class, to undercut its solidarity; its method is the random murder of innocent people."[21]

Walzer's last clause is key—*the random murder of innocent people*. That clause points to the inherent immorality of terrorism as a tactic. It involves murder of innocent people, and its very randomness intends to spread fear among other innocents as well. Furthermore, it clearly violates the restrictions central to *jus in bello*. And when we talk of a "war" against terrorism, we confuse the status of the terrorists we are fighting against. They are not soldiers/combatants that we normally confront during a war. Yes, it is true that warfare often involves attacks on noncombatants. Sometimes these attacks can be justified by the principle of double effect, a principle of JWT which permits civilian casualties when their deaths are the unintended side-effects of legitimate military operations.[22] However, when soldiers are directly responsible for noncombatant casualties (the deaths are intended), their actions fail to meet the standards of *jus in bello* and the responsible soldiers may be charged with war crimes.[23]

Terrorists are in a different category altogether. They adopt as a general tactic the random killing of civilians. Their aim is to spread fear and uncertainty for their safety among a general population in order to gain some political, economic, or religious aim.[24] The killings they perpetrate are not merely criminal deviations from the war convention. Their actions lie outside and beyond the war convention. Terrorists are criminals, and the activities they engage in, whatever their apologists might say in their defense or mitigation, are crimes of the most egregious kind. To the extent possible they should be treated as criminals under international law.[25] When captured, as with criminals everywhere, they should receive due process under the law. They are not to be tortured or otherwise mistreated, but should receive humane treatment as they await criminal proceedings. But to grant them the status of soldiers is to misrepresent their true nature.

However, the guerrilla-type insurgents that the United States and its NATO allies confront in Iraq and Afghanistan represent a different, and more recognizable category altogether.[26] These fighters hide and take refuge (and sometimes receive support) from the civilian population. They also may be less discriminate in who they target in their actions, sometimes intentionally blurring the combatant/noncombatant distinction in an attempt to get the anti-guerrilla forces to use indiscriminate attacks that harm noncombatants.[27] However, they are guerilla fighters engaged in a guerilla-type war, a category recognized by contemporary JWT and the Geneva Conventions. They therefore maintain the rights and obligations of soldiers as outlined in *jus in bello* rules. When captured they should receive treatment as prisoners of war, unless they are known to have committed criminal acts on the battlefield in contravention of the laws of war. They have a right to self-defense against other combatants, unlike terrorists, and their use of deadly force against their enemy is not considered murder.

Now this distinction between terrorists and guerrilla fighters can be a hard one to make at times. And sometimes certain individuals will occupy different categories at different times. The Afghan Taliban will operate as a guerilla force one day, and might conduct a terrorist attack against a civilian market the next. However, when the guerrilla fighter engages in indiscriminate killings, he suffers two risks: the risk of losing the support of the population upon which he depends, and the risk of forfeiting his status as a soldier and becoming a war criminal. The terrorist will also endeavor to confuse these two categories of guerilla or terrorist. He will want to claim combatant status in order to attempt to justify his actions. However, insofar as the tactics he adopts take as their general aim the random and indiscriminate killing of noncombatants, his claim to combatant status wrongly confuses his moral standing on the battlefield according to JWT. The hybrid law-war approach of the Bush administration only adds to this confusion, a confusion I believe JWT can alleviate in a helpful way.

I hope that my arguments thus far have helped to demonstrate the continuing relevance of JWT, even in the confusing realm of asymmetric warfare. In fact, as I have tried to show, I think the arguments of JWT have an important role to play in disentangling the sometimes knotty problems that lie at the heart of asymmetric warfare—the nature of the independence thesis and its recognition of the moral equality of soldiers, as well as the continuing importance of the combatant/noncombatant distinction. However, what of the future? Will the just war tradition continue to serve international society in an adequate manner? In my final section I offer some arguments that it will.

4. The continuing relevance of the just war tradition

Despite what some may believe, the purpose of JWT is not to make resort to war more likely or easy, nor is it somehow to legitimatize the horrors of war, particularly those visited upon innocent noncombatants. Rather, the overall goal of contemporary JWT and the international laws and treaties it has helped to birth remains to limit both the frequency of war and the destruction caused by war. When it comes to these two goals, JWT should continue to play a dominant role well into the future.

First, when it comes to the frequency of war, *jus ad bellum* concerns do serve to limit wars (no doubt not as much as the world would prefer). Whether they truly accept the principles of JWT or not, leaders of states and even non-state actors feel compelled to offer justifications for war that largely follow *jus ad bellum* criteria. Every side in a conflict wants to claim self-defense against aggression as the primary justification for their use of armed force. Failing to make such a case undermines their cause in the court of world opinion. The U.S. invasion of Iraq, justified using the Bush doctrine of anticipatory self-defense, makes the point. No doubt the standing of the United States around the world has suffered immeasurable harm as a result of the failure to actually find any real, imminent threat from Iraq.

Even terrorist organizations like al-Qaeda feel the need to wrap their struggle in the mantle of self-defense against aggression. As Osama bin Laden stated in his 1996 fatwa or declaration of war, "It should not be hidden from you that the people of Islam had suffered from aggression, iniquity and injustice imposed on them by the Zionist-Crusaders alliance and their collabora-tors." He goes on to claim,

> The latest and the greatest of these aggressions, incurred by the Muslims since the death of the Prophet (ALLAH'S BLESSING AND SALUTATIONS ON HIM) is the occupation of the land of the two Holy Places—the foundation of the house of Islam, the place of the revelation, the source of the message and the place of the noble Ka'ba, the Qiblah of all Muslims—by the armies of the American Crusaders and their allies.[28]

The United States' response in Afghanistan following the attacks of 9/11 similarly was cast in terms of self-defense. In his speech before Congress on September 20, 2001, President Bush clearly made this point, saying: "On September the 11th, enemies of freedom committed an act of war against our country."[29]

My point here is that just war categories remain relevant even in an era where officially declared wars are rare. And the justifications offered by the warring sides are subject to critique by the world community, a critique informed by these categories. "Reasons of state" or mere national self-interest no longer adequately justify war (if they ever really did)[30] and in the future I suspect public opinion will demand even more evidence of aggression before accepting a justification for the use of military force. This need for public support is especially critical in democratic societies, but the force of public opinion should not be underestimated in non-democratic regimes as well. The so-called "Arab Spring" of 2011 is a useful reminder of the power of the public. No doubt armed struggle and war will continue to be an all too common feature of international life, but they will be scrutinized and judged by the standards of *jus ad bellum* in ways that hopefully should work to diminish their frequency and length.

However, the case is even clearer when we consider the continuing relevance of *jus in bello* in armed conflicts. While progress has been slow and enforcement lax or sometimes non-existent, the notion of moral and legal protections for noncombatants during wartime, particularly non-combatant civilians, has come to be largely accepted in word, if not deed. While justice is not always swift, individuals who have perpetrated the intentional killing of protected persons have found themselves arrested and convicted of war crimes by the International Criminal Court in the Hague or by any number of United Nations established criminal tribunals.[31] The system is not perfect, and not all crimes and criminals are prosecuted, but that there is such a procedure of international justice at all is testament to the influence of the arguments of JWT.

Are these concerns likely to wane under the pressure of asymmetric warfare? I do not believe so. Take, for example, the relatively new and increasing use of unmanned drones by the United States in its fight against terrorists and other enemy militants (particularly those taking refuge in the northern tribal regions of Pakistan). The motivation for the use of these drone attacks comes from a number of concerns, some more laudable than others.[32] However, one compel-ling motivation is to minimize noncombatant casualties. This goal is of strategic importance if the United States is to avoid turning public opinion (both here and abroad) against its effort, and the accuracy of these strikes combined with good targeting intelligence has the potential to satisfy that goal. But this goal is also motivated in part by a genuine concern for protecting noncombatants from harm, a clear *jus in bello* consideration.

While accurate data is hard to come by, estimates indicate that, between June 2004 and April 2007, drone strikes killed 1,435 to 2,283 people with 80 to 95 percent of those killed having been identified as militants in reliable press accounts.[33] While noncombatant deaths are never desirable, if these figures are accurate then the percentage of civilian deaths to militant deaths may be morally justified under the principle of double effect. However, Washington officials have not always been forthcoming concerning noncombatant deaths, claiming that virtually all those killed in these strikes are militants. In addition, there is a lack of transparency when it comes to the rules of engagement governing these strikes. Are targets carefully identified and is due care taken to avoid killing civilians? With what rules must the operators of these drones comply? These questions are particularly difficult to ask and answer whenever the strikes are controlled by the CIA rather than uniformed military personnel, but these are the relevant questions JWT poses. Questions such as these have increased public pressure, both in the United States and abroad, to transfer responsibility for these strikes exclusively to the military where they can be more easily subject to legal review that ensures they conform to the laws of war. There have also been calls for the Pentagon to make public the rules of engagement governing these attacks so they might face moral scrutiny.[34]

My point in discussing this controversy is to highlight the way in which *jus in bello* issues frame the debate. The proscription against the intentional harming of noncombatants, so central to JWT and the international laws of war, make this a debate not about whether such harming is permissible, but whether appropriate measures are being taken to prevent and minimize that harm. In fact, no longer does it appear to be enough that combatants not intentionally harm noncombatants (the requirement of double effect), but due care must be taken that they not be harmed. Walzer made this argument for a more stringent understanding of the principle of double effect back in 1977, and it has become a central feature of our understanding of the laws of war.[35] As the drone controversy demonstrates, *jus in bello* judgments are firmly a part of the landscape of war, even in this relatively new method of war fighting.

As we look further into the foreseeable future, a new paradigm for war is starting to take shape (both in the United States and around the world), a new paradigm that is in many ways the product of JWT. This new paradigm focuses not so much on destroying enemy forces as on "compelling the enemy to accept one's interests," in the words of one writer.[36] These interests could be many things, from supporting certain international institutions and norms (e.g. embracing the rule of law concerning human rights, abiding by certain treaty obligations) to not providing support and safe haven to terrorists or insurgents. In any case, this new paradigm recognizes that success in war cannot be divorced from minimizing harm to noncombatant, civilian populations, especially when fighting asymmetric warfare.

As noted by Tony Pfaff, this paradigm shift—from a Clausewitzian way of war focused on destroying enemy forces to a more indirect approach that employs lethal as well as nonlethal means to attain one's goals—forces a greater emphasis on minimizing harm to noncombatants.[37] Weaker enemies of the United States and its allies recognize this strategic imperative, and the stronger states need to recognize it as well, says Pfaff. The supremacy of the United States in terms of conventional warfare is acknowledged by most of its current adversaries. They concede that engaging in direct combat against such a strong state is folly. For that reason they tend to adopt the more indirect approach that often involves hiding and taking refuge in the civilian population. They also rely on that population for logistical support, which can be given willingly or under duress.

In any case, success in military operations more than ever depends upon that civilian population. As I argued before, that population represents the military center of gravity in asymmetric conflict. Separate the weaker enemy from the population and the stronger side prevails. Fail to do that, and the weaker side meets with success. The indiscriminate targeting of the civilian population serves neither side's goals (as has been demonstrated in both Iraq and Afghanistan today). The lesson here is that *jus in bello* restrictions represent both a strategic as well as a moral imperative in warfare today.

5. Conclusion

In this period of sustained asymmetric conflict, I have argued that JWT considerations continue to play a central role. While some of the circumstances of war may have changed, the conceptual apparatus of JWT is more than adequate to address these changes. Part of the purpose of JWT has been to minimize the frequency and barbarity of war. Focusing on protecting the rights of both states and the individuals who make up states has served this purpose well. Additionally, many of the principles of JWT have found their way into today's international humanitarian law, particularly the Hague and Geneva Conventions. Rather than being abandoned or radically revised to accommodate changing circumstances, the limits and restrictions embodied in JWT and the international laws of war are, I believe, more relevant than ever. From both an ethical as well as a pragmatic perspective, to think otherwise would be both tragically shortsighted and morally mistaken.

Notes

1 M. Gross, *Moral Dilemmas of Modern War: Torture, Assassination, and Blackmail in an Age of Asymmetric Combat*, Cambridge: Cambridge University Press, 2009. See especially Part II, "Noncombatants and Asymmetric Warfare."

2 A. Fiala, *The Just War Myth*, Lanham, MD: Rowman and Littlefield, 2008.

3 S. Rockel and R. Halpern (eds), *Inventing Collateral Damage: Civilian Casualties, War, and Empire* Toronto, Canada: Between the Lines, 2009.

4 M. Herold, "'Unworthy' Afghan Bodies: 'Smarter' U.S. Weapons Kill More Innocents," in *Inventing Collateral Damage: Civilian Casualties, War, and Empire*, S. Rockel and R. Halpern (eds), Toronto, Canada: Between the Lines, 2009, pp. 303–27.

5 M. Walzer, *Just and Unjust Wars* NY: Basic Books, 1977.

6 Although the willingness of the stronger side, in this case the anti-guerilla, anti-terrorist forces, to respect the combatant/noncombatant distinction has often been violated by the strong as well as the weak, nonetheless it is the weak side that tends to feel more pressure to fight contrary to the standards of *jus in bello*. In fact, part of their strategy is to blur the line between combatant and noncombatant in order to force the strong side to ignore it as well, which generally redounds to their advantage as the stronger side risks losing the support of the very population they claim to be defending.

7 One critic who ventures in that direction is Michael Gross. See his *Moral Dilemmas in Modern War*, where he argues that *jus in bello* rules of warfare overly restrict the options of stronger nations like the United States, and should be reconsidered if necessary to pursue military aims (particularly in asymmetric warfare).

8 The 1957 struggle in Algeria between the National Liberation Front (FNL) and the French Army may be an example of such a scenario. Some might also argue that the insurgency in Iraq against the occupation by the United States could possibly be another example. Walzer even opens up this possibility with his notion of "supreme emergency." According to his argument a nation facing imminent defeat in which that defeat is likely to lead to a mass extermination and enslavement of its people may use unjust means, such as the intentional targeting of noncombatants, in an attempt to avoid such a fate.

9 This line of argument is pursued by David Rodin, "The Moral Inequality of Soldiers: Why *jus in bello* Asymmetry is Half Right," in D. Rodin and H. Shue (eds), *Just and Unjust Warriors*, Oxford: Oxford University Press, 2008, pp. 44-68.

10 See his *Killing in War* Oxford, Oxford University Press, 2011.

11 For additional arguments along these lines see Dan Zupan, "A Presumption of the Moral Equality of Combatants: A Citizen-Soldier's Perspective in D. Rodin and H. Shue (eds), *Just and Unjust Warriors*, Oxford: Oxford University Press, 2008, pp. 214-225.

12 Christopher Kutz makes a similar point in "Fearful Symmetry," in D. Rodin and H. Shue (eds), *Just and Unjust Warriors*, Oxford: Oxford University Press, 2008, pp. 69–88.

13 U.S. Army and U.S. Marine Corps, *Counterinsurgency*, FM 3-24/MCWP December 2006.

14 David Kilcullen, *Counterinsurgency* Oxford: Oxford University Press, 2010, p. 4.

15 His eight points were: 1) Speak politely, 2) Pay fairly for what you buy, 3) Return everything you borrow, 4) Pay for anything you damage, 5) Don't hit or swear at people, 6) Don't damage crops, 7) Don't take liberties with women, and 8) Don't ill-treat captives. See "On the Reissue of the Three Main Rules For Discipline and the Eight Points For Attention, Instruction of the General Headquarters of the Chinese People's Liberation Army," in *Selected Works of Mao Tse-tung*, 3rd edn, Vol. 4 Peking: Foreign Languages Press, 1969, pp. 155–6.

16 See the Pew Research Centers Global Attitudes Project released on May 21, 2011, "Osama bin Laden Largely Discredited Among Muslim Publics in Recent Years" at: http://pewglobal.org/2011/05/02/osama-bin-laden-largely-discredited-among-muslim-publics-in-recent-years (accessed July 11, 2011).

17 See especially Chapter 11 of M. Gross, *Moral Dilemmas in Modern War.*

18 See especially section 1.3 of J. McMahan, *Killing In War.*

19 D. Luban, "The War on Terrorism and the End of Human Rights," in James White (ed.), *Contemporary Moral Problems: War and Terrorism*, 2nd edn,. Belmont, CA: Wadsworth, 2006, p. 55.

20 D. Luban, "The War on Terrorism," p. 60.

21 M. Walzer, *Just and Unjust Wars*, p. 197.

22 In JWT the principle of double effect has four criteria that must be met before noncombatant deaths can be morally justified: 1) The action contemplated must involve a legitimate military target, 2) the bad effect of the action (civilian casualties) must not be a direct means to the good effect of attacking the military target, 3) the bad effect of civilian casualties must be an unintended side-effect, and 4) the good effect must significantly outweigh the bad effect.

23 Examples of such actions include the 1968 massacre of Vietnamese civilians at My Lai, the ethnic cleansing campaigns of various military forces in the former Yugoslavia, and cases involving U.S. Marine killings of Iraqi civilians in Haditha in 2005 and Hamdaniya in 2007. Also, the strategic bombing campaigns of the Nazis and the Allies during World War II (insofar as they intentionally targeted civilians) were and continue to be considered *jus in bello* violations by some.

24 Examples of terrorist groups include the various al-Qaeda networks, Hezbollah and Hamas, the Basque group ETA, the Shining Path movement in Peru, to name but a few. See U. S. Department of State, "Foreign Terrorist Organizations" at: http://www.state.gov/j/ct/rls/other/des/123085.htm (accessed August 17, 2011) for a further listing as designated by the United States.

25 Examples of arguments along these lines include, M. Walzer, *Just and Unjust Wars*, Chapter 12, H. Khatchadourian, "The Morality of Terrorism," in James White (ed.), *Contemporary Moral Problems: War and Terrorism*, 2nd edn., Belmont, CA: Wadsworth, 2006, pp. 34–46, V. Held, *How Terrorism Is Wrong: Morality and Political Violence*, Oxford: Oxford University Press, 2008, T. Meisels, *The Trouble with Terror: Liberty, Security, and the Response to Terrorism* Cambridge: Cambridge University Press, 2008.

26 For example, the Taliban in Afghanistan fall into this category, and the same is undoubtedly true of some of the adversaries faced by Israel in Lebanon and the Gaza Strip, as well as the Chechen rebels fighting the Russians (despite the fact that their adversaries may label these groups as terrorists).

27 This tactic is recognized and warned against by counterinsurgency experts such as Kilcullen and the U.S. military's 2006 counterinsurgency manual.

28 For a complete copy of this declaration see Bin Laden's 1996 Fatwa at PBS Newshour. Online. Available at: http://www.pbs.org/newshour/terrorism/international/fatwa_1996.html (accessed July 27, 2011).

29 See the complete text of President Bush's address to Congress on September 12, 2001 at Encyclopedia Britannica, Document: George W. Bush: Declaration of War on Terrorism.

30 See Walzer's argument against "realism" in *Just and Unjust Wars*, pp. 4–13.

31 Examples include the trials against war criminals apprehended from the sectarian fighting in the former Yugoslavia and the work of various UN tribunals for Rwanda and Cambodia, among others.

32 First, it provides a relatively risk-free method for attacking and killing these individuals. Soldiers (likely special operations soldiers) would otherwise have to enter these areas and attempt to apprehend or kill the militants, a highly risky endeavor in a very dangerous region. Second, by not apprehending these fighters, it obviates the need to deal with the politically charged problem of detaining captive militants at Guantanamo Bay or elsewhere. This motivation may or may not be a morally compelling one as

noted by David Ignatius in his opinion piece, "Our Default is Killing Terrorists by Drone Attack. Do You Care?" in *The Washington Post*, December 2, 2010.

33 P. Bergen and K. Tiedemann, "Washington's Phantom War: The Effects of the U.S. Drone Program in Pakistan" in *Foreign Affairs*, July/August 2011, p. 13.

34 P. Bergen and K. Tiedemann, "Washington's Phantom War," pp. 17–18

35 M. Walzer, *Just and Unjust Wars* pp. 152–9. Labeling his revised principle of double effect the principle of double intention, he argued that it was not enough for soldiers not to intend noncombatant deaths, but they must take "due care" to minimize those deaths, even if it meant accepting some additional risk to themselves.

36 T. Pfaff, *Resolving Ethical Challenges in an Era of Persistent Conflict*, Carlisle, PA: U.S. Army War College Strategic Studies Institute, April 2011, p. 14.

37 For more on this paradigm shift, see Pfaff, *Resolving Ethical Challenges*, pp. 9–15. Pfaff contrasts the traditional Western model of war with the model made famous by the Chinese military theoretician, Sun-Tzu.

References

Bergen, P. and Tiedemann, K., "Washington's Phantom War: The Effects of the U.S. Drone Program in Pakistan," *Foreign Affairs*, 13, 2011.

Bin Laden, O., *Fatwa*, 1996. Online. Available: http://www.pbs.org/newshour/terrorism/international/fatwa_1996.html (accessed 20 September 2012).

Fiala, A., *The Just War Myth*, Lanham, MD: Rowman and Littlefield, 2008.

Gross, M., *Moral Dilemmas of Modern War: Torture, Assassination, and Blackmail in an Age of Asymmetric Combat*, Cambridge: Cambridge University Press, 2009.

Held, V., *How Terrorism Is Wrong: Morality and Political Violence*, Oxford: Oxford University Press, 2008.

Herold, M., "'Unworthy' Afghan Bodies: 'Smarter' U.S. Weapons Kill More Innocents," S. Rockel and R. Halpern (eds), in *Inventing Collateral Damage: Civilian Casualties, War, and Empire*, Toronto, Canada: Between the Lines, 2009, pp. 303–27.

Ignatius, D., "Our Default is Killing Terrorists by Drone Attack. Do You Care?" *Washington Post*, December 2, 2010.

Khatchadourian, H., "The Morality of Terrorism," in J. White (ed.) *Contemporary Moral Problems: War and Terrorism*, 2nd edn, Belmont, CA: Wadsworth, 2006, pp. 34–46.

Kilcullen, D., *Counterinsurgency*, Oxford: Oxford University Press, 2010.

Kutz, C., "Fearful Symmetry," in D. Rodin and H. Shue (eds), *Just and Unjust Warriors*, Oxford: Oxford University Press, 2008, pp. 69–88.

Luban, D., "The War on Terrorism and the End of Human Rights" J. White, in *Contemporary Moral Problems: War and Terrorism*, 2nd edn, Belmont, CA: Wadsworth, 2006, p. 55.

McMahan, J., *Killing in War*, Oxford: Oxford University Press, 2011.

Meisels, T., *The Trouble with Terror: Liberty, Security, and the Response to Terrorism*, Cambridge: Cambridge University Press, 2008.

Pfaff, T., *Resolving Ethical Challenges in an Era of Persistent Conflict*, Carlisle, PA: U.S. Army War College Strategic Studies Institute, 2011.

Pew Research Center, "Osama bin Laden Largely Discredited Among Muslim Publics in Recent Years," *Global Attitudes Project*, May 21, 2011. Online. Available at: http://pewglobal.org/2011/05/02/osama-bin-laden-largely-discredited-among-muslim-publics-in-recent-years (accessed 20 September 2012).

Rodin, D., "The Moral Inequality of Soldiers: Why *jus in bello* Asymmetry is Half Right," in D. Rodin and H. Shue (eds), *Just and Unjust Warriors*, Oxford: Oxford University Press, 2008, pp. 44–68.

Rockel, S. and Halpern, R. (eds), *Inventing Collateral Damage: Civilian Casualties, War, and Empire*, Toronto, Canada: Between the Lines, 2009.

Tse-Tung, M., "On the Reissue of the Three Main Rules For Discipline and the Eight Points For Attention, Instruction of the General Headquarters of the Chinese People's Liberation Army," in *Selected Works of Mao Tse-tung*, 3rd edn, Vol. 4, Peking: Foreign Languages Press, 1969, pp. 155–6.

U.S. Army and U.S. Marine Corps, *Counterinsurgency*, FM 3-24/MCWP, December 2006.

U.S. Department of State, "Foreign Terrorist Organizations." Online. Available at: http://www.state.gov/j/ct/rls/other/des/123085.htm (accessed 20 September 2012).

Walzer, M., *Just and Unjust Wars*, New York: Basic Books, 1977.

Zupan, D., "A Presumption of the Moral Equality of Combatants: A Citizen-Soldier's Perspective," in D. Rodin and H. Shue (eds), *Just and Unjust Warriors*, Oxford: Oxford University Press, 2008, pp. 214–25.

3

JUST WAR THEORY

Going to war and collective self-deception[1]

Richard Werner

The truth is, there is a growing body of work coming out of psychology and cognitive science that says you have no clue why you act the way you do, choose the things you choose, or think the thoughts you think. Instead, you create narratives, little stories to explain away why you gave up on that diet, why you prefer Apple to Microsoft, why you clearly remember it was Beth who told you the story about the clown with the peg leg made of soup cans when it was really Adam, and it wasn't a clown.[2]

1. Cognitive biases and heuristics

Each of us possesses a deep desire to be correct always and to be both moral and wise. Cognitive biases and heuristics aid and abet us in pursuit of these illusions.[3] Cognitive biases are predictable patterns of thought that lead us to draw incorrect conclusions. For instance, confirmation bias leads us to look for information that confirms our beliefs and ignore information that disconfirms our beliefs, the opposite of what creates successful science.[4] We consult news sources that confirm our politics and disregard news sources to the contrary. The political slant of the news sources one consults generally track one's politics. The reasons offered for consulting the source usually cite their accuracy, whether true or not, rather than that the slant confirms our bias.[5]

Heuristics are mental shortcuts we use to solve problems. While they may speed processing of the brain, they sometimes lead us to think so fast we make mistakes. Priming is an example. For instance, if we hold a warm drink in our hand, absorb the aromas of a bakery, or find change in a telephone booth we are more likely to do a kind act. Ask us why we did the kind act and we will invent a reason unaware of the actual cause of our action.[6]

In what follows we will use the findings of contemporary psychology to explain why we are prone to self-deception through cognitive biases and heuristics and especially prone when considering war.[7] There is no need for conspiracy theories or grand theories of history to explain why recent wars failed or proved illegitimate or why our leaders and populace engage in self-deception in attempts to justify war. Indeed, our collective self-deception about recent wars may lead us to pity both them and ourselves for the harm we cause through our collective self-deception.

Self-deception is a deeply engrained part of our nature as humans. I am no exception. It may not be curable but it can be ameliorated so our ignorance need not remain eternally invincible.

Self-deception moves easily from the individual to the group through in-group-out-group bias as we will see and especially given modern media technology. In-group-out-group bias causes us to identify with and excuse those with whom we identify while denigrating and distancing ourselves from those outside our group solely because of the irrelevancy of group membership.[8] Perhaps the best example is Jane Elliot's famous story of dividing her third grade class into two groups based on eye color the day after Martin Luther King was assassinated.[9] Elliot told the blue-eyed group they were superior to the brown-eyed group and gave the blue-eyed group greater power. While bonding among themselves, the blue-eyed began to ridicule and shun the brown-eyed. Then she reversed the story and the power. Soon the brown-eyed behaved just as the blue-eyed had done. The story has been replicated many times with different groups and markers.

In war, emotionalism and exceptionalism masquerade as patriotism encouraged by in-group-out-group bias. Because of self-deception we can expect to make the same mistakes in future wars that we made in past ones: destroying undeserving nations while knowingly and directly killing millions of noncombatants, including 100,000s of children. As such, it becomes clear why the burden of proof to warrant future wars should be very heavy: war is just too dangerous and self-deception is just too deep.

1.1 Memory and multiple selves

Memories often lie. Our memories are not episodic, not pictorial, and not like a video. Memory is not a representation of the past. Memories are fragmented, incomplete. When we recall we supplement with imagination and inference to construct present memory.

As the split brain experiments reveal, the self is multiple, composed of the many different modules of the brain. The brain functions like a committee with many voices. But the conscious brain does not hear the voices, hence the success of priming. The conscious brain is unaware that it is caused to reach decisions by the unconscious brain. The decision just seems to bubble up to the conscious brain that then, mistakenly, thinks it is solely responsible for the decision.[10]

Each of us tells a narrative about our past that creates the illusion of a single self. The narrative of the slow deliberative conscious brain creates the present self but the fast automatic unconscious brain motivates the narrative. That narrative helps us to construct our memories. The conscious brain rationalizes what the unconscious brain causes the conscious brain to decide, while the narrative created by the conscious brain helps to tame the unconscious brain.[11]

Recall that when priming succeeds we invent reasons that are irrelevant to explain what are actually the effects of priming. It is how advertising, political campaigns, and subliminal messages work. When we rationalize well we form tenable beliefs and desires that give us understanding. When we rationalize poorly we form untenable beliefs and desires that lead to self-deception and misunderstanding. We can tell the difference because some webs of belief and desire are unsuccessful. Some lead to death, destitution, or misery. Webs of belief and desire that work are to be preferred. Our beliefs and desires face the tribunal of experience not singly but as a corporate body, to paraphrase W.V.O Quine's "Two Dogmas of Empiricism," and they do so continually throughout a lifetime, changing as we and the environments we inhabit change.

We build our memories to fit our narrative and our narrative to fit our memories.[12] Hindsight bias tells us that we tend to edit our memories so that when we absorb what we just learned we assume we knew it all along. We quickly confabulate our past by reorganizing our web of belief and desire so that we can maintain our over-confidence about always being correct.[13] Our memories are so fallible that eyewitnesses to murder are too frequently mistaken to be taken at their word. Murder convictions based on eyewitness testimony are routinely overturned by DNA evidence. About 75 percent of capital cases overturned by DNA evidence were based on eyewitness testimony. Because of the fallibility of eyewitness testimony New Jersey recently put restrictions on such evidence in capital cases.[14]

We tend to remember the good and forget the bad. This may allow women to have another child, runners to run another marathon, and soldiers to fight another battle. Self-serving bias tells us that we excuse our failures and focus on our successes.[15] If we honestly assessed our faults and failures, we would be overcome by doubt and fear, unable to act. So we don't honestly assess. There is survival-value in our deceived memory. When we succeed it is because we are wonderful while when we fail it is the world that is to blame. Self-serving bias leads to the illusory superiority affect: each of us believes that we are superior to those around us in everything that matters.[16] Yet that is clearly false. In-group-out-group bias is the extension of superiority affect from self to group. We confabulate our memories to fit our narrative, exaggerating the positive while exenterating the negative, causing self-deceived over-confidence about our own and our group's superiority.

1.2 *Prediction*

Worse yet we are poor predictors of the future: our own future or the future of events generally.[17] The illusion of control tells us that we often believe we have control over outcomes that are either random or too complex to successfully predict.[18] 'Magical thinking' allows us to think we can control outcomes we cannot: for example, the superstitions of athletes or fans designed to control the outcome of the sporting event. The Dunning–Kruger Effect tells us that we are generally poor predictors of our competence and the difficulty of our tasks because we are over-confident.[19] While over-confidence occasionally aids us through the self-fulfilling prophecy and explains why confabulating our memories has survival value, it too often deludes us.

Notice how easily we forget to attend to our past mistaken predictions and to continue with overly confident ones. Weak memory works to enhance weak prediction. Our narrative redescribes our failures so that we either forget them or come to remember them as successes. We do this with the wars in Southeast Asia and we will soon do it with the wars in the Middle East. We too rarely learn from our mistakes because we do not remember them as mistakes. Hindsight bias helps us forget that our predictions failed and to maintain the self-deception that we predicted correctly.

The psychologist Philip Tetlock provides perhaps the most damning evidence of the reliability of even expert predictions.

> Beginning in the 1980s, Tetlock examined 27,451 forecasts by 284 academics, pundits and other prognosticators. The study was complex, but the conclusion can be summarized simply: the experts bombed. Not only were they worse than statistical models, they could barely eke out a tie with the proverbial dart-throwing chimps. The most generous conclusion Tetlock could draw was that some experts were less awful than others.[20]

1.3 *Over-confidence*

Let's put this together. We have bad memories. We are poor predictors. Both are fed by over-confidence. We tend to be overly optimistic about the tenability and correctness of our beliefs because we are so fraught with confirmation bias that we readily ignore available evidence that renders our cherished beliefs false.[21] Our fallibility is vast but not nearly as vast as our hubris when it comes to our need to be correct. The problem is that our faith in our cherished beliefs is nothing but a feeling like anger or fear. That feeling of certainty colors the strength of the belief but it does not improve the probability of its truth. Faith in our cherished beliefs is a psychological matter, not an epistemic virtue.

Consider the second invasion of Iraq. We believed strongly at the time of the attack that we had just cause. Iraq possessed weapons of mass destruction. Iraq was aiding and abetting Al Qaeda including the 9/11 attack. Iraq was in serious violation of international treaties regarding nuclear arms. Saddam Hussein was a very bad man. With the exception of the last of these, the rest proved false. We could have known better before the invasion if we were not so fraught by collective self-deception.[22] The invasion killed tens of thousands of children and over one hundred thousand civilians[23] for reasons that proved false. The war destroyed Iraq's economy and fragmented its civil society. Yet we ignore our mistakes.

Consider the invasion of Afghanistan. The travesty of 9/11 was a criminal act, not an act of war. Al Qaeda, a gang of criminals but not a nation-state, attacked the US. Afghanistan offered to try bin Laden before we attacked (*CNN U.S.* 2001). After we attacked, they offered bin Laden for trial in a neutral country (*ABC News* 2001). We destroyed Afghanistan's economy and civil society, killing countless children and noncombatants with no tenable cause.[24]

Yet at the time of the attack on Afghanistan, and later on Iraq, the vast majority of the U.S. nation, including its leaders, were convinced that the war was justified while those who dissented were considered at best cowards or at worst traitors. We were so over-confident of the justice of our cause in both Afghanistan and Iraq that we ignored the readily available evidence that rendered both wars unjustified albeit for different reasons.[25] We looked for reasons to wage war and we found them by ignoring the better reasons to refrain from war. In short, we committed confirmation bias. We believed what made us feel good while ignoring what the evidence supported. We practiced motivated reasoning. False memory, poor prediction, and over-confidence become a lethal combination when assessing the risk of war.

Accurate recall interferes with our over-confidence, our moral righteousness, and our need to feel correct about everything. To recall would be to admit our hypocrisy, fallibility, and self-deception even when we were certain. As Mark Twain wrote, "It's not what you don't know that kills you, it's what you know for sure that ain't true."

Nor is this an isolated example. Much the same analysis can be offered about the war in Vietnam. Our initial reason for attack, the Gulf of Tonkin incident, was manufactured and then marketed to the populace.[26] We were duped by metaphors like 'communism is a cancer' and 'nations are dominoes'. We killed noncombatants not only as collateral damage but also intentionally as a means to end the war sooner. We dropped more bombs in the Quang Tri province alone than in the whole of Europe in WWII.[27] We dropped more tonnage on Cambodia than we did in all of WWII, including the two atomic bombs. Our attack on Cambodia created Pol Pot's killing fields that left over a million dead.[28] Revisionist historians and hindsight bias help us to recall that we had just cause and that we fought a just war in Southeast Asia. Such biases may even help us remember that we won when we did not.

Presently we contemplate an attack on Iran or North Korea because of their pursuit of WMDs, an attack on Syria because of human rights violations, and an attack on Pakistan because they harbor Al Qaeda. We understand that we kill innocent people such as children when we kill with drones. We are undeterred by the fact that we mistakenly attacked other nations and killed countless numbers of children because we held false beliefs not unlike those we presently hold or had irrational fears not unlike those we presently have. We believe now as then that we have warrant for our planned aggression. The attack then and now feels like self-defense because of our biases that cause self-deception. Our fallible memories and bad predictions live comfortably with our over-confidence.

2. Collective self-deception

When we move from the self-deception of individuals to that of the collective nation-state, do we commit the fallacy of composition? The fallacy of simply assuming that what is true of the parts must be true of the whole, that what is true of the individuals must be true of the nation? Recall the in-group-out-group bias. We define ourselves in terms of the groups with which we identify. We define our in-group by the creation of out-groups. We are quick to denigrate those in the out-group to identify and protect the in-group. Consider any sports rivalry. The inhabitants of some geographic area identify with their team just as the inhabitants of another identify with theirs. Citizens identify with their national team during the Olympics and derive pleasure from their team's successes and disappointment from their failures. Folks engage in serious argument about the excellence of their team and the failings of their rival ignoring the arbitrary nature of their in-group-out-group bias. Sometimes the arguments turn to violence and even to death.

The in-group-out-group bias has its way in forming our sense of nationalism in the Olympics and one can easily see how that transfers to war. Indeed, the ancient Greek Olympics were founded to lessen the frequency of Greek city-state wars and the modern Olympics were formed for similar reasons. While the bias may have had survival value on the Savannah where our instincts formed, it may no longer in the ancient world of Greek city-states let alone a globalized world of technological warfare.

Recent work examines the basis in the brain's circuitry for in-group-out-group processing. One recent study showed that the effect of in-group identification becomes even more intense when people feel mortally threatened.[29] We turn to those in our in-group when we feel that we are at risk of harm from the other. We detest and vilify those who we believe threaten us. We do this individually and collectively. Now consider war. It is essential to vilify the enemy and, if possible, dehumanize them thereby making it easier to fight and kill them. Moreover, the threat we feel the other poses to our mortality helps us bond and support one another in the fight.

The famous Milgram experiments on obedience to authority and the Stanford Prison experiment show respectively how susceptible we are to authority and how power corrupts. Both reveal how easy it is to exploit our willingness to do pointless violence to others under authority or because we are the authority. When we combine these two with the previous points about in-group-out-group bias we have a ready-made formula to explain why self-deception at the individual level helps us understand and extend our analysis of self-deception to the collective.

Recall how masterfully Hitler turned the Jews and Gypsies, the gays and lesbians, the communists and anarchists of Europe into scapegoats. They became the out-groups the Nazis claimed mortally threatened European Aryans, the rightful bearers of civilization. These out-groups became the foci of Nazi rage and hatred, promoting them to a sense of bonding around all things Aryan and with that to death and destruction of the out-groups. Recall how successful the US was at promoting racial hatred during the genocide of Native Americans, the apartheid of African-Americans, or against the Japanese in WWII, and how these aided bonding among the in-group and killing the out-group. Recall the recent wave of hatred of all things Arab and Muslim that swept the west after 9/11 and helped stoke American exceptionalism and war. Finally, recall the previously mentioned forgotten false reasons for going to war with Iraq and Afghanistan and the collective fear, hatred, and self-deception that motivated these false reasons.

We could have known better in both cases but the in-group-out-group bias helped propel us collectively into self-deception and unjust war.

Let us summarize. Cognitive biases and heuristics cause weak memories, poor predictions, deceptive over-confidence, and bias for our group and against others. At both the individual and the collective level they explain our individual and collective self-deception when we go to war. We will now turn our focus to just war theory (JWT) and the morality of war using our understanding of self-deception as background.

3. The morality of war

It is a striking fact that almost every category of self-deception we have described in this book is conducive to aggressive wars. Modern war is conducted against an out-group by powerful people who have an exaggerated opinion of themselves and their degree of morality, are overconfident, often have an illusion of control, enjoy taking risks, and are almost always male.[30]

By "modern war" I mean a technological war that involves killing numerous noncombatants including children. History shows that prior to WWI far more combatants than noncombatants died during war. Since WWII that trend is strongly reversed. The cause of the reversal is largely technological: the power and imprecision of technological warfare compared to hand-to-hand combat.

3.1 Trolley problems and war

Aren't we justified in knowingly killing some people to save a greater number from death? Doesn't that justify war when it is reasonable to believe that more lives will be saved by waging war? Trolley problem (TP) examples seem to support the conclusion. Simply imagine a TP version where one must throw a switch to divert the trolley from killing one thousand children on track A onto track B where it will kill only one child. That is the beauty of TPs. There are no epistemic problems. There is no ambiguity about consequences or ethical responsibility. Everything is straightforward. In other words, TPs are not like real life and clearly not like war, where events rarely go as planned because epistemic problems abound about the probability and the value of the consequences of action. Consider that in our wars since WWII, far more civilians were killed than anticipated. Biases impacting prediction, our over-confidence based in part on weak memory, and limits of expertise play major roles in undermining the accuracy of assessing proportionality and the likelihood of success, key criteria of JWT as well as consequentialist reasoning. We overcome our ignorance with over-confidence about both our knowledge and the justice of our cause.[31]

Recall the previous discussion of recent wars. Consider that when we attacked Vietnam and Iraq the second time, we expected these wars to be short and sweet. However, each of these wars lasted longer than any previous US war. They jointly killed over a million civilians including countless children. Vietnam led to wars in Laos and Cambodia that killed a million more civilians, mostly children.[32]

We have yet to see what the full scale of the unintended consequences of the Middle East wars will yield, but it is difficult to think that they will be optimific given the terrible state in which we leave these nations. Children are the most vulnerable during modern war, and deserve special attention. Recall that the Iraq War began in 1990 and was followed by years of devastating economic sanctions against Iraq that predated the second invasion and killed countless children. Recall that consequentialism tells us to count all of the consequences of an action when making our assessment. Recall that the most plausible versions of consequentialism tell us to act on rules general observance of which will have the best consequences. Indeed, if history is our guide, and TPs our model, then the track with the greater number of children on it, not the lesser, represents the more likely outcome when we choose to wage modern war. That is the lesson of recent war. Consequentialism comports with the notion that modern war is strongly presumptively wrong.[33] However, our individual and collective biases, particularly confirmation bias and over-confidence, limit our capacity to effectively predict these negative consequences in advance.

These issues about prediction and consequentialism are debatable. Some will argue that most recent wars were successful. They will point to different consequences or assess the stated consequences differently or conceptually carve wars differently. My actual point is that consequentialism is too pliable to be a successful guide to action,[34] a point explained in part by our vulnerability to biases and heuristics.

3.2 Consequentialism

Unlike JWT, consequentialism is a monist rather than a pluralist legalism. That is, consequentialism has a single basic principle: act solely to produce the best consequences. Given that there are not multiple principles to conflict, as there are in JWT, perhaps consequentialism is less vulnerable to such biases in practice than JWT. Consider the consequences of past wars or predictions of the consequences of future wars. The values we assign to the consequences of either past or future wars are arguable. The probabilities for consequences of past and future wars are arguable. The consequences themselves are arguable. What constitutes the particular war conceptually is arguable. The facts and concepts are arguable. What this reveals is that consequentialist moral theories can be used to justify just about any war before or after the fact simply by assigning concepts, consequences, probabilities, and their values—and by framing the issues and controlling the narrative.[35] Consequentialism is too pliable, too open to multiple interpretations to be a successful guide to action. Couple this pliability with our recognition of the capacity for self-deception, and it is a dangerous moral theory for assessing war.

3.3 Just war theory

JWT offers no decision procedure to determine which rule trumps in cases of conflict of its plurality of rules. The choice is left to reason, which is to say the slow rational conscious brain. Recall that the slow, rational conscious brain rationalizes what the fast, nonrational unconscious brain causes the conscious brain to decide. Consider how we have deceived ourselves with JWT into thinking we have justification in our recent wars when there was none. We unconsciously begin with the conclusion we intend to establish, that is to say we engage in motivated reasoning. Rationally, we play the various rules of JWT against one another to remove cognitive dissonance and provide a narrative consistent with what the unconscious causes the conscious brain to decide—that is, the one that feels best to us rather than the one suggested by reason alone. It is uncontroversial to state that just war theorists frequently disagree. Their disagreement is evidence for this claim. National leaders can then enlist the advice of the just war theorist who tells him what he wants to hear in accord with confirmation bias.

JWT contains two parts. One set of rules to assess the morality of engaging in war, *jus ad bellum*, and a second set governing the morality of waging war, *jus in bello*. Each contains a principle of proportionality that informs us that both the engaging and the waging of the war must be proportionate to our ends. These principles of proportionality in essence are consequentialist principles, allowing consequentialist reasoning to trump the other principles of JWT. This is especially so whenever we fear that the threat of not initiating war or the cost of losing the war is too great, which is to say most of the time when we wage war. Collectively, the cognitive biases and heuristics aid us to overpredict the cost of failure to attack as well as the high cost of losing the war. As we have seen with the in-group-out-group bias increases when we fear dire consequences for the in-group. National leaders help us stoke the fear of the other. It is easy to deceive ourselves with JWT by trumping with proportionality if all else fails.

When we engage JWT we are often caught in the emotionality of war and so we frame the war in terms like American exceptionalism. Recall the false fear of both WMDs and Al Qaeda that motivated our second invasion of Iraq. Or our similar false fears of the spreading cancer of communism that lead us into Southeast Asia. We lost those wars in Southeast Asia, yet less than 20 years later the Soviet Union peacefully dissolved. Our fears and exceptionalism help us dupe ourselves with JWT.

JWT allows the foreseeable but non-intentional killing of innocent civilians, so-called collateral deaths. Like many others, I do not understand how one can knowingly and directly cause the terrible deaths of thousands of children and deny both the intention to kill them and any responsibility for their deaths. I suggest that in-group-out-group bias conjoined with confirmation bias and motivated reasoning help us accept the distinction between intentional and foreseeable killing of innocents. JWT's principle of double effect sanctions knowingly and directly killing innocents, children for example. So by my lights JWT does allow the violation of persons' innocent status. Some argue that those who build highways know that people will be killed and these deaths are not morally different from collateral deaths in war. But in war one is the proximate cause of death. In the highway example one is perhaps the mediated cause, removed from the proximate cause. Others choose to drive on the highway thereby accepting the risks of death. So there is a morally relevant difference between the collateral deaths of war and those from building highways. Those who build highways don't kill those who die in highway accidents although they know that some will die in highway accidents. Those who wage war knowingly and directly kill the innocent. The former are the mediated cause of death while the later are the proximate cause of death.[36]

James Sterba and Andrew Fiala both argue that JWT strictly interpreted comports with conditional pacifism when applied to modern war.[37] Both offer many recent historical examples to support their case.[38] Yet one can find just war theorists to justify almost any war in which we have engaged. This is not surprising given our analysis that cognitive biases drive the pliability of JWT reasoning.

So while Sterba and Fiala are correct in their assessment that JWT strictly interpreted entails conditional pacifism, we have a long tradition of loose interpretation and moral casuistry with respect to JWT that makes JWT even more pliable. Taking cognitive biases seriously, we see that the traditions of loose interpretation of JWT give the desired conclusion and reason does not. Again, this is especially so during the emotionally charged times when we contemplate war. Given interpretive variability, JWT can provide a carte blanche for leaders of nations who want to start war. As Sterba and Fiala reveal, recent history teaches that much. Coupling cognitive biases with self-deceived or even unscrupulous leaders, which is to say all leaders, and their citizens, allows JWT to become a dangerous moral theory.

Consequentialism and JWT both suffer from and encourage self-deception, and thereby allow us to reach almost any conclusion we like on the morality of wars: past, present, or future. Both are a carte blanche for nations to wage wars. Both are dangerous moral theories to assess war since national leaders use both to justify any war they want. Recent history teaches as much.

3.4 *The irrationality of interventionist war*

Consider that we can no longer win the wars we are likely to fight. We can be defeated by a nonindustrialized nation of insurgents: Korea, Vietnam, Laos, Cambodia, Iraq, and Afghanistan. Our military advantage is technological. We can reduce any nation to rubble. While we can likely win a war with any of the industrialized nations, we are unlikely to go to war with them. The nations we are likely to attack know that if they are willing to suffer the punishment we will inflict technologically that they may defeat us in a long-fought asymmetric war of insurgency.

The national and global economic burdens of war are immense. Noble Prize economist Joseph Stiglitz estimates that the Iraq War will cost over $3 trillion.[39] Estimates place the combined total for Iraq and Afghanistan at $3.7 trillion and counting.[40] In adjusted dollars that is approximately the cost of WWII. The national debt is above $15 trillion and mounting for the foreseeable future. We confront serious economic stagnation and chronic high unemployment. The national infrastructure declines. Public education fails. The lack of adequate national health care is an epidemic. Climate change promises serious problems. It is the opportunity costs of war that hasten our decline.

4. Beyond just war theories: a better way

So does challenge to JWT posed by cognitive biases leave us with a potentially untenable situation of passivism? I think not, I find the ethics of modern warfare simple. It is strongly presumptively wrong knowingly and directly to kill children who present no imminent threat.[41] Call this the Principle of Innocence (PI). PI is as well understood as any belief can be. PI stands fast. It wears its warrant on its face. We cannot warrant the better known by means of the lesser known. Any reason offered for PI will be less well known than PI itself.[42] Its clarity should render PI less vulnerable to the described biases than the complex pluralism of JWT or the vague monism of consequentialism.

We understand going into modern war that we kill numerous children, kill them in a terrible manner. Given PI we should understand that modern war is strongly presumptively wrong because modern war involves knowingly and directly killing innocent children who present no imminent threat. Unlike JWT, PI is clear about the presumptive immorality of modern war. While the strong presumption against modern war may be overridden, that presumption presents a weighty burden. One instance where PI may comport with war is if one's national territory is invaded and one's besieged nation fights only to repel the invaders while refraining from acts of violence against the invader's noncombatants. PI allows defensive war as defensive war was understood before technology changed the face of war and society, stretching the notion of a just war beyond reasonable recognition. It remains an open question whether violent or nonviolent direct action of the sort the Danes used so successfully against the Nazis would be the best option for national defense.[43] This comports with the intuitions that inform existing JWT, as a self-defensive position is commonly held to be one of the strongest justifications for going to war.

We can no longer expect to win the wars that we are likely to fight and we cannot afford them. Our history evidences that we continually fight aggressive wars killing millions of innocent people, weakening our economy, fragmenting our civil society, and losing international confidence in our nation. We have no credible enemies near our borders. Anyone who attempts to mount a naval attack can be stopped long before they reach us. We remain vulnerable to air attack no matter what we do as 9/11 revealed. We can continue to do our best to subvert terrorist attack to our homeland. We no longer need to grow the military to defend ourselves successfully. Our false belief in the right to intervene in the affairs of others stokes our false belief in the need to grow the military to defend ourselves. The constant preparation for and waging of aggressive, interventionist war is irrational, based in our collective self-deception. It is time we pursue positive peace through a foreign policy of military noninterventionism. It is time we come home.

Unlike JWT, PI does not present us with options for modern preemptive or preventive wars or modern wars of so-called humanitarian intervention which through collective self-deception too frequently masquerade as wars of aggression and usually end badly. Simply consider Vietnam, Laos, Cambodia, Afghanistan, and Iraq or the Falklands, Bosnia, and Libya. Honesty and simplicity recommend we replace JWT with PI and accept that modern war is waged against civilians and especially against children and is, thereby, strongly presumptively wrong.

To say that modern warfare is strongly presumptively wrong is to say that the burden of proof is on those who would wage war rather than on those who oppose war. This reverses the traditional order in our society. It is to say that the burden of proof is a heavy burden. It involves showing why this war is different from all previous modern wars: why it won't involve the terrible deaths of countless children, why it can be expected to be better than any other available alternative, and why it is truly the last alternative. Given recent history, it is unlikely that all of these standards can be met, especially before the war begins. PI does not have the tradition of self-deceived casuistry that undermines JWT and makes it a dangerous moral theory. Moreover, collective international decision-making helps to defeat the proclivity for self-deception just as it does in science. In addition to PI, requiring a representative international association to approve war would help diminish unjust war.

5. Conclusion

Those who understand me correctly understand that the argument for military noninterventionism rests not only on PI but that it comports with political realism, consequentialism, and JWT. Political realism is consequentialism relativized to the national interest. If we frame the issue of war from the perspective of PI, then our collective self-deception is less likely to lead us to pursue aggressive war and hasten our decline. The four perspectives dovetail when we lead with PI because of the pliability of JWT, consequentialism, and realism.

I am also aware of the dangers of my own self-deception. I recommend noninterventionism as the safest position given our proclivity for collective self-deception with respect to waging terrible wars. First, do no harm. History teaches that recent wars are largely failures and that future ones will also fail. Care and safety recommend PI and noninterventionism given our history of collective self-deception and aggressive war.

Military noninterventionism is not isolationism. We are engaged in a global economy from which we cannot easily extricate ourselves. We can influence the behavior of other states in a variety of ways short of war. But in our attempts we should be mindful of how our collective self-deception will attempt to blind us both to the need in our globalized world for a just international order and to the nature of that order.

My hope is that we may understand that human nature is so prone to self-deception that we move to overcome our collective ignorance with respect to war and realize the dangers of both JWT and consequentialisms. PI is a means to that end. PI allows us rightly to defend ourselves from attack yet avoid misguided future wars that will hasten our decline. I suggest that the best means to that end is a noninterventionist foreign policy.

Notes

1 I thank Adam Henschke for invaluable advice, insight, and editorial help on the chapter. I thank Beril Esen for making me aware of the in-group-out-group bias for understanding collective self-deception in war. Mistakes remain mine.

2 D. McRaney, *You Are Not So Smart*, New York: Gotham, 2011. Kindle edition.

3 *Ibid.*

4 *Ibid.*

5 *Ibid.*

6 K. Appiah, *Experiments in Ethics*, Cambridge: Harvard, 2010.

7 R. Trivers, *The Folly of Fools*, New York: Basic Books, 2011. Kindle edition.

8 M. Sherif, O. J. Harvey, B. J. White, W. R. Hood and C. W. Sherif, *Intergroup Conflict and Cooperation: The Robbers Cave Experiment*, Norman, OK: University Book Exchange, 1961.

9 S. Whitbourne, "In-Groups, Out-Groups, and the Psychology of Crowds," *Psychology Today*, Online. Available at: http://www.psychologytoday.com/blog/fulfillment-any-age/201012/in-groups-out-groups-and-the-psychology-crowds (accessed 28 September, 2012).

10 M. Gazzaniga, *Who's In Charge?*, New York: Ecco, 2011; D. Eagleman, *Incognito*, New York: Vintage, 2011; D. Kahneman, *Thinking, Fast and Slow*, New York: Farrar, Straus and Giroux, 2011.

11 *Ibid.*

12 *Ibid.*

13 D. McRaney, *You Are Not So Smart*.

14 L. Beil, "The Certainty of Memory Has Its Day in Court," *New York Times*, New York, November 29, 2011, D1.

15 D. McRaney, *You Are Not So Smart*.

16 *Ibid.*

17 N. Taleb, 2007 *The Black Swan*, New York: Random House, 2007.

18 D. McRaney, *You Are Not So Smart*.

19 *Ibid.*

20 K. Schulz, "Why Experts Get the Future Wrong," *New York Times Sunday Book Review*, March 27, 2011, BR14. Online. Available at: http://www.nytimes.com/2011/03/27/books/review/book-review-future-babble-by-dan-gardner.html?pagewanted=all (accessed March 28, 2013).

21 R. Trivers, *The Folly of Fools*.

22 H. Blix, *Disarming Iraq*, New York: Pantheon, 2004.

23 D. Cutler, D., 2011 "US and Civilian Deaths in Iraq," *Reuters*. Online. Available at: http://in.reuters.com/article/2011/12/18/iraq-withdrawal-toll-idINDEE7BH04T20111218 (accessed 25 June, 2012).

24 J. Sterba, "The Rationale of U.S. War-Making Foreign Policy," *The Acorn* 14:2, 2011–12, pp. 15–23.

25 A. Fiala, *The Just War Myth*, Latham: Rowman & Littlefield, 2007; J. Sterba, *Justice for Here and Now*, Cambridge: Cambridge University Press, 1998.

26 D. C. Hallin, *The Uncensored War: The Media and Vietnam*, New York: Oxford University Press, 1986.

27 A. Edmonds, *The War in Vietnam*, Westport: Greenwood, 1998.

28 R. Trivers, *The Folly of Fools*.

29 E. A. Henry, B. D. Bartholow and J. Arndt, "Death on the Brain," *Social Cognitive and Affective Neuroscience* 5:1, 2010, pp. 77–87.

30 R. Trivers, *The Folly of Fools*.

31 *Ibid.*

32 *Ibid.*

33 D. Lackey, *The Ethics of War and Peace*, Englewood Cliffs, NJ: Prentice-Hall, 1989.

34 R. Werner, "Nuclear Deterrence and the Limits of Moral Theory," *The Monist*, 77:3, 1987, pp. 357–376.

35 *Ibid.*

36 R. Holmes, *Basic Moral Philosophy*, 4th edn, Belmont: Wadsworth, 2006.

37 A. Fiala, *The Just War Myth*; J. Sterba, *Justice for Here and Now*.

38 J. Sterba, "The Rationale of U.S. War-Making Foreign Policy".

39 J. Stiglitz and L. Bilmes, *The Three Trillion Dollar War*, New York: Norton, 2008.

40 D. Trotta, "The Cost of War: At Least $3.7 Trillion and Counting," *Reuters*, June 29 2011. Online. Available at: http://www.reuters.com/article/2011/06/29/us-usa-war-idUSTRE75S25320110629 (accessed 1 July, 2012).

41 R. Werner, "Pragmatism for Pacifists," *Contemporary Pragmatism* 4:2, 2007, pp. 93–115.
42 J. Murphy, "The Killing of the Innocent," *The Monist*, 57:4, 1973, 527–536.
43 R. Holmes, *On War and Morality*, Princeton, NJ: Princeton, 1989; P. Ackerman, P. and J. DuVall, *A Force More Powerful: A Century of Non-violent Conflict*, New York: Palgrave, 2001.

References

Ackerman, P. and J. DuVall, *A Force More Powerful*, New York: Palgrave, 2001.

Appiah, K. *Experiments in Ethics*, Cambridge: Harvard, 2010.

Beil, L. "The Certainty of Memory Has Its Day in Court", *New York Times*, Nov 29, 2011, D1.

Blix, H. *Disarming Iraq*, New York: Pantheon, 2004.

Cutler, D. "US and Civilian Deaths in Iraq," *Reuters*, Online. Available at: http://in.reuters.com/article/2011/12/18/iraq-withdrawal-toll-idINDEE7BH04T20111218 (accessed 25 June, 2012).

Eagleman, D. *Incognito*, New York: Vintage, 2011.

Edmonds, A. *The War in Vietnam*, Westport: Greenwood, 1998.

Fiala, A. *The Just War Myth*, Latham: Rowman & Littlefield, 2007.

Gazzaniga, M. *Who's In Charge?* New York: Ecco, 2011.

Hallin, D. *The Uncensored War*, New York: Oxford University Press, 1986.

Henry, E. A., B. D. Bartholow, and J. Arndt, "Death on the Brain," *Social Cognitive and Affective Neuroscience* 5:1, 2010, pp. 77–87.

Holmes, R. *Basic Moral Philosophy*, 4th edn, Belmont: Wadsworth, 2006.

——*On War and Morality*, Princeton, NJ: Princeton, 1989.

Kahneman, D. *Thinking, Fast and Slow*, New York: Farrar, Straus and Giroux, 2011.

Lackey, D. *The Ethics of War and Peace*, Englewood Cliffs, NJ: Prentice-Hall, 1989.

McRaney, D. *You Are Not So Smart*, New York: Gotham, 2011. Kindle edition.

Murphy, J. "The Killing of the Innocent," *The Monist*, 57:4, 1973, pp. 527–536.

Schulz, K. "Why Experts Get the Future Wrong," *New York Times Sunday Book Review*, March 27, 2011, BR14.

Sherif, M. *Intergroup Conflict and Cooperation: The Robbers Cave Experiment*, Norman, OK: University Book Exchange, 1961.

Sterba, J. "The Rationale of U.S. War-Making Foreign Policy", *The Acorn* 14:2, 2011–12, pp. 15–23.

——*Justice for Here and Now*, Cambridge: Cambridge University Press, 1998.

Stiglitz J. and L. Bilmes, *The Three Billion Dollar War*, New York: Norton, 2008.

Taleb, N. *The Black Swan*, New York: Random House, 2007.

Trivers, R. *The Folly of Fools*, New York: Basic Books, 2011. Kindle edition.

Trotta, D. "The Cost of War," *Reuters*. Online. Available at: http://www.reuters.com/article/2011/06/29/us-usa-war-idUSTRE75S25320110629 (accessed 1 July, 2012).

Whitbourne, S. "In-Groups, Out-Groups, and the Psychology of Crowds," *Psychology Today*. Online. Available at: http://www.psychologytoday.com/blog/fulfillment-any-age/201012/in-groups-out-groups-and-the-psychology-crowds (accessed 28 September, 2012).

Werner, R. "Pragmatism for Pacifists," *Contemporary Pragmatism* 4:2, 2007, pp. 93–115.

——"Nuclear Deterrence and the Limits of Moral Theory," *The Monist*, 77:3, 1987, pp. 357–376.

Jus in bello

4

The moral foundations of the *jus ad bellum/jus in bello* distinction

Steve Viner

1. Introduction

In this chapter, I examine a recent challenge to Just War Theory that concerns the commonly accepted moral separateness between the moral rules applicable to going to war, i.e. *jus ad bellum*, and the moral rules pertaining to how one should fight a war, i.e. *jus in bello*. More specifically, I inquire into why some contemporary Just War Theorists reject this moral separateness between these two sets of rules and a specific rule of war supported by this separateness often referred to as "the moral equality of soldiers."[1]

This chapter has three main sections. In Section 2, I explicate this recent criticism. In Section 3, I explain why two influential Just War Theorists, Hugo Grotius and Michael Walzer, accept this separateness and moral equality.[2] In Section 4, using insights from Section 3, I contend that the criticism fails to appreciate fully the collective moral perspective of war. This collective perspective is important for understanding some moral rules of war as not merely primary rules of justice like a right of self-defense. Rather, some, like this separateness and equality, aim at peace in addition to justice, and they can be viewed as being similar to a mixture of the primary and secondary rules of a legal system. They protect rights and aim at peace by helping to secure some fidelity to the rules of war and by helping to maintain war as a separate rule-governed activity with its own moral norms.

2. Rejecting the moral separateness and the moral equality of combatants

It is widely accepted that there is a separateness in the moral rules of war. There are moral rules regarding when a state may begin engaging in war, i.e. *jus ad bellum*, and moral rules applicable to the fighting of the war, i.e. *jus in bello*. Curiously, however, these rules, morally speaking, are considered unconnected. In other words, one does not utilize the determinations at the *jus ad bellum* level to devise the rules for how one is to fight, i.e. *jus in bello*.[3] Also, combatants on the just side are not subject to a different set of moral rules or given any advantage over the combatants on the unjust side.[4] In addition, it is generally agreed that a state could be engaged in an unjust, aggressive war, yet its combatants could fight justly, if they fight in accordance with the rules applicable to fighting. It is as if this common view clearly exempts combatants, i.e. those who kill in war, from important basic moral judgments related to the reason why they kill in the first place.

At first glance, this separateness and equality is perplexing due to its lack of concern for individual agency, rights and duties. In our lives outside of war, the fact that someone is about to kill you is not usually considered by itself enough information to conclude that you could justifiably kill that other person. More is needed. If she was a police officer and you were a bank robber attempting to kill someone while robbing a bank, the fact that she was about to kill you would not exculpate you from killing her, much less justify your killing her. At its worst, this separateness seems to say to combatants, "It does not morally matter why you are fighting or whether you kill those with a just cause. As long as you abide by these other moral rules when you kill, you act justly." At its best, it appears to say, "It would be too demanding to expect you to act differently or know if your state has a just cause and is engaged in a just war, so we can't hold you morally responsible for killing in war. If it turns out that you kill combatants with a just cause, any injustice related to their deaths will be attributed to your state not you." Both of these responses are troubling for they lessen the moral agency of combatants. Further, with this equality, combatants on the just side no longer possess a right not to be killed, a right that all others engaging in just actions possess.[5] Arguably then, this moral separateness and equality do not hold combatants, i.e. those who kill in war, responsible enough nor treat them as full moral agents.[6]

Not surprisingly, this separateness and equality has been rejected by recent criticism based on individual rights.[7] More specifically, the criticism borrows from, and relies heavily on, an individual right of self-defense, a right having deontological foundations. In his book, *Killing in War*, Jeff McMahan, a leading proponent of the criticism who I rely heavily on to articulate the criticism, clearly makes this link between an individual right of self-defense and the criticism. He states, "Thus, for example, killing in self-defense is justified not when killing the attacker would be the lesser evil than allowing the potential victim to be killed, but when the attacker has acted in such a way that makes him morally liable to defensive violence. The strategy of argument – the methodology – in this book is to extend this form of justification from these areas in which it is familiar and well understood to the context of war."[8]

The criticism can be seen as having the following two core premises:

1   Deadly force can only be used against persons who do something, or have done something, that makes them liable to such force, and
2   Being a member of a group, including a state, does not by itself exempt one from the first premise.

There are three aspects here to be highlighted. The first is that, as McMahan claims, the term "liable" in premise 1 functions as it would in a justified instance of individual self-defense. In self-defense, generally, what makes someone liable to have force used against them is that they are attempting to harm someone else who is innocent in all relevant respects. In keeping with this self-defense model for purposes of discerning liability, supporters of the criticism do not interpret "liability" in consequentialist or Utilitarian terms. In other words, for them, one is not liable to harm simply because such harm would bring about the best state of affairs or more happiness, or a swift end to the war. Rather, persons not liable to be killed are off-limits, and persons who have not done something (or have not failed to do something) that would make them morally responsible for a current or past wrong, e.g. attempting to harm an innocent person, are not liable to deadly force. The criticism can thus be seen as an absolutist position, for its prohibition on killing those not liable to deadly force.

The second aspect is the highly individualistic and interpersonal nature of this criticism, along with the epistemic demands and fine grain distinctions that come with its interpersonal nature.[9] According to premise 2, one is not exempt from moral responsibility because one belongs to a group or state. Rather, to be justified in killing other persons, one is required to look at the person (and their actions) who one is attempting to kill to determine whether that person is liable to be killed. To be justified in killing, one must do enough and what she can do to find out if the person who she is about to kill is liable to be killed.

On this view, would voluntarily wearing the uniform of the unjust side be enough to make one liable to be killed? It is not clear, probably not. Suppose that a person wearing the uniform on the unjust side were a lawyer whose main job was to prosecute members of her own military for committing sexual assaults. Clearly, there are persons who wear the uniform on the unjust side who prohibit or impede injustices by their fellow combatants and those acts could make them not liable to harm.[10] To be sure, there are enough such real examples that combatants attempting to abide by the right(s) articulated in the premises above would have a difficult time knowing if they are about to kill someone liable to be killed. If liability to be killed is judged on an individual rather than a group basis, descriptions of killings in war for moral analysis become specific or unique. Removing the collective description that functions as a moral permission to kill people within the collective makes each case of two or more persons fighting subject to a moral analysis that has specific causal chains and intentions.

It is also the interpersonal nature of the criticism that leads to its rejection of the moral separateness of the *jus ad bellum/jus in bello* distinction. On the common view, fighting on behalf of a state exempts combatants from moral responsibility when they kill each other. According to the criticism, however, rather than relieve responsibility, fighting on behalf of a state is merely evidence that is often necessary to determine whether a killing is justified. The determination of what side a combatant is on is often important for understanding and describing what a combatant is doing when she acts. According to the criticism, it seems, initially, most combatants on the unjust side are like the hit men for the mafia, and combatants on the just side are like the police trying to stop them. The criticism demands that *jus ad bellum* determinations penetrate *jus in bello* judgments because *jus ad bellum* determinations are needed for an accurate description of what a combatant is doing, a description necessary for determining whether she is engaged in committing an act that makes her liable to be killed.

The final aspect is how the criticism changes the common view of what a war is, i.e. how we understand it, the primary objectives and the primary players. On the common view, war is a rule-governed activity with three major players: states, combatants, and noncombatants (or "the innocent"). Also, one of the most important rules, if not *the* most important, is that combatants may target each other but not noncombatants (or "the innocent").[11] The criticism, however, presents us with two major players: those liable to be killed and those not liable to be killed. Because rejecting the moral separateness also rejects the moral equality between combatants, it does away with the combatant/noncombatant distinction for purposes of the rule that combatants must not target noncombatants. Also, because of its interpersonal nature, this view greatly decreases the significance of the state as a major player. Instead, it presents a picture of war in which some persons are doing, or have done, something wrong that makes them liable to be killed and other persons are victims or are trying to stop them. The state on this view is not so much a major player as a mere delineator of rights to be consulted to discover if a harm has occurred that makes one liable to be killed. As Michael Walzer states, "without an equal right to kill, war as a rule-governed activity would disappear and be replaced by crime and punishment, by evil conspiracies and military law enforcement."[12]

3. Support for the moral separateness and the moral equality of combatants

In the parts below, I offer two positions that, contrary to the view above, support the moral separateness associated with the *jus ad bellum/jus in bello* distinction and the moral equality of combatants. First, I examine Hugo Grotius's natural law view that pursues peace in addition to justice. Then, I set forth why Michael Walzer accepts this separateness and equality.

3.1 Peace versus justice? Grotius

In international law, there is a tension between peace and justice. For example, some worry that supporting the International Criminal Court and its pursuit of justice could upset international peace. Warrants for the arrest of state leaders can make those leaders more violent and reckless rather than bring them before the Court.[13] Yet, some scholars argue that international laws should still seek to fulfill the demands of justice first, and only if justice is not possible, should the laws aim at peace. Others, however, point out the difficult if not dubious problem of seeking justice between states.[14] Since, roughly, justice is usually conceived as giving each their due or what is owed them, global justice is considered dubious because as Thomas Hobbes makes clear there is no global sovereign to enforce international laws designed to ensure that all get or keep their due.[15] Without this enforcement mechanism that makes justice a real and lasting possibility, it is thought that peace is the best that can be hoped for and the proper aim of international law.[16]

Like Hugo Grotius in *On the Law of War and Peace*, the criticism rejecting the moral equality of combatants struggles with this tension between peace and justice. In this struggle, Grotius's view and the criticism are remarkably similar.[17] Not surprisingly, the criticism is reluctant to call rules of war moral if they do not adhere to the core right not to be killed when one is not liable to be killed, even if such rules bring about the best consequences given the circumstances. For example, McMahan, deems the "moral equality of combatants" morally unsupportable yet still believes that this equality should be legally recognized for pragmatic or consequentialist reasons.[18] What the law should be then, for McMahan, does not fit with what justice or morality demands (or fully demands).[19] While similar, Grotius's view looks more charitably on rules and laws that pursue peace, or conditions for peace.

Like McMahan, in *On the Law of War and Peace* Grotius appears to reject and accept the moral equality of combatants. Grotius rejects this equality in a number of places. He states that a defense by those who deserved that war be made upon them is unjustified and likens people who deserve to have war made upon them to criminals who do not "have a right to resist by force the representatives of the public authority."[20] Also, he says that those who clearly know that their cause is unjust have a duty not to fight.[21] In addition, Grotius says that all acts arising from an unjust cause, even if undertaken lawfully, are still unjust "from the point of view of moral injustice," and those who knowingly perform such acts will not be able to enter "the Kingdom of Heaven without repentance."[22]

Grotius, however, also tells us that combatants on the unjust side are "permitted" to harm the enemy subject to the same limits as those with a just cause.[23] True, this permission, for Grotius, only grants immunity from punishment.[24] However, this permission still morally obligates others to not punish unjust combatants for fighting.[25] For Grotius, then, there is a kind of moral equality between combatants because all are morally obligated to treat combatants on either side as equals with regard to punishment.[26] For Grotius, this permission and corresponding moral obligation not to punish is a "law of nations," meaning states agree on it, and, for Grotius, this mutual consent, morally speaking, places it on par with a law of nature.[27]

Why would Grotius give moral standing to a law of nations that grants a permission that is in tension with the natural law forbidding combatants on the unjust side from fighting? The answer reveals how Grotius's natural law view pursues peace *and* justice. Note first that with this permission, i.e. immunity from punishment, Grotius does not allow the law of nations to command what the natural law forbids but only allows unjust acts to go unpunished.[28] This permission accords with the natural law. Grotius tells us explicitly that, for purposes of punishment, we are to distinguish those who are responsible for the war (which are the leaders or king of the unjust state) from those who are not, and those who are not responsible should be pardoned.[29] He also says that even those who are responsible, in accordance with the natural law and mercy, may be pardoned.[30] For Grotius, pardons and mercy are a part of the natural law, for they lead to peace and less bitterness during war.

This permission is also related to the pursuit of peace in another way. For Grotius, a law of nations has moral authority in part because it is a well-tempered judgment about what rule makes for the best life for us. The mutual consent of nations is evidence that a law is an important rule necessary for peace and necessary for establishing an international legal system, which itself is necessary for peace. Grotius tells us that this grant of immunity from punishment came to be a law of nations because it was too difficult for states not a party to the war to determine which side was just, and even if this could be determined, it was too difficult to determine whether the just side had gone too far, attempted to recover too much or was attempting to exact too harsh a punishment.[31] It is the difficult fact inquiries and the absence of a global sovereign then that resulted in a law of nations allowing combatants on either side to be subject to the same limits. For Grotius, an agreement between all states,[32] like this one that is supported by common consent, is morally justified in part because it is evidence that it is something like a dictate of peace and in part because it helps establish, or acknowledges, an international rule of law, which, of course, is necessary for peace.[33]

This conclusion is not shocking. Today, we similarly allow for injustices. The maintenance of a legal system is required for peace, and laws that people agree on or support are needed for that system. The laws cannot be perfect in the sense that they guarantee perfect justice. Innocent people are prosecuted and punished even when the laws are followed. This injustice is regretful but tolerated, and it does not lead to punishing judges who follow the rules that result in innocent persons being imprisoned. Also, it often does not lead us to think that the rules themselves are morally unjustified. Rather, some injustice cannot be helped and is permitted, and the rules are considered morally justifiable because a legal system with good rules and some fidelity to them are necessary for peace. For Grotius, the natural law tells us what justice requires, and it also supports agreements between nations that help establish an international legal system and pursue peace. According to Grotius, permitting some equality between combatants, even when only one side can be truly just,[34] is such an agreement.

3.2 *Common moral perceptions and rights in war: Walzer*

Michael Walzer's support for the moral separateness of the *jus ad bellum/jus in bello* distinction and the moral equality of combatants is a clear target of the recent criticism. Walzer believes that this separateness and equality are morally justified in part because they reflect "our understanding of states and soldiers, the protagonists of war, and of combat, its central experience."[35] While, according to Walzer, the moral rules of war may not be wholly coherent, they need not be, and we should not expect them to stand up to any rigorous legal or philosophical analysis.[36] Rather, the moral rules of war should align with the common and shared moral perceptions of the community of those who argue about war.

For Walzer, the moral rules of war aim at ensuring a limited war, and they must protect individual rights. At the heart of the morality of war, for Walzer, is the moral equality of combatants and the immunity thesis, i.e. not targeting noncombatants.[37] For Walzer, these conventions make peace possible and prevent battles from becoming massacres. Without these rules or with merely Utilitarian rules, Walzer believes that peace and war as a rule-governed activity would not be possible.[38] Without these rules protecting individual rights,[39] for Walzer, the tragedy of war would be worse. In sum, according to Walzer, the moral rules of war must be of the following kind: 1) protect individual rights, 2) reinforce for us a description of war as a rule-governed activity, 3) promote peace or help make peace possible, and 4) be properly fastened or secured by reflecting our current shared moral perceptions.

Let's see what Walzer says specifically about the moral equality of combatants. Walzer claims that combatants on both sides are "victims" or, better yet, they are perceived of as victims and perceive each other as victims.[40] While not mere "pawns," they are dragged into the fight because of pride, patriotism, and training.[41] People perceive of leaders as being responsible for the war. They see combatants as doing what is told of them. People expect combatants and citizens to be loyal to their state and find it reasonable that they fight as commanded.[42] Combatants also see the war as an act of state, and the combatants themselves, even the enemy, as instruments of the state. It is precisely because enemy combatants are viewed more in an instrumental rather than a criminal light that all combatants are grouped together as victims that can defend themselves against attack.[43] For Walzer, as victims, all combatants retain a right of self-defense.[44] What is important, for Walzer, is that this perception of combatants as victims has some basis in experience and in the common understanding of how wars are fought, including by those who fight. While it cannot be false, this perception need not be wholly true or coherent. For Walzer, conventions need only to fit close enough with a concept like self-defense because their moral power is only in part derived from this concept. It is also derived from its usefulness as a commitment to individual rights and peace and the rejection of the savagery that war brings forth. The immunity thesis alongside the moral equality of combatants keeps war and those who fight from sinking further into this savagery, where rights are nonexistent and peace unattainable.

4. The moral rules of war and the collective perspective

The contrast between the recent criticism and the views in Section 3 is stark. The criticism asks "Did this person do anything to make him or her liable to harm?" An important question for Grotius and Walzer is "how can we make this tragic event better or less evil?"[45] Their "we" is a global "we" confronted with war. Their view is more forward-looking. It deems conventions moral that help bring about the best consequences, including peace. The criticism is importantly backward looking; the morality of future acts depend on whether, and to what degree, an immoral act was done. It is *quid pro quo* in that a person may engage in a violent action if done in return for, or as a result of, a previous wrongful action by another. In addition, Grotius and Walzer's views are amenable to seeing war as a separate rule-governed activity with its own moral norms. The criticism, on the other hand, supports applying the moral norms applicable to individuals in peacetime to war.[46] Finally, Grotius and Walzer give significant moral weight to norms and legal rules that pursue peace in addition to justice.[47] For them, such rules are morally on par with basic norms of justice, and arguably, the moral norm "seek peace" is stronger than some basic moral norms of justice, for it dictates whether some norms of justice should be adhered to or modified. Because the criticism sees rules that make the best of a bad situation as not belonging to the "deep morality of war,"[48] such rules if morally justifiable, are only reluctantly so.

How might we choose between these views? Any ultimate adjudication between them calls for nothing less than an international theory of justice. I cannot, of course, provide such a theory here. However, using Grotius and Walzer's insights, it appears that the answer lies in the strength that one's theory of justice attributes to the collective goal of peace, as well as whether the concept of war as a separate rule-governed activity with this separateness and moral equality likely contributes to this goal. Unlike the criticism, Grotius and Walzer's "deep morality of war" contains a significant element of peace that helps them formulate their moral rules of war, e.g. Grotius's law of nations granting immunity from punishment to all combatants. In what follows, I provide three reasons supporting their view that incorporates the pursuit of peace into "the deep morality of war."

First, the fact that peace is a foundational moral element in the rules of justice between disputes within a community is evidence that peace works similarly in international conflicts, where there is no global sovereign and the attainment of justice is more difficult. At the domestic level, the moral significance of peace is seen in the creation and maintenance of a legal system, including its laws. Clearly, most agree that a legal system is necessary for peace, and similarly, many agree that the fundamental moral norm "seek peace" forces communities to establish and maintain a legal system, even if it (its judges and rules) inevitably will not fulfill justice in every instance and basic norms of justice will be modified.[49] The need for a legal system in the pursuit of peace is that great.

Also, importantly, if they cohere with the moral purpose for the legal system, the laws pursue peace in addition to justice. Some laws hold a society together acknowledging a kind of joint venture for peace and the betterment of the community. For example, laws that require drivers to drive on the right side of the road are aimed at the collective goal of bringing about a safer, more peaceful community. Also, the fairness incorporated into such laws ("all" drivers are to be treated similarly) aids in the pursuit of peace. "Treating like cases alike" is not merely a claim about justice. It is a goal in the pursuit of peace. When one thinks others will be treated similarly, one is more likely to support that legal system. Basic norms of justice, e.g. one should be compensated for harms done, in a legal system designed for peace and justice become something like the following: one should be compensated for harms done, if those harms did not occur too long ago (statute of limitations), if the claim for compensation is filed in the proper court (jurisdictional claims), if evidence of the kind permissible in court shows that it is more likely than not that the harm occurred (evidentiary rules), and if the harm is one of a certain degree or kind (e.g. it is not merely offensive speech) that that community generally, for the betterment of the community or the protection of rights, desires to prohibit. These contingencies or contingent rules, which are also laws, that morph basic norms of justice do not always ensure that such basic norms of justice are fulfilled. On the contrary, they can impede them.

These laws or rules that morph basic norms of justice do not always ensure that such norms of justice are fulfilled. On the contrary, they can impede them. Nonetheless, they are morally justified for their role in seeking impartial judgments and adding order and fairness in the pursuit of settling disputes peacefully. Often, when basic norms of justice are modified in a forward-looking way by secondary laws or rules in a legal system, i.e. with future cases, fairness and the betterment of the community in mind, it is peace, not simply justice, at work in those modifications.

The second reason supporting Grotius and Walzer's view is that it is likely that a conception of war as a separate rule-governed activity with this moral separateness between the *jus ad bellum/jus in bello* distinction and the moral equality of combatants aids the pursuit of peace.[50] It likely aids the pursuit of peace in a number of ways. It makes it easier to forgive the violence that occurs in war. It allows a kind of acceptance between participants that helps them move forward out of, and after, war. It helps them see some acts in war, e.g. the killings of just combatants, as belonging to the war itself, and it helps those involved see some killings by unjust combatants, in a sense, as reasonable, meaning understandable and forgivable in that context. In some ways, this conception of war makes war similar to a violent game between two teams, e.g. an American football game. The violence is often attributed to the game itself, and the players' actions, if within the rules, are part of the game. Because the violence is expected and is part of the activity, the players on opposite teams, after and during the game, are more likely to show each other respect despite the violence.[51] Without this conception of war, it is more difficult to see an end to the numerous demands for justice arising from every instance of violence; it would be more difficult to forgive or forget. This concept of war helps combatants see their enemy not merely as killers but also as people like themselves, with whom they could again have peaceful relationships.

As Walzer claims, a concept of war as a separate rule-governed activity is a concept that preserves the idea of individual rights during war (even if these rights are not the rights of peacetime). This alone helps bring peace during and after war. When the violence escalates, it is easy for participants to lose sight of individual rights altogether. While Walzer is correct, it should be specifically noted how this separateness and equal right to kill focuses culpability for the war and its injustices on those who are in charge of the war, i.e. those who decide to go to war, execute the war, have the most knowledge about why the war is fought, and could stop the war. The moral equality of combatants supported by this separateness between the *jus ad bellum/jus in bello* distinction are two rules that turn our moral attention regarding responsibility for war, and the acts occurring in it, on an important few, i.e. those at the top. This focus is seen as morally acceptable certainly in part because of the power they wield, but it can also be seen as morally supportable because it aids in the possibility of peace. When those at the top are seen as holding a high degree of responsibility, those in the middle and the bottom are freer to comport with each other again as equals. It is not just that combatants on both sides have a third-party to join against and blame, it is also that these rules help them see each other as similarly situated in relation to those at the top. People in the middle and bottom, on no matter which side, share a special tie or connection. They can all appreciate the difference in power and knowledge held by those at the top, and they can relate to the difference in responsibility that should flow from such power and knowledge. This shared connection encouraged by this separateness and equality of combatants helps make peace possible.

The final reason that this separateness and equality can be considered part of the moral rules of war is that they help maintain some fidelity to this concept of war as a separate rule-governed activity, which aids in peace. This last reason builds on the other two. If we should expect peace to moderate international disputes and justice as it does in the domestic sphere and there is a concept of war that does just this, i.e. bring peace and justice to such disputes, arguably the moral norm "seek peace" informs us to maintain that concept of war. Such maintenance or fidelity comes from rules that people believe in.

An analogy with a legal system is helpful. Legal systems are morally required in part because they are necessary for peace, and a legal system is only maintained if it has enough fidelity to its laws. Its existence relies on such fidelity. Similarly, a concept of war that promotes peace is only maintained if there is enough fidelity to it, and as a result, it needs rules that people are willing to support. The third and final reason then is that the moral separateness between the *jus ad bellum/jus in bello* distinction and the equality between combatants are two such rules. People support these rules, which creates the required fidelity to this concept of war, because of the reasons related to peace stated above and because, following Walzer, they are rules that are deeply rooted in the experience of war.

This analogy with a legal system can be taken a step further. Rather than criticize this separateness and equality for not being, or conforming to, basic norms of justice, e.g. a right of self-defense, it is best to see these rules as being like a mixture of the primary and secondary rules of a legal system, hybrid rules. Like primary rules, they protect rights. Like secondary rules, e.g. a statute of limitations or an evidentiary threshold, they have communal aims, e.g. treating persons similarly, setting reasonable fact inquiries, and controlling for the lack of an appeal to a judge, which aid in the settling of disputes peacefully. As noted above, in legal systems, there are primary rules of justice, e.g. persons should be compensated for harms, and secondary rules that concern the implementation of those rules. This separateness and equality can be seen as hybrids of these two kinds of rules.[52] The recent criticism omits this adjudicative and collective, forward-looking quality found in some secondary rules from its view. Like secondary rules in legal systems that can morally obligate us (even if at times they allow those who have committed injustices to go free) because of their collective, forward-looking perspective, some moral rules of war, which are also about conduct and the settling of disputes, contain a similar moral quality.[53] The moral force then of these two rules is not simply their shaping of a certain concept of war but also their ability to create some fidelity to that concept, which makes peace possible.

The moral rules of war are often compared to the rules of crime and punishment. But, this comparison should not merely be to primary rules or principles. It should also include the secondary rules, which can have a collective, forward-looking perspective in their ability to create fairness in the administration of the primary rules. In war, this consequential, administrative quality, found in some rules of war, helps keep the notion of individual rights secure and create some fidelity to the rules in the pursuit of peace and containing the tragedy of war.

5. Conclusion

The recent criticism tells us that the moral rules of war should conform to a basic rule of justice like that of self-defense. Not surprisingly, a moral view that includes the collective goal of peace will find this criticism misguided because incomplete. As Grotius allows, the moral rules of war can have the twin moral aims of peace and justice. As Walzer advises, they should articulate rights, yet not be morally justified simply because they protect rights. They are also about fairness and importantly about how communities without a global sovereign can best maintain war as a separate rule-governed activity to keep from falling further into the savagery of war and instead find peace.

Some moral rules of war, like this separateness and equality, can be seen as a mixture of the primary and secondary rules of legal system. They are about justice, yet also have a collective, forward-looking moral quality that is found in some secondary rules of a legal system. In addition to preserving rights, they seek to contain the tragedy of war and make peace possible. It is from these important moral concerns that the separation of the *jus ad bellum/jus in bello* distinction and the moral equality of combatants are moral rules of war. In her writings on Adolf Eichmann's trial for transporting millions of Jews to death camps, Hannah Arendt reveals the banality of evil in war. Eichmann is tragic because he is ordinary. Some rules of war are morally justifiable because they are in part commitments, protecting us from this ordinary evil.

Notes

1 This phrase is used by Michael Walzer, *Just and Unjust Wars: A Moral Argument with Historical Illustrations*, 3rd edn, New York: Basic Books, 2000, p. 136. Currently, it is commonplace for the term "soldier" to denote someone in the army rather than say in the navy or air force. As a result, hereinafter, I use the more inclusive phrase "the moral equality of combatants."

2 As will be shown later, in a sense, one can say that Grotius both accepts and rejects this equality.

3 See D. Rodin and H. Shue (eds), *Just and Unjust Warriors: The Moral and Legal Status of Soldiers*, Oxford: Oxford University Press, 2008.

4 Jeff McMahan and David Rodin, J. McMahan, "The Ethics of Killing in War," *Ethics: An International Journal of Social, Political, and Legal Philosophy*, 114:4, 2004, pp. 693–733; D. Rodin, "The Moral Equality of Soldiers: Why *jus in bello* Asymmetry is Half Right," in D. Rodin and H. Shue (eds), *Just and Unjust Warriors: The Moral and Legal Status of Soldiers*, Oxford: Oxford University Press, 2008, argue that different obligations arise for soldiers depending on whether they are fighting on the just or unjust side.

5 See "The Morality of War and the Law of War," in D. Rodin and H. Shue (eds), *Just and Unjust Warriors*, pp. 21–22 and Coady "The Status of Combatants," in D. Rodin and H. Shue (eds), *Just and Unjust Warriors*, pp. 157–158.

6 But see T. Hurka "Liability and Just Cause," *Ethics and International Affairs*, 20, 2007, p. 210, where he claims that combatants "freely accept" that they may be permissibly killed by enemy combatants. If this argument is successful, then combatants are exercising their agency and are full moral agents like volunteer gladiators. For discussion on this point, see J. McMahan *Killing in War*, Oxford: Clarendon Press, 2009, pp. 52–65.

7 Some of the recent Just War Theorists that agree on, or share some version of, the "recent criticism" depicted here are Jeff McMahan, David Rodin, James Pattison, Uwe Steinhoff, Lionel McPherson, and C.A.J. "Tony" Coady.

8 J. McMahan, *Killing in War*, p. 157.

9 See J. Pattison, "When Is It Right to Fight? Just War Theory and the Individual-Centric Approach," *Ethical Theory and Moral Practice*, 26 November, 2011 pp. 1–20.

10 Ibid., Section 6.3.

11 Of course, defining the innocent or a noncombatant for purposes of immunity from being targeted is no easy task. For insightful definitions or attempts and replies, see E. Anscombe, "War and Murder," in W. Stein (ed.), *Nuclear Weapons: A Catholic Response*, London, Sheed & Ward, 1961, pp. 44–52, T. Nagel, "War and Massacre," *Philosophy and Public Affairs*, 1:2, 1972, pp. 123–144, R.K. Fullinwider, "War and Innocence," *Philosophy and Public Affairs*, 5:1, 1975, pp. 90–97, and L.A. Alexander, "Self-Defense and the Killing of Noncombatants: A Reply to Fullinwider," *Philosophy and Public Affairs*, 5:4, 1975, pp. 408–415.

12 See M. Walzer, *Just and Unjust Wars: A Moral Argument with Historical Illustrations*, 3rd edn, New York: Basic Books, 2000, p. 410. I do not here argue that this new description of war is morally speaking worse than the old description, only that I agree with Walzer that the recent criticism changes how we view war. However, clearly, war as mostly a police action brings moral difficulties or worries. Without a strong enough global state with a global police force, communities engaging in war, on their own or even some of them together, as police actions could be viewed as similar to vigilantes, and they are susceptible to, in practice, not fulfilling justice, e.g. going too far or seeking too harsh a punishment or seeking goals other than justice, as well as sparking and continuing more violence rather than achieving and ensuring peace.

13 On this point, using the example of Omar al-Bashir, the President of Sudan, see L. May, *After War Ends: A Philosophical Perspective*, Cambridge: Cambridge University Press, 2012, pp. 29–43.

14 This tension is seen in Allen Buchanan's proposal and Chris Naticchia's response to what should be the international laws applicable to recognizing a state as legitimate, See A. Buchanan, "Recognitional Legitimacy and the State System," *Philosophy and Public Affairs*, 28:1, 1999a, pp. 46–78. A. Buchanan, "Rule-Governed Institutions Versus Act-Consequentialism: A Rejoinder to Naticchia," *Philosophy and Public Affairs*, 28:3, 1999b, pp. 258–270, A. Buchanan, *Justice, Legitimacy, and Self-Determination: Moral Foundations for International Law*, New York: Oxford University Press, 2004, C. Naticchia, "Recognizing States and Governments," *Canadian Journal of Philosophy*, 35:1, 2005, pp. 27–82, and C. Naticchia, "Recognition and Legitimacy: A Reply to Buchanan," *Philosophy and Public Affairs*, 28:3, 1999, pp. 242–25.

15 See T. Nagel "The Problem of Global Justice," *Philosophy and Public Affairs*, 33:2, 2005, pp. 113–147. But see also, A. Julius, "Nagel's Atlas," *Philosophy and Public Affairs*, 34:2, 2006, pp. 176–192, and J. Cohen, and C. Sabel, "Extra rempublicam nulla justitia?" *Philosophy and Public Affairs*, 34:2, 2006, pp. 147–175.

16 This tension between peace and justice is most often found within a deontological, rights-based view like the recent criticism. Justice is a deontological notion or is at least constitutive of nonconsequentialist

moral obligations, and peace is a goal to be pursued in an imperfect world. Justice is about the natural or human rights of each person, and peace should be pursued to bring about the best possible circumstances when the world is such that obtaining justice, or protecting all such rights, is not possible or pursuing it is counterproductive.

17 As Uwe Steinhoff claims, looking closely at Grotius's *Law of War and Peace*, the recent criticism and rejection of the moral equality of combatants in some ways does not look recent or new at all, U. Steinhoff, "Rights, Liability, and the Moral Equality of Combatants," *The Journal of Ethics*, 26 February, 2012, Section 2. McMahan also acknowledges a general similarity between Grotius's view and his own view, J. McMahan, "The Morality of War and the Law of War," in D. Rodin and H. Shue (eds), *Just and Unjust Warriors*, p. 34.

18 J. McMahan, *Killing in War*, p. 95, pp. 107–110 .

19 J. McMahan, "The Morality of War and the Law of War," in D. Rodin and H. Shue (eds), *Just and Unjust Warriors*, pp. 32–43.

20 H. Grotius, *De Jure Belli ac Pacis Libri Tres*, in J. Brown Scott (ed.), trans. F. W. Kelsey, Vol. 2 of The Classics of International Law, Oxford: Clarendon Press, 1925. p. 184, Book II, Chap. I, XVIII.1 [108] (here and hereinafter, the numbers in brackets refer to the *Law of War and Peace* edition published in Amsterdam in 1646, the final edition revised by Grotius, as these page numbers are provided in the Francis W. Kelsey translation published in 1925).

21 Ibid., p. 587, Book II, Chap. XXVI, III [417].

22 Ibid., pp. 718–719, Book III, Chap. X, III [510].

23 Ibid., pp. 643–644, Book III, Chap. IV, IV [457].

24 Ibid., pp. 641–644, Book III, Chap. IV, II–IV [456–458], p. 645, Book III, Chap. IV, V.2 [458].

25 Ibid., p. 15, *Prol.*, 15–16 [ix–x] (for our obligations to the municipal law and the law of nations generally) and Grotius, p. 38, Book I, Chap. I, IX.1 [3] (on the obligation of permissions).

26 I have written elsewhere on this topic, agreeing with Grotius's conclusion that unjust combatants ought not to be liable to punishment for mere participation in an unjust war, see S. Viner, "Self-Defense, Punishing Unjust Combatants, and Justice in War," *Criminal Law and Philosophy*, 4:3, 2010, pp. 297–319.

27 For Grotius, "to abide by pacts" is a law of nature that supports the moral authority of the laws of nations, for they are rules supported by the mutual consent of nations. While Grotius, unlike past scholars, chooses to distinguish between a law of nature and a law of nations, this distinction does not remove any moral authority from a law of nations. The distinction is a difference in kind. Laws of nature and laws of nations spring both from the source of all law: the maintenance of the social order. The laws of nature are those that can be discerned "from certain principles by a sure process of reasoning," and the laws of nations are those that have their origin "in the free will of man" and human intelligence and are rules that are well-tempered judgments that secure the advantage not of any particular state but "of the great society of states." Grotius, *De Jure Belli ac Pacis Libri Tres* p.12–15, *Prol.* 8–17 [viii–xi]; Grotius, *De Jure Belli ac Pacis Libri Tres* p. 17, 20, *Prol.*, 23 [xi], 28 [xii]; Grotius, *De Jure Belli ac Pacis Libri Tres* p. 23–24, *Prol.*, 39–41[xiv–xv]; Grotius, *De Jure Belli ac Pacis Libri Tres* p. 651–652, Book III, Chap. IV, XV [461].

28 For Grotius, more generally, the law of nations cannot command what the law of nature forbids, but it can permit, i.e. grant an immunity from punishment, what the law of nature forbids. Grotius, *De Jure Belli ac Pacis Libri Tres* p. 641–646, Book III, Chap. IV, II–V [456–459] and *De Jure Belli ac Pacis Libri Tres* p. 651–652, Chap. IV, XV [461]. (See also, S. Forde "Hugo Grotius on Ethics and War," *The American Political Science Review*, 92:3, 1998, pp. 644–645.

29 Grotius, *De Jure Belli ac Pacis Libri Tres* p. 729–734, Book III, Chap. XI, V-VIII [517–520], p. 742, Book III, Chap. XI, XVII [524].

30 Ibid., p. 730, 733, Book III, Chap. XI, VI, VII.4 [517–519].

31 Ibid., p. 644, Book III, Chap. IV, IV [457].

32 Or, as Grotius also claims, "a great many states." Ibid., p. 15, *Prol.* 17 [x].

33 See Forde "Hugo Grotius on Ethics and War," pp. 646–647, for a similar conclusion.

34 Grotius, *De Jure Belli ac Pacis Libri Tres* p. 565, Book II, Chap. XXIII, XIII.2 [398].

35 Walzer, *Just and Unjust Wars*, p. 22.

36 Ibid., pp. xix, xxi, 21–22, 43, 325–327.

37 Ibid., pp. 41, 136–137.

38 Walzer, *Just and Unjust Wars*, pp. 129–133. But see, R. Brandt "Utilitarianism and the Rules of War," *Philosophy and Public Affairs*, 1:2, 1972, pp. 145–165.

39 Walzer, *Just and Unjust Wars*, pp. xxi–xxii, 136–137.
40 Ibid., pp. 30, 35–37, 45.
41 Ibid., pp. 39–40.
42 Ibid., pp. 15, 40, 127.
43 Ibid., p. 136.
44 Ibid., p. 128.
45 This is not their only "important question," but as will be argued, it is an important question for them that works alongside, or with, justice.
46 See "Do We Need a 'Morality of War'?" in D. Rodin and H. Shue (eds), *Just and Unjust Warriors*, claiming that McMahan mistakenly attempts to utilize moral rules from ordinary life and apply them to war.
47 Though beyond the scope of this chapter, one could even say that their views make less of a distinction between peace and justice.
48 Jeff McMahan and James Pattison claim that they are defending "the deep morality of war" compared to legal rules of war that can be morally justified for merely pragmatic or consequentialist reasons, McMahan, "The Morality of War and the Law of War," in D. Rodin and H. Shue (eds), *Just and Unjust Warriors*, Pattison, "When Is It Right to Fight? Just War Theory and the Individual-Centric Approach," *Ethical Theory and Moral Practice*, 26 November, 2011, Section I. Likewise, Fabre in her paper on civilian immunity or civilian liability to attack claims that she is defending the "deep morality of war," "Guns, Food and Liability to Attack in War," *Ethics*, 120:1, 2009, p. 39. For an argument rejecting this distinction between "the deep morality of war" and more consequentialist norms that are morally justifiable, see Shue "Do We Need a 'Morality of War'?" in D. Rodin and H. Shue (eds), *Just and Unjust Warriors*.
49 This view of course agrees with Thomas Hobbes's natural laws, including the first law of nature, in *Leviathan*. Hobbes's natural laws and peace do not simply call for a sovereign and a legal system, they tell us how the laws are to be adjudicated, importantly with equity and impartial arbitrators, to ensure peace.
50 Because it is likely, one could argue that supporting this concept of war is morally required similar to moral arguments pertaining to "supreme emergencies" in war. Here, war itself is a "supreme emergency," and as such, it demands that some individual rights that apply in peacetime may not be adhered to or are modified or held in abeyance, making room for other rules that best help a community emerge from that supreme emergency.
51 Of course, it can be argued, as McMahan does, that this separateness and moral equality actually leads to more acceptance of war (and thus not peace) than if there is a rule that all individuals are morally responsible for killing those who have a just cause, see McMahan, *Killing in War*, pp. 6–7. I'm not certain that this is the case, meaning I'm not sure that one or the other view actually leads to, or allows, more war overall. There are simply too many other factors why individuals become combatants. Also, this question about which rule best prevents war may not even directly change which view best captures the moral rules of war. For rules that help communities best prevent war could be seen as separate from what rules are applicable while in war. In addition, we might just think that it is not *jus in bello* rules that play a significant factor in starting and preventing war at all but rather *jus ad bellum* rules and a culture that does not hold leaders morally responsible enough for engaging in war or unjust aggression. See also, Coates, on a related claim that this separateness and moral equality does not lead to more restraint in war, Coates, A., "Is the Independent Application of *jus in bello* the Way to Limit War?" in D. Rodin and H. Shue (eds), *Just and Unjust Warriors*.
52 I have in mind here H.L.A. Hart's distinction between primary and secondary rules. The secondary rules are about the primary rules. The secondary rules that I refer to are examples of Hart's rules of adjudication, see H.L.A. Hart, *The Concept of Law*, 2nd edn, Oxford: Oxford University Press, 1994, p. 97. The thought here is that if war is recognized as a rule-governed activity, it needs rules that are supported by those for whom it is a rule-governed activity. In Hart's terms, for war to exist as such, there need to be enough states and persons that are "obliged" not merely "obligated" to those rules. This "obliging" happens in part when states (and persons) believe that all will likely be treated fairly and similarly with regard to their future actions. The secondary rules play an important role in securing this sufficient assurance of fairness in the adjudication of any facts to get the requisite fidelity to the rules, for it properly to be said that the rules are the rules of this rule-governed activity.
53 I am not claiming that all secondary rules are necessarily moral. Rather, I am claiming that there is something moral that only secondary rules can do: they can aim at the best, or a fair, implementation

of the primary rules. Rules of justice are morally important. Rules about how to best implement those rules for a collective are also morally important, especially since it is the second type that can create (or destroy) any fidelity to the first type of rule, as well as fidelity more generally to the rules being a part of the activity. When this moral quality, which looks to future implementation, mixes with a primary rule, what results is a hybrid rule that is not moral in the exact same way (or for the exact same reason) as a primary rule, nonetheless it can be a moral, or morally justifiable, rule. Also, contrary to what McMahan may claim and due to its mixed status or character, its moral force is not derived "entirely from its utility," J. McMahan, "The Sources and Status of Just War Principles," *The Journal of Military Ethics*, 6:2, 2007, p. 102.

References

Arendt, H., *Eichmann in Jerusalem: A Report on the Banality of Evil*, New York: Penguin Books, 1994.

Alexander, L. A., "Self-Defense and the Killing of Noncombatants: A Reply to Fullinwider," *Philosophy and Public Affairs*, 5:4, 1975, pp. 408–415.

Anscombe, E., "War and Murder," in W. Stein (ed.), *Nuclear Weapons: A Catholic Response*, London, Sheed & Ward, 1961, pp. 44–52.

Brandt, R., "Utilitarianism and the Rules of War," *Philosophy and Public Affairs*, 1:2, 1972, pp. 145–165.

Buchanan, A., *Justice, Legitimacy, and Self-Determination: Moral Foundations for International Law*, New York: Oxford University Press, 2004.

——"Recognitional Legitimacy and the State System," *Philosophy and Public Affairs*, 28:1, 1999a, pp. 46–78.

——"Rule-Governed Institutions Versus Act-Consequentialism: A Rejoinder to Naticchia," *Philosophy and Public Affairs*, 28:3, 1999b, pp. 258–270.

Coady, C.A.J., "The Status of Combatants," in D. Rodin and H. Shue (eds), *Just and Unjust Warriors: The Moral and Legal Status of Soldiers*, Oxford: Oxford University Press, 2008.

Coates, A., "Is the Independent Application of jus in bello the Way to Limit War?" in D. Rodin and H. Shue (eds), *Just and Unjust Warriors: The Moral and Legal Status of Soldiers*, Oxford: Oxford University Press, 2008.

Cohen, J. and C. Sabel, "Extra rempublicam nulla justitia?" *Philosophy and Public Affairs*, 34:2, 2006, pp. 147–175.

Fabre, C., "Guns, Food and Liability to Attack in War," *Ethics*, 120:1, 2009, pp. 36–63.

Forde, S., "Hugo Grotius on Ethics and War," *The American Political Science Review*, 92:3, 1998, pp. 639–648.

Fullinwider, R. K., "War and Innocence," *Philosophy and Public Affairs*, 5:1, 1975, pp. 90–97.

Grotius, H., *De Jure Belli ac Pacis Libri Tres*, in J. Brown Scott (ed.), F.W. Kelsey (trans.), Vol. 2 of The Classics of International Law, Oxford: Clarendon Press, 1925.

Hart, H.L.A., *The Concept of Law*, 2nd edn., Oxford: Oxford University Press, 1994.

Hurka, T., "Liability and Just Cause," *Ethics and International Affairs*, 20, 2007, pp. 199–218.

Julius, A., "Nagel's Atlas," *Philosophy and Public Affairs*, 34:2, 2006, pp. 176–192.

May, L., *After War Ends: A Philosophical Perspective*, Cambridge: Cambridge University Press, 2012.

McMahan, J., *Killing in War*, Oxford: Clarendon Press, 2009.

——(2008) "The Morality of War and the Law of War," in D. Rodin, and H. Shue (eds), *Just and Unjust Warriors: The Moral and Legal Status of Soldiers*, Oxford: Oxford University Press, 2008.

——"The Sources and Status of Just War Principles," *The Journal of Military Ethics*, 6:2, 2007, pp. 91–106.

——"Killing in War: A Reply to Walzer," *Philosophia*, 34, 2006, pp. 47–51.

——"The Ethics of Killing in War," *Ethics: An International Journal of Social, Political, and Legal Philosophy*, 114:4, 2004, pp. 693–733.

Nagel, T., "The Problem of Global Justice," *Philosophy and Public Affairs*, 33:2, 2005, pp. 113–147.

——"War and Massacre," *Philosophy and Public Affairs*, 1:2, 1972, pp. 123–144.

Naticchia, C., "Recognizing States and Governments," *Canadian Journal of Philosophy*, 35:1, 2005, pp. 27–82.

——"Recognition and Legitimacy: A Reply to Buchanan," *Philosophy and Public Affairs*, 28:3, 1999, pp. 242–25.

Pattison, J., "When Is It Right to Fight? Just War Theory and the Individual-Centric Approach," *Ethical Theory and Moral Practice*, 26 November, 2011, pp. 1–20.

Rodin, D., "The Moral Equality of Soldiers: Why *jus in bello* Asymmetry is Half Right," in D. Rodin and H. Shue (eds), *Just and Unjust Warriors: The Moral and Legal Status of Soldiers*, Oxford: Oxford University Press, 2008.

Rodin, D. and Shue, H., *Just and Unjust Warriors: The Moral and Legal Status of Soldiers*, Oxford: Oxford University Press, 2008.

Shue, H., "Do We Need a 'Morality of War'?" in D. Rodin and H. Shue (eds), *Just and Unjust Warriors: The Moral and Legal Status of Soldiers*, Oxford: Oxford University Press, 2008.

Steinhoff, U., "Rights, Liability, and the Moral Equality of Combatants," *The Journal of Ethics*, 26 February, 2012, pp. 1–28.

Viner, S., "Self-Defense, Punishing Unjust Combatants, and Justice in War," *Criminal Law and Philosophy*, 4:3, 2010, pp. 297–319.

Walzer, M., *Just and Unjust Wars: A Moral Argument with Historical Illustrations*, 3rd edn, New York: Basic Books, 2000.

5

JUS AD VIM AND THE JUST USE OF LETHAL FORCE-SHORT-OF-WAR[1]

S. Brandt Ford

1. Introduction

My concern in this chapter is with the moral problem that soldiers[2] face when they are expected to kill in situations that are not clearly war. Over the last twenty years or so we have witnessed increasing use of the military for purposes other than fighting conventional wars.[3] This is due in part to the emerging norm in the 1990s favouring military intervention to protect civilians whose lives are seriously threatened,[4] in part, the recognition that the military can perform a variety of political functions in peacetime,[5] and in part a response to the heightened attention to the threat from terrorism.[6] These types of military operations encompass a wide range of tasks including peacekeeping, supporting civil authorities, counter-terrorism, disaster relief, enforcement of sanctions, and so on.[7] Most of them do not require the military to use lethal force. But in some cases, because they are working in an environment of conflict, the military is expected (and prepared) to use lethal force.

Such broadening of the purpose of the military creates a moral problem in relation to the use of lethal force. The problem is that the military is expected to use its unique capabilities to apply deadly force in situations of conflict outside (what we conventionally understand as) war, where the moral grounds for their destructive actions are less clear. In war, it can be permissible for soldiers to do certain types of harms that we would not allow in any other context, especially when it comes to killing for reasons other than individual self-defense.[8] For example, soldiers fighting a war can attack and kill enemy combatants without warning (e.g. in an ambush or a missile strike). They are also permitted to do serious collateral harm, including the killing and maiming of non-combatants, providing that the military objective is important enough and the non-combatant deaths were foreseeable and not intended.[9] But in cases where soldiers are not at war (or at least there is some doubt that it is war) then how should we morally evaluate the military use of lethal force? Should we extend the boundaries of "war" to include less conventional conflicts? Is it a matter of developing a more sophisticated set of justifications based on individual killing in self-defense? Does policing[10] offer a better paradigm for judging uses of lethal "force-short-of-war?" Or is it something else?

To illustrate the problem, consider a recent example where the military have used lethal force in a context that is not conventional warfare but also could not be adequately described as killing in self-defense[11] or policing. Many people might agree that killing Osama bin Laden or

Anwar al-Awlaki was justified because they were leaders of a well-organized group of people plotting to commit mass murder.[12] But the group they led – Al Qaeda – is neither a state nor does it represent a legitimate political community.[13] If this is the case, then attacks perpetrated by Al Qaeda cannot be properly described as war and its leaders cannot, in this sense, be treated as combatants. They should be judged, instead, in the way that we would normally judge the actions of murderous criminals. This particular group of murderous criminals, however, operates outside the reach of the jurisdiction of the state (or states) whose job it is to protect the innocent victims of these aggressors. Conventional police enforcement is inadequate for such a task since these murderous aggressors can plot with impunity in some cases. Plausibly, a state that is obligated to prevent the mass murder of its jurisdictional inhabitants,[14] but whose instruments of policing are rendered ineffective, could turn to its military capabilities.

The problem then, however, is that if we choose to use military capabilities for a function that is something akin to a policing role, then we can end up transporting the military mindset about using lethal force along with the military personnel, equipment and training. If the state is using its military capabilities to fulfill a policing role, then presumably the rules of lethal force should be unlike the ones we permit in war; they should be much more restrictive. Perhaps they should not be quite as restrictive as those of the police working within a well-ordered society but they should certainly be more restrictive than we are willing to allow in war. So in situations of conflict short-of-war, where they are expected to use lethal force, the military should adjust to the fact that they are not fighting a war and be more restrained in their use of lethal force. In short, when it comes to using lethal force we need a well-reasoned "hybrid" ethical framework that draws on the appropriate moral principles of both just war theory and the policing paradigm.[15]

In this chapter, I argue that the notion which Michael Walzer calls *jus ad vim* might improve the moral evaluation for using military lethal force in conflicts other than war, particularly those situations of conflict short-of-war. First, I describe his suggested approach to morally justifying the use of lethal force outside the context of war. I argue that Walzer's *jus ad vim* is a broad concept that encapsulates a state's mechanisms for exercising power short-of-war. I focus on his more narrow use of *jus ad vim* which is the state's use of lethal force. Next I address Tony Coady's critique of *jus ad vim*.[16] I argue that Coady highlights some important problems with *jus ad vim*, but these concerns are not sufficient to dismiss it completely. Then, in the final section, I argue that *jus ad vim* provides an appropriate "hybrid" moral framework for judging the ethical decision-making outside of war by complementing other conventional just war distinctions. A benefit of *jus ad vim* is that it stops us expanding the definition of war while still providing the necessary ethical framework for examining violent conflict outside that context.

2. Walzer's *jus ad vim*

In the first section, I outline Walzer's approach to morally justifying the use of lethal force outside the context of war, which he refers to as "*jus ad vim*." His description of *jus ad vim*, or the just use of force-short-of-war, can be found in the preface to the fourth edition of his book *Just and Unjust Wars*.[17] Walzer argues that just war theory should include *jus ad vim* because he believes there is an "urgent need for a theory of just and unjust uses of force outside the conditions of war."[18] Walzer illustrates his point by describing the Iraq containment regime (1991–2003) as an example of the type of effective measures that states can use rather than going to war. From the perspective of international law, embargoes and the enforcement of no-fly zones are judged to be acts of war. But Walzer argues that it is common sense to recognize that these measures differ from actual warfare. Containment is, Walzer believes, much easier to justify than a full-scale attack.[19] The key moral point being that this type of measure is an exercise of state power that avoids the full destructiveness of war, even though it might involve the use, or the threatened use, of lethal force.

Walzer goes on to argue that for measures short-of-war to work against evil or dangerous regimes they should be the common work of a group of nations because "collective security"[20] must be a joint project.[21] He then links the limits on when *jus ad vim* can be used (and also on the ways in which it can be used) with collective security. The collective recognition by a set of states to recognize an unrealized but likely threat (such as a potential massacre or act of aggression) and to organize a response to ward off the threat, is a source of appropriate limitations on *jus ad vim* for Walzer. He contrasts this with unilateral uses of lethal force in cases where a state is permitted to intervene to stop actualized aggression or massacre.

What are we to make of Walzer's description of *jus ad vim*? First, Walzer's use of the term "*jus ad vim*" is somewhat confusing. Coady (whose critique I will consider in more detail in the next section) suggests that the Iraq containment regime, which Walzer uses as his main example to describe *jus ad vim*, included three important elements: the arms embargo; the UN inspection system; and the no-fly zone. Only one of these directly involved the use of actual violence.[22] So, pace Coady, Walzer appears to use *jus ad vim* in at least two importantly different ways. In the first sense, *jus ad vim* seems to refer to the kind of force usually reserved for war but, which due to contingent circumstances, needs to be used outside of the context of war. In the second sense, *jus ad vim* appears to refer to some kind of force that is qualitatively and/or quantitatively different from the kind of force typically used in war. Or to put the confusion in the form of a question, does "force-short-of-war" refer to the nature of the act, or does it refer to the nature of the context in which the act is carried out?[23]

Walzer is using *jus ad vim* in the first sense but he has not obviously precluded the second sense. I suspect the second sense is what Walzer means by "measures-short-of-war."[24] This then would be the broad sense of *jus ad vim* which captures all the options short-of-war available to a state in its use of power. Although discussing the full range of measures available to a state is certainly a worthy subject, it is not one I am able to tackle in this chapter. To simplify the discussion, I will assume that Walzer's *jus ad vim* offers moral guidance for the following three things: 1) actual uses of lethal force-short-of-war; 2) threats to use lethal force-short-of-war; and 3) uses of state power short-of-war that do not involve lethal force. It is this first type of *jus ad vim* – the actual uses of lethal force-short-of-war – that I will discuss here.[25] For my purposes, a *jus ad vim* use of lethal force is best described as: "an act of intentional killing of a person who is a culpable unjust threat, by a member of a military institution, acting on behalf of a legitimate political community which is not at war."

The second important point to note about Walzer's notion of force-short-of-war is his claim that there is a significant moral distinction between localized armed conflicts (where the effects are minimal) and full-scale war. Walzer argues that we approach uses of lethal force in war differently from uses of lethal force-short-of-war because of the "moral gulf" between the two types of violent conflict.[26] His point is that a full-scale war, which might involve high-intensity fighting between a number of military forces over a period of years, is much worse than a localized one-off altercation between two small groups of combatants. As such, we should recognize a moral difference between them. It is clear what Walzer is trying to get at with this point: a large amount of death and destruction is morally worse than a small amount. This difference, however, needs to be more fully explained. Let's look at an example at either end of the spectrum and compare the fighting that occurred in the Pacific against Japan's military aggression (1941–1945) with the Entebbe Operation (1976) in which an Israeli commando raid in Uganda successfully rescued 102 hostages.[27] We can say that the Entebbe incident, as a use of lethal force-short-of-war, involved intentional killing which is a serious *pro tanto* wrong if not justified. But this killing was justified by the need to rescue innocent people who were wrongfully held hostage. The fighting against Japan's aggression in World War II was also justified. But we can still conclude that the war against Japan was worse than the Entebbe Operation for three reasons. First, the Entebbe Operation consisted of one instance of low-intensity military conflict whereas the Pacific War consisted of many instances of varying levels of violent conflict. Second, the purpose of the Entebbe Operation was to rescue innocent people and lethal force was targeted at the culpable kidnappers. In contrast, the Pacific War involved killing people of varying levels of culpability, many of whom were innocent casualties. Third, the Pacific War resulted in much more overall harm than was the case in the Entebbe Operation. War in this case involved far more deaths and destruction than the use of force-short-of-war.

The third important aspect of Walzer's force-short-of-war argument is that it seemingly weakens the last-resort standard for using lethal force. That is, the threshold for permissibly using lethal force is lower in cases of *jus ad vim* than is the case for conventional just war theory. This is an issue that is of particular concern to Coady and one I will examine more fully in the next section. There are a number of reasons why we should consider the idea that the use of lethal force by the military is permissible in situations of conflict short-of-war. The first is to require us to make more effective moral judgments about the just and unjust uses of lethal force that are *already* happening outside of the context of war. The second is to ensure that the extraordinary permissions to kill that we allow in war do not become normative outside that context. The third is to apply stricter and better specified rules of engagement for soldiers in situations of conflict short-of-war.

Walzer's immediate concern in writing on *jus ad vim* was to address the question of whether the permissions of just war theory should reach to democratisation and regime change, an issue he believes is closely connected to questions about preventive war.[28] Walzer argues that while preventive war is normally not justifiable, under certain specific conditions, we might be able to justify preventive force.

> Preventive war is not justifiable either in standard just war theory or in international law, but what we might think of as "preventive force" can be justified when we are dealing with a brutal regime that has acted aggressively or murderously in the past and gives us reason to think that it might do so again.[29]

My suggestion is that we draw on Walzer's conditions for the justified use of preventive force[30] and expand them so we can say that a military use of lethal force-short-of-war is an option when we are dealing with: 1) a person or group of people (including political regimes) acting in a fashion that is brutal in that they have little or no regard for fundamental human rights or the rights of other groups; 2) the person (or group) in question has a proven track record of unjust aggression in the form of unjustly killing and maiming people in its own jurisdiction and/or the peoples of other jurisdictions; and 3) we have good reasons to conclude that this unjust aggression will continue or get worse. In short, the use of lethal force-short-of-war is a military option for dealing with serious culpable threats.

The fourth, and final, point to be made about Walzer's conception of force-short-of-war is that it constrains the permissibility of targeting using the same principle of discrimination as in the conduct of war. Conventional just war theory prohibits the intentional killing of non-combatants and, according to Walzer, force-short-of-war does the same thing. In both forms of conflict, the use of lethal force should be limited in order to protect civilians from being harmed.[31] This view, however, does not seem to go far enough. If the permissibility for targeting in *jus ad vim* is based on the same principles used in conventional just war theory then it is hard to see what makes the two distinct. More problematically, Walzer's notion of *jus ad vim* presumably leaves open the possibility of foreseeable but not intentional killing of innocent civilians. For *jus ad vim* to be worthwhile, it should require soldiers to be distinctly more restrained in their use of lethal force than is the case in conventional just war theory.

In what way might *jus ad vim* require soldiers to be more restrained in their use of lethal force? Here are some suggestions of the type of constraints that might prove useful to consider. First, we might say that foreseeable collateral deaths are either not permissible or equivalent to what we would be willing to accept in a standard policing operation. Second, we might require better standards of evidence and proof for demonstrating that a target is, in fact, a culpable threat. Third, each operation involving the military might be required to meet its own reasonable last resort test in that it must be demonstrated that other non-lethal options (such as arrest) were not available or would have been unacceptably risky. Fourth, we might choose to hold individual soldiers, who use lethal force-short-of-war, to a higher level of personal responsibility than is the case in war. This means that the individual soldier might be required to justify any personal use of lethal force. But it also means the discretionary ability to choose not to shoot.

In sum, Walzer's suggestion that we develop the notion of *jus ad vim* is a good one, so long as it means a moral framework to improve moral judgments for using lethal force-short-of-war. But the problem for Walzer's account of *jus ad vim* is threefold. It needs to explain, first of all, why the use of lethal force is justified in the first place since even a small amount of death and destruction is worse than no amount of death and destruction. War is worse than killing short-of-war because: a) the scale of permissible harm (in terms of repeated acts of death and destruction) is higher with the potential to be much higher; and b) war permits the forseeable (though unintended) killing of innocent people. Second, *jus ad vim* must give us some idea of where to draw the moral distinction between the two different types of armed conflict. *Jus ad vim* can do this because it acknowledges the need for a "hybrid" moral framework. My point here is *not* that it gives us a single moral principle (or set of moral principles) to apply in such cases. *Jus ad vim* covers a broad territory and it will end up covering a number of subcategories. The important move is to recognize that conventional just war theory alone is insufficient for judging these types of conflicts. Third, it needs to provide us with reasonable guidance for the additional constraints we apply to soldiers using lethal force-short-of-war. *Jus ad vim* is "hybrid" in that it borrows from both domestic law (the policing paradigm) and just war theory, the basic idea being that the actual use of lethal force should be more constrained than we permit in war.

3. Critiquing *jus ad vim*

In this next section I address Coady's critique of *jus ad vim* and his defence of a more conventional just war approach to conflict short-of-war. The first problem that Coady raises with *jus ad vim* is that it lowers the standard of last resort. He argues that lethal force-short-of-war should not allow us to relax the requirements of just war theory, especially that of last resort.[32] If we are talking about political violence then we neither need nor should we have some more permissive theory quite distinct from conventional just war thinking.[33] According to Coady, political violence of any sort should require satisfaction of a "genuine reluctance constraint". That is, last resort should draw attention to the need to seek realistic solutions to political problems that are *less damaging* than resort to political violence.[34] But he agrees that the wrongness of war is tied to the level of destruction that it causes. Coady argues that some wars are going to be easier to justify than others on the basis of levels of destructiveness.[35] What should count in favour of a specific use of political violence, according to Coady, is that it involves far less killing and damage than some other proposed resort to violence might.[36]

Coady has ongoing reservations about *jus ad vim*.[37] He compares it to the use of drones in targeted killings which start by claiming the high moral ground because of greater accuracy and targeting only combatants,[38] but end by escalating conflict, targeting people who have no connection with the conflict and provoking more resentful military responses. He believes *jus ad vim* is likely to do all of this and it will also make the resort to serious violence easier and less constrained which, given the inherent tendency of violence to escalate, is a bad idea. He argues that it will begin with the more powerful military powers, particularly the U.S., and will continue by encouraging other powers in the same direction where they can get away with it.[39]

I am likewise cautious about the potential consequences of a "lowering-the-threshold" argument. But I am not arguing that we should lower the threshold to full-scale war. War is a horrible thing that can only be justified in the most extreme cases because of the likelihood of widespread death and destruction.[40] Combatants in war have frequently inflicted high levels of devastation: they have laid waste to the environment, destroyed cultural heritage, wounded, maimed and killed.[41] War might be justified in some cases, but it is always a risky course of action and often costly. There should be, however, greater reluctance to engage in wholesale invasion than to send a small armed unit to effect a minimal objective. Coady argues that there are dangers in even limited military operations, as demonstrated by the botched U.S. attempt to rescue its captive diplomats in Iran during the Carter presidency.[42] Coady's view is that small-scale killing and destruction – as against available, feasible alternatives that are less damaging – needs justification.

This is correct: any use of lethal force does require the right type of justification. But Coady's point about the dangers in using a small armed unit to achieve a minimal objective is, arguably, one of military competence. The 1980 U.S. attempt to rescue its captive diplomats in Iran may have failed and it might be judged as a poor decision because it was risky. But it does not follow that risky or bold military operations are therefore always wrong. Consider again the Entebbe Operation mentioned above. The Israeli military were successful in their attempt to rescue civilian hostages in a raid into Uganda.[43] The use of lethal force-short-of-war to rescue a group of innocent people, whose lives have been unjustly threatened by a culpable group of kidnappers, appears to me to be the right type of justification.

Coady's concern is one of a slippery-slope argument because he believes that if we allow the military to use lethal force-short-of-war then the frequency of political violence will increase and inevitably the high level of destruction will follow. A key point of a slippery-slope argument is that there is no point at which one can non-arbitrarily get off the slope once one has got on to it.[44] Once we are on the slippery slope then it is likely we are heading towards a horrible result. If this is so, then I argue that *jus ad vim* works by inhibiting movement down the slippery slope. *Jus ad vim* should inhibit the slippery slope because it prevents a state from justifying higher levels of killing and damage normally permissible in war. But it does not do this if it lowers the threshold without providing additional constraints. Therefore, a *jus ad vim* moral framework must include constraints that go beyond conventional just war theory. In other words, *jus ad vim* cannot simply use the just war principles of "proportionality" and "discrimination." A successful hybrid moral framework must also draw from the principles we find in policing.

It is worth noting, however, that Walzer assumes the use of force-short-of-war "does not have war's unpredictable and often catastrophic consequences."[45] I am circumspect about Walzer's claim that using military lethal force is unlikely to be unpredictable or catastrophic. What starts out as one instance of lethal force may very well escalate or get out-of-control. Having said that, it is also possible to make a distinction between uses of lethal force that could (or are likely to) lead to war and those situations where a use of lethal force: 1) is highly unlikely to lead to war; 2) acts to greatly reduce the likelihood of war; or 3) prevents a catastrophic harm or injustice so is worth the risk of war.

The second problem with force-short-of-war, according to Coady, is that it "softens" the description of political violence. He believes terms such as "lethal force" and "force short-of-war" embody the unsatisfactory softening of terms describing political violence.[46] To Coady, the "force short-of-war" description covers a wide range of military interventions such as rocket strikes and bombing raids intended to punish, rescue or deter. He also points out that Walzer uses the term for more sustained violence such as the American "no-fly zone" bombing of Iraq carried out as part of the containment system imposed after the Gulf War.[47] As I discussed in the first section, I agree with Coady that Walzer's notion of *jus ad vim* covers a wide a range of military interventions, and is perhaps too broad. But Coady could also be accused of a similar type of "softening". He gives "political violence" a very broad remit that, much like Walzer's *jus ad vim*,[48] also covers a wide range of phenomena. I tend to agree with Coady's point that we do not want to let state actors off the moral hook by allowing them the use of self-justifying terms such as "force" while using terms that condemn the actions of non-state actors. But he does not make clear how we should treat political violence short-of-war.[49] And since it is not clear how Coady's approach is superior to Walzer's, I'm not convinced that he has effectively ruled-out *jus ad vim* as a plausible approach.

To illustrate his objection to Walzer's notion of force short-of-war, Coady makes his point using the example of the U.S. air strike against Sudan's alleged chemical weapons factory in 1998.[50] He argues that this incident could be described as a use of force short-of-war because: 1) the U.S. was not at war with Sudan at the time; 2) the incident was brief; and 3) the incident was self-contained. I have no disagreement with Coady when he argues that a declaration of war is not significant for the moral assessment of political violence. A war does not require a formal declaration to be a war.

Coady's next two claims, however, I will take issue with. First, Coady suggests that although the duration of a conflict is a morally relevant factor, it makes no difference to our fundamental assessment of war *qua* war. Short and long episodes of war have the same quality: they are both war and should be judged accordingly.[51] But it is not the duration that is constitutive of war but the repeated violent conflicts. While wars might be short (e.g. The Six Day War)[52] they can also be very long (e.g. The Hundred Years War)[53]. The point of *jus ad vim* is that it judges each incident independently. And, as I have explained earlier, we have good reason for refusing to allow all cases of political violence to be described as war: because with war we permit a wider range of destructive actions. *Jus ad vim* prevents the expansion of war. So the moral exceptionalism we allow in war is applied to fewer cases. This way, we better meet Coady's "genuine reluctance constraint" principle which I take to mean making decisions that lead to the least overall amount of political violence.

Second, Coady also argues that the target's incapacity or unwillingness to fight back does not do away with the need to justify the attack in the first place.[54] The moral standards appropriate to war should still apply in these cases. While it is true to say that the appropriate moral standards should be applied in cases where the target does not or cannot fight back, I'm arguing that in those specific cases *jus ad vim* gives us a better moral framework than does the conventional just war view. Importantly, *jus ad vim* makes a clearer distinction between the innocent civilian who has no intention of harming and a person (or group) who perhaps cannot do harm for the moment but are likely to do so when they have the opportunity. In judging the use of lethal force, *jus ad vim* increases the protections of the innocent group while still permitting the targeting of the culpable group.

The third criticism Coady has of *jus ad vim* is that some nation (or group of nations) possessing massive military superiority over an adversary will be tempted to see the resort to political violence at the less spectacular end of the scale as an example not of war but of something more like forceful correcting or policing.[55] He believes that such instances can turn into asymmetrical war where the opponent must resort to less direct forms of violence because it lacks the requisite military weaponry. I agree with Coady's assessment of what I would describe as the "policing alternative". Simply applying the policing paradigm alone is an insufficient approach for dealing with the complexity of phenomena within *jus ad vim*. For an incident to be described as a policing use of lethal force it should meet the specific criteria that apply to policing. It might seem like a straightforward solution to call anything that is not a clear-cut example of warfare a law enforcement issue by default. But just because a conflict fails to meet the criteria for warfare does not mean it automatically fits the policing paradigm.[56] As I mentioned in my introduction, the tools of law enforcement are simply not capable of dealing with many of the conflicts we find in the range of *jus ad vim*. Hence there is the necessity to use military capabilities and the requirement of a hybrid moral framework.

4. Making use of *jus ad vim*

Having examined Walzer's argument for *jus ad vim* and some of Coady's main criticisms, I now argue that *jus ad vim* has the virtue of allowing us to stop the expansion of war while still providing the necessary hybrid ethical framework for judging violent conflict outside that context. First, I will explain what I mean by a "narrow" account of war using Brian Orend's definition.[57] Then I argue that there is no need to expand war into these other areas. We should keep our definition of war suitably narrow and have a distinct hybrid ethical framework for conflicts short-of-war.

War should be understood, according to Orend, as an actual, intentional and widespread armed conflict which occurs only between political communities.[58] He argues that war is a violent way for determining formal power in a given territory and "*all warfare is precisely, and ultimately, about governance.*"[59] Orend also believes that the conflict of arms must be actual and not merely threatened for it to count as war. And this actual conflict must be both intentional and widespread. According to Orend, there is no real war until the fighters intend to go to war and until they do so with a heavy quantum of force.[60] So following Orend's definition, we can describe a narrow account of war as having the following qualities: 1) deliberate and repeated acts of serious actual conflict; 2) between two or more political communities; 3) using combatants acting on their behalf; and 4) who are acting with political goals and intentions.

Now the problem with Coady's approach to political violence is to argue that the phenomenon of force-short-of-war is of the same kind as war and so this indicates that we should apply just war principles to events short-of-war in the same way as we would to war.[61] But there is an important reason why we should refrain from doing this: to ensure that the moral exceptionalism that we grant in war remains as exceptional as possible.[62] The central moral consideration in war, narrowly defined, is not just the taking of human life but the likelihood of taking many lives, many of whom are innocent. What is most morally concerning about war is the deliberate killing of human beings, typically in vast numbers.[63] Naturally, the taking of human life in vast numbers is something we want to avoid. My main concern with the expanded approach to war, so that war encapsulates a wider range of incidents, is that it is likely to end up actually permitting more killing and destruction than is necessary. I agree with Coady's overall aim: that is, to hold state militaries to a more rigorous ethical standard in the practice of using lethal force and to minimise the overall harm caused by physical conflict. But I argue that we should be aiming to confine the "dogs of war" to the smallest range of incidents possible and apply more appropriate constraints on the military when it operates outside of that context.

5. Conclusions

In conclusion, Coady does not want to restrict the notion of political violence to the activities of non-state agents, nor to separate ethical questions concerning such activities from those having to do with war or intervention. He is unimpressed by any attempt to put a conceptual or moral gulf between the resort to lethal force for political purposes by state agencies and its political employment by non-state actors.[64] This is because he believes it gives the mistaken impression that the purposes of state violence are somehow above politics and presumptively acceptable when employed by "our" state.[65] His fear is that freeing up the power of states to deploy the sword is more likely to wreak morally objectionable damage, at least in terms of scale, than anything non-state agents can achieve.[66] But I agree with Walzer that we can (and should) make a distinction between conflict in war and conflict short-of-war. The conventional just war approach suffers from a false dichotomy where the use of lethal force by the military is judged through the lens of either no conflict whatsoever or all-out war. It seems more reasonable to suggest that situations of conflict short-of-war might require a range of moderated responses, *including* military options.

Consequently, I argue, first, that we should conclude that war (narrowly understood) is worse than lethal force-short-of-war because the scale of permissible harm is higher (with the potential to be much higher) and it permits the forseeable harm of innocent people. Second, *jus ad vim* is better than conventional just war theory alone for judging such conflicts short-of-war because it acknowledges the need for a "hybrid" moral framework that inhibits the move towards the escalating violence characteristic of war. Third, *jus ad vim* prevents the expansion of war along with its morally exceptional permissions. I agree with Coady that the distinction between state and non-state actors is not a good reason for letting state actors off the moral hook. But that is one of the reasons why I think *jus ad vim* proves its utility. It gives us a better ability to morally evaluate the actions of state actors.

Notes

1 For comments on this chapter, special thanks to Tony Coady, Larry May, John Kleinig, Seumas Miller, Ned Dobos, Ross Babbage, Christian Enemark, Levi West, Adam Gastineau, and in particular Adam Henschke.
2 I will use the term "soldiers" throughout this paper in a generic way to refer to actively serving members of a military force, including airmen, sailors, submariners, bombardiers, sappers, and so on. It does not, however, refer to civilian members of a defense organization.
3 It might be argued that the state's use of the military is merely an adaptation to the emergence of "New Wars." I tend to favour Jessica Wolfendale's argument that the character of war has not fundamentally changed. What is changing, however, is the willingness to use the military to serve a wider range of institutional roles and purposes. J. Wolfendale, ""New Wars," Terrorism, and Just War Theory," in P. Tripodi and J. Wolfendale (eds), *New Wars and New Soldiers: Military Ethics in the Contemporary World*, Aldershot: Ashgate, 2011, pp. 16–17.
4 N. Dobos, *Insurrection and Intervention: The Two Faces of Sovereignty*, Cambridge: Cambridge University Press, 2011, p. 21.
5 B.M. Blechman and S.S. Kaplan, *Force Without War: U.S. Armed Forces as a Political Instrument*, Washington, DC: The Brookings Institution, 1978.
6 F.M. Kamm, "Failures of Just War Theory: Terror, Harm, and Justice,"*Ethics* 114:4, 2004.
7 "Terms such as Gun-Boat Diplomacy, Low-Intensity Conflict (LIC), Small Scale Contingencies (SSC) and Military Operations Other Than War (MOOTW) attempt to capture the nebulous region between peace and war where civilian authorities retain significant control of the military power used to achieve political purpose." A.J. Stephenson, "Shades of Gray: Gradual Escalation and Coercive Diplomacy," DTIC Document, 2002.

8 Just war revisionists argue that killing in war should not be treated differently from any other kind of killing. I hold to the conventional just war view that wartime killing is in some way morally exceptional. But I cannot sufficiently address this debate here. See: B.J. Strawser, "Walking the Tightrope of Just War," *Analysis* 71:3, 2011; S. Lazar, "The Morality and Law of War," in A. Marmor (ed.), *The Routledge Companion to Philosophy of Law*, Abingdon: Taylor & Francis, 2012; J. McMahan, *Killing in war*, Oxford: Oxford University Press, 2009; D. Rodin, *War and Self-Defense*, New York: Oxford University Press Inc, 2003.

9 D. Luban, "The war on terrorism and the end of human rights," *Philosophy and Public Policy Quarterly* 22, 2002, p. 9.

10 I do not have the space to fully discuss the moral implications of the policing context for the use of lethal force. For a discussion of the ethics of the police use of lethal force, see: S. Miller and J. Blackler, *Ethical Issues in Policing*, Aldershot: Ashgate Pub Ltd, 2005; pp. 61–82; J. Kleinig, *The Ethics of Policing*, Cambridge: Cambridge University Press, 1996. pp. 96–122; J. Reiman, "The Social Contract and the Police Use of Deadly Force," in F. Elliston and M. Feldberg (eds), *Moral Issues in Police Work*, New Jersey: Rowman and Allanheld, 1985.

11 Self-defense is not the only justification for taking the life of another person. It may be that each of us has the right to kill in the defense of the lives of others. Furthermore, in certain roles such as that of a police officer or soldier, there might be a moral obligation to kill in the defense of the lives of others. S. Miller, *Terrorism and Counter-Terrorism: Ethics and Liberal Democracy*, Oxford: Blackwell Publishing, 2009, pp. 64–65.

12 T. Junod, "The Lethal Presidency of Barack Obama," *Esquire*, 9 July, 2012.

13 "Al Qaeda is evidently a clandestine organization consisting of elements in many countries and apparently composed of people of various nationalities; it is dedicated to advancing certain political and religious objectives by means of terrorist acts directed against the United States and other, largely Western, nations. As such, Al Qaeda does not in any respect resemble a state, is not a subject of international law, and lacks international legal personality. It is not a party to the Geneva Conventions, and it could not be a party to them or to any international agreement. Its methods brand it as a criminal organization under national laws and as an international outlaw. Its members are properly subject to trial and punishment under national criminal laws for any crimes that they commit." G.H. Aldrich, "The Taliban, Al Qaeda, and the Determination of Illegal Combatants," *The American Journal of International Law* 96:4, 2002, p. 893.

14 That is, any person who is subject to a state's jurisdiction, not only its citizens.

15 Luban's argument against what he calls the "hybrid war-law model" is his concern that 'the U.S. has simply chosen the bits of the law model and the bits of the war model that are most convenient for American interests, and ignored the rest.' Luban, "The War on Terrorism and the End of Human Rights," p. 12. But the misuse of an *ad hoc* hybrid war-law model by the U.S. does not rule out the development of a well-reasoned morally worthwhile hybrid ethical framework *per se*.

16 Outside of Coady's book, *Morality and Political Violence*, there has been seemingly little direct discussion of *jus ad vim* in the literature. C.A.J. Coady, *Morality and Political Violence*, Cambridge: Cambridge University Press, 2008.

17 M. Walzer, *Just and Unjust Wars: A Moral Argument with Historical Illustrations*, 4th edn, New York: Basic Books, 2006.

18 Ibid., xv.

19 Ibid., xiv.

20 "Collective security rests on the notion of all against one. While states retain considerable autonomy over the conduct of their foreign policy, participation in a collective security organization entails a commitment by each member to join a coalition to confront any aggressor with opposing preponderant strength … a collective security organization, by institutionalizing the notion of all against one, contributes to the creation of an international setting in which stability emerges through cooperation rather than through competition." C.A. Kupchan and C.A. Kupchan, "Concerts, Collective Security, and the Future of Europe," *International Security* 16:1, 1991, p. 118.

21 M. Walzer, *Just and Unjust Wars*, p. xiv.

22 C.A.J. Coady, *Morality and Political Violence*, p. 88.

23 Thanks to Ned Dobos for framing the problem this way.

24 M. Walzer, *Just and Unjust Wars*, p. xiv.

25 Note that I will be using the terms "force short-of-war" and "lethal force-short-of-war" interchangeably throughout the rest of this chapter.

26 M Walzer, *Just and Unjust Wars*, p. xiv.

27 M. Knisbacher, "The Entebbe Operation: A Legal Analysis of Israel's Rescue Action," *Journal of International Law & Economics* 12, 1977.

28 Walzer, *Just and Unjust Wars*, p. xv.

29 Ibid.

30 Ibid.

31 Ibid., p. xvii.

32 C.A.J. Coady, *Morality and Political Violence*, p. 93.

33 Coady's use of the expression "political violence" includes 'war as the primary instance of such violence, but it is also meant to cover other violent activities that some would not include under the heading of war. Such activities encompass terrorism, armed intervention (for "humanitarian" or other purposes), armed revolution, violent demonstrations or attacks by citizens aimed at less than the overthrow of their government, and the deployment of mercenary companies or individuals. It could also include other activities … such as certain forms of torture, assassination, and violent covert operations,' ibid., p. 3.

34 Ibid., p. 93.

35 Ibid., p. 7.

36 Ibid.

37 Coady expressed these ongoing qualms in personal communications, June 2012.

38 See: B. J. Strawser, "Moral Predators: The Duty to Employ Uninhabited Aerial Vehicles," *Journal of Military Ethics* 9:4, 2010; J.C. Galliott, "Uninhabited Aerial Vehicles and the Asymmetry Objection: A Response to Strawser," *Journal of Military Ethics* 11:1, 2012.

39 Coady says, "Given the appalling record of states in the unjustified employment of lethal force to devastate populations, economies, and cultures over the centuries, I am unimpressed by any attempt to put a conceptual or moral gulf between the resort to such force (or, as I would prefer to say, violence) for political purposes by state agencies and its political employment by nonstate actors. The tendency to talk of the state as using 'force' and of terrorists or revolutionaries as using 'violence' embodies an attempt to bring initial opprobrium upon the nonstate actors (via the negative connotations of 'violence') and to give an a priori mantle of respectability to the state actors. When the qualification 'political' is added only to the activities of the nonstate agents and withheld from the state's operations, even where the means employed are identical or similar in kind, this can suggest that the purposes of state violence are somehow above politics and presumptively acceptable, at least when employed by 'our' state." C.A.J Coady, *Morality and Political Violence*: p. 3. Since I've deliberately given myself a very restrictive focus in this chapter by only looking at the military as functionaries of the state, it might be that Coady's point about the unfairness of state versus non-state actors applies. I'm certainly sympathetic to his point. But my primary argument remains valid: that *jus ad vim* serves to morally tighten the uses of lethal force by state actors.

40 L. May, *Aggression and Crimes Against Peace*, Cambridge: Cambridge University Press, 2008, p. 23.

41 S. Lazar, "Responsibility, Risk, and Killing in Self-Defense," *Ethics*, 119:4, 2009, p. 699.

42 S. Gazit, "Risk, Glory, and the Rescue Operation," *International Security* 6:1, 1981.

43 Knisbacher, "The Entebbe Operation: A Legal Analysis of Israel's Rescue Action."

44 "It is worth distinguishing two types of slippery-slope argument. The first type – the horrible result-argument – objects, roughly speaking, to what is at the bottom of the slope. The second type objects to the fact that it is a slope: this may be called the arbitrary result argument." B. Williams, "Which Slopes are Slippery?" in M. Lockwood (ed.), *Moral Dilemmas in Modern Medicine*, Oxford: Oxford University Press, 1985.

45 M. Walzer, *Just and Unjust Wars*, p. xiv.

46 C.A.J. Coady, *Morality and Political Violence*, p. 5.

47 Ibid., p. 6.

48 Ibid., p. 3.

49 Norman concludes that moral arguments are unlikely to be advanced one way or another if they are conducted primarily in terms of the concept of "violence." He suggests this is because use of the term is likely to be determined by prior moral positions and the concept of "violence" cannot itself be used to defend these positions. R. J. Norman, *Ethics, Killing, and War*, Cambridge University Press, 1995, p. 37.

50 C.A.J. Coady, *Morality and Political Violence*, p. 6.

51 Ibid.

52 M.B. Oren, *Six Days of War: June 1967 and the Making of the Modern Middle East*, Oxford: Oxford University Press, 2002.

53 C. Allmand, *The Hundred Years War: England and France at War c.1300–c.1450*, Cambridge: Cambridge University Press, 1988.

54 C.A.J. Coady, *Morality and Political Violence*, p. 6.

55 Ibid., p. 7.

56 "[S]ystems of accountability developed to regulate the use of force domestically cannot simply be transferred to the international humanitarian law context. Consequently, both states and human rights supervisory bodies may have to readjust their understanding of the role human rights law can play in enhancing the accountability framework regarding the use of deadly force in armed conflict. No gaps in the effort to apply appropriate norms of humanity can be allowed." Kenneth Watkin, "Controlling the Use of Force: A Role for Human Rights Norms in Contemporary Armed Conflict," *The American Journal of International Law*, 98:1, 2004.

57 B. Orend, *The Morality of War*, Ontario: Broadview Press, 2006.

58 Political communities, as defined by Orend, are those entities which are either states or intend to become states, the state being the machinery of government which organises life in a given territory. Ibid., p. 2.

59 Ibid., p. 3.

60 Ibid.

61 J.A.C. Coady, *Morality and Political Violence*, p. 7.

62 By moral exceptionalism I simply mean the exceptional duties and permissions we grant soldiers in active theatres of war to use lethal force. For more on exceptionalism, see: A. Fiala, "A Critique of Exceptions: Torture, Terrorism, and the Lesser Evil Argument," *International Journal of Applied Philosophy* 20:1, 2005; F. Allhoff, *Terrorism, Ticking Time-Bombs, and Torture: A Philosophical Analysis*, University of Chicago Press, 2012, esp. Chapter 3; J.H. Marks, "What Counts in Counterterrorism," *Columbia Human Rights Law Review* 37:3, 2005.

63 R.J. Norman, *Ethics, Killing, and War*, p. 37.

64 J.A.C. Coady, *Morality and Political Violence*, p. 3.

65 Ibid.

66 Ibid.

References

Aldrich, G.H. "The Taliban, Al Qaeda, and the Determination of Illegal Combatants," *The American Journal of International Law*, 96:4, 2002, pp. 891–98.

Allhoff, F. *Terrorism, Ticking Time-Bombs, and Torture: A Philosophical Analysis*, Chicago: University of Chicago Press, 2012.

Allmand, C. *The Hundred Years War: England and France at War c.1300–c.1450*, Cambridge: Cambridge University Press, 1988.

Blechman, B.M. and S.S. Kaplan. *Force without War: U.S. Armed Forces as a Political Instrument*, Washington, DC: The Brookings Institution, 1978.

Coady, C.A.J. *Morality and Political Violence*, Cambridge: Cambridge University Press, 2008.

Dobos, N. *Insurrection and Intervention: The Two Faces of Sovereignty*, Cambridge: Cambridge University Press, 2011.

Fiala, A. "A Critique of Exceptions: Torture, Terrorism, and the Lesser Evil Argument," *International Journal of Applied Philosophy*, 20:1, 2005, pp. 127–42.

Galliott, J.C. "Uninhabited Aerial Vehicles and the Asymmetry Objection: A Response to Strawser," *Journal of Military Ethics*, 11:1, 2012, pp. 58–66.

Gazit, S. "Risk, Glory, and the Rescue Operation," *International Security*, 6:1, 1981, pp. 111–35.

Junod, T. "The Lethal Presidency of Barack Obama," *Esquire*, 9 July, 2012.

Kamm, F.M. "Failures of Just War Theory: Terror, Harm, and Justice," *Ethics*, 114:4, 2004, pp. 650–92.

Kleinig, J. *The Ethics of Policing*, Cambridge: Cambridge University Press, 1996.

Knisbacher, M. "The Entebbe Operation: A Legal Analysis of Israel's Rescue Action," *Journal of International Law & Economics* 12, 1977, pp. 57–83.

Kupchan, C.A. and C.A. Kupchan. "Concerts, Collective Security, and the Future of Europe," *International Security*, 16: 1, 1991, pp. 114–61.

Lazar, S. "The Morality and Law of War," in A. Marmor (ed.), *The Routledge Companion to Philosophy of Law*, Abingdon: Taylor & Francis, 2012.

——"Responsibility, Risk, and Killing in Self-Defense," *Ethics*, 119:4, 2009, pp. 699–728.

Luban, D. "The War on Terrorism and the End of Human Rights," *Philosophy and Public Policy*, Quarterly 22, 2002, pp. 9–14.

Marks, J.H. "What Counts in Counterterrorism," *Columbia Human Rights Law Review*, 37:3, 2005, pp. 101–61.

May, L. *Aggression and Crimes against Peace*, Cambridge: Cambridge University Press, 2008.

McMahan, J. *Killing in War*, Oxford: Oxford University Press, 2009.

Miller, S. *Terrorism and Counter-Terrorism: Ethics and Liberal Democracy*, Oxford: Blackwell Publishing, 2009.

Miller, S, and J. Blackler. *Ethical Issues in Policing*, Aldershot: Ashgate, 2005.

Norman, R.J. *Ethics, Killing, and War*, Cambridge: Cambridge University Press, 1995.

Oren, M. B. *Six Days of War: June 1967 and the Making of the Modern Middle East*, Oxford: Oxford University Press, 2002.

Orend, B. *The Morality of War*, Ontario: Broadview Press, 2006.

Reiman, J. "The Social Contract and the Police Use of Deadly Force," in F. Elliston and M. Feldberg (eds), *Moral Issues in Police Work*, New Jersey: Rowman and Allanheld, 1985, pp. 237–49.

Rodin, D. *War and Self-Defense*, New York: Oxford University Press, 2003.

Stephenson, A.J. "Shades of Gray: Gradual Escalation and Coercive Diplomacy," *DTIC Document*, 2002.

Strawser, B. J. "Moral Predators: The Duty to Employ Uninhabited Aerial Vehicles," *Journal of Military Ethics*, 9:4, 2010, pp. 342–68.

——"Walking the Tightrope of Just War," *Analysis* 71: 3, 2011, pp. 533–44.

Walzer, M. *Just and Unjust Wars: A Moral Argument with Historical Illustrations*, 4th edn. New York: Basic Books, 2006.

Watkin, K. "Controlling the Use of Force: A Role for Human Rights Norms in Contemporary Armed Conflict," *The American Journal of International Law*, 98:1, 2004, pp. 1–34.

Williams, B. "Which Slopes Are Slippery?" in M. Lockwood (ed.), *Moral Dilemmas in Modern Medicine*, Oxford: Oxford University Press, 1985.

Wolfendale, J. ""New Wars," Terrorism, and Just War Theory," in P. Tripodi and J. Wolfendale (eds), *New Wars and New Soldiers: Military Ethics in the Contemporary World*, Aldershot: Ashgate, 2011, pp. 13–30.

6

REVISIONIST JUST WAR THEORY AND THE REAL WORLD

A cautiously optimistic proposal

Bradley Jay Strawser

1. Introduction

The scholarly tradition known as just war theory has been remarkably stable. Relatively little of its primary elements have changed from its early instantiations found in the writings of Augustine all the way to its detailed exposition by Michael Walzer in *Just and Unjust Wars*.[1] Recent scholarship on the ethics of war, however, has been dominated by those critical of this tradition. These revisionist just war theorists have revolted against many of the core principles of the long-held standard view.[2] The revisionist account usually begins from a simple but powerful basis: the individual rights of all people.[3] These revisionists argue that our moral understanding of war must respect and take seriously people's rights, including the right to not be killed unjustly, just as those rights demand respect in any context other than war. They conclude that in order to do this some of the central vestments of the classic just war tradition must be discarded.

Embracing the revisionist account and attempting to wage war according to it would require rather significant changes to how war is presently waged and how *jus in bello* criteria are implemented. Indeed, *jus in bello* principles would have to be reformulated anew in many ways in order to align with the rights respecting changes proposed by the revisionists. Many have responded that, in actual practice, such changes are unworkable; that the revisionist account cannot be applied in a just way to the real world of warfare. What is needed, then, is an attempt to work out how the morality of war, properly understood by the revisionist model, might look if an honest effort were made to apply it to the realities of modern warfare. That is, the revisionists need to answer these challenges not merely by showing that the revisionist account is the better theoretical model of just war, but also by pointing to a positive vision for how war could actually be waged while following the revisionist demands. While it is only a start for such a project, that is what I aim to do in this chapter.[4] Thus, rather than argue positively for the theoretical correctness of the revisionist just war account, here I will explore how it could work were real-world militaries to actually embrace the revisionist approach when they go to war.[5]

2. The real-world objection

On traditional just war theory, a given populace in any war is divided simply and crudely between combatants and noncombatants; these are the only two categories upon which targeting decisions are to be based. If one is a combatant, one can be targeted and intentionally killed at any time and any place during war. If one is deemed a noncombatant, then one is not to be intentionally harmed or infringed upon in any way. The revisionists contend that this approach to killing in war does not properly respect the rights of many individuals involved in war. This is because some who would traditionally be labeled combatants are, in fact, not properly liable, and should not be unrestricted targets of attack. This would include both the combatants fighting for a just cause (henceforth, "just combatants"), since they have not done anything by fighting for a just cause to make themselves liable to be killed, as well as some of the less responsible combatants fighting for an unjust cause (henceforth, "unjust combatants"), since their contribution to the unjust cause is insufficient to become liable to be killed. Similarly, on the other side of the traditional view's binary divide, the revisionist's argue that a few individuals who would conventionally be labeled noncombatants are, in fact, somewhat responsible such that they should not be utterly immune from any harm and may be at least partially liable. In the revisionist vein, I hold that these deficiencies—particularly allowing people who are not in fact morally liable to be killed—demonstrate that the traditional division of target status is far too imprecise a tool for the fine-grained realities of moral responsibility in war.

This is a prime example of the ways in which the revisionist account has discarded some of the central tenets of the just war tradition in favor of a more rights respecting approach to the morality of war. The cornerstone of the traditional view here rejected by the revisionists is the doctrine known as the "moral equality of combatants thesis" (henceforth, the MEC).[6] The MEC contends that combatants on both sides of any conflict are equally legitimate targets of attack. They are considered legitimate targets not because they are engaged in wrongdoing but because they pose a threat to one another as combatants. According to the MEC, so long as these combatants follow the *jus in bello* strictures of proportionality and discrimination, just combatants and unjust combatants are moral equals: both may permissibly kill and both may permissibly be killed by the other.

The MEC's centrality for the traditional view is hard to overstate; it is in many ways the single doctrinal lynchpin of the entire just war tradition superstructure. This is because it is the MEC that allows for the division of *jus ad bellum* and *jus in bello* to begin with and, many hold, is thereby what allows for the possibility of just war at all. The MEC, by designating that combatants on both sides are legitimate targets, is also what leads to the claim that noncombatants on both sides are *not* legitimate targets. The revisionist challenge to the MEC is simple. It argues that one is not liable to be killed if one fights for a just cause. People have a presumptive right against being killed, after all, so why should a soldier fighting for a just cause lose that right for posing a *justified* threat against an unjust enemy? This is the central challenge pressed by the revisionists against the MEC and traditional just war theory more broadly. If there is no good answer forthcoming, then it seems we must reject the MEC. But doing so, and embracing the resulting revisionist position, greets its own multitude of objections and problems.

The difficulties such a change would bring to the operations of modern militaries have been the basis for much critique of the revisionist account. Seth Lazar, for example, while accepting the revisionist rejection of the MEC, argues that without it determining liability is impossible and we are left with choosing between either a form of contingent pacifism or else morally unacceptable total war.[7] Henry Shue also points to the extreme epistemic difficulties of war and contends that we must therefore retain the MEC, since it is otherwise untenable for soldiers to be able to fight justly.[8] Michael Walzer himself thinks the realities of war are such that he will not even *entertain* the possibility of what it could look like on the revisionist model. In speaking of Jeff McMahan, the scholar who has done more to advance the revisionist case than any other, Walzer dismissively wrote, "What Jeff McMahan means to provide ... is a careful and precise account of individual responsibility in time of war. What he actually provides, I think, is a careful and precise account of what individual responsibility in war would be like if war were a peacetime activity."[9] Walzer has made his opinion of the (im)plausibility of the revisionist account even more clear in spoken comments.[10]

In these debates between the traditionalists and the revisionists we can distinguish two aspects to the traditionalist critiques. In the first instance, there is usually a theoretic or technical objection to the revisionist account. But, failing that, if it is shown or granted that the revisionist theory is sound in principle, we tend to find a secondary objection which actually undergirds the broader worry against the entire revisionist project. Call this worry the "real-world objection." The objection takes on many forms, but its general outline is as follows: "I may grant that the revisionist objections to traditional just war theory's tenets (such as the rejection of the MEC) are technically correct, and I grant that the revisionist account for liability to be killed in war is morally superior. Be that as it may, there's just no way to implement the revisionist account in the real world, so it must be rejected."[11]

The real-world objection will be better illuminated with a more specific example. Return to Seth Lazar's attack on the revisionist account.[12] Lazar argued that were we to embrace the revisionist rejection of the MEC, the traditional categories of combatant and noncombatant would break down entirely. On the one hand, he argues, assignment of liability would become rampant and total war would ensue. On the other hand, restrictions on who just combatants can engage would become so great that military victory would become impossible. The problem, argues Lazar, rests in how the revisionist theory understands moral responsibility and resulting liability for a populace at war. If we raise the liability threshold too high, then many who we think ought to be legitimate targets in war will be excluded. On the other hand, if we lower the liability threshold in response to this problem, then it invites its own problem: far too many people will fall into the category of being legitimate targets than is plausible for a just war. That is, Lazar argues that the revisionist view cannot work in theory and makes just war impossible due to this supposed dilemma over the difficulty in determining liability thresholds. Elsewhere I responded to Lazar that difficulty, even extreme difficulty, in fighting war justly does not equal impossibility.[13] I showed how even if doing away with the MEC makes determination of enemy liability *difficult*, it could still be done in a reasonable way that approximates just war.

I will not return to that debate with Lazar here. Nor will I directly address any of the other currently ongoing theoretical critiques of revisionist just war theory. Rather, let us assume for the sake of argument that the revisionist account is technically correct both in its assessment of the morality of war (and the ways in which traditional just war theory gets it wrong) and that, at a theoretical level, these kinds of objections are not irresolvable. Even if that is true (if, for example, I am correct in my response to Lazar that liability attribution thresholds are not *impossible* to determine in a just way in war), the *pragmatic* challenges of actually applying revisionist just war theory to the realities of war remain daunting. This is the real-world objection that presses upon the revisionist account, even if the revisionist approach is correct in theory. This is, in fact, Lazar's underlying worry and it gives us a nice example of the real-world objection. Indeed, Lazar grants the revisionist rejection of the MEC; he is not attempting to rescue the traditional reliance upon it. Yet he doubts whether a moral understanding of war can *function* in any way resembling a just manner, even if the theoretical problem posed by his dilemma can be resolved in the ways I've argued.[14]

3. Reasonable perceived liability

How then can the revisionist account respond to the real-world objection that lies at the heart of most critiques? Not only must the theoretic model itself be defended, but a positive vision of how a revisionist approach to war could actually play out is needed. Here, then, is one such vision of how the revisionist theory could be implemented in the real world.

To align the revisionist project to targeting decisions in war, I propose tying combatant status directly to the degreed nature of liability; to re-envision combatant-hood away from an all-or-nothing condition to one of degree. McMahan writes that "the extent to which a person is excused for posing a threat of wrongful harm affects the degree of his moral liability to defensive harm, which in turn affects the stringency of the proportionality restriction on defensive force."[15] We could take this basic principle and derive *new* categories for an unjust population set that could then be applied in a given real-world war. This would mean that we need more complex categories of combatant and noncombatant status to better accommodate the realities of variable liability levels amongst any given enemy population.

Thus, rather than the binary combatant or noncombatant system of categorization traditionally used, on my proposal a conflict-by-conflict rubric could be constructed that tracks the varying levels of liability for a given set of unjust enemies based on the best possible determination of their individual moral responsibility. The distinctions could range from 1st, 2nd, and 3rd-degree combatants and the like (or more, as needed) and similar degrees for noncombatants. The basis for an adversary's degreed status would be tied to what I call "reasonable perceived liability" (RPL) rather than other less adequate metrics traditionally used (such as posing a threat, as discussed above). RPL should be understood as the best approximate determination of an enemy's degree of liability that could be reached by a just force taking all reasonable efforts to make that determination. Once broad levels of RPL were determined for a population, correlating categories of degreed combatant and noncombatant statuses could then be applied accordingly. Specialized rules of engagement (ROE) could then be created which best allow a military to achieve victory yet come as close as possible to matching the correct level of response to the RPL for each derived category.

Of course, the revisionist understanding of liability to be killed in any context is fluid dependent upon the actual degree of moral responsibility for a given individual within a population set. So, to be clear, an unjust enemy's status *should* track exactly with his or her liability on the revisionist model. That is, RPL is of a continuous nature since it is tracking liability itself. Consequently, one might object that if I am going to take the revisionist view seriously I should not generalize from distinct individual liability to categories of any kind—be it the traditional binary split or my proposed more complex divisions. I agree, in principle. Respecting each individual's moral responsibility and liability is central to the revisionist rejection of the MEC; that's precisely what the crude instrument of the binary combatant and noncombatant distinction fails to adequately do.

However, by developing complex levels of enemy status we could adequately cover the vast majority of cases such that just soldiers could engage an enemy with minimized moral risk. The primary reason for this is because there is only a limited, finite range of possible choices on how to engage any given enemy population in any given context; there are only so many things a just force can do. A force can ignore, avoid, evade, capture, shoot, bomb, and so on for any given individual within an enemy population. The options are not infinite. Thus, we could create discrete levels of enemy status derived from RPL, even if RPL is itself a non-discrete property. That is, for pragmatic reasons that do not outstrip respect for the enemies' rights, some generalizations of enemy status are permissible. The more complex divisions I'm proposing are a best approximation of what morality demands, which then serve as a heuristic for a given force's best efforts to correlate how one is treated in warfare to one's actual liability.[16]

By deriving enemy status from RPL some of those in a given population who would traditionally be labeled as simply "combatants" would instead be considered some lesser-degreed type of combatant with different correlative ROE. Similarly, the same would be done for those traditionally labeled simply "noncombatants." Narrow proportionality can press us farther than even McMahan suggests towards evermore complex and restrictive ROE resulting in a broad range of varied responses for different cases, dependent upon the given RPL. McMahan explains how the concept of narrow proportionality restricts any defensive response to "(1) the magnitude of the wrongful harm to be prevented, (2) the effectiveness of the defensive act in averting the harm, (3) the magnitude of the harm inflicted on the wrongdoer, and (4) the degree of his responsibility for the threat that he poses."[17] My proposed model takes these considerations and attempts to work them *directly* into our conception of enemy status.

Pace Lazar, under such restrictive ROE military victory could still be attainable in certain contexts. But, it must be admitted, victory will not be attainable in *all* contexts under such restrictions. However, when it is impossible to fight justly and achieve victory, it is unjust to go to war. Accepting this reality is one of the bullets we must bite in embracing revisionist just war theory. By my lights, however, this is an entirely reasonable claim when properly understood. If a given side can only achieve victory through engaging in overtly unjust practices that intentionally violate the rights of nonliable people, then any such victory, whatever else it may be, should be understood as an instance of unjust war.

RPL determination should account for factors such as epistemic limitations regarding one's cause, coercion to fight, other external pressures or confusions, and so on.[18] As noted, this RPL determination would be accomplished by a just force researching the evidence available to an enemy populace and the various options for them to take in their support, or nonsupport, of an unjust cause. While this may sound impractical at first glance, I'll show below some real-world cases of militaries making these kinds of determinations and behaving accordingly.

Further, a key piece of the RPL proposal is that that liability—even in war—need not necessarily constitute proper eligibility for *lethal* attack. Again, narrow proportionality can push just war-fighters to ever more restrictive ROE that include not only who to target, but also how to engage. This could result in a range of non-lethal responses being the best option for many cases, depending on the RPL of the enemy.[19] I argue that such ROE could be workable, reasonable, and exactly the *kind* of developments that we should expect as the just war theory tradition improves over time—ever more restrictive, striving for ever more just behavior in combat. The recent work of revisionist just war theorists can be seen as following this trajectory. Clearly, the rejection of the MEC makes fighting just war far more difficult. But if this is what morality demands of us—that is, if the revisionists are right that we should reject the MEC—then so be it. Given what war actually is, it should not be surprising that it is incredibly difficult to fight justly.

So the formal proposal for how to reconcile revisionist just war theory and the real world is that we create more categories with simplified differences in engagement for different groups in any given just war. This idea is not entirely foreign and out-of-line with the general progression of the just war canon. For example, a classic problem in traditional just war theory is how to classify people who support an unjust war effort in indirect ways such as building munitions for the unjust military. We see this in the work of both Walzer and Nagel, the two most commonly cited defenders of the traditional view. They wrestle over the question and argue it is acceptable for a just force to kill such persons while they worked but not in their homes.[20] I'm not defending their position on how to treat such noncombatants, but I raise it to show that even these traditional just war theorists recognized that liability in war is more complicated than the meager two category system can deliver. By creating more divisions within these categories, with different ROE for each, these perennial questions regarding difficult cases could be better resolved. That is precisely the kind of progress the revisionist approach aims to attain over the traditional account's weaknesses.

To see how vexing this problem is, and how badly a more complex set of wartime statuses is needed, consider the following common cases in contemporary warfare. What are we to make of a military lawyer who spends all her efforts fighting to mitigate the war crimes her unjust comrades commit? On the traditional view, as a military member her status would simply be "combatant" and she would thus be liable to be killed by an opposing force at any time. Or consider a civilian target analyst working in an unjust military's command center, making major decisions over which targets to bomb. Again, traditional just war theory would classify him as immune from harm as a "noncombatant." Compare that target analyst's contribution and liability to that of unjust soldiers who are garrisoned far in the rear, fully removed from combat, and likely to never be used to further the unjust cause. Should we treat such soldiers the same as soldiers on the frontline who are actively killing just soldiers to further the unjust cause? Moreover, compare the civilian target analyst (immune from harm on the traditional account) to unjust combatants who have been coerced into the service of the unjust cause. Whatever one's conclusions on how each should be treated in war, clearly the traditional view's binary model, by allowing for *unrestricted killing* of the coerced soldiers and *immunity* for the voluntary civilian target analyst, gets something horribly wrong. Such cases strongly suggest that more complex categories reflecting differing levels of liability are needed.

4. Deriving RPL

On my proposal, as noted, enemy soldiers under difficult epistemic circumstances for ascertaining the (in)justice of their cause, should fall into different categories than those for whom a just force had reason to believe were fighting for the unjust cause with better access to evidence for the injustice of their cause. Gerhard Overland's work, "Killing Soldiers," discusses some of the differences between various liability levels of combatants amongst an enemy population in ways that track closely with my model.[21] He argues, for example, that in the case of the US invasion of Iraq, a just force would rightly distinguish between those Iraqi soldiers who were members of the Republican Guard (a volunteer force made up of well-paid, and usually well-informed, proud partisans dedicated to Saddam Hussein) versus Iraqi soldiers who had less access to good information and were conscripted into military service under coercion and threat of death for themselves or their family.[22] A multifaceted combatant rubric like I suggest could account for these significant differences in the liability of Iraqi soldiers and varying levels of mitigating excuses. The RPL level for a member of the Republican Guard would be, presumably, quite different from that of a conscripted Iraqi soldier and would correlate to a different degree of combatant status with correspondingly different ROE.

In practical terms, this could mean that a just force engaged against the Iraqi military at that time might classify conscripted troops as, say, "3rd-degree combatants" whereas members of the Republican Guard would be "1st-degree combatants." The ROE for 3rd-degree combatants could be, perhaps, to only fire if directly fired upon, to avoid direct engagements, to seek and encourage the peaceful surrender of such enemy forces, or to seek non-lethal forms of engagement, and so on. Whereas, alternatively, ROE for 1st-degree combatants could follow more traditional just war theory guidelines for targeting.

Another important aspect to determining an enemy combatant's liability that critics of the revisionist view tend to neglect is that just war-fighters presumably take themselves to be engaged in a just war. Lazar, for example, fails to account for this as part of a given just force's apprehension of unjust soldiers' liability. He mentions this (lack of certainty knowing "that their own cause is just") as a prohibitive factor working *against* the just war-fighter's ability to discriminate. But Lazar has this reasoning backwards. *If* the set of combatants in question are *actually* just war-fighters, that then means (amongst other things) that they have the proper epistemic confidence in the justice of their cause. That is, if they are putative just combatants, then they've met whatever threshold of epistemic confidence in the justice of one's cause is required for one to permissibly engage in war. To wage war without confidence that one's cause is just is to engage in a highly morally risky activity (killing others) without the requisite epistemic diligence regarding the activity's moral permissibility. This raises the broader issue of how failing to meet certain moral epistemic demands on investigating the permissibility of one's actions can itself make one liable. I will discuss this in more detail below. The point presently is that combatant liability determination does not occur in a vacuum—"from the outside"—but by those sides already engaged in a conflict.

This means, amongst other things, that the *extent* to which just combatants are convinced of the justice of their own military undertaking would affect their ascertaining of an enemies' epistemic view of their cause. Assume that a just combatant has held herself to a highly skeptical position regarding her own side's justification for war. Yet, she attained a high-level of epistemic confidence in the justice of her cause before she decided to join the war effort.[23] From this it follows that the just combatant, in satisfying the high-level of epistemic satisfaction she would need to be justified to engage war, has at least a *prima facie* reason to hold that the enemies' side is unjust to a similar degree, at least in terms of its overall *jus ad bellum*.[24] The question of the enemies' presumed evidence for the injustice of their cause is thus colored by the just combatants' own level of epistemic certainty for the justice of their own cause.[25]

This does not settle the matter, of course, for the enemies' epistemic access (it can be assumed) will almost certainly be limited, perhaps radically so, as to the real state of affairs for their side's justification. Of course, such limitations, as best as they could be known, should be factored into RPL. But the basic idea is this: if a given population holds itself to a very high bar of healthy skepticism for themselves to be convinced that their own side is just, and then they *are* so convinced, this strongly implies that (most likely) there will be rather strong evidence making the case, such as naked aggression or genocide and so forth.[26]

McMahan makes the point that it is hard to comprehend how a German soldier invading Poland at the outset of WWII could have possibly held that his cause was just.[27] Even granting high levels of propaganda and nationalistic preference (and what Lazar calls "reasonable partiality"), it is hard to imagine one honestly believing his cause is in the right under such circumstances.[28] Far more likely is that an unjust soldier in such a case simply failed to even consider the justice of his cause. Perhaps he mistakenly thought that it was not his job to consider questions pertaining to *jus ad bellum*—as traditional just war theory has long proclaimed. This is the great hurdle the revisionist view must overcome. It argues that we must change the way soldiers approach the business of war in regard to their own participation therein.

The traditional view on this point is captured by the clichéd line from Alfred Tennyson's "Charge of the Light Brigade," that it is not a soldier's place "to make reply / Theirs not to reason why / Theirs but to do and die."[29] The thought is that it is on the soldiers' shoulders to behave justly within war; but it is not their responsibility to determine the justice of the war for which they fight.[30] The revisionist view rejects this notion and insists that a soldier must consider the justice for which they fight and kill. I admit then that a thorough-going rejection of this widespread notion in society at large will be a necessary component of any attempt to apply a revisionist just war model to the real world. That is, the revisionists must make it clear to those who consider fighting in a war that it is "theirs to question why" precisely because it is "theirs to do and die."

This leaves open an interesting question regarding excusing ignorance for moral responsibility. How should the fact that a soldier simply takes *jus ad bellum* to not be her concern affect her liability determination? Is this an excusing ignorance or is the failed moral reasoning itself something for which they can be held at least partially liable?[31]

I am not sure how we should answer this tough puzzle. A full exploration of these questions concerning excusing moral ignorance and moral responsibility lies beyond the scope of this chapter.[32] To begin, however, it seems clear that the relative accessibility or clarity of evidence that makes the unjust combatant's cause more or less manifestly unjust will run inversely correlative to how we should consider this kind of ignorance as excusing. To see why this should be our approach, note that when a cause is manifestly unjust we have historically seen soldiers drop the pretense that *jus ad bellum* was of no concern to the permissibility of their service—and this was long before the recent rise of revisionist challenges to just war theory ever surfaced. This shows that obvious and evident injustice of one's cause can lead soldiers to see through the ignorance of a strict separation of *jus ad bellum* and *jus in bello*.[33] When the injustice of a cause is less evident, then, it is presumably far easier to maintain the separation in one's mind with regard to their service therein and, thus, such ignorance would be more excusable of one's liability.

To help develop this point, McMahan offers an illuminating discussion of a Palestinian suicide bomber from Gaza.[34] Needless to say, the act the suicide bomber is carrying out is, to our eyes, a clearly wrong act. So we should consider how it is that the suicide bomber could be so mistaken and think it is permissible.[35] What are we to make of the suicide bomber in terms of his liability? Does his ignorance give him an epistemic excuse that could, even partially, excuse his liability? I do not think it does, and I do not think any plausible account of how liability is determined should be committed to this, nor any version of revisionist just war theory.[36]

McMahan argues, for example, that we can reasonably demand of someone the mere act of minimal moral reflective equilibrium. That is, that one should ask oneself if he or she would consider someone on the opposing side undertaking the same action against his or her side as just were the conditions and roles exactly reversed. McMahan argues that the Palestinian suicide bomber would almost certainly *not* hold this (that he would not think that an Israeli suicide bomber killing innocent people attending a mosque, say, would not be justified, even if the Palestinians were keeping the Israelis under their thumb in the same ways the bomber believes Israel is presently doing to them). This is a plausible assumption. And, indeed, holding that one is morally responsible to engage in at least some minimal level of moral reflection before undertaking such a morally weighty act as intentionally killing others (in war or other contexts), is likewise not a radical proposition.[37]

If one grants this, it provides a further factor to calculate RPL for a given enemy: failing to conduct even minimal moral reflection in one's actions can constitute a failing of epistemic due diligence which can be a legitimate factor for determining liability. Thus, the just combatant's apprehension of the enemy soldier proceeds through steps. If an enemy has clear evidence that demands simple moral reflection, we can rightly expect that of them (and all people, including ourselves). Ultimately all of these factors—expected moral reflection, the possibilities of epistemic limitations, coercion, reasonable partiality, and so forth—can culminate in some degree of RPL which can then map onto some degree of discrete combatant-hood. That degreed status then correlates to restrictive ROE for that status which are themselves correlative to the level of uncertainty for RPL.

In discussing people's decision to go to war Lazar writes, "It is unreasonable to expect people to formulate beliefs warranting high credence, when the moral and nonmoral evidence do not support a determinate conclusion."[38] But the revisionist view I'm defending agrees with Lazar that people should not formulate a belief warranting high credence in such a case, particularly if that belief licenses killing people. Rather, when the decision to go to war involves such uncertainty, people should remain agnostic as to whether their side is just and then err on the side of caution by not taking on the moral risk of fighting in a potentially unjust war.[39] If, however, they do have high credence for believing they are justified to go to war, this will entail that there are (most likely) some fairly obvious reasons for the opposing side to question the justice of their cause (again, think of the German soldier invading Poland or the cognitive dissonance of the Palestinian suicide bomber). And this reality will, in turn, be part of the complex calculus of RPL that a just force must make in engaging the enemy. But, again, if the just forces conclude that there are good reasons to think the epistemic constraints are such that the unjust soldier has some level of excuse mitigating their unjust actions, this will also inform their RPL and derived combatant status.[40]

5. Objections and real-world cases

Some will argue that such a scheme makes fighting war impossible by being too restrictive on the just war-fighter; that it would "tie their hands" to such an extent that they could never have military success.[41] Granted, what I am calling for places incredibly high burdens on just war-fighters; calling on them to use near Herculean strength in their self-control and self-sacrifice under some of the most extreme circumstances of duress possible. But, I contend, that is precisely what it means to be a just war-fighter, or aim to be one, at any rate. And this—the ever increasing demands placed on just war-fighters—is what we should expect as our moral reasoning regarding war improves and sharpens over time. Consider the dramatic and relatively quick moral improvements to how (purportedly) just war-fighters are expected to fight has developed over the past quarter-century alone.[42] Far more is expected of present just war-fighters with regards to behavior in combat than was ever expected of war-fighters a generation previous. This is large part because just war doctrine has become increasingly ingrained in Western militaries. We should *expect* that new developments in just war theory will elicit further developments for *jus in bello* practices.

Scholars pressing the real-world objection, however, complain that such high demands can't be expected of soldiers operating in the vagaries of modern combat. This worry is integral to the real-world objection, but I disagree with its basic premise. First, I'd ask of such scholars, "Just what do we take the aim of moral philosophy regarding just behavior in war to be?" I presume that it is to work out what morally right action in war would be, if it is even possible. If we think we have found what that is, but that it is unlikely that people will so behave, well, that is, frankly, another matter; one of how to *get* people to behave morally, not what moral behavior *is*. The job of the moral philosopher here is to work out what it *would be* to fight in war justly. Whether people will do so or not is not properly the job of a moral philosopher. Lazar argues that it is literally impossible to fight war justly given the provisions of the revisionist view. In this chapter I hope to show that he overstates that case; that it is possible and, granting the limitations soldiers face, that something like what I propose (the multifaceted system of combatant status derived from RPL with correlative restrictive ROE) is what it could look like.

Second, I am simply more optimistic of the abilities of soldiers to behave justly and follow such restrictive ROE. When Walzer challenged the realpolitik orthodoxy in 1977 with *Just and Unjust Wars*, few thought that ethical constraint in war was likely to ever gain consensus much less actionable policy changes. But the fruit of just war theory's restraining influence is now evident in much contemporary war fighting. It is indeed a difficult shift in the thinking of war-fighters, but it is undeniably occurring; and we should expect this evolution to continually occur with every new generation of war-fighter. Again, even the most "gung-ho" warrior serving in a Western nation's military today is far more aware, and most likely even deeply concerned with, being careful to do his or her best to distinguish between innocent civilians and combatants than a soldier serving in those same nation-states' militaries 100 years ago. This is true whether it is for self-interested reasons (i.e. wanting to avoid punishment) or moral ones. Indeed, today's soldier is far more concerned and careful to obey these distinctions than a soldier in the same military was even 20 years ago.

Moreover, this objection is largely discredited simply because the kind of change I'm proposing *may already be occurring*. Take NATO's recent counter-insurgency (COIN) operations in Afghanistan. Regardless of one's assessment of the overall justification for the US and NATO operations currently underway in Afghanistan, notice that COIN strategy provides an excellent example of the development I'm proposing.[43] The average soldier in this theatre undertakes extreme caution in avoiding noncombatant casualties that would have been considered unimaginable restraint even a generation ago. The soldiers have surprisingly high discipline in following incredibly restrictive ROE. Why should we not expect, or at least hope, that this trend could continue in modern warfare?

Specifically, NATO forces engage the last vestiges of al-Qaeda quite differently than they engage remnant Taliban fighters. The former they attack "with prejudice" and, where possible, kill via drone airstrike. The latter they engage more cautiously, avoid high death tolls, and use extreme restraint to avoid noncombatant casualties. The point is that they are treating distinct groups of enemy "combatants" as different *kinds* of combatants with correspondingly different ROE. Admittedly, this distinction is done in the Afghanistan campaign on purely pragmatic grounds (on the strategic hopes of not alienating certain groups for potential negotiations), but such distinctions between combatants *could* be done on the moral grounds of perceived differences in liability.

Further, recent developments in military technology strive to be ever more discriminate in war, not less. This is *contra* Lazar who believes modern warfare makes indiscriminate combat *more* likely due to long-range artillery and "dumb bomb" munitions.[44] Perhaps this was true throughout most of the twentieth century, but such forms of warfare are today becoming increasingly passé. Military weapons of the future enable more just behavior, not less, because they are far more accurate and precise. Many of these kinds of weapons are already being employed. Take, for but one example, unmanned aerial vehicles. These weapons enable forces to observe enemies for long, extended stretches of time before engaging them. This new ability would improve a just forces' accurate determination of RPL.[45]

These examples give us reason to think that modern military forces could, indeed, further restrain their behavior along the lines of the RPL model to achieve more just behavior in war. For one final example of how restrictive ROE, even if more difficult, can and are being implemented, return once again to the case of NATO's recent military action in Afghanistan. In the (now infamous) *Rolling Stone* article that led to General Staney McChrystal's ultimate removal from NATO command was this interesting comment, "'Bottom line?' says a former Special Forces operator who has spent years in Iraq and Afghanistan. 'I would love to kick McChrystal in the nuts. His rules of engagement put soldiers' lives in even greater danger.'"[46] This was from one of McChrystal's men venting frustration at the highly restrictive ROE the COIN strategy had placed on soldiers. People don't often openly complain about restrictive policies if the policies are not actually restricting their behavior. That is why the complaint is a good sign: it means the policy's aim of forcing soldiers to be ever more careful in engaging only legitimate targets is, to some extent at least, working.

Presumably an advocate for the real-world objection would argue that even if just war-fighters were actually able to behave according to the highly restrictive ROE correlated with RPL, that military victory would then be "impossible." I disagree and argue that there are many reasons to hold that military success could still be attainable under such restrictive ROE. I do admit, however, that for such a model to attain military success, tremendous asymmetry of war (in favor of the just cause) would most likely be necessary.

Many other objections to my proposal remain here unaddressed. These issues need to be worked out as part of the larger ongoing revisionist just war theory project. I'll conclude by noting that while I'm cautiously optimistic that such a proposal as sketched here could be applied in the real world and thereby, if followed, make war-fighting more just, I do not mean to minimize the real difficulties applying it would entail. Such a change in the way combatant status is understood in warfare would constitute a radical sea-change for the contemporary military mindset. Be that as it may, if the revisionist critique of traditional just war theory is correct, then we must make a serious effort at reforming not only our just war *understanding* but also our just war *practices* to better conform to the best conclusions our moral reasoning can deliver.

Notes

1 M. Walzer, *Just and Unjust Wars: A Moral Argument with Historical Examples*, New York: Basic Books, 1977. The writings of Augustine I'm referring to are, for example, his exchanges with St. Boniface, such as "Letter 189," 418 A.D. See E.M. Atkins, and R.J. Dodaro (eds), *Augustine: Political Writings*, Cambridge: Cambridge University Press, 2001, for a detailed discussion.

2 The revisionists include, at least and most prominently, Jeff McMahan, "Killing in War: a Reply to Walzer," *Philosophia*, 34:1, 2006, pp. 47–51; also his "The Ethics of Killing War," *Ethics*, 114:4, 2006, pp. 693–733, and *Killing in War*, Oxford: Clarendon Press, 2009. See also David Rodin "Superior Law," paper presented at Oxford Institute's Ethics, Law, and Armed Conflict Annual Conference, Oxford, UK, 2011, and *War and Self-Defence*, Oxford: Clarendon Press, 2003, amongst many others. I also place myself in this camp, as articulated at length in Bradley Strawser, "Moral Predators: the Duty to Employ Uninhabited Aerial Vehicles," *Journal of Military Ethics*, 9:4, 2010 pp. 342–368, and defended in "Walking the Tightrope of Just War," *Analysis*, 71:3, 2011 pp. 533–544.

3 Note: not all revisionists about just war theory are necessarily supporters of individualism about rights. I'm using "revisionists" here to refer to that specific recent camp of philosophers who reject the moral equality of combatants (as I will explain below in section 2) based on individual rights reasoning.

4 I first suggested what I argue for in this chapter in Bradley Strawser "Walking the Tightrope." That piece was a response to Seth Lazar's critique of Jeff McMahan's revisionist account of just war theory in Seth Lazar, "The Responsibility Dilemma for Killing in War," *Philosophy & Public Affairs*, 38:2, 2010, p. 180–213. At the end of my response to Lazar I briefly sketch what I explore at length in this chapter. As a result, some portions of this chapter are drawn from that work. Additionally, some of this chapter consists of revised sections of two chapters in Bradley Strawser, *The Bounds of Defense: Moral Responsibility, Autonomy, and War*, Storrs, CT: University of Connecticut, D. Phil dissertation, 2012; specifically chapter 4, "A New Proposal for Liability in War," and chapter 3 "A Defense of Revisionist Just War Theory" of that work are drawn on here at length.

5 David Rodin has made parallel first steps recently in exploring how we should change the laws of war to accord with the revisionist view of the morality of war. Here I am focusing solely on how the morality of combatant targeting should change to accord with the revisionist view, but I take my efforts here to be of a piece with Rodin's efforts on the legal side. See Rodin "Superior Law."

6 See Michael Walzer, *Just & Unjust Wars: A Moral Argument with Historical Examples*, New York: Basic Books, 1977, pp. 34–41, for the classic exposition of the doctrine.

7 S. Lazar, "The Responsibility Dilemma."

8 Henry Shue, "Do we need a 'morality of war'?" in D. Rodin and H. Shue (eds), *Just and Unjust Warriors: The Moral and Legal Status of Soldiers*, New York: Oxford University Press, 2008.

9　Michael Walzer, "Response to McMahan's Paper," *Philosophia*, 34:1, 2006, pp. 43–45.

10　Walzer has repeatedly simply dismissed the arguments of the most influential revisionist, Jeff McMahan, rather than even address his claims with counter-arguments or reasoned defense of the traditional view. I myself have witnessed such treatment of the revisionist challenge first hand. At the annual McCain Conference hosted by the Stockdale Center for Ethical Leadership, in Annapolis, Maryland, in 2011, Walzer was invited to give the keynote address. After his talk, during the question and answer session, Jeff McMahan presented a careful and well-reasoned objection, complete with a highly plausible thought experiment to make the point. Rather than consider the objection, Walzer simply replied, "I don't know Jeff. Who knows? That's a philosopher's question. And I'm not a philosopher." That claim, of course, would come as quite a surprise to many. Needless to say, in my view, such responses expose the lack of an adequate theoretical response to the challenges posed to the traditionalist by the revisionists.

11　I'm here paraphrasing the general form the objection takes, but I have heard this worry expressed in this manner countless times by those critical of the revisionist project.

12　S. Lazar, "The Responsibility Dilemma."

13　B. Strawser, "Walking the Tightrope."

14　S. Lazar has made this claim in discussion at the 2011 Annual Conference held by Oxford's Institute for Ethics, Law, and Armed Conflict, and in other personal discussion and correspondence.

15　J. McMahan, *Killing in War*, p. 156

16　That is, since the types of actions that can be taken in war are (more or less) discrete, we can have a heuristic set of distinctions based on those possible actions and how they map onto non-discrete RPL.

17　J. McMahan, *Killing in War*, pp. 196–197.

18　These limitations and difficulties are discussed and raised as challenges to the revisionist project by Lazar, "The Responsibility Dilemma," and Henry Shue, "Do We Need a 'Morality of War'?," and others in an effort to point out how hard liability determination would be in actual practice. Gerhard Overland discusses differences in liability amongst an enemy population in ways that track closely with my proposal that I will discuss below in section 5. See Gerhard Overland, "Killing Soldiers," *Ethics and International Affairs*, 20:4, 2006, pp. 455–475.

19　See J. McMahan, *Killing in War*, pp. 196–197, for a discussion of this point.

20　M. Walzer *Just & Unjust Wars*, p. 146; Thomas Nagel, "War and Massacre," *Philosophy and Public Affairs*, 1:2, 1972, pp. 123–143

21　My proposed scheme here to track degreed combatant status with RPL is, I believe, in harmony with and follows in the vein of Overland's position presented in that piece. Overland discusses more specifically how to resolve cases of innocent soldiers fighting each other. My rubric is an attempt to take this notion—that different liability levels amongst an enemy combatant population should result in different permissible responses—to an even broader scale, encompassing all of *jus in bello* practice.

22　J. McMahan argues similarly for treating the Iraqi conscripts and members of the Republican Guard differently. See J. McMahan, *Killing in War*, pp. 194–195.

23　That is, presume that she accomplished whatever epistemic due diligence was morally required for this kind of activity and rightly concluded her cause was just. Lazar suggests that this, also, cannot be done, and he offers an attack against the very possibility of a just war-fighter ever having the kind of confidence in their cause I am here suggesting as an assumption for theorizing. "Our leaders could violate at least five of the standard just war theory criteria, without anybody outside the circles of power knowing about it. They might have secretly provoked the enemy into attacking, to give the appearance of a just cause; they might have adopted a disproportionate strategy; there may have been other options besides war, thus failing last resort; their intentions may be improper, say, the pursuit of resources; and they may know our prospects of success are slim, because of classified intelligence." Lazar, "The Responsibility Dilemma," p. 194.

24　Assuming, that is, that in no war are both sides fact-relatively just in total *jus ad bellum* determinations. It is, of course, entirely possible (and probably historically highly common) that both sides of a war may be ultimately unjust, even if they each have some elements of a just cause.

25　Some critics of the revisionist approach may here object and argue that everyone is (and reasonably so) partial to their own view such that due diligence is not really possible in judging the justice of one's own cause, and then using that judgment as a partial metric upon which to determine the RPL for another's cause. I disagree. We can grant what Lazar calls "reasonable partiality" to all on each side of a conflict while still holding them to some reasonable standard of carrying out due diligence in determining whether their side is actually in the right. The success of some (albeit few) members of the German military during World War II (to give but one example) of seeing through the partiality they certainly had for their side and defecting or refusing to fight shows us that it is at least possible to do this. However, the critic could continue that, even if this possible to do, epistemic conditions for modern military actions are so complex that the only place my model would hold would be for some classical instance of a just war (particularly for a war of self-defense against aggression). This may be true but, first, even if my model could only pragmatically be true for such kinds of just war that in itself would still constitute a significant achievement for the revisionist view. Second, however, I find that the model I'm proposing here *could be* possible to apply in some contemporary instances of modern war, at least insofar as the degreed nature of liability could influence a just side's efforts at engaging an enemy population as justly as possible. The examples I give in section 5 give us some reason to think this is possible in the real world. We see this in NATO's different forms of engagement in the military operations in Afghanistan. We also see this, as just noted above, in the 1991 Persian Gulf War where the possibility existed for varied engagement tactics with units of the Iraqi Republican Guard versus units of conscripted Iraqi soldiers.

26 Notice that we do this in our *theorizing* about war. We assume "the just war-fighter" and then discuss her engagement of the enemy. But part of what it *means* to assume a war-fighter is just in the first place is that the war-fighter has proper epistemic warrant to so believe she is just and to take the moral risk of fighting in a war.

27 J. McMahan, *Killing in War*.

28 Lazar discusses the presumption in favor of one's own sources of authority, what he calls "reasonable partiality." See S. Lazar "The Responsibility Dilemma," p. 197.

29 A. Tennyson, "Charge of the Light Brigade," in *Tennyson: Selected Poems*, New York: Penguin Classics, 1995.

30 See, for example, the speech from Shakespeare's *Henry V* wherein one of the king's soldiers remarks with regard to his own culpability for the justice of their cause, "for we know enough if we know we are the King's subjects. If his cause be wrong, our obedience to the King wipes the crime of it out of us." (*Henry V*, Act IV, Scene 1.) Many thanks to Martin Cook for pointing out this passage to me and its relevance to the *ad bellum* and *in bello* distinction.

31 Cases where there is a lack of educational opportunities presents even further moral complexities. And this is no small matter since many who serve in the world's militaries often lack precisely such opportunities. It's a further question whether formal education does or should count in questions surrounding moral ignorance.

32 I explore such questions at great length in Bradley Strawser, *Bounds of Defense*. Also see A. Guerrero, "Don't Know, Don't kill: Moral Ignorance, Culpability, and Caution," *Philosophical Studies*, 136:1, 2007, pp. 59–97.

33 This also reaffirms that it is at least possible for soldiers to see through their partiality as discussed above in note 16.

34 J. McMahan, *Killing in War*, pp. 124–125.

35 Presuming, that is, that the suicide bomber thinks it's permissible; it's possible he does not take it to be permissible yet acts anyway. So let us presume here, rather, that he is mistaken in his judgment of the act's permissibility.

36 Although it is beyond the scope of this chapter, in Bradley Strawser, *Bounds of Defense*, I present my "evidence-relative" model for liability attribution which hinges heavily on the evidence available for the moral permissibility of an act to a given responsible party. Therein I craft a version of moral epistemic contextualism (following Guerrero, "Don't Know, Don't Kill") which contends that for different acts of different moral import there are correlatively different epistemic standards that one must meet before they can permissibly act.

37 Again, this demand for simple moral reflection by those who are about to kill others is part and parcel of the moral epistemic contextualism and evidence-relative account of liability attribution I argue for at length in Bradley Strawser, *Bounds of Defense*.

38 Lazar, "The Responsibility Dilemma," p. 194

39 This correlates nicely with Guerrero's "Don't Know, Don't Kill" principle found in A. Guerrero "Don't Know, Don't Kill: Moral Ignorance, Culpability, and Caution," *Philosophical Studies* 136:1, 2007, pp. 59–97

40 And there are even further limitations and factors that could mitigate an unjust soldier's liability that should also be calculated in determinations of their RPL, such as whether or not the enemy's state

allows for conscientious objector status or uses coercion to force its citizens into military service, and so forth. All of these should be included in the best effort at determining RPL.

41 It has been argued that my suggested development moves far beyond McMahanian narrow proportionality and morphs into some kind of "hyper-narrow proportionality."

42 For a good discussion on the success of just war theory to shape contemporary military practice in the United States and other Western powers, see M. Cook, *Moral Warrior*, Albany, NY: SUNY Press, 2004. Also see Michael Walzer, "The Triumph of Just War Theory—and the Dangers of Success," *Social Research*, 69:4, 2004, pp. 925–946.

43 That is, set aside for the sake of argument whether NATO's operations in Afghanistan are morally permissible to begin with. I use it as example simply to show that modern militaries are capable of applying restrictive ROE that have multiple levels of classification of an enemy population instead of merely two.

44 S. Lazar, "The Responsibility Dilemma."

45 See B. Strawser, "Moral Predators," where I discuss the potential normative advantages of UAVs at length. See also Bradley Strawser (ed.), *Killing By Remote Control: The Ethics of an Unmanned Military*, New York: Oxford University Press, 2013. I should also note that this new technology strongly points towards the kind of operational asymmetry necessary for this revisionist model as at least being possible in some cases and, perhaps, *common* in future warfare.

46 M. Hastings, "The runaway general," *Rolling Stone*, June 22, 2010.

References

Atkins, E.M. and Dodaro, R.J. (eds), *Augustine: Political Writings*, Cambridge: Cambridge University Press, 2001.

Cook, M., *Moral Warrior*, Albany, NY: SUNY Press, 2004.

Guerrero, A., "Don't Know, Don't Kill: Moral Ignorance, Culpability, and Caution," *Philosophical Studies* 136:1, 2007, pp. 59–97.

Hastings, M., "The Runaway General," *Rolling Stone*, June 22, 2010.

Lazar, S., "The Responsibility Dilemma for Killing in War," *Philosophy & Public Affairs*, 38:2, 2010, pp. 180–213.

McMahan, J., "Killing in War: a Reply to Walzer," *Philosophia*, 34:1, 2006, pp. 47–51.

—— *Killing in War*, Oxford: Clarendon Press, 2009.

—— "The Ethics of Killing War," *Ethics*, 114:4, 2006, pp. 693–733.

Nagel, T., "War and Massacre," *Philosophy and Public Affairs*, 1:2, 1972, 123–143.

Overland, G., "Killing Soldiers," *Ethics and International Affairs*, 20:4, 2006, pp. 455–475.

Rodin, D., "Superior Law," paper presented at Oxford Institute's Ethics, Law, and Armed Conflict Annual Conference, Oxford, UK, 2011.

—— *War and Self-Defence*, Oxford: Clarendon Press, 2003.

Shue, H., "Do we Need a 'Morality of War'?" in D. Rodin and H. Shue (eds), *Just and Unjust Warriors: The Moral and Legal Status of Soldiers*, New York: Oxford University Press, 2008.

Strawser, B.J., (ed.), *Killing By Remote Control: The Ethics of an Unmanned Military*, New York: Oxford University Press, 2013.

—— "Moral Predators: the Duty to Employ Uninhabited Aerial Vehicles," *Journal of Military Ethics* 9:4, 2010, pp. 342–68.

—— "The Bounds of Defense: Moral Responsibility, Autonomy, and War," unpublished dissertation, University of Connecticutt, 2012.

Strawser, B., "Walking the Tightrope of Just War," *Analysis*, 71:3, 2011, pp. 533–44.

Tennyson, A., "Charge of the Light Brigade," in *Tennyson: Selected Poems*, New York: Penguin Classics, 1995.

Walzer, M., *Just & Unjust Wars: A Moral Argument with Historical Examples*, New York: Basic Books, 1977.

—— "Response to McMahan's Paper," *Philosophia*, 34:1, 2006, pp. 43–5.

—— "The Triumph of Just War Theory – and the Dangers of Success," *Social Research*, 69:4, 2002, pp. 925–46.

Jus post bellum

7

THE PLACE OF *JUS POST BELLUM* IN JUST WAR CONSIDERATIONS

Emily Pollard

1. Introduction

The just war tradition, throughout its history, has mainly concerned itself with the ethics of declaring war and of the methods used to wage war. There is now a general acceptance of the necessity for *jus ad bellum* and *jus in bello* criteria, which a war must fulfil to be justly declared and justly fought. *Jus post bellum* considerations, on the other hand, are a relatively new aspect of the just war tradition. Many previous just war theorists have touched on them (such as Hugo Grotius,[1] who discussed principles of just war termination in *De Jure Belli ac Pacis Libris Tres*) – but only recently have some begun to consider them distinct and important enough to form a category of criteria. The idea is that, as just war theory contains categories of moral conditions for declaring war and waging war, it should also include a category for ending war; containing rules that determine when and how a war may morally be finished, and what duties the victorious country has towards the defeated (and vice versa).

Of course, given that *jus post bellum* is so recent an addition to just war theory (and not unanimously accepted), the *jus post bellum* criteria are not so established, or agreed upon, as those of *ad bellum* and *in bello*. For example, Alex Bellamy suggests that 'Under *jus post bellum*, states that embark on humanitarian interventions are required to assist the host population in rebuilding their country'[2] – which would suggest a single criterion, an obligation to ensure that the defeated people are put 'back on their feet' after the fighting. Bellamy, however, argues that his *jus post bellum* rule applies only to wars fought for humanitarian intervention – he argued it would be 'premature at present'[3] to apply it to wars with other objectives. Others disagree. One of their suggestions is, as Helen Frowe puts it, a 'minimalist'[4] account of *jus post bellum* – meaning a set of criteria limiting the rights of the victor over their defeated enemy. For instance, as Bellamy later wrote describing this view, a victorious state's post-war actions are limited to those that 'protect themselves, recover that which was illicitly taken, [and] punish the perpetrators'.[5] This means they are prohibited from 'enslaving the inhabitants of the defeated country or attempting to colonize the land'.[6] Other theorists suggest a 'maximalist' account, imposing not only limits but obligations upon the victors. Brian Orend, for example, proposes both obligations and limitations, such as:

a   Any penalties imposed upon the defeated state must observe the rule of *'discrimination'* – the victors must 'differentiate between the political and military leaders, the soldiers, and the civilian population'.[7] Civilians are 'entitled to reasonable immunity from punitive post-war measures'.[8]

b   The 'terms of peace' must be 'proportional to the end of reasonable rights vindication':[9] in short, they must be 'measured and reasonable'[10] in their efforts to successfully bring the war to an end, and they must not make unnecessary or excessive demands. Gary Bass, another proponent of *jus post bellum*, similarly claimed victorious nations have an 'obligation to exercise restraint in transforming a [defeated] society' which 'can be seen as related to the *jus in bello* requirement of proportionality that states fight limited wars, using the minimum violence necessary'.[11]

Orend also suggests that the defeated country's 'submission to reasonable principles of punishment, including compensation, *jus ad bellum* and *jus in bello* war crimes trials, and perhaps rehabilitation'[12] is necessary – the defeated country must accept terms of surrender including such 'submission' for the victor to possess 'just cause for termination'. Bass, however, argues the victorious state has a '*jus post bellum* duty to reconstruct genocidal states'[13] – in other words, when states controlled by genocidal regimes, such as Nazi Germany, are defeated then the victors must remove the genocidal regime and replace it, because in this case, merely achieving the just aims of that war (halting the genocidal regime's current atrocity-in-progress and imposing terms of surrender), will not be enough to ensure that the regime does not continue with its genocidal ambitions as soon as it feels able. Besides, as Walzer argued, governments which 'initiate massacres lose their right to participate in the normal processes of domestic self-determination';[14] or, as Bass wrote, a genocidal state has, by its actions, 'lost its claim to be recognized and respected as a state'.[15]

In this paper, it is not my intention to argue in favour of either the minimalist or the maximalist account of *jus post bellum*, or any individual's definition of it. Instead, I wish to argue that the proper place for *any* considerations of the *jus post bellum* variety, whether minimalist or maximalist, is within *jus ad bellum* and *jus in bello*; in short, there is no need for a distinct set of *jus post bellum* criteria, because *post bellum* considerations, along with any discussion of precisely what moral conditions obtain *post bellum*, should be introduced into just war theory as *part of jus ad bellum* and *jus in bello*. I submit that part of being justified in one's resort to war is the expectation or intention to behave morally towards the defeated country should one be victorious, and that waging a war justly entails ensuring that one treats the defeated country ethically even after the military conflict; and a closer examination of certain of the *ad bellum* and *in bello* criteria reveal that these criteria are not confined in their relevance to the pre-war sphere and the combat itself.

In Section 2, I argue that *jus post bellum* considerations should be included in *jus ad bellum* as an extension of the conditions of right intention and reasonable chance of success. Then, in Section 3, I demonstrate that the *jus in bello* criteria should be applied *post bellum* as well as while actual combat is in progress. Thus, *post bellum* considerations are also included in the *jus in bello* conditions. With these arguments, I hope to prove that *jus post bellum* considerations should be incorporated into *jus ad bellum* and *jus in bello*.

2. *Jus ad bellum* and *jus post bellum*

The *jus ad bellum* conditions of right intention and reasonable chance of success, as they are most commonly accepted, run as follows. The right intention criterion, in Douglas Lackey's words, 'insists that a just war be a war for the right, fought for the sake of the right'.[16] In other words, the government or ruling body declaring war must primarily intend to achieve the aims for which war is justified. If, for example, Country A invades Country B, then the government of

Country B has a generally acknowledged just cause for declaring war on Country A – namely, self-defence – but they only have *right intention* if self-defence is at least their primary motive for declaring war on Country B. If they do so because of a concealed desire to colonize Country A or to confiscate its resources, knowing that the conflict will provide the perfect excuse, then they lack right intention despite the existence of a legitimate reason for war. As Guthrie and Quinlan have observed, the right intention criterion should ensure 'that our purpose in going to war must genuinely be to help create a better subsequent peace than there would otherwise have been'.[17]

The condition that countries intending to go to war must have a reasonable chance of success requires the probability of their succeeding, that is, achieving the war's objective, to be 'reasonable': in other words, high enough to make recourse to war useful – as Richard Norman put it, 'the evils which the war is bound to involve should not be incurred if there is no hope of achieving the aim'.[18] Exactly what probability of success is 'reasonable' is a vexed question, and one I will not have time to consider in this paper.[19] Instead, I will, for the sake of argument, accept that possessing a 'reasonable chance of success' means one is at least as likely to succeed as to fail.

These criteria, however, have implications that most discussing them appear to overlook. To begin with, consider the condition of right intention. It must be the sole or primary intention of Country B, in declaring war, to 'achieve a better outcome for the people [involved] than would result from rejecting or ending combat', in Guthrie and Quinlan's words.[20] Often, this condition is taken to mean *only* that Country B must intend to achieve its just cause (self-defence). However, it seems to me that a 'right intention' is much more. The creation of 'a better subsequent peace than there would otherwise have been'[21] involves more than, for instance, a successful defence of Country B – if Country B defends itself by completely wiping out the population of Country A, then it would be difficult for any impartial observer to see this as a 'better peace'.[22] For one thing, it violates the *jus in bello* rules of discrimination and proportionality; and also, its result is no less repugnant than Country A's aim – innocent lives are lost, just as they would be should Country A wipe out Country B.[23] If the government of Country B has the sole intention of defending their nation, but intends to defend it in this manner, they do not have a 'right' intention. They intend to achieve their just cause, but they also intend to ignore *jus in bello*, and create a 'better peace' for them or their country, but *only* for them.

A right intention should be the intention to fight for the just cause in question, but also to do so wholly according to *jus ad bellum* and *jus in bello*. It should be, quite simply, the intention to fight a just war – which, as Guthrie and Quinlan observed, amounts to the intention to create a better overall situation than would otherwise have occurred. The narrower definition of right intention, that of an intention to achieve the just purpose of the war, fails by comparison, because such an intention could, as I have explained, be as unjust as the intention to fight for an unjust cause – achieving a just cause in an unjust way is condemned by just war theory. Thus, the intention to achieve a just cause in this way should be equally condemned, but only the wider definition of right intention does so.

However, once we accept this definition of right intention, it becomes clear that if 'right intention' refers to an intention to bring about a 'better peace' by waging war, then not only is the intention to act according to *jus ad bellum* and *jus in bello* required, but an important third element will be the intention to act, *post bellum*, according to the necessary moral obligations or limitations.

The intentions of a country going to war cannot be 'right intentions' if they do not intend to fight morally, or if they do not intend to act morally in victory. Supposing, for the sake of argument, that Country B had the primary purpose of self-defence (meaning they would not have fought without that reason for doing so) and, supposing they fully intended to abide by the *jus in bello* rules, nevertheless it would seem that, if they intended to declare war for a just cause, and fight justly, but, once successful, to occupy and subjugate Country A, this would not be a right intention.

There seems to be something fundamentally wrong with Country B's intention in this case. Even though their plans were to act according to all the just war criteria as they are commonly defined, they either intended their post-combat actions to create a future that favoured their ultimate agenda (which the right intention condition should avoid), or they believed the effect these actions would have was not 'their problem'. In either circumstance, their ultimate intention would not seem to be the creation of a better overall situation.

In short, if one's intention is to establish a 'better subsequent peace than there would otherwise have been',[24] then part of one's intention must be to act, *post bellum*, so as to bring this about – which may entail observing some of the possible conditions I mentioned earlier.

Ultimately, individual circumstances will determine most of the specific *post bellum* actions belligerents must perform, but I believe the right intention criterion requires, at the least, that when considering war, a nation must possess some plan for the ceasing of hostilities and its post-combat actions – a plan reasonably likely to produce the best possible situation, which they must follow as best they can. If the best possible outcome, once the war is successful, would result from leaving the defeated country at once – if, say, the aim of the war is self-defence, and the invader can be dissuaded with a minimum of force, then the plan must involve a ceasefire once the defensive aim is achieved. If, however, it is clear that Country B's defence can only be achieved after Country A has been entirely overcome by military means, then it must involve ensuring Country A is reconstructed once hostilities are over. To fulfil the right intention rule, therefore, one must work out a *post bellum* plan that, in those circumstances, can reasonably be expected to have the best possible outcome; and Country B only has right intention when it has such a plan and fully intends to implement it when the combat ends.

The common definition of reasonable chance of success can be similarly extended. Just war theorists tend to define it as the condition that there must be a possibility of military success. Nigel Dower, for instance, defends it thus: 'if there were no reasonable prospect of *winning a war*, then it would be foolhardy to embark on it, since such a war would simply involve a lot of bad consequences for no good outcome'.[25] Similarly, Frowe describes a reasonable chance of success as 'a realistic chance of winning'.[26] However, there is an underlying assumption behind arguments like Dower's that indicates the definition of 'success', in this context, is not merely military victory – namely, the assumption that 'winning a war' will mean a 'good outcome'.[27] In other words, it is assumed that military victory is synonymous with a 'good outcome', namely, success in achieving one's just cause.

This is, of course, far from indisputable. A war fought in order to defend a weaker country or vulnerable group of people from an aggressive nation might result in a resounding military victory, but end too late to achieve this – victory taking place shortly after the vulnerable people have been wiped out by the aggressor in a fit of pique. Nevertheless, this shows that the 'success' of a belligerent nation cannot be simply military success. A war may be called 'successful' if, by achieving its just cause, it creates the best possible overall outcome. If the justification for the 'reasonable chance of success' criterion is that a war cannot be just if it would result in 'bad consequences for no good outcome',[28] then, clearly, war can only be justified if this outcome is reasonably likely to be achieved.[29]

In my earlier example of a country that achieves military victory only to find that the aim of the war, the defence of the endangered group, is no longer possible, it seems that this country has fought a war with 'bad consequences for no good outcome'[30] – or, at least, no outcome good enough to warrant war. Its best consequence, the curbing of its enemy's aggressive tendencies, while no doubt good in the long term, could perhaps be achieved in other ways (such as sanctions) that have fewer 'bad consequences' like combatant and civilian casualties. This country might, before the war, foresee a reasonable chance of military success, but little chance of defending the victims of their aggressive opponent. If so, the war lacks reasonable chance of success – all the costs of war are incurred with no prospect of a 'good outcome'. Therefore, the criterion that a just war must have a reasonable prospect of success refers to a reasonable prospect of achieving the aims of the war.

Thus, I believe these *jus ad bellum* conditions impose obligations upon countries fighting a just war, obligations which they must continue to fulfil *post bellum*. I cannot provide in this paper a definitive list of which possible *jus post bellum* obligations these are; however, as I have said, it is probable that the obligations upon the victor will differ according to the foreseeable post-combat situation. If, for instance, the aim is the defence of some oppressed minority within the enemy country (often referred to as humanitarian intervention) then the intention to achieve this aim may impose obligations towards this minority. If it is necessary to stabilize the post-war situation, and ensure that the minority does not fall victim to continued oppression after the combat, the victors may be obligated to assist in the organisation of a new, non-oppressive form of government to replace the one they had cause to fight. Alternatively, if the war is a simple one of self-defence, and once the aggressor has surrendered they are in no need of aid or reconstruction and clearly have no intention of continuing their aggressions, the victors may be obligated simply to withdraw their troops and bring the post-combat phase of their campaign to a swift end.

Therefore, it is clear at the least that these two *jus ad bellum* conditions have a *post bellum* relevance overlooked by many. In order to have right intention, for instance, a country or government must intend to treat their opponent morally *post bellum*, and if one has right intention, one is obligated to act according to that intention. I would argue, therefore, that such *post bellum* obligations are in fact the domain of *jus ad bellum*.

3. *Jus post bellum* and *jus in bello*

In this section, I hope to show that the *jus in bello* conditions, discrimination and proportionality, continue to apply in the *post bellum* period. As Steven Lee wrote, although termination of hostilities 'is the end of the war in the usual way of speaking, there is a broader sense in which the war continues'.[31] Carsten Stahn similarly wrote that 'there is no (more a) clear dividing line between war and peace'.[32] Given the point that the situation immediately after combat is a part of the overall campaign of war, I hope to argue that *jus in bello* continues to apply during this part.

It is quite true, of course, that *jus in bello* is, in practice, likely to require different things in the second, post-conflict phase of a military campaign. The fact that both phases, conflict and its aftermath, should be considered part of the overall campaign does not mean both phases are identical. I should explain that when I say that a 'war' continues after the end of the physical combat between armies, I do not use the term 'war' in the sense it is often used; namely, military struggle between two armies, each fighting, with physical weapons, for their nation and their cause. I use the word as an umbrella term, meaning the entire campaign being waged in order to achieve a just cause; as Lee wrote, 'The shooting and its immediate aftermath are stages of the process of a war'.[33] In this sense, I believe 'war' very seldom ends at the same time as combat; for one thing, the realization of the victor's cause depends upon their conduct after the battle is won and they may dictate terms for the ending of the campaign.[34]

If, for instance, a country fights a defensive war, their defence fails if their enemy is embittered by the fact that, after the signing of a peace treaty, the victor failed to rebuild any of the damage caused in the conflict or support its victims, but instead withdrew, leaving them to struggle and starve, so that this enemy reinvades as soon as it regains strength. The process of achieving the aims of a war continue after the end of combat; perhaps more so in a war of humanitarian intervention, where protecting a minority from oppression and slaughter by their own government may involve assisting in the construction of a different form of government once the physical combat is over. Both phases will be necessary to achieve the just cause; however soon after the end of combat this occurs, *some* post-combat actions will be necessary, if only the instant withdrawal of all troops at the request of the defeated country. Only when the war's purpose is achieved and all actions necessary to achieve it and end the campaign are implemented is the war over – in some cases, this may be long after the victorious nation has withdrawn its troops.

As it is currently understood, *jus in bello* applies solely during an official state of war, which usually lasts from the beginning of military conflict until one armed force defeats another and the latter officially surrenders. For example, A.J. Coates refers to *jus in bello* as 'the specific requirements of just conduct [in war]',[35] and, similarly, Guthrie and Quinlan argue *jus in bello* 'concerns the morality of what is done within war – how it is to be waged'.[36] Walzer, most definitively, distinguished *jus ad bellum* from *jus in bello* by describing the former as 'the justice of war', and the latter as 'justice in war'.[37] In other words, *jus in bello* governs the ways a country in the state of 'engagement' or war may behave towards its opponent.

The official end of the fighting, however it is brought about, is not the ultimate end of the war. In the immediate aftermath of the fighting, victorious countries have certain responsibilities; not only must they assist with the organisation and enforcement of the new peace treaty, but they must decide when and how to withdraw from the combat zone, and what to do beforehand. For instance, they must decide whether to contribute to the post-combat reconstruction of the defeated country, or, if that country is utterly incapable of rebuilding, to complete the task for them. Also, if the defeated country is in a state of anarchy, the victors must decide whether they must restore order themselves and, if so, how. This cannot be considered separately; rather it is an essential part of a military campaign. In declaring war, a state acknowledges that should it win these decisions will be theirs to make, and it should therefore have a viable *post bellum* plan of action. Such actions comprise what I would call the 'post-combat' phase of a campaign of war.

During the fighting, *jus in bello* rules apply not only to the actions of armies, but to the decisions their government makes; the orders it gives concerning their campaign. During the combat phase, those government leaders and officials responsible for deciding which actions to take and directing the armed forces are as governed by *jus in bello* as the armed forces. For instance, if a dictator gives his army the order to eliminate the enemy country, combatants and non-combatants alike, as part of his military campaign, then after the end of that war, it is not (or not only) the soldiers who obeyed this instruction who may be prosecuted for war crimes. The dictator who gave that order is also liable for such a prosecution. Even though he is not a member of the armed forces, he has still broken the rule of discrimination – what he has done is both illegal and a violation of just war theory. In the same way, during the post-combat phase, the government of the victorious country is still bound to act proportionately and discriminatingly (as is that of the defeated country, but it is unlikely to be in a position to make many important post-combat decisions). The victorious government must make the decisions I just outlined, whether or not to withdraw and what to do before withdrawal, and it should, I believe, make them with an eye to proportionality and discrimination. If it does not, the military and political leaders of the victorious country should perhaps be held accountable, as they would be should they authorize a violation of *jus in bello* during combat, in which case they could be tried for war crimes like our hypothetical dictator. Ignoring *jus in bello* in the post-combat phase is still a violation of the rules of just war, and those who do so are guilty of mistreating the citizens of the defeated country.

Once their just cause is achieved, the victorious country may end the campaign, but a method of doing so must be selected, and this decision is an important part of the post-combat phase. It cannot be done in such a way as to violate the proportionality rule, which argues that, as Frowe put it, 'the harm that one inflicts must be proportionate to the good that is protected, and must be the least harmful means available of achieving the good'.[38] It would thus prohibit any treatment of the defeated nation that will cause more harm than good. For example, if the victorious country acted as an aggressive occupying force, it would break the proportionality rule by choosing a course of action that causes more harm than good. Similarly, withdrawing and ending all involvement with the defeated country at that time might cause it more harm than overall good. For instance, if withdrawing troops as soon as combat was over would result in total anarchy within the defeated country, then it might be necessary for the victorious country's armed forces to remain for some time as a peacekeeping force, or for them to solicit the help of some alternative peacekeeping force, such as the UN. Or, if a defeated country were more stable, but nevertheless desperately needed reconstruction that its own government was unable to provide (without which its people would suffer greatly), it might be morally necessary for the victors to finance, perhaps even manage, the recovery. In such circumstances, where prematurely ending the post-combat phase of a campaign would actually be a disproportionate response, that campaign must continue until such time as it can be ended (and the post-combat involvement with reconstruction finished) without violating *jus in bello*.

It might be harder to see why victorious countries should need to follow the discrimination rule in the post-combat phase. When combat has ceased, why give different treatment to combatants and non-combatants? However, as I have already pointed out, the end of the combat phase does not always signal the immediate withdrawal of the victorious country's troops – as evidenced by the recent wars in Iraq and Afghanistan. In such cases, when troops remain within the defeated country, to rebuild or ensure stability, there is a clear need for them to distinguish between fighters – insurgents or rioters, for instance – and ordinary civilians. In other circumstances, when the post-combat phase does not involve a military presence, the role of the discrimination rule is diminished, but still present. Some actions may still need to be taken as a result of the defeated country's actions during combat – such as prosecutions for war crimes, or penalties imposed as a result of damage done by that country. Any such actions must observe the discrimination rule – it would violate the spirit of just war theory to prosecute the entire country for the wartime atrocities of its government and army. Rather, such actions should be focused mainly on those who committed said atrocities, because by becoming combatants they accept not only the liabilities of battle, but the responsibility for fighting according to *jus in bello* (along with government leaders who gave orders violating *in bello* of course, since such leaders should also have been bound by these rules). However, the individual circumstances of each conflict and the situation it leaves behind may alter the nature of the constraints this condition places upon a victorious country. Discrimination will always be essential in that it is never morally right to target anyone not responsible for the activities of their country or combatants for prosecution or in battle, but the complexities of any particular situation may mean that to prosecute or fight those who *are* responsible may, under those circumstances, violate proportionality, in that it might cause more harm than good. For instance, if allowing a leader whose country were guilty of war crimes to stay in power after the defeat of that country (rather than removing him from power and prosecuting him) would prevent a long and bloody insurgency or civil war, then a case might certainly be made that proportionality necessitated leaving him untouched. The complex individual circumstances of each conflict, and the tension between prosecution and stabilisation or reconciliation, mean that no easy solution can be found. Nevertheless, the discrimination rule requires that whether or not targeting the responsible parties in a post-conflict situation is possible, targeting those who are not responsible is always out of the question.

Therefore, I would argue that *jus in bello* rules continue to apply in the *jus post bellum* period, which comes after the end of the combat phase of a campaign of war, and sometimes continues after the end of military activity. I believe the physical conflict between armies comprises just one portion of the entire campaign of war. *Jus in bello* does not solely regulate combat situations; it encompasses all dealings that are part of the overall campaign. For as long as either belligerent is engaged in activities which are part of this campaign, the rules of just conduct apply, for the same reason – the nations in question are still conducting that campaign.

For these reasons, I hold that there is a place for *jus post bellum* considerations in *jus in bello*, because the *jus in bello* conditions do not cease to apply once the fighting has been officially terminated. The necessity for just conduct *in war* applies to all phases of that war; and for this reason, the same set of rules apply to the combat and post-combat phases of war.

4. Incorporating *jus post bellum*

Finally, I must explain why I believe *jus post bellum* considerations should be considered within *jus ad bellum* and *in bello*. As I have argued, *post bellum* considerations are inextricably connected to *jus ad bellum* and *in bello*, and regarding *jus post bellum* as completely distinct from them would be to run the risk of bringing about an unnecessary separation of any discussion of *post bellum* issues from *ad bellum* and *in bello*.

The development of a distinct set of *jus post bellum* conditions would be contrary to my arguments. I argue that *jus in bello*, and certain *ad bellum* conditions, create moral obligations and limitations even after the combat phase, which is the only part of the overall conflict to which most just war theorists apply them. This puts the post-combat phase, including reconstruction, financial aid or continued military presence for stabilisation purposes, in a distinct moral domain of *jus post bellum*. I believe that post-combat activities may be regulated by moral conditions already present in *jus ad bellum* and *in bello*, which remain relevant in this post-combat phase. My further contention is that these conditions should be in the form of *jus ad bellum* and *in bello* conditions that also pertain to the post-conflict phase, rather than a distinct set of *jus post bellum* conditions derived from these *ad bellum* and *in bello* criteria, such as Orend's suggested *post bellum* rules. I have already explained why I believe they *may* be left in this form; now I shall explain why they *should*.

Jus post bellum conditions that are separate and independent from *jus ad bellum* and *jus in bello* could eventually separate any discussion and consideration of *post bellum* from that of *ad bellum* and *in bello*. It could create a gulf between them, splitting them into distinct areas, only discussed separately. I have argued (and, I hope, persuasively) in favour of connections between *post bellum* considerations and *jus ad bellum* and *in bello*; to ignore these connections would result in fragmentation of the theory.

This fragmentation is a direct result of the independence of *jus post bellum* conditions from *jus ad bellum* and *in bello*. By proposing a distinct set of conditions concerning only the post-combat phase, just war theorists such as Orend imply that this phase of the conflict is different and distinct from the earlier phases, because it needs to be governed by distinct moral rules – just as the distinct nature of the *jus ad bellum* and *jus in bello* sets of conditions means, according to most just war theorists, that the pre-war process and the combat are completely different, distinct areas of moral consideration, and that a discussion of *ad bellum* must be separate from any discussion of *in bello*. For instance, Walzer claims that *jus ad bellum* and *jus in bello* are 'logically independent', meaning that the former 'requires us to make judgements about aggression and self-defence', and the latter 'about the observance and violation of the ... rules of engagement'[39] – no overlap of these two areas of discussion is possible according to this view. In the same way, a distinct set of *post bellum* conditions would make it clear that discussion of the post-combat moral limitations or obligations of the victor must be separate from discussions of the moral rules a country must follow during the combat or leading up to it.

However, as I have argued, this is not the case. The discussion of *post bellum* considerations cannot be completely separated from discussions of *ad bellum* and *in bello*. As I pointed out, the *ad bellum* conditions of right intention and reasonable chance of success both have *post bellum* implications, and the *in bello* conditions of proportionality and discrimination are also valid after the end of combat. This continuous application cannot be replaced by a distinct set of *post bellum* conditions. Many discussions of *post bellum* questions, such as which obligations a particular victorious country might have, may need to consider or refer to both elements of the pre-combat and combat situation, and elements of the *ad bellum* and *in bello* moral conditions. This element of connection would be unavailable to just war theorists working with *post bellum* considerations separated into a distinct set of conditions, which would be dangerous because it alters the perspective used to determine the morality of many post-combat actions. Post-combat actions become viewed as part of a wholly different overall undertaking: part of the conflict's aftermath rather than the overall conflict. This would make it a lot harder to analyse the morality of such actions as, if they were distinct from wartime actions, they would require different moral rules, 'peacetime' rules – continuing the *jus in bello* rules into this domain would be unjustifiable. Not only does this disregard my earlier arguments, but it also makes it difficult to account for many post-combat situations, particularly those requiring a continued military presence. For example, if it is necessary for the victor to maintain a military presence in the defeated country as a peacekeeping force, then a separate set of *jus post bellum* rules that treat this as a completely separate situation from war may be problematic. Orend's suggested *post bellum* rules of discrimination and proportionality, because they treated the *post bellum* discussion as completely separate from *in bello* and *ad bellum*, only refer to the victorious *government's* treatment of the defeated nation and its leaders, not to the duties of combatants in a post-combat military situation; such rules are inadequate because of their separation from *ad bellum* and *in bello*. Therefore, I believe that not only is there no need for a distinct set of *post bellum* conditions, but that my arguments show they should be considered within *jus ad bellum* and *in bello*.

5. Conclusion

In my introduction, I gave a brief summary of the most important limitations and obligations which various just war theorists have suggested as a separate set of just war criteria, *jus post bellum*. Then, I endeavoured to show that a separate set of criteria is unnecessary, because the necessity to observe such *post bellum* limitations and obligations is already a necessary consequence of accepting and following *jus ad bellum* and *jus in bello*.

While these theorists disagree upon the content of *jus post bellum*, they generally agree there should be some constraints upon the permissible conduct of victorious states after combat, and some add that there must be obligations: duties which the victor is obliged to perform towards the defeated country. However, it is not always necessary for either suggestion that a distinct set of criteria be introduced into just war theory.

The *jus in bello* conditions apply not only to the portion of the war involving physical combat, but to the entire campaign of war, including the post-combat phase. The principles of conduct embedded in *jus in bello* considerations which some just war theorists, such as Bass or Stahn, claim to be part of a distinct set of *post bellum* conditions, are therefore already required *post bellum*. For instance, observing the discrimination rule during the aftermath of a conflict would prohibit the victorious nation from in any way punishing non-combatant citizens for the actions of their country – as Orend put it, this 'rules out … sweeping socio-economic sanctions as part of post-war punishment'.[40] Similarly, the proportionality rule would prohibit immediate withdrawal from a defeated country when this would result in anarchy and violence, and thus in more suffering than it would prevent.

Potential obligations towards the defeated nation (such as an obligation to ensure the defeated country can sustain itself before withdrawing) can similarly be derived from the *jus ad bellum* conditions of right intention and reasonable chance of success. Both of these conditions require, as I have shown, the intention and probability, not of winning the war or achieving the relevant just cause, but of *waging a just war*, which involves creating (or attempting to create), by fighting the war, a better overall situation than would otherwise come about, as Dower, Guthrie and Quinlan argued. Possessing such an intention and probability, and carrying out that intention, creates certain obligations after the termination of official hostilities.

Briefly, victorious countries would be obliged to ensure that their defeated opponent was not left in a position bad enough to outweigh any general benefits made possible by the war. The intended outcome of the war must be the best overall, not just best for the victorious country or for the country with a just cause. If, for instance, a government aims to defend the lives of its citizens by waging war against an aggressive invader, it should intend to achieve this defence so as to bring about the best possible overall outcome. This means that, even if it must wage war to bring about this best possible outcome, it must intend, once the war is over, to leave the citizens of its defeated adversary in the best possible situation. This might mean rebuilding the country, if necessary; or, if not, then it might mean withdrawing as soon as possible, so as not to adversely affect the recovery process. The individual circumstances would determine what actions were necessary for the best possible result, but whatever they were, the victor would be obliged to perform them. It would, as Bass suggested, be under a moral obligation to do so, as this intention is a necessary part of the justification of that war.

Thus, in conclusion, I believe *post bellum* considerations should be incorporated into *jus ad bellum* and *jus in bello*, as examination of the nature of the *jus ad bellum* conditions of right intention and reasonable chance of success, and the scope of the *jus in bello* conditions, reveals that these conditions impose limitations and obligations upon the conduct of a victorious nation towards its defeated opponent. When this is so, what need is there for a distinct set of *jus post bellum* conditions to perform the same task? There is none, and to create such a set would separate the discussion of *post bellum* considerations from the discussion of *ad bellum* and *in bello* in a way that, as I have pointed out, is very unwise. Therefore, I would argue that the most appropriate place for *post bellum* considerations in just war theory is within *jus ad bellum* and *jus in bello*.

Notes

1 H. Grotius, *De Jure Belli ac Pacis Libris Tres*, in J. Brown Scott (ed.), Francis W. Kelsey (trans.), Vol. 2 of *The Classics of International Law*, Oxford: Clarendon Press, 1925.
2 A. J. Bellamy, *Just Wars From Cicero to Iraq*, Cambridge: Polity Press, 2006, p. 214.
3 Ibid.
4 H. Frowe, *The Ethics of War and Peace: An Introduction*, London: Routledge, 2011, p. 209.

5 A.J. Bellamy, 'The Responsibilities of Victory: "Jus Post Bellum" and the Just War,' *Review of International Studies* 34(4), 2008, p. 605.

6 Frowe, *The Ethics of War and Peace*, p. 209.

7 B. Orend, "Jus Post Bellum," *Journal of Social Philosophy* 31(1), 2000, p. 129.

8 B. Orend, "Jus Post Bellum: A Just War Theory Perspective," in C. Stahn and J. Kleffner (eds), *Jus Post Bellum: Towards a Law of Transition From Conflict to Peace*, The Hague: TMC Asser Press, 2008, p. 41.

9 B. Orend, "Jus Post Bellum," *Journal of Social Philosophy* 31, 2000, p.129.

10 B. Orend, "Jus Post Bellum: A Just War Theory Perspective," in C. Stahn and J. Kleffner (eds), *Jus Post Bellum*, p. 40.

11 G. J. Bass, "Jus Post Bellum," *Philosophy and Public Affairs* 32(4), 2004, p. 390.

12 B. Orend, "Jus Post Bellum," *Journal of Social Philosophy* 31, 2000, p.128.

13 G.J. Bass, "Jus Post Bellum," p. 399.

14 M. Walzer, *Just and Unjust Wars*, New York: Basic Books, 1977, p. 106.

15 G.J. Bass, "Jus Post Bellum," p. 398.

16 D. Lackey, *The Ethics of War and Peace*, NJ: Prentice-Hall, 1989, p. 31.

17 C. Guthrie and M. Quinlan, *Just War: The Just War Tradition: Ethics in Modern Warfare*, London: Bloomsbury Publishing, 2007, p. 24.

18 R. Norman, *Ethics, Killing and War*, Cambridge: Cambridge University Press, 1995, p. 118.

19 For a more detailed discussion of reasonable chance of success, see A.J. Coates, *The Ethics of War*, Manchester: Manchester University Press, 1997, and William O'Brien, *The Conduct of a Just and Limited War*, Praeger, 1981.

20 Guthrie and Quinlan, *Just War*, p. 31.

21 Guthrie and Quinlan, *Just War*, p. 24.

22 Ibid.

23 Hypothetically, one could perhaps imagine a situation in which no 'innocent' lives would be lost in such a defensive tactic – if, thanks to a successful programme of indoctrination, the *entire* population of Country A, including children, either supported or were actively involved in the invasion of Country B, and it could be predicted that they would continue in this endeavour after the fall of their government. In response, I would say that even in such a hypothetical situation, self-defensive genocide could not be justified, as the discrimination rule requires that only combatants and leaders be targeted, even if the noncombatants are in support of the war. As I will argue later in this chapter, this rule is as valid in a post-combat situation as it is during the combat itself. An entire country without exception supporting a conflict is unlikely enough, but the population of an entire country as combatants is physically impossible – no babe in arms can be a combatant, however likely one thinks it is to grow up into one.

24 Ibid.

25 N. Dower, *The Ethics of War and Peace: Cosmopolitan and Other Perspectives*, Cambridge: Polity Press, 2009, p. 93, my italics.

26 H. Frowe, *The Ethics of War and Peace*, p. 57.

27 N. Dower, *The Ethics of War and Peace*, p. 93.

28 Ibid.

29 Incidentally, Frowe suggests a different justification for the inclusion of 'reasonable chance of success' in *jus ad bellum*. She argues that 'Leaders may not sacrifice the lives of others for hopeless causes' (Frowe, *The Ethics of War and Peace*, p. 58). However, I believe this rests on similar reasoning – if it is permissible for a government to compel their citizens to fight when 'they have a realistic chance of winning' (op. cit. p. 57) but not otherwise, then the reason must be that leaders have no right to insist their people accept the bad consequences of a war without the prospect of a good outcome.

30 N. Dower, *The Ethics of War and Peace*, p. 93.

31 S.P. Lee, *Ethics and War: An Introduction*, Cambridge: Cambridge University Press, 2012, p. 286–7.

32 C. Stahn, "Jus Post Bellum: Mapping the Discipline(s)," in C. Stahn and J. Kleffner (eds.), *Jus Post Bellum: Towards a Law of Transition From Conflict to Peace*, The Hague: TMC Asser Press, 2008, p. 99.

33 S.P. Lee, *Ethics and War: An Introduction*, p. 290.

34 For more discussions of 'war' as a process continuing, in some sense, after the end of military combat, see S.P. Lee, *Ethics and War* and, to a lesser extent, C. Stahn, *Jus Post Bellum*.

35 A.J. Coates, *The Ethics of War*, Manchester University Press, 1997, p. 209.

36 C. Guthrie and M. Quinlan, *Just War*, p. 11.

37 M. Walzer, *Just and Unjust Wars*, p. 21.

38 H. Frowe, *The Ethics of War and Peace*, p. 107.

39 M. Walzer, *Just and Unjust Wars*, p. 21.
40 Orend, "Jus Post Bellum: A Just War Theory Perspective," in C. Stahn and J. Kleffner (eds), *Jus Post Bellum*, p. 41.

References

Bass, G.J. "Jus Post Bellum," *Philosophy and Public Affairs* 32, 2004, pp. 384–412.

Bellamy, A.J. *Just Wars From Cicero to Iraq*, Cambridge: Polity Press, 2006.

Bellamy, A.J. "The Responsibilities of Victory: 'Jus Post Bellum' and the Just War," *Review of International Studies* 34, 2008, pp. 601–625.

Coates, A.J. *The Ethics of War*, Manchester: Manchester University Press, 1997.

Dower, N. *The Ethics of War and Peace: Cosmopolitan and Other Perspectives*, Cambridge: Polity Press, 2009.

Frowe, H. *The Ethics of War and Peace: An Introduction*, London: Routledge, 2011.

Grotius, H. *De Jure Belli ac Pacis Libris Tres*, in J. Brown Scott (ed.), F.W. Kelsey (trans.), Vol. 2 of *The Classics of International Law*, Oxford: Clarendon Press, 1925.

Guthrie, C. and M. Quinlan *Just War*, London: Bloomsbury Publishing, 2007.

Lackey, D. *The Ethics of War and Peace*, NJ: Prentice-Hall, 1989.

Lee, S.P. *Ethics and War: An Introduction*, Cambridge: Cambridge University Press, 2012.

Norman, R. *Ethics, Killing and War*, Cambridge: Cambridge University Press, 1995.

O'Brien, W.V. *The Conduct of a Just and Limited War*, Praeger, 1981.

Orend, B. "Jus Post Bellum," *Journal of Social Philosophy* 31, 2000, pp. 117–137.

Orend, B. "Jus Post Bellum: A Just War Theory Perspective," in C. Stahn and J. Kleffner (eds), *Jus Post Bellum: Towards a Law of Transition From Conflict to Peace*, The Hague: TMC Asser Press, 2008.

Stahn, C. "Jus Post Bellum: Mapping the Discipline(s)," in C. Stahn and J. Kleffner (eds), *Jus Post Bellum: Towards a Law of Transition From Conflict to Peace*, The Hague: TMC Asser Press, 2008.

Walzer, M. *Just and Unjust Wars*, New York: Basic Books, 1977.

8

JUS POST BELLUM

War closure in the 21st century[1]

Richard M. O'Meara

1. Introduction

There can be no Justice in war if there are not, ultimately, responsible men and women.[2]

If you break it you own it.[3]

Peace is not sought in order to provoke war, but war is waged in order to attain peace. Be a peacemaker, then, even by fighting, so that through your victory you might bring those whom you defeat to the advantages of peace.[4]

War is tough stuff. It is, at the very least, the organized projection of death and mayhem by some group against another, generally for purposes of governance.[5] Its justifications are myriad, running the gamut from self-defense, to humanitarian intervention, to national aggrandizement to whim and revenge.

Whether one argues that war is *ever* a useful project in the conduct of affairs amongst men, it appears clear that humans have a long history of its use,[6] that it is always terribly destructive, and that recourse to arms does not appear to be going away any time soon. The good news is that there is a fairly robust articulation in both law and moral philosophy regarding a political entity's right to start a war—project force—and how war is to be conducted. On the other hand, these articulations have been confounded by a bewildering set of war paradigms that do not fit neatly into these old articulations. Further, these new types of force projections never seem to end. Finally, it appears clear that failure to end a war well, to win the peace, can have catastrophic consequences and lead, even as the dead are buried, the monuments laid and the disabled march home, to future wars.[7] Getting the peace *right*, then, must be considered as important as determining when and how to fight.

2. What is war?

The use of the term *war* occurs in many contexts and can, even with the best of intentions, lead to very sloppy discussions. At one level, there are the wars on drugs, poverty and the like which seem to connote an organized and focused effort at the eradication of a particular condition. Somewhere in the middle are a whole host of definitions which come out of domestic law and are meant to trigger certain legal ramifications such as trade restrictions, immigration procedures, emergency powers for governments in the area of civil rights, or rights and responsibilities under insurance contracts. On another level are definitions of war which speak to projections of force by states, each vying with the other in relative symmetry in order to obtain a peace which conforms to the aims and desires of the victor. Finally, there are those asymmetric contests which are fought by states and non-state actors and which arise out of guerrilla wars and insurgencies, wars of intervention, wars against terrorists and terror generally and proxy guerrilla wars.[8]

A standard definition of war, one that carries with it many of the assumptions upon which the UN Charter and subsequent articulations of international law regarding constraints on war generally, appears in L. Oppenheim's treatise on International Law in 1952: 'War is a contention between two or more States through their armed forces, for the purpose of overpowering each other and imposing such conditions of peace as the victor pleases.'[9] Another commentator, Yoram Dinstein, notes that: 'There is a marked difference between war and peace: whereas it requires two States to conclude and to preserve peace … it takes a single State to embroil itself as well as its selected enemy in war.'[10]

A third commentator, Christine Gray, eschews the term *war* altogether as she discusses international law (IL) and the *use of force* generally, noting that that is the term which is used by the UN Charter in its prohibition: 'All Members shall refrain in their international relations from the threat or *use of force* against the territorial integrity or political independence of any state, or in any other manner inconsistent with the Purposes of the United Nations.'[11]

There is a recognition in the 21st century that the classical peace/war dichotomy 'has lost its *raison d'être* with the outlawry of war and the blurring of the boundaries between conflict and peace.'[12] This is especially true in internal armed violence which is reported to form, for example, 95 percent of all armed violence between 1995 and 2005.[13]

Given that *wars, conflicts, projections of force, uses of force* and *activities short of war* all have varying war aims, tend to use multiple methods of conventional and unconventional violence, have different levels of respect for civilian targets, and are fought by different groups of actors, traditional definitions of war as an activity reserved to states and constrained by state authority would appear to be less and less relevant.[14]

This is not to say, however, that all these categories of violence do not have some things in common. They all, it would appear, use levels of violence to obtain certain goals. While those goals may differ, e.g. humanitarian intervention versus terrorist bomb attacks, violence in one form or another is the primary tool. Further, these activities are carried on by political communities, seeking to impose their will on other groups through the use of violence. Finally, these activities violate the rights of others for the purpose of changing the way others operate.

Brian Orend melds these different characteristics in his definition of war as follows:

> War should be understood as an actual, intentional and widespread armed conflict between political communities … Classical war is international war, a war between different states … [B]ut just as frequent is war within a state between rival groups or communities … Certain political pressure groups, like terrorist organizations, might also be considered

'political communities' in that they are associations of people with a political purpose and, indeed, many of them aspire to statehood or to influence the development of statehood in certain lands. Indeed, it seems that *all warfare is precisely, and ultimately, about governance*.[15]

3. What is peace?

Peace is not the absence of war. As the discussion above indicates *war* is susceptible to multiple definitions and interpretations. The construct of *peace* appears to carry with it the same problems. The conclusion that peace is not a condition but an ongoing process has been bolstered in recent years by the considerable violence experienced in Iraq and Afghanistan and multiple peacekeeping operations throughout the world.[16] The cessation of widespread and organized violence, then, does not automatically signal peace and yet its achievement appears to be among humanity's highest values.[17]

Theorists from Aristotle to Michael Walzer appear to agree that the aim of war must be peace, albeit a peace defined, at least in part, by the belligerents involved.[18] There is a good deal of literature regarding the rules which might apply to the making of peace and what goals peace-making should have. These will be discussed below. It should be remembered, however, that most contemporary wars are fought by groups who have previously agreed to terms of peace in one form or another and that the 'average number of conflicts terminated per year in the 1990s was more than twice the average of all previous decades from 1946 onwards.'[19] In short, *lasting peace* is often an elusive goal. It is necessary to recognize this point, as I argue below.

3.1 *What are the rules?*

The big questions regarding war and peace have traditionally been articulated as follows:

- When is war justified and who gets to do it?
- How should we conduct ourselves as we go about the business of war?
- How should wars end and what does peace look like?

There are four traditions which dominate the response to these questions, *just war theory, international law, realist theory*, and *pacifism*. They all assume that *war*, however it is defined, is a scourge, an activity to be avoided if at all possible. Yet the first three admit to the need to conduct war in various situations and articulate rules for the conduct of war as well. Because pacifism does not admit the justification for war under any circumstances, it has very little to say about the conduct of war and its aftermath.

Just war theory

Just war theory is a theory of ethics; it is a review of norms which seeks to determine when the inception of war is *just*, that is morally permitted; what conduct during a war is *just*, that is morally acceptable or constrained; and what are the conditions for a just peace, that is what *should* a peace look like. The question here is what is humanity entitled to do *morally* when it comes to the conduct of war?

Just war theory speaks to a series of calculations regarding the conduct of war. To begin a war (*jus ad bellum*), it must be considered *just*, that is the decision must conclude that there is a *just cause;* there must be a *right intention*; it must be conducted by *proper authorities*; it must be the *last resort*; and there must be a *probability of success*. Finally, and perhaps of considerable import to the question of how to end a war, there must be a determination of *proportionality*, the idea that the universal goods to be obtained outweigh the universal evils which can be foreseen.[20] These determinations are constraints in that they: limit the use of war to a very discrete set of situations such as self-defense, the defense of others, the protection of innocents and punishment of grievous wrong doing; define who can make the determination and who will be in charge of its conduct; and require some consideration of the results of the conduct before war is initiated. Together, these determinations constitute justification for unleashing the projection of force, committing what would otherwise be held to be murder and mayhem on others. They also provide *legitimacy* for the actor in that the violence can be said to be *minimally just*.

Even if a war is determined to be *just*, there are constraints on how the war *ought* to be fought (*jus in bello*). A just actor must project violence within the constraints of morally acceptable behavior in order to insure that the violence is projected only on those who are identified as participating in the war with that degree of force necessary to accomplish the tactical and strategic tasks necessary to accomplish the just goals of the conflict. Terms such as *military necessity*, *discretion*, and *proportionality* in the use of violence help to frame this discussion. An actor, then, can be justified in the decision to project force and yet become an unjust actor by the manner in which it prosecutes that projection of force.

Just war theory does speak to the outcome of wars when it requires actors, as part of their calculus regarding the projection of force, to determine that the results reflect 'at least a *proportionality* of benefits to costs.'[21] In order to make this determination, however, the question must be answered, What is the purpose of a just war? How does one know whether the results are *so* terrible as to render the original purposes of the projection of force unjustified? Some traditionally have answered that the purpose of a just war is to reestablish the *status quo ante bellum*, that set of circumstances which existed before the war began. Walzer, and others, disagree and argue for a result which is more secure and which reflects a more just state of affairs than existed before the war began.[22] This is a key point which I will return to below.

International Law (IL)

With the growth of the nation-state system, IL has come to the forefront to answer important questions and regulate the conduct of war. First, it must be emphasized that IL is *positivist* rather than *normative;* it speaks, at its best, to the utilitarian purpose of making man-made rules which aid mankind in the conduct of war. It does not speak to what *ought* to be appropriate behavior amongst actors; rather it provides minimal standards of conduct which are adjudged by the community of international actors to be in their interest and to be useful in the constraint of the project of war. It is partially realist in that it assumes that war will occur and seeks to criminalize behavior in order to protect, where possible, the potential for peaceful relations. It is not *universal* except to the extent that all actors agree to its terms and it is not *immutable* because it accepts changes to the rules as the international community deems them appropriate through treaty agreements or customary practice.[23] As Carsten Stahns notes:

> Moral theory and legal science share distinct origins and rationales and approach the relationship between *jus ad bellum*, *jus in bello* and *jus post bellum* from different angles. Moral philosophy is primarily concerned with the moral justification of warfare ... International lawyers, by contrast, tend to view each of these categories as autonomous rules of behavior, with the aim of maximizing compliance and respect for human dignity. It is therefore not contradictory to construe *jus post bellum* differently in each discipline.[24]

IL has, however, become conflated with just war principles as well as a whole host of other human rights articulations. Just war theorists, then, are often bogged down in suggesting best practices for actors which will be *useful* and IL commentators are often heard to speak in terms of *what is fair and right*.[25]

The history of IL as it pertains to war is instructive. As nation-states eschewed normative and theological justifications in the 17th and 18th centuries, states accepted their right to conduct war as a responsibility of statehood. The justice of a state's cause in the projection of force lost a good deal of its validity; rather states conducted war as a matter of right in the exercise of their responsibility to pursue national policy.[26] The conduct of war, however, began to take preeminence, reflecting as it did age-old customary practices of warriors in the field. Purely utilitarian concerns abounded; treatment of fallen soldiers, prisoners of war, uninvolved civilians, destruction of non-military targets, use of new technologies. This movement acknowledged that *de facto* wars would continue but that if they were conducted in a particularly barbaric manner, the peaces to be obtained would not last. Revenge, rising out of the ashes of a particular conflict, might well stoke the fires of the next conflict, especially where armies were becoming democratized and ideological and states lost the ability to turn the violence on and off at will. Thus the exhortations of Abraham Lincoln during the American Civil War that

> [w]ith malice toward none; with charity for all; with firmness in the right, as God gives us to see the right, let us strive on to finish the work we are in; to bind up the nation's wounds, to care for him who shall have borne the battle, and for his widow, and his orphan—to do all which may achieve and cherish a just and lasting peace among ourselves, and with all nations.[27]

Conventions of various kinds and with various participants occurred to address a myriad of issues including what was called the *law of land warfare*. Through the Hague Conventions of 1899 and 1907 and the Geneva Conventions of 1864, 1928, 1929, 1949 and 1975 an extremely robust set of rules and proscriptions regarding conduct were enacted and ultimately agreed upon in part by most states forming the international community. Aligned with but separate from a set of rules dealing with personal human rights, this body of law has been denominated *international humanitarian law* (IHL). There are enforcement mechanisms as well including originally the Nuremburg Court system, multiple international courts and ultimately the International Criminal Court.[28]

On a separate track, and primarily as a result of the catastrophes of World Wars I and II, IL developed a response to the question regarding the justification for an actor's projection of force. Indeed, IL went well beyond the reasoning of just war theory and attempted to outlaw war altogether. For instance, the United Nation's Charter outlawed war between states except in situations of self-defense or where the international community, through the U.N. Security Council, sanctioned it.[29]

Like all systems of constraint, especially on the international stage where there are minimal means to enforce proscriptions, IL has had its failures.[30] It struggles, for example, with the reality that all actors are not sovereign states and that evolving definitions of *war* are rarely covered by its articulations. Further, in a globalized world, conflicts that have previously been considered *domestic* now clearly affect the entire global community.[31] As Bill Nash, the American General responsible for peacekeeping operations in Bosnia-Herzegovina noted, '[T]he first rule of nation-building is that everything is related to everything, and it's all political.'[32] An entire human rights regime has grown up since World War II which demands vindication not only of state's rights but individual rights during and after war is conducted. There is a growing recognition that economic and social rights are entitled to equal pride of place with political and security rights. Finally, there are a whole host of actors who refuse to pay even lip service to the proscriptions of IL as they conduct force projection on the international stage.

We should recognize that post war conduct of actors is rarely addressed in IL. There are some discussions about the Responsibility to Protect (R2P)[33] and a fairly robust set of IL requirements for states in the law of belligerent occupation[34] but these have not found their way into binding treaties or custom and only apply to a very discrete set of circumstances. Lawyers and policy-makers whose forces have undertaken these hybrid operations recognize that the rules of engagement and assumption of civil administrative responsibilities vary considerably depending on the mission. Peace keeping in Mogadishu, for example, is very different from peace keeping in Sierra Leone and Kosovo. Bosnia, Iraq and the Sinai each present significant legal challenges that IL addresses only on an *ad hoc* basis with limited success. There is a need for additional international conventions to deal with these force projections in order to insure consistency of action and accountability.

Realism

While realism has had many twists and turns in its explanations over the years, for the purposes of this paper it can be said that the doctrine has two purposes 1) to provide an explanation regarding how actors, especially states, act on the international stage and 2) to explain a set of assumptions upon which realist statesmen operate when they make decisions about when to go to war, how to conduct war, and how wars end. The doctrine has a long history ranging from Thucydides, Machiavelli and Hobbes to Hans Morgenthau, George Kennan, Reinhold Niebuhr, Henry Kissinger and Kenneth Waltz. Traditional realism speaks to power and security issues, the ability of states to survive and prosper in an anarchical world. Realists assume the appropriateness of war if *and only if* it is necessary to obtain a *national interest* and find it unreasonable for states to constrain themselves regarding the tools used to conduct wars or the ways that wars should end. Constraints and responsibilities found in just war theory and IL hold little cachet when measured against the absolute requirement for states to survive and prosper. The logic of Hobbes's dictum *Bellum omnium contra omnes*, the war of all against all, is often cited by realists to describe the state of the international community where there is no overarching governance to reign in the natural requirements of states to survive, one against the other.[35]

There is a strain of realism, however, that speaks to the efficacy of restraints in war. In a globalized international environment where states find it more and more difficult to operate unilaterally, there is an interest in developing *soft* as well as *hard* power in order to survive and prosper. Charles Krauthammer, for example, notes the problem when dealing with the domestic political debate between realists [conservatives] and idealists [liberals] in the United States:

> But here we come up against the limits of realism. You cannot live by power alone ... For most Americans, will to power might be a correct description of the world—of what motivates other countries—but it cannot be a prescription for America. It cannot be our purpose. America cannot and will not live by *realpolitik* alone. Our foreign policy must be driven by something beyond power. Unless conservatives present ideals to challenge the liberal ideal of a domesticated international community, they will lose the debate ... amongst American conservatives, another, more idealist, school has arisen that sees America's national interest as an expression of values.[36]

In essence, there are benefits to cooperation—to the adherence to multilateral organizations and international law regimes—which are either too difficult to obtain or which cannot be obtained in a unilateral fashion. Going to war within the framework of U.N. constraints, conducting war within the legal proscriptions of the various Conventions, and even finishing a war by a long and expensive round of nation-building and development aid all have ramifications which unilateral action often cannot produce. Joseph Nye argues that *soft power* which arises from the attractiveness of a country's culture, political ideals, and policies, is the ability of a state to persuade other states and actors to share its objectives or desired outcomes.[37] Adherence to restraints regarding conduct during war, for example, often benefits soldiers on the ground; adherence to treaties which ban certain types of weapons such as weapons of mass destruction can aid in the security of the domestic and foreign battlefield; and insuring that states who have lost wars are able to reenter the international community on terms beneficial to both the victor and the defeated can lessen the possibility of war for the next generation. For realists, adherence to these restraints is not based on the *normative* philosophy of how states *ought* to act, nor is state conduct restrained by the legalisms of IL. Rather, adherence is based on the assumption that cooperation with other states coupled with hard power is in the national interest, leading to the state's ability to provide security and prosperity for its citizens.[38]

4. The right way to end a war

Given the discussion above, it may be concluded that there is *no one right* way to end a war. The wide divergence in the justifications for the projection of force, the nature of the conflict, the practices used to prosecute the war, the manner in which the conflict is concluded, swift capitulation by a state, regime change, continued insurgency, aggressor victory etc., these and other multiple variables influence how the parties will act *post bellum*. The manner in which a conflict is concluded can make all the difference.

Principles regarding *jus post bellum* are at present incomplete and subject to considerable argument,[39] yet the basic premise found in *jus ad bellum* seems to apply. Before states can *morally* project force they must determine the *proportionality* of the results, that is, does the foreseeable end outweigh the damage which the projection of force will inevitably cause? This just war theory requirement seems to imply that conflict can only be initiated where an actor determines that the end result will be less traumatic, especially to the innocent who will be affected, than the benefits to be obtained. There is a further implication here: should an actor determine the necessity for conflict, it must be prepared to, and indeed has a *moral* obligation to, right the economic, social, and political trauma which its conflict will create.[40]

There is an ethical corollary to this discussion as well. Civilian policy-makers and commanders in the field have an ethical responsibility to their soldiers to project force in a manner consistent with national values.[41] David Rodin notes that

> there is good reason to believe that soldiers and statesmen will often sincerely believe their wars to be just, whether they are in fact or not. This is because ... war is so difficult, so dangerous and so costly, that it is exceptionally difficult for ordinary humans to undertake it without believing that they are in pursuit of a cause that is noble and just.[42]

Here, the status or the nature of the belligerency is of the utmost importance. Those who write rules of engagement for individual soldiers routinely characterize the conflict in order to justify their orders. The authority to fire a weapon, target a formation and detain individuals is based precisely on definitions and formulations. While the justice of a particular conflict may be left

ultimately to the court of history, there is an immediate need to sift through the various definitions of war and peace in order to promulgate orders regarding the projection of force which
advise those who do the killing what is just and what is unjust conduct.

Brian Orend asks the question, What are the ends or goals of a just war? He provides the
following answer:

> The general answer is a more secure possession of our rights, both individual and collec-
> tive. The aim of a just and lawful war, we know, is the resistance of aggression and the
> vindication of the fundamental rights of societies, ultimately on behalf of the human rights
> of their individual citizens. These values revolve around the concept of a minimally just
> and hence legitimate community. Such a community is one which does all it reasonably
> can to: i) gain recognition as being legitimate in the eyes of its own people and the inter-
> national community: ii) adhere to basic rules of international justice and good international
> citizenship, notably non-aggression; and iii) satisfy the human rights of its individual mem-
> bers (to security, subsistence, liberty, equality and recognition.[43]

Anyone who has spent any time working at peace-keeping, peace-making, nation-building or
the provision of humanitarian aid knows that the devil is in the details. The above represent a
fair checklist of discrete areas to be addressed should one actor intend to involve itself in the
project of wholesale transition of a society from one set of values and political mechanisms to
another. These are not inexpensive undertakings. As U.S. actions in Iraq and Afghanistan have
demonstrated, accomplishing the above goals can take decades, contribute to multiple additional deaths and destruction and cause cultural collisions which may never be healed. They
represent, one might argue, very Western constructions of what a minimally just society *ought*
to look like. Finally, they are open to the criticism that the enumerated responsibilities are akin
to requiring actor A who has been aggrieved by actor B to pay not only for the court proceedings used to vindicate his rights but the psychological counseling necessary to cure the malady
that caused actor B to act out in the first place.

International law, to date, does not specifically address conduct, *post bellum*, except in the
area of IHL. Here, parties to conflicts argue that their ability to regulate the conduct of actors
post-conflict is limited by the conditions on the ground, the emergent and often chaotic nature
of the environment, the breakdown in civil authority, the lack of resources to create a robust
civil society and other legal and actual constraints. There is considerable disagreement as to
whether occupiers are bound to enforce the expansive human rights found in the various
human rights treaties which bind, generally, signers of these treaties to treatment of individuals
within their jurisdictions.[44] And international criminal courts as a rule restrict their prosecu-
torial jurisdiction to *grave* breaches of IHL, leaving lesser breaches of IHL to the domestic
criminal codes of actors. Yet occupiers, in a general sense, are staying longer, projecting force
in and among civilians, and assuming responsibilities for the administration of civil society that
were not originally contemplated by IHL. This legal *black hole* has been described by Charles
Garraway as follows:

> But not only are the actors on the battlefield changing, so is the battlefield itself. Soldiers
> are now frequently involved in post-conflict situations where the international rules are
> far from clear. What is the entitlement to use force during a period of occupation? Do
> 'combat rules' apply [IHL] or have we moved to a more threat based regime? And what
> is the position where 'major combat operations' may have ceased but violence persists? In
> Helmand province, some years after the initial intervention, United Kingdom and other

NATO forces have been involved in what one senior officer described as the most intense fighting since the Korean War. But what law applies to the actions of those soldiers? On what basis are targeting decisions taken? The stark difference between status based and threat based legal regimes causes inevitable difficulties when operating in the grey area that is post-conflict ... Indeed does the Convention – or the International Covenant on Civil and Political Rights – even apply in situations of this nature where troops are operating outsides their national boundaries? These are issues over which there is strong disagreement, particularly within the United States, and yet for members of the armed forces, they are critical. They may represent the difference between a gallantry medal and a prosecution for murder.[45]

While the realist tradition might well embrace Colin Powell's maxim that an immediate and clean exit strategy after the projection of force is appropriate to the vindication of the national interest, the reality on the ground is that in a globalized international environment definitions of national interest are less clear than they have been in the past and the ramifications of force projection, no matter how small, affect multiple sets of international actors now and in the future. What is the national interest, for example, for the invasion of Iraq? There are multiple answers. One might be the destruction of Saddam Hussein's ability to foster international terrorism and the proliferation of weapons of mass destruction. Another might be regime change in order to insure that this particular dictator could no longer play havoc with the regional political order and thus disrupt the freeflow of energy, etc. A third interest might be the creation of the first Arab democracy in order to begin the development of a reasonably secure and peaceful region. Each of these tasks requires different levels of force projection, different timetables and different commitments of blood and treasure. The same analysis holds for force projection in Sierra Leone, Bosnia-Herzegovina, The Democratic Republic of Congo, Rwanda, or the Sudan.

How to use force, it is recognized, also carries with it ramifications for the future as well. No longer is the mission of the infantry always to 'close with and destroy the enemy.' The U.S. Army's Field Manual regarding the proper application of force notes:

Section V1-Rules of Engagement
2-66 The proper application of force is a critical component to any successful counterinsurgency operation. In a counterinsurgency, the center of gravity is public support. In order to defeat an insurgent force, US forces must be able to separate insurgents from the population ... Achieving the appropriate balance requires a thorough understanding of the nature and causes of the insurgency, the end state, and the military's role in a counterinsurgency operation.[46]

The lesson here is that while all politics is local, increasingly all politics is international as well, especially for those, like the United States, which benefit the most from the interconnectedness of the global economic environment.

Just war theory requires an analysis of post war ramifications in order to determine the proportional benefits of projecting force in the first place. Yet experience schools that it is difficult if not impossible to anticipate the multiple long-term unintended consequences of force projection. IHL, it can be argued, except in the very limited area of legal occupation, has no specific answer to the myriad responsibilities of states which find themselves administering to the civil needs of those they have recently conquered. There is a need for additional legal frameworks to deal with these new environments and recognition that a state which has recently undergone the scourge of war, for whatever reason, impacts the international community in very particular ways. Kosovo, Libya, Afghanistan and Syria are all examples of this premise. R2P, then, can be seen as a *post bellum* articulation as well as one of *ad bellum*.

5 How to judge a successful end to conflict?

While it may be hard to define exactly when a conflict ends, we can make some predictions about the general conditions that would bring about a successful end of war. This set of predictions accommodates the three theoretical approaches to war so described: *just war theorists* seek conditions in a *post bellum* environment which outweigh the harms caused by war (constraints on starting a war) and *international law* speaks primarily to the conduct of actors in war. However, in the future it may be the *utilitarians* or *realists* that stretch the continuum of responsibilities required of victors after the war.

Redefining national interest may well require leaving the battlefield in a state that will not require a return for the next generation: cleaning up the battle space of weapons, setting conditions for security and economic growth, and insuring that those left behind are capable of joining the international community with a degree of domestic tranquility that permits global integration. Because these projects take time, hasty judgment adds little to meaningful analysis. The condition of the *post bellum* battlefield must be considered even as policy-makers struggle with their justifications for projecting force in the first place. Actors who would wage war need to remember, however, that war, no matter how it is defined, has never been cheap. In a global world, the price of a failed peace can be even more expensive.

Notes

1 This chapter was published in earlier and somewhat modified form as R. O'Meara, "Reflections on the Right Way to End a War," *Journal on Terrorism and Security Analysis*, 6, 2011, pp. 35–45. Adapted with permission from the Student Association on Terrorism & Security Analysis.

2 M. Walzer, *Just and Unjust Wars, A Moral Argument with Historical Illustrations*, 4th edn, Basic Books: New York, 2006, p. 288.

3 Secretary of State Colin Powell's advice to President Bush regarding the pending war in Iraq, 2002, referred to generally as the *Pottery Barn Rule*, as cited by Bob Woodward. Online. Available at: http://www.buffalo.edu/ubreporter/archive/vol36/vol36n13/articles/Woodward.html (accessed 7 April 2013).

4 Augustine, "Letter 189, to Boniface," in E.L. Fortin and D. Kries (eds), *Augustine: Political Writings*, trans. M.W. Tkacz and D. Kries, Indianapolis: Hackett, 1994, p. 220.

5 Brian Orend, "War," *Stanford Encyclopedia of* Philosophy. Online. Available at: http://plato.stanford.edu/entries/war (accessed 26 March 2010).

6 See, for example, J. Keegan, *A History of Warfare*, New York: Knopf, 1993 and D. Kagan, *On the Origins of War and the Preservation of Peace*, New York: Knopf Doubleday Publishing Group, 1996.

7 Even a cursory review of the manner in which World War I ended, for example the failure to completely defeat the German army, the terms and conditions of the Treaty of Versailles, the lack of political will by the victors to enforce the terms of the Treaty, must bolster the argument that the peacemakers failed in their task of bringing World War I to a successful conclusion. See, generally, M. MacMillian, *Paris 1919*, New York: Random House 2003; M. F. Boemeke, G. D. Feldman and E.Glaser (eds), *The Treaty of Versailles: A Reassessment after 75 Years*, Cambridge: Cambridge University Press, 1998.

8 Michael L. Gross notes that the dilemmas of asymmetric warfare turn on their head the assumptions and conditions of traditional war between states.

> In general asymmetric conflicts differ as a function of the actors involved, participants' goals or war aims, and the means they use to achieve them. Actors range from guerrillas and terrorists on the weaker side to states, coalitions of states, and international forces under UN auspices on the stronger side. Goals range from maintaining the status quo to changing it, and from defeating an enemy decisively in pitched battle to simply staving off defeat in the hopes of setting incontestable

conditions for a political settlement … The means of war vary considerably. Some are conventional (missile and artillery) but many other means are unconventional and include torture, assassination, blackmail, terror, and nonlethal weapons.

M.L. Gross, *Moral Dilemmas of Modern War, Torture, Assassination, and Blackmail in an Age of Asymmetric Conflict*, New York: Cambridge University Press, 2010, p. 14.

9 L. Oppenheim, *International Law*, 7th edn. H. Lauterpacht (ed.), London: Longmans Green & Co., 1952.

10 Dinstein, Y. *War, Aggression and Self-defense*, Cambridge: Cambridge University Press, 2011.

11 C. Gray, *International Law and the Use of Force*, 2nd edn. Oxford: Oxford University Press, 2004, p. 3.

12 C. Stahn, "*Jus Post Bellum*: Mapping the Disciplines" in C. Stahn and J. Kleffner (eds), *Jus Post Bellum: Towards a Law of Transition from Conflict to Peace*, The Hague: TMC Asser Press, 2008, p. 99.

13 See Human Security Report 2005, *The Changing Face of Global Violence*, Vancouver: Human Security Report Project, p. 18.

14 M.L.Gross, *Moral Dilemmas in Modern War*, pp. 8–25.

15 B. Orend, 'War', pp. 1–2.

16 S.K. Sharma, "Reconsidering the *Jus ad Bellum/Jus in Bello* Distinction," in C. Stahn and J. Kleffner (eds), *Jus Post Bellum:Towards a Law of Transition from Conflict to Peace*, The Hague: TMC Asser Press, p. 29.

17 R.J. Rummel takes note of this occupation:

Consider: "Peace at any price." "The most disadvantageous peace is better than the most just war." "Peace is more important than all justice." "I prefer the most unjust peace to the justest war that was ever waged." "There never was a good war or a bad peace." [footnotes omitted]

Yet, we agree little on what is peace. Perhaps the most popular (Western) view is as an absence of dissension, violence, or war, a meaning found in the *New Testament* and possibly an original meaning of the Greek word for peace, *Irene*[…]

Peace, however, is also seen as concord, or harmony and tranquility. It is viewed as peace of mind or serenity, especially in the East. It is defined as a state of law or civil government, a state of justice or goodness, a balance or equilibrium.

Such meanings of peace function at different levels. Peace may be opposed to or an opposite of antagonistic conflict, violence, or war. It may refer to an internal state (of mind or of nations) or to external relations. Or it may be narrow in conception, referring to specific relations in a particular situation (like a peace treaty), or overarching, covering a whole society (as in a world peace). Peace may be a dichotomy (it exists or it does not) or continuous, passive or active, empirical or abstract, descriptive or normative, or positive or negative.

R. J. Rummel, *Understanding Conflict and War*, New York: Wiley & Sons, 1976, section 2.1, pp. 1–2.

18 B. Orend, "*Jus Post Bellum*: A Just War Theory Persepective," in C. Stahn and J. Kleffner (eds), *Jus Post Bellum*, p. 33.

19 See Human Security Report 2005, *The Changing Face of Global Violence*, Vancouver: Human Security Report Project, p. 53. Ironically, studies indicate that nationwide mortality rates overall appear to be dropping as well.

Several interrelated long-term changes have been driving this counterintuitive development:

i) The average war today is fought by smaller armies and impacts less territory than conflicts of the Cold War era. Smaller wars mean fewer war deaths and less impact on nationwide mortality rates.

ii) Dramatic long-term improvements in public health in the developing world have steadily reduced mortality rates in peacetime—and saved countless lives in wartime.

iii) Major increases in the level, scope, and effectiveness of humanitarian assistance to war-affected populations in countries in conflict since the end of the Cold War have reduced wartime death tolls still further.

Human Security Report 2009, *The Shrinking Costs of War*, pp. 1–3.

20 B. Orend, *War*, pp. 5–9; see also Y. Dinstein, *War, Aggression and Self-Defense*, pp. 63–71.

21 B. Orend, "Justice after War," *Ethics and International Affairs*, 16:1, 2002.

22 M. Walzer, *Just and Unjust Wars*, p. 119.

23 A standard definition of international law reads as follows:

[L]aw is that element which binds the members of the community together in their adherence to recognized values and standards.[…]

Similarly, the mistake of confusing international law with international morality must be avoided. While they may meet at certain points, the former discipline is a legal one both as regards its content and its form while the concept of international morality is a branch of ethics. This does not mean that international law can be divorced from its values.

M. N. Shaw, *International Law*, 6th edn. Cambridge: Cambridge University Press, 2008, p. 2.

24 C. Stahn, "*Jus Post Bellum*: Mapping the Disciplines," in C. Stahn, and J. Kleffner (eds), *Jus Post Bellum*, p. 112.

25 J. L. Goldsmith and E.A. Posner, *The Limitations of International Law*, Oxford: Oxford University Press, 2005, pp. 14–17.

26 T. W. Smith, "The New Law of War: Legitimizing Hi-Tech and Infrastructural Violence," *International Studies Quarterly*, 46:3, 2002, pp. 358–59; R. Kolb, "Origins of the Twin Terms *Jus ad Bellum*/*Jus in Bello*," *International Review of the Red Cross*, 320, 1997, p. 554; J.T. Johnson, "The Just War Idea: The State of the Question," *Social Philosophy & Policy*, 23, 2006.

27 A. Lincoln, *Abraham Lincoln's Second Inaugural Address* (March 4, 1865). Online. Available at: http://libertyonline.hypermall.com/Lincoln.lincoln-2.html (accessed 31 March, 2010).

28 See, for example, R. J. Goldstone, *For Humanity, Reflections of a War Crimes Investigator*, New Haven, Ct.: Yale University Press, 2000; O. Bartov, A. Grossman and M. Nolan (eds), *Crimes of War, Guilt and Denial in the Twentieth Century*, New York: The New Press, 2002; G.J. Bass, *Stay the Hand of Vengeance, The Politics of War Crimes Tribunals*, Princeton, NJ: Princeton University Press, 2000.

29 The UN Charter reads in pertinent part:

> Nothing in the present Charter shall impair the inherent right of individual or collective self-defence if an armed attack occurs against a Member of the United Nations, until the Security Council has taken measures necessary to maintain international peace and security. Measures taken by Members in the exercise of this right of self-defence shall be immediately reported to the Security Council and shall not in any way affect the authority and responsibility of the Security Council under the present Charter to take at any time such action as it deems necessary in order to maintain or restore peace and security.

United Nations. *Charter of the United Nations, Chapter VII: Action With Respect To Threats To The Peace, Breaches Of The Peace, And Acts Of Aggression, Article 51* (1945). Online. Available at: http://www.un.org/en/documents/charter/chapter7.shtml (accessed 30 March, 2010).

30 J. Goldsmith and R. A. Posner, *The Limitations of International Law*, pp. 225–26; D. Kennedy, "The International Human Rights Movement: Part of the Problem?" *Harvard Human Rights Journal*, 15, 2002.

31 See for example, G. R. Lucas Jr, "From *Jus ad bellum* to *Jus ad pacem*: Rethinking Just War Criteria for the Use of Military Force for Humanitarian Ends," in D. Chatterjee and D. Scheid (eds), *Ethics and Foreign Interventions*, Cambridge: Cambridge University Press, 2003.

32 Nash, quoted in Orend, "Jus Post Bellum: A Just War Theory Perspective," in C. Stahn and J. Kleffner (eds), *Jus Post Bellum*, p. 48.

33 The Responsibility to Protect (R2P) Doctrine appears to be an emerging norm which requires that when a state is either unwilling or unable to fulfill its responsibility to protect its own populations, UN members are obligated to take action to minimize human suffering. Most important, it involves the responsibility to prevent such atrocities from occurring and, if prevention fails, it requires states to react and rebuild. See, generally, G. Evans, *The Responsibility to Protect: Ending Mass Atrocity Crimes Once and For All*, Washington D.C.: Brookings Institution Press, 2008.

34 See, generally, Y. Dinstein, *The International Law of Belligerent Occupation*, Cambridge: Cambridge University Press, 2009.

> The authority of an Occupying Power is not derived from the will of the people, and democracy is not of any functional relevance to the running of an occupied territory. Belligerent occupation is not designed to win the hearts and minds of the local inhabitants; it has military—or security—objectives, and its foundation is the 'power of the bayonet.' The jurisdictional rights of the military government in an occupied territory ... stem from effective control alone. LOIAC [The Law of International Armed Conflict] offers the inhabitants of the territory vital safeguards against possible maltreatment by the Occupying Power. But belligerent occupation must be acknowledged for what it is and for what it is not.

Y. Dinstein, *The International Law of Belligerent Occupation*, p. 35.

35 V. Hanson, *Carthage and Culture: Landmark Battles in the Rise to Western Power*, New York: Random House, 2002; H. Kissinger, *Diplomacy*, New York: Simon & Schuster, 1994; S. M. Walt, "International Relations: One World, Many Theories," *Foreign Policy*, 110, 1998; H. J. Morgenthau, *Politics Among Nations*, 7th edn, New York: McGraw-Hill Companies, 2005; K. Waltz "Realist Thought and

Neorealist Theory," in C. Kegley (ed.) *Controversies in International Relations Theory: Realism and the Neoliberal Challenge*, New York: St Martin's Press, 1995; J. Mearsheimer, "The False Promise of International Institutions," *International Security* 19:3, 1994–95.

36 C. Krauthammer, *Democratic Realism, An American Foreign Policy for a Unipolar World*, Washington D.C.: AEI Press 2004, p. 13.

37 J. Nye, *Soft Power: The Means to Success in World Politics*, New York: Perseus Books Group, 2004, pp. 5–6.

38 C. Krauthammer speaks in terms of democratic realism, for example.

> And this is its axiom: We will support democracy everywhere, but we will commit blood and treasure only in places where there is a strategic necessity—meaning, places central to the larger war against the existential enemy, the enemy that poses a global mortal threat to freedom.

C. Krauthammer, *Democratic Realism*, p. 16.

39 M. Freeman and D. Djukie, "*Jus Post Bellum* and Transitional Justice," in C. Stahn and J. Kleffner (eds), *Jus Post Bellum: Towards a Law of Transition from Conflict to Peace*, The Hague: TMC Asser Press, 2008., p. 224. See also T. Seybolt, *Humanitarian Military Invention, The Conditions for Success and Failure*, Oxford: Oxford University Press, 2008.

> A great deal of ink has been spilled on this topic [human security as a justification for military intervention] already, much of it by international lawyers and moral philosophers whose legal and moral debates have shifted ground considerably since the end of the Cold War but whose arguments remain in a state of 'vincible ignorance' of empirical support.

Seybolt, *Humanitarian Military Invention, The Conditions for Success and Failure*, p.3.

See also, J.L. Holzgrefe and R. Keohane (eds) *Humanitarian Intervention: Ethical, Legal and Political Dilemmas*, Cambridge: Cambridge University Press, 2003.

40 M. Walzer, "Just and Unjust Occupation," *Dissent*, Winter, 2004 and "Regime Change and Just War," *Dissent*, Summer, 2006; S.K. Sharma, "Reconsidering the *Jus ad Bellum/Jus in Bello* distinction," in C. Stahn and J. Kleffner (eds), *Jus Post Bellum*, p. 29.

41 General David Petraeus writing to American soldiers as he took command of the Multi-National Force-Iraq in 2007 provided the following guidance, "I am confident that each of you will fight with skill and courage, and that you will remain loyal to your comrades-in-arms and to the values our nations hold so dear." D.H. Petraeus, "To the Soldiers, Sailors, Airmen, Marines, and Civilians of Multi-National Force-Iraq," Headquarters, Multi-National Force-Iraq, February 10, 2007.

42 D. Rodin, "Two Emerging Issues of *Jus Post Bellum*: War Termination and the Liability of Soldiers for Crimes of Aggression," in C. Stahn and J. Kleffner (eds), *Jus Post Bellum*, p. 71.

43 B. Orend, "Jus Post Bellum: A Just War Theory Perspective," in C. Stahn and J. Kleffner (eds), *Jus Post Bellum*, p. 39.

44 R. Wilde, "The question of the applicability of international human rights norms to situations of foreign occupation/administration, thereby forming part of the *jus post bellum* is as important as it is under-evaluated," from R. Wilde "Are Human Rights Norms Part of the *Jus Post Bellum*, and Should They Be?" in C. Stahn and J. Kleffner (eds), *Jus Post Bellum*. p. 185.

45 C. Garraway, "The Relevance of *Jus Post Bellum*: A Practioner's Perspective," in C. Stahn and J. Kleffner (eds), *Jus Post Bellum*, p. 157.

46 FMI 3-07-22 Counterinsurgency Operations. Online. Available at: http://www.fas.org/irp/doddir/army/fmi3-07-22.pdf (accessed 7 April 2013).

References

Augustine "Letter 189, to Boniface," in E.L. Fortin and D. Kries (eds), *Augustine: Political Writings*, trans. M.W. Tkacz and D. Kries, Indianapolis: Hackett, 1994.

Bartov, O., Grossman, A. and Nolan M. (eds), *Crimes of War, Guilt and Denial in the Twentieth Century* New York: The New Press, 2002

Bass, G. J., *Stay the Hand of Vengeance, The Politics of War Crimes Tribunals*, Princeton, NJ: Princeton University Press, 2000.

Boemeke, M.F., G.D. Feldman and E. Glaser (eds), *The Treaty of Versailles: A Reassessment after 75 Years*, Cambridge: Cambridge University Press, 1998.

Dinstein, Y. *War, Aggression and Self-Defense*, Cambridge: Cambridge University Press, 2011.

——*The International Law of Belligerent Occupation*, Cambridge: Cambridge University Press, 2009.

——*War, Aggression and Self-Defense*, 4th edn, New York: Cambridge University Press, 2005, 11.

Evans, G. *The Responsibility to Protect: Ending Mass Atrocity Crimes Once and For All*, Washington D.C.: Brookings Institution Press, 2008.

FMI 3-07-22 Counterinsurgency Operations. Online. Available at: http://www.fas.org/irp/dodir/army/fm13-07-22.pdf (accessed 2 April, 2010).

Freeman, M. and Djukie, D. "*Jus Post Bellum* and Transitional Justice," in C. Stahn and J. Kleffner (eds), *Jus Post Bellum*: Towards a Law of Transition from Conflict to Peace, The Hague: TMC Asser Press, 2008.

Garraway, C. "The Relevance of *Jus Post Bellum*: A Practioner's Perspective, " in C. Stahn and J. Kleffner (eds), *Jus Post Bellum: Towards a Law of Transition from Conflict to Peace*, The Hague: TMC Asser Press, 2008.

Goldsmith, J.L. and E.A. Posner, *The Limitations of International Law*, Oxford: Oxford University Press, 2005.

Goldstone, R.J. *For Humanity, Reflections of a War Crimes Investigator*, New Haven, Ct.: Yale University Press, 2000.

Gray, C. *International Law and the Use of Force*, 2nd edn, Oxford: Oxford University Press, 2004.

Gross, M.L. *Moral Dilemmas of Modern War, Torture, Assassination, and Blackmail in an Age of Asymmetric Conflict*, New York: Cambridge University Press, 2010.

Hanson, V. *Carthage and Culture: Landmark Battles in the Rise to Western Power*, New York: Random House, 2002.

Holzgrefe, J.L. and Keohane R. (eds) *Humanitarian Intervention: Ethical, Legal and Political Dilemmas*, Cambridge: Cambridge University Press, 2003.

Human Security Report, *The Changing Face of Global Violence*, Vancouver: Human Security Report Project, 2005.

Human Security Report, *The Shrinking Costs of War*, Vancouver: Human Security Report Project, 2009.

Kagan, D. *On the Origins of War and the Preservations of Peace*, New York: Knopf Doubleday Publishing Group, 1996.

Johnson, J.T. "The Just War Idea: The State of the Question," *Social Philosophy & Policy*, 23, 2006.

Keegan, J. *A History of Warfare*, New York: Knopf, 1993.

Kennedy, D. "The International Human Rights Movement: Part of the Problem?" *Harvard Human Rights Journal*, 15, 2002.

Kissinger, H. *Diplomacy*, New York: Simon & Schuster, 1994.

Kolb, R. "Origins of the Twin Terms *Jus ad Bellum/Jus in Bello*," *International Review of the Red Cross*, 320, 1997

Krauthammer, C. *Democratic Realism, An American Foreign Policy for a Unipolar* World, Washington D.C.: AEI Press, 2004.

Lincoln, A. *Abraham Lincoln's Second Inaugural Address* (March 4, 1865). Online. Available at: http://libertyonline.hypermall.com/Lincoln.lincoln-2.html (accessed 31 March, 2010).

Lucas Jr, G. R. "From *Jus ad bellum* to *Jus ad pacem*: Rethinking Just War Criteria for the Use of Military Force for Humanitarian Ends," in D. Chatterjee and D. Scheid (eds), *Ethics and Foreign Interventions*, Cambridge: Cambridge University Press, 2003.

MacMillian, M. *Paris 1919*, New York: Random House, 2003.

Mearsheimer, J. "The False Promise of International Institutions," *International Security*, 19:3 1994–95.

Morgenthau, H. J. *Politics among Nations*, 7th edn, New York: McGraw-Hill Companies, 2005.

Nye, J. *Soft Power: The Means to Success in World Politics*, New York: Perseus Books Group, 2004.

Oppenheim, L. *International Law*, 7th edn. H. Lauterpacht (ed.), London: Longmans Green & Co., 1952.

Orend, B. 'War,' *Stanford Encyclopedia of Philosophy*. Online. Available at: http://plato.stanford.edu/entries/war (accessed on 26 March 2010).

——"Justice after War," *Ethics and International Affairs*, 16:1, 2002.

——"*Just Post Bellum*: A Just War Theory Persepective", in C. Stahn and J. Kleffner (eds), *Jus Post Bellum: Towards a Law of Transition from Conflict to Peace*, The Hague: TMC Asser Press, 2008.

Petraeus, D. H., "To the Soldiers, Sailors, Airmen, Marines, and Civilians of Multi-National Force-Iraq" Headquarters, Multi-National Force-Iraq, February 10, 2007.

Rodin, D. "Two Emerging Issues of *Jus Post Bellum*: War Termination and the Liability of Soldiers for Crimes of Aggression," in C. Stahn and J. Kleffner (eds), *Jus Post Bellum: Towards a Law of Transition from Conflict to Peace*, The Hague: TMC Asser Press, 2008.

Rummel, R.J., *Understanding Conflict and War*, New York: Wiley & Sons, 1976.

Seybolt, T. *Humanitarian Military Invention, The Conditions for Success and Failure*, Oxford: Oxford University Press, 2008.

Sharma, S.K. "Reconsidering the *Jus ad Bellum/Jus in Bello* Distinction," in C. Stahn and J. Kleffner (eds), *Jus Post Bellum: Towards a Law of Transition from Conflict to Peace*, The Hague: TMC Asser Press, 2008.

Shaw, M.N. *International Law*, 6th edn. Cambridge: Cambridge University Press, 2008.

Smith, T.W. "The New Law of War: Legitimizing Hi-Tech and Infrastructural Violence," *International Studies Quarterly*, 46:3 2002.

Stahn, C. "*Jus Post Bellum*: Mapping the Disciplines," in C. Stahn and J. Kleffner (eds), *Jus Post Bellum: Towards a Law of Transition from Conflict to Peace*, The Hague: TMC Asser Press, 2008.

Stahn, C. and Kleffner, J.K. (eds), *Jus Post Bellum: Towards a Law of Transition from Conflict to Peace*, The Hague: TMC Asser Press, 2008.

United Nations, *Charter of the United Nations, Chapter VII: Action With Respect To Threats To The Peace, Breaches Of The Peace, And Acts Of Aggression, Article 51* (1945). Online. Available at: http://www.un.org/en/documents/charter/chapter7.shtml (accessed 30 March 2010).

Walt, S. M. "International Relations: One World, Many Theories," *Foreign Policy*, 110, 1998.

Waltz, K. "Realist Thought and Neorealist Theory," in C. Kegley (ed.) *Controversies in International Relations Theory: Realism and the Neoliberal* Challenge, New York: St Martin's Press, 1995.

Walzer, M. *Just and Unjust Wars, A Moral Argument with Historical Illustrations*, 4th edn, New York: Basic Books, 2006.

——"Just and Unjust Occupation," *Dissent*, Winter, 2004.

——"Regime Change and Just War," *Dissent*, Summer, 2006.

Wilde, W. "Are Human Rights Norms Part of the *Just Post Bellum*, and Should They Be?" in C. Stahn and J. Kleffner (eds), *Jus Post Bellum: Towards a Law of Transition from Conflict to Peace*, The Hague: TMC Asser Press, 2008.

Woodward B. *Pottery Barn Rule*, as cited by Bob Woodward. Online. Available at: http://www.buffalo,edu/ubreporter/archives/vol36n13/articles/Woodward.html (accessed 5 March, 2010).

9

REASONABLE CHANCE OF SUCCESS

Analyzing the postwar requirements of *jus ad bellum*

Todd A. Burkhardt

1. Introduction

Just because a war ends, it doesn't necessarily mean that the death and dying is over. Civilians are continually harmed during the postwar phase because of foreseen but unintended damages, the residual effects of war, and poorly planned occupations. Not only is it important that states realize that postwar obligations pertain to all parties, but even more so, states should be cognizant of these demanding obligations even before the fighting begins. Moreover, *jus post bellum* (justice after war/postwar) obligations needs to be considered, and not in isolation, but alongside and integrated with *jus ad bellum* (justice of war) and *jus in bello* (justice in war) considerations. Analyzing the likelihood of successful military operations as the only consideration for the *jus ad bellum* reasonable chance of success tenet is inherently shortsighted and problematic because a state can win the war but still make a moral mess of the aftermath. The benefit of incorporating *jus post bellum* obligations into a state's reasonable chance of success calculation is twofold: 1) a state could possibly curtail specific types of military operations thereby lending to that state's ability to more effectively and efficiently fulfill its postwar obligations, and 2) a state would engage in preliminary postwar scenario planning at the forefront instead of waiting until the war is over (or nearly over), which is far too late in order to deal with such a huge undertaking.

War has three distinct phases: prewar, war, and postwar. However, the importance of the postwar phase has waned over the last two centuries. Only recently (over the last decade or so) have postwar concerns taken center stage; still there is much to be done. Larry May, Brian Orend,[1] and many other scholars have done considerable work in this area. However, as of yet, there isn't any agreed upon systematic set of principles governing *jus post bellum* roles and responsibilities as there is for the prewar and war phase.[2] Michael Walzer concludes that there are three legitimate wartime ends: resist aggression, restore the peaceful status quo, and reasonably prevent future aggression.[3] However, Walzer does not expound upon any framework regarding how states should actually attempt a legitimate restoration of the peaceful status quo. It is very possible to enter a war for just reasons and fight it justly but then be morally unjustified in postwar conduct. With this in mind, the aim of this paper is to discuss what is morally required of a state *after* major conventional combat operations have ended. Not giving thought and articulation to a set of postwar considerations until after the war can have disastrous results.

The residual effects of warfare continue to harm civilians long after the fighting stops. Larry May captures an important truth about the postwar period's importance by stating, "If the object of war is a just and lasting peace, then all of Just War considerations should be aimed at this goal, and the branch of the Just War tradition that specifically governs the end of war, *jus post bellum*, should be given more attention, if not pride of place."[4] Therefore, we need to come to some resolution of what is required of the victor in regard to the vanquished before a war begins. A state resorting to war without a plan for postwar occupation and reconstruction ends up causing large amounts of suffering and loss of life, not to mention unnecessary loss of its own lives and money.

May, Orend, and Gary Bass believe that rebuilding, rehabilitating, and reconstructing (respectively) is morally required. I also agree that repairing essential infrastructure and reforming decrepit political institutions is seminal. However, something is missing in the just war literature. Some seem to suggest that postwar concerns only manifest after the war is over or coming to an end. That is, it's a sequential process—now that the fighting is over we should rebuild. For example, I'm not sure if Orend's rights vindication tenet or Bass's restraining conquest tenet really do much work. Orend mentions that, "The principle of rights vindication forbids the continuation of the war after the relevant rights have, in fact, been vindicated."[5] This seems self-intuitive, and it doesn't really express an account of what is actually needed. Similarly, Bass states that warring parties must restrain their conquest. "They should use the minimum violence necessary to achieve just ends," and "once a state has surrendered, its sovereignty must be respected again."[6] However, Bass doesn't explicate his point more than suggesting that states should fight limited and not total war, but again this seems self-intuitive.

I believe that May does a great job of capturing an essential element of *jus post bellum* by incorporating the notion of proportionality into it. May states that, "this involves the conditions necessary for achieving a just peace: they cannot impose more harm on a population than the harm that is alleviated by these post war plans."[7] May suggests that whatever harm is done during the fighting phase should be rectified (so it fits within the proportionality algorithm) in the postwar phase. However, May doesn't suggest that planning postwar obligations should be done concurrently with combat operations. Although many have discussed *post bellum* considerations, they have dealt with each phase separately. However, I want to make the case that all three phases of war need to be integrated and evaluated collectively instead of planning and dealing with postwar concerns in isolation and only once major combat operations have ended.

This paper attempts to remedy a portion of that predicament by presenting the claim that a state should not only be cognizant of its postwar obligations, but more so, that a state should factor in those obligations in its calculation of 'a reasonable chance of success' in order to bring to light the significant and challenging issues that a state will face in the postwar phase. By incorporating postwar considerations *into* a state's reasonable chance of success calculation, it forces the state to be mindful of such demands *before* it finds itself in the postwar phase with no sense of direction or that in which it somehow believed that it was not accountable for postwar harms. And by understanding what a state is responsible for in the postwar phase (to whatever extent those obligations are) even before the fighting ever begins, the state is in the best position to be prepared to undertake those demanding obligations and make better choices that facilitate obligation fulfillment.

Most refer to the *jus ad bellum* principle of reasonable chance of success as calculating a state's chances of militarily winning the conflict, but this calculation of a state's chance of success is too limited and undercuts the significant analysis that should be taken into account. I want to make the case that the *jus ad bellum* tenet of reasonable chance of success requires more than just determining the likelihood of successful military operations during the war. It is very possible for a liberal democracy[8] to resort to war for just reasons and fight the war justly, but then completely fail—make a moral mess of the postwar phase—by not fulfilling just expectations to the vanquished. To rectify this, a state needs to analyze *jus post bellum* requirements as part of the reasonable chance of success tenet of *jus ad bellum*. That is, a state should recognize that it has *ex post* responsibilities that should factor into the *ex ante* calculation of determining its reasonable chance of success, because responsibility doesn't end just because major combat operations are over. Additionally, I recommend a two-tier approach as part of a solution to effectively fulfill postwar obligations.

The responsibility to postwar rebuilding can be broken into two categories of responsibilities: 1) the just victor should be responsible for providing security to the citizens of a decimated country and 2) the international community should be responsible for the reformation of the outlaw regime's political and social institutions. This two-tier model is the best way to mitigate harms to civilians but also effectively reform the vanquished state's institutions. Fulfilling both tiers of responsibility simultaneously is the best way to achieve, restore, or redevelop a peaceful status quo.

Before explaining the two-tier model in more detail, I want to advance that I am in no way suggesting that a state has to wait to defend itself against precipitous attacks from an aggressor state until it can calculate its probability of success. In this kind of example, postwar planning must be part of the concurrent planning. Of course a state is morally and legally (U.N. Charter, art. 51) justified in stopping these attacks using defensive and offensive operations. But even if a state is defending against such attacks it should be cognizant that it still has postwar responsibilities. However, when a just state decides to preemptively (as a form of self-defense) attack another, that state should have been planning postwar operations even before the hostilities have started as opposed to initiating the planning of postwar responsibilities on the tail end of the war.

Now of course, the extent of postwar responsibilities is consistent with the degree of complexity of the war itself. If the strategic goal is only to defeat the aggressor state's offensive strike force as it rolls across the border, then there isn't really any significant postwar obligation owed by the victor, because the outlaw regime's infrastructure was not decimated. That is, only military assets (military headquarters, tanks, planes, combatants, etc.) were targeted and neutralized, defeated, or destroyed. In such a scenario, postwar considerations are still important but much less demanding. They might only include the enactment of no fly zones, a demilitarized zone, limiting weapon stockpiles, etc. which can be implemented and orchestrated by some combination of the just victor and international community. These operations are limited in scope and require few resources to accomplish them. However, pursuing unconditional surrender or a regime change requires an exorbitant amount of resources.

These operations (unconditional surrender or a regime change) are quite demanding, especially in the postwar phase, so it shouldn't come as a surprise that the victor has a morally demanding role in such a scenario. When a state's goal is to change the government of an outlaw regime, it should take steps to plan such an endeavor instead of thrusting itself into only the military operation without a plan for the follow-on operations in the postwar phase. Maybe the inherent complexity of trying to plan war and postwar operations simultaneously can seem overwhelming, so planners only focus on one phase at a time. With this in mind, planning is relegated to focusing on only how to force the enemy to capitulate, and this is usually done by incorporating a very destructive strategy without much thought about anything else.

The inherent military strategy of these operations (regime change or unconditional surrender) is to undermine a state's war-making capability (its physical ability as well as its resolve) by attacking its infrastructure. "Any act of force that contributes in a significant way to winning the war is likely to be called permissible" as long as it is consistent with the notions of military necessity and proportionality.[9] Attacking the enemy's infrastructure is considered permissible because this type of operation still targets military assets. However, these targets are classified as dual purpose targets since they also have civilian purposes. They not only serve a purpose to a state's military but also serve a purpose to the civilian population of that state as well. The bombing of electrical grids, power plants, bridges, and major highway interchanges are considered legal targets and are used as a way to significantly degrade a state's ability to wage war and undercut its center of gravity and will to fight. Armies don't have to adopt a dual purpose target bombing strategy, but they elect to do so for two reasons: 1) it brings war to the whole state, thereby crippling that state's overall ability to function and 2) this type of campaign will cause a state to sue for peace much more quickly than just striking military assets. The implication of such a strategy is that civilians will be killed. Although not intentionally attacked, civilians die from unintended results and residual effects from these operations, but "noncombatants, whatever their political affiliation, have the right not to have war waged on them."[10]

2. Empirical case

Although our moral obligations are based on rational reflection and not empirical circumstances, empirical facts are important because they provide real world situations that one can synthetically apply to practical reason. Iraq is an empirical case of what can happen when postwar considerations are not planned or thought through until major combat operations are winding down. The U.S. was so myopic in its articulation of a regime change, that it failed to develop a plan that would facilitate the rudimentary operation of the Iraqi government after its leadership had been decapitated. Richard Haas, (U.S. State Department Director of Policy Planning, 2001–2003) in regard to the 2003 Iraq invasion stated that, "The initial phase of planning for the aftermath [postwar operations] took place just before and during the war itself."[11] This is far too late in order to develop an effective plan, especially if major combat operations are going to last only six weeks.

If the State Department had initiated a thorough mission analysis regarding reconstruction, humanitarian assistance, and political governance, ideally their plan would have been much different from what unfolded as a consequence of inadequate interagency coordination, nonexistent preliminary planning, and a lack of clear strategic guidance. Instead of a solid plan addressing postwar requirements, the lack of adequate pre-planning and postwar engagement led to poor decisions that exacerbated undesirable conditions in Iraq. For example, the removal of all Ba'ath Party members from any government position, the disbanding of the civil service, as well as the dissolution of the remnants of the Iraqi Army was absolutely detrimental to any normalcy or rebuilding efforts. Additionally, Ba'ath Party members were denied any employment in government positions. The U.S. (almost overnight) created a power vacuum in Iraq. "The disqualification of so many Iraqis denied the country the experience and skills it desperately needed at the same time as it alienated many of the Sunnis who, without access to the new Iraq, supported or at least tolerated the insurgency."[12] The lack of any guidelines or framework for postwar responsibilities led to uninformed and superficial analyses: the U.S. Secretary of Defense during the George W. Bush Administration, Donald Rumsfeld, believed that there wasn't going to be a need for a large occupation force since the Iraqis would welcome the overthrow of the Saddam Hussein regime.[13] In addition, "Civilians in the Defense Department seemed determined to demonstrate that they could improve upon the previous Iraq war and in doing so render obsolete the Powell Doctrine and its call for large number of troops."[14] But this analysis by Department of Defense civilians never took into account postwar needs—because combat strength was analyzed only for the fight but not for the occupation. The Iraqis might possibly have seen the U.S. as liberators, as civilian officials believed, but this surely was not going to be the case once the U.S. produced alienation, animosity, and fear among Iraqi citizens as a result of the power vacuum it triggered.

Furthermore, the U.S. failed to abide by its own guidelines (in particular #5 and #6) of the Powell Doctrine:[15] A military force needs a coherent exit strategy with clearly defined and tenable objectives as part of a strategic end state that the president and secretary of defense formulate. Termination is critical in planning because, "it [termination] is discussed first among the elements of operational design because effective planning cannot occur without a clear understanding of the end state and the condition that must exist to end military operations."[16] Another important aspect of having postwar parameters and responsibilities is for the benefit of the Defense and State departments' planning cells. Political leaders, military advisors, and planning cells should be cognizant of the robust normative requirements obligated of the victor after the war is over before any preliminary operations even take place. Imposed postwar stipulations facilitate and enhance the planning process since certain tenets must be satisfied, and planning committees, leaders, and advisors should be familiar with these facts upfront before any planning is even initiated.

Having recognized postwar guidelines provides for unified action, synchronization, and integration of intergovernmental, nongovernmental, and federal organizations which is essential to taking advantage of the military disposition of forces—on the ground—in order to implement the postwar plan to achieve political aims and postwar stipulations, instead of the plan being reactive and military occupation forces attempting to compensate for all its shortcomings. Iraq was a case of failing to unify and synchronize action. Because planning for combat operations was never integrated with planning for postwar operations in Iraq, Haas concluded that, "Tactical and strategic decisions that made sense in one context (for example, having U.S. units move with great speed and largely avoid cities) had large and adverse consequences for the other [postwar operations] as security vacuums emerged in urban areas that were quickly filled by hostile irregular forces."[17]

The postwar stipulations are specified tasks that need to be planned, resourced, and implemented. This has multiple benefits: this puts more emphasis back on negotiations of the diplomats and world leaders because postwar stipulations drain countries of men, material, and money; military operations might be limited in scope and ambition because of the imposing postwar stipulations that are required (particularly the *jus in bello* tenet of proportionality comes to the forefront);[18] and political and civil planning would be concurrently pursued with military planning in order for an effective transition plan for postwar stability and reconstruction operations. For example, the U.S. would have had to keep units positioned near cities that were bypassed as well as keep some military units back in order to retain the ground that they had previously seized instead of moving all forces at breakneck speed toward enemy forces. This type of operation would have taken more than six weeks to complete but it could quite possibly have prevented or at least mitigated serious security vacuums. Such an implementation would not only have achieved the militarily desired end state but also set better conditions to achieve what is morally required of the postwar parameters.

It is absolutely seminal that leaders and planners critically analyze not only *jus ad bellum* and *jus in bello* requirements but also *jus post bellum* requirements before any disembarkation of troops. The main consequence from not analyzing postwar considerations as part of the *ad bellum* phase is that civilians continue to die even when the war is over, and the decimated and chaotic conditions created as a result of implementing a dual purpose target strategy becomes the perfect breeding ground for an insurgency.

3. The victor's responsibility

I mention a two-tier model of responsibilities because some obligations are not the victor's responsibility whereas others are. Just as some obligations are not the international community's responsibility whereas others are. The victor should be cognizant of the restoration owed to the vanquished on account of destroying dual purpose targets. Once the opposing force surrenders, the war might be over but civilians continue to die because of the lack of basic necessities. Andrew Altman and Christopher Wellman state that, "the risk to the safety and security of noncombatants that arise from an intervention should not be disproportionate to the rights violations that the intervention helps avert."[19] Although discussing military intervention, Altman and Wellman raise a good point about the use of force in general: Even if the victor is able to force the outlaw regime to capitulate, the very use of force could be considered disproportionate to the rights violations that the use of military force helps avert. If tens of thousands of noncombatants continue to die in a postwar situation because its state—overwhelmed and under-resourced—is unable to quickly restore essential services and the victor does nothing to alleviate the harmful situation, then this could be classified as a disproportionate use of force.

Rather than suggesting that a state shouldn't bomb dual purpose targets, after the war the victor has a responsibility to assist in repairing infrastructure that provides essential services to noncombatants. If the victor does nothing to alleviate the deleterious situation that civilians face in the postwar phase, then we can say that the victor is morally blameworthy for its failure to protect civilians. The victor is therefore morally required to assist in the repairing of infrastructure that provides essential services, e.g. electricity, potable water, trash removal, sewage disposal, shelter, and medical attention, in order to help the civilian population. Doing so is the first step toward bringing about any type of normalcy to a war torn people. Without an effective postwar plan, civilians continue to die as a result of a lack of necessities. For example, "by the end of 1992 [after Operation Desert Storm], more than a hundred thousand Iraqi civilians died from the lack of clean water and sewage disposal, and the breakdown of electrical service to hospitals,"[20] and estimates for "the loss of civilian life from the [2003] Iraqi war has concluded that at least 100,000 Iraqi civilians may have died because of the U.S. invasion."[21]

In his 1758 *Law of Nations*, Emmerich de Vattel mentions that women, children, and the infirm (of the state that one is warring with) can be classified as enemies, "but it doesn't hence follow that we are justifiable in treating them like men who bear arms, so we don't have the same rights against all classes of enemies."[22] Vattel goes on to say that, "[t]hese are enemies who make no resistance; and consequently we have no right to maltreat their persons, or use any violence against them, much less to take away their lives."[23] It is this foundation and underlying value that is the drive behind international positive law that dictates that civilians are not to be harmed during war. However, this line of thought needs to carry over into the postwar phase, because the postwar phase can be just as devastating to noncombatants as when the war is in full swing. In the postwar phase, bombs no longer kill civilians but the residual effects of bombing campaigns do.

In *The Metaphysics of Morals*, Immanuel Kant discusses the rights of states regarding war and how states have rights specific to each phase (prewar, war, and postwar). Of importance is that Kant mentions that these rights after war pronounce that, "neither the vanquished state nor its citizens [should] lose their civil freedom."[24] Kant was referring to the point that citizens of the vanquished state have the right to be free from subjugation or enslavement, but this is exactly what happens when a war torn state is left to fend for itself. Maybe those citizens are not technically being subjugated as if they were colonized. However, living in fear without access to basic necessities is definitely a form of enslavement. Civilians don't have freedom and instead are focused on mere survival, but innocent civilians—regardless of their political affiliation—should never lose their civil freedom of the right to life and liberty.

In order to attempt any type of meaningful reconciliation and return to a peaceful status quo, civilians must be secured not only against physical threats but have reasonable expectations such as the ability to return to work and for children to return to school. Firing and removing all government employees is inconsistent with this process and can often exacerbate the situation. It is essential that postwar obligations are realized and reviewed before the fighting starts in order to adequately plan and synchronize assets in the postwar phase. If a state recognizes that it has such obligations then it could very well lead to a postwar phase that is less chaotic. By doing some preliminary estimates, planning cells could (hopefully) conclude that a state cannot function without its government employees.

Disbanding the civil service completely shuts down all levels of government. In such a case, citizens cannot even apply for a driver's license since there aren't any employees working at the department of motor vehicles. Trying to hire and train new employees for all positions and at all levels of government would take months if not years. Additionally, disbanding the army (instead of using them in some type of security role and enforcing the rule of law) further exacerbates the problem. Disbanding the losing state's army creates a significant challenge since tens of thousands of young men are now unemployed, alienated, and have nothing but idle hands. "The United Nations has even expressed concern that rising numbers of Iraqi youths have been recruited into militias and insurgent groups."[25] Young men with no employment, living in decimated housing with garbage, standing sewage, and infestations provide a terrific recruitment base for insurgents and jihadists. Someone living in these conditions has nothing to lose. After all, it is very easy to understand how someone living in abject, squalid conditions could enlist as an insurgent or turn to a life of crime in order to acquire scarce resources. Tactics such as young men quickly throwing grenades at occupation forces then fading back into a crowd of civilians "has been used in fighting before but takes on added significance as the Americans have been trying to improve relations with the Iraqi public in a bid to stem support for the insurgency."[26] But it is quite impossible to improve relations when civilians live in squalid conditions and suffer due to a lack of resources.

If a legitimate war time end is to return to a peaceful status quo as Walzer mentioned,[27] then steps need to be taken by the victor to ensure this. This belief of establishing a true and lasting peace as the only reason to fight dates back to at least St. Augustine of Hippo who wrote in the *De Praesentia Dei Ep.* 187 that, "Peace should be your aim; one does not pursue peace in order to wage war; he wages war to achieve peace."[28] What Augustine was referring to was not necessarily returning to the *status quo ante bellum* (because that situation actually led to war), but a true and lasting peace as the actual aim or end of war. That is, certain conditions need to be addressed and remedied in the postwar phase as a sincere attempt to instigate a peaceful relationship that is governed by what is reasonable and right.

Winning the hearts and minds of the civilians of the war torn state is the best way to formulate any meaningful reconciliation and establish peace, and the best way to accomplish such a task is by restoring basic services, providing physical security, preventing alienation of a group or groups, and expediting employment opportunities which not only help the country return to a state of normalcy but also fulfilling such obligations contributes to significantly reducing the insurgent recruitment base. Just as the victor has certain obligations (such as mitigating the harmful effects of war during the postwar phase because these harmful effects continue to kill noncombatants even though noncombatants are not supposed to have war waged against them), so does the international community.

4. The international community's responsibility

The international community should be responsible for the reformation of the outlaw state's political regime and social institutions as well as monitoring the victor's occupation. The political organization/government of an outlaw state must change, given evidence of its external aggression to other states and/or its illegitimacy given its failings to its own citizens. With such a regime, peace among a confederation of states may not be possible, so a multilateral organizations such as the United Nations or other regional organizations or coalition of states representing the international community should be the ultimate authority and oversee postwar implementation to ensure a transition of problematic institutions as well as ensure that the victor fulfills its obligations to the civilians of the war torn state.[29]

First, with no oversight except by the victor how can justice in the postwar phase be guaranteed and if it becomes unjust what is the recourse? Regardless, if a state attacks another state without approval from the U.N., the U.N. or other another multinational union may usurp control of the aftermath. By overseeing such an endeavor, a multinational partnership could ensure that the occupation is legitimate and not self-serving in that the vanquished state is not used for the victor's gains. To guarantee future legitimate occupations, the U.N. has to convince all countries, whether directly involved in the fighting or not, that it is inherently the responsibility of all independent states as a member of the international community to oversee the postwar phase through the use of the U.N. or other multinational partnerships.

However, this is easier said than done. For example as was the case of Iraq, neither did the U.N. demand that authority be relinquished to it, nor did some U.S. officials want to relinquish authority. The U.S. State Department had mentioned that the U.N. has had a lot of experience in postconflict situations and should be given a lead role in postwar Iraq, but this suggestion "was roundly rebuffed" by the U.S. National Security Council.[30] The concern is that a hegemonic country having all the power, and no oversight during the occupation, could resist repairing essential infrastructure or force the vanquished into unfair contracts which provide kickbacks and favors to the victor's corporations, lobbying groups, government officials or even misappropriation of funds because the victor cannot properly handle the sheer scope of the operation by itself. For example, the Special Inspector General for Iraq Reconstruction (SIGIR), Stuart Bowen, "has found serious weaknesses in the government's controls over Iraq reconstruction funds that put billions of American taxpayer dollars at risk of waste and misappropriation."[31] Additionally, SIGIR's "audit of a Department of State contract for Iraqi police training program found that more than $2.5 billion in U.S. funds was vulnerable to fraud and waste as a result of poor Department of State oversight."[32] These large scale financial endeavors seem quite problematic and overwhelming to a state that attempts to do everything itself, not to mention trying to coordinate contracts with new, under-qualified, and inexperienced Iraqi government officials since the former government officials were removed from their position of employment by the U.S., which only further compounds the problems. Additionally, a single country should not have the authority to take ownership of the complete overhaul of a country. The victor should not be involved in nation building. With this type of unilateral and unchecked power coupled with the removal of government employees the victor not only has undue influence over the vanquished state but also compounds the difficulty of trying to alleviate the chaos that the war created.

Orend suggests that the U.N. should be "both watchdog and junior partner."[33] I agree with Orend that the U.N. should not only be a watchdog, but even more so it or some other multinational partnership should be the supervening authority (not a junior partner) for all postwar situations. The U.N. currently promulgates when a country has the legitimate right to resort to armed conflict and how armies should fight according to the law of armed conflict. So too, the U.N. should promulgate postwar obligations and responsibilities which could then be measured and regulated by the U.N. or by the embodiment of another multilateral configuration of states. Ideally this would be from an unbiased approach (although fallible on occasion) in order to preclude the victor from implementing unfair contracts, undue political influence, or victor's justice. Further, this should keep the postwar focus on the desired end state. A multilateral approach is also more beneficial because the outlaw regime will be assisted in reforming its political and social institutions in the way that the international community thinks is best instead of from the victor's unilateral perspective. Additionally, a multilateral approach should lessen animosity towards the victor and occupation force from not only the vanquished state but also from the international community since the victor's role would be restricted to repair and security and not the institutional changes of the defeated state. After all, "multilateralism is more and more essential, not simply as a way to get others to share burdens, but also as a way to forge global arrangements that are essential to address global challenges such as the spread of nuclear weapons, terrorism, protectionism, disease, and climate change,"[34] and reconstruction of a war torn state isn't any different.

5. Conclusion

During his Nobel Peace Prize reception address, President Obama noted that, "No matter how justified the cause, war promises human tragedy."[35] It may be true that war promises death, or as George Santayana states, "Only the dead have seen the end of war"[36] but at least we can prevent the needless deaths of many innocent civilians by declaring that states should be responsible for restoring essential services and providing physical security during the postwar phase. A step in the right direction is for states to be aware of the obligations even before any fighting starts. A significant reason for analyzing postwar requirements in the *jus ad bellum* phase is that this will, hopefully, shed light on what a country is responsible for even before a state invades or plans to invade another country. This is a huge endeavor, and it needs to be thought through and critically analyzed before any combat operations ever begin. It is far too late to think about *jus post bellum* requirements once the enemy has capitulated. I believe that incorporating postwar considerations into a state's reasonable chance of success calculation forces the state to be mindful of such demands before it finds itself in the postwar phase with no sense of direction or that it somehow believed that it is not accountable for postwar civilian deaths.

The tenet of reasonable chance of success is more demanding than just war gaming military strategies to see what might be successful. Rather, it should include the obligations that the victor has during the postwar phase. Success not only includes the fighting phase but the postwar phase as well. A state can only say that it has a reasonable chance of success by first identifying all demands then leveraging assets against them in order to determine if it can be successful. Doing so forces a state to explore preliminary considerations for postwar operations before shots are even fired.

It could be the case that the country resorting to war determines that it cannot achieve all that it is morally required to do. Maybe this is a good thing. This might send those leaders back to the drawing board—so to speak. Maybe then politicians and statesmen can determine that there are other viable elements of national power regarding flexible deterrent courses of action (diplomatic, economic, and/or informational or a combination of these) besides a military solution that ultimately can achieve what is needed. Or at least the scale of military operations might be more limited in order to accomplish what is absolutely essential and nothing more. "To say that force may sometimes be necessary is not a call to cynicism—it is a recognition of history:

the imperfections of man and the limits of reason."[37] Further recognition of history is the fact that the postwar phase can be just as debilitating for the civilians of a beleaguered nation. In order to mitigate these inherent harms and residual effects of war, the scale, duration, and intensity of the conflict should be limited to the minimum necessary in that "The means have to be commensurate with the ends, and in line with the original provocation"[38] in order not to produce more harm than not going to war would have. Sensible steps must be taken during the postwar phase to ensure that the postwar phase doesn't become a moral mess. Furthermore, a truly multilateral force like the U.N. or maybe another type of international partnership must have ultimate authority in postwar operations. First, in order to ensure the victor complies with its obligations, and second that a multilateral approach to reforming decrepit political and social institutions is the best way to foster any type of peaceful status quo as a legitimate wartime end.

Notes

1 See, for instance, L. May *After War Ends: A Philosophical Perspective*. Cambridge: Cambridge University Press, 2012, B. Orend, "Justice After War," *Ethics and International Affairs*, 16:1, 2002, p. 46, G. Bass "Jus Post Bellum," *Philosophy and Public Affairs*, 32:4, 2004, p. 390.

2 According to the U.N. Charter, states have the legal and moral right to self-defense. Additionally, armed conflict is governed by customary and positive international laws (the 1949 Geneva Convention). However, currently there isn't a set of universally recognized or instituted *post bellum* norms.

3 M. Walzer, *Just and Unjust Wars*, New York: Basic Books, 1977, p. 121.

4 L. May, *After War Ends*, p. 13.

5 B. Orend, "Justice after War," p. 46.

6 G. Bass, "Jus Post Bellum," p. 390.

7 L. May, *After War Ends*, p. 226.

8 I mention the example of a liberal democracy because we assume a peaceful liberal democracy is just, and that its action will be guided by what is right and reasonable. Furthermore, that it has resorted to war because of acts of aggression by an outlaw regime.

9 M. Walzer, *Just and Unjust Wars*, p. 129.

10 R. Miller, "Legitimation, Justification, and the Politics of Rescue," in Louis Schwartz, *Just War Reader*, 1st edn, Mason: Thomson, 2004, p. 126.

11 R. Hass, *War of Necessity, War of Choice*, New York: Simon & Schuster Inc., 2009, p. 257.

12 Ibid., p. 260.

13 "The U.S. Administration uncritically accepted what a small number of academics and exiles had told them, namely that the Iraqi people would welcome Americans as liberators and there would be no need for a heavy occupation force." Ibid., p. 254.

14 Ibid., p. 254.

15 The Powell Doctrine was named after General Colin Powell just prior to the Gulf War (1990–91). The doctrine is based in large part on the Caspar Weinberger Doctrine (Cohen, M. "The Powell Doctrine's Enduring Relevance," in *World Politics Review*, 2009. Online. Available at: http://www. worldpoliticsreview.com/articles/4100/the-powell-doctrines-enduring-relevance (accessed 3 July, 2012). Caspar Weinberger was the Secretary of Defense (1981–87) and Powell's former boss. The Powell Doctrine states that a list of questions have to all be answered affirmatively before military action is taken by the United States: 1) Is a vital national security interest threatened? 2) Do we have a clear attainable objective? 3) Have the risks and costs been fully and frankly analyzed? 4) Have all other non-violent policy means been fully exhausted? 5) Is there a plausible exit strategy to avoid endless entanglement? 6) Have the consequences of our action been fully considered? 7) Is the action supported by the American people? 8) Do we have genuine broad international support? Although it also seems that the U.S. could not answer #8 in the affirmative, this falls outside the scope of this paper. Another item that will not be addressed in the paper is if the U.S. was justified in invading Iraq. United Nations Security Council Resolution 1441 declared that Iraq was in material breach of previous U.N. resolutions and that Iraq "will face serious consequences" as a result of its continued violations of U.N. resolutions (*U.N. Security Council*, Online. Available at: http://www.un.org/News/Press/docs/2002/ SC7564.doc.htm (accessed 3 January, 2012). However, UNSCR 1441 was ambiguous about the

characteristics of the serious consequences. UNSCR 1441 did not specifically authorize the use of force to bring about Iraqi compliance. However, the U.S. policy makers believed that it did.

16 Department of Defence Field Manual, Joint Publication 5–0, *Joint Operation Planning*, 26 December, 2006, p. IV–5.

17 R. Haas, *War of Necessity, War of Choice*, p. 254.

18 I'm not suggesting that a military use limited force when engaging enemy combatants. The U.S. military's mindset is to gain the initiative and use decisive overwhelming force to impose its will on the enemy. I concur with this principle. However, what I do suggest is that operations continually be planned to mitigate, as best as possible, collateral damage as well as for combatants to accept more risks while reducing harm or potential harm to civilians on the battlefield.

19 A. Altman and C. Wellman, *A Liberal Theory of International Justice*, Oxford: University Press, 2009, p. 105.

20 G. Lopez, "Iraq and Just War Thinking: The Presumption Against the Use of Force." *Common Wealth Magazine*, 129:16, 2002, p. 17.

21 R. Stein, "100,000 Civilian Deaths Estimated in Iraq," *Washington Post*. October 29, 2004, A16. Online. Available at: http://www.washingtonpost.com/wp-dyn/articles/A7967-2004Oct28.html (accessed 10 July, 2012).

22 E. Vattel, *The Law of Nations*, London: C. G. and J. Robison Paternoster-Row, 1797, Book III (Of War), Ch V, pp. 321–22.

23 Ibid., p. 352.

24 I. Kant, *The Metaphysics of Morals*, Cambridge: University Press, 1996, p. 118.

25 NBC News, "U.S.: Insurgents using teens in Iraq attacks," 2009, p. 1.

26 Ibid., p. 1.

27 M. Walzer, *Just and Unjust Wars*, p. 121.

28 St. Augustine of Hippo, On the Presence of God: Letter 187, quoted in L. Swift, *The Earthly Fathers on War and Military Service*, Delaware: Michael Glazier Publishers, 1983, p. 114.

29 I'd like to suggest that although the U.N. has the potential to oversee the occupation and reformation of decrepit institutions, the questions still remains as to whether the U.N. is in fact such an apparatus. The U.N. has been very ineffective regarding similar past issues, so the U.N. should only be considered as one example of such a multilateral force. It is quite possible that a regional, sub-regional, or other coalition might be better suited to handle such an endeavor.

30 R. Haas, *War of Necessity, War of Choice*, p. 251.

31 J. Lee, "Iraq Auditor Questions $636m in Costs," *Iraq-Business News*. Online. Available at: http://www.iraq- businessnews.com/tag/corruption (accessed 2 July, 2012).

32 Ibid.

33 B. Orend, *The Morality of War*, Ontario: Broadview Press, 2006, p.210.

34 R. Hass, *War of Necessity, War of Choice*, p.182.

35 B. Obama, *Nobel Peace Prize Speech*, 2009. Online. Available at: http://www.huffingtonpost.com/2009/12/10/obama-nobel-peace-prize-a_n_386837.html (accessed 10 January, 2012).

36 This quote is usually misattributed to Plato. However, George Santayana is the rightful author. Santayana's remark was in response to President Wilson's comment that the First World War was the war to end all wars. G. Santayana, "Tipperary," *Soliloquies in England and Later Soliloquies*, 1922, p. 102. Online. Available at: http://plato-dialogues.org/faq/faq008.htm (accessed 10 May, 2012).

37 B. Obama, Nobel Peace Prize Speech, 2009.

38 "The Responsibility To Protect," *International Commission on Intervention and State Sovereignty (ICISS)*, Ottawa, International Development Research Centre, 2001, p.37.

References

Altman, A. and C. Wellman, *A Liberal Theory of International Justice*, Oxford: Oxford University Press, 2009.

Bass, G. "Jus Post Bellum," *Philosophy and Public Affairs*, 32:4, 2004, pp. 384–412.

Cohen, M. "The Powell Doctrine's Enduring Relevance," in *World Politics Review*. 2009. Online. Available at: http://www.worldpoliticsreview.com/articles/4100/the-powell-doctrines-enduring-relevance (accessed 3 July, 2012).

Department of Defense Field Manual, Joint Publication 5-0, *Joint Operation Planning*, 26 December 2006.

Hass, R. *War of Necessity, War of Choice*, New York: Simon & Schuster Inc., 2009.

International Commission on Intervention and State Sovereignty (ICISS). "The Responsibility To Protect," Ottawa, International Development Research Centre, 2001.

Lee, J. "Iraq Auditor Questions $636m in Costs," *Iraq-Business News*, 2012. Online. Available at: http://www.iraq-businessnews.com/tag/corruption (accessed 2 July, 2012).

Lopez, G. "Iraq and Just War Thinking: The Presumption Against the Use of Force." *Common Wealth Magazine*, 129:16, 2002, pp. 12–21.

Kant, I. *The Metaphysics of Morals*, Cambridge: Cambridge University Press, 1996.

May, L. *After War Ends: A Philosophical Perspective*, Cambridge: Cambridge University Press, 2012.

Miller, R. "Legitimation, Justification, and the Politics of Rescue," in Louis Schwartz, *Just War Reader*, 1st edn, Mason: Thomson, 2004, pp. 116–31.

Obama, B. *Nobel Peace Prize Speech*, 2009. Online. Available at: http://www.huffingtonpost.com/2009/12/10/obama-nobel-peace-prize-a_n_386837.html (accessed 10 January, 2012).

Orend, B. "Justice after War," *Ethics and International Affairs*, 16:1, 2002, pp. 43–56.

——*The Morality of War*, Ontario: Broadview Press, 2006.

Santayana, G. "Tipperary," *Soliloquies in England and Later Soliloquies*, 1922. Online. Available at: http://plato-dialogues.org/faq/faq008.htm (accessed 10 May, 2012).

Stein, R. "100,000 Civilian Deaths Estimated in Iraq," *Washington Post*. October 29, 2004, A16. Online. Available at: http://www.washingtonpost.com/wp-dyn/articles/A7967-2004Oct28.html (accessed 10 July, 2012).

Swift, L. *The Earthly Fathers on War and Military Service*, Delaware: Michael Glazier Publishers, 1983.

U.N. Security Council *Security Council Holds Iraq in 'Material Breach' of Disarmament Obligations, Offers Final Chance to Comply, Unanimously Adopting Resolution 1441*, 2002. Online. Available at: http://www.un.org/News/Press/docs/2002/SC7564.doc.htm (accessed 3 January, 2012).

"U.S.: Insurgents using teens in Iraq attacks," *NBC News*, 2009. Online. Available at: http://www.msnbc.msn.com/id/31142126/ns/world_news-mideast_n_africa/t/us-insurgents-using-teens-iraq-attacks/ (accessed 10 July, 2012).

Vattel, E. *The Law of Nations*, London: C. G. and J. Robison Paternoster-Row, 1797.

Walzer, M. *Just and Unjust Wars*, New York: Basic Books, 1977.

10

POST-WAR POLICY

Lessons for Iraq, Afghanistan, and beyond

Brian Orend

1. Introduction

Disproportionate attention, historically, has been given to the two major issues of: 1) when (if ever) one should resort to war (*jus ad bellum*); and 2) how one should best fight that war, after it has begun (*jus in bello*).[1] But a war, of course, has not only a beginning, and a middle, but also an end. What should one do at the end of armed conflict? How should nations conduct themselves during the termination phase of war (*jus post bellum*)?[2]

There is, perhaps surprisingly, very little international law regulating things in this regard. The preference, historically, has been for "the winner to enjoy the spoils of war"—i.e. for the war winner to impose whichever terms of peace it prefers upon the loser.[3] Generally, one of two approaches tends to be followed in this regard: retribution or rehabilitation. The focus of this entry shall be on explaining each of these policies—their nature, strengths, and weaknesses—looking at recent historical cases of Germany and Japan, with the aim of illustrative application to recent and ongoing case studies in Afghanistan and Iraq. The result, hopefully, will be a much fuller sense of the deep choices nations confront in the aftermath of war.[4]

2. The retribution model of post-war policy

According to "the retribution model," the basic aspects of a decent post-war peace are as follows. (Crucially, they assume that "the good side"—i.e. the countries with international law, *jus ad bellum*, and human rights on their side, at the start of the conflict—won, and that the aggressive side lost. This doesn't always happen, of course, as a matter of fact. But these are abstract models as to what states *ideally try to achieve* in the post-war period.)[5] The desired elements are:

- *Public Peace Treaty*: While it does not need to be nit-picky in detail, the basic elements of a peace agreement should be written down, and publicly proclaimed, so that: everyone's expectations are clear; everyone knows the war is over; and everyone has an idea of what the general framework of the new post-war era will be. (Sometimes, by contrast—e.g. back in medieval Europe—the most crucial parts of a peace treaty were deliberately kept secret from the public.)[6]
- *Exchange of Prisoners of War (POWs)*: At war's end, all sides need to exchange all the POWs from the armed conflict.

- *Apology from the Aggressor*: The aggressor in war, like the criminal in domestic society, needs to admit fault and guilt for causing the war by committing aggression. (And aggression, in international law, is the first use of armed force across an international border, thus violating the rights of political sovereignty and territorial integrity which all recognized countries enjoy.)[7] This may seem quaint and elemental yet, in practice, it can be quite controversial. For example, Germany has offered many, and profuse, official apologies for WWII, and especially for The Holocaust. (Germany to this day still pays an annual reparations fee to Israel for the latter). By contrast, Japan has been nowhere near as forthcoming with a meaningful, official apology for WWII (perhaps as a result of suffering the atomic bombings of Hiroshima and Nagasaki?). This reticence enrages China, in particular, which suffered mightily from Japanese aggression and expansion in the 1930s.[8]

- *War Crimes Trials for Those Responsible*: The world's first post-war international war crimes trials were held after WWII, in 1945–46, in both Nuremberg and Tokyo. The vast majority of those tried were soldiers and officers charged with *jus in bello* violations, like torturing POWs and targeting civilians. But a handful of senior Nazis were also charged with the *jus ad bellum* violation of "committing crimes against peace," i.e. of launching an aggressive war. In 1998, the international community passed the *Treaty of Rome*, creating the world's first *permanent* international war crimes tribunal. Situated mainly at The Hague, in Holland, its ambitious mandate is to prosecute *all* war crimes, committed by *all* sides in *all* wars, and to do so using lawyers and judges from countries which were *not* part of the war in question (unlike in Nuremberg and Tokyo). Recently, this new court has heard many cases from the Bosnian civil war and from various African wars. It has even put on trial former heads of state, and not just ordinary soldiers: Slobodan Milosevic of Serbia (until his death in 2006); and Jean Kambanda, the former prime minister of Rwanda during the 1994 genocide.[9]

- *Aggressor to give up any gains*: The thinking here is that the aggressor, as the wrong-doer, cannot be rewarded for its aggression and be allowed to keep any gains it may have won for itself during its aggression. For instance, during its initial campaign in 1992–94, the Serb side of the Bosnian Civil War initially conquered 70 percent of Bosnia, far beyond the area traditionally occupied by ethnic Serbs. More dramatically, during the Blitzkrieg of 1939–40, Hitler's Germany conquered Austria, Czechoslovakia, France, Poland, and the Scandinavian countries. This principle requires that, at war's end, the aggressor give back all such unjust gains.[10]

- *Aggressor must be demilitarized to avoid a repeat*: Since the aggressor broke international trust, so to speak, by committing aggression, it *cannot* be trusted *not* to commit aggression again (at least in the short term and in the absence of a change in government). The international community is entitled to some added security. The tools the aggressor has to commit aggression must thus be taken away from it, in a process known as "demilitarization." This is to say that, often, defeated aggressors lose many of their military assets and weapons capabilities, and have "caps" placed on their ability to rebuild their armed forces over time.

- *Aggressor must suffer further losses*: What makes this model one of *retribution* is the conviction that it is *not enough* for the defeated aggressor merely to give up what it wrongly took, plus some weapons. *The aggressor must be made worse off than it was prior to the war.* Why? The defenders of this model, such as Robert Nozick,[11] suggest several reasons. First, it is thought that justice itself demands retribution of this nature—the aggressor must be made to feel the wrongness, and sting, of the war which it unjustly began. Second, consider an analogy to an individual criminal: in domestic society, when a thief has stolen a diamond ring, we don't just make him give the ring back and take away his thieving tools. We also make him pay a fine, or send him to jail, to impress upon him the wrongness of his conduct. And this ties into the third reason: by punishing the aggressor, we hope *to deter or prevent* future aggression, both by him and by any others who might be having similar ideas.

But what will make the aggressor worse off? Demilitarization, sure. But two further things are frequently employed: *reparations payments* to the victims of the aggressor, plus *sanctions* imposed on the aggressor as a whole. These are the post-war equivalent of fines on all of the aggressive society. Reparations *payments* are due, in the first instance, to the countries victimized and hurt by the aggressor's aggression and then, secondly, to the broader international community. The reparations *payments* are *backward*-looking in that sense, whereas the *sanctions* are more *forward*-looking in the sense that they are designed to hurt and curb the aggressor's future economic growth opportunities, at least for a period of time (a sort of probation) and especially in connection with any goods and services which might enable the aggressor to commit aggression again.[12] (Defined, sanctions are a tool of foreign policy, signalling a move away from *positive* incentives, and mutually beneficial deal-making, and towards *negative* incentives: threats, non-cooperation, punishment, deliberately taking actions one believes will thwart the interests of the other country. Sanctions can vary in level, intensity, and effect. "Targeted sanctions" are when the measures of punishment, non-cooperation, and interest-thwarting are focused upon hurting *only* the elite decision-makers in the target country. "Sweeping sanctions" are those measures of punishment and non-cooperation which either deliberately target, or at least directly affect, *the majority* in the target country.)[13]

2.1 Two examples of the retribution model

Two of the most obvious, and infamous, historical examples of the retribution model in action concern the settlements of WWI and the Persian Gulf War.

The Treaty of Versailles ended WWI (1914–18), and is widely deemed to be a controversial failure which contributed to the conditions sparking WWII (1939–45). WWI was a disaster for perhaps all belligerents except the USA. It cost far more, and lasted so much longer, than anyone had predicted and, indeed, it only came to an end, and with victory for the Allied side, when America intervened in 1917. Because of all the cost and misery, the European powers were determined to punish Germany for invading Belgium and sparking the war to begin with. So Germany was extensively demilitarized, had all its war gains taken away and, furthermore, lost some valuable territory of its own as one aspect of punishment. Crushing reparations payments were levied upon Germany, and they would have lasted into the 1980s (!) had the peace terms stuck. But they didn't, because essentially these fines bankrupted Germany within only a few years, causing massive economic dislocation, hardship and, eventually, civil unrest. The victorious powers also tried to force elections upon Germany, but the only result was that the people there came to associate democracy with the economic problems, and they began to turn to radical, non-democratic parties promising simple solutions in a time of complex crisis. Hitler was thus able to come to power: he stopped all reparations payments; he cancelled all elections and named himself dictator; and he rebuilt the German war machine—growing the economy, short-term—and promised to get all the lost lands back. He did, or tried to, thus sparking WWII.[14]

The 1991 Treaty ending the Persian Gulf War was similarly punitive and also paved the way for a second war. The treaty called upon Saddam Hussein's Iraq to give up any claims on Kuwait (which it had invaded in 1990), officially apologize for the aggression, and surrender all POWs. Saddam was left in power, though, and no attempt was made to either change his

regime or to bring anyone to trial on war crimes charges. But Iraq *was* to be extensively demilitarized. It lost many weapons, and had strict caps put on any rebuilding. Iraq had *No-Fly-Zones*
(NFZs) imposed on it, both in the north (to protect the Kurds in Iraq from Hussein) and in
the south (to protect the Shi'ites). Hussein also had to agree to a rigorous, and UN-sponsored,
weapons inspections process. This process lasted from 1991–98, and it found and destroyed
literally tons of illegal weapons, including chemical and biological agents. After Hussein kicked
out the inspectors in 1998, this issue grew into a major factor in favour of war in 2003, as the
Americans suspected Hussein still had weapons of mass destruction (WMDs) and, moreover,
was plotting to give some to al-Qaeda to enable another 9/11-style terrorist strike on America.
Finally, and financially, Iraq had to pay reparations to Kuwait for the aggressive 1990 invasion
and, moreover, had to suffer continuing sweeping sanctions on its economy, especially on its
ability to sell oil. These sanctions devastated Iraqi civilians and did very little to hurt Hussein.
There is, in fact, evidence that the sanctions *only cemented Hussein's grip* on Iraq, as increasingly
impoverished citizens grew more and more dependent on favours from Hussein's government
in order to survive.[15]

3. The rehabilitation model of post-war policy

There is no sharp split, as if "in-kind" between the retribution and rehabilitation models. They
share commitment to the following aspects of a decent post-war settlement: the need for a
public peace treaty; official apologies; exchange of POWs; trials for criminals; some demilitarization; and the aggressor must give up any unjust gains. Where the models differ is over three
major issues. First, the rehabilitation model *rejects sweeping sanctions*, especially on grounds that
they have been shown, historically, to harm civilians. Second, the rehabilitation model *rejects
compensation payments*, for the same reason. In fact, the model favours *investing in* a defeated
aggressor, to help it rebuild and to help smooth over the wounds of war. Finally, the rehabilitation model *favours forcing regime change* whereas the retribution model views that as too risky
and costly. That it may be, but those who favour the rehabilitative model suggest that it can
be worth it over the long-term, leading to the creation of a new, better, non-aggressive, and
even progressive, member of the international community. To those who scoff that such deep-
rooted transformation simply can't be done, supporters of the rehabilitative model reply that
not only *can* it be done, it *has* been done. The two leading examples are West Germany and
Japan after WWII.[16]

3.1. Jus post bellum *in history: the reconstruction of Germany and Japan*

World War II's settlement, in 1945, was not contained in a detailed, legalistic peace treaty. This
was, partly, because Germany and Japan were so thoroughly crushed and had so little leverage.
But World War II's settlement was sweeping and profound, with immense effects on world
history. It was worked out, essentially, between the USA and USSR at meetings in Tehran and
Yalta, but with participation from the U.K., France, China, and other of the "lesser" Allies.
Both Britain and France kept control over their colonies, but everyone knew that powerful
forces of anti-colonialism—abetted by the exhaustion of England and France—would soon
cause those old empires to crumble. As for the new empires, it was understood that the USSR
would hold sway in Eastern Europe, ostensibly to serve as a barrier between itself and Germany,
preventing another Nazi-style invasion. (It also, though, provided for the export and spread
of communism the other way.) The USA, by contrast, would get Hawaii, a number of Pacific
Islands, and total sway over the reconstruction of Japan. As for Germany, it was agreed that

America, Britain, France, and Russia would split it, into Western and Eastern halves. Ditto for the German capital Berlin (which was otherwise within the Eastern, Soviet territory). Within this Soviet sphere, police-state communism came to dominate as readily as it did in Russia. But, within the West, there was a concerted effort to establish genuine free market, rights-respecting democracies. In Japan, the same experiment was undertaken, but there the US military, under the firm leadership of Douglas MacArthur, held more direct control, for longer, than it did in West Germany.[17]

The Allies, working with nationals in both countries—more so in Germany than Japan, perhaps—first undertook a purging process, which in Germany came to be known as "denazification." All signs, symbols, buildings, literature and things directly associated with the Nazis were completely destroyed. The Nazi party itself was abolished and declared illegal. Surviving ex-Nazis—but not all of them—were put on trial, put in jail, or otherwise punished and prohibited from political participation. The militaries of both Germany and Japan were completely disbanded, and for years the Allied military became *the* military, and the direct ruler, of both Germany and Japan.

After the negative purging process, the Allies in both countries established written constitutions or "Basic Law." These constitutions, after the period of direct military rule ended, provided for bills and charters of human rights, eventual democratic elections and, above all, the checks and balances so prominently featured in the American system. Since government had grown so huge and tyrannical in both Germany and Japan in the 1930s, it had to be shrunk down, and then broken into pieces, with each piece only authorized to handle its own business. Independent judiciaries and completely reconstituted police forces were an important part of this—and they went a long way to re-establishing the *impersonal* rule of law over the *personal* whims of former fascists. The executive branches, much more so than in the American system, were made more accountable to, and closely tied to, the legislative branch. The goal, of course, was to ensure that the executive couldn't grow into another dictator. By design, there were to be no strong presidents. So Germany and Japan became true *parliamentary* democracies, more in the European than American style.

Western-style liberal democracy was not the only change forcibly implemented. The education systems of both Germany and Japan were overhauled, since they played huge propaganda roles for both regimes, and the content of their curricula had been filled with racism, ultra-nationalism, and distorted ignorance of the outside world. Western experts redesigned these systems to impart the concrete skills needed to participate in reconstruction, as well as to stress a more objective content favouring the basic cognitive functions ("the three Rs") as well as critical thinking and especially science and technology. The curricula were radically stripped of political content, though of course some lessons on the new social institutions and their principles were required.

The Americans quickly saw that their sweeping legal, constitutional, social, and educational reforms would lack stability unless they could stimulate the German and Japanese economies. The people needed their vital needs met, as well as a sense of hope that, concretely, the future would get better. Otherwise, they might revolt, and the reforms fail. Instead of making the (World War I) mistake of *sucking money out* of these ruined countries through mandatory reparations payments, the Americans were the ones *who poured money into* Germany and Japan. America shunned the retribution paradigm and embraced the rehabilitative one. It was a staggering sum of money, too, channelled through the so-called "Marshall Plan." Money was needed to buy essentials, as well as to clear away all the rubble and ruined infrastructure. It was also just needed to circulate, to get the Germans and Japanese used to free market trading. Jobs were plentiful, as entire systems of infrastructure—transportation, water, sewage, electricity, agriculture, finance—had to be rebuilt. Since jobs paid wages, thanks to the Marshall Plan, the people's lives improved and the free market system deepened. But it wasn't just the money. American management experts poured into Germany and Japan, showing them the very latest, and most efficient, means of production. Within 30 years, Germany and Japan had not only rebounded economically, they had the two strongest economies in the world after America itself, based especially on quality high-tech manufacturing, for instance of automobiles.

The post-war reconstructions of Germany and Japan easily count as the most impressive post-war rehabilitations in modern history, rivalled perhaps only by America's rebuilding of its own South after the Civil War (1861–65). Germany and Japan, today, have massive free market economies, and politically remain peaceful, stable, and decent democracies. They are both very good citizens on the global stage. In addition, these countries are by no means "clones" (much less colonies) of America: they each have gone their own way, adding local colour, and pursuing political paths quite distinct from those that most interest the United States—consider especially Germany's formative role in the European Union. So we have clear evidence that even massive and forcible post-war changes need *not* threaten a nation's "character," or what makes it unique and special to its people. But such success *did* come at a huge cost in terms of time and treasure: it cost trillions of dollars; it took trillions of "man-hours" in work and expertise; it took decades of real time; it took the cooperation of most of the German and Japanese people; and, above all, it took the will of the United States to see it through. It was American money, American security, American know-how, American patience, and American generosity which brought it all into being.

3.2 Rehabilitation's principles

Based on these best-case practices, supporters of rehabilitation have devised their own list of desirable elements during the post-war period. These can simply be listed here, as they were explained above in connection with Germany and Japan. The occupying war winner, during post-war reconstruction, ought to:

- Adhere diligently to the (*jus in bello*) laws of war during the regime take-down and occupation.
- Purge much of the old regime, and prosecute its war criminals.
- Disarm and demilitarize the society.

It then ought to:

- Provide effective military and police security for the whole country.
- Work with a cross-section of locals on a new, rights-respecting constitution which features checks and balances.
- Allow other, non-state associations, or "civil society," to flourish.
- Forego compensation and sanctions in favour of investing in and rebuilding the economy.
- If necessary, revamp educational curricula to purge past propaganda and cement new values.
- Ensure that the benefits of the new order will be: 1) concrete; and 2) widely, not narrowly, distributed.
- Follow an orderly, not-too-hasty exit strategy when the new regime can stand on its own two feet.[18]

4. Application to Afghanistan and Iraq: successes

Let's examine the ongoing high-profile cases of Afghanistan and Iraq. Afghanistan has been in a period of post-war reconstruction since early 2002; Iraq since mid-2003. (These dates refer to when the regime fell in each society, as a result of American invasion, leading then to US military *occupation* (i.e. when country X's military controls the affairs of another country Y).[19] It seems true that the international community, as led by America, has—more or less—been trying to implement the above, ten-step "rehabilitation recipe" in each instance. It has been a very difficult process, in both countries, and has seen a mixture of both successes and failures.

The major post-war successes, in both nations, have been the replacement of aggressive, rogue regimes with new governments. The old regimes have been purged; and these new governments enjoy democratic legitimacy—through multiple elections, in both countries (most recently in 2010)—and are based on written, public constitutions crafted by locals. Civil society—compared to what it was under Hussein, or the Taliban—has now blossomed. The gains in terms of personal freedom, in both societies, have been huge. Also, in Afghanistan anyway, the gains in terms of gender equality have been very substantial with, for example, the international community (including Canada) building and staffing many new schools for girls and women.[20]

The problem, though, is that the evidence suggests that it's *not* things like individual liberty and gender equality which matter most when it comes to the success and durability of post-war reconstruction. The historical data suggest, rather, that the most important things are physical security (i.e. personal safety) and economic growth. Jim Dobbins, probably the leading scholar on the issue, has distilled all this data into one crystal-clear rule of thumb regarding post-war success:

> the war-winning occupier, and the new local regime, have about 10 years to form an effective partnership and to devote themselves in particular to making the average person in that society feel better off—more secure and more prosperous, especially—than they were prior to the outbreak of the war.

If they can do this, post-war reconstruction will probably succeed. If not, there will be failure, and a serious risk of back-sliding into armed conflict.[21]

Using this rule of thumb, we note that the approximate deadline for achieving this in Afghanistan would be 2012, and in Iraq, 2013. Now, the US occupation of Iraq has been declared officially over (as of December, 2011), but the reality is that a number of US troops remain indefinitely to help train the new Iraqi army, and to protect Iraqi oil infrastructure.[22] And, in Afghanistan, NATO troops have committed to being there until 2014. So, will physical security and economic improvement be achieved in the time remaining?

5. Application to Afghanistan and Iraq: challenges of security and economy

While the capital of Afghanistan, Kabul, *is* quite secure, the same *cannot* be said for the rest of the nation: there is a deep urban–rural split in this regard. Afghanistan is a highly weaponized society, with nearly all men owning guns and with local tribal leaders protecting their families' farms (and crops) with their own armed militias. The Taliban is making a comeback in rural areas by clamping down on these local tribal "war lords," and promising a return to the very strict (religious) law-and-order state they feel they achieved when in power. So, would the *average* Afghani feel they are more secure now than when the Taliban were in power? Maybe not, and this is one reason why US President Barack Obama has ordered a new surge of US troops into Afghanistan over the next few years. He has done this to: bring security; turn the tide against a resurgent Taliban; and deal more effectively with the border area, keenly focused on ensuring radical Islamic extremists don't use it to rebuild and potentially strike America once more.[23]

Things were so bad, security-wise, in Iraq during 2005–06, that experts spoke openly of there being a civil war between the three main groups: Kurd, Sunni, and Shi'ite. At the time, President George W. Bush ordered a big surge of more US troops into Iraq and, led by General David Petraeus, they have succeeded beyond anyone's expectations in cutting down group-on-group violence and in keeping the peace. (This success is what inspired Obama to order the same for Afghanistan.) But is it enough? Dobbins would remind us that more security now than in 2006 is not the same thing as more security than back when Hussein was in power in 2003. Hussein was a brutal tyrant, but he did keep law-and-order. So would the average Iraqi say they feel safer and more secure than before the war? It's hard to say, and might depend on which group one is speaking to: the Kurds and Shi'ites might well say yes, whereas Hussein's own Sunni ethnicity might say no. While there have been clear gains since 2006, all the groups are concerned as to what might happen once the US pulls out entirely.[24]

Would the average Afghani, and Iraqi, say they are more prosperous than prior to the war? Thankfully, the Americans did not implement the retribution model in either case, and instead have sent investment flowing into both countries. Iraq probably has a better shot here, as at least it has lots of oil and gas, as well as a large and reasonably educated workforce. Yet huge challenges remain. The near-constant war since 1979, plus the effects of the sanctions from 1991–2003, devastated Iraq's basic infrastructure and well-being. So much rebuilding needs to be done. Unemployment remains a terrible problem. One solution would seem to be to pay the unemployed to perform all the rebuilding, but the costs would be enormous—in the dozens of billions, or more—and the Americans have been reluctant to pay the bill all on their own. But other countries, for their part, reply that it was America's war, and so America needs to pay the price.[25]

Afghanistan is one of the world's poorest countries, where two-thirds of the population lives on $2 USD/day. The same proportion of the population is thought to be functionally illiterate, and unemployment is also thought to afflict half the workforce. Afghanistan faces the same issues of ruined infrastructure, and the brutal consequences which constant warfare has inflicted on the economy. (These consequences can be condensed as follows: *would you open a business in a war zone?*) Afghanistan's economy is a toxic mixture of war and drugs. Opium poppies grow well there, and farmers can earn much more growing them than legal crops like wheat or corn. It is estimated that one-third of Afghanistan's economy comes from poppy production, and the heroin and opium trade which comes out of it. Transforming Afghanistan's economy from one of war and drugs to a peaceful and legal economy rooted in broad-based, healthy economic growth is proving terribly hard. It's deeply unclear whether clear success will happen on this front, but at least here the Americans can count on international support, as all of NATO is involved. The UK, for example is thinking of buying Afghanistan's poppies and using them for medical-grade opiates in Western hospitals (e.g. for pain-killers). Canada and Germany are heavily involved in building and running schools for Afghan children. Even Russia, in 2010, signed an agreement to help cooperate in stopping the narcotics trade, as much of Afghanistan's drugs wind up on the streets of Moscow (as the closest major city).[26]

It's therefore clear that, if post-war reconstruction "succeeds" in Iraq and Afghanistan, it won't be anywhere near the same degree of success achieved in Japan and Germany in the

1945–55 period. This doesn't necessarily mean that these recent cases have been "failures," as this comparison is to the best cases. It's hard to beat, or match, the very best. What these complex, mixed, imperfect, contemporary cases *do* mean—for the Middle East, and the rest of the world—is, as yet, deeply unclear.[27]

6. Conclusion

This entry has examined the *"jus post bellum"* issue of what to do when war ends. Generally, there are two big policy options here, though it was noted they do share some minimal common ground. These two major post-war options are: a retribution policy; and a policy of rehabilitation. The nature, strengths and weaknesses of each of these policies were explored in detail, alongside their application to important real-world cases.

Notes

1 For perhaps the best treatment of such, see: M. Walzer, *Just and Unjust Wars*, New York: Basic Books, 4th edn, 2006.

2 An issue I first examined, inspired by Immanuel Kant, in B. Orend, *War and International Justice: A Kantian Perspective*, Waterloo, ON: Wilfrid Laurier University Press, 2000, pp. 217–67.

3 M. Reisman and C. Antoniou (eds), *The Laws of War*, New York: Vintage, 1994; A. Roberts and R. Guelff (eds), *Documentation on the Laws of War*, Oxford: Oxford University Press, 3rd edn, 2000; G. Solis, *The Law of Armed Conflict*, Cambridge: Cambridge University Press, 2010.

4 This entry draws on some material contained in Chapter 8 of B. Orend, *Introduction to International Studies*, Oxford: Oxford University Press, 2012.

5 In practice, it thus becomes an issue of trying, as best one can, to realize these ideal terms in a more complex, and often sub-optimal, real-world setting. For more on the real versus the ideal, see: J. Rawls, *The Law of Peoples*, Cambridge, MA: Harvard University Press, 1999.

6 In modern times, JFK's settlement offer to end the Cuban Missile Crisis in 1962 contained secret aspects: notably his private pledge to remove American missiles from Turkey, so long as the Russians removed theirs from Cuba. See: S. Stern, *The Week The World Stood Still*, Stanford, CA: Stanford University Press, 2005.

7 See law sources above in Note 3.

8 J. Keegan, *The Second World War*, New York: Vintage, 1990.

9 J. Persico, *Nuremburg*, New York: Penguin, 1995; T. Maya, *Judgment at Tokyo*, Lexington, KY: University of Kentucky Press, 2001; W. Schabas, *An Introduction to the International Criminal Court*, Cambridge: Cambridge University Press, 2001.

10 D. Reiff, *Slaughterhouse: Bosnia and The Failure of the West*, New York: Simon and Schuster, 1995; J. Keegan, *The Second World War*.

11 R. Nozick, *Philosophical Explanations*, Cambridge, MA: Harvard University Press, 1981, pp. 363–99.

12 B. Orend, "Justice After War," *Ethics and International Affairs*, 2002, pp. 43–56.

13 B. Orend, *Introduction to International Studies*, Chapter 4.

14 M. Boemeke (ed.), *The Treaty of Versailles*, Cambridge: Cambridge University Press, 1998; M. Macmillian, *Paris 1919*, New York: Macmillan, 2003.

15 W. Danspeckgruber and C. Tripp (eds), *The Iraqi Aggression Against Kuwait*, Boulder, CO: Westview, 1996; G. Simons, *The Scourging of Iraq*, New York: Macmillan, 2nd edn, 1996.

16 B. Orend, *The Morality of War*, Peterborough, ONT: Broadview Press, 2006, pp. 190–220.

17 Material for this section on post-war reconstruction in Germany and Japan draws upon: L.V. Segal, *Fighting to the Finish: The Politics of War Termination in America and Japan*, Ithaca: Cornell University Press, 1989; H. Schonberger, *Aftermath of War: Americans and The Remaking of Japan*, Ohio: Kent State University Press, 1989; J. Dobbins et al., *America's Role in Nation-Building: From Germany to Iraq*, Washington, DC: RAND, 2003; and E. Davidson, *The Death and Life of Germany: An Account of the American Occupation*, St Louis: University of Missouri Press, 1999.

18 J. Dobbins et al., *America's Role in Nation-Building: From Germany to Iraq*, Washington, DC: RAND, 2003; J. Dobbins and S. Jones (eds), *The United Nations' Role in Nation-Building*, Washington, DC: RAND, 2007; B. Orend, *The Morality of War*.

19 E. Carlton, *Occupation*, London: Routledge, 1995.
20 M. Tondini, *Statebuilding and Justice Reform: Post-Conflict Reconstruction in Afghanistan*, New York: Routledge, 2010; U.S. Government, *Afghanistan Reconstruction: Despite Some Progress*, Washington, DC: Books LLC, 2011; M. Lamani and B. Momani, *From Desolation to Reconstruction: Iraq's Troubled Journey*, Waterloo, ONT: CIGI, 2010.
21 J. Dobbins et al., *America's Role in Nation-Building*, pp. 8–11; J. Dobbins and S. Jones (eds), *The United Nations Role in Nation-Building*.
22 This was widely reported in December 2011, by Associated Press, along with the following figures: Iraq War lasted 9 years (2003–2011), costing over $800 billion USD, and involving 4,500 US military dead and 32,000 US military wounded. Available at: http://www.businessinsider.com/iraq-war-facts-numbers-stats-total-2013-3 (accessed 1 April, 2013).
23 U.S. Government, *Afghanistan Reconstruction*, Washington, DC: Bibliogov, 2011; D. Zakheim, *A Vulcan's Tale: How the Bush Administration Mismanaged the Reconstruction of Afghanistan*, Washington, DC: Brookings Institute, 2011.
24 U.S. Special Inspector General, *Hard Lessons: The Iraq Reconstruction Experience*, Washington, DC: US Independent Agencies and Commissions, 2009.
25 M. Lamani and B. Momani (eds), *From Desolation to Reconstruction*.
26 D. Zakheim, *Vulcan's Tale*.
27 J. Bridoux, *American Foreign Policy and Post-War Reconstruction: Comparing Japan and Iraq*, New York: Routledge, 2012.

References

M. Boemeke (ed.), *The Treaty of Versailles*, Cambridge: Cambridge University Press, 1998.

Bridoux, J., *American Foreign Policy and Post-War Reconstruction: Comparing Japan and Iraq*, New York: Routledge, 2012.

Carlton, E., *Occupation*, London: Routledge, 1995.

Danspeckgruber, W. and C. Tripp (eds), *The Iraqi Aggression Against Kuwait*, Boulder, CO: Westview, 1996.

Davidson, E., *The Death and Life of Germany: An Account of the American Occupation*, St Louis: University of Missouri Press, 1999.

Dobbins, J. and S. Jones (eds), *The United Nations' Role in Nation-Building*, Washington, DC: RAND, 2007.

Dobbins, J., J. G. McGinn, K. Crane, S. G. Jones, R. Lal, A. Rathmell, R. M. Schwanger, and A. R. Timilsina, *America's Role in Nation-Building: From Germany to Iraq*, Washington, DC: RAND, 2003.

Keegan, J., *The Second World War*, New York: Vintage, 1990.

Lamani, M. and B. Momani, *From Desolation to Reconstruction: Iraq's Troubled Journey*, Waterloo, ONT: CIGI, 2010.

Macmillian, M., *Paris 1919*, New York: Macmillan, 2003.

Maya, T., *Judgment at Tokyo*, Lexington, KY: University of Kentucky Press, 2001.

Nozick, R., *Philosophical Explanations*, Cambridge, MA: Harvard University Press, 1998.

Orend, B., *Introduction to International Studies*, Oxford: Oxford University Press, 2012.

——*The Morality of War*, Peterborough, ONT: Broadview Press, 2006.

——*War and International Justice: A Kantian Perspective*, Waterloo, ON: Wilfrid Laurier University Press, 2000.

Persico, J., *Nuremburg*, New York: Penguin, 1995.

Rawls, J., *The Law of Peoples*, Cambridge, MA: Harvard University Press, 1999.

Reiff, D., *Slaughterhouse: Bosnia and the Failure of the West*, New York: Simon and Schuster, 1995.

Reisman, M. and C. Antoniou, *The Laws of War*, New York: Vintage, 1994.

Roberts, A. and R. Guelff (eds), *Documentation on the Laws of War*, Oxford: Oxford University Press, 3rd edn, 2000.

Schabas, W., *An Introduction to the International Criminal Court*, Cambridge: Cambridge University Press, 2001.

Schonberger, H., *Aftermath of War: Americans and the Remaking of Japan*, Ohio: Kent State University Press, 1989.

Segal, L.V., *Fighting to the Finish: The Politics of War Termination in America and Japan*, Ithaca: Cornell University Press, 1989.

Simons, G., *The Scourging of Iraq*, New York: Macmillan, 2nd edn, 1996.

Solis, G., *The Law of Armed Conflict*, Cambridge: Cambridge University Press, 2010.

Stern, S., *The Week the World Stood Still*, Stanford, CA: Stanford University Press, 2005.

Tondini, M., *Statebuilding and Justice Reform: Post-Conflict Reconstruction in Afghanistan*, New York: Routledge, 2010.

U.S. Government, *Afghanistan Reconstruction*, Washington, DC: Bibliogov, 2011.

——*Afghanistan Reconstruction: Despite Some Progress*, Washington, DC: Books LLC, 2011.

U.S. Special Inspector General, *Hard Lessons: The Iraq Reconstruction Experience*, Washington, DC: US Independent Agencies and Commissions, 2009.

Walzer, M., *Just and Unjust Wars*, New York: Basic Books, 4th edn, 2006.

Zakheim, D., *A Vulcan's Tale: How the Bush Administration Mismanaged the Reconstruction of Afghanistan*, Washington, DC: Brookings Institute, 2011.

PART II

FACES OF WAR

Beyond states and soldiers

Irregular wars

11

SOFT POWER, PUBLIC DIPLOMACY AND JUST WAR

Michael L. Gross

1. Introduction

While discerning observers note the growing significance of soft power in contemporary armed conflict, just war theory and, indeed, International Humanitarian Law (IHL) and the Laws Of Armed Conflict (LOAC) are conspicuously silent and offer little normative guidance for using soft power legally and ethically. Soft power encompasses the means to obtain a political goal through attraction and persuasion rather than through threats or coercion.[1] Advocates embrace public diplomacy, economic development and public works abroad to co-opt and attract an adversary to its side. Hard power, on the other hand, is the traditional stuff of just war theory and international humanitarian law as adversaries employ, in the best case, the least destructive means necessary to disable an enemy, compel compliance and secure the political goals they seek. Accompanied by death, devastation and disease, the moral complexities of exercising hard power speak for themselves. Accompanied by publicity campaigns, humanitarian aid and ringing cultural events, the exercise of soft power seems worry free.

Closer consideration of the words and deeds that characterize public diplomacy, however, reveals that this is hardly the case. Public diplomacy, a more nuanced idiom than its older counterpart "propaganda," reflects the media efforts of any adversary to shape opinion and influence the behavior of domestic, enemy and third party audiences. Information operations, a more general category of enterprise, augments public diplomacy with staged media events, censorship and information manipulation for the benefit of one side or another. Public diplomacy also leans heavily on a wide array of public works projects. States and non-states pursue economic and medical development projects to win the hearts and minds of the local population. These projects are prime examples of soft power that together provide the means for state and non-state actors to gain crucial support at home and abroad. For non-state actors, the benefits of successful public diplomacy are even more striking, allowing such groups as the Taliban, Chechen rebels, Kosovo Liberation Army, Falintil (East Timor), the Palestinians and Hezbollah to expand their power base, form alliances, exert diplomatic pressure, recruit supporters and strengthen morale. Public diplomacy is surprisingly cheap and cost-effective and comes without the destruction and loss of life that attend kinetic means of warfare. In some cases, public diplomacy may replace hard power and successfully achieve broad national goals; in other cases, public diplomacy augments hard power by winning tactical victories no less impressive than those gained at gunpoint.

Despite these advantages, public diplomacy raises pressing concerns for *jus in bello*. How many of these soft power tactics are effective and necessary? What cost must combatants and noncombatants pay when belligerents fabricate or manipulate information, use medicine as a tool of pacification, or exploit poverty to win friends? These are not victimless or benign acts and may cause no less harm than kinetic violence during war, particularly when public diplomacy employs coercive means of persuasion. Moreover, when enemies fulminate about the lies their adversaries tell or about the way they manipulate the media or stage events for the benefit of the international community, they are appealing to some inherent norm of truth telling that people owe one another. Is truth telling a duty of any sort and, if so, is it derogable during war? Finally, consider the status of journalists and broadcasters, the foot soldiers of media warfare and public diplomacy. If soft power is as potent as hard power, are not journalists and their reporting facilities liable for harm during war? To provisionally answer these questions the sections below present a working definition of public diplomacy, several key examples of successful public diplomacy, and an analysis of the challenges these cases raise for just war theory.

2. Soft power in action

2.1 Public diplomacy

Public diplomacy is enormously variegated and multi-dimensional and captures all of a nation's (or non-state guerrilla/insurgent group's) efforts to engender material and political support among three audiences: compatriots, enemies and third party nations and organizations. Tailoring their message to each of these very different groups, states and non-states employ print media, internet, videos and DVDs, and on the ground face-to-face encounters as they extol their friends and denigrate their enemies.[2] In the process, adversaries employ a range of arguments, from the rational to the oversimplified to the *ad hominem*, to build a factual and normative narrative about what really transpired and who was responsible for praiseworthy acts of social welfare and damnable acts of terrorism and murder. Neither side is above shading the truth, manipulating or censoring information, staging media events, restricting access to journalists or attacking media facilities. Consider the following cases:

The struggle for independence, East Timor, 1991

When Indonesian troops opened fire on unarmed East Timorese demonstrators and killed 275 people in 1991 in what became known as the "Santa Cruz massacre," activists using phone, fax, and email brought details of the carnage to the immediate attention of international aid and human rights organizations. With dramatic film and still images provided by foreign journalists, the Santa Cruz massacre grew into a central theme of East Timor's public diplomacy campaign and a turning point in their efforts to gain statehood. For the first time, the world community could see the brutality that met popular demands to end Indonesian rule.[3] The campaign bore fruit. After East Timor finally gained independence in 2002 one observer enthused:

> East Timor was the first country born of the Internet Age, thanks to the sophisticated information bombardment of its committed supporters…Part of the reason for the turn of events in September 1999 when President Clinton and Prime Minister Howard relented to armed peacekeepers going to East Timor was the level of Internet outrage on embassy systems at the White House, in Portugal, and the Australian Parliament.[4]

This example of public diplomacy is potent and truthful. The telling of the massacre drew from raw footage that spoke for itself. The impact and importance of such images are not lost on any guerrilla group. Scenes of massacre, mangled corpses, dead and starving children and acres of rubble speak volumes for a guerrilla cause. These scenes reframe the narrative, lay damning blame at the feet of the enemy, paint guerrillas as saviors and offer convincing excuses for their sometimes violent response to occupation. Given sufficient force and duration, a public diplomacy campaign that exploits an adversary's killing of civilians may force an enemy to do what shells and rockets cannot: desist and stand down at little or no cost to guerrillas. As media campaigns make an increasingly important contribution to military success the question then arises: why not exploit it to the full? Why not stage events or otherwise manipulate the media?

Drone warfare in Afghanistan, 2007

Following a US aerial attack in Afghanistan's Baghni Valley that killed 154 Taliban fighters in 2007, a local Afghan news agency claimed that nearly 200 civilians (not militants) died after coalition forces bombed civilians assembled for a public event.[5] In the aftermath, a number of foreign news agencies uncritically circulated the same account with some reports still surfacing several years later.[6] Analyzing the Taliban's information coup, Rid and Hecker cite "a subsequent intelligence report" that hardly conceals its admiration:

> 'Mullah Ihklas coordinated the movement of media personnel to this remote valley ... and ensured they filmed what the Taliban wanted them to film.' The Taliban commander allegedly directed his men to get a group of 50 to 100 locals and instructed them to tell the media representatives that the bombs had hit a civilian picnic area. The U.S. report describes the incident as 'the best manipulation of the international media using video of the "locals" telling the pre-fabricated Taliban story in a multimedia interview.'[7]

In this case, as in many others, the Taliban tie their public diplomacy to images that depict American and other Western forces as foreign occupiers, a resonant and deeply rooted historical theme among the Afghan people. Exploiting the overwhelming hostility these images evoke, the Taliban successfully prevails upon villagers to fight the invaders, resist the occupation, oppose the puppet regime in Kabul, pursue martyrdom and sacrifice themselves for Islam and Afghanistan.

The Taliban campaign moves from manipulating information to its fabrication and certainly raises some ethical concerns that I will address below. Here, however, two things should be kept in mind. First, the Taliban campaign, like the others of its kind, was militarily effective and inexpensive. Second, the Taliban do not cut their story from whole cloth. Rather, they usually employ "gray propaganda," a judicious mix of truths and untruths, that exploits the uncontested fact that noncombatants often die in military attacks, however necessary and permissible those attacks may be in the view of international law.

The role of journalists

Journalists played a crucial in role disseminating information in the two cases just cited. As such, public diplomacy would fail entirely without the active participation of journalists, bloggers, writers, and TV and radio staff. Understanding the importance of media facilities and their personnel, adversaries will often try to control or manipulate the media. Knowing of Saddam Hussein's reliance on CNN, for example, the US government fed false information to the station to convince Saddam of US preparations to launch an amphibious landing to oust him from Kuwait.[8] Such efforts, like reports of WMDs in Saddam's possession, exemplify bald manipulation of the media in the name of national security. More subtly, the US perfected a system of embedded journalism that allowed certain journalists front line access during the invasion of Iraq. The investigative efforts of unapproved journalists were thwarted while critics charged that embedding stymied journalistic objectivity because embeds identified so closely with their new found comrades-in-arms as to obviate any criticism of the US military.[9] On the other side of the curtain, are the efforts of Hezbollah to carefully control media access to the battlefield in Southern Lebanon in 2006, supervise interviews with local militia, "clean up" bomb sites, doctor photographs and, in general, lead visiting journalists on what CNN's Charlie Moore called a "dog and pony" show.[10]

These three cases exemplify the poles of public diplomacy. At one end, guerrillas of East Timor prosecuted a just war with little media manipulation. At the other, the United States fought terrorism and rogue regimes while the Taliban battled foreign occupation accompanied by varying degrees of media manipulation, fabrication and censorship. In many cases, public diplomacy is impressively effective, leading some commentators to attribute the tactical retreats of the Israelis in Jenin (2002) and Southern Lebanon (2006) and the US in Fallujah (2004) to successful media campaigns by the Palestinians, Hezbollah and Taliban respectively.[11] Public works are similarly successful and similarly contentious.

2.2 Public works

Public works are a staple of guerrilla organizations trying to build support for armed resistance among their prospective constituents. Often lacking legitimate authority at their inception, guerrilla groups must provide human security, food, shelter, education, health and welfare to gain a following. Conditions vary, of course, but well-funded groups like the Taliban, Hamas and the Hezbollah maintain vibrant institutions that provide police, judicial, welfare, financial, health and educational services.[12] The impact of these services is not lost upon Western forces who often find themselves competing with insurgents to provide similar services at the behest of the local government. International Security Assistance Forces (ISAF) in Afghanistan, for example, make assiduous efforts to repair roads, maintain educational institutions, provide micro-grants and fund agricultural assistance programs.[13]

Because public work projects are inexpensive and effective, the competition between ISAF forces and the Taliban is far from friendly. Each is out to prove it can deliver more comprehensive services than its adversary. In doing so, the side offering superior services attracts support. Alternatively, the Taliban may sabotage ISAF efforts by exercising hard power and attack schools, destroy roads or threaten those utilizing ISAF services. The latter often comes in the form of "night letters" that the Taliban post to warn local villagers against collaborating with the ISAF forces or with the local government on pain of death. Actions the Taliban deem contrary to efforts to rid Afghanistan of foreign occupation and their Kabul based allies include collaboration, working for ISAF or government forces or foreign organizations and educating girls. Quite often, night letters name specific individuals. The threats are not idle: named villagers were often beaten or killed and their property destroyed while schools are often bombed and gutted. The current night letter campaign is largely successful, intimidating villagers and scaring off foreign non-governmental organizations trying to implement government welfare policies.

Threats and intimidation are no small part of the public diplomacy campaign that the Taliban employs as it competes with the local government for the loyalty and support of the people.[14]

Nor are threats and intimidation foreign to state armies. Human rights organizations have accused the Israeli government, for example, of withholding travel permits or blocking access to medical care to induce Palestinians to collaborate.[15] Less severe but no less compelling were the criticisms surrounding American medical civic action programs (MEDCAP). Providing rudimentary medical care first in Vietnam and later in strategic areas worldwide, MEDCAPs stood accused of exploiting poor health conditions by exchanging medical care for political support.[16] In all these cases, access to social services or lack thereof can significantly channel support to the government or its adversary thereby making health and welfare projects a potent tool of public diplomacy.

As these instances of public diplomacy and accompanying public works suggest, the exercise of soft power is not as benign as many think. Pulling enemies, compatriots or bystanders to one's side usually entails pushing them away from the other. The push can be gentle, infused with material and ideological incentives, or it can be rough, attended by coercion, intimidation and bald-faced lies. What are the costs of these maneuvers? What should just war theory have to say about the exercise of soft power?

3. Soft power and *jus in bello*

In the section below, I will consider several morally problematic aspects of soft power – incitement, intimidation, exploitation, lying and deception and journalist immunity – through the lenses of effectiveness, necessity and participant rights. First, a word about these principles is in order. I have long contended that just war theory and international humanitarian law overlook effectiveness, the first criteria of a permissible act of war.[17] When civilians are killed collaterally or a television station is bombed directly, commentators immediately ask: "Was this a legitimate military target?" when the first question should be "Was the attack effective?" or "Were there sufficient grounds to believe it would have been effective?" If the answer is no, then the discussion stops there. If the answer is yes, then the second question is "Was the attack necessary or were other means available to achieve the same outcome at a lower cost?" If the answer is yes, then the next question is "Did the attack violate the rights of combatants by subjecting them to inhumane harm or the rights of noncombatants by subjecting them to excessive (disproportionate) harm?" Answering the latter question will require some idea of the harms and benefits soft power brings to armed conflict.

3.1 Incitement

What little international law has to say about public diplomacy is buried in Article 20 of the *International Covenant on Civil and Political Rights* (1966). The article prohibits:

1   Any propaganda for war
2   Any advocacy of national, racial or religious hatred that constitutes incitement to discrimination, hostility or violence.

The article remains obscure and unenforced because most nations lodged reservations fearing abridgement of free speech. Nevertheless, it underscores concern about the power of propaganda and wartime public diplomacy.

In his study of this statute, Kearney interprets war propaganda as any incitement of wars of aggression.[18] Aggression, as defined by the recently amended Rome Statute comprises "the use of armed force by a State against the sovereignty, territorial integrity or political independence of another State, or in any other manner inconsistent with the Charter of the United Nations."[19] Practically, this prohibits all uses of armed force with the exception of national self-defense or humanitarian intervention sanctioned by Security Council.

Clearly there are grounds to prohibit war propaganda since wars of aggression are unlawful. Nevertheless, there are ample grounds for states and non-states to propagandize during armed conflict. This would include states defending themselves against aggression, states intervening on behalf of a persecuted people and non-states pursuing their right of self-determination against an occupying force. As such, the prohibition on war propaganda hardly affects public diplomacy in contemporary armed conflict. Still, one has to consider the limits that paragraph 2 imposes on "any advocacy of national, racial or religious hatred that constitutes incitement to discrimination, hostility or violence." Clearly, no one will countenance propaganda that exhorts civilians or military personnel to violate the rights of noncombatants by committing genocide or murder. Propaganda of this sort is condemnable because the acts they advocate are unlawful and unjust. Yet, lawful acts of a self-defensive war are the proper subject of public diplomacy. However distasteful it may seem, there are no grounds to prohibit clarion calls to ardently slaughter enemy combatants, inflict widespread collateral harm on civilians or threaten nuclear annihilation to deter an adversary from future aggression. Credible threats demand convincing propaganda, otherwise deterrence fails. Since deterrent postures as well as the other acts of war just described are lawful and ethical in the pursuit of just war, skillful public diplomacy on their behalf is likewise permissible and, indeed, laudatory. The challenge for just war theorists and jurists alike will be to draw a very firm line between war propaganda and unlawful incitement on the one hand and permissible agitation on behalf of a just war on the other.

As propaganda serves just war, other questions remain. The first returns to the question of exploitation and intimidation and the second addresses the permissibility of lying or otherwise manipulating or distorting the truth in the cause of self-defense.

3.2 Exploitation and intimidation

Public works projects that serve human security are a key feature of public diplomacy, leaving adversaries to compete intensely for the hearts and minds of the local population. When an ISAF officer says of local projects, "We tie everything back to the Afghan government. We want the people to know that their government and local governor care about them," the underlying military and political goals are not so subtle.[20] In Vietnam the term to describe this phenomenon was "pacification" and it is a far cry from the civic minded duty one expects from public officials in a well-ordered democracy. No one would expect a public official to openly admit that he is out to curry favor as he or she builds roads, hospitals or schools. ISAF officials, no less than the Taliban, on the other hand are buying support and exploiting the ills of the local population for political gain.

What might just war theory say about this? When MEDCAPs in Vietnam provided high profile, short-term care instead of basic long-term care, critics charged the US army medical corps with pursuing showmanship rather than practicing good medicine. Taken in by the dramatic results of orthopedic or plastic surgery (cleft palate repairs were a particular favorite), Vietnamese villagers were expected to fervently support the US troops and Vietnamese government that brought them these favors. The results were mixed or at best difficult to evaluate, so it remains unclear whether medical public diplomacy is effective. Military medical personnel routinely report the goodwill that comes with life-saving medical care yet it remains difficult to translate this goodwill into long-standing political support.

Whether MEDCAP infringes upon the rights of noncombatants is less difficult to pinpoint. When patients are expected to turn collaborator or spy in exchange for medical care, human dignity is radically compromised as is the basic human right to enjoy necessary medical care. When loyalty and support are a desired *byproduct* of medical care provided in the context of the lawful obligations of an occupying army, then the rights infringements are less clear. MEDCAPs may provide less than optimum care or even compromise the acceptable standard of care. Nevertheless, there is room to consider that medical care that brings significant military and political benefits will override marginal affronts to dignity and self-determination assuming that coercion is kept to a minimum.

In this regard, it should be noted that coercion, inducements or sanctions are not always impermissible. Much depends upon how coercion plays out. It is not hard to see that physical intimidation is beyond permissible bounds since no person loses his right to life or bodily integrity simply by supporting one project or shunning another. On the other hand, military organizations cannot be expected to stand by while the local population tries to make up its mind. This is a particularly acute problem for non-state military organizations who anchor their support and legitimacy in the local population. State armies have formidable tools at their disposal to coerce compliance when citizens refuse conscription or tax obligations. Men and money are the chief resources available to any army, and non-state armies must find similar means to coerce their constituents as are available to state armies. While they cannot resort to bodily harm, there is place to consider other means of coercion such as social ostracism, banishment from social services, or restricted access to the local economy, roads or other infrastructures. While occupying armies are not in a position to employ such sanctions to prevent the local population from patronizing the enemy, local forces may indeed utilize them to the extent that they are applied fairly and nondiscriminately and with some measure of consent from their constituents. This precludes night letters and assassinations but permits more subtle and less harmful forms of coercion as adversaries exercise soft power.

3.3 Lying

Commenting on Taliban propaganda successes, one observer complains how the ISAF in Afghanistan is "constrained by legal, political and ethical considerations in getting its messages across which often means that it is unable to effectively rebut or counter Taliban propaganda."[21] This is a common refrain among Western states: while non-state organizations can lie at will, state armies must tell the truth. Obviously, this is not true. I have already described how the US army fabricated information during the First Gulf War and restricted access to information in the Second. What bothers state armies seems to be that non-states, unfettered by aggressive journalists and bloggers, have more latitude to shade the truth. For the purposes of argument, I will concede this point. The real question is "So what?" What is wrong with propaganda infused with half lies and shaded truths?

Public diplomacy characterized by gray propaganda carries two dangers. In general, there is a strong aversion to government lying in democratic nations. Of course this mainly affects compatriots who expect transparency and the epistemic resources necessary to judge the workings of state. Truth is a necessary condition of solid citizenship and good government. Without the truth, citizens are denied the means to make the autonomous and judicious decisions necessary for honest and effective government.[22] During war, however, governments become less transparent as they hide information that may impair the war effort. A delicate balancing act ensues because governments bear a double burden: protecting national security and providing the information necessary so citizens can evaluate the justice, progress and cost of the war they must fight and die in. Truth telling is the norm while lying is the exception that governments must carefully justify by sustained appeals to necessity and national security. Often this accounting can only come *post bellum*.

Truth telling is an important norm that only national security can repudiate when shading the truth is effective and necessary. Lying to the enemy, however, is a different issue. After all, deception and ruses are the way of war. What ethical restrictions bind the US or Western forces as they fight in Iraq or Afghanistan? When lying to the enemy, few restrictions matter. One is perfidy, that is, a deliberate violation of the inherent trust that underlies important institutions of war.[23] Thus, exploiting a white flag of truce to draw an enemy in to better shoot him undermines the institution of surrender. A belligerent that abuses a white flag or promises of safe passage will find itself fighting to the death and without recourse to surrender.

As she considers the other costs of lying to an enemy, Sisella Bok suggests that deceit may backfire and lead to a cascade of lies that draws in friends and enemies alike or may cause "severe injuries to trust" that may impair future peace negotiations.[24] Some of these fears are overstated. It is true that lies to an enemy may rebound among compatriots who believe what they hear. On the other hand, it is unlikely that the local supporters of the Taliban, Hamas, or Hezbollah (or citizens of Israel or the US) will think any less of their leaders for their deceptive media campaigns. In fact, they would probably argue that their enemies simply *deserve* to be lied about or, in the very least, that lying is necessary for national security. The extent to which lying may affect peace negotiations is, to my knowledge, unproven. Given the grave indignities that adversaries inflict upon one another prior to pursuing peace, lying seems to be the least of all impediments to a conflict's negotiated end. This leads us to consider that reservations about lying are not directed at enemies but at third parties.

The fact remains that deceptive public diplomacy is largely directed against third parties whose right to truth telling should not be questioned. And indeed, other nations, the United Nations, the world press and international NGOs have a *prima facie* right to know the truth. However, their right seems considerably weaker than compatriots' rights. Citizens of a nation at war require the truth to fulfill their roles as dutiful citizens bound together by a social contract laden with fiduciary responsibilities. The international community is anarchic. Why should the United States tell the truth to Great Britain or to the United Nations? A major reason is simple pragmatism. Truth telling garners support for US foreign policy while lying to allies is easily counterproductive if it undermines the trust that serves mutual interests. Reducible to expediency, nations may easily trade the truth they owe other nations when lying first and apologizing later brings greater benefits.

Moreover, it is not entirely clear what "lying first" means. In the aftermath of a drone strike, for example, there is sufficient ambiguity so that the first impressions are sometimes the weightiest. This is the Taliban's or Hezbollah's true talent. They effectively spin initial events so by the time the truth emerges (if it ever does), no one particularly cares. Military necessity may override the right to know the truth when deception, manipulation and misinformation are effective, necessary, incur little cost and violate no superior rights of combatants or noncombatants as they may when lying endangers combatants through perfidy or conceals grave violations of humanitarian law.[25] These are important conditions. If the injunction against abusing the rights of combatants and noncombatants is to have any teeth at all, then violators cannot be shielded from publicity. Public diplomacy cannot hide war crimes. In many instances, however, propaganda does not cultivate perfidy or cover up crimes. Rather it plays out in the context of routine warfare. Following an airstrike that kills noncombatants, for example, a guerrilla group finds it can skillfully manipulate information to bring enough public pressure to curtail enemy operations. Guerillas stymie their enemy and win a tactical victory at little cost. Only the truth is sacrificed. Contrast this with a concerted counteroffensive that incurs heavy costs in blood and treasure to achieve the same result. Under these circumstances, necessity can be a very potent and decisive argument for a public diplomacy campaign infused with lies and half-truths.

Nevertheless, what are the concerns when the sole purpose of propaganda is to falsely incriminate an adversary? One is the import of the charge itself and while accusations of war crimes are grave they are often indeterminate. Although the Taliban most certainly exaggerated the number of noncombatant deaths resulting from drone strikes, there is often ample room for conflicting interpretations. In the aftermath of the 2009 Gaza War, for example, detailed lists documented the name and occupation of every casualty. Yet Israeli, Palestinian and independent human rights organizations reported the deaths of 295, 960 and 773 noncombatants respectively.[26] Part of this discrepancy turns on the disputed status of police officers (whom Israelis included in combatants and Palestinians placed in a separate category) and part on the status of those affiliated to the political wing of Hamas (whom Israelis classified as combatants and Palestinians as noncombatants). Thus the status of those killed in drone and other attacks is sometimes controversial, thereby leaving room for creative reporting.

Second, consider the case where the status of those killed is undisputed and one belligerent knowingly and falsely accuses another of a war crime. Here one must weigh the consequences of lying in light of the proviso that public diplomacy cannot trample superior rights. When negative consequences are marginal as they will be when fabrications are eventually exposed and criminal prosecutions stall, then military necessity outweighs the *prima facie* prohibition against lying. When the negative consequences are significant, as they will be when smear campaigns against suspected collaborators, for example, abridge their right to due process, then military necessity does not trump the ills of lying.[27] The challenge, as always, is to weigh the costs and benefits of public diplomacy and understand that the benefits, however great, cannot supersede superior rights of either combatants or noncombatants. In this regard, one is led to the next question: What rights do journalists enjoy? Are they combatants or noncombatants?

4. The status of journalists and media facilities: curbing soft power with hard

As public diplomacy gains traction and forms an increasingly significant component of contemporary warfare, weighty questions arise surrounding its practitioners. Are journalists, the purveyors of public diplomacy, liable for direct harm?

The short answer is yes. Journalists are liable for the harm they cause and the threat they pose in the service of public diplomacy. However, in contrast to armed combatants who provide war fighting capabilities, journalists only supply war-sustaining aid. The former presents a direct lethal threat; the latter only provides the means to maintain it. As such, most journalists remain liable for less than lethal harm while others might be at risk for their lives.[28] In practice this means that journalists inciting compatriots to genocide, mass rape or ethnic cleansing are liable to disabling by lethal means. On the other hand, journalists disseminating war-sustaining propaganda or non-journalists providing welfare, legal, educational or financial support during war face destruction of their infrastructures and disabling by nonlethal means that may include arrest, detention or expulsion. Most journalists and other employees of war-sustaining institutions are not liable for direct lethal harm. Nor are media, welfare, financial and other institutions sufficiently threatening to justify anything more than minimal injury to noncombatants as infrastructures are destroyed. As a result, attacks on media facilities are permissible but widespread collateral harm is not. But this argument is premature. The first question still remains "Are attacks on the media effective?"

Experience shows that they are not. In recent years the US, Russia, Israel, NATO and Syrian rebels have bombed television stations in Belgrade, Baghdad, Chechnya, Beirut, Libya and Syria with significant loss of life. In none of these cases did transmission halt for any appreciable period of time. The attacks were entirely futile and, in many cases, killed noncombatants. Nevertheless, strikes against the media are not necessarily misguided if, as argued, media targets are not immune from attack.

To illustrate this point consider NATO's account of its aerial attack on Libyan telecommunications facilities that killed three employees in 2011:

> Our intervention was necessary as TV was being used as an integral component of the regime apparatus designed to systematically oppress and threaten civilians and to incite attacks against them. Qaddafi's increasing practice of inflammatory broadcasts illustrates his regime's policy to instill hatred amongst Libyans, to mobilize its supporters against civilians and to trigger bloodshed.

In contrast, David D. Kirkpatrick of the NYT described how the goal of Libyan TV was to, "urge Libyans to resist NATO and march against the rebels … and remind [them] that [Qaddafi] is alive and in charge."[29]

These remarks are instructive in several regards. In the first description, journalists stand accused of inciting unlawful attacks against noncombatants thereby justifying the deadly strikes against media facilities and their employees. In the second, journalists are just doing their job. This renders their facility liable for destruction but should spare the employees and bystanders death and injury. As in all instances of war, the abiding challenge is to thread this needle to determine whose liability lies where. It is doubtful that everyone in the facility incited genocidal violence. Yet one should also consider whether UNESCO Director-General Irina Bokova is on solid moral grounds when she declared categorically: "media outlets should not be targeted in military actions."[30] Notwithstanding Additional Protocol I, Article 59 that affirms the civilian immunity status of journalists, belligerents should have some recourse against public diplomacy beyond simply redoubling their own propaganda efforts. Hard power is one answer but its exercise must be effective and respectful of noncombatant rights. Satisfying both NATO and UN concerns in the case above would require NATO to make a strenuous effort to effectively disable telecommunications facilities with little or no loss of life, incarcerate journalists for the duration of the war, while arresting and trying those suspected of unlawful incitement.

5. Conclusion: the allure of soft power

Although soft power is not harm free, it usually incurs significantly lower costs than the exercise of hard power. For this reason alone, an effective and well-oiled public diplomacy campaign is an ethical imperative of just war. If the last resort condition governing the use of armed force is to have any bite at all, nations must seek out alternative means to reach their objectives. Public diplomacy, propaganda and public works often fit the bill. In some cases they do the job better than hard power.

Nevertheless several caveats are in order. First, public diplomacy alone wins few wars. The challenge is always to find the right balance between hard and soft power, turning to hard power when no less destructive means are available to achieve crucial military or political goals and choosing soft power when they are not. Second, soft power and hard power, the art of attracting enemies with carrots and beating them away with sticks, sometimes reinforce one another. Militants in Israel, Lebanon and Afghanistan have shown over again that well-timed public diplomacy can act as a force multiplier, amplifying the effects of a local attack against their better armed enemies well beyond the immediate casualties or damage they caused. The interplay of hard and soft power make room for less gentle forms of persuasion – threats and intimidations – when locals refuse the entreaties of insurgent or occupying forces. Coercion, manipulation, exploitation and fabrication are a permissible component of public diplomacy when effective, necessary and respectful of fundamental human rights as a belligerent pursues a just and lawful war of self-defense or humanitarian intervention. Under these conditions journalists may permissibly propagandize and pursue public diplomacy despite codes of journalistic ethics that enjoin reporters to seek the truth and avoid "misleading re-enactments or staged news events."[31]

Notes

1 J.S. Nye Jr, "Public Diplomacy and Soft Power," *Annals of the American Academy of Political and Social Science*, 616, 2008, pp. 94–109.
2 B.D. Mor, "The Rhetoric of Public Diplomacy and Propaganda Wars: A View from Self-Presentation Theory," *European Journal of Political Research*, 46:5, 2007, pp. 661–683.
3 D.T. Hill, "East Timor and the Internet: Global Political Leverage in/on Indonesia," *Indonesia*, 73, 2002, pp. 25–51.
4 B. Connole, "Irony in the Pacific for Long-Distance Diplomat," *Australian*, June 26, 2000. Online. Available at: http://etan.org/et2000b/june/25-30/26irony.htm (accessed 20 September 2012). Cited in D.T. Hill, "East Timor and the Internet: Global Political Leverage in/on Indonesia," *Indonesia* 73, 2002, p. 46.
5 T. Rid and M. Hecker, *War 2.0: Irregular Warfare in the Information Age*, Santa Barbara, CA: Praeger, 2009, pp. 181–2.
6 D. Leigh, "US Forces Hit Target 'With No Civilian Deaths' – but Afghans Tell Different Tale: Special Forces Ensured 'No Innocent Afghans in Area', but Villagers say up to 300 Civilians Died in Attack," *The Guardian*, Monday 26 July 2010. Online. Available at: http://www.guardian.co.uk/world/2010/jul/26/afghanistan-war-logs-helmand-bombing (accessed 20 September 2012).
7 T. Rid and M. Hecker, *War 2.0: Irregular Warfare in the Information Age*, pp. 181–2.
8 P. Moorcraft and P.M. Taylor, "War Watchdogs or Lapdogs?" *British Journalism Review* 18:4, 2007, pp. 39–50, at p. 42.
9 C.J. Hamelink, "Ethics for Media Users," *European Journal of Communication*, 10:4, 1995, pp. 497–512. See also P. Moorcraft and P.M. Taylor, "War Watchdogs or Lapdogs?"; Y. Limor and H. Nossek, "The Military and the Media in the Twenty-First Century: Towards a New Model of Relations," *Israel Affairs* 12:3, 2006, pp. 484–510, at pp. 503–4; A. Banville, "Embedded War Reporting Cannot Escape its own Bias," *The Guardian*, Sunday 18 April 2010. Online. Available at: http://www.guardian.co.uk/commentisfree/2010/apr/18/embedded-war-reporting-iraq-afghanistan (accessed 20 September 2012).
10 C. Moore, "Our Very Strange Day with Hezbollah," *Anderson Cooper 360°* (blog), Sunday, July 23, 2006. Online. Available at: http://www.cnn.com/CNN/Programs/anderson.cooper.360/blog/archives/2006_07_23_ac360_archive.html (accessed 20 September 2012).
11 A. Peskowitz, "IO on the Counterinsurgency Battlefield: Three Case Studies," *Global Security Studies* l:2, 2010, pp. 100–114; K. Payne, "The Media as an Instrument of War," *Parameters*, 2005, pp. 81–93.
12 P. Ly, "The Charitable Activities of Terrorist Organizations," *Public Choice*, 131:1, 2007, pp. 177–95; A.G. Grynkewich, "Welfare as Warfare: How Violent Non-State Groups Use Social Services to Attack the State," *Studies in Conflict & Terrorism*, 31:4, 2009, pp. 350–70; S.H. Qazi, "Rebels of the Frontier: Origins, Organization, and Recruitment of the Pakistani Taliban," *Small Wars & Insurgencies*, 22:4, 2011, pp. 574–602; T.E. Nissen, *The Taliban's Information Warfare: A comparative analysis of NATO Information Operations (Info Ops) and Taliban Information Activities*, Copenhagen: Royal Danish Defence College, 2007; M. Kalb and C. Saivetz, "The Israeli–Hezbollah War of 2006: The Media as a Weapon in Asymmetrical Conflict," *The Harvard International Journal of Press/Politics*, 12:3, 2007, pp. 43–66.
13 See Afghanistan International Security Assistance Forces, (ISAF), Press Releases: N. Johnson, "Small Projects Reap Large Gains in Helmand," June, 2010. Online. Available at: http://www.isaf.nato.int/article/isaf-releases/small-projects-reap-large-gains-in-helmand.html (accessed 20 September 2012);

K. Roling, "Provincial Development Council Discusses Projects in Ghazni," n.d. Online. Available at: http://www.isaf.nato.int/article/news/provincial-development-council-discusses-projects-in-ghazni. html (accessed 20 September 2012); ISAF, "Effective Civil Partnerships: Community Project Yields Unlikely Find," August 25, 2011. Online. Available at: http://www.isaf.nato.int/article/coin/effec-tive-civil-partnerships-community-project-yields-unlikely-find.html (accessed 20 September 2012).

14 T. Rid and M. Hecker, 2009, pp. 172–4; T.H. Johnson, "The Taliban Insurgency and an Analysis of Shabnamah (Night Letters)," *Small Wars and Insurgencies*, 18:3, 2007, pp. 317–44. The IRA also used similar methods: J. Horgan and M. Taylor, "Playing the Green Card: Financing the Provisional IRA, Part II," *Terrorism and Political Violence*, 15:2, 2003, pp. 1–60.

15 R. Yaron, Physicians for Human Rights, Israel, "Holding Health to Ransom: GSS Interrogation and Extortion of Palestinian Patients at Erez Crossing," August 2008. Online. Available at: http://www. phr.org.il/uploaded/HoldingHealthToRandsom_4.pdf (accessed 20 September 2012).

16 M.L. Gross, *Bioethics and Armed Conflict: Moral Dilemmas of Medicine and War*, Cambridge, MA: MIT Press, 2006, pp. 199–210; P. Olsthoorn and M. Bollen, "Civilian Care in War: Lessons from Afghanistan," 2013, in M.L. Gross and D. Carrick (eds) *Military Medical Ethics in the 21st Century*, London: Ashgate Publishing, 2013.

17 M.L. Gross, *Moral Dilemmas of Modern War: Torture, Assassination and Blackmail in an Age of Asymmetric Conflict*, Cambridge: Cambridge University Press, 2010.

18 M. Kearney, *The Prohibition of Propaganda for War in International Law*, Oxford: Oxford University Press, 2007.

19 Annex I, Amendments to the Rome Statute of the International Criminal Court on the crime of aggression, Article 8, bis Crime of aggression, paragraph 2, 11 June 2010.

20 N. Johnson, "Small Projects Reap Large Gains in Helmand."

21 T.E. Nissen, *The Taliban's Information Warfare*, p. 11.

22 J. Black, "Semantics and Ethics of Propaganda," *Journal of Mass Media Ethics: Exploring Questions of Media Morality*, 16:2–3, 2001, pp. 121–37; P.L. Plaisance, "The Propaganda War on Terrorism: An Analysis of the United States' 'Shared Values' Public-Diplomacy Campaign After September 11, 2001," *Journal of Mass Media Ethics*, 20:4, 2005, pp. 250–68.

23 See Protocol Additional to the Geneva Conventions of 12 August 1949, Article 37 and commen-tary for a discussion on the prohibition of perfidy. International Humanitarian Law, "Protocol Additional to the Geneva Conventions of 12 August 1949, and Relating to the Protection of Victims of International Armed Conflicts (Protocol I), 8 June 1977." Online. Available at: www.icrc.org/ihl. nsf/WebART/470-750046?OpenDocument (accessed 20 September 2012).

24 S. Bok, *Lying: Moral Choice in Public and Private Life*, New York: Vintage, 1999, pp. 142–3. See also J.S Nye Jr, "Public Diplomacy and Soft Power," p. 106.

25 For a relevant case analysis see K. Slattery and E. Ugland, "Journalism Ethics in Wartime," *The Digital Journalist*, December 2004. Online. Available at: http://digitaljournalist.org/issue0412/ethics.html (accessed 20 September 2012).

26 Y. Lappin, "IDF Releases Cast Lead Casualty Numbers," *The Jerusalem Post*, March 26, 2009. Online. Available at: http//www.jpost.com/Israel/Article.aspx?id=137286 (accessed 20 September 2012); Palestinian Centre for Human Rights, "The Dead in the Course of the Israeli Recent Military Offensive on the Gaza Strip between 27 December 2008 and 18 January 2009," March 19, 2009, http://www. scribd.com/doc/22883962/The-Dead-in-the-course-of-the-Israeli-Military-offensive-on-the-Gaza-Strip-between-27-Dec-2008-and-18-Jan-2009 (accessed 20 September 2012); B'Tselem, *B'Tselem's Investigation of Fatalities in Operation Cast Lead*, September 9, 2009. Online. Available at: http://www. btselem.org/download/20090909_cast_lead_fatalities_eng.pdf (accessed 20 September 2012).

27 K. Sarma, "Defensive Propaganda and IRA Political Control in Republican Communities," *Studies in Conflict & Terrorism*, 30:12, 2007, pp. 1073–94.

28 For a more detailed discussion of this participation scale and the liability of those working for institu-tions associated with a state army or the military wing of a guerrilla organization see M.L. Gross, *Moral Dilemmas of Modern War*, Cambridge: Cambridge University Press, 2010, pp. 26–53. Liability for harm (what I refer to therein as "vulnerability") is primarily a function of the material threat one poses unre-lated to the justice of one's cause.

29 D.D. Kirkpatrick, "NATO Strikes at Libyan State TV," *New York Times*, July 30, 2011. Online. Available at: http://www.nytimes.com/2011/07/31/world/africa/31tripoli.html?_r=1&pagewanted=pr (accessed 20 September 2012). For a similar description of Hezbollah's al-Manar see: M. Dubowitz, "Watching al-Manar:

Violence in the Media," *National Review Online,* July 17, 2006. Online. Available at: http://www.national-review.com/articles/218211/watching-al-manar/mark-dubowitz# (accessed 20 September 2012).

30 UN News Centre, "UN Official Deplores NATO Attack on Libyan Television Station," 8 August 2011. Online. Available at: http://www.un.org/apps/news/story.asp?NewsID=39255&Cr=Libya&Cr1 (accessed 20 September 2012).

31 Society of Professional Journalists, *Code of Ethics.* Online. Available at HTTP: http://www.spj.org/ethicscode.asp (accessed 20 September 2012).

References

Annex I, Amendments to the Rome Statute of the International Criminal Court on the Crime of Aggression, Article 8 bis Crime of Aggression, paragraph 2, 11 June 2010.

Banville, A., "Embedded War Reporting Cannot Escape its Own Bias," *The Guardian,* Sunday 18 April, 2010. Online. Available at: http://www.guardian.co.uk/commentisfree/2010/apr/18/embedded-war-reporting-iraq-afghanistan (accessed 20 September 2012).

Black, J., "Semantics and Ethics of Propaganda," *Journal of Mass Media Ethics: Exploring Questions of Media Morality* 16:2–3, 2001, pp. 121–37.

Bok, S., *Lying: Moral Choice in Public and Private Life,* New York: Vintage, 1999.

B'Tselem, *B'Tselem's Investigation of Fatalities in Operation Cast Lead,* September 9, 2009. Online. Available at: http://www.btselem.org/download/20090909_cast_lead_fatalities_eng.pdf (accessed 20 September 2012).

Connole, B., "Irony in the Pacific for Long-Distance Diplomat," *Australian,* June 26, 2000. Online. Available at: http://etan.org/et2000b/june/25-30/26irony.htm (accessed 20 September 2012).

Dubowitz, M., "Watching al-Manar: Violence in the Media," *National Review Online,* July 17, 2006. Online. Available at: http://www.nationalreview.com/articles/218211/watching-al-manar/mark-dubowitz# (accessed 20 September 2012).

"Effective Civil Partnerships: Community Project Yields Unlikely Find," *Afghanistan International Security Assistance Forces (ISAF).* Online. Available at: http://www.isaf.nato.int/article/coin/effective-civil-partnerships-community-project-yields-unlikely-find.html (accessed 20 September 2012

Gross, M.L., *Bioethics and Armed Conflict: Moral Dilemmas of Medicine and War,* Cambridge, MA: MIT Press, 2006.

——*Moral Dilemmas of Modern War: Torture, Assassination and Blackmail in an Age of Asymmetric Conflict,* Cambridge: Cambridge University Press, 2010.

Grynkewich, A.G., "Welfare as Warfare: How Violent Non-State Groups Use Social Services to Attack the State," *Studies in Conflict & Terrorism* 31:4, 2009, pp. 350–70.

Hamelink, C.J., "Ethics for Media Users," *European Journal of Communication* 10:4, 1995, pp. 497–512.

Hill, D.T., "East Timor and the Internet: Global Political Leverage in/on Indonesia," *Indonesia* 73, 2002, 25–51.

Horgan, J. and M. Taylor, "Playing the Green Card: Financing the Provisional IRA, Part II," *Terrorism and Political Violence* 15:2, 2003, pp. 1–60.

International Humanitarian Law, "Protocol Additional to the Geneva Conventions of 12 August 1949, and Relating to the Protection of Victims of International Armed Conflicts (Protocol I), 8 June 1977." Online. Available at: www.icrc.org/ihl.nsf/WebART/470-750046?OpenDocument (accessed 20 September 2012).

Johnson, N., "Small Projects Reap Large Gains in Helmand," *Afghanistan International Security Assistance Forces (ISAF),* June 2010. Online. Available at: http://www.isaf.nato.int/article/isaf-releases/small-projects-reap-large-gains-in-helmand.html (accessed 20 September 2012).

Johnson, T.H., "The Taliban Insurgency and an Analysis of Shabnamah (Night Letters)," *Small Wars and Insurgencies* 18:3, 2007, pp. 317–44.

Kalb, M. and Saivetz, C., "The Israeli–Hezbollah War of 2006: The Media as a Weapon in Asymmetrical Conflict," *The Harvard International Journal of Press/Politics* 12:3, 2007, pp. 43–66.

Kearney, M., *The Prohibition of Propaganda for War in International Law,* Oxford: Oxford University Press, 2007.

Kirkpatrick, D.D., "NATO Strikes at Libyan State TV," *New York Times,* July 30, 2011. Online. Available at: http://www.nytimes.com/2011/07/31/world/africa/31tripoli.html?_r=2pagewanted=pr& (accessed 20 September 2012).

Lappin, Y., "IDF Releases Cast Lead Casualty Numbers," *The Jerusalem Post*, March 26, 2009. Online. Available at: http://www.jpost.com/Israel/Article.aspx?id=137286 (accessed 20 September 2012).

Leigh, D., "US Forces Hit Target 'With No Civilian Deaths' – but Afghans Tell Different Tale: Special Forces Ensured 'No Innocent Afghans in Area,' but Villagers Say up to 300 Civilians Died in Attack," *The Guardian*, Monday 26 July 2010. Online. Available at: http://www.guardian.co.uk/world/2010/jul/26/afghanistan-war-logs-helmand-bombing (accessed 20 September 2012).

Limor, Y. and Nossek, H., "The Military and the Media in the Twenty-First Century: Towards a New Model of Relations," *Israel Affairs* 12:3, 2006, pp. 484–510.

Ly, P., "The Charitable Activities of Terrorist Organizations," *Public Choice*, 131:1, 2007, pp. 177–95.

Moorcraft, P. and Taylor, P.M., "War Watchdogs or Lapdogs?" *British Journalism Review* 18:4, 2007, pp. 39–50.

Moore, C., "Our Very Strange Day with Hezbollah," *Anderson Cooper 360°* (blog), July 23, 2006. Online. Available at: http://www.cnn.com/CNN/Programs/anderson.cooper.360/biog/archives/2006_07_23_ac360_archive.html (accessed 20 September 2012).

Mor, B.D., "The Rhetoric of Public Diplomacy and Propaganda Wars: A View from Self-Presentation Theory," *European Journal of Political Research* 46, 2007, pp. 661–83.

Nissen, T.E., *The Taliban's Information Warfare: A Comparative Analysis of NATO Information Operations (Info Ops) and Taliban Information Activities*, Copenhagen: Royal Danish Defence College, 2007.

Nye Jr, J.S., "Public Diplomacy and Soft Power," *Annals of the American Academy of Political and Social Science* 616, 2008, pp. 94–109.

Olsthoorn, P. and Bollen, M., "Civilian Care in War: Lessons from Afghanistan," in M.L. Gross and D. Carrick (eds), *Military Medical Ethics in the 21st Century*, London: Ashgate Publishing, 2013.

Palestinian Centre for Human Rights, "The Dead in the Course of the Israeli Recent Military Offensive on the Gaza Strip Between 27 December 2008 and 18 January 2009, March 19, 2009." Online. Available at: http://www.scribd.com/doc/22883962/The-Dead-in-the-course-of-the-Israeli-Military-offensive-on-the-Gaza-Strip-between-27-Dec-2008-and-18-Jan-2009 (accessed 20 September 2012).

Payne, K., "The Media as an Instrument of War," *Parameters*, 2005, pp. 81–93.

Peskowitz, A., "IO on the Counterinsurgency Battlefield: Three Case Studies," *Global Security Studies* 1:2, 2010, pp. 100–14.

Physicians for Human Rights, Israel, "Holding Health to Ransom: GSS Interrogation and Extortion of Palestinian Patients at Erez Crossing," August 2008. Online. Available at: http://www.phr.org.il/uploaded/HoldingHealthToRandsom_4.pdf (accessed 20 September 2012).

Plaisance, P.L., "The Propaganda War on Terrorism: An Analysis of the United States' 'Shared Values' Public Diplomacy Campaign after September 11, 2001," *Journal of Mass Media Ethics* 20:4, 2005, pp. 250–68.

Qazi, S.H., "Rebels of the Frontier: Origins, Organization, and Recruitment of the Pakistani Taliban," *Small Wars & Insurgencies* 22:4, 2011, pp. 574–602.

Rid, T. and Hecker, M., *War 2.0: Irregular Warfare in the Information Age*, Santa Barbara, CA: Praeger, 2009.

Roling, K., "Provincial Development Council Discusses Projects in Ghazni," *Afghanistan International Security Assistance Forces (ISAF)*, n.d. Online. Available at: http://www.isaf.nato.int/article/news/provincial-development-council-discusses-projects-in-ghazni.html (accessed 20 September 2012).

Sarma, K., "Defensive Propaganda and IRA Political Control in Republican Communities," *Studies in Conflict & Terrorism* 30:12, 2007, pp. 1073–94.

Slattery, K. and Ugland, E., "Journalism Ethics in Wartime," *The Digital Journalist*, December 2004. Online. Available at: http://digitaljournalist.org/issue0412/ethics.html (accessed 20 September 2012).

Society of Professional Journalists, *Code of Ethics*. Online. Available at: http://www.spj.org/ethicscode.asp (accessed 20 September 2012).

UN News Centre, "UN Official Deplores NATO Attack on Libyan Television Station," August 8, 2011. Online. Available at: http://www.un.org/apps/news/story.asp?NewsID=39255&Cr=Libya&Cr1#.UFtsDEUx7EU (accessed 20 September 2012).

12

RETHINKING LEGITIMATE AUTHORITY

Anne Schwenkenbecher

1. Preliminaries

In its traditional form, the just war criterion of legitimate authority restricted the right to declare war to a state's legitimate representatives and the right to wage war to state agents. However, to an increasing degree, contemporary violent conflicts involve non-state actors. This has been reflected in the Geneva Convention's acknowledgement of 'armed conflict not of an international character'. Furthermore, in order to end a violent conflict involving non-state parties there is often some kind of recognition of non-state actors as legitimate negotiating partners and contract parties on the part of state actors or the international community. Former liberation movements and their leaders have in the past become internationally recognized as legitimate political forces and legitimate leaders. Such recognition has repeatedly given rise to the question of what makes it appropriate to consider particular violent non-state actors to be legitimate violent agents and others not. In just war theory, which has been both a source for international standards of war and an instance of critical reflection on those standards, there has been comparatively little debate on adjusting and reformulating the traditional criterion of legitimate authority accordingly.[1] This is why it will concern us in this article.

In recent debates surrounding the principle of legitimate authority, philosophers have invoked by and large four criteria for satisfying the principle. Some of these criteria reflect the traditional principle, while others already take the question of non-state agents in violent conflicts into account. The following criteria for legitimate authority have been put forward:

1 *Popular support and representation of a people.* This is assuming that it is morally desirable that the people on whose behalf or in whose name the violent conflict is carried out agree – in the majority – with this form of conflict resolution and its aims. It assumes that an agent that employs political violence has substantial support for this. With regard to war, Thompson says that it "cannot be waged on the whim of leaders," but "leaders of the state or organization should be acting as agents of the people."[2]

2 *Monopoly of violence and effective control over a people.* This criterion states that a violent agent must have the ability and willingness to "enforce obedience to the restrictions of just war theory."[3] And it guarantees that violence will not get out of control.[4]

3   *Adherence to international legal standards.* Janna Thompson argues that an agent must "recognise ... the restrictions of just war theory, the rights of other parties" as well as those "frameworks and institutions" that make agreements possible.[5] This will ensure that enemies treat each other with respect and will increase the chances for settling the conflict.

4   *Predisposition to strive for a lasting peace.* Janna Thompson argues that an organization in order to count as a legitimate authority must be able and willing to negotiate a peace and to keep it.[6] This clause prohibits agents to declare war on another country purely in order to profit from it financially, for instance. It also prevents wars that are not meant to settle a conflict, but to perpetuate it.

This chapter examines all four criteria for ascribing legitimate, in the sense of moral, authority to groups engaged in violent conflict – be it state or non-state agents such as terrorist actors, parties in civil wars or rebels in wars of independence. It will attempt to answer two intertwined questions:

- Are criteria (1) – (4) good criteria?
- Are there (always) good reasons to restrict the right to employ political violence to specific agents at all?

This article will show how of these four criteria only the first can be defended (part 1 and 2). It will also be illustrated that from a moral point of view non-state violent agents may perfectly well satisfy this criterion. In contrast, state actors may clearly fail in this regard. However, it will also become obvious that in exceptional circumstances agents are permitted to act without explicit approval from the people on whose behalf they employ violence. Finally, the article will argue that, in principle, *individuals* should be entitled to employ violence for political objectives (part 3).

It is important to remember, however, that establishing an agent's *legitimate* use of violence is not the same as establishing that she is *justified* in employing violence. She is justified only if meeting a number of other criteria, too. If she does not have a just cause, for instance, she would be committing a moral wrong in engaging in a violent conflict, regardless of whether she has legitimate authority.

I will begin with discussing the first criterion, followed by a short comment on the remaining criteria. Finally, I will address the question of whether the right to employ political violence – and hence the possibility of having legitimate authority – should be granted to individuals, too.

2. Popular support and representation of a people

Early in 2003 then Spanish Prime Minister José María Aznar and his conservative government decided to join the U.S.' and U.K.'s military engagement in Iraq. At that time numerous surveys confirmed what had already become visible in the form of public protests: the majority of Spaniards were opposed to that decision and saw no justification for their country's involvement in that war.[7] People took to the streets and marched against their government's decision – yet to no avail.

Clearly, the Spanish government had the formal authority to enter that war. But, while they had been elected into that role, they just as clearly acted contrary to the will of their constituency. Some might think that the Spanish government did not act wrongly, because their public role entitled them to that decision. And in a formal sense (ignoring that the invasion was not sanctioned by any international authority and ignoring that there was no just cause), that might be true. However, whether or not an agent is entitled to enter a war, or more generally employ political violence, is also a moral question. And from a moral point of view, formal authority may not be decisive.

A government's decision to go to war has an immense impact on their citizens. Taxes will be spent on the war effort and other areas of public spending will suffer cuts. Citizen soldiers will be sent to war zones; they will risk and sometimes lose their lives. These are practical implications of a decision to go to war and they deliver prudential reasons for not making that decision without seeking authorization by (a large part of) those who are paying for it. But there is more to it: when going to war, a country's armed forces kill in a people's or nation's name. It cannot be morally right that my country's armed forces kill people in my name when I have not consented to it. Not that every citizen could ever consent to everything his government does or decides. But because going to war is a decision that has serious consequences for many people's lives and because it is a morally important decision, it should only be made if there is widespread support for it among a country's population.

Let me briefly focus on a different scenario for a moment. In 1961 *Umkhonto we Sizwe (MK)*, African National Congress' (ANC) military wing, published a manifesto declaring the employment of violent means against South Africa's Apartheid regime.[8] All MK members were also members of the ANC. MK subsequently launched violent – and sometimes terrorist – attacks to support ANC's struggle against Apartheid. This struggle had overwhelming support from Black South Africans and there was growing support for using violent means too. While MK clearly had no formal authority, given that it had not undergone an established and formalized procedure, it is probably fair to say that it employed violent means in the interest and according to the will of the people represented by the ANC.

At this stage someone might argue that what was wrong with Aznar's decision in contrast to MK's decision was that the invasion of Iraq was not justified – it lacked a just cause – but the ANC's struggle against Apartheid was, overall, justified – it clearly had a just cause. However, while I agree with this judgment, I do not think it gives us any insight into the nature of legitimate authority. Rather, it seems to collapse the criterion of legitimate authority into the criterion of just cause. The decisive difference is that the political community on whose behalf Aznar's government decided to go to war did not support that decision, while MK enjoyed substantial support from the community whose interests it defended.

Does it make a difference that the Spanish government was an elected and democratically authorized agent, while MK was not? These examples suggest that it would be arbitrary to restrict the right to employ political violence to state agents for formal reasons. Especially, when we agree that non-state violence aimed at overthrowing dictatorial and oppressive regimes is sometimes justified. Instead, the right to employ violence on behalf or in the name of a political community should lie with agents that legitimately represent their community's interests and political will. This condition can be satisfied by non-state agents, as the MK example shows, while state agents that have been democratically elected and formally authorized can fail in this regard, as the Spanish example shows.

But when does a non-state agent legitimately represent the interests of a community? Lionel McPherson argued that

> [a] nonstate group may have representative authority: the group not only would take itself to act on behalf of a people but also would be acting on the people's behalf given credible measures of approval by that people. Such measures, for example, mass demonstrations, general strikes, and polling, might lie outside formal political procedures.[9]

163

There might be situations, however, in which a people or a political community are unable to express such approval. This may be the case in highly oppressive regimes. How important is the criterion of representative authority that McPherson suggests? Is it always wrong when an agent – state or non-state, military, terrorist or guerrilla – employs violence on behalf of a political community which does not agree with such violent endeavours?

In order to answer this question, it is important to distinguish two scenarios. In the first scenario, violence is employed (by a state agent or a non-state agent) with the aim of fighting against severe political injustice, such as the political oppression of ethnic, cultural or religious groups. In the second scenario, violence is employed (by a state agent or a non-state agent) to face and eventually stop crimes against humanity against the violent agent's own community or another community.

In the first scenario, independently of whether or not violence is employed to combat an injustice against one's own or a different political community or group, it seems to be crucial that the group or community on whose behalf violence is used does actually approve of such interference. Christopher Finlay has argued that "Non-state groups considering recourse to violence should therefore consult with those they claim to represent and should seek wide endorsement in order to legitimate their programmes for action."[10] Yet, clearly, this must be just as valid for state groups using violence on behalf of others. Not only should state agents consult those who they are meant to represent – their citizens – it seems that state agents too would need to consult those to whom assistance is provided.

Finlay goes on to say that there may be circumstances in which the explicit preferences of a community may be disregarded. He argues that "there may be some cases of political oppression so severe that the capacity of victims to deliberate on their situation and make decisions about those who might represent their interests is diminished or eliminated." He thinks that in such circumstances, it is acceptable if a non-state entity acts without the explicit consent of the victims of the oppression if they promote the victims' *true* interests.[11] Again, if this applies to non-state agents, there is no reason why it would not apply to state agents too. But what kinds of circumstances does Finlay have in mind?

This question takes us to the second scenario, where violent means are employed to stop or prevent crimes against humanity. In a situation where a community or people is facing such severe crimes the victim's capacity to deliberate and consent to political measures taken by others is likely to be severely limited in the way Finlay described. And indeed, it seems that this capacity or lack thereof must play a role in deciding whether agents employing violence on behalf of the victims of those crimes act legitimately.

I have argued elsewhere that an agent must have what I called *moral authority*: an agent fighting a political injustice with violent means usually has moral authority to employ violence for this end if she has explicit approval of the people on whose behalf she acts. However, no such approval is required if the injustice she fights is extremely severe, for instance, if it consists of genocide or a crime against humanity as specified in international law.[12] I think it is important to distinguish between two cases. In one case the political community or the victims of the injustice are in a position to express their political will and it is therefore possible for any agent acting on their behalf – be it a non-state agent or a state agent – to act according to a people's or community's explicit will. But there are situations where this is not possible because, as Finlay describes, the victims have no opportunity to express their political will or they have been grossly manipulated into forming a will that does not reflect their interests. Hence, it seems that under some circumstances a people's or political community's expressed will may be ignored. Or else, the lack of an expressed will may not be a reason for refraining from employing violence on their behalf.

But can we always draw a clear line between these two cases? Can we really always know what the victims' or political community's *true* interests are? What about a community that does not wish to be defended against a looming genocidal attack, but prefers dying peacefully to defending themselves or being defended by violent means? Would anyone – a domestic or international state or non-state agent – be permitted to intervene on their behalf? Is it acceptable to defend people against their will?

While in struggles of independence, and more generally for political objectives to do with a community's right to self-determination, violent interference without consent would clearly be patronizing in an unacceptable way, this is not necessarily so for extreme situations such as genocide, ethnic cleansing, etc. In these situations, no consent from those on whose behalf violence is employed is required, because a violent agent will be justified in assuming that it is not in any individual's reasonable interest to be killed, maimed, banished, etc.[13]

To sum up: in exceptional circumstances, when a humanitarian disaster is looming or when a people's or political community's ability to deliberate upon and express their political will is severely restricted the criterion of legitimate representation permits acts without the victims' approval and in disregard of a community's manipulated will. In those situations, an agent may employ violent means on their behalf without their explicit or implicit consent. But do violent agents still need to satisfy the remaining three criteria? In the following I will show that *in order to have legitimate authority* they need not have effective control over a people, comply with legal and moral standards of violent conflict or strive for a lasting peace.

3. Redundant criteria

The three remaining criteria for legitimate authority are, as the title of the section already suggests, either redundant or lack justification.

Janna Thompson in her 2005 article "Terrorism, Morality and Right Authority" has argued that a violent agent must be "able and willing to enforce obedience to the restrictions of just war theory."[14] According to Thompson, this will prevent violence from getting out of control. She argues that "[i]f violence is uncontrolled … then making and keeping the peace becomes extremely difficult." Along similar lines, but with a stronger pro-state bias, Coates has defended the public monopoly of violence as "a fundamental step in any process of pacification."[15]

Both authors emphasize how control over violence is important – or even necessary – for making peace possible. They are probably right. However, there is no reason why the capacity to achieve peace should be a necessary condition for an agent's legitimate authority to employ violent means. Just war theory attends to this problem by incorporating the criterion of prospect of success. This criterion is meant to avert the employment of violence in lost causes. It demands that a war be waged only if it is likely to succeed, that is if it is likely to achieve its intended goal. If it is improbable that violent measures will help secure this goal, then it is morally wrong to resort to such measures. Given that the criterion of prospect of success is already part of just war theory, there is no need to incorporate its central ideas into another criterion as well. Hence, "legitimate authority" should not require that an agent is only justified in resorting to violence if he has some prospect of bringing the violent conflict to a successful end, as Thompson and Coates suggest.[16]

Janna Thompson has furthermore argued that an agent in order to be a legitimate authority for employing political violence must "recognise … the restrictions of just war theory, the rights of other parties" as well as those "frameworks and institutions" that make agreements possible. A violent party, in her view, should be respecting the existence of other nations and peoples.[17] As with the previously discussed criterion, she thinks that an agent should meet this criterion if there is to be a reasonable chance that a conflict can be settled. Yet, for the same reason as above, her suggestion would already be covered by the condition of prospect of success and there would be no need for another criterion.

She also says that the agent should recognize the restrictions of just war theory. Yet this is a bit dubious because it is either a circular argument or because it makes the criterion of legitimate authority redundant. On the first interpretation, Thompson makes the satisfaction of one criterion from just war theory – legitimate authority – dependent on the satisfaction of *all* criteria – including the one that we are talking about. This would mean that an agent has legitimate authority if she has legitimate authority and a just cause, right intention, her means are proportionate, etc. This cannot be right.

On the second interpretation, she makes the satisfaction of one criterion from just war theory dependent on the satisfaction of *all other* criteria from just war theory – excluding the one that we are talking about. In the latter case, our criterion would be redundant because it would merely affirm the compliance with standards that are already covered by other components of just war such as non-combatant immunity, proportionality, or the prohibition of *mala en se* weapons. As to the question of international institutions: if adherence to international law is required for an agent in order to have legitimate authority then this begs the question against international law which may sometimes be at odds with morality. These realms should be kept separate.

Similarly, an agent's predisposition to strive for a lasting peace is usually covered by the criterion of just cause and right intention. "Right intention" specifies that the agent fight the war for the sake of the just cause, i.e. with the intention to ensure just cause. If an agent declares war purely in order to profit from it, he would be in breach of this condition. The same is true for an agent who does not aim at settling, but at perpetuating a conflict.

At this stage one might object that in my replies to Thompson I presuppose just war theory in a question-begging way. The just war tradition, one might argue, is a very heterogeneous tradition of thought under whose label philosophers have defended and defeated a range of ideas that are not always compatible. There is a lot of debate surrounding the relationship between these components, most prominently the debate surrounding the interdependence of "just cause", "non-combatant immunity" and "proportionality", with a distinctive new view put forward by Jeff McMahan.[18]

However, while it is true that just war theory is not a unified "theory", we should not forget that there is an overlapping consensus regarding which of its components are essential. And there is a division of labour between its different components. The question of legitimate authority is a specific question about who is the right agent to declare and conduct a war (or a violent conflict), assuming that only agents that qualify in some way or another should be allowed to do so. The disagreement discussed in this article this far is about how to spell out this qualification. The question of what qualifies an agent for legitimate authority is independent from the question of whether or not that agent has a just cause to resort to violence, whether she has the right intention, whether she will be likely to succeed, and so on. However, in the following part I will look into the question of whether or not there is a need for such a qualification at all.

4. Individual violent agents

Having established that a legitimate agent represents the will of a people or political community and that – in principle – both state and non-state agents can satisfy a criterion of legitimate or moral authority, the last question we have to ask is whether an individual person can ever have legitimate authority to enter and lead a violent political struggle. Cécile Fabre has, in fact, argued that this should be possible. She argues that, from a cosmopolitan point of view, individuals are the basic units of moral concern, not political communities. She holds that

> the right to protect oneself from violations of one's human rights by others is a *human* right, in the sense that it is a right to a freedom … which we need in order to lead a minimally flourishing life. By extension, the right to wage a war in defence of one's human rights should also be conceived of as human rights.[19]

Fabre basically argues that an individual person is morally entitled to go to war – in the sense of having legitimate authority to go to war. Before I discuss her main point – with which I agree – I should say two things about her argument.

First, unlike Fabre, I do not think it is helpful to speak of an individual waging war, merely because I think we should reserve the term "war" for large-scale collective endeavors.[20] But clearly, her argument does not depend on it. Second, Cécile Fabre argues that we should drop the criterion of legitimate authority, *because* it unjustifiably restricts the right to go to war to state agents. This seems to draw the wrong conclusion drawn from a correct antecedent. Why not simply adjust the criterion of legitimate authority so that it does not apply to state agents only? In fact, authors have argued for a non-state criterion of legitimate authority.[21]

However, I agree with Fabre in that there should be no principled reason for excluding individual agents from employing violence to protect their basic rights. In fact they should generally not be excluded from employing violence for a just cause, be it their own or other individuals', groups', or communities' rights.

Let me look at a number of possible objections to this claim. One may argue that clearly we would not want just any person to take up arms whenever she feels that her basic human rights have been violated. And indeed, this would be undesirable. But that a person is justified in doing so does not at all follow from what I have previously said. That an individual agent is in principle a legitimate authority for employing political violence does not mean that she is justified in doing so whenever she thinks there have been rights violations. If we look at just war theory, there are a number of other criteria that agents need to satisfy before being allowed to resort to violence. An agent must have a just cause and that cause must be weighty enough to justify the employment of violent means. An agent should furthermore only resort to violence if other – less harmful – means for resolving the conflict in question have failed. Presumably, in a democracy, there are others ways of claiming one's rights.

Furthermore, one may claim that an individual will never succeed in something like overthrowing the government, ending oppression, etc. However, this objection can be rebutted in a similar way to the previous one. In just war theory the prospect of success plays a role in justifying resort to violent means. If a violent campaign is not likely to succeed, it cannot be fully justified. It has been argued that this criterion is not independent, but should form part of proportionality considerations.[22] But regardless of whether or not "prospect of success" is independent as a criterion, it plays a decisive role in determining whether a violent effort is justified. One may object that this criterion will *as a matter of fact* render nearly all individual agents unjustified in resorting to violent means. But this does not mean that *in principle* they should be excluded as legitimate agents for resorting to violence.

Along different lines, focusing on the relation between the cause defended and the means employed one might wonder: what if an individual agent kills several people, just because she has suffered from a (comparatively minor) injustice? Surely we should not allow that one person may kill several others whenever she has suffered from rights violations.

This last worry is one about proportionality. It says that it cannot be right to cause a substantial injustice or moral wrong in response to a comparatively lesser injustice or moral wrong. And clearly, because this should not be allowed for, both traditional and non-traditional just war theories include the criterion of proportionality. According to this criterion, the positive results or moral benefits of resorting to a strategy of political violence must outweigh the negative results or moral costs. Furthermore, in the course of a single violent act, an agent must employ no more violence than necessary to achieve her objectives.[23]

If we have a proportionality criterion, we can rebut the last objection to the claim that individuals have legitimate authority to employ violence for political objectives. An individual agent resorting to violent means in reaction to a minor injustice would be unjustified in doing so if she violates the proportionality requirement. But if her violence is proportionate then the fact that she is an individual agent as such should not make her violent act or campaign unjust. In sum, none of the three objections above show that *in principle* the resort to violence should be permissible for group agents only, and not for individuals.

5. Last question

In the article I have tried to show four things: (1) that a principle of representation (in the sense of acting on the basis of a community's or people's explicit or implicit will) is the most plausible interpretation of the criterion of legitimate authority, (2) that non-state violent agents may have this kind of legitimate authority, (3) that in exceptional circumstances violent agents do not require explicit approval from the people on whose behalf they act, and (4) that – in principle – individuals are entitled to employ violence for political objectives.

This article started with observations about international law and it may be a good idea to conclude it in the same way. One might wonder whether one of the conclusions from the discussion in this article, namely that individuals are in principle legitimate agents for employing political violence, should have any bearing on national or international law. In fact, one might be worried about "legalizing" individual agent's employment of political violence. Without doubt, ethical debates have always informed national and international legislation and will continue to do so. A strong moral consensus in a society can trigger revisions of existing legislation or incorporation of new laws. The question of whether or not this is desirable for the conclusions drawn in this article is a challenging question, but unfortunately not one that has a short answer. And it is not a question that can be answered by ethical deliberation alone.

Notes

1 The exceptions being, J. Angelo Corlett, *Terrorism: A Philosophical Analysis*. Philosophical Studies Series 101, Dordrecht; London: Kluwer Academic, 2003; Anthony Joseph Coates, *The Ethics of War*, Manchester: Manchester University Press, 1997; Virginia Held, "Legitimate Authority in Non-state Groups Using Violence," *Journal of Social Philosophy* 36:2, 2005, pp. 175–193; Cécile Fabre, "Cosmopolitanism, Just War Theory and Legitimate Authority," *International Affairs*, 84:5, 2008, pp. 963–976; Christopher J. Finlay, "Legitimacy and Non·State Political Violence," *Journal of Political Philosophy*, 18:3, 2010, pp. 287–312, Anne Schwenkenbecher, *Terrorism: A Philosophical Inquiry*, Basingstoke, Hampshire: Palgrave Macmillan, 2012; Uwe Steinhoff, *On the Ethics of War and Terrorism*. New York: Oxford University Press, 2007; Janna Thompson, "Terrorism, Morality and

Right Authority," in G. Meggle (ed.), *Ethics of Terrorism and Counter-Terrorism*, Frankfurt am Main: Ontos, 2005, pp. 151–160.

2 J. Thompson, "Terrorism," p. 155. Similar views are defended by C. J. Finlay, "Legitimacy and Non-State Political Violence"; V. Held, "Legitimate Authority"; Lionel K. McPherson, "Is Terrorism Distinctively Wrong?"

3 J. Thompson, "Terrorism," p. 155

4 A.J.Coates, *The Ethics of War*, p. 124, p. 140

5 J. Thompson, "Terrorism," p. 155

6 Ibid.

7 See for instance the results of a survey by the daily newspaper EL PAÍS, 2 February 2003. Online. Available at: http://elpais.com/diario/2003/02/02/espana/1044140401_850215.html (accessed 26 March 2013).

8 Manifesto of Umkhonto we Sizwe. Leaflet issued by the Command of Umkhonto we Sizwe, 16 December 1961. Online. Available at: http://www.anc.org.za/show.php?id=77& t=Umkhonto%20 we%20Sizwe (accessed 26 March 2013).

9 McPherson, L.K., "Is Terrorism Distinctively Wrong?", p. 542. See also discussion in A. Schwenkenbecker, *Terrorism*, p. 87f.

10 C.J. Finlay, "Legitimacy and Non-State Political Violence," p. 309.

11 Ibid., p. 310.

12 A. Schwenkenbecher, *Terrorism*, p. 83 and Rome Statute of the International Criminal Court, part 2, articles 6 and 7.

13 A similar conclusion is drawn by L.K. McPherson, "Is Terrorism Distinctively Wrong?" and C.J. Finlay, "Legitimacy and Non-State Political Violence."

14 J. Thompson, "Terrorism," p. 155.

15 A.J. Coates, *The Ethics of War*, p. 124.

16 See also discussion in Schwenkenbecher, *Terrorism*, p. 96ff.

17 J. Thompson, "Terrorism," pp. 155, 156.

18 J. McMahan, *Killing in War*, Oxford: Clarendon Press, 2009.

19 Cécile Fabre, "Cosmopolitanism, Just War Theory and Legitimate Authority," *International Affairs*, 84:5, 2008, pp. 969.

20 See, e.g., Orend, Brian, "War", *The Stanford Encyclopedia of Philosophy* (Fall 2008 Edition), Edward N. Zalra (ed.); http://plato.stanford.edu/archives/fall2008/entries/war (accessed 3 May 2013).

21 J.A.Corlett, *Terrorism: A Philosophical Analysis*; Finlay "Legitimacy and Non-State Political Violence"; V Held, "Legitimate Authority"; A. Schwenkenbecher, *Terrorism*; Thompson "Terrorism."

22 A. Schwenkenbecher, *Terrorism*, pp. 96–98; Steinhoff, *On the Ethics of War and Terrorism*, p. 30.

23 Ibid.

References

Coates, A.J., *The Ethics of War*, Manchester: Manchester University Press, 1997.

Corlett, J.A., *Terrorism: A Philosophical Analysis*, Philosophical Studies Series 101, London: Kluwer Academic Publishers, 2003.

EL PAÍS, 2 February 2003. Online. Available at: http://elpais.com/diario/2003/02/02/ espana/1044140401_850215.html (accessed 26 March 2013).

Fabre, C., "Cosmopolitanism, Just War Theory and Legitimate Authority," *International Affairs*, 84:5, 2008, pp. 963–76.

Finlay, C.J., "Legitimacy and Non-State Political Violence," *Journal of Political Philosophy*, 18:3, 2010, pp. 287–312.

Held, V., "Legitimate Authority in Non–state Groups Using Violence," *Journal of Social Philosophy*, 36:2, 2005, pp. 175–93.

Manifesto of Umkhonto we Sizwe. Leaflet issued by the Command of Umkhonto we Sizwe, 16 December 1961. Online. Available at: http://www.anc.org.za/show.php?id=77& t=Umkhonto%20we%20 Sizwe (accessed 26 March 2013).

McMahan, J., *Killing in War*, Oxford: Clarendon Press, 2009.

McPherson, L.K., "Is Terrorism Distinctively Wrong?" *Ethics* 117:3, 2007, pp. 524–46.

Rome Statute of the International Criminal Court, part 2, articles 6 and 7.

Schwenkenbecher, A., *Terrorism: A Philosophical Inquiry*, Basingstoke, Hampshire: Palgrave Macmillan, 2012.

Steinhoff, U., *On the Ethics of War and Terrorism*, New York: Oxford University Press, 2007.

Thompson, J., "Terrorism, Morality and Right Authority," in G. Meggle (ed.), *Ethics of Terrorism and Counter-Terrorism*, Frankfurt am Main: Ontos, 2005, pp. 151–60.

13

FIGHTING THE HUMANITARIAN WAR

Justifications and limitations

Jennifer Mei Sze Ang

1. Introduction

With closer cooperation between nations after the Cold War, the number of peacekeeping missions increased exponentially in response to the rise in intense conscience-shocking humanitarian catastrophes in the 1990s. These missions brought to light the limitation of traditional peacekeeping principles under new circumstances and provoked an urgent response by the international community, leading to the adoption of the Responsibility to Protect (RtoP) in the 2005 World Summit. The RtoP signaled the emergence of a new international norm, one which affirms the international commitment to "never again" allow humanitarian catastrophes of such a scale to occur, while reworking existing obligations already laid down in international law.

In light of this new shift in international norm, current literature concerns itself with a few issues. The first is establishing whether we have a collective moral responsibility towards compatriots beyond our borders, and the justification and nature of these responsibilities. Some like Seumas Miller[1] argued that humanitarian intervention is a moral obligation in that we all have a collective moral responsibility towards others, while others like Fernando Tesón[2] saw it as a matter of reclaiming a violated right. The other area scholars are concerned with is the legitimacy of armed humanitarian interventions when they override state sovereignty[3] although by and large, UN members have now accepted Kofi Annan's argument that states have the responsibility to prevent any violation of the rights of its citizens.[4] But some like Edward Luck cautioned that we should not be invoking RtoP loosely lest we be too quick to justify interventions that infringe sovereignty and territorial integrity.[5] And there are also those who are concerned with the choices of operational aspects of these interventions – the timeliness of intervention, the operational strategies and technology, the role of the UN, and practicality in setting up a UN Legion.[6]

This chapter draws on familiar cases of failed and successful humanitarian interventions to deal with an essential question: how do we ensure humanitarian operations meet the aims of humanitarian interventions? Starting with a sketch of the changed circumstances affecting peacekeeping missions that led to the development of RtoP, it also discusses common challenges inherent in justifications of means in achieving these ends as well as proposes limiting means in order to achieve just aims. It fundamentally argues that for a humanitarian intervention to distinguish itself from ordinary war, humanitarian interventions must ensure that moral ends are met by moral means.

2. Towards the responsibility to protect

Peacekeeping missions carried out in the 1990s revealed that traditional peacekeeping principles were limited under changed circumstances in several ways. First, the consent from a legitimate government held little practical meaning given that some of these civil conflicts occurred as a result of a failed state in the first place. We can observe this in the instances of Liberia and Haiti. The Economic Community of West African States Monitoring Group (ECOMOG) intervention force into Liberia was commended and supported by the Security Council even when it did not act at the request of the Samuel Doe government or approval of the UN because the situation presented a threat to international peace and security. And in Haiti, the illegal replacement of the democratically elected President Jean Bertrand Aristide prompted the Security Council to authorize member states under Chapter VII to set up a Multinational Force to remove the illegal military regime. But this is not to say that all humanitarian interventions in the 1990s took place without the consent of a government. The UN Security Council responded to East Timor's invitation to intervene by first adopting Resolution 384 that recognized the inalienable right of the people of East Timor to "self-determination and independence" and deplored the armed intervention of Indonesia. Although it did not consider the invasion a violation of the UN Charter, it dispatched an election-monitoring mission to East Timor. And in Sierra Leone, the Economic Community of West African States (ECOWAS) responded to the call of the deposed democratically elected President Ahmad Kabbah to intervene and this was supported by the Security Council after the Armed Forces Revolutionary Council (AFRC) government collapsed.

Maintaining the Westphalia principles of state sovereignty and territorial integrity was also unrealistic when there was no government to request or reject humanitarian interventions. And the fact that the severity of these situations escalated into an international threat not only justified, but demanded international attention, for which, the UN was often blamed for failing to act or responding too late. Rwanda's civil war that resulted in 1 million killed, 1.2 million refugees and 2.2 million displaced was often cited as an example. An independent inquiry into the actions of the UN conducted subsequently concluded that "the United Nations failed the people of Rwanda during the genocide in 1994".[7] There was also no functioning government to request or reject interventions to stop the civil war in Somalia. But in other instances where there was explicit opposition from a recognized government, consent was not relevant because of the gravity of the situation. The action of the Iraqi government in 1991 was an example. The repression of the civilian population and 1.5 million Kurdish refugees constituted a threat to international peace and security that necessitated an intervention on humanitarian grounds.

The magnitude and intensity of these conflicts also led to a compromise in the principle of a non-use of force, and hence, also the need for authorization by the Security Council. Aimed at securing peace, peacekeeping tasks included monitoring ceasefires, protecting civilians by setting up safe havens or protected zones to maintain humanitarian corridors, protecting aid convoys, and setting up of no-fly zones. Deadly force was used as well, but only for the cantonment and demobilization of soldiers, the destruction of weapons, and the formation and training of new armed forces and existing police forces.[8] Some of the examples are the setting up of safe areas by NATO's Implementation Force and the Stabilization Force in Bosnia and Srebrenica, and no-fly zones in Iraq and recently in Libya. While the limited use of force was aligned to the UN Charter's Article 51, that outlawed the use and threat of force with the exception of self-defense, and Chapter VII, that specified the need for Security Council approval for armed intervention, the UN was criticized for doing too little and lacking in commitment to its humanitarian end on some occasions. The lack of response to the killing fields of Cambodia and genocide in Rwanda, the limited protection given to the 7,000 Muslim men and boys who were slaughtered in the presence of UN forces outside UN "safe havens" in Srebrenica and the immediate withdrawal of US forces in Somalia after the death of 18 Rangers highlighted the costs of limited commitment, support and capability of intervention forces.

Recognizing the need for UN-sanctioned military action in some circumstances and the need for a more concerted multinational effort, RtoP was a much anticipated development for pro-interventionists. However, it also drew skepticism among those who fear that this might be a pretext for armed interventions by hegemonic powers.[9] Hence, in the early stages, from its promotion and the immediate period after its acceptance, advocates dealt predominately with legitimizing armed interventions carried out without the consent from a legitimate government. This was done by identifying situations that justify armed intervention on humanitarian grounds. According to RtoP, the use of Chapter VII, that allows for "the use of all necessary means," is only justified in situations of genocide, war crimes, ethnic cleansing and crimes against humanity because they constitute threats to international peace and security.[10]

RtoP is built on three pillars: the responsibility of individual states to protect their population from genocide, war crimes, ethnic cleansing and crimes against humanity; the international community's commitment to help states fulfill these responsibilities; and finally, the international community's responsibility to respond collectively in a timely and decisive manner using a full range of diplomatic and military tools when the state in question manifestly fails to protect its population.[11] And, following the outline from the Independent International Commission on Intervention and State Sovereignty (ICISS), the aims of RtoP are a sustained effort to be achieved in three phases: the responsibility to prevent, the responsibility to react, and the responsibility to rebuild. These three phases are based on four principles modified from the just war doctrine: the primary intention for intervention must be to halt or avert human suffering; intervention can only be justified when every nonmilitary option has been explored; the scale, duration and intensity of the military intervention must be kept to a minimum; and there must be a reasonable chance of success in achieving its aim to halt or avert human suffering, with consequences of action not worse than the consequences of inaction.[12]

As of today, most debates surrounding RtoP relate to the legitimacy of intervention – as a moral obligation of the collective, and as the right to be protected from harm – and are developed from the widely accepted re-conceptualized notion of sovereignty. But there are also other important concerns regarding the moral justification of the ends of these missions and the means employed in these operations. What ends are considered morally justified in armed humanitarian interventions? What are considered morally excusable means? How do we ensure that humanitarian ends are met when justified humanitarian interventions are translated into foreign policy?

3. Justifying ends and limiting means

Humanitarian interventions motivated by RtoP have broader aims and they are to be achieved over three phases, responsibility to prevent, to react, and to rebuild. The single most important dimension of RtoP lies in the first phase, the responsibility to prevent. This is aimed at removing the root and direct causes of the man-made conflict and crisis and, arguably, more commitment and resources need to be devoted to this phase.[13] The next phase, responsibility to react, points to the response to these situations with appropriate measures such as sanctions, international prosecution and military intervention. In general, less intrusive and coercive measures are to be considered before more coercive and intrusive ones. And the last phase, the responsibility to rebuild, refers to the provision of assistance with recovery, reconstruction and reconciliation. And with close reference to just war doctrine, the same challenges present themselves in these three phases of RtoP. In the appeals made to just war doctrine in recent conflicts, what is apparent is that a war fought for a supposedly just cause without the use of just means could not claim to have been a just war. A key reason why this occurs is that ends and means were justified separately. They were often based on assessments of their probable chances of success when compared with the likely effects of alternative courses of actions and likely consequences if these ends and means in question were not chosen. Assessments were hence, largely utility-driven.

In contrast, our conceptualization of the means and ends of RtoP should not be justified simply by how effective or useful they are in overcoming humanitarian crises – in producing overall positive results or minimizing negative results – because a focus solely on the strength of these reasons may compromise or override other moral considerations. Further, there is a need to be vigilant that means contribute to ends by way of increasing the probability or degree of success, and also contribute to achieving, or at the very least not undermining, the moral aims that justified the intervention in the first place.[14] I argue that if we were to keep cognizant of the fact that moral ends define and justify means, and that the accomplishment of moral ends necessarily depends on the accomplishment of moral means relevant to its ends, we will have a better chance of ensuring moral outcomes. And this is of paramount importance if we want to maintain that armed humanitarian interventions are morally distinct from ordinary wars.

Let us start by identifying what constitutes morally right intentions in preventive actions, the first phase of RtoP. While it may be clear that the immediate aim of peacekeeping missions is to secure ceasefire and establish sustainable peace, some appeal to the broader aims of RtoP in terms of preventing its occurrence in advance. David Luban for instance, raised a pertinent point for consideration in "Preventive War." Distinguishing between preemptive strikes and preventive wars, he argued that given that enemy attack is imminent, preemptive strikes can be considered justified self-defense, but that preventive wars aimed at forestalling a distant threat are morally indefensible. However, according to Luban, this is not to say that we should do away with preventive war doctrine completely because "preventive war against serious threats posed by rogue states" and terrorists remain necessary.[15] In fact, he argued that too few preventive wars have been fought. In his example, choosing to ignore Hitler's policies and rearmament when they pointed towards imminent danger and inevitable war resulted in having to fight later and fighting on a larger scale and with worse odds. Luban's conclusion is that we should see preventive war against rogue states or states that "exhibit clear evidence of a military build-up with aggressive intentions" as justified.[16] Thus, following Luban's more restricted form of the preventive war doctrine, likely distant threats to international peace and security constitute reasonable moral justifications for the forced removal of rogue and militant states.

Yet for Luban, the 2003 Iraq war, in particular, failed to meet his restricted version of the preventive war doctrine. This is because the exaggerated threat of weapons of mass destruction did not constitute "situations in which the target poses physical threats to a state's people and homeland" nor were there any expressed threats by the Iraqi government.[17] The Iraq war was hence a pure "war of conquest" aimed at the "destruction and replacement of Iraq's government."[18] Given the fact that Luban's assessment, as with other opponents of the Iraqi war, were made from hindsight, we are still left with the fact that the right to prevent as a principle on its own is not sufficiently instructive in answering the question of whether removing distant threats constitutes justified ends. Further, there are also some like Fernando Tesón who rationalized that Saddam Hussein's tyranny warranted the use of force for humanitarian purposes.[19]

The apprehension about the misuse of RtoP hence remains valid, especially when the broader aim of RtoP is to raise matters of economic, social, cultural or humanitarian problems above domestic boundaries to the international sphere. It may be clear that situations of civil wars and forced migrations may be severe enough to prompt interventions to prevent further devastation, but we must be cautious when justifying distant threats of humanitarian catastrophes posed by a failing government, whether it is authoritarian or democratic. The slippery slope permitting preventive action is obvious here: preemptive strikes and preventive wars may be morally justified by a far distant possibility of humanitarian catastrophes arising from a deposed democratic government or failing authoritarian regime that could eventually constitute a threat to international peace and security. And this emphasis on prevention (rather than intervention) is exactly what strong RtoP supporters like Alex Bellamy advocate.[20] He argues that the "preventi[ion of] atrocities saves lives, is less expensive than reaction and rebuilding, and raises fewer difficult questions about state sovereignty and noninterference."[21]

Although there is little doubt that prevention does save lives and costs less than reaction and rebuilding, I believe that distant threats are insufficient grounds to justify compromising state sovereignty because it could be used to promote regime changes or restoration of failing democracies.

In contrast, reacting to *existing* situations of mass atrocities brought about by a rogue regime or as a result of a failing government is another matter.[22] The existing conditions of these humanitarian catastrophes attest to the reaction as necessarily moral, with primary aims of halting or averting human suffering. Hence, to morally justify preventive actions, they must be understood in terms of putting an end to the further worsening of an existing humanitarian disaster, and not to forestall distant threats to international peace and security. In this respect, the UN is also cautious in legitimating unilateral interventions or preventive wars.

But if humanitarian interventions were to depend solely on the Security Council's authorization to determine their legitimacy, I would think that RtoP has taken a step backwards. This is because the Security Council may not always render swift and decisive action when needed, just as we see in Syria's state of civil war in mid-2012. Failing to present a united front for a swift and decisive response to the 18-month civil war (that involved the use of heavy weapons, and has a high likelihood that the Assad government will deploy chemical weapons in the near future), it is difficult to argue that the importance of a UN legitimization trumps moral justifications.[23] In this case, when timely and decisive action from the UN is not forthcoming, it makes sense to use other measures to assess the legitimacy of an intervention. Not only can existing situations of grave humanitarian catastrophe justify as well as legitimize overriding state sovereignty,[24] it can also lend moral validity to the intentions of the intervention as a reaction to a crisis. In short, in times of impending catastrophes, moral justifications take precedence over formal recognition by a legitimating institution. But this gives rise to another concern: how do we ensure that these interventions meet their moral aims?

Whether interventions meet moral aims should not be assessed based on measurements of effectiveness or efficiency. This is because in practical terms, hard and fast rules are not exactly applicable. Unlike the instance of Syria, the UN acted swiftly in the case of the 2011 Libyan civil war because of different geographical and political considerations. The UN Security Council adopted Resolution 1970 as early as 26 February 2011, demanding Muammar Gaddafi put "an immediate end to the violence" and calling for "steps to fulfill the legitimate demands of the population."[25] This reaction came immediately after Gaddafi announced that "officers have been deployed in all tribes and regions so that they can purify all decisions from cockroaches" and that "any Libyan who takes arms against Libya will be executed."[26] Several resolutions were adopted soon after,[27] demonstrating that the readiness of the Gaddafi regime to use violence against its own people on top of the existing human rights violations constituted a sufficiently grave situation that morally justified armed intervention. Importantly, regime change was an effect of rather than the reason for intervention.

The timeliness and effectiveness of the means employed demonstrated the success of the intervention, but the success of moral aims must also be assessed by whether the means employed are guided by moral considerations including those that justified the intervention. Ideally, this will ensure that the means used neither compromise nor derail the moral ends of the intervention. David Rieff for instance, argues that the "RtoP is a doctrine born of good intentions, but one of its great drawbacks is that it turns war into a form of police work writ large, guided by fables of moral innocence and righteousness."[28] This might appear to be so because in reality, striking a balance between when to intervene and the appropriate types of means to employ are by no means easy. At times, interventions proved to be too little too late, and at other times, early interventions seem to be unwarranted. When the US encouraged the Kurds in northern Iraq and the Shiites of southern Iraq to rebel against Hussein's regime in the midst of the 1991 Gulf war, it also did nothing to protect them from the violent reaction from Hussein and only set up safe havens for Kurdish civilians after mounting international pressure.[29] The response in Somalia was another failure. The gravity of the situation was beyond the limited force of the United Nations Operations in Somalia (UNSOM) and US-led multinational forces. Although they were tasked with peacemaking, the disarmament of local militia and the repatriation of refugees, they lacked the necessary heavy weapons and air support. With 23 Pakistani peacekeepers and 18 US Rangers ambushed, the US forces withdrew and this led to the subsequent collapse of the UN-led mission. In these cases, it appears that too little was done to prevent the worsening of the catastrophe. However, when we turn to the case of Kosovo, it seemed that the forces deployed in NATO's unilateral attack were overwhelming. Without the Security Council's approval,[30] the US and a coalition of NATO states launched 7,000 air strikes against Serbian forces and government targets in Serbia and Montenegro, which lead to 10,000 Kosovo Albanians killed and ultimately to approximately 850,000 people being internally displaced or became refugees. As such, not only did the intervention fail to keep to the proportionality principle, its actions did not meet the end it hoped to achieve – averting a humanitarian catastrophe.

We can conclude at this juncture that while we can identify situations of grave humanitarian catastrophe, so as to lend moral justifications to humanitarian interventions in lieu of UN authorization, and recognize that the effectiveness of intervention strategies may vary from case to case, we still need to return to address Rieff's type of concern that RtoP is similar to ordinary war in terms of its "moral risks." I would argue that, given their aims, humanitarian interventions can be morally distinct from ordinary war. However, we need to ensure that the means employed do not undermine or conflict with the very humanitarian ends such interventions seek to achieve. In order to match means to ends, we need to closely observe the means–ends relation.

4. Connecting means to ends

To understand why observing limitations to the type of means used are important, I propose a return to recognizing what the destructive nature of violence implies. We understand means as contributing to ends in any human projects, but violent means in particular are capable of destroying the project. Violent means can undermine humanitarian ends and, in certain instances, replace the humanitarian ends with utilitarian ends. These in turn, justify the violent means in terms of the utility it brings to these utilitarian ends. Clearly, and in line with *jus in bello*, keeping humanitarian interventions morally justified requires keeping its means morally acceptable.

Reaffirming the means-ends relation in humanitarian interventions, I assert, is the only response to Rieff's type of concern. To him, "even when [RtoP] is applied well, it carries moral risks" since wars "always involves a descent into barbarism." [31] In particular, NATO's response in Libya became distorted, and he concluded that RtoP "is not a needed reform to the international system, but a threat to its legitimacy."[32] But in arguing so, Rieff is not acknowledging that there is a middle-ground between pacifism and realism – a blind moral alley – that we need to stand on.[33] Here I put forth a distinction between moral justification and moral excusability. In arguing that conscience-shocking situations morally justify intervention, I mean that given the situation there are morally good reasons for intervention. We can still recognize that military solutions, as with any instances of force or violence used, only bring about morally undesirable consequences (and in Rieff's example, Gaddaffi's death) by seeing armed interventions in such situations as a necessary evil. In this instance, armed interventions belong to the category of moral excusability – excusable because of the situation establishes this morally undesirable course of action as necessary. Importantly, not all types of means are morally excusable as we must still discriminate between means that reaffirm and those that undermine or replace moral ends. In other words, the means-ends relation must guide our identification of means that are morally excusable.

Means that undermine or derail the moral ends of the intervention can be easy to spot. For instance, in carrying out airstrikes that incur massive civilian casualties, the moral ends – the aversion of further human death and suffering – have been compromised. Operation Enduring Freedom may have appealed to moral claims – to destroy Al-Qaeda's terrorist base of operations and military capability so as to replace the oppressive Taliban regime with a viable democratic government. But the fact that the coalition forces conducted the war through air campaigns with indiscriminate targeting compromised the moral claims it advanced.[34] It had compromised thousands of civilian lives, with tens and thousands more deaths indirectly brought about by the lack of medical help, diseases, exposure, displacement and lawlessness, and continued its air campaigns in spite of President Hamid Karzai's protests against these air strikes.

By comparison, it is harder to identify means that alter or replace original ends. Often, when violent means conflict with humanitarian ends, violent means alter or replace original humanitarian ends with utilitarian ends. In turn these means are justified according to the utility they achieve in line with the newly posited ends. An example is that justification of the use of heavy weapons redefines the original aim of forestalling further humanitarian crisis with the aim of regime change. Operation Iraqi Freedom may have set out to destroy weapons of mass destruction, cease Iraqi support for Al-Qaeda and put an end to human rights abuses. But as the war unfolded, regime change *became* the fundamental end that was used to justify the choice of weapons and indiscriminate targeting. These means were not necessary if we defined them according to the first set of aims, but they were explained away by the necessity of regime change. What we see here is a case where the humanitarian ends of the war conflict with the intended strategy, and this original end is replaced with a supposedly more important emergency – that is, the threat of Hussein's government to global security – so that these new means become not only necessary, but also justified in yielding a better outcome. In this way, violent means undermine, derail or replace the original humanitarian means by appealing to utilitarian calculations rather than moral deliberations as the conflict continued. Thus, the intervening force may win the war, but not on its own stated moral aims.

RtoP's adoption of just war principles in its second phase appears to include these considerations. The responsibility to react maintains that interventions can only be justified when every nonmilitary option has been explored, and the scale, duration and intensity of military operations must be kept to a minimum. Furthermore, there must be a reasonable chance of success in the intervention's humanitarian aims, with consequences not worse than consequences of inaction. However, RtoP's adoption of *jus in bello* also faces similar problems as utilitarian deliberations often dominate decision-making.

The discrimination condition forbids intending the deaths of noncombatants as an end but admits the unforeseen side effect of civilian deaths if attacks are directed at legitimate military targets. It follows that indiscriminate bombing or terror bombing is forbidden, but accidental massive civilian deaths or collateral damage can be justified provided they were not the direct targets. This means that so long as area bombing was not directed at the civilian population but to disrupt communications and destroy industrial production, the strategy of area bombing met the condition of discrimination since these were legitimate targets by definition.

We also observe similar latitude in the interpretation of the necessity condition. The necessity condition prohibits the killing of soldiers and civilians if they serve no military purpose. According to William O'Brien, the principle of military necessity aims to outlaw military actions or tactics that are of no use to the achievement of legitimate ends although the assessment of necessity weighs on the potential for achieving the results, and not to consider it legal because that was a successful military campaign.[35] Conversely, means that result in civilian deaths that are out of proportion to the relevant good are considered excessive and unnecessary. And in weighing the cost and benefit of alternative courses of action, armed humanitarian interventions can justify most types of means given that the calculation of the equation will always weigh more on one side. Yet, we are fully aware that the most effective and efficient means to achieve the best results for the situation do not always mean they are morally justified. As such, in assessing the permissibility of means according to how useful they are to the achievement of legitimate ends, we may fundamentally leave the moral dimension of means unaddressed because ends justify any means so long as they are effective, not moral.

This latitude is especially a cause for concern because authorizing Chapter VII can be permitting too much, beyond the morally justified ends. Although the current RtoP specifies that we should exhaust all possible means before military interventions, it still leaves an opportunity for means to posit ends that are absolute, such that any means are possible. Hence, the use of means by interventionist forces must be justified on its own moral considerations, and its effectiveness be assessed based on its achievement of moral ends. This is what we find when we compare Operation Unified Protector (OUP) with Operation Iraqi Freedom. The former was mandated under Chapter VII of the UN Charter. It emphasized traditional peacekeeping tasks such as monitoring ceasefires, establishing no-fly zones and safe havens, imposing an arms embargo, carrying out asset freezes and bans on flights, while maintaining the capacity to use deadly force for the cantonment and demobilization of soldiers, the destruction of weapons, and the formation and training of new armed forces and existing police forces. Clearly, the type of means reaffirms the intent of humanitarian protection as they are not focused on military options and the choice of military weapons and strategies is limited by the condition of keeping the scale, duration, and intensity of military intervention to a minimum, and averting massive human suffering. OUP shows that military means can reaffirm the ends of humanitarian protection when they exercise restraint in causing civilian casualty. But humanitarian interventions can also justify the use of certain means as military necessity (such as air strikes) by positing an end that is absolute (such as the regime change). Thus maintaining an absolutist limitation on the choice of targets and choice of weapons ensures that we are more likely to end up with the humanitarian missions. James Pattison also made similar observations – that "if regime change was the primary objective initially, the coalition would have bombed Gaddafi's troops wherever they were likely to be found, with less regard for civilian casualties."[36]

Humanitarian ends can also help us identify measures that constitute recovery, reconstruction and reconciliation in the exceptionally difficult and long-drawn final phase – the responsibility to rebuild. The International Force for East Timor, INTERFET, is an Australian-led multi-nation force that was highly successful in restoring peace and security and the establishment of a UN peacekeeping force that aided in the successful transition to independence for East Timor.[37] Not only was the UN swift in authorizing international force three days after the Indonesian government agreed to allow international force into East Timor, INTERFET was deployed five days after UN resolution 1264 was approved, in time to prevent exacerbation of the already severe humanitarian crisis. Within a month of deployment, INTERFET successfully reduced the power of the militia, and restored basic infrastructure and services. After the withdrawal of the National Troops of Indonesia and Indonesian government officials at the end of the month, INTERFET had effectively established the security of the country and started to provide peacekeeping support for the UN Transitional Administration (UNTAET) created in Security Council Resolution 1272. After 157 days, INTERFET not only secured law and order, but also supported the UNTAET in reconstructing governance and administration as well as aiding in the investigations of crimes against humanity.[38] As such, not only did INTERFET respond in a timely and decisive fashion to the existing humanitarian violations, it also dealt with the broader duties of restoration and rebuilding effectively.

The Australian government argued on grounds of humanitarian protection for the East Timorese and the defense of their desire for independence, yet some remained doubtful of the altruistic actions of Australian government, questioning the extent to which those actions were truly driven by humanitarian motives. They cited the likely security-political threat of a fragmented Indonesia to Australia and Southeast Asia in terms of social unrest, outflow of refugees, trade disruption and economic gains.[39] In the first place, it is clear from the start that intervention, and especially the occupation of East Timor, would not have constituted a prudent move for Australia because it will jeopardize its diplomatic relations with Indonesia. Furthermore, we have also seen that true intentions are better reflected in the means employed than by the justification of causes alone. The Australian-led forces stayed for a period just sufficient to establish law and order necessary for the East Timorese to hold their elections, and when compared to the U.S.'s unfair oil-for-blood approach in the Middle East and its continued presence since the 1991 Gulf War, there are little grounds to suspect Australia of imperialist intentions. The choice of means and length of stay were indicative of their intention and commitment to establish and secure peace, law and order by removing root causes of the humanitarian crises so as to achieve independence for East Timor.

Intervention in Kosovo yielded very different results. Responding to the inter-ethnic killing between the Kosovo Liberation Army (KLA) and Yugoslav armed forces, the Security Council adopted Resolution 1199 and Chapter VII demanding a ceasefire from all parties. In the event that Slobodan Milosevic refuses to comply with the resolution, NATO was to issue an "activation warning" the very next day, and hence went ahead to prepare for a phased air campaign without the authorization from the Security Council. However, as the resolution was already on the side of the KLA, the peace talk in March 1999 was set to fail right from the beginning.[40] NATO began its air campaign against Yugoslavia a day later, leading to a humanitarian disaster because Yugoslav forces set off an onslaught on Albanian civilians as part of the pogrom of ethnic cleansing.[41] In addition to the questionable legitimacy of NATO's air campaign, the use of depleted uranium ammunition and cluster bombs aimed at oil refineries, chemical plants, selected state-owned factories, civilian infrastructures and media stations were also morally questionable. The long-term cost to the environment and economy was obvious, but what was even worse was the cost to the lives of Albanians who were killed by Yugoslav forces and hundreds of thousands refugees – a result of NATO's intervention. Instead of averting human suffering, it achieved the opposite effects.

After the war, the governance of Kosovo was transferred to the 50,000-strong NATO-led Kosovo Force (KFOR), under the Kumanovo agreement to establish security. This led to a large number of Serbs and non-Albanians fleeing in order to avoid reprisals by returning Albanian refugees and members of the KLA. These refugees lived in temporary camps and shelters in Serbia proper and Montenegro, with many remaining displaced within Kosovo. In fact, returning refugees found themselves unable to inhabit their original homes, and more Serbs continued to leave when Albanians started pogroms against the Serbs. KFOR was unable to establish protection for Kosovo's ethnic minorities, who were killed, abducted, detained and abused, and had their property destroyed and taken over by ethnic Albanians – all with the aim of revenging the atrocities committed by Serb forces and to drive them out of Kosovo.[42] And when Kosovo declared independence in 2008, it faced divided international opinions.

Hence, unlike the case of East Timor, not only was security not established effectively to aid reconciliation and restoration efforts, the intervention was also unsuccessful in facilitating a political solution. Making comparisons between Kosovo and East Timor, we need to recognize that political conflicts require political solutions, and these are unique to the conditions of each state. A fine balance must thus be drawn between imposing a standard solution that the intervening force thinks might benefit the peoples they were protecting and facilitating a solution that respects the sovereign decisions of these peoples.

5. Concluding remarks

The starting point of the RtoP is the moral responsibility we have to others in need. To justify overriding international law on state sovereignty and territorial integrity, RtoP appeals to impartial assessments of four situations – genocide, war crimes, ethnic cleaning and crimes against humanity. Aside from the issues of legality, I have argued that it is essential to ensure that interventions achieve the moral aims they have set out. To this end, I have argued that only when means reaffirm moral ends can they be considered morally excusable and permitted. But when strategies that incur collateral damage with massive civilian casualties are employed or when measures taken do not aid in restoration efforts, they compromise moral ends and are hence morally unjustified. By recognizing just how the means are justified, and the importance of limiting means to achieve the moral ends, humanitarian interventions are more likely to achieve their moral aims and not be reduced to just another armed intervention.

Notes

1 S. Miller, "Collective Responsibility and Armed Humanitarian Intervention," in T. Coady and M. O'Keefe (eds), *Righteous Violence: The Ethics and Politics of Military Intervention*. Victoria: Melbourne University Press, 2005. pp. 51–71.

2 F. Tesón, "Ending Tyranny in Iraq," *Ethics and International Affairs*, 19:2, 2005, pp. 1–20.

3 Gareth Evans and Alex Bellamy, for instance, dealt with the issue of sovereignty in their early works. See G. Evans, *The Responsibility to Protect: Ending Mass Atrocity Crimes Once and for All*. Washington: Brookings Institution Press, 2008; A. Bellamy, *Responsibility to Protect: The Global Effort to End Mass Atrocities*. Cambridge: Polity Press, 2009. Jennifer M. Welsh and Maria Banda examined the legality of the obligations and responsibility of RtoP. See J. M. Welsh, and M. Banda, "International Law and the Responsibility to Protect: Clarifying or Expanding States Responsibilities?" *Global Responsibility to Protect*, 2:2, 2010, pp. 213–231.

4 K. Annan, "Two Concepts of Sovereignty," *The Economist* 1999. 16 September, 1999. Online. Available at: http://www.economist.com/node/324795 (accessed 27 March, 2013). To quote Kofi

Annan at length here: "States are now widely understood to be instruments at the service of their peoples, and not vice versa. At the same time individual sovereignty — by which I mean the fundamental freedom of each individual, enshrined in the charter of the UN and subsequent international treaties — has been enhanced by a renewed and spreading consciousness of individual rights. When we read the charter today, we are more than ever conscious that its aim is to protect individual human beings, not to protect those who abuse them."

5 C.E. Luck, "The United Nations and the Responsibility to Protect," *The Stanley Foundation Policy Analysis Brief*, August 2008. Online. Available at: http://humansecuritygateway.com/documents/TSF_theUNandR2P.pdf (accessed 4 August, 2012). Luck warned that commentators should not extend RtoP to the 2008 Cyclone Nargis in Myanmar.

6 L. Lutz Unterseher for instance, explored the creation of a UN Legion. See "Domesticating Military Interventions and the Creation of a UN Standing Force," in T. Coady and M. O'Keefe (eds), *Righteous Violence*, Victoria: Melbourne University Press, 2005, pp. 137–59. Some others who dealt with the development of precision weapons and its implication for the battle field for example are Henry Shue and Michael Schmitt. See H. Shue, "Targeting Civilian Infrastructure with Smart Bombs: The New Permissiveness," *Philosophy and Public Policy Quarterly*," 30, 2012, pp. 2–7, and M. N. Schmitt, "Precision attack and international humanitarian law," *International Review of the Red Cross*, 87, 2005, pp. 445–66.

7 United Nations General Assembly, "2009 Report: Implementing the Responsibility to Protect," 12 January, 2009. Online. Available at: http://responsibilitytoprotect.org/SGRtoPEng%20(4).pdf (accessed 30 April, 2012).

8 T. G. Weiss, *Humanitarian Intervention*. Cambridge: Polity Press, 2007, p. 9.

9 Besides Edward Luck who warned against commentators that extended the type of situations justified under RtoP (such as including natural disasters like the 2008 Cyclone Nargis), there are also others such as Lee Feinstein and Anne-Marie Slaughter that expanded the duty to prevent to include preventive wars. See L. Feinstein and A-M. Slaughter, "A Duty to Prevent," *Foreign Affairs*, 83:1, 2004, pp. 136–150. Thomas Weiss also pointed out that the consensus building around RtoP must be understood in the context of the 2003 invasion of Iraq. The UN was sidelined in the war against Iraq, and it could not impede U.S. hegemony, and also could not approve requisite action against Saddam Hussein. See T.G. Weiss, "R2P after 9/11 and the World Summit," *Wisconsin International Law Journal*, 24:3, 2006, pp. 741–760. Online. Available at: http://hosted.law.wisc.edu/wordpress/wilj/files/2012/02/weiss.pdf (accessed 4 August 2012).

10 2005 World Summit Outcome document states: "Section IV. Human rights and the rule of law: 138. Each individual State has the responsibility to protect its populations from genocide, war crimes, ethnic cleansing and crimes against humanity. This responsibility entails the prevention of such crimes, including their incitement, through appropriate and necessary means. We accept that responsibility and will act in accordance with it. The international community should, as appropriate, encourage and help States to exercise this responsibility and support the United Nations in establishing an early warning capability. Section 139. The international community, through the United Nations, also has the responsibility to use appropriate diplomatic, humanitarian and other peaceful means, in accordance with Chapters VI and VIII of the Charter, to help protect populations from genocide, war crimes, ethnic cleansing and crimes against humanity. In this context, we are prepared to take collective action, in a timely and decisive manner, through the Security Council, in accordance with the Charter, including Chapter VII, on a case-by-case basis and in cooperation with relevant regional organizations as appropriate, should peaceful means be inadequate and national authorities manifestly fail to protect their populations from genocide, war crimes, ethnic cleansing and crimes against humanity. We stress the need for the General Assembly to continue consideration of the responsibility to protect populations from genocide, war crimes, ethnic cleansing and crimes against humanity and its implications, bearing in mind the principles of the Charter and international law. We also intend to commit ourselves, as necessary and appropriate, to helping States build capacity to protect their populations from genocide, war crimes, ethnic cleansing and crimes against humanity and to assisting those which are under stress before crises and conflicts break out." United Nations General Assembly, 2005 World Summit Outcome. 15 September, 2005. Online. Available at: http://responsibilitytoprotect.org/world%20summit%20outcome%20doc%202005(1).pdf. (accessed 4 April, 2012).

11 B. Ki-Moon, *Implementing the Responsibility to Protect*, A/63/677, 12 January, 2000.

12 ICISS, The Responsibility to Protect, 2005. Online. Available at: http://responsibilitytoprotect.org/ICISS%20Report.pdf (accessed 30 April, 2012).

13 Ibid.
14 T. Hurka, "Proportionality in the Morality of War," *Philosophy and Public Affairs*, 33, 2005, p.37. Interestingly, Hurka emphasized this relationship between means and ends in just war theory. Outlining a measurement of relevant good and relevant evil, he suggested that the proportionality principle can help assess if a course of action can bring about a reasonable chance of success as well as determine the last resort by weighing the probable effects of alternatives that are not chosen as well as the magnitude of evils the war prevented. Further, he proposed that particular acts in a war should only be evaluated as a relevant good when it contributes to just causes, by way of increasing the probability or degree of the achievement of these causes. This would mean that whether "an act in war is *in bello* proportionate depends on the relevant good it does, which in turn depends on its *ad bellum* causes" because we cannot maintain independence between *ad bellum* and *in bello* when considering morality of war and not matters of legality.
15 D. Luban, "Preventive War," *Philosophy and Public Affairs*, 32(3), 2004, p. 209.
16 Ibid., p. 230.
17 Ibid., p. 210.
18 Ibid., p. 214.
19 F. Tesón, "Ending Tyranny in Iraq." Tesón viewed the regime change in Iraq as just cause for humanitarian intervention, while most supporters of the Iraq war, like Michael Walzer, advanced arguments of self-defense in the face of weapons of mass destruction as just cause.
20 Alex Bellamy outlined the common preventive agenda of RtoP to consist of structural, direct and escalation prevention and argued that it is not possible to identify a narrower set of measures that targets the prevention of mass atrocities. I think structural prevention is still dangerously permissive according to my argument because they can be used to justify regime changes. A more detailed discussion is unfortunately beyond the scope of this chapter. See A. Bellamy, "Mass Atrocities and Armed Conflict: Links, Distinctions, and Implications for the Responsibility to Prevent," *The Stanley Foundation Policy Analysis Brief*, February 2011. Online. Available at http://www.stanleyfoundation.org/publications/pab/BellamyPAB22011.pdf (accessed 20 April, 2012).
21 Ibid.
22 Tesón on the other hand would argue that the Iraq intervention is humanitarian by intent, even if it is not apparent that its motive is humanitarian in nature. I am unfortunately unable to address this argument in detail for the purpose of this discussion here.
23 Since the adoption of the Six-Point Proposal of the Joint Special Envoy of the United Nations and the League of Arab States spelt out by the Security Council Resolution 2042 (2012) on 14 April, the envoys led by Kofi Annan have been unable to obtain any positive outcome from their mediation efforts since the conflict began. The Security Council members remain divided over which measures may make the Syrian government carry out UN demands. To date, Russia and China have vetoed three Security Councils and this disagreement eventually led to the resignation of Kofi Annan as the international peace envoy to Syria. Already, the U.S., the U.K. and France are considering a coalition of the willing in light of the gravity of the situation at the time of writing. See Security Council resolution 2042 (2012) of 14 April. Online. Available at: http://www.un.org/en/peacekeeping/documents/six_point_proposal.pdf (accessed 7 August, 2012).
24 Under Chapter VII of the UN Charter, the Security Council has the authority to "determine the existence of any threat to the peace, breach of the peace, or act of aggression and shall make recommendations, or decide what measures shall be taken in accordance with Articles 41 and 42, to maintain or restore international peace and security." One of the six *jus ad bellum* principles also requires that for a war to be considered just it must be waged by a legitimate authority.
25 Security Council SC/10187/Rev.1. 26 February, 2011. Online. Available at: http://www.un.org/News/Press/docs/2011/sc10187.doc.htm (accessed 4 April, 2012).
26 Barbara Miller, "Defiant Gaddafi Issues Chilling Threat," ABC (Australia), February 23, 2011. Online. Available at: http://www.abc.net.au/worldtoday/content/2011/s3146582.htm (accessed 4 April, 2012).
27 Resolution 1973 adopted on 17 March considers "the widespread and systematic attacks [currently] taking place in the Libyan Arab Jamahiriya against the civilian population [as] amount[ing] to crimes against humanity." The UN demanded immediate ceasefire and stressed the need to intensify efforts to find a solution. Spelling out a range of nonmilitary options (enforcing a no-fly zone, assets freeze, arms embargo, and bans on flights), it determined that "the situation in the Libyan Arab Jamahiriya continues to constitute a threat to international peace and security," and authorized Member States "to

take all necessary measures … to protect civilian and civilian populated areas under threat of attack in the Libyan Arab Jamahiriya, including Benghazi, while excluding a foreign occupation force." On 16 September, it adopted Resolution 2009 that established a UN Support Mission to Libya and unanimously reaffirmed NATO's mandate to protect civilians in Libya.

28 David Rieff, "R2P, R.I.P," *The New York Times*, 7 November, 2011. Online. Available at: http://www.nytimes.com/2011/11/08/opinion/r2p-rip.html?pagewanted=all (accessed 4 August, 2012).

29 The Security Council passed resolution 688 declaring the situation as constituting a threat to international peace and security, and demanding an end to the repression only after mounting international pressure. Despite international pressure, the Security Council did not authorize the use of force and instead authorized Operation Provide Comfort to set up safe havens.

30 The UN Security Council twice condemned the situation in Kosovo as a threat to international peace and security, but did not authorize the use of force or intervention. NATO justified this unilateral attack on humanitarian grounds in spite of the absence of *opinion juris* necessary to endorse state practice of this nature.

31 D. Rieff, "R2P, R.I.P," *The New York Times*, 7 November, 2011, Online. Available at: http://www.nytimes.com/2011/11/08/opinion/r2p-rip.html?pagewanted=all (accessed 4 August, 2012).

32 Ibid. Alex Bellamy and Tim Dunne understood Rieff's criticism slightly differently. They agreed with Rieff that supporters of RtoP ought to be mourning rather than celebrating because "intervention is only needed when prevention has failed". See A. Bellamy and T. Dunne, "'Responsibility to Protect' on Trial – or Assad?" *Ethics and International Affairs*, 2012. Online. Available at: http://www.ethicsand-internationalaffairs.org/2012/responsibility-to-protect-on-trial-or-assad-3/ (accessed 4 April, 2012).

33 Thomas Nagel in "War and Massacre" explained the blind moral alley as a moral dilemma of dirty hands – one between utilitarian computations of *what will happen* (weighing between choice of action based on postulated outcome) and an absolute prohibition of certain actions being carried out to achieve any of these ends. Nagel argues, "[u]tilitarianism gives primacy to a concern with what will *happen*. Absolutism gives primacy to a concern with what one is *doing*. The conflict between them arises because the alternatives we face are rarely just choices between total outcomes: they are also choices between alternative pathways or measures to be taken. When one of the choices is to do terrible things to another person, the problem is altered fundamentally; it is no longer merely a question of which outcome would be worse." T. Nagel, 'War and Massacre," in *Mortal Questions*, Cambridge: Cambridge University Press, 1991, p. 54.

34 Amnesty International, *Annual Report 2012*. Online. Available at: http://www.amnesty.org/en/region/afghanistan/report-2012 (accessed 4 August, 2012).

35 According to William V. O'Brien in W.V. O'Brien, "The Meaning of Military Necessity in International Law," *1 World Polity 109*, 1957, p. 113, military necessity is defined as consisting of "all measures immediately indispensable and proportionate to a legitimate military end, provided that they are not prohibited by the laws of war or the natural law, when taken on the decision of a responsible commander subject to a judicial review."

36 J. Pattison, "The Ethics of Humanitarian Intervention in Libya," *Ethics and International Affairs*, 2011, pp. 1–7. Other observations made by Pattison that further support my argument that the operation was for humanitarian ends and not regime change include: 1. military targets selected for bombing were largely those that were a clear threat to civilians, 2. the coalition did not arm the rebels or deploy ground troops that would have been necessary for regime change, and 3. a limited scope of intervention was observed.

37 "East Timor – UNMISET – Background." Online. Availble at http://www.un.org/en/peacekeeping/missions/past/unmiset/background.html (accessed 4 August 2012).

38 It was also successful on other fronts. There were no other Western powers ready to take on the lead with US, and the UK was heavily engaged in Kosovo. Not only did Australia take the lead, it was also able to gather a multinational force and financial assistance from other countries. Domestically, it also received strong support from the Australian public.

39 A.A. Lachica, "Humanitarian Intervention in East Timor: An Analysis of Australia's Leadership Role," *The Peace and Conflict Review*, 5:2, 2001. Online. Available at: http://www.review.upeace.org/index.cfm?opcion=0&ejemplar=22&entrada=113 (accessed 30 July 2012).

40 It demanded for the Yugoslav military and police presence in Kosovo to return to pre-war levels, to allow monitoring by 2,000 international inspectors, known as the Kosovo Verification Mission (KVM), and to allow for NATO to make reconnaissance flights. However, the KLA on the other hand, was not bound to the ceasefire provisions of Resolution 1199.

41 U.S. Department of State "Erasing History: Ethnic Cleansing in Kosovo" *Report released by the U.S. Department of State*, 1999. Online, available at: http://www.state.gov/www/regions/eur/rpt_9905_ethnic_ksvo_toc.html (accessed 4 August, 2012).

42 Human Rights Watch, "Abuses against Serbs and Roma in the New Kosovo" *Human Rights Watch*, 11:10, 1999. Online. Available at: http://www.hrw.org/reports/1999/kosov2/ (accessed 4 August, 2012).

References

Amnesty International, *Annual Report 2012*. Online. Available at: http://www.amnesty.org/en/region/afghanistan/report-2012 (accessed 4 August, 2012).

Annan, K., "Two Concepts of Sovereignty," *The Economist*, 16 September, 1999. Available at: http://www.economist.com/node/324795 (accessed 27 March, 2013).

Bellamy, A. "Mass Atrocities and Armed Conflict: Links, Distinctions, and Implications for the Responsibility to Prevent," *The Stanley Foundation Policy Analysis Brief*, 2011. Online. Available at: http://www.stanleyfoundation.org/publications/pab/BellamyPAB22011.pdf (accessed 20 April, 2012)

Bellamy, A., *Responsibility to Protect: The Global Effort to End Mass Atrocities*. Cambridge: Polity Press, 2009.

Bellamy, A. and Dunne, T. ""Responsibility to Protect" on Trial – or Assad?" *Ethics and International Affairs*, 2012. Online. Available at: http://www.ethicsandinternationalaffairs.org/2012/responsibility-to-protect-on-trial-or-assad-3 (accessed 4 April, 2012).

Coady, T. and O'Keefe, M. (eds), *Righteous Violence: The Ethics and Politics of Military Intervention*. Victoria: Melbourne University Press, 2005.

Evans, G., *The Responsibility to Protect: Ending Mass Atrocity Crimes Once and for All*. Washington: Brookings Institution Press, 2008.

Feinstein, L. and A.-M. Slaughter, "A Duty to Prevent," *Foreign Affairs*, 83:1, 2004, pp. 136–150.

Hurka, T. "Proportionality in the Morality of War," *Philosophy and Public Affairs*, 33(1), 2005, pp. 34–66.

ICISS, *The Responsibility to Protect*, 2005. Online. Available at: http://responsibilitytoprotect.org/ICISS%20Report.pdf (accessed 4 April, 2012).

Ki-Moon, B., *Implementing the Responsibility to Protect*, A/63/677, 12 January, 2000.

Lachica, A.A., "Humanitarian Intervention in East Timor: An Analysis of Australia's Leadership Role," *The Peace and Conflict Review*, 5:2, 2001.

Luban, D., "Preventive War," *Philosophy and Public Affairs*, 32, 2004, pp. 207–248.

Luck, C.E., "The United Nations and the Responsibility to Protect," *The Stanley Foundation Policy Analysis Brief*, August 2008. Online. Available at: http://humansecuritygateway.com/documents/TSF_theUNandR2P.pdf (accessed 4 August, 2012).

Miller, B., "Defiant Gaddaffi Issues Chilling Threat," ABC (Australia), 23 February, 2011. Online. Available at http://www.abc.net.au/worldtoday/content/2011/s3146582.htm (accessed 4 April, 2012).

Miller, S., "Collective Responsibility and Armed Humanitarian Intervention," in T. Coady and M. O'Keefe (eds), *Righteous Violence: The Ethics and Politics of Military Intervention*. Victoria: Melbourne University Press, 2005. pp. 51–71.

Nagel, T., "War and Massacre," in *Mortal Questions*, Cambridge: Cambridge University Press, 1991.

O'Brien, W.V., "The Meaning of Military Necessity in International Law," *1 World Polity 109*, 1957, pp. 109–176.

Pattison, J., "The Ethics of Humanitarian Intervention in Libya," *Ethics and International Affairs*: 2001, pp. 1–7.

Rieff, D. "R2P, R.I.P", *The New York Times*, 7 November, 2011. Online. Available at: http://www.nytimes.com/2011/11/08/opinion/r2p-rip.html?pagewanted=all (accessed 4 August, 2012).

Security Council SC/10187/Rev.1. 26 February 2011. Online. Available at: http://www.un.org/News/Press/docs/2011/sc10187.doc.htm (accessed 4 April, 2012).

Security Council SC/10200. 17 March 2011. Online. Available at: http://www.un.org/News/Press/docs/2011/sc10200.doc.htm#Resolution (accessed 4 April, 2012).

Security Council SC/10389. 16 September 2011. Online. Available at: http://www.un.org/News/Press/docs/2011/sc10389.doc.htm (accessed 4 April, 2012).

Security Council Resolution 2042 (2012) of 14 April. Online. Available at: http://www.un.org/en/peacekeeping/documents/six_point_proposal.pdf (accessed 7 August, 2012).

Schmitt, M.N., "Precision Attack and International Humanitarian Law," *International Review of the Red Cross*, 87, 2005, pp. 445–66.

Shue, H., "Targeting Civilian Infrastructure with Smart Bombs: The New Permissiveness," *Philosophy and Public Policy Quarterly*," 30, 2012, pp. 2–7.

Tesón, F., "Ending Tyranny in Iraq," *Ethics and International Affairs*, 19:2, 2005, pp. 1–20.

United Nations General Assembly, 2005 World Summit Outcome. 15 September 2005. Online. Available at http://responsibilitytoprotect.org/world%20summit%20outcome%20doc%202005(1).pdf (accessed 4 April, 2012).

United Nations General Assembly, "2009 Report: Implementing the Responsibility to Protect," 12 January 2009. Online. Available at http://responsibilitytoprotect.org/SGRtoPEng%20(4).pdf (accessed 30 April, 2012).

UNMISET, "East Timor – UNMISET – Background." Online. Available at: http://www.un.org/en/peacekeeping/missions/past/unmiset/background.html (accessed 4 August, 2012).

U.S. Department of State "Erasing History: Ethnic Cleansing in Kosovo," 2009. Online. Available at http://www.state.gov/www/regions/eur/rpt_9905_ethnic_ksvo_toc.html (accessed 4 August, 2012).

Weiss, G. T., *Humanitarian Intervention*. Cambridge: Polity Press, 2007.

——"R2P after 9/11 and the World Summit," *Wisconsin International Law Journal*, 24:3, 2006, pp. 741–760. Online. Available at: http://hosted.law.wisc.edu/wordpress/wilj/files/2012/02/weiss.pdf (accessed 4 August, 2012).

Welsh, J. M. and M. Banda, "International Law and the Responsibility to Protect: Clarifying or Expanding States Responsibilities?" *Global Responsibility to Protect*, 2:2, 2010, pp. 213–231.

14

PEACEKEEPER VIOLENCE

Managing the use of force[1]

Daniel H. Levine

1. Introduction

[T]he images of war handed to us, even when they are graphic, leave out the one essential element of war—fear.[2]

Peacekeeping Operations (PKOs) are authorized to use force and violence to consolidate peace. One reaction to this is to dismiss it as an oxymoron. A different approach, more common among analysts and defenders of peacekeeping, is to see peacekeeping as a limited form of war, distinguished from other forms of warfare by its object rather than by its nature.

In this chapter, I hope to show that both viewpoints are problematic, but a careful conceptualization of violence in peacekeeping missions is possible, and should impact on the way peacekeepers conduct themselves.

My argument has two parts. First, I will discuss the ways in which violence impacts not only the armed groups against which peacekeepers may wield it, but the broader population. Then I will argue that peacekeepers cannot eliminate the trauma that their use of violence, however controlled it may be, tends to inflict, but must recognize its effects in order to maintain a morally acceptable and practically effective relationship with the people among whom they operate.

Peacekeepers must worry about sowing fear, chaos, and non-political violence in a way that few warfighters must, because of the nature of their task. The goal of peacekeepers is not, or should not be, simply to "pacify" an area. Rather, given their goal of long-term stability and respect for human rights, they should aim at "participatory peace," characterized not only by a lack of violence, but at least "a minimal degree of political assent and participation."[3] Such peace involves the creation of social bonds and relationships that bind former enemies into a unified polity. As a result, peacekeepers who use violence should engage in relationship-restoring practices of communication and mourning aimed especially at the groups and individuals they target.

2. What is peacekeeping?

I use the United Nations' (UN) "capstone doctrine" definition of peacekeeping.[4] "Peacekeeping is a technique designed to preserve the peace, however fragile, where fighting has been halted, and to assist in implementing agreements achieved by the peacemakers ... [it incorporates] a complex model of many elements—military, police and civilian—working together to help lay the foundations for sustainable peace."[5] Peacekeeping is distinct from peace*making* (primarily diplomatic efforts to resolve a conflict) and post-conflict peace*building* (long-term enhancement of state capacities to prevent future violence).

PKOs are complex operations, comprising everything from diplomatic, humanitarian, and legal personnel to military and police. In this chapter, since I am interested in the use of violence, I will focus on peacekeeping *troops*, armed soldiers deployed with PKOs. Some of my remarks may also be relevant to police with an executive mandate, especially para-military "formed police units."[6]

In practice, and for purposes of this discussion, the most important and trickiest distinction is between peace*keeping* and peace *enforcement*, which is the use of military force to compel an end to a conflict. Peacekeepers are often authorized "to 'use all necessary means' [the standard UN jargon for the authorization to use force] to deter forceful attempts to disrupt the political process, protect civilians under imminent threat of physical attack, and/or assist the national authorities in maintaining law and order." PKOs are still distinguished from peace enforcement, in principle at least, by the fact that peacekeepers are authorized to use force only at the "tactical" and not the "strategic" level. The doctrine does not precisely define the distinction, but explicates it by saying that "[t]he ultimate aim of the use of force is to influence and deter spoilers working against the peace process or seeking to harm civilians; and *not to seek their military defeat*."[7] In Sir Brian Urquhart's words, "peacekeeping forces [have] no 'enemies,' just a series of difficult and sometimes homicidal clients."[8]

The ultimate goal of a PKO is not to bring about any particular resolution to the conflict, but to work with locals to create a new political situation in which differences are resolved otherwise than through the use of force. This is as much a moral recognition of the right of self-determination as a practical consideration.

A cooperative perspective does not require peacekeepers to be *neutral*, in the sense of not criticizing or acting against any party, but it does require a degree of *impartiality*. The UN doctrine defines "impartiality" as an even-handed adherence to the mandate, and a willingness to take action to stop threats to the peace process.[9] The centrality of the peace process, however fragmentary or fragile, to the concept of impartiality drives home that, even when action may be taken against a party, it is in the context of an aspiration to cooperation with them. The parties, at least tentatively and conditionally, have taken their own steps toward peace that peacekeepers support by serving as impartial guarantors.[10] Because this aim extends to including the "homicidal clients" in the new order, it means that peacekeepers do not simply use force for different or more limited goals than warfighters do. They use force in the context of a radically different relationship to the targets of that force, and one that gives them different collateral obligations to the use of violence than warfighters have. Violent incident-by-incident peacekeeping may look much like war; the difference should be in what surrounds those incidents.

3. Violence in peacekeeping

While no just war theorist could be accused of ignoring the badness of killing or death, it easily fades into the background in favor of discussions of liability, military advantage, and the like. When Walzer writes that "[w]ar kills; that is all it does," it is to quickly move on to a discussion of how we cannot dwell on the fact that war kills but must ask whether the good it achieves outweighs the death.[11] When Coady updates Walzer's quip to, "[w]ar kills, sure enough; but it also maims, distorts, and injures in many complex, enduring ways," he too "intends to show the horror of war," but does so in the context of explaining why, despite this, there would be a demand for just war theory—a demand the remainder of his book aims to satisfy.[12] Both Walzer's and Coady's books are exemplary pieces of just war theory, but tend to de-center and abstract from the actual violence of warfare.

Peacekeepers, unlike warfighters, commonly undertake tasks in which violence very much *is* beside the point, tasks that are crucial to the mission but are only violent if they are opposed by a spoiler group.

Peacekeepers may help deliver food, reconstruct roadways, and the like. Though these are non-military tasks, military peacekeepers may have an advantage in performing them. The fact that peacekeepers are *able* to use violence to defend themselves may make them able to conduct such activities in areas where violence is still endemic. We should also remember that military units may be conceptually characterized by their access to the tools of violence, but in reality they often have logistical capacities available to few other actors—military peacekeepers may be the best people to deliver food because they have the best access to heavy cargo vehicles.

There are *literal, physical* ways to enforce outcomes that inherently involve confrontation as well. Peacekeepers may be able to halt or mitigate attacks on civilians by building a literal wall around them, or creating checkpoints where weapons can be physically removed with (if all goes well) minimal violence. Armed opposition forces can be disarmed. Peacekeepers can create alternate patterns of movement for civilians, using either their military intelligence or practical know-how, to keep them out of the line of fire. For instance, a Rwandan officer told me with pride how, as a member of the African Union Mission in Sudan (AMIS), he taught internally displaced women how to build more fuel-efficient Rwandan-style ovens so that they would have to make fewer vulnerable trips for firewood.[13]

It is important to distinguish these operations that may involve *coercion* and *force* from the use of *violence* because violence is specially problematic for peacekeepers.

As Scarry emphasizes, physical violence is central to military operations—at their heart is "the body maimed, the body in pain, the body dead and hard to dispose of … the sheer material weight of multitudes of damaged and opened human bodies."[14] If we pretend that it is not, we will miss important aspects of the moral analysis. We should not pretend that military confrontation usually proceeds by threatening one side until it complies, with actual violent clashes only a marginal issue, and so think only in terms of the balance of incentives and how spoilers can be induced to stop their activities. In fact, analysts often criticize peacekeepers for focusing on "deterrence through presence" (i.e., the idea that merely having peacekeepers present will cause spoilers to stand down, even if the PKO may not be prepared to win a fight), remarking that the needed credibility for such a strategy is often only established through the actual use of violence.[15]

For PKOs, the basic issue is that violence is *traumatizing*—it inflicts psychological damage on both its direct targets and the broader political communities in which it operates that disrupts their social bonds. This is not a marginal effect that can be, at least in principle, entirely eliminated. It is precisely the damage to social bonds both within the combatant groups directly targeted and the political communities that support them that erodes their cohesion and ability to fight, giving violence its particular power.[16] But this psychological impact undermines the peacekeeper's goal of helping to build a new, cohesive political community capable of operating peacefully.

4. War as mass trauma

In order to understand the traumatic impact of violence, it helps to start with the most "desirable" site of that trauma (for those dishing it out, at least), the disruption of combatant groups.

Soldiers do not give up a fight because they have changed their beliefs—their beliefs may be inchoate while they fight, and they may bitterly resent defeat. Soldiers are instead overcome by fear of death, fear of "letting others down" (and the related fear of or actual collapse of the military social group), loss of hope and frustration at the perceived futility of their mission, sheer physical exhaustion, and the psychologically draining effects of guilt, horror, and hatred.[17,18] Much of this has little to do with belief (e.g. soldiers experience guilt and horror even when they believe their cause is just) and is instead a matter of creating psychological barriers to further action, that function on a level below conscious will.

4.1 Political trauma

Ultimately, war is not about the soldiers, but about the political entity that stands behind them. Disrupting the morale of soldiers, making them into "psychiatric casualties," can win *battles*, but the *war* is not ended until the polity supporting the military ends it. In principle, new soldiers can always be thrown into the breach, whether the old are killed or incapacitated. Of course, this rapidly becomes inefficient, and it is easier and easier to slaughter enemy combatants as the social and material base behind them degrades, and each wave is more poorly trained and more poorly equipped—but we never get to the point of literal inability to fight until the polity is completely annihilated (or, perhaps, reduced to young children and the elderly).

Using violence to change the behavior of organized groups is not an exact science, however.

At least since the Greeks portrayed Ares as accompanied by Eris, it has been a commonplace that violence is chaotic. Clausewitz claimed that "[n]o other human activity is so continuously or universally bound up with chance."[19] And Arendt: "nowhere does Fortuna, good or ill luck, play a more fateful role in human affairs that on the battlefield, and this intrusion of the utterly unexpected does not disappear when people call it a 'random event' … nor can it be eliminated by simulations, scenarios, game theories, and the like."[20] I see no reason to doubt these claims.

The chaos of violence has two aspects. First, the effect even on its intended targets is not simple. Trauma disrupts social connections (more on this below) but can also create new, unpredictable ones. Fear can cause people to cling to primary identities in a way that they did not when other connections were intact. Anger can be a source of shared purpose that may cause new violent groups to form, or previously non-violent groups to turn on peacekeepers or others in society. Even if the power and coherence of a group is shattered, some other group can take advantage, or a crowd or mob with limited cohesion and unpredictable and often violent character can form.[21]

These side effects may be irrelevant to the goal of defeating an organized enemy, and may be morally beside the point for a warfighter—if banditry and revenge killings become widespread after a war, a military intent on repulsing interstate aggression may not care. But peacekeepers are as concerned with the post-conflict order that emerges as with breaking down hostile/obstructionist centers of order in the conflict.

Second, even with the most circumspect weaponry, the psychological impacts will reverberate down social connections. Deterrence through changing incentives can be relatively narrowly focused on particular acts. And this is *part* of what violence does. But an important part of what distinguishes violence from other sorts of violence is that its traumatizing psychological impact undermines social cohesion more generally.

As Arendt puts it:

> the danger of violence … will always be that the means overwhelm the end. If goals are not achieved rapidly, the result will be not merely defeat but the introduction of the practice of violence into the whole body politic. Action is irreversible, and a return to the *status quo* in case of defeat is always unlikely. The practice of violence, like all action, changes the world, but the most probable change is to a more violent world.[22]

These are not just philosophers' laments. Doyle and Sambanis' statistical analysis of peacekeeping and peacebuilding efforts in civil conflicts found that the numbers of people killed and displaced in a war had a negative, statistically significant effect on the likelihood that the area would be at peace two years after the peacekeeping intervention ended.[23] Homicide rates in post-conflict nations rise.[24] Civilians affected by war have significantly elevated levels of Acute Stress Disorder and Post-Traumatic Stress Disorder (PTSD).[25]

These psychological impacts have physical and social repercussions. Fear and reflexive responses to it—hair loss, ulcers, and the like—were so embedded in the body politic of London during World War II that advertisers used it to sell products. "(1) Do you jump when a bus backfires? (2) Does worry bring sleepless nights? (3) Are you spotty? (4) Are the whites of your eyes muddy? (5) Are you puffed out after running upstairs?" asked a 1940 laxative advertisement.[26]

The fear in London also exacerbated racial and class tensions, with contemporary accounts often expressing anxiety that Jews or working-class Londoners would sow seeds of panic.[27] Trauma seems to exploit social ties at the same time that it undermines them. Kosovar civilians who lost family members during the 1990s wars showed statistically significantly higher rates of psychological damage, including PTSD, than "non-bereaved" individuals, even when controlling for number and severity of direct wartime trauma.[28]

These wounds make it difficult to maintain communal action. Characteristic symptoms of PTSD are emotional numbness, hopelessness, and difficulty maintaining relationships.[29] Experiences of pain, fear, and violence, seem to shape the way individuals interact with other human beings. The subject of violence will shrink reflexively from those she perceives as able to use further violence. But she is also likely to model violent domination of those weaker than she is, having had more pro-social patterns of behavior partly or completely beaten out of her, thus "infecting" others with social models ripe for numbed obedience but damaging to collective action and identity. In discussing the use of corporal punishment on children, Ruddick argues that "the social construction of a child's body as a vulnerable locus of pain seems a preparation for later public domination and submission."[30] She echoes this comment later in discussing the body in war: "[t]he salient feature of war's body is its susceptibility to pain and damage that lead to surrender."[31]

4.2 Violence and embodiment

One of the reasons that the effects of violence are so difficult to precisely contain, and so dangerous for peacekeepers, is that "psychological" trauma operates on an emotional and even physiological level not fully subject to conscious control. Just as soldiers can experience trauma from killing even if they believe fully in the righteousness of their cause, part of what makes violence specially effective and specially problematic is that its traumatic effects operate on a sub-rational and non-rational level. Conceived in terms of pure utility calculations, a person can probably do as much damage (if not more) to me by, say, firing me from my job as by shooting me in the arm. But pulling a gun will secure most people's immediate compliance, before they even calculate the odds—the exceptions being individuals like soldiers who are *trained* to have different automatic responses to violence and the threat of violence.[32]

Violence's involvement of the *body* should make its non-rational impacts unsurprising. Understanding the interplay of the psychological, social, and bodily in violence (the theme of this section) will set us up to say something useful about how peacekeepers can address the trauma of their violence (the theme of the next).

A field anecdote drives home the fact that violence is effective on a deep, non-rational level that crosses the "mind" and the "body." A Ghanaian member of the UN staff told me about his encounter with an elderly Darfuri woman during his service in AMIS:

> And, I remember we brought an aircraft, I think AN-12 [an Antonov cargo plane, similar to those used by the Sudanese government to bomb civilian areas] or something, and the lady, one old lady who lived in the IDP [internally displaced person] camp was weeping, she wanted to come and touch it … She touched it and she started crying … She only knew what Antonov had done to her. So when we brought this in, because this flies over the village, the sound was very familiar. Then she was going to hide when her niece told her, no no no no no, this is for the African Union. It's here for peace. She says she doesn't believe it. So they brought her, and she said she wanted to know what type of thing they were using to, you know, kill their people. And I was thinking, that's the first time she was able to touch that.[33]

Violence functions as an element of "political physiology," to use Protevi's term. Political physiology is the "direct interaction of the social and the somatic, skipping the subjective level."[34] Political physiology enters play when, for instance, we are exhausted from witnessing another's grief. Its sub-rational effects are clearest in cases where our emotional response is at odds with our conscious attitudes, such as when we react to facial cues from other human beings as if the human possessed full personhood even if we know intellectually that their brains have been severely damaged and the facial cues are simply involuntary tics.[35]

Violence against bodies damages social connections in part because they are built in an embodied way.

We only think of political communities as voluntary and conscious contracts if we forget we were born. "[B]irthing," Ruddick writes, "is indelibly a social relation, a fact that only a radical distinction between mind and body can disguise."[36] The process by which human relationships are created is one in which total bodily union eventually gives way to individuation, but an individuation that is never totally independent. The ideal of a body fully under control of a will is at best only imperfectly realized by human beings who depend on support networks, who get sick, who act on emotions spurred by biological systems, and who die.[37] And the ability to build and maintain those support networks and connections has its substrate in the combined physical and social relationships exemplified by birthing, mothering, and sexuality, as well as less charged physical rituals, like sharing meals.

In a traumatized polity, the experience of violence, transmitted through proximity and social relations, disrupts processes that allow corporate action on a physical–psychological level. Individuals who may once have been willing to risk death or sacrifice to feed their polity's war machine find their reserves of adrenaline hammered through the stress of warfare and exposure to violence—and may even find them depleted by proxy reactions to seeing injured comrades, losing family members to violence, etc.—a physical limit they experience as fear, exhaustion, or war-weariness.

5. Peacekeepers and traumatic violence

5.1 Humanizing violence

As noted above, one of Ruddick's insights is that the construction of the body as a site of pain, either in child abuse or war, is preparation for relationships of domination and submission. This is the ramification of violence down embodied social connections. Traumatized bodies, and bodies adapted to situations of domination and violence have had undermined their ability to engage in the "active connectedness" that Ruddick (persuasively) identifies with peace, people "resist[ing] others' violence and their own temptations to abandon or assault, persisting in relationships that include anger, disappointment, difference, conflict, and nonviolent battle."[38] That active connectedness is undermined by fear that the physical proximity involved in social connection will lead to vulnerability to violence, and habituation to the non-rational immediate obedience that violence can obtain. It is also a good description of what peacekeepers aim at.

Part of the insight of this description of peace is that it centrally recognizes that peace is not a matter of harmonious fellow-feeling, but precisely of finding ways to build relationships in the face of power-undermining emotions and reflexes. Though she presents mothering as a paradigm of peaceful practice, Ruddick *opens* her substantive account of mothering with violence—telling an anecdote of a mother so overwhelmed by frustration, sleep-deprivation, isolation, and the demands of her infant that she bundles the child up and takes it on the bus in the middle of the night, because she will not be able to give in to her temptation to violence in public.[39] The human condition of relationships is that we recognize and deal with our temptations to hurt and dominate others, not that we become saints incapable of violence—and that we realize that others who do give in to these temptations are humans and not monsters.

Peacekeepers may come to relate to armed individuals primarily as sources of unreasoning violence, such as in Gen. Cammaert's "armed groups who have conducted barbaric attacks with guns, spears and/or machetes."[40] It is difficult to read graphic accounts of rapes, mutilations, and other atrocities in Bosnia, Sierra Leone, Liberia, or the DRC, and then imagine the perpetrators (mostly, but not exclusively men) as young boys, nursing from their mothers or giggling with other children. Yet they were, and even after becoming combatants, they are not murderous all day, every day—they may fall in love, they may eat with friends, they may laugh and play with their own children. If peacekeepers do not recognize this, a relationship with such individuals may become near literally "unthinkable," because of the way that the emotions that structure our thinking interfere. Yet, an undistorted picture of peace may need to involve building relationships that include such abusers and certainly needs to understand the relationships that they have with other people in the society.

What peacekeepers need is some way of *re-humanizing* the enemy in the context of violence—in their own minds, and the society—even when they must kill.

As mortal beings, we have many social resources for humanizing the injured and dead, as long as we know where to look. There is a tendency to think of death as a transcendent, totally individuating moment, but this is at least partly another fantasy of disembodiment. Of course, there is something unsharable in the very moment of death (as there is in the very moment of giving birth or being born). But real human deaths are extended, messy, and tightly interwoven into social practices.[41] As Ruddick puts it:

> A full appreciation of the capacity rooted in birth includes an understanding that death must be tended and cared for. A death that is cared for is actively non-violent. Those who mitigate pain and assuage fear are engaged in a discipline of intellect and action contradictory to the planned cruelty of a claymore mine or a napalm bomb. Tended deaths, like

war deaths, are neither romantic nor heroic. Dying bodies stumble, smell, forget, leak, fester, shake, and gasp ... whereas military strategies note the body's vulnerabilities merely to exploit them ... caretakers perceive pain and decay accurately to comfort an embodied being.[42]

In the peacekeeping context, a big part of humanizing the targets of violence is recognizing that even the "barbaric" enemies peacekeepers face leave behind friends, kin, acquaintances, co-religionists, enemies, etc. who will be bereaved, sickened, angered, elated, or frustrated at their passing—and that they themselves die in ways that reflect the physical vulnerability we share. Violence works precisely by exploiting this physical vulnerability that embeds us in social ties.[43] Our embodiment, of course, gives a vector for physical violence and makes us vulnerable. Our embodied connections to others also transmit the fear and anger that make violence unpredictable and effective. The effect of these deaths, especially if "untended," cannot be completely silenced by the peacekeepers' abstract moral justification.

These ties also give a vector for responding to violence. The trick is to make the deaths of those peacekeepers must kill "grievable." Butler focuses on the obituary as a piece of public mourning that, crucially, *particularizes* the dead. "[T]o be an obituary, there would have had to have been a life, a life worth noting, a life worth valuing and preserving, a life that qualifies for recognition."[44] Peacekeepers may not use the Western-culture bound obituary, but it is an example of a broader family of practices of recognizing the particular humanity of the dead and the tragedy of their passing.

5.2 The tactics of mourning

The core way that peacekeepers can and should respond to their own use of violence is to engage in rituals of recognition that the violence is tragic. In the abstract, it is hard to say more—the appropriate rituals may well be very context- and culture-specific (like obituaries). Learning how they can express mourning in their particular context should be considered an obligation of peacekeepers that use or may use violence. But there are likely to be certain common elements, such as refraining from triumphalism about those peacekeepers kill (straightforwardly identifying a willingness to kill members of spoiler groups with "protecting civilians" is problematic) and publicly extending the possibility to renew relationships to individuals and groups that have been the subject of peacekeeper violence. In general, peacekeepers should remember the insights of Ruddick and the woman who needed to touch the Antonov—beliefs and attitudes are not enough, but rituals must be observed and concrete action taken. Even the obituary is not just an abstract "narrative"; the fact that it is a widely reproduced cultural item is important. Butler does not linger on it, but the obituary is also tied up with other acts of mourning and grief. It is something that the bereaved can read to reaffirm the feeling that the dead mattered, and it is an artifact they can show to others as an act of communicating their grief. In the culture I share with Butler, it is a form of communal recognition, of a piece with the creation of spaces where it is socially acceptable for people to cry and in other ways give voice to the pain of their loss. Peacekeepers may need to cry with people (see below), or share food with their kin, or let them touch the machines whose violent power is now being put aside.

Two more specific examples, of general applicability, are the use of graduated force and the creation of communicative spaces. These are *graduated force* and *active communication*.

Recognizing the importance of violence's tragic nature provides a non-instrumental reason to use *graduated force*. Graduated force is the use of carefully escalated force in response to a threat— typically beginning with shouted warnings, escalating through displays of weaponry and warning shots, and reserving lethal fire not only for a last resort, but a last resort after all other levels have actually been used. It is itself a kind of ritual. While graduated force may operate at least in part through fear, it provides a way to both rein in the effects of fear and create a communicative context between the peacekeepers and their opponents. Using graduated force sends a message that peacekeepers are committed to not killing if they can avoid it—we should not simply assume that all spoiler groups trust that this is peacekeepers' stance without it being communicated.

But peacekeepers can and should also surround their use of violence with *active communication* aimed at reconciliation with the targeted groups, and drawing them into a new power structure rather than just trusting in the effects of fear and trauma. This communication should be *active* in distinction to public information efforts, like the creation of mission radio stations—public information efforts are valuable and critical, but recognition of humanity in one's opponents requires a two-way communication. Communication that the violence is regrettable and regretted is itself a form of mourning.[45]

Consider the case of the Unified Task Force (UNITAF).[46] While Somalia is often cited as a classic case of a peacekeeping failure, it was mostly in the follow-on mission, UNOSOM II, that things went infamously wrong.[47] The story of the US/UN operation in Somalia often focuses on the confrontation that built between the US and UN forces there and the Somali National Army (SNA) of Mohammed Farah Aideed, culminating in the withdrawal of the US forces and then of the UN mission.[48]

But an earlier confrontation between Aideed and the US went very differently. Early on, UNITAF, under the US Special Envoy Robert Oakley, established the US Liaison Office (USLO), which facilitated regular "joint security committee" (a faction initiative) meetings with representatives of the Aideed and Ali Madhi factions (the other main contender in Mogadishu) throughout the UNITAF deployment.[49] These meetings, as well as general coordination between UNITAF and the factions, via the USLO, significantly smoothed and pacified interactions between the US/UN forces and the local militants.

The USLO and the joint security committee paid off when UNITAF ended up in conflict over a SNA weapons site. Members of the militia had fired on UNITAF troops, despite warnings, and Anthony Zinni, UNITAF's Director for Operations, informed the security committee that the site would be destroyed in six hours. UNITAF surrounded the site, and responded to resistance with lethal force, killing seven.[50] UNITAF called in the security committee immediately after the attack.

> It was a really solemn meeting, Zinni recalls. I said, "General [Aideed], here is the point. We are either at war or we put this behind us." They got together and talked amongst themselves and they came back and said, "We want to put this behind us." Zinni adds: There was a forum to deconflict.[51]

Incidents continued, but similar procedures were followed, and the overall level of violence and confrontation was kept from escalating too much. As UNOSOM I and UNITAF were replaced with UNOSOM II, the meetings did not continue, and "tension mounted."[52] Both the fact of the space for continued conversation and the very solemnity of UNITAF's response to the deaths of Aideed's combatants were important.

Unfortunately, while some of these approaches were promising, and their successes support the idea that communication, empathy, and relationship-building are important, the approach did not pervade the mission, and was even less present in UNOSOM II. While members of UNITAF and the USLO met with various local leaders, there still seems to have been a focus on the elites (perhaps out of necessity), exemplified in UNOSOM II by the fact that only faction leaders signed the first major peace agreement in March 1993.[53] Admiral Howe, the retired US military officer appointed as Special Representative of the Secretary General (SRSG, the head of the mission) for UNOSOM II took an "arms-length" approach to the faction leaders from the start, in line with the hard-line approach to Aideed that the new head of the USLO took at the close of UNOSOM I.[54] Howe did not seem to appreciate the way in which his sincere commitment to peace in Somalia might not be enough to render the issues of violence moot; he recalled telling the press that it "would be crazy for anyone to test us. The UN is here solely to support the peace and recovery of the Somali people."[55] At the moment of transition, political contact with the main faction leaders was interrupted as Aideed and Ali Madhi were out of the country from March–May, and then the deputy Howe, assigned to be "czar" of the political effort, went on leave for six weeks on their return.[56]

The shift in attitude in UNOSOM II towards the faction leaders, particularly Aideed, was cemented in June 1993, when Pakistani peacekeepers were ambushed after inspecting another SNA cache, near the militia's radio station. Some UNITAF officials argued that a lack of communication may have led the SNA to believe the UN was about to shut down its radio station, or that its heavy-handed approach may have provoked resistance. The SNA was condemned by name for the attacks, and UNOSOM II was authorized to take "all necessary measures" against them.[57] Maj. Gen. Montgomery, the deputy force commander, declared that after an attack such as this "there can be no doubt in your mind that you've got an enemy out there."[58] The enmity with Aideed would ultimately lead to the aforementioned confrontation and withdrawal of US/UN forces. A quieter development, ominous from the point of view of an approach concerned with mourning, was that the UN declined to even count Somali casualties.[59]

I mean only to point out the positive contribution of relationship-building activities in the face of violence; UNOSOM II may have had such serious obstacles that it could not have succeeded even with the best approach possible. And there were criticisms of the elements of UNOSOM I's approach that I praise, because it was seen as "legitimizing" the warlords.[60]

If it seems morally right that peacekeepers not grieve those that they have killed in justified acts of violence, I think this is an effect of forcing members of spoiler groups into an abstract role as beasts or evildoers. Even the worst perpetrators of atrocities are human beings. One member of the US Africa Command (AFRICOM) civilian staff I interviewed, who had worked with members of the DRC military involved in systematic rape as part of the DRC conflict, told me that she found herself in the course of her work comforting men who would break down in tears thinking about their actions in the war.[61] And there are many relationships that one can have with human beings—not all of them need be unequivocally positive. For instance, consider the relationship that one might have with an ex-spouse with whom one must raise children.[62] Building and maintaining relationships with people, and recognizing them as human beings whose lives have meaning to themselves and others, and who are vulnerable to bodily pain and emotion, does not mean that we cannot morally criticize them. In fact, one virtue of Oakley's intimate involvement with the Somali warlords was that he "could scold them and chew them out and they would sit like little school boys and accept it."[63]

6. Conclusion

The moral paradox of peacekeeping is not that they must use violence to promote peace. Rather, it is that they must build relationships at the same time as they are destroying them. I have argued that this is possible if peacekeepers understand the emotional, embodied impact of violence and take the practical steps necessary to mourn that violence and rebuild relationships damaged by it.

Perhaps surprisingly, as far as my argument goes, peacekeepers are not essentially bound to *limit* their use of force. Often, limiting the use of violence will, naturally, be the best way of reining in its bad side effects. But not always—especially if some other group is looking to damage the ability of people to come together powerfully by using its own violence and trauma. More important than the *amount* of violence is the *attitude* peacekeepers take to it, and what they do *besides* use violence. Even if peacekeepers wield the sword with one hand, they should always—in real, practical terms, like UNITAF's consultations and engagement in public mourning—extend the other cooperatively.

Notes

1 Many thanks to Nick Evans, Nancy Gallagher, Max Kelly, Joshua Miller, and Dwight Raymond for their comments on earlier drafts of this piece. I have benefited greatly from their insights, and any remaining errors are my own. Support for field research cited in this chapter was provided by a Smith-Richardson Foundation Young Faculty Fellowship and a summer research grant from the Maryland School of Public Policy. In mourning, Lauren Fleming (1980–2011).

2 Chris Hedges, *War is a Force That Gives Us Meaning*, First Anchor Books Edn, New York, NY: Anchor Books, 2003, p. 83.

3 This definition is from Michael W. Doyle and Nicholas Sambanis, *Making War & Building Peace: United Nations Peace Operations*, Princeton, NJ: Princeton UP, 2006, p. 18.

4 The UN is not the only organization that deploys PKOs, but UN PKOs have been at the center of analysis and development of peacekeeping, and the concepts developed to understand and structure them have cast a long shadow on non-UN peacekeeping. So my discussion will tend to focus in general on UN operations while, hopefully, remaining relevant to non-UN ones.

5 UN Department of Peacekeeping Operations, *United Nations Peacekeeping Operations: Principles and Guidelines*, United Nations, January 18, 2008, p. 18.

6 To avoid repetition of a qualifier, I will simply use the term "peacekeepers" here to refer specifically to the military elements. To designate armed personnel not engaged in peacekeeping, I will use "warfighters."

7 UN Department of Peacekeeping Operations, *United Nations Peacekeeping Operations*, 34–35, emphasis mine.

8 Brian Urquhart, *A Life in Peace and War*. New York, NY: Harper & Row, 1987, p. 293.

9 UN Department of Peacekeeping Operations, *United Nations Peacekeeping Operations*, pp. 33–34. This distinguishes peacekeepers from counterinsurgents, who are arguably trying to build a new peaceful political order, but who are definitely on the side of the government against insurgents, rather than trying to bring things to an even-handed resolution.

10 I discuss the concepts of neutrality and impartiality at length—and propose an understanding at odds with at least some mainstream ones—in Daniel H. Levine, "Peacekeeper Impartiality: Standards, Processes, and Operations," *Journal of International Peacekeeping* 15, 2011, pp. 422–450.

11 Michael Walzer, *Just and Unjust Wars: A Moral Argument With Historical Illustration*, 4th edn, New York, NY: Basic Books, 2006, p. 109.

12 C.A.J. Coady, *Morality and Political Violence*, New York, NY: Cambridge UP, 2008, pp. 9–10.

13 Confidential interview, Washington, DC, October 2009.

14 Elaine Scarry, *The Body in Pain: The Making and Unmaking of the World*. New York, NY: Oxford UP, 1985, p. 62.

15 See, for example, Max Kelly and Alison Giffen, *Military Planning to Protect Civilians: Proposed Guidance for United Nations Peacekeeping Operations*, Washington, DC, September 2011, p. 30. http://www.stimson.org/images/uploads/research-pdfs/3_-_Military_Planning_To_Protect_Civilians_2011.pdf (accessed 14 August, 2012).

16 I develop this argument more fully in Daniel H. Levine, *Morality for Peacekeepers*. Edinburgh, UK: Edinburgh UP, forthcoming. Note also that "support" here means acquiescence and cooperation—which are often given to armed groups out of fear, coercion, and motivations other than "support" in the sense of agreement with goals.

17 Dave Grossman, *On Killing: The Psychological Cost of Learning to Kill in War and Society*. First Paperback Edn, Boston, MA: Back Bay Books, 1996, §II, chs. 2–5; Bruce Allen Watson, *When Soldiers Quit: Studies in Military Disintegration*, Westport, CT: Praeger, 1997, pp. 158–164.

18 Frustration at futility is perhaps especially relevant to peacekeepers, and an example I owe to Dwight Raymond.

19 Carl von Clausewitz, *On War*, Trans. by Michael Howard and Peter Paret. Originally published 1832. Princeton, NJ: Princeton UP, 1976, p. 85.

20 Hannah Arendt, "On Violence," in *Crises of the Republic*, New York, NY: Harcourt Brace Jovanovich, 1972, p. 106.

21 On crowds in the wake of military breakdowns, see Watson, *When Soldiers Quit*, pp. 164–170. This effect is echoed by the "splintering" of irregular armed groups that tends to follow both military confrontations and peace negotiations.

22 H. Arendt, "On Violence," p. 177

23 M. W. Doyle and N. Sambanis, *Making War & Building Peace*, pp. 94–95, 97–99.

24 Dane Archer and Rosemary Gartner, "Violent Acts and Violent Times: A Comparative Approach to Postwar Homicide Rates," *American Sociological Review* 41:6, December 1976, pp. 937–963; Ember, Carol R. and Melvin Ember, "War, Socialization, and Interpersonal Violence," *The Journal of Conflict Resolution*, 38:4, December 1994, pp. 620–646.

25 Rivka Yahav and Miri Cohen, "Symptoms of Acute Stress in Jewish and Arab Israeli Citizens During the Second Lebanon War," *Social Psychology and Psychiatric Epidemiology* 42:10, 2007, pp. 830–836; Denise Michultka, Edward B. Blanchard, and Tom Kalous. "Responses to Civilian War Experiences: Predictors of Psychological Functioning and Coping," *Journal of Traumatic Stress* 11:3, 1998, pp. 571–577; Patrick A. Palmieri, Daphna Canetti-Nisim, Sandro Galea, Robert Johnson, Stevan Hobfoll, "The Psychological Impact of the Israel-Hezbollah War on Jews and Arabs in Israel: The Impact of Risk and Resilience Factors," *Social Science & Medicine* 67:8, 2008, pp. 1208–1216.

26 Amy Bell, "Landscapes of Fear: Wartime London, 1939–1945," *Journal of British Studies* 48, 2009, pp. 160–161, 165–168, quote from p. 160.

27 Ibid., p. 156.

28 Nexhmedin Morina, Konrad Reschke, and Stefan G. Hofmann. "Long-Term Outcomes of War-Related Death of Family Members in Kosovar Civilian War Survivors," in *Death Studies* 35:4, 2011, pp. 365–372.

29 Mayo Clinic Staff, *Post-traumatic Stress Disorder (PTSD): Symptoms*. April 8, 2011. Online. Available at: http://www.mayoclinic.com/health/post-traumatic-stress-disorder/ds00246/dsection=symptoms (accessed 7 September, 2012).

30 Sara Ruddick, *Maternal Thinking: Toward a Politics of Peace*. First Digital-Print Edn. Originally published 1989. Boston, MA: Beacon, 2002, p. 167.

31 Ibid, p. 200.

32 On immediate compliance, see H. Arendt, "On Violence," p. 140.

33 Confidential interview, New York, NY, May 2009.

34 J. Protevi, *Political Affect*, loc. 707. Note that Protevi uses "political" in a broad sense of having to do with human collectives—political physiology need not be about "politics" in the sense of contests for control of state institutions, etc.

35 J. Protevi *Political Affect*, ch. 5 explores this case in an extended discussion of the case of Terri Schiavo.

36 S. Ruddick, *Maternal Thinking*, p. 191.

37 Ibid, pp. 206–217.

38 Ibid, pp. 183–184.

39 Ibid., pp. 66–77.

40 Patrick C. Cammaert, *Learning to Use Force on the Hoof in Peacekeeping: Reflections on the Experiences of MONUC's Eastern Division*, Situation Report. Pretoria, South Africa: Institute for Security Studies, 3 April 3 2007, p. 6. Online. Available at: http://www.iss.co.za/uploads/MONUCSITREPAPR07. PDF (accessed 9 June, 2012).

41 Even an "instantaneous" death involves a quick cessation of life processes in the individual body but an extended series of practices of mourning and grief in people connected to the person who has died.

42 Ruddick, *Maternal Thinking*, p. 215.

43 Judith Butler, *Precarious Life: The Powers of Mourning and Violence*, Brooklyn, NY: Verso, 2004, p. 27.

44 Ibid., p. 34.

45 Though I do not have the space to develop the thought here, of course peacekeepers should not allow public performance of mourning at the fate of violent individuals they may target eclipse a clear message that the deaths those groups themselves cause are cause for mourning.

46 UNITAF was the UN designation for the US military mission co-deployed with the first United Nations Mission in Somalia (UNOSOM I). The US designation for the same mission was Operation Restore Hope.

47 For some overviews, see William J. Durch, "Introduction to Anarchy: Humanitarian Intervention and 'State Building' in Somalia," in William J. Durch (ed.) *UN Peacekeeping, American Policy, and the Uncivil Wars of the 1990s*, New York, NY: St Martin's Press, 1996, pp. 311–366; Susan Rosegrant and Michael D. Watkins, *A "Seamless" Transition: United States and United Nations Operations in Somalia—1992–1993 (A)*. Kennedy School of Government Case Study C09-96-1324.0. 1996; and *A "Seamless" Transition: United States and United Nations Operations in Somalia—1992–1993 (B)*. Kennedy School of Government Case Study C09-96-1325.0. 1996.

48 Rosegrant and Watkins, *A "Seamless" Transition (B)*, p. 15; W.J. Durch, "Introduction to Anarchy," pp. 347–350.

49 W.J. Durch, "Introduction to Anarchy," p. 324; John L. Hirsch and Robert B. Oakley, *Somalia and Operation Restore Hope: Reflections on Peacemaking and Peacekeeping*, Washington, DC: United States Institute of Peace, 1995, p. 58.

50 Mark Fritz, "U.S. Forces Kill Seven Somalis in Attack on Two Clan Camps," *The Associated Press*, Januay 8, 1993.

51 Rosegrant and Watkins, *A "Seamless" Transition (A)*, p. 25.

52 J.L. Hirsch and R. B. Oakley, *Somalia and Operation Restore Hope*, p. 58.

53 S. Rosegrant and M. D. Watkins, *A "Seamless" Transition (A)*, p. 36.

54 W.J. Durch, "Introduction to Anarchy," pp. 341–342

55 Quoted in S. Rosegrant and M.D. Watkins, *A "Seamless" Transition (A)*, p. 42.

56 S. Rosegrant and M. D. Watkins, *A "Seamless" Transition (B)*, p. 4.

57 S. Rosegrant and M. D. Watkins, *A "Seamless" Transition (B)*, pp. 6–7; United Nations Security Council, S/RES/837. June 6, 1993, pp. 1–2.

58 Quoted in S. Rosegrant and M. D. Watkins, *A "Seamless" Transition (B)*, p. 7

59 W. J. Durch, "Introduction to Anarchy," p. 343.

60 Rosegrant and Watkins, *A "Seamless" Transition (A)*, p. 26.

61 Confidential interview, Stuttgart Germany, July 2010

62 I am indebted to Nancy Gallagher for this example.

63 Confidential interview, Stuttgart, Germany, July 2012.

References

Archer, D. and R. Gartner, "Violent Acts and Violent Times: A Comparative Approach to Postwar Homicide Rates," *American Sociological Review*, 41:6, 1976, pp. 937–963.

Arendt, H., "On Violence," in *Crises of the Republic*. New York, NY: Harcourt Brace Jovanovich, 1972.

Bell, A., "Landscapes of Fear: Wartime London, 1939–1945," *Journal of British Studies* 48, 2009, pp. 153–175.

Butler, J., *Precarious Life: The Powers of Mourning and Violence*. Brooklyn, NY: Verso, 2004.

Cammaert, P.C., *Learning to Use Force on the Hoof in Peacekeeping: Reflections on the Experiences of MONUC's Eastern Division*. Situation Report. Pretoria, South Africa: Institute for Security Studies, 3 April, 2007, Online. Available at: http://www.iss.co.za/uploads/MONUCSITREPAPR07.PDF (accessed 9 June, 2012).

Coady, C.A.J., *Morality and Political Violence*. New York, NY: Cambridge UP, 2008.

Doyle, M.W. and N. Sambanis, *Making War & Building Peace: United Nations Peace Operations*. Princeton, NJ: Princeton UP, 2006.

Durch, WJ., "Introduction to Anarchy: Humanitarian Intervention and 'State Building' in Somalia," in W.J. Durch (ed.), *UN Peacekeeping, American Policy, and the Uncivil Wars of the 1990s*. New York, NY: St Martin's Press, 1996, pp. 311–366.

Ember, C.R. and M. Ember, "War, Socialization, and Interpersonal Violence," *The Journal of Conflict Resolution*, 38:4, 1994, pp. 620–646.

Fritz, M., "U.S. Forces Kill Seven Somalis in Attack on Two Clan Camps," *The Associated Press*, January 8, 1993.

Grossman, D., *On Killing: The Psychological Cost of Learning to Kill in War and Society*. First Paperback Edn, Boston, MA: Back Bay Books, 1996.

Hedges, C., *War is a Force That Gives Us Meaning*. First Anchor Books Edn, New York, NY: Anchor Books, 2003.

Hirsch, J.L., and R. B. Oakley *Somalia and Operation Restore Hope: Reflections on Peacemaking and Peacekeeping*. Washington, DC: United States Institute of Peace, 1995.

Kelly, M. and A. Giffen, *Military Planning to Protect Civilians: Proposed Guidance for United Nations Peacekeeping Operations*. Washington, DC, September, 2011. Online. Available at: http://www. stimson.org/images/uploads/research-pdfs/3_-_Military_Planning_To_Protect_Civilians_2011.pdf (accessed 14 August, 2012).

Levine, D.H., "Peacekeeper Impartiality: Standards, Processes, and Operations," *Journal of International Peacekeeping* 15, 2011, pp. 422–450.

——*Morality for Peacekeepers*. Edinburgh, UK: Edinburgh UP, forthcoming.

Mayo Clinic Staff, *Post-traumatic Stress Disorder (PTSD): Symptoms*. April 8, 2011. Online. Available at: http://www.mayoclinic.com/health/post-traumatic-stress-disorder/ds00246/dsection=symptoms (accessed 7 September, 2012).

Michultka, D., E.B. Blanchard and T. Kalous, "Responses to Civilian War Experiences: Predictors of Psychological Functioning and Coping," *Journal of Traumatic Stress* 11:3, 1998, pp. 571–577.

Morina, N., K. Reschke and S.G. Hofmann, "Long-Term Outcomes of War-Related Death of Family Members in Kosovar Civilian War Survivors," *Death Studies* 35:4, 2011, pp. 365–372.

Palmieri, P.A., D. Canetti-Nisim, S. Galea, R. Johnson and S. Hobfoll, "The Psychological Impact of the Israel-Hezbollah War on Jews and Arabs in Israel: The Impact of Risk and Resilience Factors," *Social Science & Medicine* 67:8, 2008, pp. 1208–1216.

Protevi, J., *Political Affect: Connecting the Social and the Somatic*. Kindle Edn, Minneapolis, MN: University of Minnesota Press, 2009.

Rosegrant, S, and M.D. Watkins, *A "Seamless" Transition: United States and United Nations Operations in Somalia—1992–1993 (A)*. Kennedy School of Government Case Study C09-96-1324.0. 1996.

——*A "Seamless" Transition: United States and United Nations Operations in Somalia—1992–1993 (B)*. Kennedy School of Government Case Study C09-96-1325.0. 1996.

Ruddick, S., *Maternal Thinking: Toward a Politics of Peace*. First Digital-Print Edn. Originally published 1989. Boston, MA: Beacon, 2002.

Scarry, E., *The Body in Pain: The Making and Unmaking of the World*. New York, NY: Oxford UP, 1985.

UN Department of Peacekeeping Operations. *United Nations Peacekeeping Operations: Principles and Guidelines*. United Nations, January 18, 2008.

United Nations Security Council. S/RES/837. June 6, 1993.

Urquhart, B., *A Life in Peace and War*. New York, NY: Harper & Row, 1987.

von Clausewitz, C., *On War*. Trans. by M. Howard and P. Paret. Originally published 1832. Princeton, NJ: Princeton UP, 1976.

Walzer, M., *Just and Unjust Wars: A Moral Argument With Historical Illustration*, 4th edn, New York, NY: Basic Books, 2006.

Watson, B.A., *When Soldiers Quit: Studies in Military Disintegration*. Westport, CT: Praeger, 1997.

Yahav, R. and M. Cohen., "Symptoms of Acute Stress in Jewish and Arab Israeli Citizens During the Second Lebanon War," *Social Psychology and Psychiatric Epidemiology* 42:10, 2007, pp. 830–836.

Terrorism and counterterrorism

15

THE WAR ON TERROR AND THE ETHICS OF EXCEPTIONALISM[1]

Fritz Allhoff

1. The war on terror

Since 9/11, we have been told that the nature of war has changed and that our approaches to it must be updated lest we be unable to defend ourselves.[2] Traditional wars, including ones as recent as the United States' first incursion in Iraq, have tended to be fought on battlefields. The distinction between combatants and noncombatants has been clear, not least because combatants wore uniforms whereas noncombatants did not. Civilians have been largely exonerated from risk during these conflicts: while collateral damage has always been a part of warfare, the risk to civilians was unintended but foreseen. The non-involvement of civilians was effected not just by clear identification thereof, but also by the abovementioned separation between them and the conflict. Wars were fought between state actors with transparent chains of command, a high degree of centralization, and obvious diplomatic and political outlets. To be sure, there are numerous exceptions to these features of conflicts, though it is uncontroversial that they have, historically, been largely instantiated in those conflicts. Not only have we been able to characterize conflicts in these ways, we have adopted norms that explicitly require many of them to be characterized in this way; these have been codified both legally and in the just war tradition.[3]

The contemporary advent of terrorism, however, compromises all of these features.[4] Wars are not fought on conventional battlefields but rather in urban centers. The combatant/non-combatant distinction has become blurred, at least insofar as combatants are no longer readily identified. Certainly, they commonly lack military uniforms but the distinction has been further blurred insofar as noncombatants often provide material support for combatants through positioning, sustenance, communication, and so on. Can these noncombatants be justly targeted? Are they properly designated as noncombatants? Not only do such people, whether willing or unwilling, become complicit in some of these cases, but noncombatants on the other side become targets. In fact, the targeting of noncombatants is one of the hallmarks of terrorism.[5] So, again, the effects that terrorism has on the combatant/noncombatant separation is two-fold: terrorists incorporate noncombatants on their side into the conflict while, at the same time, threatening noncombatants on the other side.[6] Finally, terrorists are (usually) not state actors. It is therefore often unclear what their command structures are, and they are usually decentralized. And traditional tools, such as diplomacy and other political interventions, are less effective insofar as we often would not even know who to approach in the first place, and, regardless, the ideological commitments of terrorist groups could render such measures futile.[7] Given that terrorists change the landscape of warfare, we can then ask whether those who attempt to combat these terrorists are justified in changing their tactics as well. Does the fact that terrorists are no longer playing by the traditional rules license the terrorists' opponents to play by different rules as well? If so, what should the new rules be? How do we justify them?

Before moving forward, let us identify some archetypical practices that have catalyzed new discussion vis-à-vis their role in the opposition to the war on terror: torture (especially interrogational variants), assassination, and enemy combatancy/prisoner of war (POW) status.[8] None of these is a historically novel issue, but each had a reasonably clear status in pre-9/11 norms (both in the US and abroad). Since 9/11, however, the associated norms have come under pressure and/or been subject to violation.

Torture, for example, has been widely decried as a violation of basic human rights as well as of international law. The opposition to torture has been codified in various declarations and conventions, including, but not limited to: §5 of the Universal Declaration of Human Rights (1948);[9] §3.1a, §17, §87, and §130 of the Third Geneva Convention (1949);[10] the Declaration of Tokyo (1975);[11] and the Convention against Torture and Other Cruel, Inhuman or Degrading Treatment or Punishment (1975/1987).[12] However, since 9/11, the torture debate has resurfaced. While few have overtly called for the legitimization of torture, the strategy employed by the Bush Administration bears notice. For example, §17 of the Third Geneva Convention says that "[n]o physical or mental torture, nor any other form of coercion, may be inflicted on prisoners of war to secure from them information of any kind whatever."[13] By denying suspected terrorists prisoner of war status (see below), §17 would seemingly not apply. The Bush Administration has also endorsed coercive techniques that, in its estimation, nevertheless fall short of torture.[14] Furthermore, the Bush Administration employed counsel, John Yoo, whose infamous "torture memos" sought to give legal grounding to torture or torture-like techniques.[15]

The purpose of this essay is not to evaluate the policies of the Bush Administration, but it bears notice that, post-9/11, proscriptions on torture have been debated, both morally and legally. And, lest we lay this wholly at the feet of an unpopular administration, it is worth noticing that, as recently as 2005, the majority of Americans thought that the torture of terrorists was justifiable in some situations.[16] Why would anyone think this? The putative answer is that, without torture, we leave ourselves more vulnerable to terrorist attacks and more susceptible to the harms that they portend. Whether such an answer succeeds is, for now, beside the point,[17] which is simply that terrorism puts pressure on existing moral and legal norms, of which those pertaining to torture are an example.[18]

Let me raise two other practices that are similar to torture in the sense that proscriptions against them have been revisited in light of the war on terror. First, consider assassinations.[19] Historically, these have played an important role in warfare and in thinking about warfare:[20] Sun Tzu mentions assassinations in his *Art of War*;[21] Machiavelli discusses the importance of protecting against them in *The Prince*;[22] and Thomas More wrote about the potential moral advantages of assassination in terms of effecting a quicker end to hostilities.[23] Pre-9/11, though, assassination was clearly not allowed in the US, nor by its agents operating abroad. In 1976, President Ford issued Executive Order 11905 which stated (in §5g, "Restrictions on Intelligence Activities") that "[n]o employee of the United States Government shall engage in, or conspire to engage in, political assassination."[24] This apparent ban on assassination was reaffirmed in subsequent executive orders by President Carter in 1978[25] and President Regan in 1981.[26] However, just weeks after 9/11, President Bush signed an intelligence "finding", which authorized "lethal covert action" against Osama Bin Laden.[27] While the word "assassi-nation" is not explicitly used here, it is reasonable to interpret this action from Bush as relaxing the strictures earlier emplaced by Ford.

As in the torture case, the argument for assassination derives from a post-9/11 climate: ter-rorists, especially high-impact ones, can effect a tremendous amount of damage and take many civilian lives. Assassination can neutralize the targeted terrorists and, perhaps, save many lives. And, in this climate, the legitimacy of assassination has again become a prominent issue.[28] Why not use regular law enforcement to apprehend and prosecute those terrorists? This is an impor-tant question being discussed in the literature, and I do not plan to address it here.[29] Suffice it to say that at least part of the answer has to do with expediency: assassinations might be carried out faster than law enforcement and the judicial process can operate. Furthermore, we also may not always have the diplomatic or jurisdictional avenues that would otherwise empower law enforcement, thus rendering that option moot. It is also worth noticing that the executive orders from 1976–1981 were during the Cold War, particularly when the USSR thought that we might have been plotting assassinations of Fidel Castro; our presidents' actions were at least as much to allay Cold War hostilities as with any other concern. Therefore, at least part of the historic impetus against assassination lies in antiquated concerns.

Finally, consider the treatment of POWs. The Third Geneva Convention clearly delimits how POWs can and cannot be treated; we have already seen above that any sort of coercive interrogation is clearly proscribed, though other issues are addressed as well.[30] The detention facilities at Guantánamo and Abu Ghraib almost certainly failed to live up to these require-ments. This was not, however, from some sort of mere complacency on the behalf of the Bush Administration, but rather followed from a position that the Convention does not apply. As has now become controversial, the Administration applied "enemy combatancy"—as opposed to POW—status to the detainees, thus abrogating substantial restrictions on their treatment. However, despite widespread opinion, the Bush Administration did not create this status, which was originally proffered in a 1942 Supreme Court case, *Ex Parte Quirin*. The ruling held that:

> the law of war draws a distinction between the armed forces and the peaceful populations of belligerent nations and also between those who are lawful and unlawful combatants. Lawful combatants are subject to capture and detention as prisoners of war by opposing military forces. Unlawful combatants are likewise subject to capture and detention, but in addition they are subject to trial and punishment by military tribunals for acts which render their belligerency unlawful. The spy who secretly and without uniform passes the military lines of a belligerent in time of war, seeking to gather military information and com-municate it to the enemy, or an enemy combatant who without uniform comes secretly through the lines for the purpose of waging war by destruction of life or property, are familiar examples of belligerents who are generally deemed not to be entitled to the status of prisoners of war, but to be offenders against the law of war subject to trial and punish-ment by military tribunals.[31]

Under the Bush Administration, this legal category effectively allowed foreign detainees to be held indefinitely, both without Geneva Convention protections *and* without access to the (civilian) legal system[32,33]—or at least it did before being eroded by two Supreme Court deci-sions.[34] As a justification for this approach, we were told by White House Counsel Alberto Gonzales that the war on terror constitutes a "new paradigm" and "renders obsolete Geneva's strict limitations on questioning of enemy prisoners and renders quaint some of its provisions."[35]

Similar sentiments were expressed by Major General Geoffrey Miller, the former commanding officer at Guantánamo, who said: "[Joint Task Force] Guantánamo's mission is to detain
enemy combatants and then to gain intelligence from them to be able to win the global war
on terrorism. And so we are detaining these enemy combatants in a humane manner … and in
accordance, as much as we can, with the Geneva Convention."[36] This emphasis on intelligence
and the defeasible commitment to the Geneva Convention is endemic of the post-9/11 era.[37]
Myriad moral and legal issues are raised by these practices,[38] though their contribution to our
discussion is to provide a third example of a way in which terrorism, or at least our response to
it, has challenged pre-existing norms. Having now sketched how some of those norms— i.e.,
those pertaining to torture, assassination, and enemy combatancy status—have come under
pressure post-9/11, let us now move on to a more general and theoretical discussion of exceptionalism (Sections 2–5) and its ethical upshots (Section 6).

2. Exceptionalism

In this section—and incorporating the abovementioned and other examples—I will develop
a general and theoretical account of exceptionalism. By this I mean that the war on terror,
through its novel face and extreme stakes, suggests to some that we need to make exceptions
to traditional norms.[39] In Section 6, I will consider some of the ethical issues that attach to this
discussion, but the intermediate sections are largely conceptual. Surprisingly, the literature bears
little work on the doctrine of exceptionalism, a deficiency that this chapter aims to ameliorate.[40]
In particular, there are four elements that an account of exceptionalism should provide. First, it
should tell us what the exception is *to*. Second, it should tell us *what* is being excepted. Third, it
should properly delimit the *scope* of the exceptions. Fourth, it should tell us *why* the exception
is being made.

Let me briefly expand on each of these elements before moving forward. The semantics of
"exceptionalism" mandate that something is being excepted vis-à-vis some category. Consider,
for example, some school rule which holds that all students must be in the classroom except
those with a hall pass. The exception, then, is to the otherwise inflexible stricture that all students must be in the classroom (element 1). When we talk about what exceptions are to, we are
looking for some sort of stricture that would apply in absence of the exception. The strictures
that we are primarily interested in are moral and legal ones, so I will most commonly just refer
to "norms," which we can take to be usefully ambiguous between either of these two classes;
nothing in the following analysis hangs on the various distinctions between them.[41]

Second, we have to be precise about what is being excepted (element 2), which, in the
above example, it is those students who hold hall passes. Importantly, the exceptions have to
be granted to a proper subset of whatever the norm binds (including the empty set).[42] So, for
example, teachers are not excepted from the norm that all students must be in the classroom
since they are, *ex hypothesi*, not students. Regarding teachers, the norm simply *does not apply*,
and that is relevantly different from it having an exception. Therefore, what gets excepted must
be something to which the norm otherwise would have applied absent the exception.

Our third element pertains to scope, and I think scope can be understood in various sorts
of ways. Let me herein mention three; these will be discussed in greater detail in subsequent
sections.[43] First, imagine that we can park on the street except on Tuesdays (when street cleaning takes place). In this case, the scope of the exception is *temporal*: the norm applies at all *times*
except Tuesdays. Second, consider that Americans can have wine directly shipped from wineries in California except those who live in Montana (among some other states).[44] In this case, the
scope of the exception is *spatial*: people who occupy certain spaces have one set of privileges,

while those that occupy some other spaces lack those privileges. Third, consider that all children in Prince George's County, Maryland were required to be vaccinated against Hepatitis B, except those whose families could demonstrate certain religious beliefs.[45] In this case, the scope is *group-based* since some groups (namely, those lacking certain religious beliefs) are bound by the stricture, whereas others (namely, those having certain religious beliefs) are excepted.

Let me make several other points regarding scope. First, there need not be *single* classes of exceptions, but exceptionalism is rather fully consistent with the following: "All Xs can/cannot/must ϕ, except for Ys and Zs." In the wine shipping case, Montana residents are restricted, but so, at time of writing, are residents of just over a dozen other states. Each of these states is then an exception to the norm, and it is irrelevant to their status vis-à-vis that norm what other states' statuses are. In the vaccination case, those with certain religious beliefs were excepted, but so were those with certain medical conditions. And, second, these scopes need not be mutually exclusive: some norm could bind pursuant to two of the above requirements being met and otherwise be excepted. For example, I once lived on a street in Pittsburgh where you could park only on one side of the street (spatial) on Tuesdays (temporal). If it was not Tuesday or if there was a spot on the permitted side of the street, then the stricture was excepted. The interplay among these different scopes can give rise to more complex norms and exceptions but, conceptually, such interplay is straightforward.

In addition to the above comments regarding scope, there is a further consideration which is more pragmatic than conceptual. To wit, it should be the case that there are fewer exceptions to the norms than cases in which the norms apply. Again, this is not conceptually required, but failing this desideratum would otherwise give rise to poorly specified norms. For example, we could have a "norm" which says that everyone must serve on university service committees, except those that do not work at universities. And, undoubtedly, this is true. But it is not useful, and the problem lies in scope. The proper norm is not this one, but rather that all university employees must serve on university service committees: the people that are "excepted" from the first norm never should have been included in its scope in the first place.

Finally, there must be reasons for the exceptions (and for the norms), lest they be arbitrary or capricious. This issue of justification will be deferred until Section 6 when we consider the ethics of exceptionalism, though I certainly take it to be part of the conceptual requirements that we are discussing here. And, in every one of the cases above, we can easily supply reasons for both the norms and the exceptions, while withholding judgment on their relative merits.

Let us now take the above framework and return to a discussion of exceptionalism as pertains to the war on terror in particular. In a recent essay, Jonathan Marks writes about the history that "compartmentalization" has had on various military conflicts; his compartmentalization bears on my group-based exceptionalism insofar as both effect varying treatments for some groups. Marks argues that:

> The wars between the city-states of ancient Greece, as well as war waged by Alexander the Great against the Persians, were marked by respect for the life and personal dignity of war victims. Temples, embassies, and priests of the opposing side were spared and prisoners of war were exchanged. Yet both the Greeks and Romans failed to demonstrate similar respect for those regarded as barbarians … More recently, Nazi doctors perceived Jews as *Untermenschen* (or sub-humans) who were, by reason of this categorization, not protected by the 1931 *Reichsgesundheitsrat* regulations prohibiting human experimentation that was fatal, disabling, or conducted without the voluntary consent of the subject.[46]

These are some pre-9/11 examples of group-based exceptionalism: whether the "barbarians" are excepted from certain forms of respect or the Jews were excepted from legal protections, the examples are ones in which group membership changed the norms that were afforded to some population. And, as I will argue below, most of the significant exceptionalisms that are endemic in the post-9/11 era are group-based exceptionalisms, as opposed to temporally- or spatially-based ones.

3. Temporal exceptionalism

Before turning to that argument, though, let us consider some post-9/11 exceptionalisms that are not group-based, as these are worth considering. So, for example, consider the USA PATRIOT Act,[47] which I take as an example of temporal exceptionalism, as does Marks. In this original legislation, there were various provisions—so-called "sunset provisions"—that were to expire on December 31, 2005, unless they were reauthorized by Congress.[48] In fact, most of these provisions were made permanent by Congress; only §206 and §215 were left as sunset provisions, now set to expire on June 1, 2015. Some other provisions were slightly modified.[49] As originally legislated, the gist of the PATRIOT Act was that Americans were to have such and such liberties, *except* for the dates between its being signed into law (October 26, 2001) and its then prospective expiration (December 31, 2005). Since dates are delimiting when the exceptions are in play, this is an example of temporal exceptionalism. However, temporal exceptionalism is not all that significant in the war on terror. For one, there are very few cases that are overt ones of temporal exceptionalism; probably the PATRIOT Act is the only substantial one. And, of course, the bulk of the PATRIOT Act was made permanent, so it is hardly delimiting temporal exceptions any more. §206 and §215 are the only sections that are still temporally delimited, and they may yet be made permanent. If they are, then none of the sunset provisions will have actually expired.

But it is also unlikely that temporal exceptions are ever what legislators will really be after. In the wake of 9/11, the Bush Administration presented a controversial legislation that, even in that political climate, would have been hard to make permanent. To my mind, the sunset provisions are more of a test run or political compromise than an end in themselves, as the now permanence of most of the PATRIOT Act indicates. This is probably not always the case for sunset provisions, though the exceptions are strange cases.[50] For example, John Adams and the Federalist Party passed the Alien and Sedition Acts (1798), which were meant to limit political opposition to an undeclared naval war on France.[51] However, this act expired at the end of Adams's presidency such that the Democratic-Republicans (the then political rivals of the Federalists) could not similarly limit opposition against their own agendas. More typical would be something like the Federal Assault Weapons Ban, which was a subtitle of the Violent Crime Control and Law Enforcement Act of 1994, signed into law by President Clinton. This provision was set to expire in 2004, if President Bush did not renew it. He did not, and the provision expired. But certainly the advocates of the ban wanted it to be renewed or made permanent and, as with the PATRIOT Act, the sunset provision on the ban was a political compromise in order to gain temporary legislation as permanent legislation would have been less politically viable.

Of course, there are differences between having sunset provisions and simply repealing laws. Consider, for example, Prohibition in the United States.[52] The Eighteenth Amendment, which prevented the sale, manufacture, and transportation of alcohol for consumption, went into effect in early 1920. The Twenty-First Amendment then repealed the Eighteenth Amendment in late 1933, thus restoring the previously precluded practices. However, this is not properly understood as a case of exceptionalism in the sense that the PATRIOT Act was originally conceived. The latter had explicit provisions for the cessation of its provisions, whereas the Eighteenth Amendment did not. It is true that Americans have had various liberties with respect to alcohol *except* during (most of) 1920–1933, though this exceptionalism only makes sense *ex post* (i.e., once the liberties are restored). This is importantly different from the PATRIOT Act, which said, *ex ante*, that Americans would (not) have certain liberties from part of 2001 until the end of 2005. Or, to put it another way, a repeal just means that some legislature has changed its mind (or that some new legislature disagrees with its predecessor and legislates accordingly). Temporal exceptionalism, on the other hand, means that the same legislature is effecting different legislation at different times and not that that legislature (or any other) has changed its mind on appropriate legislation. This, then, is another reason that temporal exceptionalism is not likely to be extremely prevalent as many of the instances that we might appeal to are, properly understood, ones of repeal rather than of (*ex ante*) exceptionalism.

We have therefore amassed several reasons to think that temporal exceptionalism will not be common, whether generally or as pertains to the war on terror. First, it will often/typically be the intent (or at least, the hope) that the exceptions are made permanent. The assault weapons ban is perhaps even more clear in this regard than the PATRIOT Act: it is certainly not the case that those legislators thought that assault weapons would be any better in 2004 than they were in 1994, though a different administration intervened against their aspirations. Second, and similarly, exceptions *are* made permanent, at least some of the time (cf., most sections of the PATRIOT Act). In these cases, there are no temporally delimited exceptions; rather, there is ongoing legislation, though legislation whose status has changed (i.e., from provisional to permanent). Note, though, that it hardly matters to whoever would have been affected as there is no practical difference between a temporary status being made permanent and a permanent status being assigned from the outset. (This is not to say that there are not psychological or political differences in these legislative schemes, just no significant practical differences aside from reauthorization.) Third, many cases that might otherwise look like temporal exceptionalism are better understood as ones of legislative *change* rather than exceptionalism, strictly speaking.

4. Spatial exceptionalism

As mentioned in Section 2, exceptionalism could also occur along some spatial axis: remember our friends from Montana who cannot receive wine directly from California wineries. So here we have some norm which applies to everyone *except* those who occupy some particularly delimited space. And this suggests the generalized conception of spatial exceptionalism: "All Xs can/cannot/must ϕ, except those who are in S (where S is some location)." Unlike temporal exceptionalism, there is undoubtedly a lot of spatial exceptionalism: every time local norms deviate from some more widely held norms, spatial exceptionalism exists. Something would have to be said about how to individuate locations, particularly nested ones, but we shall not pursue that here. For this project, though, the question is whether the war on terrorism gives rise to spatial exceptionalism. And I do not think that it does, at least not in the relevant sense. Before seeing the argument for that, let us consider Marks, who argues for the contrary.

Marks points to enemy combatancy status, which was discussed in Section 1; we can therefore skip the details of that status. Let me say from the outset that this is probably the most plausible example of spatial exceptionalism in the war on terror and that, if it does not withstand scrutiny, then it is unlikely that spatial exceptionalism is significant in this regard. Marks writes of "*spatial* or *geographic* exceptionalism, in which physical locality is relied upon to justify the non-application of protective norms and procedures. A good example of this is Guantánamo, selected by the administration in an effort to keep detainees beyond the *habeas corpus* jurisdiction of federal courts."[53,54] Marks thinks that this is an example of spatial exceptionalism on the grounds that certain norms (do not) apply, based on location. The norm, then, could be something like: "All those held in US custody have the right to *habeas corpus*, except those held at Guantánamo (and, perhaps, some other places)."

I do not disagree that this statement is true, nor do I disagree that the Bush Administration specifically chose Cuba precisely because they could assign such status to the detainees held there. But this does not seem like an example of spatial exceptionalism, at least once we look at it more closely. Return to the case of the Montanan who cannot directly order Californian wine. In that case, there is nothing about the Montanan *himself* that does any of the motivating work for the legislation. If the Montanan moves south to Wyoming, he can order wine, and this would be of vanishingly little interest to the Montanan legislature. Their law is precisely designed to govern a *space*, irrespective of whoever occupies that space. If all of the residents of Montana and Wyoming traded states, the legislation would continue unaffected. This is therefore a perfect example of spatial exceptionalism.

Contrast that case with Guantánamo. The practices at Guantánamo are not motivated by the space over which they are operative, but rather by the people who occupy that space (namely, the detainees). If the detainees were to swap spots with a couple hundred residents from Florida, the US government, unlike the Montana legislature, would not have any reason to maintain its practices in Cuba. Furthermore, it might have a reason to try to change some of the norms that thereafter applied to those detainees who were now in Florida.

So the appropriate test to distinguish between true spatial exceptionalism and would-be cases is to ask whether it is the *space* that matters or else the *group* that is in the space. Imagine that the Bush Administration could deny *habeas corpus* to suspected terrorists (or allies who might have critical intelligence) *regardless* of where they were. In such a scenario, there would be no reason to create Guantánamo; there is no independent reason to exercise control over that space. Of course, *habeas corpus* probably cannot be denied in, say, Florida, so the administration has a reason to keep the detainees away from there. Again, the interest is in affecting the status of the *group*, not the space. So, unlike the example with Montana—which is a true instance of spatial exceptionalism—the treatment of the enemy combatants at Guantánamo is effectively group-based exceptionalism masquerading as spatial exceptionalism. This is not, though, to prejudge the morality of the practices, only to identify the proper avenue for that inquiry. Let us now take up group-based exceptionalism directly.

5. Group-based exceptionalism

In Section 3, I denied that temporal exceptionalism was an important facet of the war on terror and, Section 4, I argued that the war on terror's most compelling example of spatial exceptionalism was more properly understood as a group-based exceptionalism. In this section, I will argue that the most significant exceptionalisms in the war on terror are, in fact, group-based; in the next section, we will see the ethical implications of this result. Let us now return to the three cases identified as archetypical in the war on terror: torture, assassination, and enemy combatancy status. The identification of enemy combatancy status as group-based exceptionalism was already made above, but more should be said about torture and assassination in this regard.

Starting with torture, this is clearly an example of group-based exceptionalism. But what is the group that is receiving different treatment? And what is the norm to which the exception is being made? Roughly, it looks something like this: "Do not torture, except when it is necessary to prevent greater harms." Putting aside the associative moral and empirical issues that I have discussed elsewhere, this is a reasonable approximation of the idealized torture exception as some endorse to fight the war on terror.[55] Again, this is not to prejudge the morality or efficacy of the exception, merely to try to get clear on its proposed structure; let us therefore consider a couple of remarks on this proposal.

First, nobody would seriously argue that torture is justified unless it prevents some greater harm. Torturing of prisoners and political dissidents, for example, is patently impermissible and there is little to no philosophical merit to having a discussion about these sorts of practices.[56] (Though there might be practical merits in terms of abrogating such practices where they continue.) Second, this norm seems to be of the right sort insofar as its starting point is *not* to torture, and then to allow the exceptions to come in. Alternatively, it could say something like: "torture should be practiced, except when ..." but this formulation would violate the pragmatic constraint on exceptionalism postulated above insofar as the exceptions should be rarer than the non-exceptions. Even those who defend torture, including me, only do so in limited cases, such that the excepted norm would be one prohibiting torture rather than one allowing it.

Now the question is what the relevant axis of exception is in the abovementioned norm. It is not spatial: there is no *space* outside of which one norm applies and inside of which a different one applies. Or, if there is, this space delimitation is derivative (cf., the above argument regarding enemy combatancy status). Similarly, there is no time at which torture is licensed as against other times or, if there were, it would again be derivative. For example, we might say that torture is licensed only at *times* during which it would be expedient, but the only reason that those times are relevant is because there are *people*, at those times, who are unwilling to surrender lifesaving intelligence. This proposal, then, is that the exception for torture could be predicated only on there being people from whom we might extract important information. These people, actual or hypothetical, therefore form the *group* that is relevant to the exceptions to our norm against torture: the people with lifesaving intelligence that cannot be expediently obtained in any way other than torture.

The point of this essay is not to assess whether such groups exist, or whether, even if they did, torture would be permissible. Certainly critics object to the exception on either of these two grounds: some say that the relevant preconditions will never be met, whereas others say that, even if they were, torture is categorically impermissible.[57] Regardless, the present objective is to figure out the structure of the exceptions, though more general comments will be made in the following section regarding some of the moral issues that follow. I take it, though, that torture could only be a sort of group-based exceptionalism, and, as discussed above, the same goes for enemy combatancy status.

Furthermore, assassination occupies a similar sphere. Again starting negatively, the norms against assassination are not tied to specific places: it is not the case that assassination is normalized in place A and not normalized in place B (from the point of view of US agency/ involvement, let us say). If we were attempting to assassinate someone, we would not care much where he happened to be, at least not for reasons other than prudence and efficacy. We might care, for example, whether the target was in a crowded place, at an embassy, in some place where the assassin might be noticed, and so on, but all of these features are again derivative of the class of persons that we want to assassinate. Temporal-based exceptionalism is also not appropriate: the would-be assassinated is not off the hook when the clock strikes midnight, or at any other time. The circumstances might change such that we no longer pursue assassination at some time but, in that case, the driving feature is the circumstances themselves, not the temporal features of the case.

Rather, the norm against assassination looks something like: "Do not assassinate, except when it is necessary to prevent greater harms." The exceptions to this norm are going to be *people* who are effecting great evils and who cannot be accessed diplomatically or politically. There are probably two classes of people to which assassination could be the most appropriate—which is not to say that it is necessarily appropriate at all— and those are terrorists and despotic, genocidal leaders. If, for whatever reason, these groups cannot be directly engaged by military action, then there are at least *prima facie* compelling reasons to target them. Again, this discussion is not to render any commentary on the morality of assassination, but rather to locate it under the category of a group-based exceptionalism: the putative exceptions to the norms against assassination would be the groups of people that comprise the terrorists and leaders who the world would be better off without.

Having already discussed enemy combatancy status in Section 4, I will not say more about it, other than to reiterate that it was, like torture and assassination, appropriately categorized as group-based exceptionalism. Therefore, *all* of the examples that we have considered as archetypical in the war on terror are of this sort. Furthermore, as argued in previous sections, there are no other examples in the war on terror where different kinds of exceptionalism are likely to play a significant role. Having now located the sort of exceptionalisms suggested by the war on terror, let us discuss the ethics of exceptionalism.

6. The ethics of exceptionalism

In this final section, let us consider some of the ethical features that are germane to the exceptionalisms presented above. While the most interesting discussion will pertain to group-based exceptionalism, let us start with the ethics of temporal and spatial exceptionalism. From the outset, let me say that I consider these the most benign and group-based exceptionalism more perilous.

Taking temporal-based exceptionalism first, the idea here was that some norms applied at some times and not at others. Again, this sort of exceptionalism is not particularly relevant to the war on terror (though see Section 3 for a discussion of the PATRIOT Act). But, even if it were, it could be carried out in a morally sensible sort of way. More generally, imagine that there is some national emergency.[58] This could be war, some infectious disease, a national disaster, or whatever. In these cases, the public good is quite often going to be pitted against the rights of some individuals. We can see this in the public health case, for example, by considering quarantine and forced immunization.[59] In other cases, we might see it in rationing.[60] In all of these cases, though, it at least seems reasonable that we might restrict some liberties, so long as such restrictions were necessary, served the greater good, and were lifted when advisable. Certainly some people might deny this position, though I will not defend it here.[61]

What are debatable, of course, are the sorts of empirical claims that motivate the restrictions on offer. For example, imagine the claim that we need electronic surveillance to conduct the war on terror, thus violating the privacy rights of at least some. Objections to this line of thought are more often made on the grounds that the results of such surveillance are not likely to be of any use to the war on terror; such restrictions therefore incur costs without providing countervailing benefits.[62] Civil libertarians certainly like to invoke rights to privacy but if they actually believed that, absent such restrictions, our society were in serious risk of destruction, then it would be unreasonable of them to persist in their objections. Rather, I assert that the empirical basis for restricting liberties is sometimes unsound, not that, in theory, there is any serious moral objection to the sorts of reasonable restrictions that well-founded empirical prognoses would suggest.

Moving on to spatial exceptionalism, I again do not find this to be that worrisome. Or at least, I think this insofar as we are considering genuine instances of spatial exceptionalism and not the sorts that are more properly understood as group-based exceptionalism (cf., Guantánamo). Again, return to the example of the Montana legislature excepting its citizenry from norms governing other locales. It seems perfectly acceptable as a premise of self-governance that local legislatures be able to set the parameters by which they govern, and some of these parameters may give rise to spatial-based exceptionalisms. To be sure, there are constitutional considerations that come into play, such as the Fourteenth Amendment and the Commerce Clause, that are relevant; the Commerce Clause, for example, is being interpreted in ways inconsistent with legislation banning direct wine shipments, which means that the Montana law might soon fall.[63] But *in principle* there is nothing wrong with norms applied to certain geographic zones, so long as those norms do not run afoul of broader considerations (e.g., constitutionality). We certainly do not want it to be the case that local norms are arbitrary or capricious; but, if they were, the problem would be the caprice or arbitrariness and not, intrinsically, the spatial-based exceptionalism that they characterized.

But what about group-based exceptionalism? Again, this is the most substantial form of exceptionalism suggested by the war on terror. And, unfortunately, it is the most perilous of all the forms described in this chapter. Why? There are obvious cases of group-based exceptionalism which are completely immoral and rank among the greatest injustices humanity has perpetuated. We hardly need to catalogue these but consider, for example, slavery or genocide. In both of these cases, certain norms applied, except to some group. These norms could range from freedom to vote to even the liberty not to be killed. In the Holocaust, Jews were deprived of practically everything (often including their lives) merely because of their association with some group; the same is true with American slaves and countless other tyrannized groups. The mere fact that some of these horrors are straightforward instantiations of group-based exceptionalism should give us pause when considering the whole category.

Or should it? Just as there are horrible cases of group-based exceptionalism, there are also completely innocuous ones. For example, consider collegiate admissions, which except one group from some outcome (e.g., acceptance or rejection) based on features that it has (e.g., grade point average, SAT scores, etc.). All American citizens can vote, except convicted felons—or at least those not residing in Maine or Vermont—and those under the age of eighteen. This former exception strikes many of us as problematic, but little seems wrong with the latter. We except the group of people that have been in car accidents or otherwise have poor driving records from the car insurance rates to which the rest of us have access. So there certainly seem to be unproblematic group-based exceptionalisms. What, then, is the difference between the acceptable and unacceptable forms? And, for present purposes, where do our archetypes from the war on terror fall?

The first thing to say here is that the relevant differentia is *not* what norm the exception is from, which might seem an intuitive way to go. Take some norm such as: "None should be enslaved, except those of African descent." The reason that this exception is morally problematic does not, strictly speaking, have to do with allowing exceptions to a particular norm. It might be the case that there are exceptions to the norm (e.g., those that consent to being sold into slavery) or it might not. But it is the *exceptions* that matter, not just the norms, in determining the moral status of the exceptionalism.

To see why this is the case, consider the norm of allowing citizens to vote. As mentioned above, there are and have been exceptions to this norm. For example, children cannot vote in the US, and women did not, nationally, gain the right to vote in the US until the ratification of the Nineteenth Amendment in 1920. Consider some time before 1920, when neither women nor children had the right to vote. Granting that one of these exceptions is morally permissible and the other one morally impermissible, it therefore follows that it cannot be the *norm* that drives the permissibility, but rather the *group* that is excepted from the norm. I do not deny that it depends on the group *in relation to the norm*, such that some group might be reasonably excepted from some norm (e.g. women's access to men's restrooms) while that same group might not be reasonably excepted from another (e.g. women's right to vote). However, the norms, independently of the groups to which the exceptions would apply, are not the proper objects of moral evaluation.[64]

If this is right, we must look at the groups that would be excepted from the norms. Using the suffrage case again, there is no moral reason to exclude women from a political process to which men have access: whatever the morally relevant features are that ground men's claim to voting are similarly held by women. As this illustrates, we have to think not only about the group that is to be excepted, but we also have to think about the relationship that group shares *to the other groups that are not excepted*. We need to treat like cases alike, though we have to specify the dimensions of similarity that matter in each case. Unlike the gender difference in voting, though, we can locate a relevant difference between children and adults, thus grounding the exception made against children's right to vote. Namely, we want our electorate to have a certain level of rationality, capacity for acquisition and processing of information, etc., and there is no doubt that young children lack this. (I take no position on whether the age of eighteen is the appropriate cutoff.)

Now let us return to the cases presented in the context of the war on terror, looking specifically at the groups that stand to be excepted and the relationship that those groups bear to the groups that will not be excepted. Furthermore, let us consider whether there are morally relevant differences between these groups that might serve to ground differential moral statuses. Both of the groups that are affected by exceptions made for torture and enemy combatancy status are, ideally, those that have critical intelligence.[65] And those that are targeted for assassination are similar insofar as they are assessed to pose threats, whether now or in the future. There might be a difference in these cases insofar as the former groups' crimes could be of omission (i.e., by not revealing the information), while the latter group's crimes would be of commission (i.e., by effecting the harms directly). I am not sure this is right though and, regardless, the distinction is orthogonal to our discussion. Rather, what matters is that all of those groups excepted are responsible, actively or passively, for some threat and, through their agency, can abrogate the threat.

An obvious objection to this claim is that it is simply false: many of those subject to detention or torture, in fact, have no critical intelligence, and some are not even terrorists at all.[66] It might even be the case that those targeted for assassination are not bad people, though I find this less likely: it is more likely that we disagree about what "bad" means and/or whether there are other options available. Regardless, at least this first claim is certainly true. What are its implications for our analysis? To my mind, it does not have important implications for the morality of group-based exceptionalism. The reason is that it just shows we are applying the exceptions to the *wrong group*: a group that includes, not just the people that we should be excepting, but rather a group that (maybe) includes those people, as well as others to whom the exceptions should not apply. That we have our groups delimited improperly says nothing about the status of exceptionalism, *as applied to the proper groups*.

The waiting objection now is that, pragmatically, it is somewhere between hard and impossible to make sure that we have the right groups. First, I do not think that this is completely true: our military intelligence just has to do a good job in classifying people appropriately. There is no doubt that this is a challenge, and probably no doubt that it could have been done better than has been since 9/11. But I certainly think that we can get it mostly right and, given the complexities of warfare and some of the latitudes that must be therein conferred, this is close enough (cf., collateral damage).[67] Second, this really is meant to be a theoretical project, and we need to work out our theoretical commitments before turning to practice.[68]

Where we now stand is that we have an (idealized) account of exceptionalism wherein we are excepting groups who pose harms from various protections. What is the moral status of such an account? As indicated above, one of the criteria is to compare the moral status of the excepted groups to the non-excepted groups. In these cases, there is at least one morally relevant difference between those groups, which is complicity or agency in imminent or otherwise future harms. For simplicity, let us just call this something like (partial) responsibility. The notion of responsibility certainly has hardly gotten a free ride in the philosophical literature, though I will not have anything substantive to say about it here.[69] Rather, I will just observe that we obviously treat responsible parties differently from non-responsible parties, as evidenced by our systems of praise and blame, and as is codified in our moral and legal systems.[70] And there are certainly good reasons for this.

So there are relevant differences between these would-be excepted groups and their contraries. Are they sufficient to warrant exceptions to the norms? People will disagree strongly about this, and I cannot hope to settle the debate, so much as to offer the framework in which it should be considered. I think that what ultimately matters is whether the practices are effective. It either is or is not the case that we gain critical intelligence by holding detainees indefinitely (i.e., without affording them due process) and/or by torturing them. Critics are surely skeptical in both cases, though I am more sanguine vis-à-vis torture than indefinite detention insofar as detention probably offends a higher rate of innocents; escalating the treatment of some within that group to another group subject to torture would hopefully only be done with good reason (e.g., reasonable expectation that critical intelligence could be gleaned). This is not to suggest that torture always—or even most of the time—reveals critical intelligence, but rather that we must discriminate more precisely when we consider torture than when we consider (mere) detention since the former portends a greater and more irreversible moral harm. Finally, assassinations either avert worse harms in the future or they do not, and it is these proclivities by which their merits should be judged.

Note that I have intentionally used vague concepts, such as "effective," "better," and "worse." The reason that I do this is not to waffle, but rather to appreciate that different people understand these terms differently and that the above account is compatible with variable conceptions in this regard. We could make these evaluations in terms of consequences, human rights, dignity, or whatever. The upshot of this chapter, however, is meant to be that there is nothing inherently wrong with group-based exceptionalism. Nor is there anything wrong with exceptionalism merely in virtue of the norms that are being excepted. Both of these conclusions, I think, would have been counterintuitive. Rather, we gauge the ethics of exceptionalism by focusing on the *groups* that are excepted and by looking for differentia between those groups and other groups that are not excepted. Ideally, I think that the exceptions that we have considered can be justified. As those exceptions have actually been practiced in the war on terror, I am less certain. Regardless, I see no in-principle objection to these sorts of group-based exceptionalisms or others that would employ similar strategies.

Notes

1 This chapter was published earlier and in somewhat different form as F. Allhoff, "The War on Terror and the Ethics of Exceptionalism," *Journal of Military Ethics*, 8:4 2009, pp. 265–288. Adapted with permission.

2 See, for example, N. Crawford, "Just War Theory and the US Counterterror War," *Perspectives on Politics*, 1:1, 2003, pp. 5–25.

3 See, for example, M. Walzer, *Just and Unjust Wars*, 4th edn, New York, NY: Basic Books, 2006. Also, see the classic treatment of just war theory by T. Aquinas in *Summa Theologica*, trans. by the Fathers of the English Dominican Province, New York, NY: Benziger Books, 1948, Question 40, esp. Article 1. See also B. Orend, "War," *Stanford Encyclopedia of Philosophy*. Online. Available at: http://plato.stanford.edu/entries/war (accessed 18 July, 2012).

4 See, for example, T. Shanahan (ed.), *Philosophy 9/11: Thinking about the War on Terror*, Peru, IL: Open Court Publishing Company, 2005. For skepticism on the distinctiveness of terrorism, see L.K. McPherson, "Is Terrorism Distinctively Wrong?" *Ethics* 117, 2007, 524–46.

5 For more discussion, see F. Allhoff, *Terrorism, Ticking Time-Bombs, and Torture*, Chicago: University of Chicago Press, 2012, §1.3.

6 For more discussion, see T. Meisels, "Combatants—Lawful and Unlawful," *Law and Philosophy*, 26:1, 2007, pp. 31–65.

7 For more discussion, see Allhoff, *Terrorism, Ticking Time-Bombs, and Torture*, §1.4.

8 Michael Gross has also discussed blackmail as such a practice, though I will not consider it here. See M. L. Gross, *Moral Dilemmas of Modern War: Torture, Assassination, and Blackmail in an Age of Asymmetric Conflict* Cambridge: Cambridge University Press, 2009, esp. ch. 7. The development of chemical and biological weapons might also be visited in this context. See M. Cooper, "Pre-Empting Emergence: The Biological Turn in the War on Terror," *Theory, Culture, and Society* 23:4, 2006, pp. 113–35. Cooper is especially interested in germ warfare and the US military's growing interest in biodefense research. See also F. Allhoff (ed.), *Physicians at War: The Dual-Loyalties Challenge*, Dordrecht: Springer, 2008a, esp. Part III.

9 Universal Declaration of Human Rights. 1948. Online. Available at: http://www.un.org/en/documents/udhr/ (accessed 18 July, 2012).

10 Third Geneva Convention. 1949. Online. Available at: http://www.icrc.org/ihl.nsf/7c4d08d9b287a4 2141256739003e636b/6fef854a3517b75ac125641e004a9e68 (accessed 18 July, 2012).

11 Declaration of Tokyo (1975). Online. Available at: http://www.cirp.org/library/ethics/tokyo/ (accessed 18 July, 2012).

12 The Convention against Torture, and Other Cruel, Inhuman or Degrading Treatment or Punishment (CAT). Online. Available at: http://treaties.un.org/doc/Publication/UNTS/Volume%201465/volume-1465-I-24841-English.pdf (accessed 18 July, 2012). CAT has a somewhat complicated legislative history, thus making it unclear how to date it. The General Assembly of the UN adopted CAT in 1975. It was then opened for ratification by signatory countries in 1985; CAT entered into force once it was ratified by the 20th country, which happened when Canada ratified it in 1987. 1975 and 1987 are therefore both commonly listed as dates, depending on what the date is meant to represent.

13 Third Geneva Convention. Online. available at: http://www.icrc.org/ihl.nsf/7c4d08d9b287a421412 56739003e636b/6fef854a3517b75ac125641e004a9e68 (accessed 18 July, 2012).

14 See, for example, J. Wolfendale, "Torture Lite and the Normalization of Torture," *Ethics & International Affairs* 29:1, 2009, pp. 47–61.

15 Henceforth, I shall just use "torture," though I mean it to include most sorts of coercive interrogations. This locution is not meant to morally load those practices, but rather is undertaken for facility and in concordance with common usage. For more discussion, see F. Allhoff *Terrorism, Ticking Time-Bombs, and Torture*, §4.1.

16 Associated Press, "Poll Finds Broad Approval of Terrorist Torture," December 9, 2005. Online. Available at: http://www.msnbc.msn.com/id/10345320/ (accessed 18 July, 2012). I suspect that public sentiment against torture has been rising in the past couple of years, though that is just a hypothesis; I could not find more recent data. Regardless, polls are fickle, so we should not take them too seriously.

17 For more discussion, see F. Allhoff *Terrorism, Ticking Time-Bombs, and Torture*, esp. ch. 7.

18 Just to be clear, I am not proposing that existing norms are necessarily revised in light of terrorism; my proposal is far more modest and simply suggests that the norms are subject to review. Certainly this review might ultimately reaffirm those norms, even if they are liable to revision.

19 In the literature, we see the term "assassination" alongside the closely-related "targeted killing," though these distinctions are never made clear. According to Michael Gross (personal communication, 5 May, 2008), assassination is linked to "perfidious killing in war", while "targeted killing" lacks this connotation; it is therefore less morally loaded. However, some interpret "targeted killing" as being a sort of extra-judicial execution, and therefore more appropriate to law enforcement rather than to

armed conflict. I shall use "assassination" for my discussion, though take it that discussion would apply equally to targeted killing.

Regarding "assassination" itself, Franklin Ford defines it as "the intentional killing of a specified victim or group of victims perpetrated for reasons related to his (her, their) public prominence and undertaken with a political purpose in view." F.L. Ford, *Political Murder: From Tyrannicide to Terrorism*, Cambridge, MA: Harvard University Press, 1985, p. 2. For some other conceptual work on assassination see H. Zellner (ed.), *Assassination*, Cambridge: Schenkman, 1974. Especially helpful is James Rachels, "Political Assassination," in H. Zellner (ed.) *Assassination*, Cambridge: Schenkman, 1974, pp. 9–21.

20 A good historical account of assassinations is Ford *Political Murder: From Tyrannicide to Terrorism*.

21 Sun Tzu, *Art of War*, trans. L. Giles, 1910, esp. Ch. XIII. Online. Available at: http://www.gutenberg.org/etext/132 (accessed 18 July, 2012).

22 N. Machiavelli, *The Prince*, trans. W.K. Marriott, 1908, esp. Ch. XIX. Online. Available at: http://www.constitution.org/mac/prince00.htm (accessed 18 July, 2012).

23 Thomas More, *Utopia*, New York: Appleton-Century-Crofts, 1949, p. 65. Referenced in A. Altman and C.H. Wellman, "From Humanitarian Intervention to Assassination: Human Rights and Political Violence," *Ethics* 118 2008, pp. 251–252.

24 G.R. Ford, "Executive Order 11905: United States Foreign Intelligence Activities", 18 February 1976. Online. Available at: http://www.fas.org/irp/offdocs/eo11905.htm (accessed 1 April, 2013).

25 J. Carter, "Executive Order 12036: United States Foreign Intelligence Activities." 24 January 1978. Online. Available at: http://www.fas.org/irp/offdocs/eo/eo-12036.htm (accessed 18 July, 2012).

26 R. Reagan, "Executive Order 12333: United States Intelligence Activities," 4 December 1981. Online. Available at: http://www.fas.org/irp/offdocs/eo12333.htm (accessed 18 July, 2012).

27 B. Woodward, "CIA Told to Do 'Whatever Necessary' to Kill Bin Laden," *Washington Post*, 21 October 2001: A01.

28 W. Thomas, "The New Age of Assassination," *SAIS Review* 25, 2005, pp. 27–39. See also Gross (unpublished).

29 For discussion of this question see, for example, Altman and Wellman "From Humanitarian Intervention to Assassination: Human Rights and Political Violence;" S.R. David, "Israel's Policy of Targeted Killing," *Ethics and International Affairs*, 17:1, 2003, pp. 111–26; M.L. Gross, "Assassination and Targeted Killing: Law Enforcement, Execution, or Self-Defence?" *Journal of Applied Philosophy*, 23:3, 2006, pp. 323–335; A. Kasher and A. Yadlin, "Military Ethics of Fighting Terror: An Israeli Perspective," *Journal of Military Ethics*, 4:1, 2005, pp. 3–32; S. Kershnar, "Assassination and the Immunity Theory," *Philosophia* 33:1–4, 2005, pp. 129-47; T. Meisels, "Targeting Terror," *Social Theory and Practice*, 30:3, 2004, pp. 297–326; and D. Statman, "Targeted Killing," *Theoretical Inquiries in Law*, 5:1, 2004, pp. 179–198.

30 See the complete text of the Third Geneva Convention. Online. Available at: http://www.icrc.org/ihl.nsf/7c4d08d9b287a42141256739003e636b/6fef854a3517b75ac125641e004a9e68 (accessed 18 July, 2012).

31 *Ex Parte Quirin*, 317 US 1 (1942). Online. Available at: http://caselaw.lp.findlaw.com/scripts/getcase.pl?navby=CASE&court=US&vol=317&page=1 (accessed 18 July, 2012). The case upheld the jurisdiction of a United States military tribunal over a group of German saboteurs who had been apprehended in the US, two of whom were American citizens.

32 See, for example, S.D. Murphy (ed.), "Ability of Detainees in Cuba to Obtain Federal *Habeas Corpus* Review", *American Journal of International Law*, 98:1, 2004, pp. 188–190. For critical discussion, see T. Gill and E. van Sliedregt "Guantánamo Bay: A Reflection on the Legal Status and Rights of 'Unlawful Enemy Combatants,'" *Utrecht Law Review*, 1:1, 2005, pp. 28–54.

33 I thank Don Scheid (personal communication, 16 December, 2009) and Jonathan Marks (personal communication, 18 December, 2009) for helpful discussions on enemy combatancy status. As Professor Marks pointed out, enemy combatancy status is not recognized in international law, nor in the Third Geneva Convention (which post-dated *Quirin*).

34 See *Hamdan v. Rumsfeld* 548 U.S. 557 (2006). Online. Available at: http://www.law.cornell.edu/supct/html/05-184.ZS.html (accessed 18 July, 2012). See also *Boumediene v. Bush* 553 U.S. 723 (2008). Online. Available at: http://www.law.cornell.edu/supct/html/06-1195.ZS.html (accessed 18 July, 2012). President Bush signed the Military Commissions Act of 2006 (MCA) into law following an unfavorable ruling in *Hamdan*; *Boumediene* found the §7 of the MCA—which denied *habeas corpus* to unlawful enemy combatants—unconstitutional. See also note 50 below.

35 A. R. Gonzales, Memorandum for the President, January 25, 2002. Online. Available at: http://www. gwu.edu/~nsarchiv/NSAEBB/NSAEBB127/02.01.25.pdf (accessed 18 July, 2012). Cited in J. Marks, "9/11+3/11+7/7=?: What Counts in Counterterrorism," *Columbia Human Rights Law Review*, 37:3, 2006, pp. 101–161, p. 118.

36 E. Gandini and T. Saleh (Directors), *Gitmo: The New Rules of War* [Motion Picture], Sweden: Atma Media Network, 2005, 22:58–23:21.

37 Following his service at Guantánamo, Major General Miller was sent to Abu Ghraib, where it is widely believed that he transformed the interrogation program to include some of the more aggressive techniques practiced at Guantánamo. For more discussion of these techniques, see J. Wolfendale "Torture Lite and the Normalization of Torture."

38 See, for example, M.W. Brough, "Legitimate Combatancy, POW Status, and Terrorism," in T. Shanahan (ed.), *Philosophy 9/11: Thinking about the War on Terror*, Peru: IL Open Court Publishing Co. pp. 205–222. See also note 34 above.

39 For a contrary position, see A. Fiala, "A Critique of Exceptions: Torture, Terrorism, and the Lesser Evil", *International Journal of Applied Philosophy*, 20:1, 2006, pp.127–142. Fiala is worried that exceptions can ultimately normalize immoral behavior. This seems a misplaced worry to me insofar as the exceptions that are of interest to us are the ones that are morally justifiable; there is no reason to consider morally unjustifiable exceptions. Therefore, what we are normalizing is not immoral behavior, but rather behavior that, in other contexts, was not necessary. If the worry is that the normalized behavior would persist if and when the present context reverted to the earlier one, then this becomes more interesting legislatively than philosophically. Philosophically, there would no longer be any justification for the exception, so the unexcepted norm should be restored. Exceptions in war are also considered in D. Rodin, "The Ethics of War: State of the Art," *Journal of Applied Philosophy*, 23:3, 2006, pp. 241–246.

40 There is a growing literature on moral particularism, though much of it is orthogonal to the present project. In its more extreme forms, moral particularism denies that there are moral principles. More conservatively, it admits of moral principles, but denies the preeminence of these principles. See, for example, B. Hooker and M. Little (eds), *Moral Particularism*, Oxford: Oxford University Press, 2000, and J. Dancy, *Ethics without Principles*, Oxford: Clarendon Press, 2004. See also J. Dancy, "Moral Particularism," *Stanford Encyclopedia of Philosophy*. Online. Available at: http://plato.stanford.edu/entries/moral-particularism/ (accessed 18 July, 2012). Some of this literature mentions exceptions. See, for example, J. Dancy, "Defending Particularlism," *Metaphilosophy*, 30:1–2 1999, pp. 25–32 and A. H. Goldman, *Practical Rules: When We Need Them and When We Don't*, Cambridge: Cambridge University Press, 2001.

41 Note, though, that exceptionalism can be construed even more generally than moral and legal norms. Consider, for example, Mendel's Second Law (the Law of Independent Assortment), which holds that the inheritance pattern of one trait will not affect the inheritance pattern of another trait. However, this is not quite right: this "law" is true except when genes are linked to each other (as might happen with genes proximally situated on the same chromosome such that they might segregate together during meiosis), in which case it is not. Again, the exception is to some stricture (namely, that independent assortment is required), and what is being excepted is some phenomena (namely, transmission of linked genes). My analysis can similarly accommodate these examples as well, though the emphasis will be on exceptions to moral and legal norms.

42 For example, consider: "All Xs must ϕ, except Ys." This norm does not imply that there are Ys; rather, it implies only that, if there were any Ys, they would not have to ϕ. This is still a well-formed excepted norm, even if there might not be any Ys at present.

43 These examples will motivate distinctions similar to those suggested in Marks "9/11+3/11+7/7=?: What Counts in Counterterrorism," esp. pp. 119–120. We both derive spatial and temporal exceptionalisms, and his collective exceptionalism is similar to my group-based exceptionalism. Further discussion of his account will appear below.

    Marks's taxonomy also includes "*interpretive exceptionalism*, in which norms are reinterpreted in order to narrow the scope of the protection conferred or of the conduct that is prohibited" (ibid. p. 121; author's emphasis). His example of this includes (re-)interpretation of torture as that which requires pain "equivalent in intensity to the pain accompanying serious physical injury, such as organ failure, the permanent impairment of a significant bodily function, or even death," J.S. Bybee, 2002, "Memorandum for Alberto R. Gonzales Counsel to the President, Re: Standards of Conduct for Interrogation under 18 U.S.C. §§2340-2340A," August 1, 2002, Washington, DC: US Department of Justice.

Another example he uses is the view once expressed by Department of Defense officials that medically-trained personnel assigned to develop interrogation strategies at Guantánamo and Abu Ghraib were not acting as physicians and, therefore, not subject to the strictures of medical ethics. See M.G. Bloche and J.H. Marks, "When Doctors Go to War," *New England Journal of Medicine*, 352:3, 2005, pp. 3–6.

There are a few different reasons that I do not bring his interpretive exceptionalism into my account. First, interpretive exceptionalism seems necessarily *post hoc*, and therefore not very philosophically interesting: of course people should not change their conceptions of something merely because it is convenient or expedient. What is interesting, in both the torture and physician cases, is to *acknowledge* that we have torture or physicians, and then to talk about whether these things are acceptable or not; mere semantic recourse to move the bar somewhere else just seems disingenuous rather than philosophically suggestive. Second, the interesting facets of the interpretive approach—if there are any—can be subsumed under another form of exceptionalism, most likely group-based exceptionalism. In the torture case, for example, there would be a certain group of people, namely the interrogatees, who are excepted from protections against some practices. In the physician case, there would be a certain group of people, namely medically-trained interrogators, who are excepted from medical duties. His interpretive exceptionalism can therefore be subsumed under my group-based exceptionalism (see section 6, this chapter).

44 Wine shipping laws are available from the Wine Institute. Online. Available at: http://www.wineinstitute.org/initiatives/stateshippinglaws (accessed 18 July, 2012). For discussion, see D. Massey, "Shipping across State Lines: Wine and the Law," in F. Allhoff (ed.), *Wine & Philosophy*, Oxford: Blackwell Publishing, 2008, pp. 275–287.

45 S. Abruzzese, "Maryland Parents Told to Have Children Immunized," *New York Times*, 18 November, 2007. Online. Available at: http://www.nytimes.com/2007/11/18/us/18vaccine. html (accessed 18 July, 2012)). See also G.R. Chaddock, "One Maryland County Takes Tough Tack on Vaccinations," *The Christian Science Monitor*, 19 November 2007. Online. Available at: http://www.csmonitor.com/2007/1119/p02s04–ussc.html (accessed 18 July, 2012).

46 J. Marks "9/11+3/11+7/7=?: What Counts in Counterterrorism," p. 119. See also: D. Fleck (ed.), *Handbook of Humanitarian Law in Armed Conflicts*, New York: Oxford University Press, 2000, p. 13; R. Baker, "A Theory of International Bioethics: Multiculturalism, Postmodernism and the Bankruptcy of Fundamentalism," *Kennedy Institute of Ethics Journal*, 8:3, 1998, pp. 201, 211. Both cited in Marks "9/11+3/11+7/7=?: What Counts in Counterterrorism," p. 119.

47 Uniting and Strengthening America by Providing Appropriate Tools Required to Intercept and Obstruct Terrorism (USA PATRIOT Act) Act of 2001, Pub. L. No. 107-56, 115 Stat. 272. Online. Available at: http://www.fincen.gov/statutes_regs/patriot/index.html (accessed 18 July, 2012).

48 For list of these provisions, see C. Doyle, "Patriot Act Sunset: Provisions that Expire on December 31, 2005," Washington, DC: Congressional Research Service. 2004. Online. Available at:http://www. fas.org/irp/crs/RL32186.pdf (accessed 18 July, 2012). They include: §201 (wiretapping in terrorism cases); §202 (wiretapping in computer fraud and abuse felony cases); §203(b) (sharing wiretap information); §203(d) (sharing foreign intelligence information); §204 (Foreign Intelligence Surveillance Act (FISA) pen register/trap and trace exceptions); §206 (roving FISA wiretaps); §207 (duration of FISA surveillance of non-US persons who are agents of a foreign power); §209 (seizure of voice-mail messages pursuant to warrants); §212 (emergency disclosure of electronic surveillance); §214 (FISA pen register/trap and trace authority); §215 (FISA access to tangible items); §217 (interception of computer trespasser communications); §218 (purpose for FISA orders); §220 (nationwide service of search warrants for electronic evidence); §223 (civil liability and discipline for privacy violations); and §225 (provider immunity for FISA wiretap assistance. Cited in Marks"9/11+3/11+7/7=?: What Counts in Counterterrorism," p. 121.

49 The PATRIOT Act was renewed and amended through three subsequent pieces of legislation. The first was the USA PATRIOT Improvement and Reauthorization Act of 2005, 109–333, H.R.3199. Online. Available at: http://thomas.loc.gov/cgi-bin/cpquery/R?cp109:FLD010:@1(hr333) (accessed 18 July, 2012). The second was the USA PATRIOT Act Additional Reauthorizing Amendments Act of 2006, 109–178, S.2271. Online. Available at: http://www.intelligence.senate.gov/laws/pl109-178. pdf (accessed 18 July, 2012). For analysis, see C. Doyle, "USA PATRIOT Act Reauthorization in Brief," Washington, D.C.: Congressional Research Service (August 2005). Online. Available at: http:// fpc.state.gov/documents/organization/51133.pdf (accessed 18 July, 2012). The third was PATRIOT Sunsets Extension Act of 2011, Pub. L. no. 112–114, 125 Stat 216 (2011). Online. Available at: http://

www.gpo.gov/fdsys/pkg/PLAW-112publ14/pdf/PLAW-112publ14.pdf (accessed 31 July 2012). For analysis, see E. Liu, "Amendments to the Foreign Intelligence Surveillance Act (FISA) Extended Until June 1, 2015," Washington, D.C.: Congressional Research Service, June 16, 2011. Online. Available at: http://www.fas.org/sgp/crs/intel/R40138.pdf (accessed 31 July, 2012).

50 For a more comprehensive discussion of sunset provisions than can be offered here, see L.A. Davis, "Review Procedures and Public Accountability in Sunset Legislation: An Analysis and Proposal for Reform," *Administrative Law Review*, 33, 1981, pp. 393–402. For a recent proposal to apply a sunset provision model to judicial decisions, see N. Katya, "Sunsetting Judicial Opinions", *Notre Dame Law Review*, 79:4, 2003, pp. 1237–1246.

51 US Congress "Alien and Sedition Acts," 1798. Online. Available at: http://www.loc.gov/rr/program/bib/ourdocs/Alien.html (accessed 18 July, 2012).

52 For discussion, see D. Massey "Shipping across State Lines: Wine and the Law."

53 Marks "9/11+3/11+7/7=?: What Counts in Counterterrorism," p. 120 (emphasis in original). Marks also mentions CIA interrogation centers in Eastern Europe that "were established in order to circumvent the ban on cruel, inhuman, and degrading treatment, pursuant to the administration's view that the ban did not apply to aliens held outside the United States." (Ibid.) I will not discuss this example in particular, though my forthcoming discussion applies, *mutatis mutandis*, to it.

54 Note that, while the Bush Administration is routinely criticized for denying *habeas corpus* to detainees, Bush's was certainly not the first presidency to restrict or undermine this protection. (It further bears notice that, according to the US Constitution, the protection is hardly unalienable. According to Article I, Section 9, Clause 2: "The Privilege of the Writ of Habeas Corpus shall not be suspended, unless when in Cases of Rebellion or Invasion the public Safety may require it." This clause, of course, does not grant the *President* the right to suspend it, of which more shortly).

During the Civil War, President Lincoln suspended *habeas corpus* several times. The first took place after the attack on Fort Sumter in April 1861 and applied to the military line between Philadelphia and Washington, DC. This action was challenged and overturned in *Ex Parte Merryman*, in which Supreme Court Chief Justice Roger Taney held that only Congress, not the President, could suspend the writ. Lincoln went on to ignore Taney's order to restore it. For more details, see *Ex Parte Merryman*, 17 F. Cas. 144 (1861). Online. Available at: http://www.tourolaw.edu/Patch/Merryman (accessed 18 July, 2012). The suspension ended in February 1862, though was reissued—this time over the entire North—that September. Congress then passed the Habeas Corpus Act in 1863, which was meant to indemnify the President against judicial challenges as had arisen in *Merryman*. President Johnson then restored the writ state-by-state between December 1865 and August 1866. In the early 1870s, President Grant suspended it in nine South Carolina counties as part of action against the Ku Klux Klan. See A. Johnson, "Habeas Corpus," in J. J. Lalor (ed.), *Cyclopaedia of Political Science*, New York: Maynard, Merrill, and Co., 1899. Online. Available at: http://www.econlib.org/library/YPDBooks/Lalor/llCy521.html (accessed 1 April, 2013).

In 1987, President Reagan refused to ratify Protocol I, an amendment to the Geneva Conventions that the US had signed in 1977. At stake primarily was Article 44, Paragraphs 3–5; Reagan interpreted these paragraphs as extending protections to terrorists. By not ratifying the Protocol, the US would not owe those fighters the judicial provisions made in Article 3(1)(d) of the Third Geneva Convention, thus, effectively, denying them *habeas corpus*. Despite having been ratified by over 160 countries, the US has still not ratified it, whether under Reagan or any subsequent administration. (Iran, Iraq, and Israel are other notable exceptions.) See R. Reagan, "Message to the Senate Transmitting a Protocol to the 1949 Geneva Conventions," 29 January, 1987. Online. Available at: http://www.reagan.utexas.edu/archives/speeches/1987/012987b.htm (accessed 18 July, 2012).

President Clinton signed into law the Antiterrorism and Effective Death Penalty Act of 1996, in which §101 set a statute of limitations for the request of *habeas corpus* and further limits the power of federal judges to grant relief. See Antiterrorism and Effective Death Penalty Act of 1996 (AEDPA), Pub. L. No. 104-132, 110 Stat. 1214, 1996. Online. Available at: http://www.gpo.gov/fdsys/pkg/PLAW-104publ132/html/PLAW-104publ132.htm (accessed 18 July, 2012).

There have also been various Supreme Court cases which have upheld the limitation of *habeas corpus*. *Ex Parte Quirin* (1942)—discussed in Section 1—held that the enemy combatants could be denied *habeas corpus*. *Johnson v. Eisentrager* denied *habeas corpus* to nonresident aliens captured and imprisoned abroad. See *Johnson v. Eisentrager*, 339 U.S. 763 (1950). Online. Available at: http://supreme.justia.com/cases/federal/us/339/763 (accessed 1 April, 2013). However, some important decisions have asserted *habeaus corpus* protection, including *Hamdan* and *Boumediene*; see note 34 above. See also

Hamdi v. Rumsfeld 542 U.S. 507 (2004). Online. Available at: http://caselaw.lp.findlaw.com/scripts/getcase.pl?court=US&vol=000&invol=03-6696 (accessed 18 July, 2012).

55 For more discussion, see F. Allhoff *Terrorism, Ticking Time-Bombs, and Torture*, esp. pts. II–III.

56 For more discussion, see F. Allhoff *Terrorism, Ticking Time-Bombs, and Torture*, §4.2.

57 For example, Michael Davis does not think there are any conditions that would justify torture whereas Vittorio Bufacchi and Jean Maria Arrigo think that, even if torture were permissible in theory, it would never be so in practice. (This is an extension of dialectical charity as, I suspect, they otherwise agree with Davis.) See M. Davis, "The Moral Justifiability of Torture and Other Cruel, Inhuman, or Degrading Treatment," *International Journal of Applied Philosophy*, 19:2, 2005, pp. 161–178. See also V. Bufacchi and J. M. Arrigo, "Torture, Terrorism, and the State: A Refutation of the Ticking Time-Bomb Argument," *Journal of Applied Philosophy*, 23:3, 2006, pp. 355–373. For a response, see F. Allhoff *Terrorism, Ticking Time-Bombs, and Torture*, esp. ch. 6.

58 It is worth noting that constitutional provisions have already been explored in this regard as pertains especially to terrorist attacks. See Bruce Ackerman, "The Emergency Constitution," *Yale Law Journal* 113, 2004b, pp. 1029–1091. For a less technical discussion, see B. Ackerman, *Before the Next Attack: Preserving Civil Liberties in an Age of Terrorism*, New Haven, CT: Yale University Press, 2004a.

59 See, for example, M. K. Wynia, "Ethics and Public Health Emergencies: Restrictions on Liberty," *American Journal of Bioethics*, 7:2, 2007, pp. 1–5. See also M. J. Selgelid, "Ethics and Infectious Disease," *Bioethics*, 19:3, 2005, pp. 272–289.

60 Rationing can take place in different contexts, but consider food rationing in the US during World War II. See, for example, A. Bentley, *Eating for Victory: Food Rationing and the Politics of Domesticity*, Urbana-Champaign, IL: University of Illinois Press, 1998. Also, see I. Zweiniger-Bargielowska, *Austerity in Britain: Rationing, Controls, and Consumption 1939–1955*, Oxford: Oxford University Press, 2000. There is also a literature about rationing in medicine; a classic is N. Rescher, "The Allocation of Exotic Medical Lifesaving Therapy," *Ethics*, 79:3 1969, pp. 173–186.

61 For discussion of such rights in the time before WWII, see C.B. Swisher, "Civil Liberties in War Time," *Political Science Quarterly*, 55:3, 1940, pp. 321–447. For a recent opinion against the suspension of such rights for the greater good, see E. Cassel, *The War on Civil Liberties: How Bush and Ashcroft Have Dismantled the Bill of Rights*, Chicago, IL: Lawrence Hill Books, 2004. For a general overview of such issues, see C. Duncan and T. Machan, *Libertarianism: For and Against*, Lanham, MD: Rowman & Littlefield, 2005.

62 For discussion, see N. C. Henderson, "The Patriot Act's Impact on the Government's Ability to Conduct Electronic Surveillance of Ongoing Domestic Communications," *Duke Law Journal*, 52:1, 2002, pp. 179–209.

63 See D. Massey "Shipping across State Lines: Wine and the Law."

64 As a counter example to this claim, we might postulate some norm which could bear no exceptions, such as: "None may be subjected to genocide, except …" I still think that, logically, it matters what the group is that is being excepted and, even if no exceptions are justified, that the analysis must include the groups. For example, imagine a case in which the world will be destroyed unless some group is subjected to genocide. I think that it is an open question whether genocide is justified in such a case, and we would want to think about the group to be excepted. Maybe it turns out to be the case that no exception is justified, but we would have to consider the groups who were candidate exceptions. The other alternative, then, is that there *are* exceptions to every norm, whether actually or possibly, and this is the view that I would be more inclined to endorse. If this is true, then, *ex hypothesi*, the groups matter.

65 Note that the group subject to torture is probably a subset of those classified as enemy combatants; it is probably unreasonable to think that most enemy combatants are tortured, though this presumably depends on the definitions that we employ.

66 For more discussion, see F. Allhoff *Terrorism, Ticking Time-Bombs, and Torture*, ch. 7. See also: L. Baldor, "More Than Half of Guantánamo Detainees Not Accused of Hostile Acts," Associated Press, 9 February, 2006; D. Rejali, *Torture and Democracy*, Princeton, NJ: Princeton University Press, 2007, p. 510.

67 This discussion typically starts with the doctrine of double effect; see P. Foot, "The Problem of Abortion and the Doctrine of Double Effect," *Oxford Review*, 5, 1967, pp. 5–15. For discussion pertaining to the war and terrorism context in particular, see G.D. Brown, "Proportionality and Just War," *Journal of Military Ethics*, 2:3, 2003, pp. 171–185; B. Haydar, "The Ethics of Fighting Terror and

the Priority of Citizens," *Journal of Military Ethics*, 4:1, 2005, pp. 52–59; and F.M. Kamm, "Terror and Collateral Damage: Are They Permissible?" *Journal of Ethics*, 9:3–4, 2005, pp. 381–401.

68 For more discussion of torture in practice, see Allhoff *Terrorism, Ticking Time-Bombs, and Torture*, ch. 7.

69 A conspicuous beginning to this discussion was in J.J. Thomson, "A Defense of Abortion," *Philosophy and Public Affairs*, 1:1, 1971, pp. 47–66. More recently, see P. Pettit, "Responsibility Incorporated," *Ethics*, 117, 2007, pp. 171–201 (esp. §1). For discussion in the context of war, see H. Ingierd and H. Syse, "Responsibility and Culpability in War," *Journal of Military Ethics*, 4:2, 2005, 85–99.

70 See, for example, R. J. Wallace, *Responsibility and the Moral Sentiments*, Cambridge, MA: Harvard University Press, 1994. See also G. Sher, *In Praise of Blame*, Oxford: Oxford University Press, 2005. For a discussion relating responsibility to politics and law, see M. Matravers, *Responsibility and Justice*, Malden, MA: Blackwell Publications, 2007.

References

Abruzzese, S. "Maryland Parents Told to Have Children Immunized," *New York Times*, 18 November, 2007. Online. Available at: http://www.nytimes.com/2007/11/18/us/18vaccine.html (accessed 18 July, 2012).

Ackerman, B. *Before the Next Attack: Preserving Civil Liberties in an Age of Terrorism* New Haven, CT: Yale University Press, 2004a.

——"The Emergency Constitution," *Yale Law Journal*, 113, 2004b, pp. 1029–1091.

Allhoff, F. *Terrorism, Ticking Time-Bombs, and Torture* Chicago, IL: University of Chicago Press, 2012.

——"The War on Terror and the Ethics of Exceptionalism," *Journal of Military Ethics*, 8:4, 2009, pp. 265–288.

——(ed.) *Physicians at War: The Dual-Loyalties Challenge*, Dordrecht: Springer, 2008a.

——(ed.) *Wine & Philosophy* Oxford: Blackwell Publishing, 2008b.

Altman, A. & Wellman, C.H. "From Humanitarian Intervention to Assassination: Human Rights and Political Violence," *Ethics*, 118, 2008, pp. 228–257.

Antiterrorism and Effective Death Penalty Act of 1996 (AEDPA), Pub. L. No. 104-132, 110 Stat. 1214, 1996. Online. Available at: http://www.gpo.gov/fdsys/pkg/PLAW-104publ132/html/PLAW-104publ132.htm (accessed 18 July, 2012).

Aquinas, T. *Summa Theologica*, trans. Fathers of the English Dominican Province, New York: Benziger Books, 1948.

Associated Press "Poll Finds Broad Approval of Terrorist Torture," December 9, 2005. Online. Available at: http://www.msnbc.msn.com/id/10345320/ (accessed 18 July, 2012).

Baker, R. "A Theory of International Bioethics: Multiculturalism, Postmodernism and the Bankruptcy of Fundamentalism," *Kennedy Institute of Ethics Journal*, 8:3, 1998, pp. 201–231.

Baldor, L. "More Than Half of Guantánamo Detainees Not Accused of Hostile Acts," *Associated Press*, 9 February, 2006.

Bentley, A *Eating for Victory: Food Rationing and the Politics of Domesticity*, Urbana-Champaign, IL: University of Illinois Press, 1998.

Bloche, M.G. & Marks, J.H. "When Doctors Go to War," *New England Journal of Medicine*, 352:3, 2005, pp. 3–6.

Boumediene v. Bush 553 U.S. 723, 2008. Online. Available at: http://www.law.cornell.edu/supct/html/06-1195.ZS.html (accessed 18 July, 2012).

Brough, M. "Legitimate Combatancy, POW Status, and Terrorism," in: T. Shanahan (ed.), *Philosophy 9/11: Thinking about the War on Terror*, pp. 205–222, Peru, IL: Open Court Publishing Co, 2005.

Brown, D.G. "Proportionality and Just War," *Journal of Military Ethics*, 2:3, 2003, pp. 171–185.

Bufacchi, V. & Arrigo, J.M. "Torture, Terrorism and the State: A Refutation of the Ticking Time-Bomb Argument," *Journal of Applied Philosophy*, 23:3, 2006, pp. 355–373.

Bybee, J.S. "Memorandum for Alberto R. Gonzales Counsel to the President, Re: Standards of Conduct for Interrogation under 18 U.S.C. §§2340–2340A," August 1, 2002. Washington, DC: US Department of Justice.

Carter, J. "Executive Order 12036: United States Foreign Intelligence Activities," 24 January, 1978. Online. Available at: http://www.fas.org/irp/offdocs/eo/eo-12036.htm (accessed 18 July, 2012).

Cassel, E. *The War on Civil Liberties: How Bush and Ashcroft have Dismantled the Bill of Rights*, Chicago, IL: Lawrence Hill Books, 2004.

Chaddock, R.G. "One Maryland County Takes Tough Tack on Vaccinations," *The Christian Science Monitor*, 19 November, 2007. Online. Available at: http://www.csmonitor.com/2007/1119/p02s04-ussc.html (accessed 18 July, 2012).

Cooper, M. "Pre-empting Emergence: The Biological Turn in the War on Terror," *Theory, Culture, and Society*, 23:4, 2006, pp. 113–135.

Crawford, N. "Just War Theory and the US Counterterror War," *Perspectives on Politics*, 1:1, 2003, pp. 5–25.

Dancy, J. "Moral Particularism," *Stanford Encyclopedia of Philosophy*. Online. Available at: http://plato.stanford.edu/entries/moral-particularism (accessed 18 July, 2012).

——*Ethics without Principles*, Oxford: Clarendon Press, 2004.

—— "Defending Particularism," *Metaphilosophy*, 30:1–2, 1999, pp. 25–32.

David, S.R. "Israel's Policy of Targeted Killing," *Ethics and International Affairs*, 17:1, 2003, pp. 111–126.

Davis, L.A. "Review Procedures and Public Accountability in Sunset Legislation: An Analysis and Proposal for Reform," *Administrative Law Review*, 33, 1981, pp. 393–402.

Davis, M. "The Moral Justifiability of Torture and Other Cruel, Inhuman, or Degrading Treatment," *International Journal of Applied Philosophy*, 19:2, 2005, pp. 161–178.

Declaration of Tokyo (1975). Online. Available at: http://www.cirp.org/library/ethics/tokyo/ (accessed 18 July, 2012).

Doyle, C. "Patriot Act: Sunset Provisions that Expire on December 31, 2005," Washington, DC: Congressional Research Service, 2004. Online. Available at: http://www.fas.org/irp/crs/RL32186.pdf (accessed 18 July, 2012).

Doyle, C. (August 2005) *USA PATRIOT Act Reauthorization in Brief* (Washington, DC: Congressional Research Service). Online. Available at: http://fpc.state.gov/documents/organization/51133.pdf (accessed 18 July, 2012).

Duncan, C. & Machan, T. *Libertarianism For and Against*, Lanham, MD: Rowman & Littlefield, 2005.

ex Parte Merryman 17 F. Cas. 144, 1861. Online. Available at: http://www.tourolaw.edu/Patch/Merryman (accessed 18 July, 2012).

ex Parte Quirin 317 US 1, 1942. Online. Available at: http://caselaw.lp.findlaw.com/scripts/getcase.pl?navby=CASE&court=US&vol=317&page=1 (accessed 18 July, 2012).

Fiala, A. "A Critique of Exceptions: Torture, Terrorism, and the Lesser Evil," *International Journal of Applied Philosophy*, 20:1, 2006, pp. 127–142.

Fleck, D. (ed.), *Handbook of Humanitarian Law in Armed Conflicts*, New York: Oxford University Press, 2000.

Foot, P. "The Problem of Abortion and the Doctrine of Double Effect," *Oxford Review*, 5, 1967, pp. 5–15.

Ford, F.L. *Political Murder: From Tyrannicide to Terrorism* Cambridge, MA: Harvard University Press, 1985.

Ford, G.R. "Executive Order 11905: United States Foreign Intelligence Activities," 18 February, 1976. Online. Available at: http://www.fas.org/irp/offdocs/eo11905.htm (accessed 1 April, 2013).

Gandini, E. & Saleh, T. (Directors) *Gitmo: The New Rules of War* [Motion Picture], Sweden: Atma Media Network, 2005.

Gill, T. & van Sliedregt, E. "Guantánamo Bay: A Reflection on the Legal Status and Rights of 'Unlawful Enemy Combatants'," *Utrecht Law Review*, 1:1, 2005, pp. 28–54.

Goldman, A.H. *Practical Rules: When We Need Them and When We Don't*, Cambridge: Cambridge University Press, 2001.

Gonzales, A.R. "Memorandum for the President," 25 January, 2002. Online. Available at: http://www.gwu.edu/~nsarchiv/NSAEBB/NSAEBB127/02.01.25.pdf (accessed 18 July, 2012), cited in J. Marks "9/11+ 3/11+7/7?: What Counts in Counterterrorism?" *Columbia Human Rights Law Review*, 37:3, pp. 101–161.

Gross, M. *Moral Dilemmas of Modern War: Torture, Assassination, and Blackmail in an Age of Asymmetric Conflict*, Cambridge: Cambridge University Press, 2009.

——"Assassination and Targeted Killing: Law Enforcement, Execution, or Self-Defence?" *Journal of Applied Philosophy*, 23:3, 2006, pp. 323–335.

Hamdan v. Rumsfeld 548 U.S. 557, 2006. Online. Available at: http://www.law.cornell.edu/supct/html/05-184.ZS.html (accessed 18 July, 2012).

Hamdi v. Rumsfeld 542 U.S. 507, 2004. Online. Available at: http://caselaw.lp.findlaw.com/scripts/getcase.pl?court=US&vol=000&invol=03-6696 (accessed 18 July, 2012).

Haydar, B. "The Ethics of Fighting Terror and the Priority of Citizens," *Journal of Military Ethics*, 4:1, 2005, pp. 52–59.

Henderson, N.C. "The Patriot Act's Impact on the Government's Ability to Conduct Electronic Surveillance of Ongoing Domestic Communications," *Duke Law Journal*, 52:1, 2002, pp. 179–209.

Hooker, B. & Little, M. (eds), *Moral Particularism*, Oxford: Oxford University Press, 2000.

Ingierd, H. & Syse, H. "Responsibility and Culpability in War," *Journal of Military Ethics*, 4:2, 2005, pp. 85–99.

Johnson, A. "Habeas Corpus," in J. J. Lalor (ed.), *Cyclopaedia of Political Science*, New York: Maynard, Merrill, and Co, 1899. Online. Available at: http://www.econlib.org/library/YPDBooks/Lalor/llCy521.html (accessed 1 April, 2013).

Johnson v. Eisentrager 339 U.S. 763, 1950. Online. Available at: http://supreme.justia.com/cases/federal/us/339/763 (accessed 1 April, 2013).

Kamm, F.M. "Terror and Collateral Damage: Are They Permissible?" *Journal of Ethics*, 9:3–4, 2005, pp. 381–401.

Kasher, A. & Yadlin, A. "Military Ethics of Fighting Terror: An Israeli Perspective," *Journal of Military Ethics*, 2005, 4:1, pp. 3–32.

Katya, N. "Sunsetting Judicial Opinions, *Notre Dame Law Review*, 79:4, 2003, pp. 1237–1246.

Kershnar, S. "Assassination and the Immunity Theory," *Philosophia*, 33:1–4, 2005, pp. 129–147.

Liu, E. "Amendments to the Foreign Intelligence Surveillance Act (FISA) Extended Until June 1, 2015," Washington, D.C.: Congressional Research Service, June 16, 2011. Online. Available: http://www.fas.org/sgp/crs/intel/R40138.pdf (accessed 31 July, 2012).

Machiavelli, N. *The Prince*, trans. W.K. Marriott, [1515] 1908. Online. Available at: http://www.constitution.org/mac/prince00.htm (accessed 18 July, 2012).

Marks, J. "9/11+3/11+7/7=?: What Counts in Counterterrorism," *Columbia Human Rights Law Review*, 37:3, 2006, pp. 101–161.

Massey, D. "Shipping across State Lines: Wine and the Law," in F. Allhoff (ed.), *Wine & Philosophy*, Oxford: Blackwell Publishing, 2008, pp. 275–287.

Matravers, M. *Responsibility and Justice*, Malden, MA: Blackwell Publications, 2007.

McPherson, L. "Is Terrorism Distinctively Wrong?" *Ethics*, 117, 2007, pp. 524–546.

Meisels, T. "Targeting Terror," *Social Theory and Practice*, 30:3, 2004, pp. 297–326.

——"Combatants—Lawful and Unlawful," *Law and Philosophy*, 26:1, 2007, pp. 31–65.

More, T. *Utopia*, New York: Appleton-Century-Crofts. [ca. 1516], 1949.

Murphy, S.D. (ed.), "Ability of Detainees in Cuba to Obtain Federal *Habeas Corpus* Review," *American Journal of International Law*, 98:1, 2004, pp. 188–190.

Orend, B. "War," *Stanford Encyclopedia of Philosophy*, 2005. Online. Available at: http://plato.stanford.edu/entries/war (accessed 18 July, 2012).

PATRIOT Sunsets Extension Act of 2011, Pub. L. no. 112–114, 125 Stat 216, 2011. Online. Available at: http://www.gpo.gov/fdsys/pkg/PLAW-112publ14/pdf/PLAW-112publ14.pdf (accessed 31 July, 2012).

Pettit, P. "Responsibility Incorporated," *Ethics*, 117, 2007, pp. 171–201.

Rachels, J. "Political Assassination," in H. Zellner (ed.), *Assassination*, Cambridge: Schenkman, 1974, pp. 9–21.

Reagan, R. "Message to the Senate Transmitting a Protocol to the 1949 Geneva Conventions," 29 January, 1987. Online. Available at: http://www.reagan.utexas.edu/archives/speeches/1987/012987b.htm (accessed 18 July, 2012).

Reagan, R. "Executive Order 12333: United States Intelligence Activities," 4 December, 1981. Online. Available at: http://www.fas.org/irp/offdocs/eo12333.htm (accessed 18 July, 2012).

Rejali, D. *Torture and Democracy*, Princeton, NJ: Princeton University Press, 2007.

Rescher, N. "The Allocation of Exotic Medical Lifesaving Therapy," *Ethics*, 79:3, 1969, pp. 173–186.

Rodin, D. "The Ethics of War: State of the Art," *Journal of Applied Philosophy*, 23:3, 2006, pp. 241–246.

Selgelid, M. "Ethics and Infectious Disease," *Bioethics*, 19:3, 2005, pp. 272–289.

Shanahan, T. (ed.), *Philosophy 9/11: Thinking about the War on Terror*, Peru, IL: Open Court Publishing Co, 2005.

Sher, G. *In Praise of Blame*, Oxford: Oxford University Press, 2005.

Statman, D. "Targeted Killing," *Theoretical Inquiries in Law*, 5:1, 2004, pp. 179–198.

Swisher, C.B. "Civil Liberties in War Time," *Political Science Quarterly*, 55:3, 1940, pp. 321–447.

"The Convention against Torture, and Other Cruel, Inhuman or Degrading Treatment or Punishment (CAT)," 1987. Online. Available at: http://treaties.un.org/doc/Publication/UNTS/Volume%201465/volume-1465-I-24841-English.pdf (accessed 18 July, 2012).

"Third Geneva Convention," 1949. Online. Available at: http://www.icrc.org/ihl.nsf/7c4d08d9b287a42 141256739003e636b/6fef854a3517b75ac125641e004a9e68 (accessed 18 July, 2012).

Thomas, W. "The New Age of Assassination," *SAIS Review*, 25, 2005, pp. 27–39.

Thomson, J.J. "A Defense of Abortion," *Philosophy and Public Affairs*, 1:1, 1971, pp. 47–66.

Tzu, Sun. *Art of War*, trans. L. Giles, [ca 600 BCE], 1910. Online. Available at: http://www.gutenberg. org/etext/132 (accessed 18 July, 2012).

"Universal Declaration of Human Rights," 1948. Online. Available at: http://www.un.org/en/ documents/udhr/ (accessed 18 July, 2012)

US Congress "Alien and Sedition Acts," 1798. Online. Available at: http://www.loc.gov/rr/program/ bib/ourdocs/Alien.html (accessed 18 July, 2012).

USA PATRIOT Act Pub. L. No. 107-56, 115 Stat. 272, 2001. Online. Available at: http://www.fincen. gov/statutes_regs/patriot/index.html (accessed 18 July, 2012).

USA PATRIOT Act Additional Reauthorizing Amendments Act of 2006, 109–178, S.2271, 2006. Online. Available at: http://www.intelligence.senate.gov/laws/pl109-178.pdf (accessed 18 July, 2012).

USA PATRIOT Improvement and Reauthorization Act of 2005, 109–133 H.R.3199. Online. Available at: http://thomas.loc.gov/cgi-bin/cpquery/R?cp109:FLD010:@1(hr333) (accessed 18 July, 2012).

Wallace, R.J. *Reponsibility and the Moral Sentiments*, Cambridge, MA: Harvard University Press, 1994.

Walzer, M. *Just and Unjust Wars*, 4th edn, 2006. New York: Basic Books.

Wine Institute (no date) "State Shipping Laws." Online. Available at: http://www.wineinstitute.org/ initiatives/stateshippinglaws (accessed 18 July, 2012).

Wolfendale, J. "Torture Lite and the Normalization of Torture," *Ethics & International Affairs*, 29:1, 2009, pp. 47–61.

Woodward, B. "CIA Told to Do 'Whatever Necessary' to Kill Bin Laden," *The Washington Post*, 21 October, 2001, A01.

Wynia, M.K. "Ethics and Public Health Emergencies: Restrictions on Liberty," *American Journal of Bioethics*, 7:2, 2007, pp. 1–5.

Yoo, J. "Memorandum for William J. Hynes II, General Counsel of the Department of Defense, Re: Military Interrogation of Alien Unlawful Combatants Held Outside the United States, 14 March," Washington, DC: US Department of Justice, 2003.

Zellner, H. (ed.), *Assassination*, Cambridge: Schenkman, 1974.

Zweiniger-Bargielowska, I. *Austerity in Britain: Rationing, Controls, and Consumption 1939–1955*, Oxford: Oxford University Press, 2000.

16

JUST WAR THEORY AND COUNTERTERRORISM

Seumas Miller

1. Introduction

This chapter is concerned with the application of just war theory (hereafter JWT) to a species of armed conflict, namely armed conflict between liberal democratic states and terrorist groups. Historically, such armed conflicts have involved the use on the part of such states of morally problematic strategies to combat terrorism, notably indefinite detention, targeted killing and torture. In the context of the application of a normative theory of armed conflict (JWT), the most salient of these counter-terrorism strategies is targeted killing. At any rate, my principal focus in this chapter will be on the implications of JWT for liberal democratic states engaged in armed conflict with terrorist organizations and, more specifically, in the targeted killing of terrorists.

My discussion proceeds on the assumption that targeted killing (and, for that matter, other counter-terrorism strategies) are potentially to be deployed by liberal democratic states against non-state terrorist groups engaged in the intentional killing of innocent civilian members of these states. So I will not discuss state terrorism (e.g. that of the Soviet Union under Stalin) or non-terrorist (non-state) groups engaged in armed conflict (e.g. the African National Congress during the apartheid years in South Africa).[1]

Accordingly, the USA, UK and other liberal democratic states' counter-terrorist initiatives against Al Qaeda are paradigmatic of the kind of armed conflict I have in mind. Moreover, the counter-terrorism measures in question, and targeted killing in particular, are to be understood as in large part pursued for the purpose of protecting the lives of US, UK and other citizens.

I take it that these counter-terrorism measures are morally problematic because they involve the infringement (if not the violation) of human rights, specifically the right to life in the case of targeted killing. Notwithstanding the need to give security agencies additional specific powers, e.g. in relation to intelligence/evidence gathering, the morally legitimate actions of a liberal democratic state are significantly constrained by the human rights of its own individual citizens and, for that matter, the human rights of non-citizens. Accordingly, there are a range of in-principle moral limits to counter-terrorism strategies adopted by a liberal democratic state to protect the lives of its citizens; it is not simply a matter of weighing up, or trading off, the right to life of some citizens against the rights to freedom of others in the abstract. To put matters somewhat crudely, there are significant in-principle limits on what a liberal democratic state is entitled to do, even in order to protect the lives of its citizenry. It is presumably morally unacceptable, for example, to intentionally kill or torture innocent persons (whether citizens or non-citizens), even if this might be an efficient and effective counter-terrorism strategy.

In applying JWT to armed conflict between liberal democratic states and terrorist groups it is important not to confuse the following three different contexts: (1) a well-ordered, liberal democracy enjoying peacetime conditions within its borders; (2) a liberal democracy under a state of emergency, and; (3) a theatre of war. Confusing these contexts leads to a dangerous blurring of the distinctions between, for example, what is an appropriate response to a terrorist-combatant in a theatre of war as opposed to a terrorist suspect under normal peace-time conditions.[2]

Presumably, in a well-ordered, liberal democracy enjoying peace-time conditions within its borders, e.g. the UK in 2012, a terrorism-as-crime framework ought to be applied; that is, terrorists ought to be treated as criminals (but not as combatants) and brought to justice after due process of law. However, matters are somewhat different for a liberal democracy operating in an area under a state of emergency, such as India-controlled Kashmir, or against terrorists in a *de facto* theatre of war, such as parts of Afghanistan.

A liberal democracy might justifiably be operating under a state of emergency in one or more of its cities or regions because it is confronting a one-off disaster (e.g. the 9/11 attack on the World Trade Centre), and/or because of a serious, ongoing, internal armed struggle (e.g. the IRA's campaign of violence in Northern Ireland in the 1970s).

If a state of emergency is to be morally justifiable it must be comprehensively legally circumscribed, both in relation to the precise powers granted to the government and its security agencies, and in relation to the termination of those powers and their judicial oversight while in use.

A liberal democracy might be engaged in an armed conflict with a non-state actor in a theatre of war because of serious, ongoing, terrorist attacks on the part of an external, non-state actor, e.g. Hezbollah's rocket attacks on Israeli towns. Arguably, in theatres of war, terrorists are *de facto* military combatants (terrorist-combatants). Moreover, since terrorist organizations are, or ought to be unlawful, terrorist-combatants are unlawful combatants. Since a terrorism-as-war framework (as opposed to a terrorism-as-crime framework) applies to theatres of war, it may be morally justifiable to implement, say, a shoot-on-sight policy in relation to known terrorists. Naturally, this depends on the specifics of the terrorism-as-war framework to be applied, the JWT framework being the one of interest to us here.

Notwithstanding the possible moral acceptability of such counter-terrorism measures in a theatre of war and/or under a state of emergency (but not otherwise during peace-time), fundamental moral principles concerning human rights must be respected. In particular, it is not morally permissible for a government to discount the lives of innocent non-citizens in favor of protecting the lives of its own non-combatant, let alone combatant, citizens (as has been argued by some theorists in relation to the Israeli counter-terrorism strategy). Nor is it morally permissible for a government to possess the legal power, say, to intentionally kill one cohort of its (innocent) citizens in the service of some (alleged) larger purpose, such as, say, the protection of a second, but larger, cohort of its (innocent) citizens. Someone might suggest that a government ought to have the legal power to order the mid-air destruction of an aircraft under the control of terrorists but whose passengers are innocent civilians, if the government deemed this necessary to prevent the aircraft crashing into a large building and killing a much larger number of innocent civilians. Such scenarios raise the related questions of the moral permissibility of legalizing: (a) the unintended (but foreseen) killing of persons known to be innocent, and; (b) the intentional killing of persons known to be innocent. Perhaps the legalization of (a), but not (b), is (under certain circumstances) morally acceptable.

Let me now turn to the construction of a suitably revised version of JWT before applying it to targeted killing.

2. Just war theory

Recently JWT has been receiving considerable attention both in respect of the question of its viability as a theory, and as a means for determining the justifiability of particular armed conflicts.[3] However, the application of JWT to armed conflicts involving non-state actors, including terrorist groups, raises particular problems.

While we are in this chapter adopting traditional JWT as a set of guidelines, we should not be constrained by all its tenets, and in their every detail. In particular, traditional JWT principally concerns itself with wars between states, as opposed to armed conflicts involving non-state actors, and has as a condition that the war be conducted under lawful authority, and therefore in effect under the authority of the state. But clearly such a condition would automatically rule out any internal war against the state (e.g. a revolutionary war) or other armed conflict involving a non-state actor (e.g. armed conflicts against international terrorist groups), and for this reason ought not to be made a necessary condition of a *general* theory of just war. This is not to say that wars waged by non-state actors against nation-states may not for a variety of reasons be especially difficult to justify, nor is it to deny that some suitably adjusted notion of legitimate authority might be required for (morally legitimate) armed conflicts involving non-state actors, but it is to say that in principle armed conflict conducted by a non-state actor could be morally justified (e.g. the ANC's armed struggle), and that therefore it cannot be a necessary condition for a just war that it be fought under the authority of the state. In fact historically many just war theorists allowed for the possibility of a just rebellion and for the possibility of removing a tyrant.[4] Indeed political theory in general, including liberalism, admits of the moral possibility of a just internal war, and this is because there are limits to the obligation to obey the state, and because the state itself has obligations the discharging of which is part of the ground of its legitimacy.

Before presenting a version of JWT appropriate to armed conflict between nation-states and terrorist organizations, there are a number of preliminary definitions and distinctions that need to be introduced. These are as follow.

First, let us assume that wars are large-scale, ongoing, armed conflicts involving the use of violence and waged between corporate entities. The violence in question would consist of destroying and damaging property (as well as perhaps the physical environment) and the injuring and killing by members of one corporate entity of members of the other corporate entity or entities—normally by the use of arms, armaments, etc.

Second, assume that corporate entities are organized, political entities. More specifically, a corporate entity is a group of individuals such that: (a) they have a structure of practices, including rule-governed practices, and a network of *political* beliefs held in common; (b) there is a set of interlocking *political* collective ends to which these practices are directed; (c) the rules which govern some of these practices provide for a differentiated and hierarchically ordered— though not always clearly defined—set of roles for the individuals; and (d) the individuals see themselves as owing allegiance to the group and its political ends as a whole, and perhaps they actually belong to the group, or, if not, they at least view themselves as having to comply with the dictates of the leaders of the group. Moreover, at least some of the members of such an entity (the armed forces) have been organized for the purpose of coordinated, ongoing and (in principle) reciprocated acts of violence against the members of some other (at least notional) corporate entity. Note that in the case of Al Qaeda the political beliefs/ends in question are evidently grounded in religious ones and the organization is relatively loosely structured.

Third, assume that for two (or more) corporate entities to be at war is for the armed forces of one corporate entity to be actually performing acts of violence against the members of another corporate entity; so war in my sense is *de facto* as opposed to being merely *de jure*. And in so acting these armed forces are: (a) instruments of the leadership of the corporate entity to which they belong, (b) performing their actions on behalf of this corporate entity, and (c) using violence against members of the opposing corporate entity *qua* members of that opposing corporate entity.

On this account, the mob violence perpetrated by soccer hooligans is not war since such violence, even if organized and lethal, is not political in character; on the other hand, an armed revolution may well be war, notwithstanding that one of the protagonists is not a state.

Fourth, it seems that many wars are waged under a claim of legal right, and are fought in accordance with some (perhaps quite minimal) set of laws and conventions. But that conflict be conducted under such a claim of right is not necessary for it to be war in my sense; nor is it necessary that one or both protagonists accept that there be at least some laws and conventions governing the conflict. Armed conflict conducted by warriors who accepted that they were acting illegally and who refused to abide by any conventions governing the conduct of war, e.g. the convention or law not intentionally to kill innocent civilians, could still be war on this account.

On this account of war an internal armed conflict (e.g. the English civil war) could be a war, as could a revolutionary war (e.g. the American Revolution). Again, on this account, an armed conflict between a liberal democratic state and an international terrorist group, such as Al Qaeda, could be a war.

Let us then turn to the matter of constructing our account of JWT suitable for application to terrorism. I provide an account which consists of a set of conditions which are jointly (morally) sufficient for engaging in armed conflict; I do not offer a set which is jointly (morally) necessary. Moreover, my account only provides a set of conditions under which a corporate entity is morally entitled to engage in armed conflict, as opposed to a set of conditions under which it is morally obliged to do so.

The definition is as follows. Corporate entity A (a liberal democratic state), is morally entitled (though not necessarily morally obliged) to engage in war (and thus use lethal violence) against corporate entity B (a terrorist group) in a context C—if (though not necessarily, if and *only if*):

(1) B is violating the rights of members of A (notably by killing innocent civilian members of A);
(2) There is no alternative non-violent method by which A could prevent this violation;
(3) A has a reasonable chance of ending this violation by using violence;
(4) It is probable that if A uses violence the consequences, all things considered, will be better than if A does not;
(5) A uses violence only to the end of bringing about the cessation of B's violation of the rights of members of A; and
(6) A only uses violence: (i) of a type that is morally legitimate; (ii) which is necessary and proportionate to the end in question, and; (iii) against members of B who are combatants or the leaders of combatants.

Earlier we distinguished between three different contexts (context = C in the above definition): (1) a well-ordered, liberal democracy enjoying peace-time conditions within its borders but confronting a terrorist threat; (2) a liberal democracy under a state of emergency by virtue of terrorist activities; and (3) a theatre of war. Accordingly, let us refer to these three contexts as (respectively), C1, C2 and C3. I take it that C in the above definition of JWT should refer to C3, and perhaps C2, but not C1.

Under what conditions would a context C1 come to be a context C2 or C3? Presumably, the terrorism-as-crime framework of the liberal democratic state in question cannot adequately contain serious and ongoing terrorist attacks and, therefore, either a state of emergency has been put in place or the region in question has become a *de facto* theatre of war (whether or not a state of emergency has been put in place). Moreover, the abandonment of the terrorism-as-crime framework in favor of the JWT terrorism-as-war framework is to be applied only to an extent (e.g. with respect to a specific theatre of war but not necessarily to all areas that have suffered, or might suffer, a terrorist attack), and over a period of time, that is necessary. These points are to a degree reflective of the intent of clause (2) in the above definition.

Further, the consequences mentioned in clause (4) are the overall consequences of waging war—as opposed to the consequences attached to the option(s) of not doing so—and would include the loss of life, restrictions on freedoms, economic impact, and institutional damage. Arguably, for example, the US and her allies response to Al Qaeda has only exacerbated the situation; perhaps the overall consequences would have been better if Iraq and Afghanistan had not been invaded.

In addition, clause (6) refers to the standard conditions of the so-called *jus in bello*, i.e. the legitimate methods (e.g. not biological warfare) and targets in war (e.g. not innocent children). Finally, notice that on the basis of clause (1), and the assumption that a political authority must enforce and not violate rights if it is to be legitimate, B is not a legitimate political authority. But we need to assume in respect of the above account that: (a) there is no additional corporate entity A1 which could count as the legitimate political authority of A; and (b) A, or at least its political leadership, is not itself illegitimate as it would be if, for instance, it consistently violated the rights of its constituency or if its constituency did not (at least tacitly) consent to this leadership.

So much for our revised account of JWT and its general applicability to an armed conflict between a liberal democratic state and a terrorist organization. Let us now turn directly to the specific applicability of JWT (or, at least, of a number of its constitutive principles) to targeted killing *qua* counter-terrorist strategy.

3. Targeted killing

In this section I describe the phenomenon of targeted killings and differentiate it, in particular, from assassinations.[5]

The term, "targeted killing," has recently come into general use in relation to the state-sanctioned killing by state operatives of members of non-state terrorist groups, most recently and spectacularly in the case of Osama bin Laden by US special forces, but also (notably) of PLO and Hamas members by Mossad operatives.

Indeed, in Afghanistan and in the tribal areas of Pakistan (e.g. Wazuristan and Quetta) and in Afghanistan, the US military has engaged in a sustained campaign of targeted killing by means of UAVs (unmanned aerial vehicles) or drones. The US has also initiated its so-called Kill/Capture campaign in Afghanistan whereby named Taliban and Al Qaeda leaders and others are targeted.

One could take the term "targeted killing" in a highly generic sense. Then it would simply mean the premeditated, freely performed, intentional killing of an uniquely identified individual person who is not an imminent threat. The fact that the threat is not imminent enables targeted killing to be premeditated. Roughly speaking, a uniquely identified individual person is a named person, e.g. Mahatma Gandhi, or a person identified by a uniquely identifying description, e.g. the President of the USA. However, given our purposes here we need a more specialized sense of targeted killing. In particular, we need to differentiate targeted killing from assassination.

One way of differentiating targeted killings from assassination is to restrict the former to armed conflicts, including conventional wars, non-conventional (so-called) wars of liberation and armed conflicts involving terrorist groups. Under this restriction the assassination of President Kennedy or Mahatma Gandhi would be assassinations, but not targeted killings.

A second restriction would be one that excluded the killing of political figures who were not in the chain of command of the armed force conducting the war or terrorist attacks. Under this restriction the assassinations of black township mayors who were collaborating with the South African apartheid government would not be targeted killings.

A third way of distinguishing targeted killings from assassinations would be to include among targeted killings the killing of terrorists who were not leaders and, *a fortiori*, not political leaders.

A fourth way of distinguishing between assassination as it is traditionally understood and targeted killing as it has come to be pertains to the scale of the killing. For targeted killing is being used by US armed forces to inflict relatively heavy casualties on the enemy and, thereby, disable it, e.g. in Afghanistan and Pakistan by the use of unmanned drones and by the Kill/Capture program involving US special forces, such as JSOC (Joint Special Operations Command). According to *Frontline*, there have been 225 drone strikes since 2009 and they have killed between 1,100 and 1,800 militants.[6] The Kill/Capture program has targeted thousands of militants in the last couple of years, many of whom have been killed. The US military is targeting not simply the Taliban and Al Qaeda senior leadership and other "high value" targets, but also middle-level commanders. Accordingly, this strategy is arguably much closer to the conventional military strategy of inflicting heavy casualties on enemy forces (on "the body," so to speak) than it is to the decapitation strategy (targeting "the brain") normally associated with targeted killings (and, for that matter, assassinations).

Whatever the strategic virtues of this strategy, it comes at a moral cost. For commensurate with the increase in the numbers of targeted killings, the quantum of collateral damage in the form of civilian casualties seems bound to increase sharply.

4. Targeted killing and the principles of JWT

In this section I discuss the moral principles standardly deployed in the justification of targeted killing, and especially those which are in part constitutive of JWT.

Let us first assume that the targeted killing in question is of terrorist leaders and/or terrorist-combatants belonging to a terrorist group engaged in an armed conflict—appropriately described as a war (see above)—and is undertaken by members of the security forces of the liberal democratic state engaged in that war.

By our definition of terrorism, the terrorist group in question is violating the rights of members of the liberal democratic state in question (notably by killing innocent civilians). So clause (1) is satisfied. As indicated above, there are a variety of circumstances in which the targeted killing of terrorists by liberal democratic states might take place and which bear on its legality and morality. For the sake of simplicity let us assume that the targeted killings in question take place either: (1) in a *de facto* theatre of war, albeit war against a non-state actor (i.e. a context C3 above), or (2) in a setting outside the liberal democratic state in question and in which there is no effective enforcement of the law in relation to terrorists perpetrating ongoing, serious terrorist attacks against said liberal-democratic state. Accordingly, I am not considering targeted killing of terrorist suspects in cities or regions of well-ordered, liberal democratic states enjoying peace-time conditions, i.e. contexts C1 (or, for that matter, in cities or regions under a state of emergency, i.e. contexts C2, since this raises additional morally complex questions).

For the targeted killing of terrorists to be morally justified, the war in which they take place must meet the various other conditions of JWT and, in particular, clauses (2) (no alternative to violence), (3) (the violence is effective), (4) (good consequences, all things considered), and (5) (violence only used as means to bring cessation of rights violations). Evidently, it is possible, at least in principle, that these conditions be met.

Thus in relation to clause (5) it is conceivable that the violence, including the targeted killing, is principally undertaken for purposes of self-defense (e.g. to prevent future lethal terrorist attacks, as opposed to, for example, as retribution). That is, the required justification is essentially prospective in character.

It is in relation to clause (6) that the objections to targeted killing in the context of an otherwise morally justified war against a terrorist group are most likely to be raised. Specifically, it might be argued that targeted killings do not comply with the JWT principles of necessity, proportionality and/or discrimination. (Recall that the principle of discrimination forbids the killing of non-combatants). No doubt it is true that many instances of targeted killing of terrorists do not in fact comply with one or more of these principles; but surely some do, and it is evident that targeted killings could in principle comply with all these principles.

Accordingly, at least at the level of theory, there do not seem to be good and decisive reasons to believe that targeted killing of terrorists could not be morally justified by the lights of JWT. However, there are a number of arguments that are made at this point to the effect that there are specific features of targeted killing that render it morally unacceptable as a practice, these theoretical claims regarding terrorism and JWT notwithstanding.

One such argument rests on the danger of mistakes being made, given that terrorist combatants often blend in with civilians and are not readily identifiable as combatants, e.g. by virtue of wearing uniforms. This point has been made in relation to the targeted killing of Taliban leaders in Afghanistan by NATO forces; it is suggested that the intelligence on which the identification of persons as terrorists is based is often of poor quality and provided by local Afghanis with questionable motives. Moreover, it is argued that the problem is compounded, given the lack of accountability when mistakes in war are made.

In response to this it can be said that this is not an in-principle problem since there are a set of subordinate principles which deal with this kind of problem and which could be complied with. These principles include: (1) The target is a well-known terrorist figure, e.g. bin Laden, whose identify is confirmed by several reliable sources and forms of evidence, e.g. photographic and eye-witness evidence; (2) the decision has been authorized at an appropriate political level (e.g. by the US President or the Israeli Prime Minister); and (3) the decision is subject to accountability mechanisms of some sort (e.g. judicial oversight).

Another familiar argument is that targeted killing of terrorists cannot be justified since they have not been found guilty according to a court of law. However, it is quite clear that there are many instances of morally justifiable killing, e.g. in self-defense, that do not require, indeed cannot require, prior adjudication by a court of law. Accordingly, if it is known with certainty that a person is a terrorist and the terrorist cannot be apprehended, tried and punished, then arguably—other things being equal—it is morally permissible to kill the terrorist in order to save the lives of the terrorist's future victims (although not necessarily to punish the terrorist). More generally, the argument does not apply to terrorist-combatants. Thus if a given area is a *de facto* theatre of war then justifiably there might be rules of engagement permitting the shooting on sight of persons reasonably and rightly taken to be terrorist-combatants. Targeted killing of persons outside *de facto* theatres of war is a different matter. However, it might be justified, if the persons in question were members of an organization that was perpetrating serious and ongoing terrorist attacks, the persons themselves were perpetrating serious and ongoing terrorist attacks, and it was not possible to bring either the organization or these individuals to justice. (More on this below.)

A further argument appeals to ineffectiveness (clause (3) in the above definition of JWT). For example, the argument that targeted killing of some terrorists might not reduce terrorist attacks, since others take their place. While this might be true in some cases it is not necessarily the case with respect to high value targets, such as bin Laden. Moreover, it is not an argument against the strategy of high volume targeted killings described above. It seems that, while each of these particular arguments against targeted killing might apply in particular instances, they do not constitute *in-principle* problems with targeted killings; they do not demonstrate that targeted killing is always or necessarily morally unjustified. I conclude that targeted killing may well be in principle morally permissible by the lights of widely accepted moral principles, notably those in part constitutive of JWT.

Let us now turn to a specific application of JWT, namely to the targeted killing of Osama bin Laden. Let us assume for the purposes of this discussion that by the lights of JWT there is a morally justifiable war being waged against Al Qaeda by western liberal democratic states. This is a very large and controversial assumption, to say the least, but it allows us to focus without distraction on the specifics of the targeted killing of bin Laden.

Let us first consider the context in which bin Laden was killed and do so in the light of our above discussion of the three different contexts for the use of lethal force.

Recall that targeted killing in C1 contexts cannot be, at least in general, morally justified by the lights of JWT (as construed above) since in C1 contexts the terrorism-as-crime framework applies. Consider in this connection the shooting of de Menezes—the innocent Brazilian student—by UK security agencies in a London underground station in 2005. De Menezes was shot under conditions in which the police believed (falsely as it turned out) that he was a suicide bomber about to trigger a bomb on his person. This lethal shooting did not take place according to the principles governing targeted killing, but rather according to the much more restrictive principles governing police use of deadly force, e.g. necessity and imminent threat to life. Yet an innocent person was, nevertheless, shot dead. I take it targeted killing is not justified in such well-ordered contexts in liberal democratic states and certainly not by JWT since, apart from any other consideration, JWT is a theory which is intended to apply only to wars.

Perhaps the firing of a rocket by a US unmanned aircraft in Yemen in 2002 that killed six Al-Qaeda operatives is an instance of targeted killing in a context in which there is no effective law enforcement in relation to terrorists conducting attacks on liberal democratic states; likewise the use of UAVs in the tribal areas of Pakistan.

The targeted killing of bin Laden in a well-ordered, urban setting in Pakistan provides a different kind of case to that of de Menezes, the Yemen killings or targeted killing by drones of Taliban and Al Qaeda militants in the tribal areas of Pakistan. Certainly, it was not done in a theatre of war. Moreover, it was a setting in which there was enforcement of the law; indeed, a setting in which the state enforcing the law (Pakistan) was an ally of the liberal-democratic state suffering terrorist attacks (USA). However, law enforcement in relation to bin Laden in particular, and perhaps Al Qaeda in general, was evidently ineffective due to, presumably, the unwillingness of the Pakistani state to enforce their own and/or international law or, at least, to comply with the applicable moral principles, e.g. to arrest and try him in a court of law or hand him over to another appropriate jurisdiction to do so. Nevertheless, by the lights of our account (and JWT, in particular), the targeted killing by the Pakistan government of one of its residents in an urban setting under its effective control would be morally unacceptable.

Moreover, again by the lights of JWT, the targeted killing of a terrorist on foreign soil and in an area in which there is effective law enforcement is not permitted. Of course, it might be argued that the Pakistan state, although able to arrest the terrorist bin Laden and, thereby, apply or facilitate an appropriate judicial process, was unwilling to do so and that this Pakistani unwillingness justified the targeted killing of bin Laden by US forces (or, at least, his capture). Whatever the merits of this argument it is not justified by JWT (as outlined above). For JWT does not countenance the possibility of the targeted killing of civilians in areas in which there is effective law enforcement. Rather the law enforcement model is to be preferred.

Leaving aside the question of the context for the application of the principles of JWT, what of the substantive principles themselves; what of the justice, so to speak, of the matter?

From a retrospective moral perspective, killing bin Laden is held by many to be an act of substantive justice. Indeed, given bin Laden's responsibility for the murder of numerous US and other citizens, the relevant moral principle in play here may well be the principle of reciprocity understood as simple retribution ("an eye for an eye and a tooth for a tooth"). However, such a retrospective perspective is not that embodied in JWT; JWT is, as discussed above, prospective in character.

By contrast with substantive justice, procedural justice—at least as it is understood in criminal justice contexts—requires arrest and a fair trial. It might be responded that substantive justice ultimately trumps procedural justice on the grounds that the latter is in large part the means to realize the former. Or it might be responded that bin Laden resisted arrest, and deadly force can be justifiably used against those resisting arrest for very serious offences, such as murder, if it is necessary to do so. One problem with the latter claim is that bin Laden was apparently unarmed when cornered and it seems, therefore, unlikely that the use of deadly force was necessary.

From the prospective moral perspective of JWT, killing bin Laden might be justifiable. For it was arguably an act of self-defense, assuming he continued to constitute a threat to the lives of innocent Americans (and others). At the time of his death he was apparently playing a much less central operational role in Al Qaeda than previously. However, the point could be made that the terrorist organization, Al Qaeda, constitutes an ongoing deadly threat to Americans (and others) and bin Laden remained an important member of that organization, symbolically and in other ways—sufficiently important for his targeted killing to count as an act of self-defense against the organization.

Moreover, in the case of the killing of bin Laden there was apparently no so-called "collateral damage," at least of innocent civilians (clause (6) of JWT). On the other hand, perhaps an analogous point might be made in relation to ineffectiveness. The considerations in play here are complex. Certainly, the killing of bin Laden is symbolically important, given bin Laden's key role in Al Qaeda's terrorist activity especially on 9/11. It constitutes a major symbolic victory for the US and its allies and, to that extent, weakens Al Qaeda and the cause of global terrorism more generally (clause (4) of the above definition of JWT). A counter-point here is that it might galvanize bin Laden's followers and provide further impetus to terrorism. Here the bystander role of Al Qaeda in the popular uprisings in Libya, Egypt, Tunisia and elsewhere in the Arab world is salient. Perhaps the death of bin Laden will have little effect in these Muslim countries. A further dimension to the issue is US-Pakistan relations and, relatedly, Pakistani government-Pakistani citizenry relations. As already stated: even if it is (all things considered) morally permissible for the US to engage in the targeted killing of terrorists in a foreign state if the state in question is unwilling or unable to apprehend these terrorists, it is not morally permissible for the Pakistan government to engage in targeted killing of its citizens/residents in areas under its effective control and, *a fortiori*, it is not permissible for it to allow foreign states to do so. This raises the more general questions as to whether, on balance, the killing of bin Laden will further destabilise Pakistan or not—given that perhaps Pakistanis are unsupportive of Al Qaeda, notwithstanding their hostility to the US.

5. Conclusion

In this chapter the following tasks have been completed: (1) A version of JWT applicable to wars involving non-state actors has been outlined; (2) A characterization of targeted killing has been provided; one which enables us to distinguish between assassination and targeted killing; (3) JWT (appropriately modified and extended) has been applied to the practice of targeted killing and it has been concluded that targeted killing is, at least in principle, morally justifiable; (4) JWT has been applied to the killing of Osama bin Laden and it has been concluded that that particular killing is probably not justified by the lights of JWT, although this is not to say that, all things considered, it might not have been morally justified.

Notes

1 S. Miller "Just War Theory—The Case of South Africa," *Philosophical Papers*, xix:2, August, 1990, pp.143–161
2 S. Miller *Terrorism and Counter-terrorism: Ethics and Liberal Democracy*, Oxford: Blackwell, 2009, Chapters 4 and 5.
3 A good deal of the impetus for this was initially provided by Michael Walzer's *Just and Unjust Wars: A Moral Argument with Historical Illustrations*, New York: Basic Books, 1977.
4 F. H. Russell, *Just War in the Middle Ages*, Cambridge: Cambridge University Press, 1975.
5 See Haig Khatchadourian, "Is Political Assassination ever Morally Justifed?'" in H. Zellner (ed.), *Assassination*, Cambridge, MA: Schenkman, 1974; D. Kretzmer, "Targeted Killing of Suspected Terrorists: Extra-Judicial Executions or Legitimate Means of Defence?" *The European Journal of International Law*, 16:2, pp. 171–212, 2005; and S. Miller, *Terrorism and Counter-terrorism*, Chapter 5.
6 Frontline video, *Kill/Capture*, 10 May, 2011. Online. Available at: frontline@pbs.org (accessed 3 March 2013).

References

Frontline video, *Kill/Capture*, 10 May 2011. Online. Available at: http://frontline@pbs.org (accessed 3 March 2013).

Khatchadourian, H. "Is Political Assassination ever Morally Justifed?" In H. Zellner (ed.), *Assassination*, Cambridge, MA: Schenkman, 1974.

Kretzmer, D., "Targeted Killing of Suspected Terrorists: Extra-Judicial Executions or Legitimate Means of Defence?" *The European Journal of International Law*, 16:2, pp. 171–212, 2005.

Miller, S.,"Just War Theory—The Case of South Africa," *Philosophical Papers*, xix:2, August, 1990, pp.143–161.

——*Terrorism and Counter-terrorism: Ethics and Liberal Democracy*, Oxford: Blackwell, 2009.

Russell, F. H., *Just War in the Middle Ages*, Cambridge: Cambridge University Press, 1975.

Walzer, M., *Just and Unjust Wars: A Moral Argument with Historical Illustrations*, New York: Basic Books, 1977.

17

PUNITIVE WARFARE, COUNTERTERRORISM, AND *JUS AD BELLUM*

Shawn Kaplan

1. Punitive warfare

It should also be accepted that the best defense against terrorism, assuming competent passive defense, may be deterrence based upon preventive/attrition operations.[1]

The above passage reflects a series of all too common confusions. I am not referring to the author's position regarding the best response(s) to terrorism but to the conceptual confusions that are present in the statement. In one sentence, defense is equated with both deterrence and preventive tactics. Regardless of whether viewed from the perspective of international law or just war theory, theorists have traditionally preserved distinctions between the three modes of warfare alluded to above: defensive, punitive and preventive.[2] These three categories are broadly distinguished along temporal lines. Defensive warfare aims to repulse ongoing or imminent acts of aggression in the present, whereas punitive warfare (regardless of whether it aims at deterrence, retribution, or reform) responds to past acts of aggression or 'wrongdoing', and preventive acts, of course, aim to thwart threats of future aggression. Punitive warfare today may include: belligerent reprisals, targeted killings, punitive interventions, and full-scale punitive war.[3] While all of these practices can have the retrospective focus of punitive warfare, some—e.g. targeted killings—can also have a preventive employment insofar as they aim to lessen an adversary's capacities for future attacks.

The recent tendency to blur the line between all three and to characterize punitive and preventive acts as defensive apparently is the result of two other factors.[4] First, under contemporary international law as stated in the UN Charter, only defensive warfare is legally permitted (unless the Security Council approves the use of military force for humanitarian purposes). Similarly, a dominant strain of recent just war theory follows international law's presumption against war except in cases of national or other defense as well as humanitarian interventions. One consequence of the current 'legalist paradigm' is that nearly all attempts to either legally or morally justify military action couch the conflict in terms of national or collective defense. It ought to be noted, however, that this greatly restricts the range of justifiable warfare since just war theory has traditionally permitted some punitive wars.[5]

The second contributing factor towards blurring these traditional distinctions is the nature of contemporary international security threats. Many contemporary threats to national security come from sporadic attacks by various non-state terrorist or militant groups whose individual acts of violence often fall short of war. Faced with security threats from such intermittent attacks, states have claimed that the only military means by which to defend the lives and property of their citizens is to either: deter future attacks by retaliating, coercively reform 'rogue' states as well as states that tolerate or shelter militant groups operating within their borders, or to preventively reduce the militant's capabilities via attrition.[6]

While in such instances states make an appeal to *defending* their citizens' lives and property from unlawful attack, this sense of defense is much broader than what is meant by defensive warfare. I will use some domestic analogues to clarify the differences. When individuals are deterred from committing violent crimes by punishments resulting from fair trials, the state's judicial system cannot be said to be defending citizens from ongoing or imminent acts of aggression. Rather, the state is making its citizens safer in important ways. Similarly, when domestic law enforcement agencies capture weapons cached by some gang or kill its known members or leadership while attempting to apprehend them, citizens may be made safer from the gang's reasonably anticipated violence but these agencies are not defending anyone's life or property in the strict sense of repulsing an ongoing or imminent attack. While in the domestic context we tend not to blur the lines between defensive actions and punitive deterrence or preventive reductions to security threats, this may be because we have not made defensive action the only permissible use of domestic force for the state. In contrast, the dominant legalist paradigm has done exactly this within the international context.

Instead of conflating punitive retaliation or preventive warfare with defensive warfare, greater clarity will be attained by an analysis of the possible justifications for punitive or preventive warfare in their own rights. To be open to such possibilities would mark a significant turn away from the legalist paradigm but would also allow for a more relevant discourse on the permissible means of addressing contemporary security threats. In effect, describing punitive retaliation or preventive warfare as acts of national defense is an attempt to force these square pegs into the legalist paradigm's round hole.[7] By examining whether these non-defensive military measures can be justified within a broader just war framework, my aim is neither to be an apologist for current counterterrorist military tactics nor to univocally condemn them. Instead, I hope to articulate those factors relevant for making such moral evaluations.

More specifically, in this chapter, I will focus upon the question of punitive warfare and its potential justifications when aimed at either deterrence, reform, or the enforcement of international law.[8] Unlike preventive warfare, punitive warfare has long found justifications amongst just war theorists.[9] The legalist paradigm's rejection of punitive warfare is largely based upon the presumption that states *always* lack proper authority to punish other international agents given the existence of international legal institutions (ILIs) that can adjudicate and punish in a less biased fashion. Though one might reasonably be skeptical of the efficacy and fairness of current ILIs, the question of how a nation-state can have the proper authority to punish other international agents remains key to the debate over justified punitive warfare.[10]

The next section will outline accounts from Augustine, Locke, and Grotius for how punishment can serve as a justifying aim for war as well as how each account attempts to establish the proper authority of states to punish other international agents. Whether any agent can ever have the proper authority to punish within 'international society' will depend upon how the legal and political order of this society is understood. Accordingly, special attention will be paid to the corresponding images of international order presumed within each account of justified punitive warfare. The goal of this examination will be to determine whether any of these three historical approaches can provide a basis for justifying punitive warfare today. I will assume that the relative success of each of the justifications of punitive warfare will depend, in part, upon how realistically their images of international order reflect our contemporary situation. However, mere resemblance to our contemporary international order is insufficient for establishing a satisfactory justifying argument. The basis of a state's authority to punish other international agents must be strong enough to produce broad affirmation in international society and avoid being a fundamentally contested form of authority. Lastly, if a plausible model for a state's valid authority to punish international agents can be found, I will consider what punitive aims it can support and what challenges such punitive warfare would have in satisfying other *jus ad bellum* conditions.

2. Augustine, Locke and Grotius on punitive warfare

2.1 *Augustine on punitive warfare as a means to restore well-ordered peace*

Augustine originates a tradition of justifying punitive wars within just war theory: "As a rule just wars are defined as those which avenge injuries, if some nation or state against whom one is waging war has neglected to punish a wrong committed by its citizens, or return something that was wrongfully taken."[11] Unlike a theory based upon a natural right of self-defense which would hold the preservation of individual lives to be fundamental, Augustine's justified punitive warfare is fundamentally aimed at re-establishing a justly ordered peace. A nation or state which fails to either punish its own citizens for their international transgressions or which fails to return what has been wrongfully taken has disrupted the *tranquillitas ordinis*—the divinely ordained, well-ordered concord between man and man.[12] When a well-ordered peace is disrupted, punishment from a proper authority is required to correct the transgressor and, thus, restore order.

Augustine makes this point most clearly in what he takes to be the analogous case of domestic peace being disturbed.

> And if any member of the family interrupts the domestic peace by disobedience, he is corrected either by word or blow, or some kind of just and legitimate punishment, such as society permits, that he may himself be the better for it, and be readjusted to the family harmony from which he had dislocated himself … To be innocent, we must not only do harm to no man, but also restrain him from sin or punish his sin, so that either the man himself who is punished may profit by his experience, or others be warned by his example.[13]

Following Augustine's analogy of domestic punishment, a nation seeking justice against injuries committed by another nation must through its punishment seek to 'readjust' the transgressing nation to the ordered harmony between nations. While defensive wars aim at re-establishing peace by repelling aggression, on Augustine's account, they may not attain a well-ordered peace if they fail to establish a true concord by either rehabilitating the aggressor or deterring others from future transgressions. Just as a truly harmonious agreement in the domestic context can only emerge from individuals being corrected by the patriarch and having their moral characters reformed, Augustine's political authorities must play a similarly patriarchal role by correcting and rehabilitating neighboring states so that a well-ordered concord can be attained.

In Augustine, both the family's patriarch and the nation's ruler have the authority to punish based upon the natural order. In fact, this natural order is what is preserved in the Augustinian well-ordered peace. "The peace of all things is the tranquillity of order. Order is the distribution which allots things equal and unequal, each to its own [natural] place."[14] Just as Augustine assumes it is the natural place of the patriarch to punish family members to help reform their characters, he claims in *Against Faustus the Manichean* that "the natural order of mortal things, ordained for peace, demands that the authority for making war and inflicting punishment should rest with the ruler."[15] This is not merely to avoid private wars but Augustine echoes St Paul's *Letter to the Romans* (13:4) as the ruler has authority to carry out punitive wars "for he is the minister of God" and His tool to punish and reform those "evildoers" who violate the tranquility of order.

To contemporary readers, Augustine's views on both domestic punishment and punitive warfare may appear to be archaic. That a *tranquillitas ordinis* has been divinely ordained and that patriarchs and rulers have a morally privileged perspective regarding who violates this order and is owed punishment is difficult to accept. I will simply mention two possible sources of significant skepticism. On the one hand, Augustine seems to assume that a singular well-ordered global whole can be united under a common morality (and, if possible, that this is even desirable). Given the great diversity of complex and rich value systems, why assume either that such a singular tranquil order is possible or that one's own perspective is morally privileged in determining what disturbs such peace and who is rightly due punishment? Second, not only is an appeal to a natural patriarchal authority within the family or state arbitrary but it is circular reasoning to ground a state's authority to preserve the natural order via punishment by an appeal to that same order.

However, neo-Augustinians attempt to eliminate these more problematic elements and to emphasize the moral obligation of legitimate states (and their leaders) to address grave injustices in the world by militarily punishing those rogue nations or responsible militant groups.[16] Instead of appealing to a natural order to establish the authority of state leaders to punish other states, Elshtain claims that the authority of then President Bush to begin a punitive war against Afghanistan was grounded in sanctions received from the US Congress and the UN.

> The right authority criterion was met when both houses of the US Congress authorized statutes and appropriated monies for the war effort. To this we can add the right authority enshrined in Article 51 of the United Nations Charter on self-defense. The Bush administration honored the charter's requirement by giving advanced notification to the UN Security Council of its intention to use armed force to punish aggression.[17]

Unfortunately, Elshtain fails to address how democratic legislation could ever establish the legitimate authority of that state to punish *other* international agents who in no way fall under its jurisdiction. If one assumes that a legislative body gains its authority from being elected, then it is hard to fathom how it can legitimately wield that authority over members of *other* political communities when they are not within jurisdictional boundaries. In addition, Elshtain's appeal to Article 51 makes the familiar conflation between defensive and punitive warfare. The aim of punishing aggression is not the same as defending against an ongoing or imminent attack (which Article 51 states is an inherent right). In the same text, Elshtain elaborates in very Augustinian terms how the US war in Afghanistan was a punitive response to an injury and that it aimed to restore tranquillity:

> Indeed, when a wound as grievous as that of September 11 has been inflicted on a body politic, it would be the height of irresponsibility and a dereliction of duty for public officials to fail to respond … Such an act of terrorism aims to disrupt fundamental civic peace and tranquility. Good is forced into hiding as we retreat behind closed doors. Preventing further harm and restoring the preconditions for civic tranquillity is a justifiable *casus belli*.[18]

Elshtain may be correct that public officials have an obligation to 'respond' to a terrorist attack upon its citizens. However, since this broad obligation can be satisfied in numerous ways, including tightening national security and engaging in international policing efforts, it is not a clear basis for those public officials to have the rightful authority to wage punitive warfare against another state and its citizens.[19]

It seems that Elshtain's neo-Augustinian argument supporting punitive warfare is bound to fall prey to one of two broad problems. Like Augustine's own argument, she appears to affirm some arbitrary factor—e.g. being the wounded party or receiving congressional approval—as being sufficient for establishing a morally privileged perspective on whom is in need of correction and ought to be punished in the name of civic tranquility. Though she rejects Augustine's patriarchal model of natural authority, her own proposed grounds for establishing the authority to punish international agents are just as arbitrary as Augustine's dogma of the natural role of patriarchs and rulers since congressional approval cannot *in principle* establish punitive jurisdiction over other political communities. Alternatively, her appeal to UN Charter Article 51 as grounds for establishing the authority of states to wage punitive wars leads her to conflate defensive and punitive warfare. Not only does she not provide a satisfying answer to why one nation-state can have the authority to punish other international agents by means of warfare, she presents a confused image of our current international order—one where the authority for punitive warfare can be established both by a state's legislative approval and by international laws permitting *defensive* measures against aggression.

2.2 Locke on punitive warfare in the state of nature

In his *Second Treatise on Government*, John Locke famously asserts that within the State of Nature[20] every individual has equal authority to punish others who violate the Law of Nature by harming another's life, liberty, bodily integrity, or property.[21] Prior to establishing a commonwealth, *"every Man hath a Right to Punish the Offender, and be the Executioner of the Law of Nature."*[22] Rightful punishment must be both proportionate and serve the legitimate ends of reparation or restraint. In contrast to self-defense, punishment restrains by means of either direct or indirect deterrence. The natural right to punish for the sake of restraint belongs to everyone, not merely to the victim for whom reparations are also due.[23] Locke reasons that if anyone in the State of Nature has the right to protect his natural rights by means of punishing transgressors, then "in that State of perfect Equality, where there is no superiority of jurisdiction of one over another, what any may do in Prosecution of the Law, every one must needs have a right to do."[24] In contrast to the common view that punishment requires a superior authority imposing penalty, Locke's State of Nature is one of perfect equality where the authority to punish is rooted in everyone's natural right to protect life, liberty, and property.

Since truly independent states cannot bind themselves by mutual consent into a single body politic, they remain perpetually in the State of Nature for Locke.

> [A]ll *Princes* and Rulers of *Independent* Governments all through the World are in a State of Nature … For 'tis not every Compact that puts an end to the State of Nature between Men, but only one of agreeing together mutually to enter into one Community, and make one Body Politick.[25]

Hence, while states can mutually establish trade agreements and other limited compacts, such contracts do not terminate the State of Nature. In parallel to individuals prior to forming a commonwealth, states are perfectly equal in their authority to enforce the Laws of Nature whenever they are violated and regardless of who is the victim.

Locke's image of the international order certainly appears less archaic than Augustine's. Regardless of whether one embraces social contract theorizing, states are typically viewed as having an obligation to protect their citizens' basic rights to life, liberty, bodily integrity, and property. It is not altogether inconceivable that this fundamental obligation could ground a state's right to punish those international parties who have violated the basic rights of its citizens in order to deter them and others from doing so in the future or in order to coerce reparations for its citizens.[26]

However, without embracing Locke's absolute Laws of Nature, it will be more difficult to establish the authority of *all* states to punish those groups who violate the rights of other state's citizens—especially if the conflict is a distant one that poses little immediate threat to the rights of its own citizens. More often, punitive military responses to violations of foreign citizens' rights are supported as acts that enforce international law as opposed to the Laws of Nature. There is, however, no place for international law within Locke's depiction of the international order as the State of Nature. While one might agree with Locke that independent states could never subordinate themselves to an international legal order without establishing a united body politic with all other nations, there is no middle ground between a global state and the State of Nature for Locke. That is, there is no room in Locke to consider the role of a primitive international legal order based upon convention and lacking a centralized authority to enforce it.

2.3 Grotius on punitive warfare and international law enforcement

Hugo Grotius directly addresses the role of punitive warfare within a primitive international legal order. He asserts that within an international order lacking a centralized authority, sovereigns "have a Right to exact Punishments, not only for Injuries committed against themselves, or their Subjects, but likewise, for those which do not peculiarly concern them, but which are, in any Persons whatsoever, grievous Violations of the Law of Nature or Nations."[27] According to Grotius, each sovereign nation is at liberty to exercise its decentralized authority to uphold either natural law or the conventional laws of nations. Though Grotius' version of natural law grounded in our supposed natural desire to live in a peaceful international society is intriguing, its strong naturalist assumptions would be unacceptable for justifying punitive warfare today.[28] However, Grotius' laws of nations are less controversial as they are the product of the common consent of most nations and do not require a centralized coercive authority.

> But the *more extensive* Right, is the *Right of Nations*, which derives its Authority from the Will of all, or at least of many, Nations. I say *of many*, because there is scarce any Right found, except that of Nature, which is also called the Right of Nations, common to all Nations ... Now the Proofs on which the Law of Nations is founded, are the same with those of the unwritten Civil Law, namely continual Use, and the Testimony of Men skilled in the Laws.[29]

Grotius' account of international law and right coincides with the contemporary, skeptical outlook that the UN Charter and its resolutions are fundamentally conventional or customary forms of international law. According to this outlook, these documents are binding only to the extent that most nations consent to them as being to the general advantage of all nations and this accurately fits Grotius' definition of international law as the laws of nations: "[T]here are, *some Laws agreed on by common Consent, which respect the Advantage not of one Body in particular, but of all in general. And this is what is called the Law of Nations.*"[30]

Whereas the inability of contemporary ILIs to judicially enforce their own laws is posed as a fundamental flaw by their critics, Grotius presumed that "*War is made against those who cannot be restrained in a judicial Way. For judicial Proceedings are of Force against those who are sensible of their Inability to oppose them; but against those who are or think themselves of equal Strength, Wars are undertaken.*"[31] Since members of international society view themselves as equals, the Grotian outlook would expect that the enforcement of human rights or of UN resolutions will not come from judicial proceedings but via punitive warfare. Given that the laws of nations gain their authority through general consent and in the absence of a centralized power to enforce them, any member of international society is permitted to enforce them by means of punitive warfare. In addition, while the wrongs being punished must be grievous, they by no means must amount to international aggression in the sense of violating a state's right to territorial integrity or sovereignty.

A prime example that Grotius makes use of is piracy. If the laws against piracy are conventions consented to by most states out of the belief that they serve the general interests of all states, then any state has the authority—following Grotius—to punish those guilty of piracy. This is not equivalent to the right to defend oneself from piracy but the permission for any state to seek out 'known pirates' and carry out a punitive retaliation. Furthermore, if any state is an accomplice to the international crime, they too are liable to punishment from any member of international society. Grotius envisions a relatively wide array of circumstances in which states are liable to punishment for being accomplices to international crimes.

> They therefore who command a wicked Action; who consent to it, when their Consent is necessary for committing it; who afford their Assistance; who shelter the Author of the Action, or are in any other Respect accessary to it, either in advising, commending, or encouraging the Fact; they who prevent it not, when under a strict Obligation of so doing … These are all justly liable to punishment.[32]

Though states may directly order or support acts of piracy (or militant attacks by third parties), Grotius supposes that most cases involve states either sheltering or tolerating international criminals.[33] If the state knows of the illegal acts being launched from within its borders but fails to either punish or extradite those responsible, then it may be liable to punishment for sheltering the criminals.[34] However, toleration of the criminal act establishes liability *only if* the state has both the obligation *and* the power to stop the criminal acts.[35] The state's obligation arises from widely held and continuously used international laws; whereas the power to stop the acts depend upon the state's strength of sovereignty in two senses. First, can the state overcome the combative strength of the criminals? Second, does the state have sufficient political support of its citizens to oppose the criminal group working within its borders? The state that incurs liability by directly ordering or supporting piracy or by sheltering or tolerating pirates in the ways just outlined ought to make reparations; however, if it cannot or refuses to make reparations, Grotius claims that a resort to punitive warfare is justified.

According to Grotius, the legitimate aims of punishment are threefold: to reform the criminal, to protect the victim's liberty and rights by either killing, disempowering or directly deterring the criminal from repeating the offense, or to make an example of the criminal for the sake of deterrence that protects the broader public.[36] Yet, insofar as states that either shelter or tolerate international criminals operating within their borders partake in the crime, for Grotius their punishment must also serve one of these three aims.[37] Here, the full breadth of the decentralized authority Grotius bestows on every sovereign state comes into clearer focus. First, any sovereign state may punish groups directly engaged in international crimes. Additionally, they may carry out punitive military strikes against states that sponsor, shelter or tolerate international criminals within their borders but fail to make reparations, turn over the criminals, or prosecute and punish the criminals when they have the power to do so. Furthermore, insofar as state accomplices can be punished for three diverse ends, a Grotian may support punitive warfare to either: coercively 'reform' another regime's policies vis-à-vis international criminals, or to reform them more radically to the point of forcing regime change,[38] or to protect the liberties and rights of victims by disempowering the international criminals and the states which either sponsor, shelter or tolerate international criminals, or to deter other states from taking a lax attitude vis-à-vis international criminals within their own borders.

Though Grotius' image of international order does not include the existence of ILIs, it does not exclude the possibility of centralized institutions which either articulate conventional international norms or pass judgment on when these conventional laws have been violated. However, he would not hold out hope that these laws could be enforced by a centralized authority. First, as states and even militant groups view themselves as equals to other members of international society, they will not submit themselves to the authority of a judicial institution; hence, punitive warfare would be required to enforce international law. Second, even if ILIs 'authorized' punitive warfare in order to enforce international law and deter future violations, it still requires willing states to carry out the punitive warfare and for other states to generally view the law being enforced to be in the interest of all and not just in the interest of those states carrying out the punishment. As soon as members states are either unwilling to carry out the enforcement or fail to see how the law's enforcement serves the interest of all in general, both the law and the ILIs' claims for enforcement lose their authority. In these senses, the authority to enforce international law via punitive warfare must remain decentralized from a Grotian standpoint.[39]

3. A state's limited authority to punish international agents

Though some may be optimistic that a centralized authority for the punitive enforcement of international law can be established, the Grotian image of decentralized authority resembles in many ways the current international legal and political order. Importantly, however, it also reflects key problems with the current absence of (or extreme weakness of) a centralized authority to adjudicate and punish violators of international laws. Decentralized authority within international society will *in principle* most often amount to the contested authority of its various members. As suggested above, uncontested authority to enforce international law via punitive warfare in a decentralized system can, at best, emerge from the members of the international community generally agreeing that the punitive act is in the interest of all generally and not solely in the interest of those carrying out the punishment. Though such broad agreement is not theoretically impossible, the current configuration of ILIs cannot produce a meaningful agreement of this kind nor legitimately censure members who unilaterally enforce international laws via punitive warfare. First, given the UN Security Council's bias due to the veto power of a handful of nations, this ILI cannot produce meaningful agreement to sanction punitive warfare. On the other hand, the General Assembly lacks the authority to approve military action; it can only vote to censure or refuse to censure members for the unilateral actions they take. These votes are highly politicized and, thus, the results are generally contested by the participants as being shaped by concerns other than justice. Again, in the decentralized authority structure of our international legal and political order, contested authority to carry out punitive warfare as a means of international law enforcement will necessarily be the norm and contested authority is not sufficient to underwrite the case for justified punitive warfare.

The authority of the UN to censure members for unilateral punitive attacks has been contested by an alternative and rather Lockean image of authority. In the absence of ILIs ensuring the security of their citizens' rights to life and property from intermittent cross-border militant attacks, states have claimed the right to punitively retaliate against both the militants and the states that shelter or tolerate their operations.[40] While such arguments do not presume the existence of Locke's international State of Nature, they do suggest that, given 1) an unwillingness or inability of ILIs to take measures that will deter future attacks by militants across borders and 2) the state's obligation to secure its citizens' lives and property, states have the authority to punitively retaliate against the militants as well as against those who shelter or tolerate their activities. The aim here is the deterrence of future attacks from the same or other militant groups by means of punitive warfare.

To help contrast the image of a state's limited authority for punitive warfare at work here with other possibilities, a brief consideration of why states may or may not have an exclusive authority to carry out domestic punishment is in order. Though the exclusive authority of states to domestically punish criminals often goes unquestioned, A. John Simmons problematizes the state's *exclusive* authority to punish.[41] Following a Lockean premise that state authority arises from consent, Simmons is skeptical that citizens in fact ever grant the state the exclusive authority to punish acts that are *mala in se* and, thus even within a commonwealth, individuals maintain their natural right to punish violators of natural laws.[42] Following Simmons in our context of punitive warfare would seemingly give rise to a system where all parties (i.e. states, ILIs and private parties) would hold the non-exclusive authority to punish *anyone* who violates anyone's natural rights to life, liberty, bodily integrity or property—regardless of state jurisdiction and regardless of whether ILIs are willing or capable of punishing them. Such an international order would be too permissive as it would allow interventions by any interested party (public or private) and no matter what the severity of rights violations.

In order to avoid Simmons' anarchistic conclusion against the exclusivity of state punishment, Christopher Wellman argues that legitimate states can maintain an exclusive authority to punish their own citizens but only on the pragmatic grounds that they have an unparalleled ability to accomplish the legitimate aims of punishment when compared to individual citizens.[43] If a state lacks this unparalleled ability to accomplish the aims of punishment, then that state would relinquish its exclusive authority to punish to both individual citizens and international agents. Applying Wellman's view to our question, one can argue that when ILIs are unwilling or incapable of taking deterrent measures against international militants or terrorists, it would be impossible for them to maintain exclusive authority for international punishment on analogous pragmatic grounds. Following Wellman's forfeiture theory of punishment, a non-exclusive authority to punish the cross-border militants or terrorists would be established since they would have forfeited their right not to be punished by anyone.

Though this is a promising line of support for the argument proposed above, Wellman's theory of rights forfeiture is controversial.[44] None the less, it is still possible to support a state's proper authority to carry out deterrent retaliations against cross-border militants without attempting to defend rights forfeiture (a project far beyond the bounds of this work). In my more limited argument, the victim state is viewed as having the authority to punish the cross-border militants or terrorists due to its obligation to protect its citizens' basic rights from such attacks. If deterrent retaliation is a *necessary* means for preserving these rights, then the state's fundamental obligation to preserve its citizens' basic rights would establish the moral permission (i.e. authority) to carry out the punitive warfare.[45] If states are granted the authority to protect their citizens' basic rights, then they cannot reasonably be denied the authority to pursue the necessary means for doing so. The authority described here has exclusivity for the specific state(s) whose citizens have been attacked and whose obligation it is to protect them from repeated militant or terrorist violence. It ought to be remembered, however, that granting the proper but limited authority of states to carry out deterrent retaliations against cross-border militants or terrorists does not imply that such military acts will pass other *jus ad bellum* conditions.

Since this image of limited authority is rooted in the state's obligation to protect its citizens' basic rights, it fails to directly support punitive warfare with the broader aims of international law enforcement or rehabilitating rogue groups or states.[46] Given this second limitation, the authority to carry out punitive warfare against a state that shelters or tolerates a militant group is more controversial than directly targeting the militants. A belligerent reprisal against such states or their citizens seems better characterized as an attempt to coercively reform their lax policies towards militants within their own borders rather than as a deterrent against militant violence. Though the international community may contest whether a specific act of punitive retaliation against a militant group is either discriminate, a last resort, proportionate, or likely to succeed as a deterrent, less often is the state's authority to secure its citizens' lives and property by means of deterring future attacks contested.

Though beyond the scope of this chapter, it should be noted that similar Lockean arguments can be offered in support of attacks that aim to lessen future threats from militants by means of general attrition, or by the targeted elimination of leadership or skilled members. These arguments propose that due to each state's obligation to protect its citizens' rights and given the inability or unwillingness of ILIs to address security threats posed by terrorists and militants as well as an inability to capture militants or terrorists without killing them, states have the authority to carry out targeted strikes within foreign territories against known terrorists or militants to lessen their capabilities. I mention this related argument for two reasons. First, both the punitive and preventive arguments are regularly offered in conjunction to justify the same anti-terrorist operations. Second, both rationales face similar complications and controversies in regard to the *jus ad bellum* requirements of reasonable likelihood of success and proportionality.

In regard to defensive warfare, reasonable likelihood of success sets a limit on what political authorities can justifiably risk in the name of preserving territorial integrity and sovereignty; citizens cannot be justifiably commanded to fight a war with no reasonable chance of repelling the aggression. When considering a punitive retaliation aimed at deterring terrorist or militant violence or a preventive mission aimed at reducing such security threats, success would need to be measured in terms of protecting citizens' basic rights from terrorist or militant violence. However, the reasonable likelihood of successful deterrence or reduction of security threats opens many complicated empirical questions. Will retaliatory strikes deter future attacks or will they strengthen the militant's resolve, increase recruitment, and generate greater local support? Similarly, will preventive strikes that eliminate militant resources, leadership, or skilled members reduce security threats or lead to a backlash in terms of increased violence, recruitment, commitment, and local support? While reasonable likelihood of success does not require proof of effectiveness beyond a reasonable doubt, recent history provokes concerns that both punitive and preventive strikes promote greater dangers to citizens from backlash as opposed to deterrence or reduction of security threats.[47] In addition, unlike the typical application of this principle to defensive wars against aggression, the aims of deterrence and reduction of security risks have an indeterminate timeframe. Even if punitive or preventive anti-terrorist tactics are met with a backlash and escalation that further endangers citizens' basic rights, it has been argued that in the 'long term' it is reasonable to believe that greater security will be achieved.[48] While this claim is not easily dismissed, its acceptance may gut the reasonable likelihood of success condition of any sort of stringency. Without any determinate temporal limit for success, counterproductive warfare can claim justification from the viewpoint of the 'long war.' Hence, *if* punitive or preventive warfare can be justified, it might require a rethinking of this *jus ad bellum* standard.

Similarly, novel complications emerge for the application of the *jus ad bellum* principle of proportionality to punitive retaliations aimed at deterrence and preventive warfare aimed at reducing terrorist threats. First, in contrast to defensive warfare that aims to protect national sovereignty from aggression, the degree of danger posed by terrorist and militant groups is often a matter of debate. Second, given what has just been discussed regarding the effectiveness of punitive and preventive tactics and the indeterminate scope of the 'long war,' proportionality also faces the possible loss of stringency. Will the harms to noncombatants, one's own military, and one's own citizens due to backlash and escalation be outweighed by the long-term deterrence and reduction of security threats from punitive and preventive tactics? This question can become empty of meaning by allowing the temporal scope of the proposed benefits to extend into the indeterminate future.

4. Concluding comments

Though we have found one plausible account of a state's authority to carry out punitive warfare, it limits the permissible aims to deterrence while excluding both punitive enforcement of international law and reforming rogue members of international society. Additionally, the same obligation of the state to protect its citizens' basic rights from militant or terrorist violence that grounds this model of authority can lend justificatory support to preventive warfare aimed at attrition. However, the potential shift away from the legalist paradigm's strict limits to include as justified ends the deterrence of militant or terrorist violence or the attrition of militant or terrorist capabilities, produces troubling possibilities for the *jus ad bellum* principles of reasonable likelihood of success and proportionality. Given the temporal indeterminacy of these alternative ends, the options are either: to allow these two *ad bellum* conditions to lose their stringency, to reject as a form of evasive rhetoric the move to measure likelihood of success and proportionality in the scope of the 'long war', or to reformulate (if possible) the two *ad bellum* conditions to limit the temporal indeterminacy associated with the 'long war' and preserve a significant degree of stringency. While a limited conception of punitive warfare can plausibly overcome the legalist paradigm's presumption that states *always* lack proper authority to punish other international agents, fully embracing the deterrence of militant or terrorist violence as a justified end would likely require a more radical revision of just war theory that could greatly undermine its stringency.

Notes

1 W.V. O'Brien, *Law and Morality in Israel's War with the PLO*, New York: Routledge, 1991, p. 124.
2 I am using the term 'warfare' to refer to a broad range of military activities many of which fall short of full-scaled war. Theorists who preserve this threefold distinction include: L. de Molina, "On justice and law," in G. Reichberg, H. Syse and E. Bebgy (eds), *The Ethics of War*, Oxford: Blackwell Publishing, 2006, pp. 333–38; R. Falk, "The Beirut raid and the international law of retaliation," *The American Journal of International Law*, 63, 1969, pp.415–43; M. Walzer, *Just and Unjust Wars*, 3rd edn, New York: Basic Books, 2000, pp. 51–85; D. Rodin, *War and Self-Defense*, Oxford: Oxford University Press, 2002; J. McMahan, *Killing in War*, Oxford: Oxford University Press, 2009.
3 For a characterization of punitive interventions, see A.F. Lang Jr, "Punitive intervention: enforcing justice or generating conflict?" in M. Evans (ed.), *Just War Theory: A Reappraisal*, New York: Palgrave Macmillan, 2005, p. 50.

4 For recent examples of this tendency, see: R.W. Tucker, "Reprisals and self-defense: the customary law," *The American Journal of International Law*, 66, 1972, pp. 586–96; Y. Dinstein, *War, Aggression and Self-Defence*, Cambridge: Cambridge University Press, 1988, pp. 202–3; W.V. O'Brien, *Law and Morality in Israel's War with the PLO*; K. W. Kemp, "Punishment as just cause for war," *Public Affairs Quarterly*, 10, 1996, p. 344; and D. Luban "War as punishment," *Philosophy & Public Affairs* 39(4), 2012, p. 330.

5 Notable just war theorists who have found justification for punitive wars include: Augustine, "Questions on The Heptateuch," in G. Reichberg, H. Syse and E. Bebgy (eds), *The Ethics of War*, Oxford: Blackwell Publishing, 2006, p. 82; T. Aquinas, *Summa Theologiae* II–II, Q40; F. Suarez, "On war," in G. Reichberg, H. Syse and E. Bebgy (eds), *The Ethics of War*, Oxford: Blackwell Publishing, 2006, pp. 339–53; J.B. Elshtain, *Just War Against Terror*, New York: Basic Books, 2003, pp. 50–8; and J.T. Johnson, *The War to Oust Saddam Hussein*, Lantham, MD: Rowman & Littlefield, 2005.

6 While the rhetoric of defense by means of deterrent retaliation was used by Israel to justify its 1968 Beirut Raid (see R. Falk, "The Beirut raid," pp. 415–43), the language of deterring and reforming 'rogue states' emerged during the Clinton administration and gained favor in the rhetoric of both Tony Blair and George W. Bush. For a useful overview of these later trends, see A.F. Lang, "Punitive intervention," pp. 54–8. The shift to equating defense with the preventive tactic of reducing terrorist threats was championed by the Bush administration's mission to 'take the fight to the terrorists' before they could amass the means to attack the US again and continues within the justifications for the ongoing drone strikes by both the US and Israel.

7 In a recent article, David Luban explicitly proposes such a move: "Some nonretributive arguments for punishment [by means of warfare] may be accepted if we recast them as arguments grounded in self-defense." D. Luban, "War as Punishment," p. 330.

8 I will not take up the question of punitive warfare as a means of retribution, since it has often been pointed out that war is too blunt and indiscriminate an instrument for just retribution. For a thorough critique of retributive war, see D. Luban, "War as Punishment," pp. 299–330.

9 See note 5.

10 It should be noted that the *exclusive* authority of states to punish their own citizens has also been called into question by recent authors. See, A.J. Simmons, "Locke and the right to punish," *Philosophy & Public Affairs*, 20(4), 1991, pp. 311–49 and C.H. Wellman, "Rights and state punishment," *The Journal of Philosophy* 106(8), 2009, pp. 419–39.

11 Augustine, "Questions on The Heptateuch," p. 82.

12 Augustine, *City of God, Book XIX*, Ch. 13. Online. Available at: http://www.newadvent.org/fathers/120119.htm (accessed 19 June 2012). In this passage, Augustine depicts the *tranquillitas ordinis* as a broadly ordered peace between *all* things, including: the parts of each individual's soul, family members, rulers and ruled, nations, man and God, etc.

13 Augustine, *City of God, Book XIX*, Ch. 16.

14 Augustine, *City of God, Book XIX*, Ch. 13.

15 Quoted in C. O'Driscoll, *The Renegotiation of the Just War Tradition in the Twenty-First Century*, New York: Palgrave Macmillan, 2008, p. 63.

16 Two such neo-Augustinian projects can be found in J. B. Elshtain, *Just War Against Terror*, pp. 50–8 and O. O'Donovan, *The Just War Revisited*, Cambridge: Cambridge University Press, 2003, pp. 22–3.

17 Ibid., p. 61.

18 Ibid., p. 59.

19 A further controversy in this case is how indiscriminate this punitive war was when generally targeting Afghanistan and not specifically the terrorists within its borders.

20 Note that I will use 'State of Nature' to refer to Locke's particular conception of the state of nature.

21 J. Locke, *Two Treatises of Government*, P. Laslett (ed.), Cambridge: Cambridge University Press, 1988, pp. 271–2.

22 Ibid., p. 272. (Emphasis is in the original text.)

23 Ibid., pp. 272–3.

24 Ibid., p. 272.

25 Ibid., p. 276.

26 This line of argument is supported by R. Falk, "The Beirut raid," p. 430.

27 H. Grotius, *The Rights of War and Peace, Vol. 2*, R. Tuck (ed.), Indianapolis: Liberty Fund, 2005. Online. Available at: http://files.libertyfund.org/files/1947/1032-02_LFeBk.pdf (accessed 19 June 2012).

28 For Grotius' account of natural law and its grounds, see H. Grotius, *The Rights of War and Peace, Vol. 1*, R. Tuck (ed.), Indianapolis: Liberty Fund, 2005. Online. Available at: http://files.libertyfund.org/files/1425/1032-01_LFeBk.pdf (accessed 19 June 2012).

29 Ibid., pp. 162–3.

30 Ibid., p. 94. (Emphasis is in the original text.)

31 Ibid., p. 101. (Emphasis is in the original text.)

32 Grotius, *The Rights of War and Peace, Vol. 2*, pp. 1053–5.

33 Ibid., p. 1056.

34 Ibid., p. 1062.

35 Ibid., p. 1056.

36 Ibid., pp. 961–76.

37 Ibid., pp. 1053–5.

38 A.F. Lang, "Punitive intervention," p. 50.

39 It is also conceivable for the Grotian that if ILIs are unwilling for political reasons to sanction punitive warfare that aims to enforce international law and deter future violations, they would lack the authority to justifiably stop a member state from doing so unilaterally.

40 For a history of such claims, see D. Bowett, "Reprisals involving recourse to armed force," *The American Journal of International Law*, 66, 1972, pp. 1–36.

41 A. J. Simmons, "Locke and the right to punish."

42 Ibid., 344–9.

43 C.H. Wellman, "Rights and state punishment," pp. 427–31. When Wellman discusses international punishment, he focuses solely on cases of systematic human rights violations when no border has been crossed. He argues that the authority to intervene for humanitarian purposes is not exclusive to any state or institution due to the lack of pragmatic grounds. Ibid., pp.433–8. One might counter, however, that humanitarian interventions are attempts to rescue people from *ongoing* rights violations and, thus, are not truly punitive in nature.

44 For Wellman's defense of his forfeiture approach, see C.H. Wellman, "The rights forfeiture theory of punishment," *Ethics*, 122:2, 2012, pp. 371–93.

45 I do not in this chapter discuss the *jus ad bellum* condition of necessity in regard to punitive warfare aimed at deterrence. However, insofar as it is assumed that the basic rights of citizens are not being protected from international militants or terrorists by either ILIs or the state governments where the militants are operating and that these militants cannot be captured without undue risk to one's own soldiers, then one can argue that the necessity condition for punitive strikes is satisfied. This is not to suggest that these assumptions are born out in actual cases.

46 In contrast, Wellman uses his forfeiture theory to defend the proper authority of all states to enforce international human rights conventions via humanitarian interventions. C.H. Wellman, "Rights and state punishment," pp. 436–8. In opposition to Wellman's characterization, wars of law enforcement that are in response to *ongoing* violations of international human rights law are not properly punitive in nature as they lack the retrospective quality required.

47 Though the reliability of terrorist recruitment statistics is controversial, an IISS study showed a spike in al Qaeda recruitment after the US invasion of Iraq which could be characterized as a being punitive towards Iraq. The results were reported in T. Karon, "Why al-Qaeda thrives," *Time*, 26 May, 2004. Online. Available at: http://www.time.com/time/world/article/0,8599,642825,00.html (accessed 19 July 2012). Similar concerns have been raised about the ongoing drone attacks which aim to prevent future terrorist attacks by means of attrition: I. Mothana, "How drones help al Qaeda," *The New York Times*, 13 June, 2012. Online. Available at: http://www.nytimes.com/2012/06/14/opinion/how-drones-help-al-qaeda.html (accessed 19 July 2012).

48 D. Statman, "Targeted killing," *Theoretical Inquiries in Law*, 5, 2004, p. 192.

References

Aquinas, T. *Summa Theologiae* II-II, Q40.

Augustine "Questions on The Heptateuch," in G. Reichberg, H. Syse and E. Bebgy (eds), *The Ethics of War*, Oxford: Blackwell Publishing, 2006.

——*City of God, Book XIX*, Ch. 13, Online. Available at: http://www.newadvent.org/fathers/120119.htm (accessed 19 June 2012).

Bowett, D. "Reprisals involving recourse to armed force," *The American Journal of International Law*, 66, 1972, pp. 1–36.

Dinstein, Y. *War, Aggression and Self-Defence*, Cambridge: Cambridge University Press, 1988.

Elshtain, J.B. *Just War Against Terror*, New York: Basic Books, 2003.

Falk, R. "The Beirut raid and the international law of retaliation," *The American Journal of International Law*, 63, 1969, pp.415–43.

Grotius, H. *The Rights of War and Peace, Vol. 1*, R. Tuck (ed.), Indianapolis: Liberty Fund, 2005. Online. Available at: http://files.libertyfund.org/files/1425/1032-01_LFeBk.pdf (accessed 19 June 2012).

——*The Rights of War and Peace, Vol. 2*, R. Tuck (ed.), Indianapolis: Liberty Fund, 2005. Online. Available at: http://files.libertyfund.org/files/1947/1032-02_LFeBk.pdf (accessed 19 June 2012).

Karon, T. "Why al-Qaeda thrives," *Time*, 26 May, 2004. Online. Available at: http://www.time.com/time/world/article/0,8599,642825,00.html (accessed 19 July 2012).

Kemp, K.W. "Punishment as just cause for war," *Public Affairs Quarterly*, 10, 1996, pp. 335–53.

Lang Jr, A.F. "Punitive intervention: enforcing justice or generating conflict?" in M. Evans (ed.), *Just War Theory: A Reappraisal*, New York: Palgrave Macmillan, 2005.

Locke, J. *Two Treatises of Government*, P. Laslett (ed.), Cambridge: Cambridge University Press, 1988.

Luban, D. "War as punishment," *Philosophy & Public Affairs*, 39, 2012, pp. 299–330.

Johnson, J.T. *The War to Oust Saddam Hussein*, Lantham, MD: Rowman & Littlefield, 2005.

McMahan, J. *Killing in War*, Oxford: Oxford University Press, 2009.

de Molina, L. "On justice and law," in G. Reichberg, H. Syse and E. Bebgy (eds), *The Ethics of War*, Oxford: Blackwell Publishing, 2006.

Mothana, I. "How drones help al Qaeda," *The New York Times*, 13 June, 2006. Online. Available at: http://www.nytimes.com/2012/06/14/opinion/how-drones-help-al-qaeda.html (accessed 19 July 2012).

O'Brien, W.V. *Law and Morality in Israel's War with the PLO*, New York: Routledge, 1991.

O'Donovan, O. *The Just War Revisited*, Cambridge: Cambridge University Press, 2003.

O'Driscoll, C. *The Renegotiation of the Just War Tradition in the Twenty-First Century*, New York: Palgrave Macmillan, 2008.

Rodin, D. *War and Self-Defense*, Oxford: Oxford University Press, 2002.

Simmons, A.J. "Locke and the right to punish," *Philosophy & Public Affairs*, 20, 1991, pp. 311–49.

Statman, D. "Targeted killing," *Theoretical Inquiries in Law*, 5:192, 2004, pp. 179–98.

Suarez, F. "On war," in G. Reichberg, H. Syse and E. Bebgy (eds), *The Ethics of War*, Oxford: Blackwell Publishing, 2006.

Tucker, R.W. "Reprisals and self-defense: the customary law," *The American Journal of International Law*, 66, 1972, pp. 586–96.

Walzer, W. *Just and Unjust Wars*, 3rd edn, New York: Basic Books, 2000.

Wellman, C.H. "The rights forfeiture theory of punishment," *Ethics*, 122:2, 2012, pp. 371–93.

——"Rights and state punishment," *The Journal of Philosophy*, 106, 2009, pp. 419–39.

Warfighters and moral agency

18

RE-EVALUATING THE STATUS OF NONCOMBATANTS IN JUST WAR THEORY AND TERRORISM[1]

Jason P. Blahuta

1. Introduction

The idea that "innocent" noncombatants are deserving of immunity from attack is emotionally comforting, after all, no one wants to think that those who fight on their behalf would intentionally kill or maim those who are undeserving of such a fate. But noncombatant immunity is a big assumption, premised on the interpretation of noncombatants as innocent *qua* harmless. However, an analysis of this claim quickly shows that while on a *prima facie* level noncombatants deserve immunity from attack, this status needs to be justified not just on the basis of innocence *qua* harmless, but on the basis of innocence *qua* blameless as well. The results of such an analysis reveal that, in principle, noncombatants are not always as innocent *qua* harmless as they appear, and rarely are they innocent *qua* blameless. Thus, subject to a variety of contingent factors, their right to immunity from attack is significantly eroded or collapses altogether. A successful re-evaluation of noncombatant claims to immunity from attack has a profound impact on discussions of terrorism, for in many asymmetrical conflicts the smaller party is labeled terrorist precisely because of the noncombatant casualties they generate. In light of the in principle moral justification of noncombatant deaths, other criteria must be used to distinguish when noncombatants can be legitimately targeted, namely when doing so is a justifiable part of an asymmetric conflict, and when it is unjustifiable and therefore an act of terrorism. The criteria of just cause, supreme emergency, legitimate authority, the use of violence as a last resort, and that the violence employed has a reasonable chance of success can accomplish this.

2. Innocence and noncombatants

In his seminal piece on the topic, *Just and Unjust Wars*, Michael Walzer points to several classes of individuals that qualify as noncombatants—the unarmed soldier, the civilian working in a munitions plant but who is off duty at home, and the civilian working in a food processing plant—and places varying restrictions on if and when they may be targeted.[2] The rationale Walzer offers for attacking soldiers, even those who are not expecting the attack, is that they belong to a class that is dedicated to being a threat. However, when the soldier is unarmed, she is no longer a threat, even though she belongs to a class that is. In the case of civilians, Walzer maintains that they are noncombatants, and decries attempts to include civilians in the class of combatants.

Being harmless entails neither innocence nor blamelessness; and a defensible blanket right to immunity from attack needs to be grounded in being both. To be truly innocent requires being blameless; a murderer who lays down her weapon when confronted by the police is innocent *qua* harmless, but not innocent *qua* blameless. Innocence *qua* harmless is enough to secure an immunity from attack in cases where the enemy has equally viable alternative options, but in cases where other options are too risky or run afoul of military expediency and the stakes are extremely high, noncombatants must establish that they are not only harmless, but blameless too if they are to maintain a right to immunity from attack.

A. J. Coates defends the conception of innocence *qua* harmless, arguing that interpretations of innocence *qua* blameless risk either being useless when applied to individuals because combatants rarely have fine-grained knowledge about their targets, or undermine "all attempts at discrimination"[3] when applied to groups, for attributing guilt to a people is essentially a declaration of total war. Coates's characterization of innocence *qua* blame as subjective or excessive is perhaps too quick. While those who make military decisions can never really know if a target is deserving of blame, reflective conceptual analysis can provide reliable guidance for determining whether noncombatants can be targeted, are acceptable collateral damage, or how much of an obligation one has to avoid harming them.

3. Noncombatants under democratic regimes

The claim that civilian populations of democratic regimes are not directly engaged in combat or in oiling their state's war machine, are therefore innocent and possess a blanket right to immunity from attack does not hold for several reasons. In democracies, citizens have (a) consented to their government, rendering soldiers agents acting on their behalf; citizens are thus (b) the ultimate moral authority of their government's actions. They also (c) constitute the economic and physical infrastructure of their government, and even if this were not the case, as it is with children, democratic citizens are (d) the beneficiaries of their government's actions.

3.1 *Consent and moral authority*

At the core of democratic theory is the assumption that the government represents the people, so it is unfathomable that a democracy that declares war could argue that its citizens have done nothing to lose their right to immunity from attack. Even if the electorate did not want the war, such as was the case with recent wars in Iraq and Afghanistan where significant numbers of Americans did not support their government's actions, two remaining factors implicate the citizenry. The first is that democracies do not require plebiscites on every issue, but operate with public officials acting as agents on behalf of the electorate, even those who did not vote for them. "Buying into the system" is sufficient to undermine a noncombatant's right to immunity from attack. Furthermore, given the division of powers and other checks and balances characteristic of democratic political structures, the ability of the head of a democratic state to go to war without broad-based support of other elected officials is nil. The second factor is that the electorate remains the moral authority of the government, even between elections, and is capable of influencing government decisions through communication with elected officials via traditional and social media, public dialogue, and public protests. In short, the very nature of the democratic system makes the electorate the moral power behind the government's actions. However, this also assumes that the democracy is functioning in a proper, transparent manner; there will be instances where a democracy becomes corrupt and information relevant to public support for a conflict is intentionally obfuscated or suppressed by a democratic regime. In such cases, the culpability of citizens, and whether they have done anything to lose their right to immunity from attack, becomes questionable.

One may reverse the moral authority, and argue that in light of the government's vast resources it is better equipped to make morally reliable decisions about *jus ad* bellum and *jus in bello* issues than ordinary citizens and soldiers, and therefore these persons are morally obligated to obey their government's decisions even if they disagree with them. Assumedly, this deferral to a more epistemically reliable source would absolve citizens of any blame. However, as Jeff McMahan aptly points out, "democratic decision-making procedures do not offer even a presumption that the *morality* of a democratic government's decision to resort to war has been subjected to any kind of epistemically reliable deliberation or scrutiny whatsoever."[4] The upshot is that there is no reason to think governments produce moral decisions that are more reliable or have more epistemic authority than those made by individuals and so noncombatants, if they wish to maintain that they are innocent *qua* blameless and deserving of a right to immunity from attack, need to think carefully and rigorously about their obedience to the government and their participation, however indirect it may be, in their nation's or group's military activities.

3.2 Noncombatants as economic and physical infrastructure

Noncombatants also constitute the economic and physical infrastructure of their government, so even if they disavow its actions, their participation in the economy provides their government with the means to carry out those actions. Against this position, Walzer defends noncombatants on the grounds that they are not threats if they are not directly engaged in the military aspect of the war machine, arguing that "[a]n army, to be sure, has an enormous belly, and it must be fed if it is to fight. But it is not its belly but its arms that make it an army. Those men and women who supply its belly are doing nothing peculiarly warlike. Hence their immunity from attack: they are assimilated to the rest of the civilian population."[5]

However, Walzer's argument does not hold up well. Consider the following example: Bob lives in a desert and is located far from his enemy Betty, who has repeatedly announced in deed and word her intention to kill Bob. At his disposal, Bob has an armed Predator drone, but Betty is exceptionally clever at covert operations and can evade the drone. Betty's problem is that while she can carry her weapons and ammunition with her, the trip from her secret base to Bob's base is so long that she cannot carry enough supplies with her. It is when she has to resupply at the last trading post en route to Bob's location, buying water and foodstuffs from the proprietor Dave, that she is vulnerable to the drone. Dave listens well to his customers, and knows what Betty is planning, but still sells to her, perhaps out of a desire for profit, perhaps out of fear that she will harm him if he refuses to deal with her. Walzer maintains that using the drone to kill Betty is fair game, but that Dave's death would be unacceptable, for Dave is no threat to Bob and is not selling the tools of war to Betty. In fact, he is selling only food and water. But does this entitle Dave to immunity from Bob's attack? Under the scenario described, it does not. Yes, Dave is selling what any human being *qua* human being, needs, but Betty needs these supplies and cannot complete the long journey to reach Bob without them. In effect, there is no difference between Dave selling Betty armaments and ammunition or water and foodstuffs, in each case, Dave's resupplying of Betty is a necessary condition of Betty being able to reach Bob and carry out her attack. Only after Dave has completed his transaction with Betty can he claim to be no threat to Bob, and since his death at that point will not affect Betty's ability to attack Bob, any strike against him at this point would be purely retributive. During and before the transaction, Dave is a legitimate target. Thus Walzer's distinction between civilians who provide the necessities of life and those who provide the weapons of war, does not always hold.

The situation becomes murkier when industrialized warfare, with the multipurposed nature of parts and the multifaceted nature of production facilities, is taken into consideration. Not only can the same production facility make a variety of products, some destined for civilian use while others are earmarked for military use, but a production facility can also produce a single part that has multiple applications, as indeed do many electrical and computer components. Clearly, there are degrees of involvement, and discerning involvement depends on accurate intelligence reports regarding many contingencies such as whether soft targets are acting knowingly, how necessary their actions are to the war machine, the chances of success that various different modes of attack promise, and how much noncombatant damage vis-à-vis other soft targets would occur if an attack was launched. Case in point: if a production facility that assembles fighter jets is too heavily defended to be successfully attacked, but softer targets such as suppliers that provide key components can be attacked, their involvement in the plant's activities makes them sufficiently culpable to undermine their claim to immunity from attack. The community college where the welders who may some day help assemble these fighter jets are trained and where a variety of other students are trained for peaceful occupations, is less essential to the production process, possesses less culpability, and carries with it a higher likelihood of unrelated noncombatant casualties. Given these considerations, it would be easy to justify attacking the supplier because of its more direct involvement with military production, but less so the community college.

3.3 Noncombatants as beneficiaries

Even if the members of the electorate are ignorant of their government's actions, as is often the case in modern democracies where apathy and ignorance abound, these persons are still arguably the beneficiaries of their government's actions. Any benefit the state acquires through military action, be it new territory, access to another state's natural resources, or the removal of an international competitor, is enjoyed by the aggressor state's populace. Obviously the gains of a conflict are rarely shared equally across a society, just as the distribution of the costs incurred are rarely born equitably. However, collectively the class of all citizens benefits or is harmed, even if distributively this is not the case. States often herald this in their war commemoration ceremonies, in which the young are rightly told that the freedoms they presently enjoy were made possible by the sacrifices of their nation's soldiers. Fair enough, but if the war did not have a just cause, the citizens of that democracy are essentially living off the proceeds of crime, which makes them complicit in the unjust activities of their military, and shreds their right to immunity from attack in future conflicts related to the original war. Ignorance may be bliss, but it is not without blame, especially when that ignorance is willful.

Children pose a special problem for anyone trying to justify noncombatant casualties, and for obvious reasons. With the exception of child soldiers, children are clearly noncombatants; additionally, children do not vote and therefore cannot consent to any government nor can they be the moral authority of their government's actions. However, children remain the beneficiaries of their government's actions; if children are part of a regime involved in an unjust war, they are still living off the proceeds of crime.

To illustrate both the typical view of children as innocent as well as how children can be beneficiaries of war, consider the example of a mismatched boxing match put forth by Shannon French. French suggests the pairing of a heavy-weight champion at the top of his game versus the stereotypical ninety pound weakling. The weakling's only chance of victory is to fight dirty and French is willing to allow this to underdogs in asymmetric conflicts in general: they can flout the rules when engaging the enemy, and as the stakes get higher, more underhanded tactics become justifiable. However, French refuses to allow underdogs carte blanche in terms of targeting noncombatants.[6] Instead, French restricts the weakling's options thusly: "[W]e could quite rightly find a great deal of fault with the underdog if he tried to overcome his disadvantage by kidnapping the champion's child and lighting the infant on fire just outside the boxing ring in order to destroy his opponent's concentration and will to fight (a horrific act of terror)."[7] The rationale French offers for not attacking the heavyweight's child is standard: the child is not a threat to the ninety pound weakling. However, what if the ninety pound weakling cannot win, even by using dirty tricks in the ring, but the stakes are such that if the heavyweight wins the fight, his prize is the ability to forcibly harvest the organs, specifically the heart, of the ninety pound weakling's child? The recipient of the heart will be the heavyweight's child who is gravely in need of a heart transplant and is ignorant of the lengths her father is going to in order to secure her the organ. Under such circumstances it is not obvious that the heavyweight's child should enjoy immunity from an attack. In fact, as the beneficiary of the heavyweight's efforts, she is very much part of the conflict and her receiving the heart makes her culpable whether she knows it or not. If there is no way the ninety pound weakling can win, even by cheating during the fight, but an attack on the heavyweight's child could break his opponent's will, momentarily distract him enough that a victory may be possible, or remove the motivation for the fight, it becomes arguable given the high stakes that the heavyweight's child is fair game.

This example is both contrived and extreme, but a similar conclusion could easily be reached and justified if the stakes were enslavement of the loser's child as opposed to organ harvesting. And when one considers that underdogs in many asymmetric conflicts may see their situation in such terms—it seems plausible that Palestinians and apartheid-era black South Africans would see their respective conflicts in terms commensurable with this scenario—even the targeting of children is no longer an unquestionable taboo, but can in principle and under certain circumstances be justified.

Being blameful does not justify all attacks on noncombatants, only those which are required by military expediency. If other options are available, they are preferable from a moral perspective. Should soldiers, generals, and their political masters choose options which entail significantly more risk, that is certainly a laudable and honorable decision, but it is also not necessitated by the mere fact that noncombatants are innocent *qua* harmless. The resulting in principle loss of noncombatant immunity is subject to an analysis of numerous contingencies which it must pass before the targeting of noncombatants can be morally justified. It is quite likely, given the probability of options other than targeting noncombatants, that this in principle loss of the immunity to attack would not survive such an analysis and carry over into practice, but the moral culpability of noncombatants still poses a serious problem for conventional just war theory.

4. Moral responsibility of noncombatants under nondemocratic regimes

As is the case with citizens of democratic states, noncombatants of nondemocratic regimes (a) are the economic and physical infrastructure of their government, and (b) may stand to benefit from the regime's actions. This is sufficient reason to render these noncombatants legitimate targets of violent action on the grounds of self-defense. However, citizens of nondemocratic regimes cannot meaningfully consent to their government. Such nations often limit the ability of their citizens to emigrate to other countries, so even tacit consent cannot be attributed to these persons. This is the strongest defense of such noncombatants: their lack of political and civil freedoms render whatever their participation in their nation's war effort coerced and mitigates their responsibility for it.

Lorraine Besser-Jones offers an intuitive view of moral responsibility based on intentionality and makes it the basis for self-defense, arguing that "in cases where acts of self-defense are truly warranted and so justifiable, the aggressor must have been committing the act of aggression based on her own free will and thereby forfeiting one or more of *her* rights."[8] This argument is problematic, for it assumes two things without warrant: (a) that lack of intention renders one blameless, and (b) that the use of violence is a luxury, that there are always other options that allow for defense without significant increases in risk or loss.[9]

Unfortunately, these assumptions rarely correspond with the reality of the world we live in. Consider the following scenario: the dictator of an enemy nation has abducted a number of "innocent" noncombatants and sequestered them on an island where she is using some as hostages and some as forced labor to build a weapon of mass destruction (a really big cannon, similar to the ones commissioned by Saddam Hussein) that she plans on using on a neighboring country. These noncombatants have no interest in this dictator or her dispute with the other country, and they are not complying with her instructions willingly, but have loved ones threatened or abducted and now fear for their safety. The dictator and military elite reside in a series of impenetrable shelters buried deep beneath the island, but the forced laborers live in buildings susceptible to conventional attacks.

That these noncombatants are not acting of their own free will is irrelevant to whether they should enjoy immunity from attack, the reality is that they are helping the regime construct a weapon of mass destruction that will be used against the neighboring state, and since the dictator and military leadership are unreachable, the noncombatants can be targeted on the grounds of self-defense. Even if these noncombatants are acting under duress and sympathize with the neighboring state, the fact is that they made a choice—they chose to place their lives or those of their loved ones before others whom they are willing to put at risk. While it is understandable that they would make this choice, it raises the prospects of a double standard that lies at the heart of Walzer's argument. Walzer modifies the intentionality clause of traditional just war theory (the caveat that harm to innocents must not be intentional in any way) by rightly insisting that mere lack of intention is an empty criterion that can be satisfied far too easily to be of any practical use. Instead, Walzer insists that "[w]hat we look for in such cases is some sign of a positive commitment to save civilian lives."[10] The problem is not with the higher standard Walzer invokes, but that he does not apply this standard to the class of noncombatants as well as the class of soldiers, for their decision places the lives of others at risk too.

Even Walzer allows for a limited defense of noncombatant casualties when the stakes are high enough, as is evidenced by his support of British bombing of German cities in World War II, a defense which as Coates observes, ignores the fact that earlier decisions grounded in the British experience of trench warfare from the first World War shaped, if not created, the situation the British found themselves in and which they used to justify their bombing campaigns.[11]

It must also be remembered that there are those who are in fact blameless. The illiterate rural farmer, ignorant of her government's activities and largely unaware of the larger political sphere—not out of apathy or convenience but by the nature of her location, lack of education, and poverty—who has her crops seized by the military, cannot be called a beneficiary of a regime that clearly mistreats her in the same way that a farmer who sells her crops to the military can be. Any minority that lacks political power and is seriously oppressed by a nondemocratic regime, such as the Kurds in Iraq, would fall into this category. Their children also cannot be said to be beneficiaries of the regime, a knowing part of its infrastructure, or a source of its moral authority.

Oppression is not enough, however, to claim a right to immunity from attack, for oppressed groups in democratic states can still be beneficiaries. Homosexuals, for instance, are oppressed in many democratic regimes—in some jurisdictions they are legally discriminated against in a variety of ways or are otherwise denied the same privileges as heterosexuals—but they can still be classified as beneficiaries of the democratic regime that oppresses them, because they enjoy many other political and civil rights, and many physical and monetary privileges, even in the face of their oppression. Similar arguments can be put forth for women and ethnic minorities, despite the historical and contemporary injustices they face under democratic regimes.

5. Distinguishing terrorism from asymmetrical conflicts

Citing "innocent" noncombatant casualties is often used as a means of vilifying an enemy, and in the case of asymmetrical conflicts, is often sufficient justification for labeling the other side as terrorist. Given that the preceding analysis has demonstrated that the innocent *qua* harmless are often not innocent *qua* blameless and thus in principle and under certain circumstances can be targeted, the line between terrorism and asymmetrical warfare needs to be redrawn. If intentional noncombatant casualties are insufficient to mark the distinction between these phenomena, other criteria are needed for determining whether an organization is terrorist or simply pursuing a just cause by whatever means available. Fortunately, just war theory does have other criteria which can do precisely this, namely (a) that the group has a just cause, (b) that a supreme emergency exists, (c) that the use of violence is their last resort to attaining the group's goals, namely serious attempts at diplomacy are futile or have failed to date, and (d) that the group is a legitimate authority, meaning that they have a defensible claim to representing a significant number of persons united by their cause. Additionally, and apart from standard accounts of just war theory, (e) the criteria of reasonable chance of success—namely the violence used must be a plausible means of achieving their stated goals, irrespective of its actual efficacy—needs to be included.

5.1 Just cause and supreme emergency

For the most part, it is easy to determine whether the just cause criteria has been met. Wars of aggression cannot be deemed to have a just cause, which leaves only defensive wars, wars of liberation, and arguably humanitarian interventions. Although typically treated separately, the idea of supreme emergency also plays a role in the discussion of just cause. One cannot simply be fighting a defensive war, the threat one faces must be significantly serious and imminent to justify the targeting of noncombatants who are innocent *qua* harmless, even if they are not innocent *qua* blameless. Thus Walzer condemns the nuclear attacks against Hiroshima and Nagasaki as misapplied utilitarianism; the deaths of so many noncombatants cannot be justified because at the time of the attacks Japan no longer posed a significant or imminent threat to the United States.[12]

The apartheid-era ANC and the provisional IRA sought, and the Palestinians currently seek, specific goals of correcting oppression or having independent territories, and so have strong arguments in favor of having satisfied the just cause criteria. These conflicts, even though they utilize tactics typically seen as terrorist, are better characterized as asymmetric wars of liberation. Revolutionary movements have less of a case that they are involved in a just cause, unless they can establish that they also possess legitimate authority. Al Qaeda too has a weak argument for pursuing a just cause. Part of the problem with both revolutionaries and Al Qaeda are that their fights are based on ideologies as opposed to concrete goals such as political independence of a specific geographic region or political rights for a particular population. The more abstract the goals become, the more difficult it is to establish all the players involved (who is responsible, who is represented, etc.) and that the goals constitute a just cause. The Taliban in Afghanistan appear to be an odd case, for they were a toppled power. This means they could argue to be fighting a war of liberation against foreign aggressors, but their lack of legitimate authority both while they were in power and afterwards throws doubt on any claim that they are motivated by a just cause.

5.2 Legitimate authority

The purpose of the legitimate authority criterion is to distinguish between war and the private use of violence; it determines that a conflict is, in fact, a war, and not a private criminal activity, and it does this by making war lawful through defining war as part of the coercive power of the state as it acts in an international context.[13] This criterion is generally interpreted in two ways: *de facto* authority and *de jure* authority. Despite the strengths of each interpretation, both have weaknesses that a "plausible claim" approach could avoid.

De facto authority claims that those who have power at the moment have the necessary authority to declare war. As Besser-Jones observes, the danger inherent in such an interpretation is that it allows for any group to self-authorize itself.[14] However, what Besser-Jones overlooks is that this is often how things work in the absence of an established political order. Not only do victors proclaim their authority to be legitimate after messy civil wars, but one generation's warlord can become the next generation's member of parliament in areas where democracy is being transplanted by the international community.

The *de jure* interpretation requires that for authority to be legitimate it must be grounded in the rule of law, both internally and externally, the latter meaning the international community. To accommodate this and still allow for non-state groups to possess legitimate authority, Besser-Jones sponsors a conception of legitimate authority grounded in the fact that persons deferred to that authority, creating a common way of life.[15] But such a conception does not adequately distinguish the *de facto* interpretation from the *de jure* interpretation of legitimate authority, for persons obviously defer (even if under duress) to warlords and organized crime. There are two further drawbacks to the *de jure* interpretation which undermine it: (a) internally, rule of law may not be possible in areas of conflict or where a group is oppressed or denied statehood, and (b) externally, rule of law has little credibility internationally. A quick look at the inability of the United Nations Security Council to unanimously condemn recent violence in Syria and the fact that United Nations Human Rights Council typically has states renowned for human rights abuses as sitting members shows that the recognition of the international community is neither a ringing endorsement nor objective, but is fraught with conflicts of interest and a variety of competing political agendas that do not necessarily have the good of the international community as their guiding principle.

A plausibility standard for legitimate authority steers a middle path between the *de facto* and *de jure* interpretations, and would extend legitimate authority to some non-state groups while avoiding self-authorization. Andrew Altman and Christopher Heath Wellman sponsor a version of legitimate authority premised on whether a regime respects human rights, defined as those rights which are "generally needed against the standard and direct threats to leading a minimally decent human life in modern society."[16] This resonates well with a plausibility standard, for it is hard to take seriously an organization's claim to legitimate authority if the group violates the rights of those they claim to represent. An important aspect of Altman and Wellman's argument is that democracy is not tied to political legitimacy, nor is the efficiency of the group,[17] namely a group does not lose its legitimacy merely because another group or political system could do a better job; what does cost a group its political legitimacy is its failure to respect human rights. In short, groups that oppress, intimidate, or terrorize those they profess to represent have no claim to legitimate authority. Altman and Wellman go to considerable lengths to establish this point by distinguishing between a human right, which is directly linked to leading a minimally decent life, and a human rights-based claim, a claim to something which would enhance one's likelihood of receiving or ability to enjoy a human right, but which itself is not a human right and is only indirectly linked to leading a minimally decent life.[18] Additionally, what makes a claim plausible, in part, is the size of the group and the geographic dimensions of it. All such persons or groups will purport to have political goals, but illegitimate groups either lack the critical mass or necessary structure to be a real organization, or they claim to represent a group of people that they clearly cannot truly represent. Any legitimate group must possess a plausible claim to representing the people they claim to represent both in geographic scope and morally through respecting their human rights or clearly serving interests these people recognize as their own.

Persons or groups who obviously have no plausible claims to legitimate authority include Timothy McVeigh and the Unabomber. Revolutionary groups who claim to represent people who disavow the revolution also lack any plausible claim to legitimate authority; any group which claims to be advancing the interests of others who suffer from some form of false consciousness must be viewed with the highest degree of skepticism.

When dealing with groups such as the provisional IRA and the apartheid-era ANC it can be easy to identify who these groups represent, but even then, a claim to represent a group is not the same as representing that group. If there are no elections, such claims quickly become murky. Reliable polling also does not exist in areas of conflict, although rough estimates of support can be arrived at through attention to important relevant facts. Case in point: reports of intimidation by the provisional IRA cast doubt on how much of the Catholic population in Northern Ireland that they claimed to represent really supported them, and a bombing in Warrington that killed two children clearly hurt their support throughout the rest of Ireland. The fact that Sinn Féin began to see significant electoral results only after agreeing to ceasefires also testifies to the fact that while their cause had widespread support, their violent methods did not enjoy the same level of support.

The apartheid-era ANC was initially classified as a terrorist group by both South Africa and the United States, and while it is a typical rhetorical maneuver in an asymmetric conflict to label one's opponents terrorist as South Africa did, the American response was driven by Cold War concerns that the ANC had links to communism.

The Taliban in Afghanistan could only offer a *de facto* claim to legitimate authority, lacking the rule of law internally as well as enjoying only minimal recognition internationally. Their rule before Western military powers entered their country in 2001 was marked by widespread corruption, the serious oppression of women, and ethnic cleansing of minorities. Since the Taliban were removed from power and became an insurgency, they have repeatedly targeted the people any claim to legitimate authority would require them to represent. The fact that they are no longer the *de facto* power in Afghanistan removes the only claim they could advance to being a legitimate authority.

When groups become global, such as Al Qaeda, their ability to represent anyone becomes even more problematic. Clearly, as the aftermath of 9/11 showed, Al Qaeda did not represent Muslims around the world. Many Muslims condemned the events of 9/11, and aside from fringe groups already inclined to Bin Laden's way of thinking, there was no great rallying around Bin Laden afterwards. Certainly mainstream Muslims in North America and Europe did not view him as representing their interests. Regardless, it is implausible that Muslims worldwide, a group that transcends national, economic, social, and gender boundaries, could be represented by such a radical organization.

5.3 Last resort

The last resort clause requires diplomacy to have been tried or be futile before violence can be justified. To this end, both the provisional IRA and the apartheid-era ANC possessed political wings as well as military wings. The political branches of these organizations allowed for negotiations to take place and, in fact, they were instrumental in securing a peace plan in Northern Ireland and ending apartheid in South Africa. While it will always remain debatable whether diplomacy is truly exhausted before any group resorts to violence, it cannot be denied that diplomacy was the first option of the ANC. In the case of the provisional IRA, its political wing Sinn Féin developed after the military, so clearly violence was not the last resort. Even with this failing though, the fact that a political organization was created to make negotiations possible lends credence to the idea that even if chronologically the provisional IRA employed violence first, they would have preferred a peaceful solution.

While the Taliban cannot be faulted for not engaging in negotiations, for they were the *de facto* power when Western forces removed them from power in 2001, they can however be blamed for refusing to seriously negotiate since becoming an insurgency. The lack of negotiations and their quick and indiscriminate use of violence undermines any pretense that violence was their last resort.

Al Qaeda never attempted diplomatic negotiations with any of the nations it targeted before attacking them, but it is implausible, given the organizational structure of Al Qaeda and the world-wide persons and interests it professes to represent, that meaningful diplomacy could have been possible in the years leading up to the 9/11 attacks. In the aftermath of its top leadership being decimated by the war on terror, its organizational structure has continued to devolve and it now currently operates even more as a series of loosely connected franchises. This means that while historically it lacked the sufficient organizational structure to engage in negotiations, it now also lacks the control over its membership necessary to make them respect the outcome of any negotiations.

5.4 Reasonable chance of success

Violence for the sake of violence may satisfy a group's bloodlust, but it can never be justified morally or under just war theory. Thus, violence that targets noncombatants, if it stands any hope of being morally justified, must have a reasonable chance of success.[19] This criterion relates back to geography very quickly, for the geographic proximity of the apartheid-era ANC to the white minority in South Africa, the provisional IRA to Northern Ireland and Britain, and the Palestinians to Israel means that all these groups could wage long, drawn-out campaigns of violence. The ability to conduct such a protracted campaign is vital to its chances of success, and it is a credit to the Israeli population's steadfastness and resolve that they have not given way to the prolonged campaigns of Palestinian fighters. Yet, the Palestinians have every reason to think that such a drawn-out siege would eventually produce results. Similar campaigns of violence have been waged with greater success by the apartheid-era ANC, the provisional IRA, and by the Taliban insurgency in Afghanistan. Ten years after the arrival of Western military forces, very little progress has been made in securing Afghanistan, and while the Afghan insurgency has not won, it endures and appears to have a resilient and robust health capable of reasserting significant control over the country once Western powers leave.

The same cannot be said of the Oklahoma City bombing or the 9/11 attacks. The bombing of the Alfred P. Murrah Federal Building in 1995 was an isolated event and could not reasonably be expected to do anything other than draw attention to Timothy McVeigh and his concerns; no one-off act of violence, no matter how large, can reasonably be expected to change a nation's policies.

The 9/11 attacks were also essentially a singular event. Even if the horizon was broadened to include other Al Qaeda operations such as the attacks on U.S. embassies in Kenya and Tanzania in 1998 and the targeting of the U.S.S. Cole in 2000, Al Qaeda never produced enough violence with enough regularity to provide a reasonable chance of success. As psychologically devastating as 9/11 was, it did absolutely nothing to impede the U.S.'s ability or determination to continue with the activities to which Al Qaeda objected. Even including the real death toll from the 9/11 attacks—the long-term health impacts and premature deaths of rescue and recovery workers, and the thousands of citizens exposed to the toxic fallout from the collapse of the World Trade Center towers—9/11 was still a singular event, more akin to the attack on Pearl Harbor than a prolonged campaign. The fact that Al Qaeda has targeted several countries only weakens any claim they could make that their violence would be effective, for the more spread out their violence becomes, the less influence it will exert on any one nation. Engaging in violence without any reasonable chance of success is not only morally unjustifiable, but reprehensible as well.

6. Conclusion

In the end, innocent noncombatants are not so innocent after all. Once the concept of innocence is extended from innocence *qua* harmless to innocence *qua* blameless, their culpability can be seen to be rooted in consent to their government, being the moral authority behind their government's actions, supporting their government economically and physically, and being the beneficiary of their government's actions. Thus, subject to a variety of contingent factors, they remain, in principle, legitimate targets of violent action on the grounds that they have either forfeited their right to immunity from attack or on the grounds of self-defense.

The implications of this for discussions of terrorism are significant for, if noncombatant casualties can be morally justified in principle, then they cannot be used to label a group terrorist, which is typically what happens in asymmetric conflicts. Instead, other criteria, namely just cause and supreme emergency, a plausible claim to legitimate authority, the use of violence as a last resort, and a reasonable expectation that violence will be efficacious, must be used in making the determination between legitimate fighters engaged in an asymmetric conflict and terrorists.

Notes

1 I would like to thank the editors of this volume for their feedback, especially Adam Henschke for his many detailed comments on earlier versions of this essay and David Ratz, sessional lecturer of military history at Lakehead University, for helpful discussions about the specific examples of terrorism and asymmetrical warfare.
2 Michael Walzer, *Just and Unjust Wars: A Moral Argument with Historical Illustrations*, 4th edn, New York: Basic Books, 2006, pp. 138–147.
3 A.J. Coates, *The Ethics of War*, New York: Manchester University Press, 1997, p. 235.
4 Jeff McMahan, *Killing in War*, New York: Oxford University Press, 2009, p. 76.
5 M. Walzer, *Just and Unjust Wars*, p. 146.

6 Shannon E. French, "Murderers, Not Warriors: The Moral Distinction Between Terrorists and Legitimate Fighters in Asymmetric Conflicts," in James P. Sterba (ed.), *Terrorism and International Justice*, New York: Oxford University Press, 2003, pp. 35–36.

7 Ibid., p. 36.

8 Lorraine Besser-Jones, "Just War Theory, Legitimate Authority, and the 'War' on Terror," in Timothy Shanahan (ed.), *Philosophy 9/11: Thinking about the War on Terrorism*, La Salle: Open Court, 2005, p. 138.

9 It should also be noted that Besser-Jones rejects this conception of responsibility later in the same essay when ascribing legitimate authority to nondemocratic regimes, claiming that deferral to authority is indicative of a shared way of life, which legitimizes said authority. L. Besser-Jones, "Just War Theory, Legitimate Authority, and the 'War' on Terror," in Timothy Shanahan, *Philosophy 9/11*, p. 143.

10 M. Walzer, *Just and Unjust Wars*, pp. 155–156.

11 A.J. Coates, *The Ethics of War*, pp. 253–254. Coates points out that the British concentrated on developing a fleet of bombers with the intent of ignoring the trenches and hitting production facilities behind enemy lines well before their emergency situation came to be.

12 M. Walzer, *Just and Unjust Wars*, p. 268.

13 A.J. Coates, *The Ethics of War*, pp. 126–127.

14 L. Besser-Jones, "Just War Theory, Legitimate Authority, and the 'War' on Terror," in Timothy Shanahan, *Philosophy 9/11*, p. 133.

15 Ibid., p. 143.

16 Andrew Altman and Christopher Heath Wellman. *A Liberal Theory of International Justice*, New York: Oxford University Press, 2009, p. 2.

17 Ibid., p. 41.

18 Ibid, pp. 33–34.

19 Unlike Kai Nielsen, who in a discussion of revolutionary movements maintains the thoroughly utilitarian perspective that successful violence is justifiable (see his "Violence and Terrorism: Its Uses and Abuses," in B.M. Leiser (ed.), *Values in Conflict*. New York: Macmillan, 1981, p. 446). I argue that justifiable violence need not be actually effective, but it must be accompanied by a reasonable expectation of efficacy.

References

Altman, A. and C.H. Wellman, *A Liberal Theory of International Justice*, New York: Oxford University Press, 2009.

Besser-Jones, L., "Just War Theory, Legitimate Authority, and the 'War' on Terror," in T. Shanahan (ed.), *Philosophy 9/11: Thinking about the War on Terrorism*, La Salle: Open Court, 2005.

A.J. Coates, *The Ethics of War*, New York: Manchester University Press, 1997.

French, S. E., "Murderers, Not Warriors: The Moral Distinction Between Terrorists and Legitimate Fighters in Asymmetric Conflicts," in J.P. Sterba (ed.), *Terrorism and International Justice*, New York: Oxford University Press, 2003.

McMahan, J., *Killing in War*, New York: Oxford University Press, 2009.

Nielsen, K., "Violence and Terrorism: Its Uses and Abuses," in B.M. Leiser (ed.), *Values in Conflict*, New York: Macmillan, 1981.

Walzer, M., *Just and Unjust Wars: A Moral Argument with Historical Illustrations*, 4th edn, New York: Basic Books, 2006.

19

ENDANGERING SOLDIERS AND THE PROBLEM OF PRIVATE MILITARY CONTRACTORS

Ned Dobos

1. Introduction

Soldiers are routinely exposed to risk. Sometimes commanding officers put their rank-and-file troops in danger because this is necessary to achieve military objectives. Sometimes they do it to minimise the chances of unintended civilian harm. We feel that this is perfectly justified. Indeed, according to just war theory, endangering combatants to protect non-combatants is something that the commander is *obliged*, not merely permitted, to do. We are told that this is consistent with the rights of the soldiers because they have in fact surrendered (or "exchanged") their rights by enlisting. The consent of the soldier squares his endangerment with his moral status.

If we shift our focus from military to occupational ethics, however, the right to workplace health and safety is usually treated as *inalienable*; as something that cannot be validly relinquished through contract. This raises the question: If other classes of employees cannot waive their right to safety, why should things be any different for military personnel?

One way forward is to identify some relevant difference that makes the normal standards of occupational ethics inapplicable to the profession of arms. What sets the soldier apart on most accounts is the special bond that he shares with the state and the "common life" that it protects. As we shall see, this might offer some explanation for why soldiers can give up their rights even though other kinds of employees cannot. The problem with this approach, however, is that it has no purchase on private military and security contractors. Taking this path, then, threatens to yield asymmetric standards for the treatment of national soldiers and mercenaries, with the latter being entitled to greater care and protection than the former. I will suggest an alternative approach to justifying soldier endangerment that avoids this unattractive corollary.

2. Enlistment and the alienation of rights

Even the most fundamental human rights can be forfeited, as when an individual culpably or negligently threatens the life of another, and thus renders himself liable to defensive violence. Arguably, human rights can also be voluntarily *waived* or *relinquished* by the bearer of those rights. According to Michael Walzer this is precisely what happens when one joins the military profession. More accurately, soldiers are said to *exchange* their human rights – to life, liberty etc.

– for a different set of rights: what Walzer calls "war rights". The list of war rights is a short one. It includes a liberty to do the things that combatants are meant to do, and a right to be treated as the POW conventions require if captured. The soldier loses his rights to life and physical safety, but thereby gains a right to compromise the safety and take the lives of others.[1]

Walzer is not entirely clear on how this exchange is registered. In one place he says that a soldier surrenders his human rights "simply by fighting". In another he says it is by becoming a "dangerous man": one who "bears arms effectively". In yet another he says it is simply by enlisting or joining the class of combatants. The trouble is that these three criteria do not always overlap.[2] One can be a member of the combatant class without being a "dangerous man": the new recruit who is still unable to bear arms competently or the soldier who knows how to use his rifle, but psychologically cannot bring himself to do it in the heat of battle.[3] One can also be an effective arms-bearer without actually fighting. Walzer's famous example of the naked soldier illustrates the point well. As long as Walzer wants to insist that all soldiers in combat have the same complement of rights and duties, no matter how few bullets they fire or how few items of clothing they wear, it seems he must ultimately identify enlisting itself as the act by which the soldier's rights are exchanged.

If all soldiers have indeed waived their right to safety, there is nothing that their endangerment could be said to infringe. Though Walzer does acknowledge that exposing troops to danger can constitute wrongdoing in some circumstances, importantly this is not because the soldiers themselves are wronged in any sense. On Walzer's view the soldier is an asset to be managed, an instrument to be used in the pursuit of the state's objectives. Accordingly a commander who wastes his soldiers' lives, or recklessly endangers them, is guilty of *poor resource management*. He is akin to the corporate CEO who carelessly squanders his company's money or who puts its capital to inefficient use. It is the shareholders of the company who are wronged here; the money itself is not an object of moral concern. Similarly, there may be something objectionable about a commander exposing his troops to undue risk on Walzer's account, but it is not the troops that have the grounds for complaint, it is the political community to which these assets belong.[4]

Walzer admits: "I don't think it can ever be impermissible for an officer to send his soldiers into battle: that is what he is for and that is what they are for."[5] What Walzer seems to mean is that it is never impermissible to send soldiers into battle *on the grounds that they have some justified moral claim that would be infringed by this*. Sending soldiers into battle is always consistent with their rights, no matter how high the probability of death; how weak the prospect of success; how negligible the military advantage sought, and so on.

This position is far from idiosyncratic. In fact Colm McKeogh sees it as the dominant view of military service:

> Western culture accepts that, in the special circumstances of war, some people can have their human status suspended. Military personnel in war, and until such time as they become *hors de combat* through wounds, shipwreck or being taken prisoner, may be treated as non-persons, instruments, as means to a military or political objective … Once in the role of combatant, it is accepted that a person's life can be treated as of instrumental value, both to his commanders and to the enemy … [Soldiers] have given up their right to be treated as persons.[6]

But should the consent of the soldier be treated as sufficient to divest him of his rights? To see why the question needs to be asked let us turn our attention briefly to the field of occupational ethics. Here one finds two sharply contrasting views on the subject of employee rights. For a rare few, the rights of workers are limited to those specified in their contract. In other words, the employee possesses whatever claims and entitlements have been successfully negotiated with the employer as a condition of taking on the position, but nothing more. All other rights are waived in exchange for the job. This position is itself justified by appeal to the rights of employees. As one of its staunchest advocates, Ian Maitland, puts it, "to set up a class of moral rights in the workplace invades workers' rights to freely choose the terms and conditions of employment they judge best."[7] If someone is happy to trade away their safety and liberty in return for better pay and other perks, standing in their way by prescribing and enforcing a set of employee rights and labour standards is objectionably paternalistic.

On the alternative and by far the dominant account, employees have (at least some) rights that cannot be relinquished or surrendered through contract. That is, there are some employee rights that are *inalienable*. Des Jardins and McCall, for instance, defend a conception of workers' rights "as presumptive entitlements *not subject to bargaining within the employment agreement*" (emphasis added).[8] This explains certain widely shared and deeply felt intuitions. Racism in the workplace is clearly abhorrent. But what if the victim signs a contract stipulating that ongoing racial vilification is a condition of his employment? To any right-thinking person it hardly makes a difference; the victim remains a victim. Any contract he may have signed waiving his right not to be racially abused is void. In other words, the right against racial harassment and discrimination imposes moral constraints on the content of one's contract of employment.

Some such position can be defended either by showing that certain rights are *intrinsically* inalienable, or by showing that they are *contingently* inalienable.[9] A right is *contingently* inalienable if the conditions necessary for its alienation do not obtain, even though that right can be relinquished in theory. For instance in circumstances where there is coercive pressure or an absence of vital information, we might say that rights are inalienable because consent to waive one's rights must be both voluntary and fully informed in order to be valid. On the other hand if it is logically or morally impossible to waive a right no matter the circumstances, that right is inalienable not just in fact but in principle. It is *intrinsically* inalienable.

I will not bother to rehearse the standard arguments for why employee rights cannot be contracted away. I will simply assume the prevailing view for the sake of discussion: employees have a set of inalienable rights against their employers, and workplace safety features in that set. The question that I want to address is this: *If* we concede this point with respect to ordinary civilian employees, why should things be any different for armed forces personnel? We saw in the previous section that soldiers are understood to give up their human rights by enlisting, thereby ceasing to be persons and becoming instruments or assets. But if men and women in other occupations cannot surrender their rights and objectify themselves in some such way simply through an act of consent, why should things be any different for soldiers?

3. The common life and private contractors

What we need is to identify some morally relevant difference between military service and other occupations. On most accounts, what sets the military apart, morally, is its unique function of defending and preserving the state. What sets the state apart, morally, is its unique function of protecting and indeed expressing the "common life" of its citizens: their shared customs and traditions, their inherited culture, their "national soul". Without this common life – this "moral and collective body" – Rousseau tells us that the individual citizen is "worse than dead". "If the citizen is alone he is nothing; if he has no more country, he has no existence."[10]

Because the state is a thing of such superlative value, any suggestion that its entrusted guardians are simply "doing a job" is vehemently resisted. Sir John Hackett describes the military as something more akin to a holy order than an occupation, and Hackett is not alone in this regard.[11] Samuel Huntington characterises the military professional as "one who pursues a '*higher calling*' in the service of society" (emphasis added).[12] The analogy with the priesthood is carried further in the recent revision of SLA Marshall's classic *The Armed Forces Officer*. Clergy and combatant are said to be alike in that both answer a call "to serve others, to sacrifice self, and to be about something larger than one's own ambitions and desires, something grander than one's own contributions and even one's own life".[13] For the clergy, the "larger" and "grander" thing in question is the divine. For soldiers it is the closest thing on earth to divinity: the state.

This "high moral purpose" of the military places its members in a "unique moral world", according to Martin Cook: a world governed by norms quite unlike those applicable in ordinary civilian life.[14] But does any of this give us grounds for thinking that soldiers (and only soldiers) can contract away their rights? Perhaps it does.

If we accept Rousseau's point about death being a fate preferable to statelessness, it seems that risking one's life for the state – and indeed dying for it – is not an unreasonable or irrational thing to do.[15] The political subjugation of the state or the conquest of its territory threatens to dispossess the citizen of his common life. This is the worst thing that could possibly happen to someone, and so defending the state with life and limb represents a sound choice. By contrast, other occupations are geared towards ends that are far less exalted than the preservation of the common life, so sacrificing one's most fundamental interests (life, health, liberty) for *their* sake might be seen as inherently irrational.

This is important if we think that the reasonableness or rationality of consent has some bearing on its validity. Consent in ignorance or under coercive pressure is void, but plausibly so is any act of consent that is not minimally rational, in some suitably precise sense of that word. This premise underpins standard philosophical objections to voluntary self-enslavement. It is not that the would-be slave is ill informed or acting under duress, necessarily; it is that being enslaved so contradicts basic human interests that consenting to it indicates an impairment of one's rational faculties, or at least suggests an isolated and temporary malfunction. Opponents of assisted suicide and euthanasia often defend their position in a similar way: by insisting that anyone who consents to being killed cannot possibly be expressing his or her "true desires", since death is the ultimate harm that permanently precludes the enjoyment of all other goods.

So, our argument might look like this: 1) Consenting to something that is inherently irrational is invalid; 2) There is nothing irrational about sacrificing one's basic interests – life, health, liberty – for the sake of the state, given the importance of the common life; 3) There *is* something inherently irrational in sacrificing these same interests for the ends that most ordinary occupations are geared towards. The upshot is that *the considerations which make rights contingently inalienable with respect to other occupations have no purchase (or less purchase) in relation to military service.*

There are clearly a number of problems with, or gaps in, this argument. First, it all rests on the premise that individual death is not the ultimate loss. But this, of course, is controversial. Hobbes denies it, and thus reaches a conclusion in stark contrast to the one Rousseau's conception of political community lends itself to. Hobbes sees individual self-preservation as the highest value, and the justification for all political institutions rests ultimately on this. A corollary is that sacrificing oneself for the state *is* inherently irrational, and because it is irrational consent to do it cannot be binding.[16] It is precisely to preserve their lives and liberties that individuals submit to a sovereign power to begin with, Hobbes tells us. Any agreement to give up one's life for the sake of, or at the behest of, the sovereign power is incoherent; it gives up the end for the sake of the means. Walzer summarises Hobbes' position with typical flair:

> A man who dies for the state defeats his only purpose in forming the state: death is the contradiction of politics. A man who risks his life for the state accepts the insecurity which it was the only end of his political obedience to avoid: war is the failure of politics.[17]

Setting all this aside, however, even if the argument under consideration is persuasive as far as it goes, it seems to have a particularly troubling implication. Essentially, the argument says that a soldier can validly surrender his rights because it is not irrational to sacrifice one's most basic interests for the state. It is not irrational because the state is where one's other, more valuable life – the common life – is embodied. But where does this leave the growing mass of private military contractors?

Today, private military and security companies (PMSCs) offer services ranging from strategic advice and consulting, to training and tactical military assistance, including actual combat services. To date they have plied their trade in over 50 countries, on every continent on Earth except for Antarctica. In Iraq alone there were at one point over 60 such firms employing 20,000 personnel – roughly equal to the number of personnel provided by all of the US's coalition partners combined. (Singer calls it the "coalition of the billing".)[18] Their clientele includes nation states, NGOs, the UN, drug cartels, rebel groups, and (allegedly) even jihadist movements.

PMSC employees are not in the business of defending their common lives. They do not take a sacred oath to the state, but simply exchange their services for financial reward.[19] As Huntington points out, for the mercenary military service is not a calling; it is a business. The special bond that is said to exist between the state and national soldiers does not seem to extend to private contractors. But this special bond is what we just said makes it possible for soldiers to give up their rights in the service of the state.[20]

One might simply bite the bullet and accept that private contractors cannot surrender their rights in the same way that national soldiers can. But insofar as this implies that PMSC employees – even those engaged in combat – have more rights or are entitled to greater protections than their national counterparts, it strikes me as unacceptably counter-intuitive. In the following and final section of the chapter, I briefly outline an alternative approach to justifying soldier endangerment: one that does not rely on the premise that soldiers have waived their rights, and one that can equally account for why PMSC employees may be knowingly exposed to risk.

4. An alternative approach

It is commonly held that soldiers surrender or exchange their rights by enlisting. If we reject this, it might seem to imply that soldiers have their rights violated whenever they are knowingly endangered – a *reductio ad absurdum*. But this, I think, is mistaken.

To claim that an employee has an inalienable right to occupational health and safety is not to say that his employer is obliged to create zero-risk working conditions. That would be impossibly demanding, and "ought implies can". The standard most occupational ethicists agree upon is a more modest one: employers must eliminate risks and hazards as far as is "reasonably practicable" in the circumstances. Or, equivalently, employees have a right to the highest measure of occupational health and safety that is reasonably practicable for their particular line of work.

In cases where exposing soldiers to risk is necessary for the achievement of legitimate military objectives, averting the risk is simply not practicable in the relevant sense: it is something that cannot be realised without thereby compromising the ability of the military to fulfil its function. Eliminating the risk effectively means crippling the institution. In these cases, the endangerment of the soldier is consistent with his rights, not because he has surrendered his right to be protected by his employer, but because the content of that right is always constrained by the purpose of the institution in question.

Notice this is a far cry from Walzer's claim that sending soldiers into battle is always consistent with their rights. The infantry charges of the First World War saw scores of young men sent over the trench walls to certain death, to fight battles that would have achieved close to nothing even if they did stand a chance of success. On Walzer's view the troops whose lives were so squandered could not have mounted a sound moral objection; after all "that is what they are for". But if we deny the premise that soldiers waive their rights, clearly these infantrymen were not shown the reasonably practicable level of care to which they were entitled.

As noted earlier, however, sometimes soldiers are exposed to risk not for the sake of military objectives but for the sake of minimising harm to civilians. To be sure, these two aims will regularly coincide, especially in modern day asymmetric wars and counterinsurgencies where there is little hope of winning without first winning hearts and minds. Nevertheless, there will be cases where there is no military utility in protecting enemy civilians. In these cases, one might ask, is it not true that endangering soldiers to protect civilians amounts to imposing on those soldiers risks that it is reasonably practicable to avoid? After all, avoiding these risks by allowing the civilians to bear them would, *ex hypothesi*, not in any way compromise the military's ability to fulfil its purpose.

While avoiding the risks to soldiers may be practicable in these cases – in the sense that it would not impair the military's ability to perform its legitimate function – it would not necessarily be *reasonably* practicable.

David Luban introduces the idea of a "risk-transfer ratio" as a way of evaluating the inevitable trade-offs that must be made between force protection and the minimisation of civilian casualties.[22] If a soldier reduces the amount of risk to which he is exposed by X units, and this increases the risk borne by civilians by exactly that same amount, X, then the risk-transfer ratio is 1. Luban's argument, crudely put, is that any risk-transfer ratio greater than 1 fails to treat civilians as their moral equality demands. It means that soldiers are imposing greater risks on civilians in order spare themselves proportionately smaller risks.

This *devalues* the lives of the civilians in question. Luban rightly suggests that soldiers who shift risks from themselves onto civilians will often contravene this standard simply because:

> Professional soldiers are better armed and armored, better trained, better disciplined, better conditioned, better able to function in coordinated teams, and better supported than their adversaries, including in the crucial matter of medical care if they are wounded. Everyone in their units is pledged never to leave them fallen on the field; their buddies have their backs. In every respect, they are simply better able to protect themselves than are noncombatants (or even irregular adversaries).[23]

This makes it more likely than not that a soldier will exceed the allowable ratio of 1 when he offloads risks to civilians. Otherwise put, the risk that a soldier assumes by adopting tactics that better safeguard civilians will typically be small compared to the risk that he spares civilians by so doing.

Now, when a soldier is forced to bear some such additional risk by his commanding officer, it seems to me he cannot claim that his right to workplace safety has been infringed. This is because safeguarding the soldier any further – by allowing the civilians to bear the risk – effectively treats those civilians as though their lives are of lesser value than that of the soldier. For the soldier to demand that others be devalued in this way for the sake of his safety is not a reasonable demand. The soldier cannot plausibly claim, then, that the level of care he is being given while on the job is something less than what is *"reasonably* practicable".

There is clearly a lot more to be said in this connection. All I hope to have shown with these cursory remarks is that, in order to explain why force protection can legitimately be compromised for the sake of civilian protection, we need not rely on the premise that soldiers surrender their rights by enlisting.

5. Conclusion

Business and professional ethicists say that individuals cannot waive their rights by signing a contract of employment, while military ethicists say that individuals waive their rights by joining the armed forces. Coherently endorsing both views requires identifying some relevant difference between workers and soldiers. The special bond that exists between soldiers and the "common life" that the state embodies might be entrusted with this normative task. One purpose of this paper has been to draw attention to a particular danger inherent in this approach: it threatens to yield asymmetric standards of treatment for national military personnel and private contractors, insofar as there is no such special bond between the state and PMSC employees. I have suggested that one way to avoid this is simply to deny that soldiers have waived their rights; to think of them just as we would ordinary workers. As long as we understand that the content of employee rights is always context-dependent, recognising that even soldiers have an inalienable right to occupational health and safety need not have the counter-intuitive implications that one might fear.

Notes

1 M. Walzer, *Just and Unjust Wars: a Moral Argument with Historical Illustrations*, New York: Basic Books, 1977, pp. 136 and 145.

2 For a full discussion of this point, see J.M. Dubik, "Human Rights, Command Responsibility, and Walzer's Just War Theory", *Philosophy and Public Affairs*, 11:4, Autumn 1982, pp. 359–62.

3 General S.L.A. Marshall, an official U.S. historian of World War II, interviewed thousands of soldiers, asking them what it was they did in battle. The results were consistent: only 15 per cent to 20 per cent of the American riflemen in combat fired at the enemy.

4 As James Dubik puts it, on Walzer's theory "any limit set on the amount of risk to which this asset [soldiers] may be exposed is set by virtue of the principle of efficient management". J.M. Dubik, "Human Rights", p. 370.

5 M. Walzer, *Just and Unjust Wars*, pp. 20–21.

6 C. McKeogh, *Innocent Civilians: the Morality of Killing in War*, Houndsmills, Basingstoke: Palgrave Macmillan, 2002, p. 12.

7 I. Maitland, "Rights in the Workplace: A Nozickian Argument", *Journal of Business Ethics* 8:12, December 1989, p. 951.

8 Joseph R. Des Jardins and John J. McCall, "A Defence of Employee Rights", *Journal of Business Ethics*, 4:5, 1985, p. 367.

9 Some such distinction is drawn by a number of authors, including J. Feinberg, "Voluntary Euthanasia and the Inalienable Right to Life", *Philosophy and Public Affairs*, 7:2, Winter 1978, pp. 93–123.

10 J.-J. Rousseau, *Considerations on the Government of Poland*, chapter 4 in *Political Writings*, trans. Frederick Watkins, Edinburgh: Thomas Nelson and Sons, 1953.

11 Sir J. Hackett, *The Profession of Arms*, London: Book Club Associates, 1983, p. 9.

12 S.P. Huntington, *The Soldier and the State: the Theory and Politics of Civil-Military Relations*, Cambridge, Mass: Harvard University Press, 1957, p. 8.

13 U.S. Department of Defense, *The Armed Forces Officer*, Washington: Potomac Books, National Defense University Press, 2007, p. 13.

14 M.L. Cook, *The Moral Warrior: Ethics and Service in the U.S. Military*, Albany, NY: State University of New York Press, 2004, pp. 41 and 123.

15 See Michael Walzer, *Obligations: Essays on Disobedience, War and Citizenship*, Cambridge Mass.: Harvard University Press, 1970, p. 93.

16 T. Hobbes, *Leviathan*, chapter 14 (any edition).

17 M. Walzer, *Obligations*, p. 82.

18 P. W. Singer, "Outsourcing War", *Foreign Affairs*, March/April 2005.

19 Huntington, *The Soldier and the State*, p. 20.

20 A number of theorists have suggested that private contractors cannot be obliged to make the ultimate sacrifice in the same way that national soldiers can. For two of the most interesting discussions on this point, see J. Pattison, "Deeper Objections to the Privatisation of Military Force", *The Journal of Political Philosophy*, 18:4, 2010, pp. 440–43; and D.-P. Baker, "To Whom does a Private Military Commander Owe a Moral Duty? Reflections on the Trustworthiness of Private Warriors", in P. Tripodi and J. Wolfendale (eds), *New Wars and New Soldiers: Military Ethics in the Contemporary World*, London: Ashgate, 2011.

21 See R. Johnstone, "Paradigm crossed? The Statutory Occupational Health and Safety Obligations of the Business Undertaking", *Australian Journal of Labour Law*, 12:2, 1999.

22 D. Luban, "Risk Taking and Force Protection", Georgetown Public Law and Legal Theory Research Paper No. 11–72, 2011, in Itzhak Benbaji and Naomi Sussman (eds), *Reading Walzer*, London: Routledge, 2013. Available online at: http://scholarship.law.georgetown.edu/facpub/654/ (accessed 16 July 2012).

23 D Luban, "Risk Taking", pp. 28–29.

References

Baker, D.-P., "To Whom does a Private Military Commander Owe a Moral Duty? Reflections on the Trustworthiness of Private Warriors", in P. Tripodi and J. Wolfendale (eds), *New Wars and New Soldiers: Military Ethics in the Contemporary World*, London: Ashgate, 2011.

Cook, M.L., *The Moral Warrior: Ethics and Service in the U.S. Military*, Albany, NY: State University of New York Press, 2004.

Des Jardins, J.R. and J.J. McCall, "A Defence of Employee Rights", *Journal of Business Ethics*, 4, 1985.

Dubik, J.M., "Human Rights, Command Responsibility, and Walzer's Just War Theory", *Philosophy and Public Affairs*, 11:4, 1982.

Feinberg, J., "Voluntary Euthanasia and the Inalienable Right to Life", *Philosophy and Public Affairs*, 7:2, Winter 1978.

Hackett, Sir J., *The Profession of Arms*, London: Book Club Associates, 1983.

Hobbes, T., *Leviathan*, any edition.

Huntington, S.P., *The Soldier and the State: the Theory and Politics of Civil-Military Relations*, Cambridge, Mass: Harvard University Press, 1957.

Johnstone, R., "Paradigm crossed? The Statutory Occupational Health and Safety Obligations of the Business Undertaking," *Australian Journal of Labour Law*, 12:2, 1999.

Luban, D., "Risk Taking and Force Protection," Georgetown Public Law and Legal Theory Research Paper No. 11–72, 2011, in I. Benbaji and N. Sussman (eds), *Reading Walzer*, London: Routledge, 2013.

Maitland, I., "Rights in the Workplace: A Nozickian Argument", *Journal of Business Ethics* 8:12, December 1989.

McKeogh, C., *Innocent Civilians: the Morality of Killing in War*, Houndsmills, Basingstoke: Palgrave Macmillan, 2002

Pattison, J., "Deeper Objections to the Privatisation of Military Force", *The Journal of Political Philosophy*, 18:4, 2010, pp. 440–43.

Rousseau, J.-J., *Considerations on the Government of Poland*, chapter 4, in *Political Writings*, Edinburgh: Thomas Nelson and Sons, 1953.

Singer, P.W., "Outsourcing War", *Foreign Affairs*, March/April 2005.

U.S. Department of Defense, *The Armed Forces Officer*, Washington: Potomac Books, National Defense University Press, 2007.

Walzer, M., *Just and Unjust Wars: a Moral Argument with Historical Illustrations*, New York: Basic Books, 1977.

——*Obligations: Essays on Disobedience, War and Citizenship*, Cambridge Mass.: Harvard University Press, 1970.

20

THE AGENCY OF CHILD SOLDIERS

Rethinking the principle of discrimination

Tor Arne Berntsen and Bård Mæland

1. Introduction

Anybody that can shoot a little kid and not have a problem with it, there is something wrong with them. Of course, I had a problem with it. After being shot all day, it didn't matter if you were a soldier or a kid.[1]

One of the most disturbing trends of modern warfare has been the increased use of children as combatants. Children have historically been recognized as the most innocent and vulnerable members of society. When children are trained and equipped with modern weapons, their effect on the battlefield can be devastating.[2] Although not a new phenomenon historically, the widespread and systematic use of child soldiers in today's military conflicts can be regarded as an attempt at "tactical innovation," as it is used strategically not only to recruit soldiers but also to increase fighting opportunities against regular military forces.[3]

The use of children as soldiers poses compelling ethical problems with profound implications, not least from a military perspective. When children are armed with weapons that make them just as lethal as adult combatants, how should this affect their traditionally protected status as non-combatants?

Moreover, it seems that based on a critique of liberal, mostly western notions of childhood and its accompanying sense of children's innocence and lack of agency, one risks not heeding sufficiently the willful and active participation of children in war.[4] This kind of critique may be raised both from the perspectives of cultures other than western ones, and also of children who have taken part in war. Lastly, the criticism may also be raised from a normative view-point, which we will return to later in this article.[5]

If these child soldiers can be said to exercise some kind of political and moral agency, should this affect the way we perceive the issues of discrimination and combatancy, with the consequences this may have for restraints or lack thereof in fighting children who have taken up arms? Or does the principle of discrimination imply a denial of the agency of children participating in armed conflict?

In addressing these questions, this article will explore the challenge that the use of child soldiers in contemporary conflicts presents to the continued development of just war theory.

2. Innocence, agency and the principle of discrimination

The principle underlying the "discrimination" criterion of *jus in bello* holds that while it is impermissible for combatants intentionally to attack non-combatants, some people may be legitimate targets of attack during armed conflict while others should not be. Richard Regan argues that innocence, understood as the absence of "wrongdoing," can be the adjudicator of who should fall into each of these categories. He writes,

> Just warriors may directly target personnel participating in the enemy nation's wrongdoing but should not directly target other enemy nationals. The reasoning behind the principle is twofold: On the one hand, the enemy nation's wrongdoing justifies the victim nation's use of military force to prevent or rectify wrongdoing. On the other hand, enemy nationals not engaged in the war or contributing to waging it are committing no wrong against the victim nations, and so the victim nation has no just cause to target such nationals.[6]

Regan suggests that the actions of some people in warfare can cause them to lose their "innocence" which makes it morally permissible to kill them. Combatants normally fall into this group. Conversely, other people retain their innocence by not participating in combat and there should be a moral presumption against killing them. Those who traditionally have fallen into this category include non-combatants, wounded soldiers, and prisoners of war. Within this line of thought, all enemy combatants can become legitimate targets, irrespective of whether they have a just cause for fighting and irrespective of whether they have some form of moral agency and can be held morally responsible for their actions.

Another way of thinking about who should enjoy non-combatant protection in war has less to do with actions and more to do with identity. Many societies throughout history have believed that, in war, there are certain people who should be presumed to be innocent by virtue of their inherent vulnerability and, thus, should not be attacked. Traditionally, these people have included elderly, the infirm, and children.

Children are of particular concern in this regard. Their vulnerability lies not only in their physical weakness relative to adults, but also in their impressionable emotional state as well as in their general immaturity. For these reasons, children have traditionally been presumed to be amongst the most innocent and should thus enjoy special protection in armed conflicts.

There is a growing literature that does not emphasize the victimcy and innocence of children, but their moral agency, development and responsibility, yet often heavily constrained and limited, e.g. where moral sensitivity and political "imaginations" still may display limited mental capacities.[7]

With some inclination to rational choice theory, Alice Schmidt, for example, maintains that children often participate in war, "maximising their opportunities to help themselves and their families when faced with violent conflict … creatively engaging with their situation and constructively managing their risk."[8] Exploring representations of (ex)child soldiers, she concludes that they seem closer to "real" volunteerism than "coerced choice." Children are resourceful, and they use their talents, creativity and initiatives in times of war, when amidst armed groups, as well as for the benefit of their successful rehabilitation and reintegration.

A profound ethical dilemma exists, however, when children participate in war. If a person can lose his or her "innocence" by participating in warfare and thus become a legitimate object of attack, then a child who engaged in armed violence during war can be killed with no further moral consequences than killing an adult combatant. Yet such an implication seems to go against not only our most basic instincts to protect children from harm, but also the traditional view that children should enjoy non-combatant protection by virtue of their identity as vulnerable children, even when they engage in behavior that may be dangerous to themselves or others.

Interestingly, in an article on the moral conundrums child soldiers may present to US soldiers, Robert Tynes has contextualized this dilemma within the operational theatre of Iraq in 2003 as well as within the moral tradition of just war:

> When US troops invaded Iraq, they not only had to consider facing chemical and/or biological weapons but also (and more realistically) had to accept that they may have to fire at children. This would not necessarily be an insurmountable problem, were it not for the fact that American troops are steeped in the just-war tradition.[9]

It remains the ambition of this article to discuss this interpretation of the just war tradition, simply because it is not unambiguous as to how one should approach the issue of children as combatants normatively.

The cultural difference as to how children are perceived in terms of maturity, social status and moral responsibility in different cultures also forms part of this discussion. Whereas chronology and age is a main component in the view of liberal and mainly western cultures' view of the progress from childhood through youth to adulthood, other cultures may emphasize matters such as cultural rites of passage, physical size, gender, belonging (to someone), place in family, as well as participation in war.[10]

3. The use of child soldiers in contemporary conflicts

Armed conflict has always had deleterious effects on children. In countries plagued by war, children suffer from poverty, malnutrition, disease, lack of educational and economic opportunities. But in the last ten years, in countries where the adult population, including parents and community leaders, has been diminished by these conditions, children have been forced to undertake adult responsibilities. One of the most horrific phenomena of modern warfare has been the use of and reliance on child soldiers.

While the use of child soldiers is certainly not a new battlefield strategy, the use of child soldiers has become increasingly more systematic and widespread in the intrastate wars of the last decade.[11] Hundreds of thousands of children are used as soldiers in virtually every current conflict waged around the world. Rebel groups, guerrilla armies, militias, and armed gangs utilize child soldiers in their violent conflicts against each other, against the state, or to gain control of resources and power. Many of these armed groups would be unable to wage war without the added force provided by child soldiers.

There is no universally accepted definition of child soldiers, but most experts agree that child soldiers are "any person under the age of 18 who is a member of or attached to government armed forces or any other regular or irregular armed force or armed group, whether or not an armed conflict exists."[12] Not all child soldiers are direct combatants, and while some children wield assault rifles on the front lines, others are used in combat support roles, or even as sex-slaves to their military "husbands."

While child soldiers serve alongside adult soldiers, they often face dissimilar treatment on the battlefield. Child soldiers are seen as expendable and are forced to do the most dangerous tasks, such as walking across the field to clear landmines or serving as human shields. In addition to rape, child combatants may also face dehumanizing treatment, such as torture and various forms of psychological abuse, at the hands of their adult commanders or other child soldiers.

In the literature, both popular and scholarly, children are often depicted either as "super-victims," based on the way they have been forcibly abducted and treated as soldiers, or as "monsters." In the latter case, child soldiers have often been described as drug addicts, as ruthless soldiers committing atrocities against family members, more dangerous than regular soliders, and sometimes even "contaminated" by evil spirits of the persons they may have killed, and hence beyond the common imagination of what a regular soldier is expected to be.[13] Especially, the representation of young African men as irrationally violent may fuel not only the understanding of Africa in general, but also of child soldiers as the "wholly other," similar to "The New Barbarism" thesis by Paul Richards.[14]

A way to move beyond the stereotyping of either kind is to analyze the political and moral agency of the children who have been recruited into armed irregular groups. Already related to the recruitment issue lies an important perspective on this issue as most children (see Schmidt, 2007) have joined armed groups voluntarily for reasons such as vengeance on the enemy, personal protection, national liberation, protection of a clan or community, or to turn one's marginalized self into a empowered and viril self.[15]

4. Children's protection and agency in international law

Despite the widespread use of child soldiers in armed conflicts around the world, children enjoy the status in international law as protected in armed conflicts. The 1949 Geneva Conventions and the additional Protocols I and II (1977) protect children from use in war. Protocol II, in particular, prevents children under the age of 15 from being recruited for or used in armed hostilities. In 1989 these same standards were reinforced in the UN Convention on the Rights of the Child (CRC). While the CRC defined a child as any person under the age of 18, Article 38 established 15 as the minimum age for allowing children to serve as combatants, consistent with the standards set out in the additional protocols to the Geneva Convention.

In July 1998, the statute of the International Criminal Court (ICC) established, under Article 8, that it was a war crime to conscript or enlist children below the age of 15 into the armed forces or groups or use them to participate actively in hostilities. In addition, the June 1999 International Labor Organization (ILO) Convention 182 included child soldiers among the worst forms of child labour banned by the Treaty, prohibiting forced recruitment of children under the age of 18 for use in armed conflict.

In May 2000 the UN General Assembly adopted the Optional Protocol to the Convention on the Rights of the Child on the Involvement of Children in Armed Conflict to pursue a higher standard for the protection of children in conflict. The Protocol requires states to "take all feasible measures" to ensure that members of their armed forces under the age of 18 years do not participate in hostilities; prohibits the conscription of anyone under the age of 18 into the armed forces; requires states to raise the age of voluntary recruitment from the existing age of 15 and to deposit a binding declaration of the minimum age for that country's recruitment into its armed forces; and prohibits the recruitment or use in hostilities of children under the age of 18 by rebel or other nongovernmental armed groups and requires states to criminalize such practices.

Regional agreements, including the African Charter on the Rights and Welfare of the Child (1990), have also encouraged states to "take all necessary measures" to avoid the recruitment or use of children under 18 in combat.

In the Rome Statute of the International Criminal Court, it is regarded as a war crime to conscript and enlist "children under the age of fifteen years into the national armed forces or using them to participate actively in hostilities."[16] Furthermore, the Court has no jurisdiction over persons who were below the age of 18 when the alleged crime took place.[17] On the issue of involvement of children in armed conflict, this parallels the Optional Protocol to the Convention on the Rights of the Child (2002). Children are thus exempted from indictment.

Another expression of a similar point can be found in Article 53 (2.c) of the Rome Statute, which mentions that, even when it is apparent that genocide, crimes against humanity or war crimes have taken place, the Prosecutor may decide not to prosecute if "a prosecution is not in the interests of justice, taking into account all the circumstances, including the gravity of the crime, the interests of victims and the age or infirmity of the alleged perpetrator, and his or her role in the alleged crime."

In the Statutes of the Special Court of Sierra Leone, the ad-hoc tribunal for war crimes after the end of hostilities in Sierra Leone, the legal situation has been slightly different as it included anyone over the age of fifteen.[18] However, the Special Court Prosecutor chose not to prosecute any children, arguing that "the children of Sierra Leone have suffered enough both as victims and perpetrators."[19]

5. Child soldiers as a challenge for military ethics

The *jus in bello* principle of discrimination holds that actors in war can be categorized as combatants and non-combatants. As noted previously, such categorization can be based on the actions of an individual or on the individual's inherent identity as one who is in need of protection and thus should not be targeted.

Child soldiers present a morally complex problem because they defy such a strict distinction with regard to the principle of discrimination. On the one hand, their actions can make them deadly adversaries on the battlefield and classify them as combatants who may be targeted. On the other hand, their identity as children suggests that they are individuals in need of special protection who should not be the object of attack.

The child soldier challenges the *jus in bello* principle of "discrimination," which holds that a person is either a combatant or a non-combatant and that there are no degrees of combatancy.[20] The simplest account of operating with a strict demarcation between combatants and non-combatants is that the principle of non-combatant immunity is, as mentioned above, not only a component of the just war tradition, but is also embodied in modern international law. Moreover, the just war principle of discrimination is often understood as a distinction between civilians who are "harmless" and combatants who are engaged in an activity of harming others. Thomas Nagel attempts to link this idea to the traditional language of "innocence." He says that "innocent" does not mean "morally innocent" but "currently harmless."[21]

One way of solving this ethical conundrum is to view the action/identity dichotomy as a hierarchy rather than a juxtaposition of two equally important criteria. That is, individuals who are protected in warfare by virtue of their identity will retain their special status until their actions characterize them as combatants, when they will accordingly lose their protection. The innocent child should be protected from the violence of combat, until he participates in combat himself and poses a threat to just combatants.

The modern law of war reflects this hierarchical approach to the discrimination principle. Article 50 of the 1977 Additional Protocol I to the 1949 Geneva Conventions essentially says that any person who is not a combatant, "shall be considered to be a civilian." Article 51 of the 1977 Additional Protocol I goes on to say: "Civilians shall enjoy the protection afforded by this Section, unless and for such time as they take a direct part in hostilities."[21]

In some senses, the ethical challenge posed by child soldiers is no different from that of other ethical conundrums created by the nature of modern warfare. If resort to warfare is justified by protecting those who are innocent and attacking those who are not, the deliberate taking of innocent lives in combat poses a moral dilemma. Traditional approaches to just war theory deal with these problems through the *jus in bello* principle of proportionality and through the doctrine of double effect.

They do so, however, by simultaneously recognizing the innocence of non-combatants who may be killed and reconciling it with the greater importance of the military objective sought (in the case of proportionality) or with intent of the person who takes such lives (in the case of double effect). The fact that a child is killed in a bombing raid may be morally justified because she may be in close proximity to the enemy's headquarters, the destruction of which might bring great military advantage, or because her death was unintended by the bombardier.

The problem of child soldiers is unique, however, because the presumed innocence of children is made ambiguous by their military conduct. The child soldier is what Jeff McMahan calls a "nonresponsible threat." Unlike adult non-combatants who take up arms and thus immediately lose their legal and moral protected status, virtually every cultural norm, as well as soldiers' codes, suggests that children require special protection.

Yet there is nothing in *jus in bello* that explicitly suggests taking particular care toward a certain group of combatants. The discrimination criterion only presumes a combatant/non-combatant distinction, which lays the foundation for the combatant's privilege to kill other combatants during war.

By this logic combatants could kill child soldiers at any time, so long as it was clear that they were combatants. This, however, is not fully satisfactory with respect to child soldiers. The same is the case with the proportionality criterion which traditionally has applied only to cases of complete innocence on the part of the noncombatants affected when trying to balance the harm done to them against the military necessity of the situation. Furthermore, the doctrine of double effect is not of much help with regard to child soldiers because, presumably, a regular combatant intends to do harm in such cases, however regrettable they may be.

Therefore, the principal question that child soldiers create for military ethicists is the problem of providing special protection for a particular group of combatants. In other words, can the combatant's privilege be circumscribed in order to prevent unnecessary harm to child soldiers? If so, what are the criteria that would comprise such constraints and what are the implications for the conduct of warfare?

Even if one accepts that child soldiers still require extra protection given their status as children, this almost necessarily means that adult combatants may have to take additional risks to their own lives in order to protect a child that is also a potentially lethal adversary. In fighting child soldiers, just combatants must exercise restraint and accept greater risk to themselves in order to minimize harm on child soldiers.

What, then, should be the limits of those risks? In the view of McMahan, "The commander of a force fighting against a unit of child soldiers might be morally required to order his own soldiers to fight in a way that would predictably cause them [the soldiers] to suffer great casualties, and even a greater number of deaths."[23] However, how do you judge such a risk? Must child soldiers pose a clear and imminent danger to the life of an adult combatant before the latter is morally justified in killing the former? Or is it enough for a child soldier to be armed and identified with an enemy force during times of hostilities for their killing to be morally justified? Should such judgments be prudential considerations on the part of an adult combatant or should they be morally required?

There is no other category of combatants with whom other combatants are morally expected to take similar risks. However, there may also be reasons to resist or, at least, challenge the claim that child soldiers are completely without moral agency. How about children who have voluntarily enlisted in insurgencies against government forces, and who are aware of their responsibility and choices, though often very difficult ones?

McMahan's point is not that of the agency of the child soldiers *per se*, but the conception of child soldiers as being innocent. In that case, it will be of help for the soldier who is to fight armed children to think of them as non-responsible for the threats they pose. This may justify combating them if the threats are real and imminent, but also inspire them to show constraints if there is only a slight possibility for that, even at the cost of increased risk to themselves. It seems that the bottom line of argument runs thus: These children, who have already been deeply exploited and deprived, should be given another chance by sparing their lives.

Robert Tynes, who has discussed this dilemma which provides a special status to children as combatants, admits that this "may be the most complicated of all rationalizations for how to treat child soldiers."[24]

6. Killing child soldiers?

As argued so far, children are in need of special protections, even if they take up arms in the context of warfare. Furthermore, their immaturity and vulnerability to manipulation make them fundamentally different from adults who would normally be protected but who lose their special status when taking up arms. Hence, child soldiers constitute a category of "protected combatants" who should be treated with particular care.

However, though they are of a special category, the protection afforded to child soldiers must not be absolute. The idea that soldiers must exercise restraint against child soldiers because of their protected status can also be challenged. Their potential lethality means that they can be just as dangerous as adult soldiers, or sometimes even more so. Since soldiers must be able to defend themselves against threats on the battlefield, it follows that child soldiers must not have an uncontested ability to kill other soldiers in combat by virtue of their special status. Neither should commanders be able to employ children in combat with a reasonable assurance that they will not be engaged. Such a situation would only encourage the recruitment and use of minors, creating a perverse moral hazard for those who try to treat child soldiers in an ethical manner.

As difficult as it may be, adult combatants can justify the application of lethal force against child soldiers. Just combatants should show restraint against child soldiers, not primarily because the child soldiers are lacking responsibility for their actions, but rather because of their special vulnerability to exploitation and loss.

In the context of warfare, soldiers need not determine that regular adult combatants pose an imminent threat to their lives in order to be morally and legally justified in killing them. Their very identity as soldiers implies that they are a threat to an enemy force, regardless of whether they take on ancillary or combat roles. The same assumption, however, should not be made for child soldiers. This is not because their age makes them any less lethal than regular soldiers, but because applying the same logic that is applied to adults about why they pose a threat would necessarily permit a much wider scope of hostile action toward children than would seem to be morally appropriate. As McMahan argues:

> If the child soldiers are morally responsible even to a minimal degree for the unjust threat they pose, and if the just combatants are in no way at fault for the threat they face, it does not seem that justice should require even one just combatant to allow himself to be killed in order to spare the life of a child soldier.[25]

Rather than assuming that children pose a threat, adult combatants should consider whether the child soldier possesses the capabilities to mount a lethal attack and demonstrates a hostile intent that creates a circumstance in which there is no time for any other reasonable action than engaging the child with hostile force. Under these circumstances a child may be killed in self-defense.

Another general just war principle that should be considered with regards to child soldiers is proportionality. As noted earlier, proportionality is not primarily applied to combatants, but rather to non-combatants who may be subject to harm in the course of combat operations aimed at the enemy. According to the principle of proportionality, it is both legally and morally required that an attacking force weigh the military advantage that will likely come from an attack against the anticipated harm that it will cause to non-combatants. To improve the protections of child soldiers, the concept of proportionality should be applied. For example, an attacking force should consider whether the military advantage from assaulting an ammunition dump is worth the deaths that will result from the child soldiers who are guarding it.

It may very well be that the answer to such considerations, tragically, would be yes. By adhering to this criterion, however, two results would follow. First, it would minimize unnecessary loss of life among children in an enemy force. Second, by permitting an attack to occur if the advantage was great, it would prevent an enemy from gaining special protection for an objective by their use of child soldiers as some kind of "live shields," thus discouraging their use in such circumstances.

Examples of practical suggestions for approaching child soldiers with restraint also include contextualized tactical measures, such as more use of nonlethal weaponry and psychological operations (in order to persuade children to put down their arms and enter a safe-haven environment).[26] Long-term measures to combat child soldiering, directed towards the recruitment problem, may include removal of adult leaders who are reponsible for the recruitment and securing recruitment zones. Combating child soldiers should thus involve a broad-spectrum approach of both military and civilian actors.

Finally, rather than being prudential in nature, consideration of such a moral framework should be incumbent upon every adult combatant who encounters a child soldier on the battlefield. This would make the application of these principles less arbitrary and more likely to save the lives of children forced to engage in war.

7. Conclusion

The use of children as soldiers poses important ethical problems with profound implications, not least from a military perspective. That child soldiers may be considered as legitimate targets goes against our most basic human intuition of protecting the lives of children.

Soldiers must therefore exercise restraint and accept greater risk to minimize the harm inflicted on child soldiers, not because they are not moral agents, but because of their vulnerability and protected status as children.

Even though the killing of child soldiers who pose a threat to other combatants may be morally and legally permissible, it nevertheless presents a psychological problem to conventional military forces. In his book *On Killing*, Dave Grossman writes:

> Being able to identify your victim as a combatant is important to the rationalization that occurs after the kill. If a soldier kills a child, a women, or anyone who does not represent a potential threat, then he has entered the realm of murder (as opposed to a legitimate, sanctioned combat kill), and the rationalization process becomes quite difficult. Even if he kills in self-defense, there is enormous resistance associated with killing an individual who is not normally associated with relevance or payoff.[27]

In other words, while the actions of child soldiers may make them combatants who may be legitimately killed, their presumed identity as innocent children who should be protected creates a powerful psychological barrier for the moral warrior who must confront them on the battlefield. This barrier can have significant tactical consequences as soldiers try to decide when, and how, to engage child soldiers in combat.

Lastly, the death of child soldiers in a war zone could possibly undermine the strategic objectives that are the basis of the use of force. Television images of children dead on the battlefield can directly undermine the legitimacy of a military operation even though those children have been combatants. We therefore need a profound understanding of the complexity of this phenomenon, and an ethical framework that takes into account both the necessity of protecting and engaging children in war.

Notes

1 P.W. Singer, *Children at War*. Berkeley; Los Angeles: University of California Press, 2006, p. 170.

2 T. A. Berntsen, "Negotiated identities: The discourse on the role of child soldiers in the peace process in Northern Uganda," in B. Mæland (ed.), *Culture, Religion, and the Reintegration of Female Ex-child Soldiers in Northern Uganda*, New York: Geneva: Peter Lang, 2010, p. 43.

3 R. Tynes, "Child soldiers as tactical innovation," *Air & Space Power Journal*, 2008. Online. Available at: http://www.airpower.maxwell.af.mil/apjinternational/apj-s/2008/1tri08/tyneseng.htm (accessed 24 June, 2012).

4 A. Schmidt, "Volunteer child soldiers as reality: A development issue for Africa," *New School of Economic Review*, 2:1, 2007.

5 Cf. McMahan, J., "An Ethical Perspective on Child Soldiers," in S. Gates and S. Reich (eds) *Child Soldiers in the Age of Fractured States*. Pittsburgh: Pittsburgh University Press, 2009, pp. 27–36.

6 R. J. Regan *Just War: Principles and Cases*, Washington, D.C: The Catholic University of America Press, 1996, p. 87.

7 See A. Schmidt, "Volunteer child soldiers as reality"; J. Boyden, "The moral development of child soldiers: What do adults have to fear?" *Peace and Conflict: Journal of Peace Psychology* 9:4, 2003, pp. 343–362; K. Hoffman. "The ethics of child-soldiering in Congo," *Young: Nordic Journal of Youth Research* 18:3, 2010, pp. 339–358; B. Mæland "Constrained but not choiceless: On moral agency among child soldiers," in Bård Mæland (ed.), *Culture, Religion, and the Reintegration of Female Ex-child Soldiers in Northern Uganda*, New York; Geneva: P. Lang, 2010, pp. 57–74; S. Shepler, "The rites of the child: Global discourses of youth and reintegrating child soldiers," *Journal of Human Rights* 4, 2005, pp. 197–211; M. Wessells, *Child Soldiers: From Violence to Protection*. Cambridge, Mass. and London: Harvard University Press, 2006, p. 143.

8 A. Schmidt, "Volunteer child soldiers as reality," p. 61.

9 R. Tynes, "Child solders as tactical innovation."

10 A Schmidt, "Volunteer child soldiers as reality," p. 58f.

11 P.W. Singer, *Children at War*.

12 Optional Protocol to the Convention on the Rights of the Child on the Involvement of Children in Armed Conflict. United Nations. Online. Available at: http://www2.ohchr.org/english/law/crc-conflict.htm (accessed 30 June, 2012).

13 J. Boyden, "The moral development of child soldiers," p. 345; B. Mæland, "Constrained but not choiceless," p. 57.

14 Reference to Richards made in K. Hoffmann, "The ethics of child-soldiering in Congo," p. 342.

15 K. Hoffmann, "The ethics of child-soldiering in Congo"; I. Cohn, and G. S. Goodwin-Gill, *Child Soldiers: The Role of Children in Armed Conflicts*, Oxford: Oxford University Press, 1994; S. Shepler, "The rites of the child," Wessells, *Child Soldiers*, p. 143.

16 Rome Statute of the International Criminal Court, United Nations, 1998, Art. 8.2.b.xxvi. Online. Available at: http://untreaty.un.org/cod/icc/statute/romefra.htm (accessed 25 June, 2012).

17 Rome Statute, Art. 27.

18 See the Statute of the Special Court for Sierra Leone, Article 7 ("Jurisdiction over persons of 15 years of age"). Online. Available at: http://www.sc-sl.org/LinkClick.aspx?fileticket=uClnd1MJeEw%3d&t

abid=70 (accessed 9 August, 2012). See also T. Allen, *Trial Justice: The International Criminal Court and the Lord's Resistance Army*. London: Zed Books, 2006: p. 92.

19 "Special Court Prosecutor Says He Will Not Prosecute Children," press release 2 November 2002. Online. Available at: http://www.sc-sl.org/LinkClick.aspx?fileticket=XRwCUe%2baVhw%3d&tabid=196 (accessed 9 August, 2012).

20 J. McMahan, "Child soldiers," p. 34.

21 Protocol Additional to the Geneva Conventions of 12 August 1949, and relating to the Protection of Victims of International Armed Conflicts (Protocol I), Geneva, 8 June 1977, Article 51(3). Online. Available at: http://www.icrc.org/customary-ihl/eng/docs/v2_rul_rule6 (accessed 26 March, 2013).

22 T. Nagel, "War and massacre," in C. R. Beitz, M. Cohen, T. Scanlon, and J. Simmons (eds), *International Ethics*. Princeton, NJ: Princeton University Press, 1985, p. 69.

23 J. McMahan, "Child soldiers," p. 33.

24 R. Tynes, "Child soldiers as tactical innovation."

25 J. McMahan, "Child soldiers," p. 36.

26 T.A. Berntsen, "Den uskyldige fiende: Militæretiske perspektiver på bekjempelse av barnesoldater" (Norw. "The innocent enemy: Military-ethical perspectives on fighting child soldiers"), in K. Firin, K. Hellemsvik and J. Haarberg (eds), *Kryssild: militært lederskap i en ny tid*. Trondheim: Tapir, 2007, pp. 109–128; R. Tynes, "Child soldiers as tactical innovation."

27 D. Grossman, *On Killing: The Psychological Cost of Learning to Kill in War and Society*, New York: NY, Little, Brown and Company, 1995, pp. 174–175.

References

Allen, T., *Trial Justice: The International Criminal Court and the Lord's Resistance Army*. London: Zed Books, 2006.

Berntsen, T.A., "Den uskyldige fiende: Militæretiske perspektiver på bekjempelse av barnesoldater" (Norw. "The innocent enemy: Military-ethical perspectives on fighting child soldiers"), in K. Firin, K. Hellemsvik and J. Haarberg (eds), *Kryssild: militært lederskap i en ny tid*. Trondheim: Tapir, 2007, pp. 109–128.

——"Negotiated identities: The discourse on the role of child soldiers in the peace process in Northern Uganda," in B. Mæland (ed.), *Culture, Religion, and the Reintegration of Female Ex-child Soldiers in Northern Uganda*. New York; Geneva: Peter Lang, 2010, pp. 39–56.

Boyden, J., "The moral development of child soldiers: What do adults have to fear?" *Peace and Conflict: Journal of Peace Psychology*, 9:4, 2003, pp. 343-362.

Cohn, I., and G.S. Goodwin-Gill, *Child Soldiers: The Role of Children in Armed Conflicts*. Oxford: Oxford University Press, 1994.

Grossman, D., *On Killing: The Psychological Cost of Learning to Kill in War and Society*, New York: NY, Little, Brown and Company, 1995, pp. 174-175.

Hoffmann, K., "The ethics of child-soldiering in Congo," *Young: Nordic Journal of Youth Research*, 18:3, 2010, pp. 339-358.

McMahan, J., "An Ethical Perspective on Child Soldiers," in S. Gates and S. Reich (eds) *Child Soldiers in the Age of Fractured States*. Pittsburgh: Pittsburgh University Press, 2009, pp. 27–36.

Mæland, B., "Constrained but not choiceless: On moral agency among child soldiers," in B. Mæland (ed.), *Culture, Religion, and the Reintegration of Female Ex-child Soldiers in Northern Uganda*. New York; Geneva: Peter Lang, 2010, pp. 57–74.

Nagel, T., "War and massacre," in C.R. Beitz, M. Cohen, T. Scanlon, and J. Simmons (eds), *International Ethics*. Princeton, NJ: Princeton University Press, 1985, pp.53–74.

Optional Protocol to the Convention on the Rights of the Child on the Involvement of Children in Armed Conflict, 2000. United Nations. Online. Available at: http://www2.ohchr.org/english/law/crc-conflict.htm (accessed 30 June, 2012).

Protocol Additional to the Geneva Conventions of 12 August 1949, and relating to the Protection of Victims of International Armed Conflicts (Protocol I), Geneva, 8 June 1977, Article 51(3). Online. Available at: http://www.icrc.org/customary-ihl/eng/docs/v2_rul_rule6 (accessed 26 March, 2013).

Regan, R.J., *Just War: Principles and Cases*. Washington, D.C: The Catholic University of America Press, 1996.

Rome Statute of the International Criminal Court, 1985. United Nations. Online. Available at: http://untreaty.un.org/cod/icc/statute/romefra.htm (accessed 25 June, 2012).

Schmidt, A., "Volunteer child soldiers as reality: A development issue for Africa," *New School of Economic Review*, 2:1, 2007, pp. 49–76.

Shepler, S., "The rites of the child: Global discourses of youth and reintegrating child soldiers," *Journal of Human Rights* 4, 2005, pp. 197–211.

Singer, P.W., *Children at War*. Berkeley; Los Angeles: University of California Press, 2006

"Special Court Prosecutor Says He Will Not Prosecute Children," press release 2 November 2002. Online. Available at: http://www.sc-sl.org/LinkClick.aspx?fileticket=XRwCUe%2baVhw%3d&tabid=196 (accessed 9 August, 2012).

Statute of the Special Court for Sierra Leone, Article 7 ("Jurisdiction over persons of 15 years of age"). Online. Available at: http://www.sc-sl.org/LinkClick.aspx?fileticket=uClnd1MJeEw%3d&tabid=70 (accessed 9 August, 2012).

Tynes, R., "Child soldiers as tactical innovation," *Air & Space Power Journal*, 2008. Online. Available at: http://www.airpower.maxwell.af.mil/apjinternational/apj-s/2008/1tri08/tyneseng.htm (accessed 24 June 2012).

Wessells, M., *Child Soldiers: From Violence to Protection*. Cambridge, Mass. and London: Harvard University Press, 2006.

PART III

TECHNOLOGIES OF WAR

The future of fighting

Technology and just war theory

21

EMERGING TECHNOLOGIES AND JUST WAR THEORY[1]

Braden Allenby

1. Introduction

It is elementary that technologies fundamentally impact military operations and practice, as well as society as a whole. Indeed, technological evolution and military activity have been linked throughout history. The relationship is not, however, straightforward. The existential challenge to society represented by warfare, combined with the immediate advantage that new technology can deliver, tends to accelerate technological innovation and diffusion; the inherent conservatism of military personnel, the emphasis on tradition and culture that marks many military organizations, and the high costs of experimentation in conflict environments, serve as a powerful brake on technological evolution. Similarly, the relationships between military and security technology systems, and consequent institutional, cultural, and social changes, are profound, complex, unpredictable, and often subtle. Many technologies of sufficient power to be of interest militarily have at least the potential to be deeply destabilizing to existing economic, social, and technological systems, especially as they are introduced into civil society.[2] As military RFID and sensor systems, and robots and cyborgs at many different scales, are shifted from theatre intelligence and combat to civil society environments, for example, the implications for privacy, and for the balance between national security and civil rights, could be substantial. Technologies that can accelerate the development of human varietals within the overall population could be very effective for warriors, but raise difficult issues for social stability (many cultures, after all, do not deal very gracefully or equitably with the race, gender, and sexual preference differences that have long been part of the human story).[3] Equally important, emerging technologies are likely to have similar destabilizing effects within the military as well, potentially affecting not just operations, but also military culture and organization. A military leadership class which has developed in traditional combat environments will not have the same values, nor behave in the same way, as a military leadership class selected for its ability to play video games in high school (an issue that Singer, 2009, points to as the US Air Force leadership, at present consisting almost entirely of pilots, is affected by incoming gamers who are proficient at flying unmanned aerial vehicles (UAVs)).

Equally important, it is clear that leading contenders for great power status – including at least the US, the BRICS (Brazil, Russia, India, China, and, to some, South Africa), the EU and certain member states, and perhaps others such as Indonesia, Turkey, Iran, and Mexico – realize that scientific and technological capability is a critical competency for achieving and defending such a position. This is not just true in the obvious terms of economic performance and in the less obvious but equally critical realm of "soft power,"[4] but in a purely military sense as well. Especially as more traditional great power conflicts, such as that between the rising power of China and the existing power of the United States, are reframed informally or formally as confrontations that must be engaged across all domains of culture and society,[5] the importance of broad technological competence and innovation is enhanced.

Such issues are particularly pertinent given the accelerating technological change that characterizes the current era, combined with the changes in military operations discussed below and elsewhere in this volume, particularly Part III. Accordingly, this chapter will provide an overview of emerging technologies, the environment within which such technologies are being developed, and suggest some of the concomitant implications for just war theory. It should be emphasized, however, that because of the complexity and unpredictability necessarily associated with such an evolutionary process, any such effort should be regarded as illustrative and partial, rather than predictive (as many reviews of the implications of emerging technology for the military and security domains have emphasized)[6].

2. Technology systems and Kondratieff waves

It is very common for both technologists and social scientists to misunderstand both the essence, and the implications, of technology systems. To begin with, technology systems are not just artifacts; rather, they are integrated cultural, social, psychological, economic, institutional, and built phenomena.[7] Moreover, any technology system of more than trivial power tends to be profoundly destabilizing of existing institutions, norms, and power relationships – as well as of the technology systems that it replaces, along with the firms and employment patterns built on the now-obsolete technologies. This is the well-known capitalist "gale of creative destruction," as the Austrian economist Joseph Schumpeter famously put it; it is a major reason that emerging technologies tend to generate substantial and potentially powerful opposition.[8] In societies where conservative forces are able to dominate, they are therefore highly likely to impede technological evolution, thus creating less competitive cultures; whether a culture will evolve technologically may therefore depend to a large extent on whether conservative forces are able to merely hinder technological evolution, or whether they can stifle it completely.[9] Third, technology systems are complex adaptive systems, which means that trying to predict their future evolution, as opposed to exploring possibilities through techniques such as scenario analysis, is essentially impossible. One can prepare for the future by, for example, creating agile institutions through war gaming and scenario exercises; one cannot predict it.[10]

Consider the seemingly simple and mundane example of the railroad. To moderns railroad technology may be trite, but it was a devastating technological juggernaut to the societies it affected in the early 1800s. Remembering that technologies are co-evolving parts of complex adaptive systems, rather than causal mechanisms, the breadth of change of which railroads were a major forcing component is still remarkable. For example, the modern structure and sense of time is to a large extent a product of railroad technology. Before railroads local times were isolated and unsynchronized: London time was four minutes ahead of Reading, and fourteen minutes ahead of Bridgewater.[11] But railroads required a uniform, precise system of time that was coextensive with, and matched to the characteristics of, the physical network.[12] Similarly, railroad operations also require coextensive signaling and communications systems, and thus provided not just a convenient right of way, but also a raison d'être, for telegraph technology.[13]

But this by no means exhausts the social and cultural impacts of railroad technology. Before railroads, local, fairly isolated economic institutions were the norm. Rail technology, however, created regional and economies of scale in industrial operations, and thus fundamentally changed economic and power structures. More subtly, railroads enabled a fundamental cultural shift: not just economic but cultural power passed to industrial firms from agriculture as the yeoman farmer was replaced by the urban factory worker and the capitalist.[14] Agriculture itself changed from an individual, small unit, subsistence activity to industrial scale, and in doing so altered entire continental ecologies.[15] Similarly, the unprecedented scale and complexity of railroad operations called forth the financial and managerial institutions of industrial capitalism, replacing the simpler practices of earlier factory capitalism.[16]

Readers of this volume no doubt already realize that the military and national security implications of the railroad were not trivial. The logistical and industrial benefits the North realized during the American Civil War as a result of its substantial superiority in rail technology are well known.[17] Less familiar, perhaps, is the role of railroad technology in the rise of Prussia. Unlike Russia, Austria, and to some extent France, the Prussians realized early on the strategic importance of railroad technology.[18] Thus, for example, Prussian commercial railroad cars were explicitly designed so that in addition to their routine commercial purpose they could carry soldiers, horses, military supplies, and military equipment if necessary, and Prussian civilian railroad stations were designed with dual use military functionality in mind. The results became obvious in 1866 at the battle of Koniggratz, where the upstart Prussians stunned and essentially destroyed the Austrian Empire. Of course, railroads were not the only factor. In this case, for example, the Prussians also had the needle gun, arguably the most advanced rifle in Europe; world class military management (no one else had von Moltke); highly advanced training; and more effective administration, an underappreciated military competence. In the event, as Austria fell, Prussia rose, and Koniggratz marked Prussia as a European power.

In this systemic restructuring of society and its institutions, railroads are not unique. Economic historians have developed a theory of "long waves" or "Kondratieff waves" of innovation, where periods of economic expansion are driven by constellations of technologies and institutions that form around core technology systems, with concomitant social, cultural, legal, psychological, technological, and economic change. This is a theory of developed, industrialized systems, so the first Kondratieff wave is generally understood to involve the mechanization of textile manufacture, the basis of the Industrial Revolution in the UK.[19] Although this is not something about which the literature is exact, subsequent examples might include: railroads and steam technology, which powered a wave from about 1840 to 1890; followed by a wave from about 1890 to 1930, which developed around steel, heavy engineering, and electricity; and an automobile, fossil fuel, and aviation wave from about 1930 to 1990.[20] Each wave is characterized by co-evolution of the core technology cluster with institutional, organizational, economic, cultural and political institutions and systems, leading to profound and unpredictable change, as the railroad example illustrates. Thus, for example, some have suggested that modern developed economies are reacting to an information and communication technology wave by shifting from a mass production, heavy industry paradigm of specialized professional managerial systems and associated "Taylorism" industrial efficiency techniques to a far more networked, adaptive, and flexible structure characterized by, for example, virtual offices and informal and protean regional and global information networks.[21]

Technology systems, both in the limited context of military operations and national security, and across social and cultural systems generally, are not just profoundly destabilizing. Rather, they define new Earth-system states; they change and integrate built, human, and natural systems and networks in unpredictable, contingent, and fundamental ways.[22] The observations about some of the impacts of railroad technology may seem trivial, but that is only because the backward looking perspective of history hides the traumas, conflicts, confusion, and dislocations experienced by contemporaries of that technology. More recently, anthropogenic climate change, a product of a global civilization based on fossil fuel technology; major shifts in nitrogen and phosphorous cycles, products of the agricultural revolution (specifically, fertilizer production and use); and cultural phenomenon such as the environmentalist and sustainability discourses all illustrate the continuing transformative power of human technologies. That being the case, it is sobering to realize that at this point in human history it is not one or two core technologies that are undergoing rapid evolution, but five: The Five Horsemen of emerging technologies: nanotechnology, biotechnology, robotics, information and communication technology (ICT), and applied cognitive science (NBRIC).[23]

Taken as a whole, the NBRIC technologies in some ways are the logical end of the chapter of human history that began 2,500 years ago with the Greeks, the human effort to rationally understand and control physical reality (which has now been extended to synthetic realities, combining virtual and real realities in different patterns). Nanotechnology extends human will and design to the molecular and atomic level. While it is certainly true that the complexity of biological systems remains daunting, biotechnology is rapidly providing new tools and knowledge that will enable the extension of human design to the level of genes and proteins, so that life can be designed and controlled at scales from the molecular to the cell to the organism to the community to the global (e.g. extinction events). Advances in robotics continue to provide not just enhanced mechanical power and functionality (e.g. manufacturing robots in factories, UAVs), but to blur the line between human and biological systems, and mechanism (for example, the "ratbot," a hardware robot guided by hybrid rat neuron/chip configurations consisting of some 300,000 rat neurons in a soup).[24] ICT is a somewhat more complicated set of technologies, but its rapid evolution, from computer to Internet, is undeniable; less obvious, but perhaps more potent, is the vast increase in information technological advances have generated. Eric Schmidt, the CEO of Google, famously noted that in today's world more information is created every two days than was created in the entire of human history up until 2003 – whether that is a technically correct statement is, inevitably, contested; that it is directionally correct is not.[25] Some effects of globalizing interconnectivity are illustrated when publication of a few cartoons in a small country in Europe results in riots and deaths around the Islamic world, or when radical elements that ordinarily would have been isolated in their geographical communities link across the Internet to form terrorist or activist networks. This is especially the case when changes in ICT are coupled to accelerating changes in applied cognitive science. For example, the need for rapid, comprehensive cognition in complex and chaotic environments is pushing the development of "augmented cognition," where elements of the cognitive function that were previously performed by individuals are built into technology networks within which humans function.[26] This may be a fundamental shift in the way humans integrate with technology, but it is also quotidian, as the development of familiar smart car technology demonstrates. Indeed, the ability to couple with ambient technology systems is perhaps an underappreciated aspect of being human; that coupling to potent ICT technologies, so closely associated with cultural and psychological dimensions of the human, should be particularly potent should be no surprise.

It is not just that each one of these technology systems is powerful in itself (and of course there is an element of arbitrariness in what technology system is identified as core, and how that system is bounded for purposes of analysis). Rather, it is that they are being combined, and enable each other's development, in complex and unpredictable ways. The ratbot, combining robotics with biotechnology, has already been mentioned; augmented cognition, where different aspects of cognition (memory, perception, response to immediate environment) are dispersed across technology networks rather than centered in the Cartesian individual, is another. A third example, involving a number of different foundational scientific and technological domains, is the possibility of radical human life extension. This is an active area of research and, like any emerging technology that is not yet clearly demonstrated, is best regarded as a scenario, rather than a prediction. That said, there are some who believe that, given the progress being made in genetics, biotechnology, and other enabling fields, the first people to live to 150 years, with a high quality of life, have already been born in developed economies;[27] more dramatic claims of "functional human immortality" within fifty years, either as a result of biotechnology, or downloading of human consciousness into information networks, have also been made.[28] Such predictions are viewed by other experts as highly unlikely. Nonetheless, there is some evidence that substantial extensions of average lifespan, with a high quality of life, are achievable. In this regard it is notable that, at least initially, military researchers and organizations are among the institutions most interested in enhancing humans, and human design, for better performance.

It is entirely premature to speculate as to what effects the NBRIC Kondratieff Wave will generate. But one thing is clear. Powerful technologies destabilize psychological, institutional, social and cultural systems; the combination of NBRIC technologies taken as a whole, and the demographic and economic growth of the past 200 years, suggest that most of the assumptions that underlie current systems are now contingent. The Earth is now a continuing experiment in terraforming (e.g. anthropogenic climate change; perturbations to the hydrologic, nitrogen, sulphur, phosphorous, and other systems; urbanization and life extension); the human is becoming a design space to a far greater degree than in the past. It is therefore not inappropriate to wonder whether emerging technologies are, in fact, destabilizing the traditional laws of war. To that question we now turn.

3. Emerging technologies and the laws of war

For purposes of this discussion, the "laws of war" will be treated as a comprehensive, albeit informal, corpus that has developed, particularly in the West, over many centuries and which, in complicated and sometimes partial ways, governs the behavior of most states to some degree as they contemplate, conduct, and conclude combat activities.[29] Moreover, as the previous discussion will have made clear, a focus only on the physical technologies themselves will be entirely inadequate to consideration of deeper questions of technological impact. In the instant case, for example, it is impossible to understand the implications of planned or potential military and security technologies without a deeper initial understanding of the cultural, operational, and institutional frameworks within which the technologies are being conceived, and will be used.

It is axiomatic given the competition implicit in warfare that technological change is endemic to the domain. It is also apparent, however, that modern conflict exhibits both an accelerated rate of change, and increased complexity, when compared to historical eras.[30] For example, the sorts of conflicts that developed countries have engaged in most recently – Libya, Afghanistan, Iraq, Bosnia, United Nations interventions in African conflicts – are very different from the European continental and religious wars of the past centuries, the Napoleonic Wars, or World Wars I and II, not just in conduct, but in intent (recent European, American, and UN conflicts have not been for conquest of territory or establishment of colonies, but to achieve ideological aims and defeat disfavored elites). More fundamentally, the Iranian-Israeli conflict has to date occurred primarily in cyberspace, where the relationship between the physical and the ethereal, and hence the relatively clean assumptions of the laws of war (e.g. you know when aggression occurs and who is responsible, because it is physically obvious, as opposed to cyberconflict, where attribution of an attack, even if it can be ascertained that it has occurred, is difficult if not impossible) are brought into question. Even in the case of Afghanistan, a more traditional conflict, the geographical boundaries of the battlefield become vague when US attacks with Predator unmanned aerial vehicles are guided from sites outside Las Vegas, Nevada.

It appears to be a sociological truism that, the more complex a situation, the more desirable technological fixes appear to be. This has certainly been the case with climate change, where both the policy framework and the proposed technological responses are dysfunctionally simplistic (geoengineering as a "silver bullet" response to climate change has been seriously questioned).[31] Similarly, the Prussian example discussed above, as well as the US experience in Iraq, suggest that there appears to be a tendency for leaders of technologically superior military forces to rely overmuch on the (unquestioned) advantages their technology provides them. Indeed, while it is rare for any nation to achieve unquestioned dominance in conventional military technologies, the US experience suggests a danger of misperceiving true sources of power under such conditions – perhaps even more dangerous if such a country has a technologically optimistic culture.

But over-reliance on technology and under-appreciation of soft power is not the only trap posed by modernity.[32] The entire environment within which conflict occurs is changing in fundamental ways. Figure 21.1 presents one, highly schematic, framework for conceptualizing this complex domain. Initially, it is apparent that many if not most of the working assumptions that have been stable over much of the past centuries are stable no more. The Libyan intervention, for example, demonstrates the increasing emphasis on "Duty to Protect," which is clearly in conflict with the recent historical assumption that the internal activities of states directed against their minorities are not subject to intervention by the international community.[33] Global terrorist networks put paid to another significant historical assumption: states are clearly no longer the only operational entities in international conflicts (contrary to the 1648 Treaties of Westphalia and subsequent international law). Is a soldier sent to Afghanistan there to conduct combat operations, to conduct espionage, or to police? Those are very different missions requiring very different cultures, training, and, importantly, technology. An incapacitating directed energy weapon used to control and disperse unruly crowds is a police weapon, not a combat weapon. Moreover, the legal and ethical frameworks within which each of those missions occurs is profoundly different. For example, applicable military law would not permit an American soldier to deliberately target a civilian whereas policing activities necessarily target civilians. So not only is the system as mapped highly complex and unpredictable, but the domains are not independent as Figure 21.1 might suggest; indeed, they interact in many new and uncertain ways.[34]

That said, consider the four major domains given in Figure 21.1. The first, Revolutions in Military Technology, or RMT, is the traditional technology dimension. It is the one that seems most obvious and simple, although as the discussion of Kondratieff Waves has suggested, that is not necessarily the case because it is the cumulative implications of entire suites of technologies taken across the technological frontier as a whole that poses such a difficult conceptual and analytical problem.[35] The second realm is that of Revolutions in Nature of Conflict, or RNC. Fundamental change is occurring in this domain as well. The "Duty to Protect" is an example; it suggests that nations are permitted under applicable international law to intervene in the internal affairs of other countries under certain circumstances. This remains a new, ill-defined, and contentious principle opposed by a number of countries that have difficult internal conflicts of their own such as China and Russia, but it is increasingly the basis of armed intervention in what until now would have been regarded as unfortunate civil wars.[36] The movement away from the state as sole actor is reflected in the rise of counterinsurgency, policing actions, violent non-governmental regional and global networks, and other models of conflict (sometimes combining in different ways, as states project their power using actors that are not part of the formal military establishment, a pattern that appears to characterize the current cyberconflict

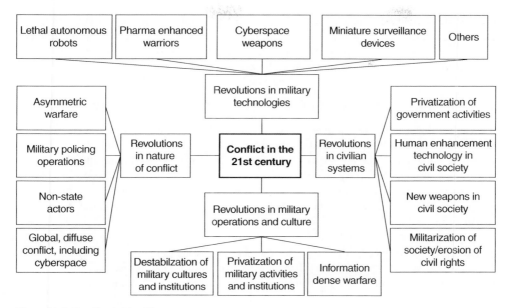

Figure 21.1 Conflict in the 21st century

environment, and is perhaps not unlike the use of privateers in an earlier age).[37] The US dominance of conventional military technologies actually complicates this space; not only can it lead
to dangerous hubris, but it encourages potential adversaries to invest heavily in asymmetric
warfare. The US and to some extent Europe, for example, are asymmetrically highly vulnerable
to cyberattack because of their reliance on Internet functionality.[38]

The third realm, Revolutions in Civilian Systems or RCS, is also undergoing unpredictable
and accelerating change. Consider, for example, the implications of the ongoing privatization of
conflict, such as has characterized the US experience in Iraq and Afghanistan over the period of
more than a decade.[39] Additionally, many technologies that have highly positive implications in
a military context, and thus are likely to be funded, are at least more problematic if introduced
into civic society: UAVs may erode privacy and civil rights; pharmaceuticals that enhance performance may become endemic at college campuses; non-lethal weapons developed for use in
military policing environments will become domestic technological staples not just for police
but for civil society given US culture.

Finally, one would be remiss not to point out that technologies do not just interact with
civic society, but also have profound effects on military organization and structure – hence,
Revolutions in Military Operations and Culture, or RMOC. This is not a trivial issue; after all,
a significant reason some countries are prone to coups while others are not is military culture.
The stirrup, the cross-bow, the handgun, and field artillery all dramatically changed military
tactics, strategies, logistics, and balances of power, both between militaries and within military
organizations.[40] Here one also sees interactions with changes in mission: policing operations
not only require different technologies, but different training, a different attitude towards the
indigenous civilian population, different institutional cultures – one reason why crack soldiers
are seldom good policemen – and why it is extremely difficult, if not impossible, to be both
at the same time, or switch rapidly from role to role. Similarly, the rapid introduction of
unmanned aerial vehicles – UAVs – creates deep cultural strains as US Air Force officers who

have absorbed military culture for many years as they worked their way through the ranks find themselves managing (and sometimes competing with) geek gamers, and military personnel in active combat situations in Afghanistan are augmented with remote control operators who go to their homes in American suburbs when their day is done.[41]

4. Thoughts on the continuing validity of the laws of war

It is against this background of co-evolving complexity and destabilization in not just a single domain, but across RMT, RNC, RCS, and RMOC taken both individually and together, that one must ask whether the laws of war, conceptually and as embodied in existing treaties and agreements, are adequate. Given the changes occurring across the relevant landscape, and the nascent state of the dialog, any discussion at this point should be regarded as preliminary and tentative – indeed, what is sketched out here in rough outline is more a research agenda than any sort of substantive analytical effort.

But there are a few thoughts that are (probably) reasonably robust. Most importantly, it is doubtful that the answer to the question as to the continuing applicability and efficacy of the laws of war is a simple "yes" or "no." It is unlikely that fundamental and pervasive change across virtually all relevant domains will not affect in some meaningful way doctrines and principles that were formulated and tested under very different, and in relevant ways less complex, conditions. If nothing else, many of the deep assumptions underlying the laws of war, such as the primacy of the state and the physical nature of warfare – and, indeed, that a condition called "war" is still separable from other conditions of conflict and conflict management – are being destabilized. On the other hand, very few human systems change discontinuously, and even fundamental change, upon inspection, has roots deep in the past, and occurs far more gradually than a superficial inspection might indicate. Moreover, the laws of war have been developed over a long period, with commentary and input from many cultures (including Christian, Islamic, and Chinese thinkers, for example), and it is unlikely that a body of work that is so robust has suddenly become completely inapplicable to present conditions. After all, many argue that the embodiment of the laws of war in humanitarian law, treaties, and institutions such as the United Nations is one of the great, albeit imperfect, strides in human civilization, and that such an achievement should not be jettisoned lightly (others, of course, might take issue with this, arguing that the laws of war and modern humanitarian law are a Western framework, and thus merely superficially universal, when in fact they constitute continuing Western imperialism).[42]

If one is to devise a research and dialog agenda, therefore, the more pertinent question is to what extent, and where, the existing formulation of the laws of war should be revised, or even rejected, and what should take the place of the doctrines that currently exist? In addressing this question, one must also recognize that, regardless of what may be happening in new domains such as cyberconflict, there remain a number of "traditional" situations where the laws of war remain applicable. Moreover, one may well have conditions where traditional and non-traditional conflict coexist, raising difficult analytical challenges, but perhaps not fundamentally challenging the applicability of the laws of war, at least to specific aspects of operations. Thus, for example, the Afghanistan/Pakistan (AfPak) war includes traditional ground combat operations, where the laws of war presumptively are fully applicable (at least to NATO operations); policing activities where the laws of war may not be entirely appropriate; espionage and sabotage operations (e.g. UAV flights over Pakistan operated by the CIA, not by military institutions), which are not governed by the laws of war; and privatized military operations, which are also not governed by the laws of war. If these were completely separate operational domains, there might be less of a problem, but the fact that they overlap considerably in practice makes analysis difficult.

More subtly, AfPak also raises difficult issues of weaponization of the laws of war, in that they, or at least alleged violations of them, are converted to effective operational and propaganda weapons against Western forces. This also leads to interesting questions as to whether, or how, the laws of war, modern conflict, and soft power considerations should be integrated: one of the main arguments against alleged American mistreatment of prisoners is that it led to loss of the moral high ground against terrorists, which is a soft power argument (e.g. that America gains strength from maintaining the moral high ground that should not be undermined by its own actions even for some (alleged) short-term operational benefit). Note this latter case suggests at least two different if intertwined research questions: first, to what extent is morality an operational component of the exercise of power (a realist sort of inquiry); and second, what is the proper ethical framework from a philosophical and moral perspective (a normative inquiry).

Similarly, for purposes of clarity one must be careful to differentiate between traditional critiques of the laws of war, and new conditions which may call their applicability into question. For example, realists have consistently questioned whether the very idea of "laws of war" is viable, given that states engaging in warfare are usually doing so for fundamental values that cannot be defended by anything short of total war (and the more basic argument that states are not moral agents, but can, and should, care only about their interests and their power). On the other side, pacifists have argued that no war, no matter what the rationale or how conducted, can be moral; "laws of war," therefore, is oxymoronic, an attempt to pretend that the initiation, conduct, and termination of war may be under some conditions just.[43] These arguments and others – John Keegan's argument, for example, that war has over thousands of years become a habit that can no longer be tolerated because humans have developed such effective weaponry and a capability to push war beyond savagery to extremes (consider World War II's air wars against civilian targets, and what nuclear war would do if it ever happened) – are important ones,[44] and they indeed affect the way one might consider the viability and desirability of the laws of war, but they are not new.

A research and dialog agenda around the current status of the laws of war should therefore differentiate between their philosophic and cultural underpinnings and justification, which remains a legitimate and contentious arena, and the different and less explored question of whether changes in the nature of conflict, military and security technologies, and the environment within which conflict is conducted, have at least in some cases rendered the laws of war inapplicable not because they are philosophically questionable but because they are obsolete, and thereby dysfunctional.

As this chapter has suggested, to begin to explore this latter question requires a more sophisticated understanding of technology systems and their far-reaching implications than is usually brought to the table. It is still necessary to understand the engineering, operational, and tactical implications of new military artifacts as they are introduced to the battlefield, but as the battlefield, civil societies and cultures, and the technologies mutate in unpredictable and complex ways, it is no longer sufficient. It is not a choice to have to do this; it is a requirement for military and strategic adequacy in the modern world of conflict, war, and competition.

Notes

1 This chapter is excerpted from a longer article, "The Implications of Emerging Technologies for Just War Theory," currently in review at *Public Affairs Quarterly*.
2 B.R. Allenby and D. Sarewitz, *The Techno-Human Condition*, Cambridge, MA: MIT Press, 2011.
3 G. Riddihough, G Chin, E. Culotta, B. Jasny, L. Roberts and S. Vignieri (eds), "Human conflict: Winning the peace (special section)," *Science* 336, 2012, pp. 819–884.
4 J.S. Nye Jr, *The Future of Power*, Philadelphia, PA: Perseus Books Group, 2011.

5 Q. Liang and W. Xiangsui, *Unrestricted Warfare*, Beijing: PLA Literature and Arts Publishing House, 1999 (CIA translation).

6 U.S. National Research Council, *Avoiding Surprise in an Era of Global Technology Advances*, Washington, DC: National Academy Press, 2005; U.S. National Research Council, *Persistent Forecasting of Disruptive Technologies*, Washington, DC: National Academy Press, 2010.

7 W.E. Bijker, T.P. Hughes, and T. Pinch (eds), *The Social Construction of Technological Systems*, Cambridge: MIT Press, 1997.

8 J. Schumpeter, *Capitalism, Socialism, and Democracy*, London: Routledge Press, first published 1943, paperback edn 1994.

9 D.S. Landes, *The Wealth and Poverty of Nations*, New York: W.W. Norton and Company, 1998; D. Acemoglu and J.A. Robinson, *Why Nations Fail*, New York: Crown Business, 2012.

10 B.R. Allenby, *The Theory and Practice of Sustainable Engineering*, Upper Saddle River, NJ: Pearson/Prentice-Hall, 2011.

11 W. Schivelbusch, *The Railway Journey: The Industrialization of Time and Space in the 19th Century*, Berkeley: University of California Press, 1977.

12 N. Rosenberg and L.E. Birdzell Jr., *How the West Grew Rich: The Economic Transformation of the Industrial World*, New York: Basic Books, 1986.

13 A. Grubler, *Technology and Global Change*, Cambridge: Cambridge University Press, 1998.

14 L. Marx, *The Machine in the Garden: Technology and the Pastoral Ideal in America*, Oxford: Oxford University Press, 1964; D.E. Nye, *American Technological Sublime*, Cambridge: MIT Press, 1994.

15 W. Cronon, *Nature's Metropolis: Chicago and the Great West*, New York: W.W. Norton and Company, 1991.

16 D.E. Nye, *America as Second Creation: Technology and Narratives of New Beginning*, Cambridge: MIT Press, 2003; C. Freeman and F. Louçã, *As Time Goes By: From the Industrial Revolutions to the Information Revolution*, Oxford: Oxford University Press, 2001.

17 D.E. Nye, *America as Second Creation*; J. Keegan, *A History of Warfare*, New York: Vintage Press, 1993; Acemoglu and J.A. Robinson, *Why Nations Fail*.

18 M. Boot, *War Made New*, New York: Gotham, 2007.

19 N. Rosenberg and L.E. Birdzell, *How the West Grew Rich*.

20 C. Freeman and Louçã *As Time Goes By*.

21 M. Castells, *The Rise of the Network Society* (2nd edn), Oxford: Blackwell Publishers, 2000.

22 Allenby, *The Theory and Practice of Sustainable Engineering*.

23 Allenby, *The Theory and Practice of Sustainable Engineering*; Allenby and Sarewitz, *The Techno-Human Condition*.

24 P. Marks, "Rat-brained robots take their first steps," *New Scientist* 199:2669, 2008, pp. 22–23.

25 K. Finley, "Was Eric Schmidt wrong about the historical scale of the Internet?" ReadWriteWeb. Online. Available at: www.readwriteweb.com/cloud/2011/02/are-we-really-creating-as-much.php#.T9PaRW-w8Q (accessed June 2012).

26 M.L. Bernard, C.M. Vineyard, S.J. Verzi, S.E. Taylor, I. Dubicka, and T.P. Caudell, *Augmented Cognition Tool for Rapid Military Decision Making*, Sandia Report SAND2011-7337, October 2011, prepared by Sandia National Laboratories, Albuquerque, New Mexico, USA.

27 A. De Grey and M. Rae, *Ending Aging: The Rejuvenation Breakthroughs that Could Reverse Human Aging in Our Lifetime*, New York: St Martin's Press, 2007.

28 H. Moravec, *Mind Children: The Future of Robot and Human Intelligence*, Cambridge: Harvard University Press, 1988; R. Kurzweil, *The Singularity is Near*, New York: Viking, 2005.

29 B. Orend, *The Morality of War*, Peterborough, Ontario, Canada: Broadview Press, 2006; J.A. Bovarnick, J.P. Harlow, T.A. Rush, CR. Brown, J.J. Marsh, G.S. Musselman, and S.R. Reeves, *Law of War Deskbook*, Charlottesville, VA: International and Operational Law Department, The Judge Advocate General's School, U. S. Army, 2010.

30 J. A. Tainter, *The Collapse of Complex Societies*, Cambridge: Cambridge University Press, 1988; J. Keegan, *A History of Warfare*; J.S. Nye Jr, *The Future of Power*.

31 B.R. Allenby, "Durban: Geoengineering as a response to cultural lock-in," *Proceedings* of the IEEE Annual Symposium on Sustainable Systems and Technology, May 2012.

32 J.S. Nye Jr, *The Future of Power*.

33 B. Orend, *The Morality of War*.

34 B.R. Allenby, *Theory and Practice of Sustainable Engineering*.

35 NRC, 2005, op. cit.; NRC, *Persistent Forecasting of Disruptive Technologies*.
36 Orend, *The Morality of War*.
37 U.S. Army, *The U. S. Army/Marine Corps Counterinsurgency Field Manual (USAFM 3-24; MCWP 3-33.5)*, Chicago: University of Chicago Press, 2007.
38 Liang and Xiangsui, *Unrestricted Warfare*.
39 P.W. Singer, *Corporate Warriors: The Rise of the Privatized Military Industry*, Ithaca: Cornell University Press, 2003, updated 2008.
40 W.H. McNeill, *The Pursuit of Power: Technology, Armed Force, and Society Since A.D. 1000*, Chicago: University of Chicago Press, 1982; G. Parker, *The Cambridge History of Warfare*, Cambridge: Cambridge University Press, 2005.
41 P.W. Singer, *Wired for War: The Robotics Revolution and Conflict in the 21st Century*, New York: The Penguin Press, 2009.
42 S.P. Huntington, *The Clash of Civilizations and the Remaking of World Order*, New York: Simon & Shuster, 2011.
43 B. Orend, *The Morality of War*.
44 J. Keegan, *A History of Warfare*.

References

Acemoglu, D. and J.A. Robinson, *Why Nations Fail*. New York: Crown Business, 2012.

Allenby, B.R. "Durban: Geoengineering as a response to cultural lock-in," *Proceedings* of the IEEE Annual Symposium on Sustainable Systems and Technology, May 2012.

Allenby, B.R. *The Theory and Practice of Sustainable Engineering*. Upper Saddle River, NJ: Pearson/Prentice-Hall, 2011.

Allenby, B.R. and D. Sarewitz, *The Techno-Human Condition*. Cambridge, MA: MIT Press, 2011.

Bernard, M.L., Vineyard, C.M., Verzi, S.J., Taylor, S.E., Dubicka, I., and Caudell, T.P. *Augmented Cognition Tool for Rapid Military Decision Making*, Sandia Report SAND2011-7337, October 2011, prepared by Sandia National Laboratories, Albuquerque, New Mexico, USA.

Bijker, W.E., T.P. Hughes and T. Pinch (eds), *The Social Construction of Technological Systems*. Cambridge: MIT Press, 1997.

Boot, M. *War Made New*. New York: Gotham, 2007.

Bovarnick, J.A, P. Harlow, T.A. Rush, C.R. Brown, J.J. Marsh, G.S. Musselman and S.R. Reeves, *Law of War Deskbook*. Charlottesville, VA: International and Operational Law Department, The Judge Advocate General's School, U. S. Army, 2010.

Castells, M. *The Rise of the Network Society* (2nd edn). Oxford: Blackwell Publishers, 2000.

Cronon, W. *Nature's Metropolis: Chicago and the Great West*. New York: W. W. Norton and Company, 1991.

De Grey, A. and M. Rae, *Ending Aging: The Rejuvenation Breakthroughs that Could Reverse Human Aging in Our Lifetime*. New York: St Martin's Press, 2007.

Finley, K. "Was Eric Schmidt wrong about the historical scale of the Internet?" 2011. ReadWriteWeb. Online. Available at: www.readwriteweb.com/cloud/2011/02/are-we-really-creating-as-much.php#.T9PaRW-w8Q (accessed June 2012).

Freeman, C. and F. Louçã, *As Time Goes By: From the Industrial Revolutions to the Information Revolution*. Oxford: Oxford University Press, 2001.

Grubler, A. *Technology and Global Change*. Cambridge: Cambridge University Press, 1998.

Huntington, S.P. *The Clash of Civilizations and the Remaking of World Order*, New York: Simon & Shuster, 2011.

Keegan, J. *A History of Warfare*. New York: Vintage Press, 1993.

Kurzweil, R. *The Singularity is Near*. New York: Viking, 2005.

Landes, D.S. *The Wealth and Poverty of Nations*. New York: W. W. Norton and Company, 1998.

Liang, Q. and W. Xiangsui, *Unrestricted Warfare*. Beijing: PLA Literature and Arts Publishing House, 1999. CIA translation.

Marks, P. "Rat-brained robots take their first steps," *New Scientist*, 199:2669, 2008, pp. 22–23.

Marx, L. *The Machine in the Garden: Technology and the Pastoral Ideal in America*. Oxford: Oxford University Press, 1964.

McNeill, W.H. *The Pursuit of Power: Technology, Armed Force, and Society Since A.D. 1000*. Chicago: University of Chicago Press, 1982.

Moravec, H. *Mind Children: The Future of Robot and Human Intelligence*. Cambridge: Harvard University Press, 1988.

NRC (U.S. National Research Council). *Avoiding Surprise in an Era of Global Technology Advances*. Washington, DC: National Academy Press, 2005.

NRC (U.S. National Research Council). *Persistent Forecasting of Disruptive Technologies*. Washington, DC: National Academy Press, 2010.

Nye, D.E. *America as Second Creation: Technology and Narratives of New Beginning*. Cambridge: MIT Press, 2003.

Nye, D.E. *American Technological Sublime*. Cambridge: MIT Press, 1994.

Nye Jr, J.S. *The Future of Power*. Philadelphia, PA: Perseus Books Group, 2011.

Orend, B. *The Morality of War*. Peterborough, Ontario, Canada: Broadview Press, 2006.

Parker, G. *The Cambridge History of Warfare*. Cambridge: Cambridge University Press, 2005.

PSRM (Pacific Southwest Railway Museum). *Railroad History: Important Milestones in English and American Railway Development*, 2012. Online. Available at: www.sdrm.org/history/timeline (accessed May 2012).

Riddihough, G., G. Chin, E. Culotta, B. Jasny, L. Roberts, and S. Vignieri (eds), "Human conflict: Winning the peace (special section)," *Science* 336, 2012, pp. 819–884.

Rosenberg, N. and L.E. Birdzell Jr. *How the West Grew Rich: The Economic Transformation of the Industrial World*. New York: Basic Books, 1986.

Schivelbusch, W. *The Railway Journey: The Industrialization of Time and Space in the 19th Century*. Berkeley: University of California Press, 1977.

Schumpeter, J. *Capitalism, Socialism, and Democracy*. London: Routledge Press, first published 1943, paperback edn 1994.

Singer, P.W. *Wired for War: The Robotics Revolution and Conflict in the 21st Century*. New York: The Penguin Press, 2009.

——*Corporate Warriors: The Rise of the Privatized Military Industry*. Ithaca: Cornell University Press, 2003, updated 2008.

Tainter, J.A. *The Collapse of Complex Societies*. Cambridge: Cambridge University Press, 1988.

U. S. Army. *The U. S. Army/Marine Corps Counterinsurgency Field Manual (USAFM 3-24; MCWP 3-33.5)*. Chicago: University of Chicago Press, 2007.

22

MINIMIZING HARM TO COMBATANTS

Nonlethal weapons, combatants' rights, and state responsibility[1]

Chris Mayer

1. Introduction

It is uncontroversial that it is immoral for combatants to intentionally harm noncombatants. This concept, commonly referred to as noncombatant immunity,[2] forbids combatants from targeting noncombatants, even if the harm to the noncombatants enables the combatants to complete their mission. This prohibition is codified in the Law of Armed Conflict (LOAC), and it is commanders' responsibility to ensure that their subordinates do not intentionally harm noncombatants. Noncombatant immunity does not, however, deem any action that causes harm to noncombatants as impermissible. It is recognized that unintentional harm will often come about as the result of military operations, and the doctrine of double effect provides a means of determining whether this unintentional harm is morally permissible. Wanting to offer further protection for noncombatants, Michael Walzer revises the doctrine of double effect to require due care to be taken when combatants' actions are likely to cause unintentional harm to noncombatants.[3] Exercising this due care may require combatants to assume more risk to themselves in order to protect noncombatants. Thus, combatants are not only prohibited from intentionally harming noncombatants, but they must actively seek to minimize unintentional harm. This move by Walzer makes clear the rights that noncombatants possess and the obligation that combatants have to respect them.

A related question concerns what sort of care is due to enemy combatants; that is, do combatants have a responsibility to minimize harm they cause to their enemy? I am not referring to the harming of the wounded or prisoners, former combatants who gain noncombatant status because they are incapacitated or in custody. The protection of these groups is already codified in just war theory and the LOAC. Instead, what I want to explore is whether it is ever morally impermissible to use lethal force against combatants who are not wounded or prisoners. This investigation will have to begin with why it is permissible to harm combatants in war in the first place, the types of rights maintained by combatants, and what combatants owe their enemies. First, however, it is necessary to describe the technology that makes this issue so important to address.

The development and increased effectiveness of nonlethal weapons should change how we think about the issues I raise above, and it is necessary to consider the effect of this increased effectiveness on the permissibility of the harm combatants inflict upon their enemy. If nonlethal technology is ever developed to the degree where nonlethal weapons become as (or almost as) effective[4] as lethal weapons (in terms of nonlethal weapons' capability to allow combatants to accomplish their mission), then it becomes necessary to consider what sorts of claims combatants have over their enemies. What I will argue below is that just war theory, in its current state, deems it morally impermissible to employ lethal weapons against a combatant when nonlethal weapons can accomplish the mission just as effectively. This suggests that combatants who are not wounded and not prisoners retain some of their rights, even though just war theory allows them to be harmed in order to accomplish the mission.

My claim (that combatants retain some of their rights) is compatible with principles articulated in the *jus in bello* area of just war theory. As I will argue below, just war theory condemns intentional harm that is not necessary for the accomplishment of the mission, proposing that military forces should not employ disproportionate force against enemy combatants. Instead, combatants do retain some right not to be harmed when this harm does not do anything to further mission accomplishment. The availability of effective nonlethal weapons makes it even more important to establish how combatant rights restrict military forces.

If the availability of effective nonlethal weapons requires a rethinking of combatant rights and what is prohibited in war, it also brings up another, and certainly more difficult and complex, area of concern focused on a higher level. Must states, especially technologically advanced ones, invest the resources necessary to produce effective nonlethal weapons in a large enough quantity to minimize harm to enemy combatants? That is, if combatants do maintain certain rights in war, and the widespread use of effective nonlethal weapons would better promote the respecting of these rights, does this mean that states have an obligation to devote the necessary resources to develop such weapons? It is much clearer and far less controversial to argue that conceptions of proportionality and permissibility of harming require the use of effective nonlethal weapons (when available) against combatants than it is to suggest that states have an obligation to devote resources to the development and deployment of nonlethal technology so that their military forces are able to accomplish their missions with minimal loss of not only noncombatant life, but also of enemy combatant life. I will devote the end of the paper to this difficult question.

In what follows I intend to frame future discussion about, and investigation of, these two questions, and suggest what a clear articulation of combatant rights and advanced nonlethal technology mean for just war theory. Before I begin, however, it is necessary to establish what I mean by effective nonlethal weapons. By effective, I mean that these weapons have the ability to accomplish the mission in a manner similar to that of lethal weapons. This need not be exactly to the same degree, but these nonlethal weapons should reliably provide effects similar (in terms of allowing combatants to accomplish their mission) to those attained by lethal weapons.[5] In a given situation, whether combatants employ lethal or nonlethal weapons does not make much difference (in a practical sense) as both provide the capability needed for the combatants to accomplish their mission.

What I am imagining here is the possibility of a weapon that enables a state's military forces to disable enemy combatants without employing lethal force. That is, these nonlethal weapons allow military forces to target enemy combatants and incapacitate them to such a degree that the nonlethal weapons make victory possible without much or any use of lethal weapons. How could this be possible? If nonlethal weapons enabled military forces to put large numbers of their enemy to sleep and disable their equipment for extended periods of time, combatants would have the capability to achieve victory without extensive use of lethal weapons. Once this was done, military forces could enter the country, taking the sleeping soldiers prisoner and permanently disabling the military equipment.[6] Or, imagine that this weapon did not exist on such a grand scale, but that some combatants were able to employ it during engagements, subduing enemy combatants and putting their equipment out of commission without employing lethal force. Such weapons might possess a stun setting like the weapons on Star Trek; this would allow combatants to render those they target unconscious or temporarily impair them to such a degree that combatants would be able to accomplish their mission without having to kill or seriously wound those they target.

While the capabilities I mention above are not yet available, much progress has been made with nonlethal weapon development. The United States military has a dedicated organization (the Joint Non-Lethal Weapons Directorate) to manage and develop nonlethal weapons, and there are currently many nonlethal weapons available in the American military forces' inventory. For example, the X26 Taser, which is used by many police departments, provides the capability to disable individuals for an extended period of time, allowing police or military forces to restrain the individual (without employing lethal force) and minimize his ability to harm others.[7] There is also the FN-303 Less Lethal Launching System, which fires a blunt projectile that can suppress targeted individuals.[8] In certain situations, employment of enhanced versions of these weapons might enable military forces to engage their enemy without killing them. That is, they disable enemy combatants long enough to enable mission accomplishment.

There are also weapons under development that offer a greater capability than those I mentioned above. The 40mm Human Electro-Muscular Incapacitation Projectile provides taser-like incapacitation without the tether, enabling it to be fired from further distances.[9] Used in mass, this weapon might be able to disable a large number of enemy combatants, allowing the combatants who fired the weapons the opportunity to capture their enemy. Another weapon under development, Active Dermal Technology, "emits a focused beam of wave energy that travels at the speed of light and produces an intolerable heating sensation that causes targeted individuals to flee."[10] This would allow combatants to push their enemy off of a position without having to employ lethal force. There is also the Multi-Frequency Radio-Frequency Vehicle Stopper, which produces aimed microwaves that have the capability to disable engines. If a military unit were equipped with enough of these weapons, it would be able to significantly undermine its enemy's ability to fight without having to resort to destroying vehicles and killing the combatants in them.[11]

Further enhancement of the nonlethal weapons in the inventory of many militaries has the potential to offer military forces the capability to accomplish their mission with minimal harm to combatants; however, much more work needs to be done to ensure that the weapons reliably allow mission accomplishment without additional risk to the combatants using the weapons. If this could be achieved, it would mean that wars could be fought with only a fraction of the death currently experienced.[12] What I argue, then, is that such weapons would change the obligation of combatants in a dramatic way. I will begin my examination of these questions with a look at why killing in war is generally thought to be permissible.

2. Justification for intentional harm to combatants and the obligation to use nonlethal weapons

Killing is generally prohibited; there has to be a good reason for intentionally inflicting lethal harm on another person. It is commonly accepted that defending yourself against unjust aggression provides a reason to inflict potentially lethal harm on another person. This conception of self defense has been used by some to justify the use of lethal and nonlethal harm by combatants during war. What I want to do now is lay out in detail this idea of how self defense provides justification for the harm intentionally inflicted by combatants. Using the ideas behind this justification as a starting point, I will then move to develop the claim that combatants have an obligation to employ nonlethal weapons if these weapons enable the combatants to accomplish the mission without employing lethal force. I will also show how this fits into the self-defense justification.

John Lango addresses the permissibility of intentionally harming combatants when he proposes the combatant nonimmunity principle, which is: "In the conduct of war, the intentional targeting of enemy combatants is morally permitted."[13] This formulation nicely captures the idea that combatants are different from noncombatants because combatants may be harmed. Yet, this principle does not allow unlimited harm to combatants, but instead is constrained by what Lango calls the minimum force principle, which he articulates as follows: "In the conduct of war, it is morally obligatory to use the minimum force necessary to realize a military objective."[14] Lango proposes that this principle "is different from the *jus in bello principle* of proportionality,"[15] that it goes beyond the proportionality principle in limiting the harm that may be done to combatants. He suggests that when it is possible to stop combatants with nonlethal weapons, then "the use of nonlethal weapons would be morally obligatory, because of the minimum force principle."[16] I agree with Lango that it is impermissible to harm combatants any more than required; that is, if other alternatives exist to stop enemy combatants that are less lethal, then combatants are obligated to employ these means.[17] Where I part ways with Lango is that I think that more can be said about why this is so and that the *jus in bello* proportionality requirement does more work than Lango gives it credit for doing. Additionally, I will argue that the state's obligation to develop such weapons may not be as easily determined as Lango proposes. First, however, it is necessary to explore why just war theorists have justified intentional harm to combatants and what this might mean for the obligation to use nonlethal weapons.

In *Just and Unjust Wars*, Michael Walzer claims that "The first principle of the war convention is that once war has begun, soldiers are subject to attack at any time (unless they are wounded or captured)."[18] He relies a great deal upon the idea of human rights and how the possession of these rights restricts the actions of others. These rights, however, do not apply to the combatant. Walzer believes that combatants may be attacked at any time because combatants "lose the rights they are supposedly defending. They gain war rights as combatants and potential prisoners, but they can now be attacked and killed at will by their enemies."[19] They have lost these rights "Simply by fighting" and because the combatant has "allowed himself to be made into a dangerous man."[20] For Walzer, then, the training and status of the combatants makes it permissible to harm them, even with lethal force, at any time during the war, except, of course, when they are prisoners and wounded. Walzer appears to be describing a complete forfeiture of rights; however, his other views qualify this claim, and it is this qualification that provides an opening for the idea that it is obligatory to use nonlethal weapons during war. I will discuss this in greater depth below.

Brian Orend takes the approach that a legitimate target (something or someone that may legitimately be intentionally harmed during war) "is anyone or anything engaged in harming."[21] This does not mean that the person or thing has to actually be in the act of harming at the time to be a legitimate target; what it relates to is the person or thing's capability to inflict harm that makes it a legitimate target. The target's capability to harm is what makes it permissible for combatants to inflict lethal harm. This forfeiture of rights comes from consenting to be a combatant and allowing oneself to become a dangerous person by being trained and equipped to inflict harm in the name of the state. David Rodin thinks that this sort of justification (one based on self defense that involves the forfeiture of right) is relevant only for individual harm, but not necessarily for harm on the international level, meaning that combatants engaging other combatants cannot use the same reasoning that is employed to justify individuals harming individuals. Despite this difference, it is worth noting Rodin's discussion of the justification for individual self defense as it provides a nice illustration for the justification of self defense and the reason that this justification does not lead to a complete forfeiture of rights for the attacker.

Rodin suggests that defensive rights are grounded in a "complex set of normative relationships between four entities: the subject (the holder of the right), the content (the defensive act), the object (the party against whom the right is held), and the end (the good or value which the defensive actions seek to protect or preserve)."[22] When the object does not respect the right of the subject, the right to which the subject is entitled, then it becomes permissible for the subject to inflict harm against the object in order to protect this right. The object's actions (failure to respect the subject's right) make it permissible for the subject to perform "an action which would otherwise be impermissible."[23] This action is inflicting intentional harm on the object; if necessary, this harm may be lethal. Rodin only thinks that this justifies individual self defense and does not provide justification for combatants to harm other combatants; however, as I mentioned above, this is still a useful illustration of the right to self defense. What makes Rodin's views different from cases in war are that the subject still maintains the right not to be harmed, whereas the combatant does not have this right (if Walzer is correct). Yet, what makes it similar is the identification of the particular action committed by the object (the object attempting to violate the rights of the subject); for Walzer, this entails allowing oneself to become a dangerous man and adopting combatant status, and for Orend, this involves assuming a role (combatant), the purpose of which is to engage in harm. While neither Walzer nor Orend believe that the combatant has a right not to be harmed, they do agree with Rodin that the actions of the attacker are important in the justification for intentional harm.

Jeff McMahan presents an interesting discussion on this matter as well. He distinguishes between a person deserving to be harmed and being liable to be harmed. If a person deserves to be harmed, McMahan suggests that "Giving him what he deserves is an end in itself."[24] That is, if Joe deserves to be harmed, then harming him is the end no matter what other consequences come about; one need not look any further to see any consequences that came about because of the harm inflicted. If a person is merely liable to be harmed, McMahan claims that harming is permissible "only if harming him will serve some further purpose."[25] Thus, if John is attacking you unjustly, he becomes liable to be harmed; the purpose of this harm is to defend yourself against John and end the unjust aggression. You may harm only to the extent necessary to achieve this goal; once this goal is achieved, it is no longer permissible to harm John. In terms of harming in war, McMahan suggests that in defensive war the goal is "to prevent the achievement of an unjust cause, and to defend people from harms that would otherwise be inflicted by unjust combatants in their efforts to achieve an unjust cause."[26] Once this goal is achieved, unjust combatants are no longer liable to be harmed.[27]

It is worth noting here that Walzer, Orend, Rodin, and McMahan, while having differing views, especially regarding the moral equality of soldiers, all seem to suggest that the harm that the combatant is about to cause provides strong support for the justification for harming the combatant. Walzer goes the furthest in linking the right to harm a person to this person's identity or role as a combatant; however, I think that even he would agree that what matters is that the person occupying the role has become dangerous (and it is a role linked to harming), and if it is possible to stop this danger or potential harming without killing this person, then this ought to be done. Thus, what makes it permissible to intentionally harm a combatant is the harm that he has the potential to and is likely to cause. The goal is to end the potential or likelihood of the combatant causing harm, not to kill the combatant. If a method allows for the achievement of this goal without killing (or risking killing) the combatant, then this method must be employed.

The permissible harm that may be inflicted upon attackers is not meant to be a punishment, meaning that the person who is inflicting unjust harm does not deserve to die and should not be killed when they can be otherwise prevented from carrying out the harm. What matters is that the harm is stopped. It seems required, then, that if it is possible to stop the perpetrator of the unjust harm with nonlethal weapons, allowing the perpetrator to be stopped and taken into custody, then this is a requirement. We can see this view in the concept of proportionality, which is a widely accepted tenet of the *jus in bello* area of just war theory.

Disproportionate force is impermissible because it is not necessary to accomplish the goal (stop unjust aggressors). McMahan writes: "if attacking him [the aggressor] is unnecessary for the prevention of or correction of a wrong for which he is responsible, or if it would cause him harm that would be excessive in relation to the achievement of one of those aims, then he is simply not liable to attack."[28] According to McMahan, it is not always permissible, even for combatants on the just side, to kill any combatant or to use lethal force in every situation. It is only permissible to employ the force necessary to prevent the wrongdoing. David Rodin argues this point as well, highlighting the importance of proportionality, when he writes that the liberty to inflict harm is constrained by three considerations, one of which is: "the defensive act is a proportionate, necessary response to an imminent threat of harm."[29] This constrains combatants by limiting the type of harm they may inflict.

Thus, even the fact that the subject's rights are being violated does not allow the subject to inflict disproportionate harm. The subject is limited to doing only what is necessary to secure his rights. As I mentioned above, this only applies to individual self defense (Rodin's case), but the point is still an important one to make as it suggests a limit to what may be done to an aggressor.[30] So, if one accepts the self-defense justification for intentional harm to combatants during war, this suggests that if enemy combatants may be stopped by dropping flyers (if, for example, previous experience has shown this tactic to be effective), and dropping flyers is something that your forces has the capability to do, then this must be done, rather than killing these combatants. Thus, even if combatants forfeit their rights not to be harmed by allowing themselves to be trained and equipped as members of a military force, they may not be harmed unnecessarily. They can only be harmed in order to accomplish certain goals, which are usually limited to certain military objectives and do not necessitate the death of the combatant. This goes beyond the prohibitions against harming prisoners of war and the wounded; it suggests that healthy combatants engaged in an attempt to harm their enemy, who can be stopped without performing an action that risks the death of these combatants, must be stopped by their enemy using this nonlethal method.

Walzer provides another example of proportionality that Orend describes and responds to in a manner that highlights the rights that combatants possess, even when they are still considered to be in the fight. Orend recalls Walzer's discussion of the "Highway of Death" in Kuwait where American and other allies targeted fleeing Iraqi forces who were returning to Iraq, most likely with the intent to establish a defensive line against the invading allied forces. Walzer suggests that this was excessive and disproportionate force; it was perhaps technically permissible because the Iraqis were combatants and had not surrendered, but the force was disproportionate because, as Orend describes it, the action was a "bloodbath."[31] What this example suggests, besides bolstering the intuition that the *jus in bello* proportionality requirement is a legitimate concept, is the idea that combatants, even ones who are still dangerous, have rights. Certainly these rights are not as strong as those of noncombatants; however, they are real and are of the sort that the use of nonlethal weapons would respect, assuming that the nonlethal weapons allowed military forces to accomplish their mission.

Beyond proportionality, Michael Walzer offers additional discussion that provides insight on the idea of combatant rights in his section entitled "Naked Soldiers." In it, he discusses five situations where it seems impermissible to attack and inflict lethal harm on enemy combatants, yet Walzer suggests that inflicting this harm is actually permissible. One instance involves a German soldier who, because he looked "funny" at the time when British soldiers had an opportunity to shoot him, escaped harm; the British soldiers could not bring themselves to shoot him. Walzer suggests that "A soldier who looks funny is not at that moment a military threat," or at least does not appear so.[32] Another case involved a naked soldier. Walzer quotes from *Goodbye to All That* in which Robert Graves writes that he had a clear shot at a German soldier taking a bath however he did not fire because he "disliked the idea of shooting a naked man."[33] Rather than fire, Graves gave the sniper rifle to the soldier next to him. Walzer also provides details of cases where an enemy combatant is not shot because his trousers were falling down,[34] sleepwalking,[35] and enjoying a cup of coffee in the morning.[36] All of these cases illustrate hesitation on the part of combatants to engage the enemy when the enemy is doing something that illustrates their humanity. This hesitation occurs even on the battlefield, when the enemy combatants who were not engaged would likely be a threat later that day or even minutes from the time they were first spotted.

Walzer proposes that their unwillingness to engage seems to "fly in the face of military duty"; additionally, he claims that "They are acts of kindness, and insofar as they entail any danger at all or lower minutely the odds for victory later, they may be likened to supererogatory acts."[37] Walzer claims that these actions do not "involve doing more than is morally required; they involve doing less than is permitted."[38] It was permissible for the combatants in the above scenarios to engage enemy combatants, as the enemy combatants were on the battlefield and were not wounded or prisoners. Yet combatants were hesitant to engage their enemy. This hesitation highlights an intuition, which grounds the above discussion on proportionality, that suggests that combatants maintain much of their humanity and its associated rights, even when engaged in combat. It highlights the difficulty that combatants have harming other combatants, which suggests the principle that combatants should not be unnecessarily harmed. In the cases above, it was certain that military necessity support harming the combatants; however, the difficulty experienced by those who had clear shots emphasizes the idea that even though these combatants were likely to be a threat, it was difficult to shoot them at a moment when they do not appear to be. The aim of targeting enemy combatants is not to kill or harm them; instead, it is to prevent the harm they are capable of causing so that one's mission may be accomplished. Mission accomplishment does not necessarily require lethal force. It only requires that the enemy be rendered incapable of inflicting harm and accomplishing their mission. If nonlethal weapons provide this capability, then it seems to violate the proportionally requirement and the rights that combatants possess as humans if the enemy is targeted with lethal weapons.

The justification for killing, the proportionality requirement, and the hesitation of combatants to harm others suggests that the possession of combatant status does not mean that a combatant may be targeted with lethal harm at any time. Involvement in war as a combatant does not eliminate all rights that the combatant possessed prior to adopting the combatant role. If effective nonlethal weapons became available in large numbers, then combatants would be required to use these nonlethal weapons instead of relying on lethal weapons. To use lethal weapons would be disproportionate and unnecessary to stopping enemy combatants. Combatants are owed respect as they maintain the right not to be disproportionately harmed, meaning that the use of a lethal weapon instead of a nonlethal one could be a violation of the combatant's rights.

Therefore, while a combatant does appear to forfeit his rights to a degree, this forfeiture does not appear to be absolute; combatant status does not automatically and absolutely make combatants liable to be killed at any time during the war. This means that combatants must not cause disproportionate harm to their enemy, which, in many circumstances, would require the use of nonlethal weapons if they are available. Questions remain, however, such as the risk that combatants must take to minimize harm. Are combatants, in a way that Walzer claims they are with noncombatants, required to assume some risk in seeking to minimize harm to noncombatants? Similarly, how much of a lower probability of mission accomplishment are combatants required to accept when choosing between lethal and nonlethal weapons? Another question concerns how we should view a combatant who engaged an enemy with a lethal weapon when it was clear that an available nonlethal weapon would have enabled the mission to be accomplished just as successfully. Is this combatant responsible for murder, or is it called disproportionate force and considered not as morally objectionable as murder? Finally, the scope of combatant rights would need to be laid out regarding how much is owed to them and how the responsibility they possess for allowing themselves to become dangerous men minimizes the rights they possess. The advances in the capabilities of nonlethal weapons suggest that further exploration of these questions is necessary if just war theory is to be relevant.

3. The obligation of the state

If combatants are required to use nonlethal weapons (rather than lethal weapons) when they are effective and allow for mission accomplishment, then another question that arises is whether states, especially technologically advanced ones, are obligated to invest the necessary resources into developing adequate numbers of effective nonlethal weapons. That is, if empirical evidence exists that it is possible to develop the types of nonlethal weapons that I have described, then are states doing something wrong by not investing adequate resources to produce such weapons? This second question focuses on the responsibility of the state and in a broad way considers what states owe enemy combatants in terms of reducing harm to them. If states recognize the importance of the issues I raise above, they acquire an obligation to commit resources to developing effective nonlethal weapons. A conflicting obligation, and a more important one for the state, is its responsibility to defend its citizenry, sovereignty, and territory.

To subscribe to any sort of contractarian view of political legitimacy means to accept the view that a state's citizens give up certain liberties when they submit to state authority in order to preserve certain rights. The liberties citizens give up include such things as the ability to do what one pleases, take what one wants, and harm others to promote one's self interest. Citizens also give up their own resources to the state, usually in the form of money that they earned through their labor. What citizens expect in return are, at a minimum, protection from each other and protection from other states. States that cannot do this lose legitimacy; when this happens, citizens are released from their obligation to obey the state's political authority because their contract with the state is void. We see this view especially in John Locke's approach to the social contract, but can also see it in Orend's idea of a minimally just state, where states are required to "make every reasonable effort to satisfy the human rights of their citizens."[39] States that are unable to do this are no longer legitimate.

One right that citizens possess is the right to live in communities free from interference from another state; consequently, the state's responsibility is to protect its citizens from other states. To provide the protection needed to secure this right, states collect taxes to create and sustain military forces. Because resources are limited (states must provide an array of services besides defense), there is only a finite amount of resources that can be spent on the creation and sustainment of military forces. Given the state's purpose, and the fact that citizens give the state resources to provide a national defense, these funds must be spent wisely and effectively. The state must provide training and weapons that allows its military forces to fulfill the state's defense needs. Right now, lethal weapons are the most effective and cost efficient manner of providing military forces with the means to meet the state's defense needs; these are the weapons that are in states' inventories, and these are the weapons that have the most research behind them.

Given the financial limitation to which states are subject, investing large amounts of their resources in developing effective nonlethal weapons (for the purpose of minimizing harm to enemy combatants) risks leaving the state unable to accomplish its purpose of defending itself and securing the rights of its citizens. That is, during the time it would take to develop effective nonlethal weapons with the capability and in sufficient amounts to minimize harm to enemy combatants, a state could possibly make itself vulnerable to attack. This constitutes a failure of the state to fulfill its obligation to its citizens, and this obligation certainly overrides any obligation the state has to minimize harm to enemy combatants. The state owes its citizens protection; to do this, it has to provide its military forces with the sorts of weapons these forces need to defend the state. If a state committed to the sort of effort needed to produce large quantities of effective nonlethal weapons, it is possible that the state would not fulfill this obligation. Additionally, the state also owes its military members (who are citizens of the state) some degree of protection on the battlefield; its combatants should not be required to accept unnecessary risk to minimize harm to the enemy's combatants. This state obligation to its military members might also be violated during the period when nonlethal weapons were being deployed due to neglect of the lethal weapons inventory.

Even if one argues that states are obligated to minimize harm to their opponents' noncombatants, possibly requiring states to invest heavily in nonlethal weapon, it is not clear that this obligation can best be fulfilled by the widespread use of nonlethal weapons. Protection of noncombatants can be accomplished by precision weapons, which many military forces already use, and restrictive rules of engagement, which many military forces already have in place. Therefore, it seems uncontroversial that if combatants can accomplish their mission by using nonlethal weapons against enemy combatants, they ought to. However, it is not clear that states have a strong obligation to minimize harm to enemy combatants, as this obligation is certainly overridden by the obligation to protect the state and its citizens, as well to provide the types of weapons its military forces need to accomplish the mission without excessive risk.

Given the responsibilities of the state that I propose above, a state would only be obligated to pursue nonlethal capability to the degree needed to minimize harm to enemy combatants on a large scale only if that state has an abundance of resources available for defense spending. A state, however, is not obligated to commit the resources necessary to achieve this capability if doing so will hinder its ability to fulfill its primary responsibility. This is the situation in which states find themselves given their numerous obligations to their citizens. However, the obligation to seek to minimize harm to enemy combatants still exists, and states should, in some way, conduct research on these types of weapons and consider the possibility of their widespread use. Consequently, while states may possess the obligation to take efforts to minimize the harm to combatants, fulfilling this obligation completely through the development of nonlethal weapons may not be achievable for the foreseeable future.

Further exploration of the state's responsibility will have to consider what exactly states owe to enemy combatants regarding minimizing harm to this group and how this relates to the development of nonlethal weapons. This obligation to enemy combatants will have to be balanced against the state's primary responsibility to its citizens and its military members. Another concern, which I noted in note 12, is whether this sort of development would have the practical effect of making wars more likely given that these weapons do not cause the sort of destruction and death that lethal weapons have previously caused. If the widespread development of these sorts of weapons makes war less appalling, thus promoting more unjust aggression, then perhaps this undermines the case that states have an obligation to develop them. Finally, when states go to war, there is a great deal of concern over probable noncombatant harm, but not much regarding harm caused to enemy combatants as well as the numbers of enemy combatants harmed. Is this appropriate, or should, even in a world with lethal weapons, enemy combatant harm be a factor in deciding whether or not to go to war? That is, if engaging in a war will most likely result in the death of large numbers of enemy combatants, should this be considered in terms of the proportionality criterion of *jus ad bellum*?

Technological advances promise to stretch, alter, and possibly undermine just war theory. Improved effectiveness of nonlethal weapons is one technological advance that will refocus the issues considered important for just war theorists. These weapons will elevate the importance of combatant rights and bring to the forefront the question of what combatants owe their enemies in terms of care as well as what states are required to do to minimize harm to the military forces that are opposing its forces.

Notes

1 The views expressed in this paper are those of the author and do not reflect the official policy position of the United States Government, the Department of Defense, the Department of the Army, or the United States Military Academy.
2 M. Walzer, *Just and Unjust Wars: A Moral Argument with Historical Illustrations*, 4th edn, New York: Basic Books, 2006, chapter 9; B. Orend, *The Morality of War* Toronto: Broadview Press, 2006, pp. 106–107.
3 M. Walzer, *Just and Unjust Wars*, p. 155
4 From this point when I designate nonlethal weapons as effective, I will mean as or almost as effective as lethal weapons.
5 From this point on, I will only use the term "nonlethal weapons," with the assumption that they are effective.
6 While I grant that such technology is not yet available, I do not think such a thing is impossible. Again, what I am assuming is that such technology would be as, or almost as, effective as lethal technology, allowing military forces to achieve victory with some or no additional risk.
7 United States Department of Defense Non-Lethal Weapons Program *X26 Taser*, 2012. Online. Available at: http://jnlwp.defense.gov/current/TaserX26.html (accessed 8 September, 2012).
8 United States Department of Defense Non-Lethal Weapons Program, *FN-303 Less Lethal Launching System*, 2012. Online. Available at: http://jnlwp.defense.gov/current/FN303.html (accessed 8 September, 2012).
9 United States Department of Defense Non-Lethal Weapons Program, *40mm Human Electro-Muscular Incapacitation Projectile*, 2012 Online. Available at: http://jnlwp.defense.gov/developing/40mmHEMI.html (accessed 8 September, 2012).
10 CNN, *L.A. Jail Tests "Intolerable Heat" Beam on Brawling Inmates*. Online. Available at: http://news.blogs.cnn.com/2010/08/24/l-a-jail-tests-intolerable-heat-beam-on-brawling-inmates (accessed 27 March, 2013).
11 United States Department of Defense Non-Lethal Weapons Program, *Multi-Frequency Radio-Frequency Vehicle Stopper*, 2012. Online. Available at: http://jnlwp.defense.gov/future/MultiFreq_RFVS.html (accessed 8 September, 2012).
12 One possible negative effect of these sorts of weapons would be that they make war more frequent, given that a war fought with lethal weapons would not be as devastating as it is now. This is certainly a consideration as to whether widespread effective nonlethal weapon availability is desirable.
13 J. Lango, "Nonlethal Weapons, Noncombatant Immunity, and Combatant Nonimmunity: A Study of Just War Theory," *Philosophia*, 38:3, 2010, p. 478.
14 Ibid., p. 482.
15 Ibid.
16 Ibid., p. 487.
17 I thank Nick Evans for his recommendation to clarify my point regarding the permissibility of seriously harming combatants when other alternatives exist.
18 M. Walzer, *Just and Unjust Wars*, p. 138
19 Ibid., p. 136
20 Ibid., p. 145
21 B. Orend, *The Morality of War*, p. 107

22 D. Rodin, *War & Self-Defense* Oxford: Oxford University Press, 2002, p. 99
23 Ibid.
24 J. McMahan, *Killing in War* Oxford: Clarendon Press, 2009, p. 8
25 Ibid.
26 Ibid.
27 I will remain agnostic on the idea that only combatants on the just side have the right to inflict harm in war, I will focus on the type of harm inflicted, which means that even combatants on the just side have an obligation to employ nonlethal force. Additionally, as I note about Rodin's argument, it seems morally preferable for the unjust side to use nonlethal force (as opposed to lethal force) if McMahan's argument is true,
28 J. McMahan, *Killing in War*, p. 10
29 D. Rodin, *War & Self-Defense*, p. 99
30 If Rodin is right regarding the morally problematic nature of harm in war, then this makes it all the more important to employ nonlethal weapons. Nonlethal harm, while still wrong, seems morally preferable to lethal harm.
31 B. Orend, *The Morality of War*, p. 119
32 M. Walzer, *Just and Unjust Wars*, p. 139
33 Ibid., p. 140
34 Ibid.
35 M. Walzer, *Just and Unjust Wars*, p. 141
36 Ibid., p. 143
37 Ibid.
38 Ibid.
39 B. Orend, *The Morality of War*, p. 36

References

CNN, *L.A. Jail Tests "Intolerable Heat" Beam on Brawling Inmates*. Online. Available at: http://news.blogs. cnn.com/2010/08/24/l-a-jail-tests-intolerable-heat-beam-on-brawling-inmates (accessed 27 March, 2013).

Lango, J. "Nonlethal Weapons, Noncombatant Immunity, and Combatant Nonimmunity: A Study of Just War Theory," *Philosophia*, 38:3, 2010, pp. 475–497.

McMahan, J. *Killing in War* Oxford: Clarendon Press, 2009.

Norma, R. *Ethics, Killing and War* Cambridge: Cambridge University Press, 1995

Orend, B. *The Morality of War* Toronto: Broadview Press, 2006.

Rodin, D. *War & Self-Defense* Oxford: Oxford University Press, 2002.

United States Department of Defense Non-Lethal Weapons Program, *40mm Human Electro-Muscular Incapacitation Projectile*. 2012. Online. Available at: http://jnlwp.defense.gov/developing/40mmHEMI. html (accessed 8 September, 2012),

United States Department of Defense Non-Lethal Weapons Program *FN-303 Less Lethal Launching System*. 2012. Online. Available at: http://jnlwp.defense.gov/current/FN303.html (accessed 8 September, 2012).

United States Department of Defense Non-Lethal Weapons *Multi-Frequency Radio-Frequency Vehicle Stopper*. 2012. Online. Available at: http://jnlwp.defense.gov/future/MultiFreq_RFVS.html (accessed 8 September, 2012).

United States Department of Defense Non-Lethal Weapons Program *X26 Taser*. 2012. Online. Available at: http://jnlwp.defense.gov/current/TaserX26.html (accessed 8 September, 2012).

Walzer, M. *Just and Unjust Wars: A Moral Argument with Historical Illustrations*, 4th edn, New York: Basic Books, 2006.

23

EDUCATIONAL IMPLICATIONS OF THE POTENTIAL FOR HOSTILE APPLICATIONS OF ADVANCES IN NEUROSCIENCE

Malcolm Dando

1. Introduction

Quietly, out of public attention, the hopes, indeed the expectations, of many of those involved in the Seventh Five-Year Review Conference of the Biological and Toxin Weapons Convention (BTWC) for a significant strengthening of the regime preventing the hostile misuse of the modern life sciences did not come to fruition in the modest result achieved in December 2011.[1]

It might be argued, nevertheless, that the agreement to have a "Review of developments in the field of science and technology related to the Convention" as one of the three new Standing Agenda Items (SAIs) for the annual meetings at Expert and State Party levels through to the next Review Conference in 2016 was a step forward.[2] Thus the two sub-items under this SAI on:

(d) voluntary codes of conduct and other measures to encourage responsible conduct by scientists, academia and industry; [and]
(e) education and awareness-raising about risks and benefits of life sciences and biotechnology;

could indeed, if used well, help to strengthen the prohibition regime.

Given that some 12 countries, including the UK and USA Depositary States, had clearly recognized the deficiency in awareness and education of life scientists in an official Working Paper for the Review Conference by stating that:

7(b) While the existence of a well-developed sense for aspects related to (bio-) safety among students and practising life scientists has been repeatedly confirmed, there is, in general, a limited level of awareness of the risk of malevolent misuse of the biological sciences.
(c) Life scientists do not often consciously consider the possibility that their specific work could be of relevance to a biological weapons programme or otherwise misused to cause harm to people, animals, or plants or to render critical resources unusable.[3]

it seemed likely that the SAI would be used to correct this deficiency.

The Working Paper also recalled the agreement in 2008 on a series of measures that could be used to achieve this aim through activities that, for example, would include:

(i)   explaining the risks associated with the potential misuse of the biological sciences and biotechnology;

(ii) covering the moral and ethical obligations of Convention incumbent on those using the biological sciences;

(iii) providing guidance on the types of activities which could be contrary to the aims of the Convention and relevant national laws and regulations and international law.

So there also appeared to be a well thought through path that could be followed by States Parties in their deliberations and that "Best Practice" could quickly evolve and be implemented around the world.

Yet the history of the very slow progress in engaging the life science community in protecting their work from hostile misuse since bioterrorism and biowarfare again became a major concern for States following 9/11 and the anthrax letter attacks in the USA strongly suggests that, on the other hand, it was unlikely that any change of great significance would be seen by the time of the Eighth Review Conference of the BTWC in 2016.[4] Planning for such a continuation of this "very slow progress" scenario may, however, have to be radically revised following the shambles that the international scientific community made of dealing with the publication of work that led to the creation of a mammalian-transmissible lethal H5N1 influenza virus in late 2011 and early 2012.

2. H5N1 influenza

By April 2012 602 cases of human infection with highly pathogenic avian influenza H5N1 virus had been confirmed by laboratory analysis and 355 of these people had died.[5] However, sustained human-to-human transmission of the virus had not been found and thus the potential for a major pandemic, whilst of concern, was not an immediate threat. Then, in late 2011 papers were submitted for publication by groups in the United States and The Netherlands that demonstrated how the virus could be modified to make it contagious through the air in mammals. Given the rather obvious security implications the papers were referred to the US National Science Advisory Board for Biosecurity (NSABB) which had been set up to deal with such problems after the "Fink Report" on *Biosecurity Research in an Age of Terrorism* in 2004.[6] The Fink Report had, in part, suggested that at least seven classes of experiment raised such dual-use concerns that they should be reviewed for their *biosecurity* implications. These experiments:

1.   Would demonstrate how to render a vaccine ineffective.
2.   Would confer resistance to therapeutically useful antibiotics or antiviral agents.
3.   Would enhance the virulence of a pathogen or render a nonpathogen virulent.
4.   Would increase the transmissibility of a pathogen.
5.   Would alter the host range of a pathogen.
6.   Would enable the evasion of diagnostic/detection methodologies.
7.   Would enable the weaponization of a biological agent or toxin.

The NSABB deliberated over the two H5N1 papers for many hours in late 2011 and decided that they should not be published in full. As the Chair stated, "If this virus were to escape by error or terror, we must ask whether it would cause a pandemic."[7] The experiments clearly fell into the fourth of the Fink categories and, given the difficulty of quickly producing quantities of vaccine, there was a possibility of a pandemic.

Subsequently, a meeting of experts at the World Health Organization (WHO) disagreed with the NSABB. When the Board considered amended papers again it agreed to their publication—in the case of The Netherland's work, only by a split vote—and they were duly published in the prestigious journals *Nature* and *Science*. However, events were by then moving beyond the scientists; the US National Institutes of Health had funded both projects and no concerns had been raised until the publication stage. A senior Congressman, Jim Sensenbrenner, directed a series of searching questions to the White House science advisor:

1. How does NSABB weigh the potential risks and benefits of dual use research? When does it advocate against publication?
2. What systems exist to identify and, if necessary, control early stage dual use research?
3. What is the government's current system for disseminating legitimate dual use research worldwide? How is that system being implemented with respect to the articles [on H5N1] in question?
4. Is the NIH's review system adequate to identify potentially dangerous dual use research? Why did it fail to identify the avian flu research until it was completed and submitted for publication? [8]

These are indeed very difficult questions and show why the NSABB members had deliberated for such a long time over the H5N1 papers.

Interestingly, in 2007 the NSABB had published a major paper, *Proposed Framework for the Oversight of Dual Use Life Science Research: Strategies for Minimizing the Potential Misuse of Research Information*. It is important here to stress the broad scope of the NSABB's concerns:

> Because arguably *most life sciences research has some potential for dual use*, the NSABB strove to delineate a threshold that would identify that subset of life science research with the highest potential for yielding knowledge, products, or technology that could be misapplied. [9]

Furthermore, the board added that they were concerned with "the potential for threats to public health and safety, agricultural crops and other plants, animals, the environment, and/or materiel."

The *experiments* of concern described by the Fink Report were the starting point for the Board's own system, but it must be stressed that the NSABB's own categories "are descriptors of information, products, or technologies that, *if produced from life science research*, might define that research as meeting the criterion for being dual use research of concern." The NSABB categories are therefore knowledge, products or technologies resulting from research that could:

1. Enhance the harmful consequences of a biological agent or toxin.
2. Disrupt immunity or the effectiveness of an immunization without clinical and/or agricultural justification.
3. Confer to a biological agent or toxin, resistance to clinically and/or agriculturally useful prophylactic or therapeutic interventions against that agent or toxin or facilitate their ability to evade detection mmethodologies.
4. Increase the stability, transmissibility, or the ability to disseminate a biological agent or toxin.
5. Alter the host range or tropism of a biological agent or toxin.
6. Enhance the susceptibility of a host population.
7. Generate a novel pathogenic agent or toxin or reconstitute an eradicated or extinct biological agent. [10]

So rather than applying to a set of mainly microbiology/immunology experiments these categories appear to be the result of an attempt to generalise the system across a much wider range of the life and associated sciences. In Appendix 4 to the report the NSABB also provided a list of "Points To Consider in Risk Assessment and Management of Research That Is Potentially Dual Use of Concern."[11]

In the event the US Government moved quickly in the spring of 2012 following the decision on the amended H5N1 papers and issued a new United States policy on oversight of life science dual-use research of concern. The purpose of this policy was stated to be "to establish regular review of United States Government funded or conducted research with certain high-consequence pathogens and toxins for its potential to be dual use research of concern."[12] So, for the moment, the impact of this policy might be seen as being restricted to a sub-set of the life sciences. However, the policy "will be updated, as needed, following domestic dialogue, engagement with our international partners, and input from interested communities including scientists, national security officials, and global health specialists."[13] Now, as the H5N1 experiments are most unlikely to be the last to be of dual-use concern it can be reasonably expected that this US policy will evolve and expand to other countries (for example, through meetings at the BTWC in regard to the new SAI on science and technology).

Dual-use research of concern has been defined by the NSABB as:

> Research that, *based on current understanding, can be reasonably anticipated* to provide knowledge, products, or technologies *that could be directly misapplied by others* to pose a threat to public health and safety, agricultural crops and other plants, animals, the environment, or materiel.[14]

So not only is the current US policy restricted to a sub-set of life science research, but also to a sub-set of that sub-set which based on our understanding today can reasonably be expected to be directly misapplied.

The question that naturally arises, then, is what has all of this to do with neuroscientists? One point of clarification is needed before turning to that issue: "toxin," in the perspective of the BTWC, does not mean what most scientists would understand. As the World Health Organization noted, the Convention does not define "toxin" but "its travaux préparatoires shows that the term is intended to mean toxic chemicals produced by living organisms." Thus:

> there are chemicals that occur naturally in the human body that would have toxic effects if administered in large enough quantity. Where a scientist might see a bioregulator, say, the treaty would see a poisonous substance produced by a living organism, in other words a toxin.[15]

Thus many signalling molecules, such as neurotransmitters and their analogues, would come under the purview of the prohibition embodied in the BTWC and be regarded as toxins if they were subject to misuse.

3. Neuroweapons

Of course, it is our artificial system of classification that separates the nervous system from the endocrine (hormonal) and the immune systems. The body functions as a whole and disturbance of one of these systems likely will affect the others, for example in the fever induced by many infections. Thus the list of biological and toxin agents that can interfere with the operations of the nervous system is extensive.[16] Some of these agents, such as Venezuelan Equine Encephalitis (VEE), and toxins, such as Botulinum neurotoxin, were certainly weaponized in the huge offensive biological weapons programmes of major states in the last century.[17] Moreover, Botulinum neurotoxin and toxin-producing strains *of Clostridium botulinum* are clearly listed as being within the scope of the new US oversight system.[18]

Despite its weaknesses—in the lack of a verification system and major international organisation—the BTWC does provide a strong basis for a prohibitory norm in its Article I, which states:

> Each State Party to this Convention undertakes never in any circumstances to develop, produce, stockpile or otherwise acquire or retain:
>
> (1) Microbial or other biological agents, or toxins whatever their origin or method of production, of types and in quantities that have no justification for prophylactic, protective or other peaceful purposes;
>
> (2) Weapons, equipment or means of delivery designed to use such agents or toxins for hostile purposes or in armed conflict.[19]

Yet if neurotechnology is going to be the basis of a major industrial revolution this century, as indeed appears possible, the upholding of this prohibitory norm cannot be guaranteed.[20]

Then, as Professor Meselson, the eminent Harvard University biologist who has long worked to help preserve the non-proliferation norm, argued in 2000, a wide range of grim possibilities would arise. As he wrote "A world in which these capabilities are widely employed for hostile purposes would be a world in which the very nature of conflict had radically changed. Therein could be unprecedented opportunities for violence, coercion, repression, or subjugation."[21] And it is not difficult to find official concerns over the potential malign implications of advances in neuroscience. For example, the UK's contribution to the background paper on science and technology for the Seventh Review Conference of the BTWC stated, in a section on neuroscience:

> Developments in this area could also result in the identification of compounds with potential for misuse as biological or toxin weapons agents since drugs acting on the brain to produce toxic or incapacitating effects could also have utility in a BW programme. Methods to facilitate delivery of such agents could also be exploited for harmful purposes, for example, to facilitate the entry of peptide neurotoxins across the BBB [Blood Brain Barrier].[22]

More specifically, as is well known, the US report, *Emerging Cognitive Neuroscience and Related Technologies*, gave examples such as:

> Pharmacological agents are not used as weapons of mass effect, because their large-scale deployment is impractical: it is currently impossible to get an effective dose to a combatant. However, technologies that could be available in the next 20 years would allow dispersal of agents in delivery vehicles that would be analogous to a pharmacological cluster bomb or a land mine.[23]

Nevertheless, as the UK's paper noted, "many of the benefits and risks of advances in neuroscience lie in the future." So, "it is timely to consider issues related to the governance of this dual-use technology area."

Unfortunately, it is not possible to be as sanguine about the immediate impact of advances in neuroscience in regard to the more recent—and widely considered to be stronger—Chemical Weapons Convention (CWC). Like the BTWC, the CWC appears to contain a sweeping prohibition of the hostile misuse of chemistry. Article I of the CWC states "1. Each State Party to this Convention undertakes never under any circumstances: (a) To develop, produce, otherwise acquire, stockpile or retain chemical weapons, or transfer, directly or indirectly, chemical weapons to anyone."[24] Article II then defines chemical weapons, in part, as: "(a) Toxic chemicals and their precursors, except where intended for purposes not prohibited under this Convention, as long as the types and quantities are consistent with such purposes." The Article goes on to define a toxic chemical as:

> Any chemical which through its chemical action on life processes can cause death, temporary incapacitation or permanent harm to humans or animals. This includes all such chemicals, regardless of their origin or method of production, and regardless of whether they are produced in facilities, in munitions or elsewhere.

There seems, therefore, to be an overlap in that both the BTWC and the CWC cover toxins (broadly defined).

One might think that this apparent overlap between the BTWC and the CWC should strengthen the prohibition; in fact, there has been considerable concern that a potential loophole in the CWC will, in fact, greatly weaken the prohibition against chemical (and biological) weapons. This arises because Article II.9(d) states that one peaceful, and therefore allowable, purpose is: "Law enforcement including domestic riot control." Now the use of standard riot control agents for domestic purposes is certainly allowed, but "law enforcement" is not defined. Some people have therefore argued that a wider category of incapacitating law enforcement chemical agents—such as the fentanyl(s) used to break the 2002 Moscow theatre siege—could also be legal. This idea, if accepted, would mean that advances in neuroscience could be exploited to develop new kinds of law enforcement agents, and this would surely weaken the prohibition as a whole.[25] How, for example, would an offensive CW programme be distinguished from a law enforcement programme?

The dangers here were well illustrated in a recent publication by the NATO Standardization Agency. This stated:

> *Incapacitating agents.* These agents cause temporary disabling conditions which can be either physical or mental and can be viewed normally as non-lethal … Incapacitating agents are not, by their legal definition, considered to be chemical agents when used for law enforcement purposes, such as riot control.[26]

In other words, law enforcement agents—novel incapacitants—are legal under the CWC, according to this document.

While the prohibitory norm against the development and use of chemical and biological weapons is embodied in the BTWC and CWC at the international level it has to be reinforced by national implementation of the Conventions, export controls, biodefense, and, as has become increasingly clear, the development of means to prevent misuse of ongoing civil research. For this reason effective engagement of life scientists is clearly needed. We do not have detailed studies of what neuroscientists know about the BTWC and CWC and about their responsibilities under these conventions. However, it is clear that, as for most life scientists, these security issues are rarely covered in their education and thus they are unlikely to be aware of these dangers and of the need to lend their expertise to supporting and developing the prohibitions embodied in the conventions.[27]

Whilst biological pathogens, toxins and certain chemical agents may be the most obvious means that could be used to target the nervous system, unfortunately for neuroscientists, and the neuroethicists who might wish to help them, chemical and biological weapons are not the only systems that could be employed today. The UK Royal Society's Brian Waves Module 3, on *Neuroscience, Conflict and Security*,[28] concentrated its attention on neuropharmacological agents, in view of the pressing policy issues related to the CWC, but it also noted concerns about other so-called non-lethal weapons such as the Active Dermal System (ADS) "which employs a millimetre wave beam to heat the skin and cause a painful burning sensation." Another such weapon is the Long Range Acoustic Device (LRAD), which can produce powerful and painful sound at a distance. Though the development of these weapons is not related directly to current advances in neuroscience, they certainly depend on the nervous system for their action. According to the BBC, an LRAD device, which has been deployed in other such situations, was to be deployed at the London Olympic Games.[29]

However, States do not have the right to deploy any weapon they wish. Indeed, as the Royal Society Brain Waves Module 3 explains, there is a complex set of international laws which apply to weapon systems deployment and use. International Humanitarian Law (IHL), or the laws of war, apply to international armed conflicts and to armed conflicts of a non-international type. IHL has a set of general rules such as: "the use of weapons which are by their nature indiscriminate is prohibited" and "the use of means and methods of warfare which are of a nature to cause superfluous injury or unnecessary suffering are prohibited."[30] It is not difficult to see how large-scale beaming of microwaves and high intensity sound could raise questions in regard to these rules. Also, IHL applies to all situations and involves, for example, the right to freedom from torture and there have been considerable concerns expressed over the potential misuse of so-called "non-lethal" weapons in this regard.

So although a weapon system may not be subject to a specific treaty such as the BTWC or the CWC it cannot be assumed that it is not subject to regulation or that the legal and ethical arguments concerning the development and use of such weapons are simple to resolve. Yet it is against that background that the increasing understanding of the nervous system and the development of new neurotechnology—that could have other than beneficial purposes—have to be approached.

4. Future neuroweapons?

In the first module of the UK Royal Society's Brain Waves project an attempt was made to "provide a primer of current developments in neuroscience and highlight interesting issues and questions for society and policy." The module ended with an essay by Professor Andrew Stirling on the "Governance of Neuroscience: Challenges and Responses." In the essay Stirling suggested that past experience in governance of emerging technologies had led to the recognition of characteristic syndromes such as "See no evil" (that is, to focus only on the beneficial impacts of these new technologies). As he noted: "A particular technology may realise its initial promise, but this very feasibility may itself create opportunities for deliberate or inadvertent misuse."[31] Significantly, he continued: "Although readily foreseeable in the same terms as benign uses, malign applications are typically understated in regulatory assessment ... Yet easily anticipated effects may be of a magnitude that seriously jeopardises overall benefits." So it is necessary to be very careful not to treat possible misuses of advances in neuroscience lightly. In that regard it is clear that the term "dual-use" does not really capture all of the possibilities that need to be considered. For example, advances in neuroscience may not lead to weapon systems but to insights that allow intelligence or battlefield domination. Also, advances in neuroscience that find application in military neurotechnology may cause problems in civil society through what has been called "the reverse dual-use dilemma."[32] Perhaps then, in discussing the potential for the future misuse of advances in neuroscience, it is better to have a concept of multi-use (for both civil and military spheres) in mind.

It is certainly not difficult to see how some of the advances likely to arise in coming decades could be subject to misuse. For example, Steven Rose, in his study of the *Prospects and Perils of the New Brain Sciences: a twenty year timescale*, had these in a list of nine probably significant outcomes:

1   Development of human-machine interfaces, implanted chips and prostheses and methods of focussed transcranial brain stimulation.
3   Increased use of brain imaging techniques both for diagnostic and prognostic purposes and surveillance, for both civil and military purposes.
5   New and better targeted psychoactive drugs to treat neurological diseases such as Alzheimer's as well as depression, anxiety and related conditions, based on greater insights into these disorders through advances in neurogenetics and neurochemistry.[33]

And in the study edited by Jonathan Tucker on *Innovation, Dual Use and Security: Managing the Risks of Emerging Biological and Chemical Technologies* both of the two historical case studies and three of the fourteen contemporary case studies clearly related directly to advances in neuroscience.[34]

More specifically, in a recent survey paper Tennison and Moreno have suggested that Brain-Computer Interfaces, Warfighter Enhancement, Neuroscientific Deception, Detection and Interrogation are all subjects that should come under scrutiny in considerations of "Neuroscience, Ethics, and National Security,"[35] and Zilinskas has raised concerns about possible Russian interest in novel psychotronic weapons.[36] And that is to leave out the more far-reaching possibilities of advances being used to develop autonomous killing machines that can make "moral" decisions in warfare.[37] In short, could we be moving, without full consideration of the consequences, into a period of "neurowars," which:

would engage cognitive forces, minds-in-conflict over a landscape of virtual spaces where there is only virtuality, digital worlds, or pure consciousness, yet the manifestations and artifices of such combat occur in the realm of the material.[38]

But that could be the road on which we are moving unless careful consideration is given to the potential misuse of such emerging technologies as neuroscience.

5. Responsible conduct of research

It can be reasonably argued that the scientific community has begun to take more seriously what might be called the "internal" aspects of responsible conduct of research such as data acquisition and management, human subjects, animal welfare and research misconduct.[39] However, it is also clear that the community has not yet faced up to what might be called the "external" aspects of responsible conduct: how to communicate to non-scientists, how to act responsibly as an advocate for science, and how to deal with emerging technologies—including when there is a possibility of misuse for hostile purposes.

When one of the two H5N1 papers that had caused the extensive debate about oversight was eventually published in *Science* there were a set of accompanying commentary papers, and amongst these was one concerned with the problems and prospects of implementing the new US policy for dealing with dual use.[40] Whilst not avoiding the arguments that had been made for and against the new policy the author argued strongly for avoiding polarisation of the debate about oversight once again in the future. And in this regard the paper ended on a positive note: "The proposed modification to the Select Agent Rule adds additional requirements for biosafety and biosecurity training for those personnel with access to these dangerous pathogens." As the institutions dealing with dangerous pathogens already carry out extensive training for personnel, the author added: "it does not seem unreasonable to add a discussion of the risks of dual-use research as a component of that required training."

Gradually, also, there are a number of open-source resources that can be used for such training being made available on the web. Certainly, it seems necessary to underpin the development of oversight systems or codes of conduct that are found necessary in different countries with educational measures that ensure that the scientific community is able to engage effectively in the process of producing and implementing such systems.

On first sight it might indeed look like a relatively simple task to develop and implement such educational material. If the security community involved in the international and national aspects of the chemical and biological non-proliferation regime and the growing community of neuroethicists and neuroscientists were in good communication with each other it would surely be possible, for example, to devise an open-source educational module that could be made available so that lecturers in universities around the world would simply have to add such material, as they found appropriate, to their university courses. However, the polarised debate over the publication of the H5N1 papers illustrates all too clearly how little communication there is between scientists, ethicists and the security community in regard to biosecurity.

Moreover, the material that has been developed to help with awareness-raising and education about dual-use issues for life scientists has obviously so far been directed predominantly at microbiologists,[41] and it cannot be assumed that such material will be effective in engaging a different specialist community like neuroscientists—in fact it should be assumed that it will not work well.

So what kind of material might have to be developed to engage the interest of neuroscientists? First, surely, it is necessary to acknowledge that the problem of dual use could be much more complex in regard to neuroscience than in regard to microbiology as hostile misuse could be directed at psychological damage as well as at physiological harm. Nevertheless, it seems possible that the same general approach as was taken for the Bradford Education Module Resource might be effective. This approach is very broad, not seeing the problem as one of bioterrorists misusing high technology today, but rather advances in modern biology becoming more and more used for hostile purposes over coming decades, first by states and then by sub-state groups. Thus the problem is seen to require not just control of individual dual-use experiments but the effective implementation of the chemical and biological nonproliferation regime that is embodied in the BTWC and the CWC and bolstered by a web of associated policies at the national and international level.

This approach has the advantage that the lecture series can begin with a selection of the history of misuse focused on the scientific aspects (such as lethal and incapacitating chemical and biological weapons) that will be of most immediate interest to the specialist group of neuroscientists. That can then be followed by an outline of how the nonproliferation regime has evolved, and then, in that context, the current focus on the problem of dual use and of responsible conduct of research can make much more sense. Following these sections of the lecture series the idea of the need for the continuing development of the regime and how that can best be done may sensibly be discussed to provide a basis for scientists' longer term engagement throughout their careers.

6. Conclusion

The Chairman of the first Experts Meeting of the 2012–2015 Inter Sessional Process (ISP) of the BTWC suggested in a letter of June 2012 to State Parties that the two sub-topics of the science and technology SAI agreed at the Seventh Review Conference in December 2011 on codes and oversight, and education and awareness-raising should be dealt with in the meetings of 2012, 2013 and 2015. Thus, even given the crowded agenda of these annual meetings, there should be enough time for State Parties to examine a wide variety of approaches to oversight and education. No doubt some States will follow the US in instituting oversight systems that will need improved levels of awareness and education. Yet even those States that decide to move more slowly on codes and oversight would do well to embark on enhanced education on dual use for their neuroscientists either as a useful measure of biosecurity itself or as a means of laying the basis for further action that may be deemed necessary later as the revolution in neuroscience continues.

Notes

1 G.S. Pearson and N.A. Sims, *The BTWC Review Conference: A Modest Outcome*. Review Conference Paper No. 31, University of Bradford, March 2012.
2 State Parties to the Convention on the Prohibition of the Development, Production and Stockpiling of Bacteriological (Biological) and Toxin Weapons and on Their Destruction, *Final Document of the Seventh Review Conference*, BWC/CONF.VII/7, United Nations: Geneva, 2011. Available at: http://daccess-dds-ny.un.org/doc/UNDOC/GEN/G12/600/60/PDF/G1260060.pdf?OpenElement (accessed 21 August 2012).
3 Australia, Canada, Japan, New Zealand, Republic of Korea and Switzerland (on behalf of the "JACKSNNZ") and Kenya, Sweden, Ukraine, the United Kingdom of Great Britain and Northern Ireland and the United States of America, *Revised: Possible Approaches to Education and Awareness-raising among Life Scientists*, BWC/CONF.VII/WP.20/Rev.1, United Nations: Geneva, 2011.
4 Royal Society, *Neuroscience, Conflict And Security*, Brain Waves Module 3, Royal Society, London, 2012.
5 T. Novossiolova, Minehata, M. and Dando, M.R., "The Creation of a Contagious H5N1 Influenza Virus: Implications for the Education of Life Scientists," *The Journal of Terrorism Research*, 3:1, 2012, pp. 39–51.
6 Committee on Research Standards and Practices to Prevent the Destructive Application of Biology, *Biotechnology Research in an Age of Terrorism*. Washington, DC: National Academies Press, 2004.
7 T. Novossiolova et al., "The Creation of a Contagious H5N1 Influenza Virus."
8 D. Malakoff, "Senior U.S. Lawmaker Leaps into H5N1 Flu Controversy. *Science Insider*," 4 March 2012. Available at: http://news.sciencemag.org/scienceinsider/2012/03/senior-us-lawmaker-leaps-into-h5.html (accessed 21 August 2012).
9 National Science Advisory Board for Biosecurity, *Proposed Framework for the Oversight of Dual Use Life Science Research: Strategies for Minimizing the Potential Misuse of Research Information*, NSABB: Washington, DC, 2007 (emphasis added), p. 16.
10 National Science Advisory Board for Biosecurity, *Proposed Framework* (emphasis added), pp. 18–19.
11 National Science Advisory Board for Biosecurity, *Proposed Framework*, pp. 51–52.
12 United States Government Policy for Oversight of Life Sciences Dual Use Research of Concern. Online. Available at: http://oba.od.nih.gov/oba/biosecurity/pdf/united_states_government_policy_for_oversight_of_durc_final_version_032812.pdf (accessed 21 August 2012).
13 Ibid.
14 National Science Advisory Board for Biosecurity, *Proposed Framework*, p. 17 (emphases added).

15 World Health Organisation, *Public Health Response to Biological and Chemical Weapons*, 2nd edn, WHO: Geneva, 2004. See Annex 2: Toxins, pp. 214–216.
16 For a detailed listing of agents and effects see J. Giordano and R. Wuzman, "Neurotechnologies as Weapons in National Intelligence and Defense—An Overview," *Synthesis: A Journal of Science, Technology, Ethics and Policy*, 2012, T:55–T:71.
17 M.R. Dando, *Biological Warfare in the 21st Century: Biotechnology and the Proliferation of Biological Weapons*, Brassey's, London, 1994.
18 See the list of agents and toxins under Section III: Scope, National Science Advisory Board for Biosecurity, Proposed Framework, p. 2.
19 For official documentation on the BTWC see http://www.opbw.org (accessed 21 August 2012).
20 R.H. Carlson, *Biology is Technology*, Cambridge, MA: Harvard University Press, 2010.
21 M. Meselson, "Averting the Hostile Exploitation of Biotechnology," *The CBW Conventions Bulletin*, 48, 2000, pp. 16–19.
22 State Parties to the Convention on the Prohibition of the Development, Production and Stockpiling of Bacteriological (Biological) and Toxin Weapons and on Their Destruction, *New Scientific and Technological Developments Relevant to the Convention*, BWC/CONF.VII/INF.3/Add.1, United Nations: Geneva, 2011, pp. 21–38.
23 Committee on Military and Intelligence Methodology for Emergent Neurophysiological and Cognitive/Neural Science Research in the Next Two Decades, *Emerging Cognitive Neuroscience and Related Technologies*, National Academies Press, Washington: DC, 2008, p. 137. Chart 5–2.
24 For official documentation on the CWC see http://www.opcw.org (accessed 21 August 2012).
25 A. Kelle, K. Nixdorff and M.R. Dando, *Controlling Biological Weapons: Adapting Multilateral Arms Control for the 21st Century*, Basingstoke: Palgrave, 2006.
26 NATO Standardization Agency, *Allied Joint Doctrine for Chemical, Biological, Radiological, and Nuclear Defence*, AJP-3.8, Edited Version 1, NATO: Brussels, 2012 (emphasis added).
27 Royal Society, *Neuroscience, Conflict and Security*, Royal Society of London, 2012. Online. Available at: http://www.royalsociety.org/uploadedFiles/Royal_Society_Content/policy/projects/brain-waves/2012-02-06-BW3.pdf (accessed 21 August 2012).
28 Ibid.
29 BBC, "Sonic Device Deployed in London during Olympics," *BBC News*, 12 May 2012. Online. Available at: http://www.bbc.co.uk/news/uk-england-london-18042528 (accessed 21 August 2012).
30 S. Casey-Maslen, *Non-kinetic-energy Weapons Termed 'Non-lethal': A Preliminary Assessment under International Humanitarian Law and International Human Rights Law*, Geneva Academy of International Humanitarian Law and Human Rights: Geneva, October 2010.
31 A. Stirling, "Governance of Neuroscience: Challenges and Response," in Brain Waves Module 1: *Neuroscience, Society and Policy*, Royal Society: London, 2011, pp. 87–97.
32 G. Marchant and L. Gulley, "National Security Neuroscience and the Reverse Dual-Use Dilemma," *AJOB Neuroscience*, 1:2, 2010, pp. 20–22.
33 S.P.R. Rose, *Prospects and Perils of the New Brain Sciences: a twenty year timescale*, Royal Society Policy Lab, Royal Society, London, 2009. Available at: http://royalsociety.org/policy/policylab (accessed 21 August 2012).
34 J.B. Tucker (ed.), *Innovation, Dual Use and Security: Managing the Risks of Emerging Biological and Chemical Technologies*. Cambridge, MA: The MIT Press, 2012.
35 M.N. Tennison and J. D. Moreno, "Neuroscience, Ethics, and National Security: The State of the Art," *PLoS Biology*, 10:3, 2012.
36 R. Zilinskas, "Take Russia to 'Task' on Bioweapons Transparency," *Nature Medicine*, 18:6, 2012, p. 14.
37 M.S. Pritchard, "Moral Machines?" *Science and Engineering Ethics*, 18:2, 2012, pp. 411–417.
38 J. Conton, "Forward: Toward Our Neurofuture: Challenges, Risks, and Opportunities," in J. Giordano (ed.), *Neurotechnology: Promise, Potential, and Problems*, Boca Raton: CRC Press, 2012, pp. xiii–xvii.
39 M.S. Frankel, "Regulating the Boundaries of Dual-Use Research," *Science*, 336:6088, 2012, pp. 1523–1526.
40 C.D. Wollinetz, "Implementing the New U.S. Dual-Use Policy," *Science*, 336:6088, 2012, pp. 1525–1527.
41 See, for example, Bradford University's Education Module Resource at www.brad.ac.uk/bioethics (accessed 21 August 2012).

References

Australia, Canada, Japan, New Zealand, Republic of Korea and Switzerland (on behalf of the "JACKSNNZ") and Kenya, Sweden, Ukraine, the United Kingdom of Great Britain and Northern Ireland and the United States of America, *Revised: Possible Approaches to Education and Awareness-raising among Life Scientists*, BWC/CONF.VII/WP.20/Rev.1, United Nations: Geneva, 2011.

Biological and Toxin Weapons Convention (BTWC) see http://www.opbw.org (accessed 21 August 2012).

Carlson, R.H., *Biology is Technology*, Cambridge, MA: Harvard University Press, 2010.

Casey-Maslen, S., *Non-kinetic-energy Weapons Termed 'Non-lethal': A Preliminary Assessment under International Humanitarian Law and International Human Rights Law*, Geneva Academy of International Humanitarian Law and Human Rights: Geneva, October 2010.

Chemical Weapons Covention (CWC) see http://www.opcw.org (accessed 21 August 2012).

Committee on Military and Intelligence Methodology for Emergent Neurophysiological and Cognitive/ Neural Science Research in the Next Two Decades, *Emerging Cognitive Neuroscience and Related Technologies*, Washington, DC: National Academies Press, 2008.

Committee on Research Standards and Practices to Prevent the Destructive Application of Biology, *Biotechnology Research in an Age of Terrorism*, Washington, DC: National Academies Press 2004.

Conton, J., "Forward: Toward Our Neurofuture: Challenges, Risks, and Opportunities," in J. Giordano (Ed.) *Neurotechnology: Promise, Potential, and Problems*, Boca Raton: CRC Press, 2012, pp. xiii–xvii.

Dando, M.R., *Biological Warfare in the 21st Century: Biotechnology and the Proliferation of Biological Weapons*, Brassey's, London, 1994.

Frankel, M.S., "Regulating the Boundaries of Dual-Use Research," *Science*, 336:6088, 2012, pp. 1523–1526.

Giordano, J. and R. Wuzman, "Neurotechnologies as Weapons in National Intelligence and Defense— An Overview," *Synthesis: A Journal of Science, Technology, Ethics and Policy*, 2012, T:55–T:71. Online. Available at: www.synthesisjournal.com/vol2_no2_t1/GiordanoWuzman_2011_2_1.pdf (accessed 21 August 2012).

Kelle, A., K. Nixdorff and M.R. Dando, *Controlling Biological Weapons: Adapting Multilateral Arms Control for the 21st Century*, Basingstoke: Palgrave, 2006.

Malakoff, D., "Senior U.S. Lawmaker Leaps into H5N1 Flu Controversy. *Science Insider*," 4 March 2012. Online. Available at: http://news.sciencemag.org/scienceinsider/2012/03/senior-us-lawmaker-leaps-into-h5.html (accessed 21 August 2012).

Marchant, G. and L. Gulley, "National Security Neuroscience and the Reverse Dual-Use Dilemma," *AJOB Neuroscience*, 1:2, 2010, pp. 20–22.

Meselson, M., "Averting the Hostile Exploitation of Biotechnology, *The CBW Conventions Bulletin*," 48, 2000, pp. 16–19.

National Science Advisory Board for Biosecurity, *Proposed Framework for the Oversight of Dual Use Life Science Research: Strategies for Minimizing the Potential Misuse of Research Information*, NSABB: Washington, D.C., 2007.

NATO Standardization Agency, *Allied Joint Doctrine for Chemical, Biological, Radiological, and Nuclear Defence*, AJP-3.8, Edited Version 1, NATO: Brussels, 2012.

Novossiolova, T., M. Minehata and M.R. Dando, "The Creation of a Contagious H5N1 Influenza Virus: Implications for the Education of Life Scientists," *The Journal of Terrorism Research*, 3:1, 2012, pp. 39–51.

Pearson, G.S. and N.A. Sims, *The BTWC Review Conference: A Modest Outcome*. Review Conference Paper No. 31, University of Bradford, March 2012.

Pritchard, M.S., "Moral Machines?" *Science and Engineering Ethics*, 18:2, 2012, pp. 411–417.

Rose, S.P.R., *Prospects and Perils of the New Brain Sciences: a twenty year timescale*, Royal Society Policy Lab, Royal Society, London, 2009.

Royal Society *Neuroscience, Conflict And Security*. Brain Waves Module 3, Royal Society, London, 2012.

State Parties to the Convention on the Prohibition of the Development, Production and Stockpiling of Bacteriological (Biological) and Toxin Weapons and on Their Destruction, *Final Document of the Seventh Review Conference*, BWC/CONF.VII/7, United Nations: Geneva, 2011.

——*New Scientific and Technological Developments Relevant to the Convention*, BWC/CONF.VII/INF.3/ Add.1, United Nations: Geneva, 2011, pp. 21–38.

Stirling, A., "Governance of Neuroscience: Challenges and Response," in Brain Waves Module 1: *Neuroscience, Society and Policy*, Royal Society: London, 2011, pp. 87–97.

Tennison, M.N. and J.D. Moreno, "Neuroscience, Ethics, and National Security: The State of the Art," *PLoS Biology*, 10:3, 2012.

Thomas, G., "Sonic Device Deployed in London during Olympics," *BBC News*, 12 May 2012. Online. Available at: http://www.bbc.co.uk/news/uk-england-london-18042528 (accessed 21 August 2012).

Tucker, J.B. (ed.), *Innovation, Dual Use and Security: Managing the Risks of Emerging Biological and Chemical Technologies*. Cambridge, MA: The MIT Press, 2012.

United States Government Policy for Oversight of Life Sciences Dual Use Research of Concern. Online. Available at: http://oba.od.nih.gov/oba/biosecurity/pdf/united_states_government_policy_for_oversight_of_durc_final_version_032812.pdf (accessed 21 August 2012).

Wollinetz, C.D., "Implementing the New U.S. Dual-Use Policy," *Science*, 336:6088, 2012, pp. 1525–1527.

World Health Organisation, *Public Health Response to Biological and Chemical Weapons*, 2nd Edition, WHO: Geneva, 2004. See Annex 2: Toxins, pp. 214–216.

Zilinskas, R., "Take Russia to 'Task' on Bioweapons Transparency," *Nature Medicine*, 18:6, 2012, p. 14.

Uninhabited and autonomous military systems

24

UNMANNED DRONES AND THE ETHICS OF WAR

Christian Enemark

1. Introduction

Over the century since Italian army pilot Giolio Gavotti threw four bombs out of his Blériot XI monoplane's cockpit onto two Turkish-held oases in Libya in 1911,[1] air power technology has advanced steadily, but a concern has endured that novel uses of force should be driven not only by what is possible but also by what is permissible. A useful tool for ethical assessment is the centuries-old legitimization framework known as the just war tradition. This framework, incorporating contemporary international laws on the use of force, is comprised of two strands: *jus ad bellum* (the justice of going to war) and *jus in bello* (the just conduct of war). This chapter explores the relationship between just war principles and the new technology of armed, uninhabited aerial vehicles ("hunter-killer drones"). The focus is on the US Government because it has recently engaged in the most extensive use of this technology (in Afghanistan, Iraq, Libya, Pakistan, Somalia and Yemen). The first half of the chapter assesses drone use in the light of principles governing the resort to force: such action should have a just and proportionate cause, be properly authorized and motivated by right intention, have a reasonable prospect of success, and be a last resort. The second half examines whether drone strikes satisfy the *jus in bello* requirements that force be used only in a manner that discriminates between combatants and non-combatants, and that generates harm proportional to the expected military benefit. The overarching question is whether (or the extent to which) drone technology unjustly increases the incidence and/or lethality of armed conflict.

2. *Jus ad bellum*

A state seeking to resort to armed force has the onus of proving that the justice of its cause outweighs the inevitable calamity that war would bring.[2] The cause of a state seeking to wage war is just if it appeals to a moral principle higher than mere self-interest. A desire to exact revenge, greed for more territory, or simple aggression can all be motivating forces for going to war, but none of them qualifies as a just cause. Currently, international norms and practices indicate that only two justifications for using force have the potential to pass muster from an ethical perspective: self-defense; and military intervention to prevent or mitigate a large-scale, deliberately-caused humanitarian disaster.

Regarding self-defense, a restrictive view (based on strict adherence to the wording of Article 51 of the United Nations Charter) is that the right of self-defense may only be invoked and acted upon after an armed attack has taken place. A more permissive view (based on customary international law) is that the right of self-defense may also be exercised against a real and imminent threat when the necessity of that self-defense is instant, overwhelming, and leaves no choice of means and no moment of deliberation.[3] The most permissive view contemplates the use of force even when a threat is not imminent and where uncertainty remains as to the time and place of the enemy's attack. The latter view currently has no foundation under international law, although the necessity (for 'War on Terror' purposes) of establishing a new norm of "preventive war" is hotly debated.[4] Reasoning from the view of self-defense most widely subscribed to (the restrictive view), the United States arguably has a just cause for using force, including via armed drones, in Afghanistan on the grounds of self-defense. As US State Department lawyer Harold Koh stated in 2010: "as a matter of international law, the United States is in an armed conflict with al-Qaeda, as well as the Taliban and associated forces, in response to the horrific 9/11 attacks, and may use force consistent with its inherent right to self-defense under international law."[5]

By contrast, it is less easy to characterize US drone strikes (or any other use of force) in Iraq as being essentially defensive in an overall sense. This is because the Iraq War as a whole was one started pre-emptively by the United States rather than in response to an armed attack against it by Iraq. Likewise, drone strikes in Pakistan, Yemen and Somalia are pre-emptive rather than defensive and thus they arguably lack a just cause. Alternatively, if pre-emptive use of force is to be regarded as legitimate, it may be that some individuals are more legitimate targets than others for the purposes of forceful self-defense. For example, regarding drone strikes carried out in Yemen and Somalia, there is debate within the US Government about the scope of its fight against Islamist militants. On the one hand, there is a view (taken by the US State Department) that the United States may only target those few high-level militant leaders who are personally linked to plots to attack the United States. On the other hand, the US Defense Department reportedly insists that force may also be used against the thousands of low-level militants whose concerns are local (i.e. to control territory on either side of the Gulf of Aden).[6] The narrow view is more easily defensible because individuals who are actively plotting to attack the United States more obviously attract defensive action than do individuals who are merely "against Americans in a general sense."[7]

In Libya in 2011, although US use of armed drones was not for self-defense, there was nevertheless arguably a just cause in the form of humanitarian intervention. There is a widespread and long-prevailing attitude that military action of this kind violates the fundamental principle of state sovereignty which underpins international stability. However, an emerging and strengthening view in the international community is that intervention is acceptable if civilians are faced with the threat of serious and irreparable harm in the form of genocide, war crimes, ethnic cleansing and crimes against humanity.[8] By the middle of March 2011, the government forces of Libyan leader Muammar Gaddafi had been about to attack the rebel-held city of Benghazi and, as threatened, to clear its population of one million people "house by house".[9] Under such circumstances, the prevention or mitigation of such a disaster was a just cause for the use of force. In response to this imminent attack, on 17 March 2011 the UN Security Council (UNSC) authorized the use of "all necessary measures ... to protect civilians and civilian populated areas under threat of attack ... while excluding a foreign occupation force of any form on any part of Libyan territory" (UN Security Council Resolution 1973). As such, air power (rather than ground troops) was the military instrument of choice, and the United States chose to restrict itself to drones.

At the international level, the passage of Resolution 1973 – the first occasion the UNSC had authorized the use of force in a state, and against the wishes of that state, for civilian protection purposes – arguably bestowed Right Authority for, *inter alia*, the US use of drones in that conflict. At the domestic level, however, the exclusive deployment of this particular technology appears to have precipitated a shift in the kind and degree of authorization bestowed. In 2002, Paul Kahn warned

> Riskless warfare … may take the destructive power of war outside of the boundaries of democratic legitimacy, because we are far more willing to delegate the power to use force without risk to the [US] president than we are a power to commit the nation to the sacrifice of its citizens.[10]

Nine years later, the promise that US deployment of drones to Libya would be casualty free fed into an argument that the usual rules for congressional authorization did not apply. The White House instead argued in June 2011 that Congress did not need to authorize US military operations in Libya extending beyond the 60 days already authorized at the President's discretion because

> U.S. operations do not involve sustained fighting or active exchanges of fire with hostile forces, nor do they involve the presence of U.S. ground troops, U.S. casualties or a serious threat thereof, or any significant chance of escalation into a conflict characterized by those factors.[11]

At least two conclusions could be drawn from such an assertion being accepted: either that the standard for authority to wage war had been lowered; or that authority was unnecessary for something that did not really count as "war" in the first place. On the latter point, according to Martin van Creveld, "War does not begin when some people kill others; instead, it starts at the point where they themselves risk being killed in return."[12] If one assumes, for the sake of argument, that risk-free warfare is not an insurmountable paradox, it nevertheless raises questions about the relationship between combatant risk and Right Authority. For example, if drone operators are at no risk of retaliation, why should special permission for them to use force be necessary?

Any lowering or removal of the authorization standard for using force is also relevant to the *jus ad bellum* principle of war as a last resort. This principle supports the notion that recourse to violent action must only occur after every other reasonable, non-violent way of achieving a political aim has proven to be unavailable or ineffective. One concern might be that drones, as a technology for eliminating risk (to the user) somehow lowers the threshold for using force and thus is likely to increase its frequency. Indeed, risk-free drone strikes perhaps enable less anxious contemplation by politicians about using force to solve political problems, since the traditional countervailing moral considerations as regards one's own side (deaths, injuries, grieving families, etc.) no longer apply. A precedent supporting such a view may be found in the 1999 US-led intervention in the Serbian province of Kosovo – an air-only campaign which suffered not a single pilot casualty in combat. The US Air Force subsequently reported:

> The air war over Serbia offered airmen a glimpse of the future, one in which political leaders turned *quickly* to the choice of aerospace power to secure the Alliance's security interests without resorting to more costly and hazardous alternatives that would have exposed more men and materiel to the ravages of war.[13]

The resort to air power might be quick, but it is difficult to draw an ethical line between "quick" and "too quick". Lowering the threshold for political decisions to use force is not necessarily a bad thing; if the cause for war is just, why not hasten in its pursuit? However, if such lowering is the result of civilian disengagement from the war-making process (because imaginations are not excited at the prospect of physical risk and personal sacrifice), doubts might arise as to whether there is sufficient civilian authorization for the use of force. As Michael Ignatieff wrote after the Kosovo intervention, "If war becomes unreal to the citizens of modern democracies, will they care enough to restrain and control the violence exercised in their name?"[14] Even when, in respect of drones, a nation's leader claims (as above) that there is no "significant chance of escalation," it is the immutable nature of war that all risks cannot be predicted and eliminated. As such, a state that would wage war in the name of its citizens, thus potentially exposing them to the dangers of escalation and blowback, arguably requires their consent. If so, the lack of a blessing from Congress for the US use of drones in Libya in 2011 may constitute a deficit of Right Authority.

A decision to use armed drones – for a just cause, properly authorized, and as a last resort – must also be proportionate to the harm suffered (or anticipated) and motivated by Right Intention. To the extent that drones facilitate the restrained and precise application of force, and where their use does not amount to an overreaction, this is consistent with the principle of proportionality. It may also reflect a just desire to bring about a post-war peace that is not haunted by excessive physical damage and aggravated popular resentment against an overzealous intervener. Nevertheless, when contemplating *jus ad bellum* in the context of a campaign which involves only drones, one criticism might be that such use of force is about wanting to respond only to "little things". In an uncontested or poorly contested air space especially, it might appear that the deployment of uninhabited aircraft reflects a desire to use force in the pursuit only of causes that are not worth dying for. Eliot Cohen has written that "air power is an unusually seductive form of military strength, in part because, like modern courtship, it appears to offer gratification without commitment."[15] In like fashion, Ignatieff has described the 1999 Kosovo intervention as "the kind of war a nation fights when it wants to, not when it must, when values rather than survival are on the line; when commitment is intense but also shallow."[16] These factors, real or perceived, might militate against satisfying the ethical requirement that the use of force should have a reasonable prospect of success.

It is an important principle within the Just War tradition that, because death and destruction inevitably result from war, there should be a reasonable chance that a would-be user of force will be victorious and thus succeed in bringing about a better peace than what currently exists. To wage war in the knowledge that the damage caused is likely to be in vain is unjust. Regarding the limited and precise application of force using drones, is this likely to be seen as a sign of strength – the restraint of the powerful deciding not to be as heavy-handed as they could towards an adversary? Or is it a sign of weakness – the restraint of the risk-averse deciding not to place their military personnel in harm's way? Is the remote-controlled, risk-free application of air power a foretaste of worse things to come and thus dissuasive of enemy action, or is it indicative of a reluctance to use force at all and thus an encouragement for an enemy to continue? Where there is doubt on such questions, a drone campaign is vulnerable to strategic failure.

Niccolò Machiavelli wrote in *The Prince*:

> Men ought either to be well treated or crushed, because they can avenge themselves of lighter injuries, of more serious ones they cannot; therefore the injury that is done to a man ought to be of such a kind that one does not stand in fear of revenge.[17]

In its use of drones in and around the Middle East, the US Government exhibits an intention not to crush its enemies but rather merely to decapitate them (i.e. deprive them of leaders). In 2009 the then director of the US Central Intelligence Agency (CIA), Leon Panetta, stated that drone strikes in Pakistan are "the only game in town in terms of confronting or trying to disrupt the al Qaeda leadership."[18]

Another view is that decapitation strikes are likely to be strategically successful only if one "assumes a meritocratic system in which the leaders are the most talented rather than the most ideologically committed; in actuality, their replacements could turn out to be more talented and more skilful leaders."[19] Findings based on empirical data have been mixed. One study of leadership decapitations, published in 2009, adds weight to the notion that drone strikes are ineffective or even counterproductive.[20] More recently, however, a pair of studies concluded that killing or capturing the leaders of militant organizations can reduce the effectiveness of those organizations or even cause them to disintegrate.[21] An important caveat on such findings is that they illustrate only a correlation between decapitation and organization survival; this is not evidence of causation. It is presently no straightforward matter, therefore, to establish that a campaign of drone strikes against militant leaders has a reasonable prospect of success.

If one could be certain that those individuals killed in drone strikes were in fact militant leaders, and that no person other than a militant leader had been killed, there would arguably be no need to take this ethical discussion any further. Unfortunately, there is and can be no such certainty. In 2010, White House counterterrorism adviser John Brennan stated that the US Government "will take the fight" to extremists "wherever they plot and train in Afghanistan, Pakistan, Yemen, Somalia and beyond." He acknowledged that "an action that eliminates a single terrorist but causes civilian casualties can, in fact, inflame local populations and create far more problems - a tactical success but a strategic failure."[22] The likelihood that drone strikes will bring strategic success for the US Government is closely connected to the manner in which these strikes are conducted, and so this discussion necessarily turns from *jus ad bellum* to *jus in bello* principles.

3. *Jus in bello*

In 1932 former British prime minister Stanley Baldwin alluded to the deliberate targeting of civilians when he said: "I think it is well also for *the man in the street* to realise that there is no power on earth that can prevent him from being bombed. Whatever people may tell him, the bomber will always get through."[23] Today, the reverse attitude holds sway, as reflected in the near-universal commitment by states to Article 51(2) of the 1977 Additional Protocol (I) to the 1949 Geneva Conventions which provides: "The civilian population as such, as well as individual civilians, shall not be the object of attack." Article 57(2)(iii) of the Protocol, reflecting commitment to the principle of proportionality, prohibits attacks "which may be expected to cause incidental loss of civilian life, injury to civilians, damage to civilian objects, or a combination thereof, which would be excessive in relation to the concrete and direct military advantage anticipated." These principles are victim-oriented rather than weapon-specific, and they apply regardless of whether force is used by land, sea or air. To the extent that drone technology deserves special consideration from a *jus in bello* perspective, however, some of its attributes ought to facilitate more discriminate and proportionate application of force.

The norm against indiscriminate uses of force has strengthened as powerful states have acquired the technological wherewithal to be more precise. As Alex Bellamy has observed, "the advent of PGM [precision guided munition] warfare has significantly increased societal expectation about the minimization of non-combatant casualties."[24] In this context, the killing of non-combatants is tragic in itself, as well as being bad for business strategically. So when Panetta described drone strikes as "the only game in town," he also offered the assurance that they are "very precise" and "very limited in terms of collateral damage."[25] Similarly, in a live internet forum in January 2012, US President Barack Obama said: "drones have not caused a huge number of civilian casualties ... For the most part they have been very precise precision strikes against Al Qaeda and their affiliates."[26] Such statements notwithstanding, the actual balance of combatant and non-combatant casualties resulting from drone strikes is far from clear, so arriving at a *jus in bello* assessment is difficult. In all the places where the US Government uses hunter-killer drones, it faces the challenge of confronting a non-uniformed enemy, so discrimination between combatants and non-combatants can only occur on the basis of intelligence or interpretation of someone's observed actions (such as firing a weapon). But poor intelligence and misinterpretation of actions can and does result in harm to non-combatants. In June 2002, for example, manned US aircraft were dispatched, on the basis of erroneous information, to strike what they believed to be a Taliban headquarters in Afghanistan but what was in fact a wedding party. After shots were fired into the air, as commonly occurs at Afghan weddings, the American pilots overhead mistook this for anti-aircraft fire and responded with lethal force.[27] Arguably, such mistakes are less likely to occur when drones are used instead of manned aircraft.

A common criticism of bombing from a high altitude has been that it necessarily involves transferring risk from the bomber crew above to non-combatants below. For example, Walzer's position is that we should be prepared to place combatants in harm's way in order to reduce the risks to enemy non-combatants.[28] Similarly, Bellamy asks: "What level of risk should [pilots] accept in order to increase the chances of distinguishing between combatants and non-combatants?"[29] Their assumption is that discrimination is enhanced by physical proximity; by taking on more risk, the users of force can better avoid causing non-combatant deaths. However, the real enabler of discriminate application of force is accurate visual identification, and drones are technically capable of achieving this notwithstanding the fact that they fly at high altitude and their ground-based operators assume no risk. In other words, drone technology breaks the traditional nexus between the visual and the physical when it comes to discrimination; the proximity of the operator need not be a factor as regards target identification and strike accuracy. Because drones can hover undetected over an area for long periods of time while relaying imagery back to base, they are a means of obtaining a superior picture of what usually happens (and of any unusual happenings) in that area. This is a much stronger basis for applying force in a discriminate manner to persons more readily identifiable as either combatants or non-combatants. Insofar as superior imagery enables more discriminate use of force, the use of drone technology ought generally to be a mode of warfare ethically superior to other forms of ranged weaponry (for example, manned aircraft, missiles and artillery), at least in theory.

In practice, the empirical picture is murky. This is due to a dearth of reliable data on combatant and non-combatant casualties resulting from drone strikes. In Pakistan, where the United States has engaged in drone strikes most extensively, unofficial assessments of the casualty impact have relied largely on sketchy reports in the local and international media. It is difficult to know the ratio of combatants to non-combatants killed, not least because in many cases there has been no positive identification of bodies. According to records maintained by the *Long War Journal* since 2006, at the time of writing there had been 2312 "leaders and operatives from Taliban, Al Qaeda, and allied extremist groups" killed, and 138 civilians killed.[30] This indicates that, on average, around 5.6 percent of those killed by drones have been non-combatants. By contrast, according to the New America Foundation's data, there had been between 1851 and 2843 total deaths from drone strikes, including between 293 and 471 "non-militant" deaths.[31] This indicates a much higher average ratio (around 16 percent) of non-combatant deaths; a figure more likely to be regarded as excessive. Figures emanating from US Government sources suggest that drone strikes have been much more discriminate, but inconsistent accounts do little to inspire confidence. For example, in April 2011, US officials were reported as claiming that "about 30" Pakistani civilians had died in drone strikes between August 2009 and August 2010. But a year later, the *New York Times* reported that a senior Obama administration official had claimed that the total number was in the "single digits."[32] The confusion is compounded by uncertainty over who the US Government counts as a non-combatant in the first place. In May 2012, several White House officials were reported as claiming that President Obama had embraced a method of counting casualties that "in effect counts all military-age males in a strike zone as combatants … unless there is explicit intelligence posthumously proving them innocent."[33] Such a counting method, and the physical difficulty of gathering evidence of identity following a drone strike, might well explain US Government claims of extremely small numbers of non-combatant deaths.

Closely related to the ethical requirement of discrimination, drone strikes need to be proportionate in order to constitute a just use of force. That is, the anticipated harm resulting from using drones in pursuit of a legitimate military objective must not be excessive in relation to the expected military benefits. In a general sense, the putative benefits of US drone strikes are the general disruption of militant activity and the undermining of enemy organizations through leadership "decapitation." Weighing against these benefits, the degree of harm (including non-combatant deaths) resulting from drone strikes might be regarded as either acceptable or excessive depending on which unofficial body count is regarded as most accurate.

A *New York Times* investigation, involving interviews with dozens of current and former officials within the Obama administration, revealed in May 2012 that the President had been personally involved in drone strike decisions at weekly counterterrorism meetings in the White House Situation Room. Moreover, the journalists found that "When a rare opportunity for a drone strike at a top terrorist arises – but his [the terrorist's] family is with him – it is the president who has reserved to himself the final moral calculation."[34] Without explanation by the US Government, one can only speculate as to the existence of some kind of decision-making algorithm to guide proportionality calculations. In an attempt to kill a top-level enemy combatant, is it worth carrying out an attack in circumstances where there is a high risk of harm to, say, up to 10 non-combatants? If the enemy combatant is only mid level, however, could an attack proceed only if there is a high risk of harm to five or fewer non-combatants? And if the enemy is only a low-level combatant, would a high risk of harm to just one non-combatant be enough to preclude an attack? Presumably, the calculation of proportionality would differ also in circumstances of only moderate or low risk of harm to a particular number of non-combatants. Other relevant factors when weighing the relative value of anticipated harm and expected benefit might include the drone operator's level of confidence that the right person is in the crosshairs. Given that DNA analysis of bodies has sometimes revealed that the intended target was not present at the time and place of some drone strikes, it has been suggested that "the target value must be weighted by a probability of presence/absence."[35]

Even if proportionality calculations are made in this way, there remains the problem of whether leadership decapitations are really as militarily beneficial as the US Government seems to think. If the benefit is only slight, the permissible degree of expected but unintended harm to non-combatants would need to be much reduced, possibly to the point of not allowing any such harm at all. However, the US Government appears rather to have extended the rationale for leadership decapitations to embrace a wider range of targets. In 2008, as part of a dramatic expansion of the Pakistan drone campaign, the CIA was reportedly authorized to attack not only high-value individuals whose names are on an approved list ("personality" strikes) but also suspected militants of lower value whose names are not known.[36] The expanded authority for these "signature" strikes, granted by President George W. Bush and maintained by the Obama administration, permits the CIA to rely on so-called pattern-of-life analysis, using evidence about individuals and locations collected by surveillance cameras on drones and from other sources. In the words of one senior US official (speaking anonymously): "We might not always have their names but ... these are people whose actions over time have made it obvious that they are a threat."[37] Seen in terms of proportionality, the targeting of low-level militants who exhibit an apparently threatening pattern of life might constitute excessive use of force if the damage caused includes unintended non-combatant deaths. Even if the US Government could plausibly characterize its objective overall in Pakistan as a legitimate (self-defense) response to the terrorist attacks of 11 September 2001, it is difficult to see how it measurably furthers that objective to kill individuals who are engaged in localized insurgent activities but are not actively planning to attack the United States. However, even if there is a slight benefit in carrying out such killings, it is worth asking whether it outweighs the cost of causing harm (albeit unintended) to even one Pakistani non-combatant.

4. Conclusion

In April 2012, when John Brennan described those within the Obama administration as "very mindful that, as our nation uses this [drone] technology, we are establishing precedents that other nations may follow," he warned that "not all of those nations ... share our interests or the premium we put on protecting human life, including innocent civilians."[38] Already, dozens of other states – among them, states that the United States would regard as actual or potential adversaries – use unarmed drones for surveillance purposes, although currently only the United States, Britain and Israel are known to have used armed drones. The technology of remote-control air power is bound to proliferate, however, as its apparent operational advantages become more widely attractive. Some states are almost certainly pursuing their own hunter-killer drone capacity, while some of America's allies (Australia, Italy and Turkey) appear to be interested in acquiring such a capacity from the United States. Under these circumstances, there needs to be greater ethical consideration of drone technology – commensurate with the degree of military consideration – so as to guard against any unjust increase in the incidence and/or lethality of armed conflict.

There is a plausible danger that drone technology will enable an increase in the overall quantum of force being used in the world inasmuch as force (even if small-scale and precise) could be used more easily and thus more often. From a *jus ad bellum* perspective, such an increase would be unjust if force was resorted to without a just cause. The recent record of drone use has included the US Government's interventions in Libya for humanitarian purposes and in Afghanistan for self-defense purposes, but elsewhere its pre-emptive use of armed drones is less easy to justify. In addition, if the risk-free nature of drone-based killing sees citizens disengaging from the wars waged in their name by their governments, it is worth asking whether such use of force has Right Authority and whether it is truly a last resort. If drone technology enables small-scale and precisely-applied uses of force in response to minor threats, and if this is done with the intention of forestalling the emergence of major threats, this would appear to satisfy ethical requirements that force be resorted to in a proportionate fashion and with a desire to achieve a better post-war peace. However, recent empirical analyses leave room for doubt about whether limiting drone strikes to the decapitation of militant leaders is likely to bring strategic success in the long term. Expanding the range of targets to include low-level fighters might work better, but in this approach there is also greater potential to generate non-combatant casualties.

From a *jus in bello* perspective, any drone-driven increase in the lethality of armed conflict is unjust to the extent that more non-combatants are being deliberately killed in drone strikes or unintentionally killed to an excessive degree. Drone technology, incorporating powerful target identification capabilities, has the theoretical capacity to enable greater levels of discrimination and proportionality than those achievable using other military platforms. In practice, however, reported statistics differ markedly on the ratio of combatant to non-combatant deaths resulting from drone strikes. This makes it difficult to render a *jus in bello* judgment, especially when there is uncertainty over what kinds of people get counted as non-combatants in the first place. Clearly, more government transparency on the US drone program is needed to substantiate President Obama's claim that "this thing is kept on a very tight leash."[39]

Notes

1 A. Gropman, "Aviation at the Start of the First World War," *U.S. Centennial of Flight Commission.* Online. Available at: http://archive.is/T00r (accessed 27 April, 2012).
2 M. Quinlan, "Justifying War," *Australian Journal of International Affairs*, 58:1, 2004, pp. 7–15.
3 M. Walzer, *Just and Unjust Wars: A Moral Argument with Historical Illustrations*, 4th edn, New York: Basic Books, 2006, p. 74.
4 See, for example: A. M. Dershowitz, *Preemption: a Knife that Cuts Both Ways*, New York: Norton, 2007; B.M.J. Szewczyk, "Pre-emption, Deterrence, and Self-Defence: A Legal and Historical Assessment," *Cambridge Review of International Affairs*, 18:1, 2005, pp. 119–135; and T. Taylor, "The End of Imminence?" *The Washington Quarterly* 27: 4, 2004, pp. 57–72.
5 H. Hongju Koh, "The Obama Administration and International Law." Speech at the Annual Meeting of the American Society of International Law, Washington DC, 25 March, 2010. Online. Available at: http://www.state.gov/s/l/releases/remarks/139119.htm (accessed 12 January 2011).
6 Charlie Savage, "At White House, Weighing Limits of Terror Fight," *New York Times*, 16 September, 2011, p. A1.
7 Ibid.
8 International Commission on Intervention and State Sovereignty, *The Responsibility to Protect*, Ottawa: ICISS, 2001, p. 32; United Nations General Assembly, "World Summit outcome," A/RES/60/1, 24 October 2005.
9 D. Fisher and N. Biggar, "Was Iraq an Unjust War? A Debate on the Iraq War and Reflections on Libya," *International Affairs*, 87:3, 2011, pp. 687–707, at p. 701.
10 P. Kahn, "The Paradox of Riskless Warfare," *Philosophy and Public Policy Quarterly*, 22:3, 2002, pp. 2–8, at p. 4.
11 White House, "United States Activities in Libya," *Washington Post*, 15 June, 2011. Online. Available at: http://www.washingtonpost.com/wp-srv/politics/documents/united-states-activities-libya.html (accessed 8 August, 2011).
12 Cited in P. W. Singer, *Wired for War: The Robotics Revolution and Conflict in the 21st Century*, New York: Penguin, 2009, p. 432.
13 Cited in T. Mahnken, *Technology and the American Way of War since 1945*, New York: Columbia University Press, 2008, p. 187. Emphasis added.
14 M. Ignatieff, *Virtual War: Kosovo and Beyond*, New York: Picador, 2000, p. 4.
15 Cited in T. Mahnken, *Technology and the American Way of War since 1945*, p. 179.
16 M. Ignatieff, *Virtual War*, p. 4.
17 N. Machiavelli, *The Prince*, trans. W.K. Marriott, London, J.M. Denet and Sons, 1958, p. 13.
18 Anonymous, "U.S. Airstrikes in Pakistan Called 'Very Effective'," *CNN News*, 18 May, 2009. Online. Available at: http://articles.cnn.com/2009-05-18/politics/cia.pakistan.airstrikes_1_qaeda-pakistani-airstrikes?_s=PM:POLITICS (accessed February 23, 2011).
19 N. Sharkey, "Death Strikes from the Sky: The Calculus of Proportionality," *IEEE Technology and Society*, Spring 2009, pp. 16–19, at p. 19.
20 J. Jordan, "When Heads Roll: Assessing the Effectiveness of Leadership Decapitation," *Security Studies*, 18:4, 2009, pp. 719–755.
21 B.C. Price, "Targeting Top Terrorists: How Leadership Decapitation Contributes to Counterterrorism," *International Security*, 36:4, 2012, pp. 9–46; P.B. Johnston, "Does Decapitation Work? Assessing the Effectiveness of Leadership Targeting in Counterinsurgency Campaigns," *International Security*, 36:4, 2012, pp. 47–79.

22 K. deYoung, "Obama redefines national security strategy, looks beyond military might," *Washington Post*, 27 May, 2010. Online. Available at: http://www.washingtonpost.com/wp-dyn/content/article/2010/05/27/AR2010052701044.html (accessed 29 June, 2012).

23 Cited in T. Garden, "Air Power: Theory and Practice," in J. Baylis, J. Wirtz, E. Cohen and C.S. Gray (eds), *Strategy in the Contemporary World*, Oxford: Oxford University Press, 2002, p. 150. Emphasis added.

24 A.J. Bellamy, *Just Wars: from Cicero to Iraq*, Cambridge UK: Polity, 2006, p. 185.

25 Anonymous, "U.S. Airstrikes in Pakistan Called 'Very Effective'."

26 S. Shane, "U.S. Drone Strikes Are Said to Target Rescuers at Sites," *New York Times*, 6 February, 2012: p. A4.

27 A. Bellamy, *Just Wars*, p. 189.

28 M. Walzer, *Just and Unjust Wars*, p. 156.

29 A. Bellamy, *Just Wars*, p. 182.

30 B. Roggio and A. Mayer, "Charting the Data for US Airstrikes in Pakistan, 2004–2012," *Long War Journal*, 26 June, 2012. Online. Available at: http://www.longwarjournal.org/pakistan-strikes.php (accessed 27 June, 2012).

31 P. Bergen and K. Tiedemann, "The Year of the Drone: An Analysis of US Drone Strikes in Pakistan, 2004–2012," *New America Foundation*, 26 June, 2012. Online. Available at: http://counterterrorism.newamerica.net/drones (accessed 27 June, 2012).

32 J. Elliott, "Washington's Silence Creates Doubt on Deaths," *Sydney Morning Herald*, 23 June, 2012, p. 22.

33 J. Becker and S. Shane, "Secret 'Kill List' Proves a Test of Obama's Principles and Will," *New York Times*, 29 May, 2012: A1.

34 Ibid.

35 Sharkey, "Death Strikes from the Sky," p. 18.

36 D. Cloud, "CIA Allowed to Kill Terrorist Suspects Without Identification," *Sydney Morning Herald*, 7 May 2010. Online. Available at: http://www.smh.com.au/world/cia-allowed-to-kill-terrorist-suspects-without-identification-20100506-uh33.html (accessed 8 November, 2010).

37 Ibid.

38 A. Entous, "U.S. Plans to Arms Italy's Drones," *Wall Street Journal*, 29 May, 2012: p. A1.

39 M. Landler, "Civilian Deaths Due to Drones Are Not Many, Obama Says," *New York Times*, 31 January, 2012: p. A6.

References

Anonymous, "U.S. Airstrikes in Pakistan Called 'Very Effective'," *CNN News*, 18 May, 2009. Online. Available at: http://articles.cnn.com/2009-05-18/politics/cia.pakistan.airstrikes_1_qaeda-pakistani-airstrikes?_s=PM:POLITICS (accessed February 23, 2011).

Becker J. and S. Shane, "Secret 'Kill List' Proves a Test of Obama's Principles and Will," *New York Times*, 29 May, 2012: A1.

Bellamy, A. J. *Just Wars: from Cicero to Iraq*, Cambridge UK: Polity, 2006.

Bergen P. and K. Tiedemann, "The Year of the Drone: An Analysis of US Drone Strikes in Pakistan, 2004–2012," *New America Foundation*, 26 June, 2012. Online. Available at: http://counterterrorism.newamerica.net/drones (accessed 27 June, 2012).

Cloud, D. "CIA Allowed to Kill Terrorist Suspects Without Identification," *Sydney Morning Herald*, 7 May, 2010. Online. Available at: http://www.smh.com.au/world/cia-allowed-to-kill-terrorist-suspects-without-identification-20100506-uh33.html (accessed November 8, 2010).

Dershowitz, A. M. *Preemption: a Knife that Cuts Both Ways*, New York: Norton, 2007.

deYoung, K. "Obama Redefines National Security Strategy, Looks Beyond Military Might," *Washington Post*, 27 May, 2010. Online. Available at: http://www.washingtonpost.com/wp-dyn/content/article/2010/05/27/AR2010052701044.html (accessed 29 June, 2012).

Elliott, J. "Washington's Silence Creates Doubt on Deaths," *Sydney Morning Herald*, 23 June, 2012: p. 22.

Entous, A. "U.S. Plans to Arms Italy's Drones," *Wall Street Journal*, 29 May, 2012: p. A1.

Fisher D. and N. Biggar, "Was Iraq an Unjust War? A Debate on the Iraq War and Reflections on Libya," *International Affairs*, 87:3, 2011, pp. 687–707.

Garden, T. "Air Power: Theory and Practice," in J. Baylis, J. Wirtz, E. Cohen and C.S. Gray (eds), *Strategy in the Contemporary World*, Oxford: Oxford University Press, 2002.

Gropman, A. "Aviation at the Start of the First World War," *U.S. Centennial of Flight Commission*. Online. Available at: http://www.centennialofflight.gov/essay/Air_Power/Pre_WWI/AP1.htm (accessed 27 April, 2012).

Hongju Koh, H. "The Obama Administration and International Law." Speech at the Annual Meeting of the American Society of International Law, Washington DC, 25 March, 2010. Online. Available at: http://www.state.gov/s/l/releases/remarks/139119.htm (accessed 12 January, 2011).

Ignatieff, M. *Virtual War: Kosovo and Beyond*, New York: Picador, 2000.

International Commission on Intervention and State Sovereignty, *The Responsibility to Protect*, Ottawa: ICISS, 2001.

Johnston, P.B. "Does Decapitation Work? Assessing the Effectiveness of Leadership Targeting in Counterinsurgency Campaigns," *International Security* 36:4, 2012, pp. 47–79.

Jordan, J. "When Heads Roll: Assessing the Effectiveness of Leadership Decapitation," *Security Studies*, 18:4, 2009, pp. 719–755.

Kahn, P. "The Paradox of Riskless Warfare," *Philosophy and Public Policy Quarterly*, 22:3, 2002, pp. 2–8.

Landler, M. "Civilian Deaths Due to Drones Are Not Many, Obama Says," *New York Times*, 31 January, 2012: p. A6.

Machiavelli, N. *The Prince*, trans. W. K. Marriott, London, J.M. Denet and Sons, 1958.

Mahnken, T. *Technology and the American Way of War since 1945*, New York: Columbia University Press, 2008.

Price, B.C. "Targeting Top Terrorists: How Leadership Decapitation Contributes to Counterterrorism," *International Security* 36:4, 2012, pp. 9–46.

Quinlan, M. "Justifying War," *Australian Journal of International Affairs*, 58:1, 2004, pp. 7–15.

Roggio B. and A. Mayer, "Charting the Data for US Airstrikes in Pakistan, 2004 – 2012," *Long War Journal*, 26 June, 2012. Online. Available at: http://www.longwarjournal.org/pakistan-strikes.php (accessed 27 June, 2012).

Savage, C. "At White House, Weighing Limits of Terror Fight," *New York Times*, 16 September 2011, p. A1.

Shane, S. "U.S. Drone Strikes are Said to Target Rescuers at Sites," *New York Times*, 6 February, 2012: p. A4.

Sharkey, N. "Death Strikes from the Sky: The Calculus of Proportionality," *IEEE Technology and Society*, Spring, 2009, pp. 16–19.

Singer, P.W. *Wired for War: The Robotics Revolution and Conflict in the 21st Century*, New York: Penguin, 2009.

Szewczyk, B.M.J. "Pre-emption, Deterrence, and Self-Defence: A Legal and Historical Assessment," *Cambridge Review of International Affairs*, 18:1, 2005, pp.119–135.

Taylor, T. "The End of Imminence?" *The Washington Quarterly* 27:4, 2004, pp. 57–72.

United Nations General Assembly, "World Summit outcome," A/RES/60/1, 24 October, 2005.

Walzer, M. *Just and Unjust Wars: A Moral Argument with Historical Illustrations*, 4th edn, New York: Basic Books, 2006.

White House, "United States Activities in Libya," *Washington Post*, 15 June, 2011. Online. Available at: http://www.washingtonpost.com/wp-srv/politics/documents/united-states-activities-libya.html (accessed 8 August, 2011).

25

AUTONOMOUS ROBOTS AND THE FUTURE OF JUST WAR THEORY[1]

Keith Abney

1. Introduction

The history of just war theory has demonstrated the power of the "ought implies can" principle in ethics. For, as technological capacities have changed over time, the traditional moral strictures of just war theory have adapted. For instance, one traditional tenet claims just wars must be fought in self-defense—understood as being after an actual (unjust) attack has begun. In a time of massive armies marching across plains to join battle, this requirement made sense. But with the development of long-range weapons and the reliable use of remote means of detecting attack preparations, this requirement changed: 20th century just war theory legitimates the use of force in self-defense against an "imminent attack"—when one can detect that the enemy's attack will begin very soon.

The development of international non-state terrorism led to nation-states focusing military activity on denying smaller groups obtaining WMDs. Hence, the 21st century idea of self-defense morphed once more, to the "Bush Doctrine" of preemptive or preventive war. As Bush put it, "Facing clear evidence of peril, we cannot wait for the final proof, the smoking gun that could come in the form of a mushroom cloud."[2] Whether or not this particular doctrine is morally defensible, a watershed has passed; given "ought implies can," tactical and technical changes in the capabilities of groups smaller than nation-states to wage war has led to changes in just war theory.

The Bush Doctrine is but one example of such changes. The wars of the early 21st century have launched other attempts to justify warfare that nonetheless apparently violate traditional just war doctrine: from those that downplay the principle of discrimination, such as the Putin Doctrine[3] or the "Sri Lanka option,"[4] to those that address the new warfare of drone strikes and the "responsibility to protect" of the Blair Doctrine[5] and the Obama Doctrine.[6]

So, developments in policy and technology ineluctably drive changes in our understanding of crucial moral concepts. These new capabilities transform not only the conduct of war, but also the very understanding of what war is, and when and how it ought (not) to be waged. Accordingly, such innovations require clarifications, if not wholesale revisions, to ethical concepts and theories. The just war tradition is particularly affected by such changes, as military activity is perhaps at the forefront of technological innovation as well as deep moral dilemmas.

One technological development in particular promises to revolutionize just war theory: the rise of lethal autonomous robots. Herein, I first examine some details of how just war theory has been reinterpreted in the light of post-9/11 developments, and then focus on the ramifications of the rise of lethal autonomous robots for further challenges to just war theory.

2. Traditional just war theory[7]

What is war? For a long time, such a question was not theoretically contentious. A recent definition, one that captures well the old understanding, defines war as "actual, intentional, and widespread armed conflict between political communities."[8] But there is a problem: on a straightforward understanding of this concept of war, a drone strike may loosely be termed an "attack" or even "armed" conflict, but it would not count as a war. And of course, on this definition, the "War on Terror" is not a war, not least because "Terror" is not the name of a political community.

But suppose we broaden and redefine the concept of war in such a way as to make the "War on Terror" no longer so oxymoronic, perhaps involving violent coercion by recognized groups across national borders. There remains an international consensus that acts of war legally must adhere to international humanitarian law (IHL), otherwise known as the laws of war. These laws include the Geneva and Hague Conventions and other international agreements. Much of IHL is rooted in just war theory, the philosophical tradition meant to establish the moral boundaries of warfare.[9] To begin this discussion, I briefly explain traditional just war theory, including a moral justification for the very existence of war. I then will discuss some of the novel tensions autonomous robots pose for it.

2.1 How can war be moral?[10]

War, however regrettable, has been an inescapable aspect of human life. To understand the nature of war, we can see it as a type of forcible coercion that nations engage in as a means of attaining their political goals. Naturally, if some states are engaged in legitimate forcible coercion in order to deter or punish illegitimate coercion by other states, then there must be some means of distinguishing legitimate from illegitimate coercion amongst states. This is called "just war theory," and is divided into three basic categories:

- *Jus ad bellum*: Law concerning acceptable justifications to declare war.
- *Jus in bello*: Law concerning acceptable conduct in war, once begun.
- *Jus post bellum*: Law concerning acceptable conduct following the official or declared end of a war.

These three categories are typically (but not always) asserted to be independent; so, the morality and legality of a state deciding to go to war (*jus ad bellum*)—typically a political decision made by a state's political leadership—have long been considered independent of the morality and legality of one's actions in waging war (*jus in bello*); the latter is typically the province of a state's professional military, not its political leadership.

2.2 *Just war theory:* jus ad bellum

Principles of jus ad bellum

A recent analysis[11] insists on six necessary conditions for *jus ad bellum*:

- *Proper authority and public declaration*: War must be waged by a competent authority for a publicly stated purpose, i.e. "secret wars are immoral."
- *Just cause*: There must be sufficient and acceptable justifications for entering war; the war must be in self-defense, against unjust attacks on innocent citizens or states, to restore rights wrongfully denied and/or to re-establish a just order.
- *Proportionality*: The good(s) achieved by war (presumably, securing the just cause) must be proportional to the evil of waging it.
- *Last resort*: Peaceful means of avoiding war have been exhausted, e.g. negotiations must have been tried and have failed.
- *Reasonable probability of success*: There is no point fighting a war one cannot possibly win; one is morally compelled to resist in some other way.
- *Right intention*: One must have morally correct motivation in engaging in war, rather than illegitimate ulterior motives, such as property acquisition.

Just war theory insists all six criteria must each be fulfilled for a particular declaration of war to be morally justified; they are individually necessary, and only jointly sufficient. Three of these six rules are deontological requirements, or "first-principle" requirements.[12] The other three requirements are broadly consequentialist: one must also consider the expected costs and benefits (to all sides) of launching a war. So, just war theory combines both deontological and consequentialist considerations in determining whether declaring war is just.

Accordingly, critiques of just war theory can take either of two basic approaches: following deontology, they can claim traditional just war theory imposes not truly necessary, but merely *prima facie* duties; or, perhaps the duties have changed or are even defunct in the light of technological development. Alternatively, a consequentialist critique could claim traditional just war theory should be ignored, perhaps even flagrantly violated, for the greater good. Now, how does the rise of autonomous robots affect such critiques?

Autonomous robots and jus ad bellum

Peter Asaro, Robert Sparrow, and Noel Sharkey[13] all raise a similar *jus ad bellum* objection to the use of autonomous robots: such use illegitimately emboldens political leaders to wage war, because it lowers barriers to entering a war, given reduced human casualties and therefore political cost. Michael Ignatieff[14] reiterates this point, claiming using robots eliminates the "blood sacrifice" that formerly restrained democracies.

Note this argument is indirect: no one seriously contends the robots themselves will be directly effecting *jus ad bellum* violations. Rather, autonomous robots, with their promise of fewer human casualties, will make war less terrible and therefore more tempting, plausibly enticing political leaders to wage war more readily. But such an argument has multiple flaws.

First, to claim that developing lethal autonomous robots (LARs) will cause terrible consequences for the tendency to declare war on insufficient grounds is a consideration that could be handled by the nonconsequentialist requirements for declaring a just war: using robots or not presumably makes no difference as to whether the war is (a) in self-defense, (b) for a just cause, (c) a last resort, and so forth. If these necessary nonconsequentialist conditions are not met, then traditional *jus ad bellum* would simply maintain a war is immoral, regardless of the (net positive) consequences.

Second, history shows that the increasing technical sophistication of war has reinforced the need for *jus ad bellum* and *jus in bello* restrictions, not undermined them; technological innovation in weapons from the crossbow to chemical agents and WMDs have driven new international agreements on restrictions. The advent of autonomous robots will cause further development in such just war considerations and potentially could make war ever more ethically waged.

Third, there is a complaint that using autonomous robots will avoid the necessary "blood sacrifice"[15] that just war requires. But the already extant use of remotely piloted drones already enables "casualty aversion," at least as long as drone pilots in Nevada are effectively immune to return fire from those they attack halfway around the world. Under current technical and real-world capabilities, giving the drones more autonomy over firing decisions, so as to no longer require a "human in the loop," would not appreciably alter the casualty aversion of the side employing the drones. So the move to greater autonomy for such drones adds nothing new to such *jus ad bellum* worries that do not already exist for drone use.

But what if the development of autonomous drones nonetheless makes it easier to sell a war that violates *ad bellum* restrictions to the public? If such wars becomes more pervasive as a result, isn't that a lamentable consequence? In response, we can acknowledge that war is terrible and ought normally to be avoided; but perhaps the rise of autonomous robots in fact means a greater proportion of wars fought will be just, given the greater *"reasonable probability of success,"* which may actually reduce the incidence of war in long run. After all, the "deterrence" strategy to avoid war is to create such an overwhelmingly powerful and technologically superior military force that no rational adversary ever dares to attack us. Granted, perhaps this goal is unrealistic; perhaps it will merely spark an arms race. But history attests that (so far) this approach seems to be working reasonably well with nuclear weapons.

It remains plausible, however, that such overwhelming deterrence, while lessening full-scale wars, has contributed to creating the ubiquity of a new kind of conflict, asymmetric warfare; when the consequences of full-scale war between nation-states are too devastating, the result may be a series of proxy conflicts (as the Cold War demonstrated). The implications of this development are further examined in the final section.

2.3 Robots and *jus in bello*

There are serious problems with traditional *jus ad bellum*, and the doctrine will continue to evolve as the technology and asymmetric nature of contemporary warfare change. But given that robots for the foreseeable future will not be in a position to declare wars (or even inadvertently start one), but will only fight them, *jus ad bellum* issues in the rest of this essay will be examined only insofar as they affect the *jus in bello* or *jus post bellum* use of robots.

Total war doctrine: is there really a jus in bello?

"War is hell," said US Civil War Union General Sherman—and he burned to the ground the cities and farms of Georgians on his march to the sea.[16] Sherman believed that, given his just cause, he was permitted nearly any means to victory. By World War II, this "total war" doctrine was espoused by those who saw nothing wrong with launching V-2 rockets on London citizens, or firebombing Dresden or Tokyo, or dropping A-bombs on Hiroshima and Nagasaki. Through this doctrine, one may do anything to win the victory in a just war; one's enemies have forfeited their right to any consideration by unjustly beginning their forcible coercion, and deserve whatever they get.

But this view appears both unrealistic and morally indefensible. While it is true that the international arena is not yet sufficiently similar to a well-governed state such that wars are simply considered to be international crimes and soldiering is merely international police work, it is also true that international relations are hardly a Hobbesian "war of all against all."[17] This trend toward seeing war as an activity with rules or virtues that sanction proper and improper behavior has only gained strength as states have acquired an institutional professional military, especially one independent of those making *jus ad bellum* decisions. Instead, professional soldiers have a code of conduct that details their proper and improper functioning in their various roles, just as other professions do. Given "ought implies can," they cannot be meaningfully held responsible for decisions by politicians over which they have little to no control; but they can be held responsible for performing their roles in war in a way the international community recognizes as legitimate and avoiding illegitimate means of performing those roles.

Traditional jus in bello

Much of the just war tradition[18] asserts only two basic necessary conditions for the external rules of *jus in bello*: proportionality and discrimination and non-combatant immunity. The military ends must be proportionate to the means: harms to the enemy must be proportionate to one's military goal, but only the minimal level of force is justified. To satisfy this constraint, autonomous robots would need to learn how to apply force proportionate to their goal, using some operational program that involved properly computing the minimal force necessary for military success. After sufficient testing, robots could perform at least as well as humans in deploying no greater violent force than needed, and thereby passing the "military Turing test"[19] for moral deployment.

Under proportionality, Michael Walzer[20] and others also include other aspects of traditional *jus in bello* that reject any means "*mala in se*"—that is, evil in themselves—because they violate human rights whenever used, such as rape.[21] Robots presumably can be programmed to avoid any such means; robots can not only do dirty, dangerous, and dull tasks in war that humans cannot, they can also do so dispassionately,[22] avoiding the problems of bloodlust, the quest for revenge, scenario fulfillment, and the other human characteristics that lead to war crimes.

Whatever the exact laws of war amount to in these cases, programming robots to obey them poses no special problems over and above the basic problem of robot discrimination and classification of humans into their proper *jus in bello* categories, and then meting out the appropriate treatment. Thus, we see the next requirement may be trickier for robots.

On discrimination and non-combatant immunity, one must attempt to discriminate between combatants and noncombatants (civilians), and noncombatants must not be intentionally killed. Hence, we can see that *jus in bello* prohibits weapons that are intrinsically disproportionate, such as thermonuclear weapons in conventional wars, or those that fail to discriminate between combatants and civilians, such as most biological or chemical weapons—and perhaps even many modes of "cyberattacks" on computer networks.[23]

The doctrine of the double effect

We should note that conventional requirements of civilian immunity require merely that noncombatants must not be intentionally killed or harmed, not that they must not be harmed at all. The latter requirement in practice would lead directly to pacifism, as no war yet fought or practically imagined could guarantee a complete absence of civilian casualties. But if non-combatants can never be legitimate targets, how can it be morally legitimate to harm and even kill them? The usual way out of this problem of "collateral damage"—that in practice, all those who wage war foresee that some noncombatants will inevitably be harmed—is to use a time-honored ethical principle (originating from natural law ethics) called the Doctrine of the Double Effect (DDE).

In the DDE, an action may be morally permissible, even if it is foreseen that it will cause a bad effect, if certain conditions are met:[24]

- The act itself is not morally wrong (e.g. killing combatants in wartime);
- The good effect is produced directly by the action, and not by the bad effect (e.g. winning is produced by killing the enemy combatants, not by terrorizing or murdering civilians);
- The good effect is sufficiently desirable to compensate for allowing the bad effect (winning is worth killing civilians); and,
- The bad effect must not be intended, but merely foreseen and permitted (e.g. the US would be happy if all Afghani noncombatants escape the drone strike, but alas, one foresees they all will not, and US weapons never intentionally target them).

The principle of the double intention

Ronald Arkin[25] appropriates an aspect of Walzer's work in his work on devising methods of programming ethical autonomous robots, and in particular endorses Walzer's[26] version of the DDE known as the Principle of the Double Intention (PDI), which is essentially the DDE plus a further ("double") intention that combatants are not only to refrain from intending harm to civilians, but they are also to take precautions to reduce risk to civilians, even at the expense of increased risk to themselves. Arkin[27] highlights the possibility that robots with an "ethical governor" will outperform human soldiers at satisfying the PDI—especially when humans are (understandably) reluctant to minimize foreseen harm to others at a greater risk to themselves, but selfless robots will not prioritize their own continued existence over obeying their ethical programming.

Immediate questions are raised by the PDI: what does it mean to intend to reduce civilian risk, and how much should civilian risk be reduced?[28] Walzer's PDI gives no clear answer, unfortunately. The principle Walzer appeals to is one from liability law—the "principle of due care"—that is, that one exercised due care (including potentially creating some risk to oneself) before targeting the enemy, and hence did not heedlessly attack civilians. But what level of reliability and accuracy constitutes "due care"? A robot's programming must specify some answer.

2.4 Summary of challenges posed by robots to just war theory
Attack decisions and the issue of latency

For current tele-operated military robots, such as the Predator UAV, the current understanding of the requirement of discrimination involves the need for "eyes on target": the weapon cannot fire until and unless the human tele-operator has the target firmly acquired in its sights, and no civilians are in the bullseye. But the time lag (termed "latency") between remotely pulling the trigger and the weapon actually firing, along with all the vulnerabilities in the satellite and electromechanical connections in between, mean that eventually a robot with real-time decision-making capability—a sufficiently autonomous robot—should be able to do as well or better than a human operator in such discrimination. Closer to the target, with faster reaction times, the robot likely could become more effective in preventing unintended deaths. At that point, it seems *jus in bello* would permit or even demand that such LARs be used, and the requirement of human eyes on target—i.e. that robots be tele-operated—would be morally scrapped, as the best means of employing the principle of discriminating between combatant and non-combatant targets can then be done by a machine.

Imprecision in Laws of War and Rules of Engagement

A robot's target-identification module—assuming it has been sufficiently tested for accuracy—programmed by engineers thus could outperform human eyes. A requirement for 100 percent accuracy in target identification is overly burdensome, inasmuch as we do not require that of human soldiers before deployment. We already accept that, due to gravitational forces and biological limitations, computers can fly in situations that humans cannot; it is plausible they will soon make better, more moral targeting decisions as well.

But robots still may need specificity in their rules that have never been fully specified for human soldiers, who traditionally rely instead on vague constructs like "military necessity." For instance, the general LOW and ROE for minimizing collateral damage is vague: is the rule that we should not attack a position if civilian deaths are expected to be greater than combatant deaths? Are we permitted to kill one (high-ranking) combatant, even if it involves the death of ten civilians—or $10M in unnecessary damage? What about 20 civilians, or $100M? And how are robots to accurately calculate these expected results, even if the laws are clearly specified? Of course, these problems regarding incommensurable values afflict human implementation of these rules as well. Is it possible to specify vague rules in a way that LARs can follow them as well as humans? My final section will explore how.

3. Why current just war theory fails the novel challenges posed by robots

3.1 Problems endemic to the terminology of the debate

What is clear from these examples of the new capabilities of autonomous bots is that the ethical discussion is treading new ground, and previous versions of IHL are simply inadequate to deal with the new realities. For example, articles 3 and 41 of the UN Charter deal with the use of force and armed attack—but do these articles legislate for autonomous robots/bots (cyberwar) or not? The questions raised defy easy answer: for example, is any use of force (even a cyberattack that involves no apparent kinetic force) equivalent to an armed attack? Is using a robot to kill another robot, in hand to (robot) hand combat, an armed attack? What about merely the use of information/programming—i.e. hacking? How shall we understand (ro)bot activity in the context of traditional problems like espionage, perfidy, etc.?

In fact, some of the questions involving the use of robots in war highlight the most fundamental questions of just war theory: e.g. whether a state of war exists (or even can exist) using robots instead of troops between the United States and Yemen, or Libya, or Pakistan—or the transnational group al Qaeda; or, whether or not we term it "war," does the "zone of conflict" in Afghanistan legitimately extend into another state, Pakistan, with whom the US has no declaration of war; or, can we properly term robots or other non-state agents a "combatant," and what rights and responsibilities they would have under IHL. If they are not "combatants," then what are they?

These problems already exist in the "War on Terror" when human forces are used in situations admitting terminological ambiguity; the use of robots merely exacerbates the moral and legal confusions. For example, Kai Ambos and Josef Alkatout[29] claim that nothing in existing UN Security Council resolutions on terrorism explicitly allows for cross-border raids without the permission of the territorial state: "Quite the contrary, the relevant-antiterrorism resolutions … confirm the need for respect of the integrity of the territorial state concerned." Hence, they are skeptical that the mere presence of Taliban or al Qaeda forces in Pakistan, up to and including bin Laden himself, create a threat immediate enough to trigger the US right to self-defense and allow a violation of Pakistan's sovereignty. Their arguments, if taken at face value, would mean all US drone attacks (as well as SEAL team 6's assassination of bin Laden) within Pakistan are violations of IHL.

But in response, David A. Wallace[30] insists that the Pakistani government's inability or unwillingness to deal with resident terrorists rendered the bin Laden operation perfectly legal: "the raid … did not violate Pakistan's sovereignty because Pakistan was unable or unwilling to prevent bin Laden from hiding in its territory and planning future attacks against the United States." The same analysis would, by analogy, make US drone attacks perfectly legal under existing IHL. But what degree of unwillingness or inability permits such raids? How much antiterrorism assistance must Pakistan provide before the US is not allowed to violate its sovereignty? Again, vague rules require clarification, especially when followed by literal-minded robots. And current just war theory has not too few, but instead too many answers to such questions.

3.2 The challenge: how now to assess the ethics of robots in war

So what is the status of robots in war, and how must they change just war theory? Interim solutions may include a kind of quarantine, in which some of the contentious issues involving autonomous robots or cyberbots are reframed away from a military and just war approach altogether, perhaps using extant civilian international law, or in its absence, even a "stand your ground" approach.[31] Such an approach may allow private entities to engage in retaliation without fear of punishment in the absence of a third party (government) capable of enforcing norms, gradually creating a "Wild West" style version of frontier justice. If, for example, Baidu's (ro)bots attacked Google, perhaps it is best to allow Google to counterattack and leave it to the private parties to sort things out. But such stopgap solutions inevitably will prove problematic at best, and clearly will be insufficient when at least one of the actors employing such autonomous robots is the government of a traditional nation-state engaging in warlike activities, such as the US drone strikes.

Another approach, for those wishing to simply make the problem go away, is to advocate a complete ban on all autonomous lethal robots,[32] perhaps by suggesting that there is a human duty to never make such machines,[33] or there is a human right not to be killed by an autonomous robot.[34]

But international agreements[35] have a dismal track record at turning back the clock on new technology and enforcing a lasting peace. The arms race of warfare will not end with unilateral abandonment of autonomous robots in the foreseeable future, especially when such technical superiority has made the US military the unquestioned current master of all symmetric warfare it engages in. That superiority guarantees America's competitors, including (but not limited to) China, Iran, Russia, and other nations, will seek drones and other autonomous weapons of their own. In the long run, abolition appears to be an even more hopeless goal for autonomous robots than it is for nuclear weapons. So, human policymakers must decide on a new just war theory that takes into account the novel capabilities of warfighters who are no longer merely human.

What would those new policies look like? How can we plan for an acceptable future that includes lethal, autonomous robots? One (admittedly speculative) future scenario forms my conclusion.

4. Final conclusions: an end of war, and eternal robotic peace(keeping)?

4.1 Ethics requires virtue, and a hybrid approach to robots

There is a foundational critique of all procedural ethics, i.e. any approach that claims morality is determined by following the proper rules. Hursthouse[36] claims that all procedural ethics fail, because these requirements cannot be met: (a) the rules would amount to a decision procedure for determining what the right action would be in any particular case; and (b) the rules would be stated in such terms that any non-virtuous person could understand and apply them correctly.

A rules-based approach for robots devised for civilian contexts, such as Asimov's Three (or Four) Laws, usually has a further problem for military robots: we would not want them to always act altruistically towards some humans. In fact, we would want them to be able to kill the right humans—but not the wrong (friendly) ones. Therefore, we need an approach that enables machines to use a basic top-down program plus bottom-up machine learning to be able to function excellently in its military roles and without malfunctioning; it should be fierce towards its enemies, helpful to its allies, and reliable in discerning the difference, including in situations unforeseen by its programmers. What ethical approach can accomplish all this?

Perhaps the most viable hybrid approach that avoids the conflict between duties and consequences, and incorporates both warrior fierceness towards enemies and a gentle kindness towards comrades, is virtue ethics: an approach that sees ethics, not in terms of what rules should be followed, but in terms of what kind of character an agent has—does one have a virtuous character, or is one full of vice? The proper moral question is not "what rule should I follow?" or "what rules apply to this act?" but instead "what would performing this action reveal about my character? How can I properly function in my proper role(s)?"

All human institutions require rules, but robots, like lawyers, need more than rules to be virtuous. Someone motivated to bend the rules for their own benefit, and sufficiently clever, will inevitably find the loopholes and unintended consequences of any finite set of rules. Robots would be particularly prone to this, as they (for now) lack the "common sense" virtues required to properly apply top-down rules. This problematizes any pure Kantian (merely rule-following) robot; and the impossibility of calculational accuracy in any rich context also largely rules out general-purpose utilitarian robots. Instead, robot ethics will ineluctably lead to a requirement for bottom-up machine learning as well as top-down rules (perhaps phrased as hypothetical, not categorical, imperatives)[37] in order to obtain acceptable outcomes.

4.2 Postmodern war?

I believe the result of these considerations will be an ethics of "Postmodern War," as argued by George Lucas.[38] Lucas asserts that the development of military robotics (along with the advent of nanotechnology, bio-psychological enhancement, nonlethal weapons, and cyber warfare) have created a "diffuse, decentralized, 'neoconnectionist' vision of warfare in the post-Clausewitzian, postmodern world that Eco prophesied."[39] Echoing the criticisms of Sharkey, Asaro, et al., Lucas avers that these technologies threaten to make war ever more ubiquitous as the path of least resistance, rather than the option of last resort, for resolving political conflict. However, these same technologies offer hope for lessening the indiscriminate destructiveness of war, and make likelier the gradual evolution from conventional war to more discriminating law enforcement, ideally undertaken by international coalitions of peacekeepers.

If Lucas (as I believe) is correct, then I contend the key issue of the replacement for just war theory is a new theory of legitimate forcible coercion; the issue of whether we should call such forcible coercion "war" may be politically important, but may in the end mask ethical issues—for the real moral question in our new reality is when and by whom forcible coercion is morally permissible. Robots are merely another means for such forcible coercion: a means that offers new possibilities, and so raises new ethical dilemmas that should not be confused by outmoded concepts and theories.

I believe the proper result of such considerations for robots is not to press for *complete* bans (abolition) on LARs; such an official ban will not eradicate the technology, but merely push development to the unscrupulous borders of society, with first mover technical advantages further accruing to the least morally punctilious parties, quite probably including criminals and terrorists. A world in which the Mafia and al Qaeda and the like are the only groups with lethal autonomous robots is a possible (if unintended) consequence of such naïve do-gooding.

Instead of bans, I believe that effective arms control comes from enforceable agreement between the most technologically sophisticated and powerful parties on proper regulation of the weapon's use. Hence, there will need to be new arms control agreements regarding the permissible use of LARs. To that end, just war theory will need to be gradually updated, not completely replaced, in a piecemeal fashion that keeps up with technical developments—as ought implies can, so moral consideration about what ought (not) be allowed needs to follow step by step with near-term changes of capabilities, and programmed into the character of virtuous robots. Our new legal regime will still need rules, as laws should neither be based on any simplistic act-utilitarian calculus, nor allowed to be determined by vested interests such as the military-industrial complex. Some think teaching autonomous robots the virtues may be hopeless, but just as human children need education into a virtuous way of life, so autonomous robots will require machine learning into an "art of war." The result, after significant and realistic training and simulated battle, will be that such properly trained robots obey the evolving mores of our new *jus in bello*/international peacekeeping, and an international agreement can be made that minimizes the impact of this new means of forcible coercion on innocent civilians.

4.3 The future: autonomous robots fight … only each other?

Could the eventual result be that robots may morally fight only other robots? This scenario has been called a *reductio ad absurdum* of the entire enterprise of robot ethics. But, hopefully, serious international agreement may turn the apparent *reductio* into a reality of perpetual peace.[40] That is, as just war theory slowly reacts to the novel capabilities of autonomous robots to kill humans, I have hope that the international community will slowly create a moral and legal structure of additions to IHL that will increasingly reduce the circumstances under which humans (rather than robots) will be a permissible target within *jus in bello* and *jus post bellum*, as well as increasing the requirement of discrimination to gradually reduce the allowable harm to noncombatants (also called "collateral damage") to zero.

In my hoped-for future, through this slow, piecemeal process, one day it will come to pass that robots will do all the dying for us, and humans will never be legitimate targets (or even legitimate "collateral damage") in any war. War will become a merely economic and mechanical battle, much like the "trade wars" that already exist. An international consensus will gradually develop to the effect that humans are never legitimately harmed in battle; so that even if occasional lapses occur, they are always to be morally condemned—not unlike the international attitude towards human slavery today, as opposed to the international moral dissensus over slavery 200 years ago.

At some point soon after that, as the world community begins to accept the robotic UN peacekeepers which continuously survey all public spaces and autonomously attack any weapon aimed at humans, perhaps our dream of eternal and lasting peace may be realized, as people realize their political and economic and legal disagreements must always be settled by political and economic and legal means, and never by coercive violence against fellow humans. Autonomous lethal robots could herald, not a Terminator scenario of the "rise of the machines" and the death of humanity, but an enforceable and lasting peace, based on an international moral consensus that disagreements are always to be resolved by negotiations or robotic "proxy wars," and never by coercive violence against humans. But that bright future depends on our willingness to create a new just war theory for autonomous robots, regulating (but not forbidding) the conditions of their use.

Notes

1 Some parts of this chapter have been adapted from past and pending collaborations, and I'd like to express my appreciation to those collaborators for their input (while in no way blaming them for any errors of fact or omission contained herein): they include Maxwell Mehlman, Fritz Allhof, George Bekey and, most especially, Patrick Lin.

2 G.W. Bush, "Don't Wait for Mushroom Cloud," *From Speech in Cincinnati*, Ohio, October 6, 2002. Online. Available at: http://edition.cnn.com/2002/ALLPOLITICS/10/07/bush.transcript/ (accessed 14 July, 2012).

3 A. Glucksman, "The Putin Doctrine," *Forbes.com*, 22 October, 2008. Online. Available at: http://www.forbes.com/2008/10/21/putin-doctrine-europe-oped-cx_ag_1022glucksmann.html (accessed 25 September, 2012).

4 Economist "The 'Sri Lanka option': The Rush to Learn Lessons from the Obliteration of the Tamil Tigers," *Economist* May 20th 2010. Online. Available at: http://www.economist.com/node/16167758 (accessed September 25, 2012).

5 S. Lendman, "Opposing Doctrines: Putin v. Obama," *theintelhub.com, Civilian Intelligence Agency*, June 2, 2012. Online. Available at: http://theintelhub.com/2012/06/03/opposing-doctrines-putin-v-obama/ (accessed 14 July, 2012).

6 B. Obama, "Renewing American Leadership," *Foreign Affairs*, July/August, 2007, Council on Foreign Relations. Online. Available at: http://www.foreignaffairs.com/articles/62636/barack-obama/renewing-american-leadership (accessed 14 July, 2012).

7 This section is adapted in part from P. Lin, F. Allhoff and K. Abney "Is Warfare the Right Frame for the Cyber Debate," in L. Floridi and M. Taddeo (eds), *The Ethics of Information Warfare*, Springer, accepted and forthcoming in 2013.

8 B. Orend, "War," in E. N. Zalta (edn), *Stanford Encyclopedia of Philosophy*, Stanford University, 2005. Online. Available at: http://plato.stanford.edu/ entries/war (accessed 25 September, 2012).

9 T. Aquinas, *Summa Theologica*. Translated by Fathers of the English Dominican Province. New York: Benziger Books, 1948; M. Walzer, *Just and Unjust Wars: A Moral Argument with Historical Illustrations*, 4th edn, New York: Basic Books, 2006.

10 Much of the rest of section 2.1 is adapted from P. Lin, G.A. Bekey and K. Abney, "Autonomous Military Robotics: Risk, Ethics, and Design" *DTIC Document*, California Polytechnic State University San Luis Obispo, 2008.

11 B. Orend, "War."

12 Ibid.

13 P. Asaro, "Remote-Control Crimes," *Robotics & Automation Magazine, IEEE*, 18:1, 2011, pp. 68–71; P. Asaro, "Robots and Responsibility from a Legal Perspective," *Proceedings of 8th IEEE 2007 International Conference on Robotics and Automation: Workshop on RoboEthics*, Rome, 14 April, 2007; R. Sparrow, "Can Machines Be People," in P. Lin, K. Abney and G. A. Bekey (eds), *Robot Ethics: The Ethical and Social Implications of Robotics*, Massachusetts: MIT Press, 2012; R. Sparrow, "Killer

Robots," *Journal of Applied Philosophy*, 24:1, 2007, pp. 62–77; N. Sharkey, "Automated Killers and the Computing Profession," *Computer*, 40:11, 2007.

14 M. Ignatieff, "Drones Give Democracies No Cause for War," *Financial Times*, June 12, 2012. Online. Available at: http://www.ft.com/intl/cms/s/0/10a03278-b3b3-11e1-a3db-00144feabdc0.html#axzz2 OfezfLVw (accessed 26 March, 2013).

15 M. Ignatieff, "Drones Give Democracies No Cause for War."

16 B. Davis, *Sherman's March: The First Full-Length Narrative of General William T. Sherman's Devastating March through Georgia and the Carolinas*, New York, NY: Random House, 1980.

17 T. Hobbes, *Leviathan*, New York, NY: Penguin Group, 1651, 1982 edn.

18 For example, W.V. O'Brien, *The Conduct of Just and Limited War*, New York, NY: Praeger Publishers, 1981.

19 C. Elliott, "'Military Turing Test' Would Make War Robots Legal," *Proceedings of RUSI*, reprinted in *New Scientist*, February 2008. Online. Available at: http://www.newscientist.com/blog/technology/2008/02/military-turing-test-would-make-war.html (accessed 14 July, 2012).

20 M Walzer, *Just and Unjust Wars*.

21 B. Orend, *Michael Walzer on War and Justice*, Montreal, Quebec: McGill-Queen's University Press, 2001.

22 G. Veruggio and K. Abney, "Roboethics: The Applied Ethics for a New Science," in P. Lin, K. Abney and G.A. Bekey (eds), *Robot Ethics: The Ethical and Social Implications of Robotics*, Cambridge, MA: MIT Press, 2012, pp. 347–364.

23 P. Lin, F. Allhoff and K. Abney, "Is Warfare the Right Frame for the Cyber Debate."

24 A. McIntyre, "Doctrine of Double Effect," in E. N. Zalta (ed.), The *Stanford Encyclopedia of Philosophy*, 2004, Fall 2008 Edition. Online. Available at: http://plato.stanford.edu/archives/fall2008/entries/double-effect/ (accessed on September 15, 2008).

25 R. Arkin, *Governing Lethal Behavior: Embedding Ethics in a Hybrid Deliberative/Reactive Robot Architecture*, Technical Report GIT-GVU-07-11, 2007. Online. Available at: http://www.cc.gatech.edu/ai/robot-lab/online-publications/formalizationv35.pdf (accessed 26 March, 2013).

26 M. Walzer, *Just and Unjust Wars*.

27 R. Arkin, *Governing Lethal Behavior*.

28 S. Lee, "Double Effect, Double Intention, and Asymmetric Warfare," *Journal of Military Ethics*, 3:3, 2004, pp. 233–251.

29 K. Ambos and J. Alkatout "Has 'Justice Been Done'? The Legality of Bin Laden's Killing Under International Law," *Israel Law Review*, 45:2, 2012, pp. 341–366.

30 D.A. Wallace "Operation Neptune's Spear: The Lawful Killing of Osama Bin Laden," *Israel Law Review*, 45:2, 2012, pp. 367–377.

31 For example, see P. Lin, F. Allhoff and K. Abney, "Is Warfare the Right Frame for the Cyber Debate?"

32 For example, W. Wallach, "The Case Against Autonomous Killing Machines," interviewed by G. Dvorsky, 2012. Online. Available at: http://io9.com/5920084/making-the-case-against-autonomous-killing-machines (accessed 25 September, 2012).

33 For example, G. Veruggio and K. Abney, "Roboethics: The Applied Ethics for a New Science," in P. Lin, K. Abney and G.A. Bekey (eds), *Robot Ethics*, pp. 347–364.

34 P. Asaro, "Remote-Control Crimes," pp. 68–71.

35 For example, see the Kellogg-Briand Pact, Kellogg-Briand Pact of 1928. Online. Available at: http://history.state.gov/milestones/1921-1936/Kellogg (accessed 25 September, 2012).

36 R. Hursthouse, "Virtue Ethics," in E. N. Zalta (ed.), The *Stanford Encyclopedia of Philosophy*, Summer 2012 Edn. Online. Available at: http://plato.stanford.edu/archives/sum2012/entries/ethics-virtue/ (accessed September 25, 2012.

37 For example, P. Foot, "Morality as a system of hypothetical imperatives," *The Philosophical Review*, 81:3, 1972, pp. 305–316.

38 G. Lucas, "Postmodern War," *Journal of Military Ethics*, 9:4, 2010, pp. 289–298.

39 G. Lucas, "Postmodern War," pp. 289–298.

40 I. Kant, *Perpetual Peace: A Philosophical Essay*, Trans., Introduction and Notes by M. Campbell Smith, Preface by L. Latta, London: George Allen and Unwin, 1917.

References

Ambos, K. and J. Alkatout "Has 'Justice Been Done'? The Legality of Bin Laden's Killing Under International Law," *Israel Law Review*, 45:2, 2012, pp. 341–366.

Aquinas, T. *Summa Theologica*. Translated by Fathers of the English Dominican Province. New York: Benziger Books, 1948.

Arkin, R. *Governing Lethal Behavior: Embedding Ethics in a Hybrid Deliberative/Reactive Robot Architecture*, Technical Report GIT-GVU-07-11, 2007.

Asaro, P. "Remote-Control Crimes," *Robotics & Automation Magazine, IEEE*, 18:1, 2011, pp. 68–71.

Asaro, P. "Robots and Responsibility from a Legal Perspective," *Proceedings of 8th IEEE 2007 International Conference on Robotics and Automation: Workshop on RoboEthics*, Rome, 14 April, 2007.

Bleek, P. C. 2000. "Putin Signs New Military Doctrine, Fleshing Out Security Concept" *Arms Control Today*, 2000. Online. Available at: http://www.armscontrol.org/act/2000_05/ru2ma00 (accessed 14 July, 2012).

Bush, G.W. "Don't Wait for Mushroom Cloud," *from speech in Cincinnati*, Ohio, October 6, 2002. Online. Available at: http://edition.cnn.com/2002/ALLPOLITICS/10/07/bush.transcript/ (accessed 14 July, 2012).

Cheney, R. 2003. "Vice President Tells West Point Cadets 'Bush Doctrine' is Serious," *American Forces Press Service*, June 2, 2003. Online. Available at: http://www.defense.gov/news/newsarticle.aspx?id=28921 (accessed 14 July, 2012).

Davis, B. *Sherman's March: The First Full-Length Narrative of General William T. Sherman's Devastating March through Georgia and the Carolinas*, New York, NY: Random House, 1980.

Elliott, C. 2008. "'Military Turing Test' Would Make War Robots Legal," *Proceedings of RUSI*, reprinted in *New Scientist*, February 2008. Online. Available at: http://www.newscientist.com/blog/technology/2008/02/military-turing-test-would-make-war.html (accessed 14 July, 2012).

Economist "The "Sri Lanka Option": The Rush to Learn Lessons from the Obliteration of the Tamil Tigers," *Economist* May 20, 2010. Online. Available at: http://www.economist.com/node/16167758 (accessed September 25, 2012).

Foot, P. "Morality as a System of Hypothetical Imperatives," *The Philosophical Review*, 81:3, 1972, pp. 305–316.

Glucksman, A. "The Putin Doctrine," *Forbes.com*, 22 October, 2008. Online. Available at: http://www.forbes.com/2008/10/21/putin-doctrine-europe-oped-cx_ag_1022glucksmann.html (accessed 25 September, 2012).

Hobbes, T. *Leviathan*, New York, NY: Penguin Group, 1651, 1982 edn.

Hursthouse, R. "Virtue Ethics," in E. N. Zalta (ed.), *The Stanford Encyclopedia of Philosophy*, Summer 2012 Edn. Online. Available at: http://plato.stanford.edu/archives/sum2012/entries/ethics-virtue/ (accessed September 25, 2012.

Ignatieff, M. "Drones Give Democracies No Cause for War," *Financial Times*, June 12, 2012. Online. Available at: http://www.ft.com/cms/s/0/10a03278-b3b3-11e1-a3db-00144feabdc0.html#axzz2LI4lNVaM (accessed 14 July, 2012).

Kant, I. *Perpetual Peace: A Philosophical Essay*, Trans., Introduction and Notes by M. Campbell Smith, Preface by L. Latta, London: George Allen and Unwin, 1917.

Kellogg-Briand Pact of 1928. Online. Available at: http://history.state.gov/milestones/1921-1936/Kellogg (accessed 25 September, 2012).

Lee, S. "Double Effect, Double Intention, and Asymmetric Warfare," *Journal of Military Ethics*, 3:3, 2004, pp. 233–251.

Lendman, S. "Opposing Doctrines: Putin v. Obama," *theintelhub.com, Civilian Intelligence Agency*, June 2, 2012. Online. Available at: http://theintelhub.com/2012/06/03/opposing-doctrines-putin-v-obama/ (accessed 14 July, 2012).

Lin, P., F. Allhoff and K. Abney "Is Warfare the Right Frame for the Cyber Debate?" in L. Floridi and M. Taddeo (eds), *The Ethics of Information Warfare*, Springer, accepted and forthcoming in 2013.

Lin, P., G.A. Bekey and Abney, K. "Autonomous Military Robotics: Risk, Ethics, and Design" DTIC Document, California Polytechnic State University San Luis Obispo, 2008.

Lucas, G. "Postmodern War," *Journal of Military Ethics*, 9:4, 2010, pp. 289–298.

Mazzetti, M. "The Drone Zone," *NY Times*, 6 July, 2012. Online. Available at: http://www.nytimes.com/2012/07/08/magazine/the-drone-zone.html?_r=2&smid=tw-nytimesworld&seid=auto&pagewanted=all (accessed 14 July, 2012).

McIntyre, A. "Doctrine of Double Effect," in E. N. Zalta (ed.), *The Stanford Encyclopedia of Philosophy*, 2004, Fall 2008 Edition. Online. Available at: http://plato.stanford.edu/archives/fall2008/entries/double-effect/ (accessed on September 15, 2008).

Obama, B. "Renewing American Leadership," *Foreign Affairs*, 1 July, 2007. Online. Available at: http://www.foreignaffairs.com/articles/62636/barack-obama/renewing-american-leadership (accessed 14 July, 2012).

O'Brien, W.V. *The Conduct of Just and Limited War*, New York, NY: Praeger Publishers, 1981.

Orend, B. "War," in E.N. Zalta (ed.), *Stanford Encyclopedia of Philosophy*, Stanford University, 2005. Online. Available at: http://plato.stanford.edu/ entries/war/ (accessed 25 September, 2012).

Orend, B. *Michael Walzer on War and Justice*, Montreal, Quebec: McGill-Queen's University Press, 2001.

Saletan, W. "Slipping With the Yemenis," *Slate Magazine*, 26 April, 2012. Online. Available at: http://www.slate.com/articles/news_and_politics/human_nature/2012/04/yemen_s_drone_war_is_mission_creep_drawing_us_into_a_civil_war_.html (accessed 14 July, 2012).

Schell, J. "Say What You Will, It's a War in Libya," *LA Times*. 21 June, 2011. Online. Available at: http://articles.latimes.com/2011/jun/21/opinion/la-oe-schell-war-powers-20110621 (accessed 14 July, 2012).

Sharkey, N. "Automated Killers and the Computing Profession," *Computer*, 40:11, 2007.

Sparrow R. "Can Machines Be People" in P. Lin, K. Abney and G. A. Bekey (eds), *Robot Ethics: The Ethical and Social Implications of Robotics*, Massachusetts: MIT Press, 2012.

Sparrow, R. "Killer robots," *Journal of Applied Philosophy*, 24:1, 2007, pp. 62–77.

Thiessen, M. "The Obama-Bush doctrine," *Washington Post*, 31 May, 2012. Online. Available at: http://www.washingtonpost.com/opinions/the-obama-bush-doctrine/2012/05/31/gJQAGZmM4U_story.html (accessed 14 July, 2012).

Trenin, D. "The Forgotten War: Chechnya and Russia's Future," *Carnegie Endowment for International Peace*, Policy Brief, 2003, pp. 4–5. Online. Available at: http://www.carnegieendowment.org/files/Policybrief28.pdf (accessed 14 July, 2012).

Veruggio, G. and K. Abney "Roboethics: The Applied Ethics for a New Science," in P. Lin, K. Abney and G.A. Bekey (eds), *Robot Ethics: The Ethical and Social Implications of Robotics*, Cambridge, MA: MIT Press, 2012, pp. 347–364.

Wallace, D.A. "Operation Neptune's Spear: The Lawful Killing of Osama Bin Laden," *Israel Law Review*, 45:2, 2012, pp. 367–377.

Wallach, W. "The Case Against Autonomous Killing Machines," interviewed by G. Dvorsky, 2012. Online. Available at: http://io9.com/5920084/making-the-case-against-autonomous-killing-machines (accessed 25 September, 2012).

Walzer, M. *Just and Unjust Wars: A Moral Argument with Historical Illustrations*, 4th edn, New York: Basic Books, 2006.

26

KILLING IN WAR

Responsibility, liability, and lethal autonomous robots

Heather M. Roff

1. Introduction

> To operate in complex and uncertain environments, the autonomous system must be able to sense and understand the environment … The perception system must be able to perceive and infer the state of the environment from limited information and be able to assess the intent of other agents in the environment. This understanding is needed to provide future autonomous systems with the flexibility and adaptability for planning and executing missions in a complex, dynamic world.
>
> United States Department of Defense (DoD) "Unmanned Systems Integrated Roadmap FY 2011–2036"

The DoD's goal of creating an autonomous system that is able to assess the intent of other agents on the battlefield may not be in the distant future, as we are already at a critical juncture for the development of autonomous systems. Recently, Georgia Tech researchers fielded two pilotless planes and one driverless vehicle that gathered information about a target, shared and communicated the information with each other and then located the target.[1] These machines determined their own routes and achieved their goal without human direction. Yet what is to stop us from arming such autonomous and interoperable systems, thereby placing the power of life or death with them? Such a question is not far off base, as all branches of the U.S. military are seeking to do exactly that. We must, then, attempt to locate moral and legal responsibility for killing in war when the warfighter targeting and firing is no longer a human being but an autonomous machine. While many keep warning that such weapons are "a long way off," and so any deep philosophical consideration can be shelved for a later date, Georgia Tech's success and the DoD's goals tell a different tale.[2] The future for fully autonomous weapons is nearer than we would like to admit.

This chapter seeks to meet the challenge by addressing questions of moral responsibility and legal liability for killing in combat when the warfighter is not a human being but a lethal autonomous robot (LAR). I argue that we must engage with the traditional definitions and ideas about autonomy if we are to have any moral guidance when it comes to LARs. Especially if we view LARs as not simply weapons but a class of combatants. Furthermore, I contend that when we hand over the decision to target and to fire to a machine, we jeopardize a moral bedrock of just war theory, for we move from the central question of "who is responsible" to

352

"is there any potential of responsibility?" I suggest that LARs will never be truly autonomous in the philosophical sense of the word, and because of this, the degree to which they can act without human control threatens to undermine the moral equality of soldiers, thus placing any hope of accountability or responsibility for killing on *jus ad bellum* considerations. Finally, I counter objections that responsibility and liability for LARs automatically lies with the software programmers, politicians and military commanders.

2. Autonomy v. autonomous

The possibility for moral responsibility derives from a capacity for freedom. That is, acts that agents undertake must be voluntary for those acts to be imputable. As Kant reminds us, "imputation (*imputatio*) in the moral sense is the judgment by which someone is regarded as the author (*causa libera*) of an action."[3] By being an author of an action, there is no other cause (such as the will or act of another person or a physical hindrance) that can be attributed to it. When an agent decides to undertake an action, she exercises her will. That is, she exercises her "faculty of choosing."[4] Only when one exercises this faculty, free of any other determining force, can we call that act "free."[5] This freedom, in the philosophical (moral) sense, is called "autonomy."[6]

Autonomy is the principle of morality because through it we require agents to do or forbear from particular actions. We can require this of agents by way of a reciprocal recognition of another's freedom. For instance, I understand that I have the capacity to choose to do X, and I see that Jane, like me, also has projects she would like to pursue, so I reason that she too has the capacity to choose.[7] I recognize that all other agents with this capacity are like me: they do not want their freedom or choices hindered.[8] From this basic tenet, we can derive principles of morality to which we can then attach moral evaluations of praise or blame. But the point is the same: for any action to be imputed to me (with the attending moral evaluations), that action must be freely undertaken. Moreover, by freely choosing an action, I am intending that act. It is not merely accidental.

Robotic "autonomy" is, however, considered differently. Some view robotic autonomy as "the capacity to operate in the real-world environment without any form of external control."[9] This definition is rather broad and opens the door for differing levels of autonomous action, such as a plane landing and taking off on its own or elevators or trains operating without human conductors. This definition, though, misses more nuanced levels of uncontrolled action. Therefore others make the distinction between "automatic systems" and "autonomous" ones. Automatic systems, like the train mentioned above, "are fully preprogrammed and act repeatedly and independently of external influence or control," and can be "self-steering or self-regulating" but cannot "define" or "dictate" their own paths.[10] "Autonomous" machines on the other hand, are "self-directed toward a goal in that they do not require outside control," *and* are "able to make a decision on a set of rules and/or limitations" based on information that they deem important to the decision process.[11] Making such decisions about rules, however, is accomplished by way of programming algorithms into a software program, where the machine can "learn" and thus "choose" which means to use or perhaps goals to pursue based on the different types of programming platforms and approaches and a series of information inputs over repeated experiences of interactions.[12] With an autonomous machine, the machine is merely finding a route that it deems correct, given its programming structures and experience.

Machine autonomy is therefore fundamentally different than philosophical or moral autonomy. Machine autonomy is merely the ability to act in the world without someone or something immediately directing that action.[13] There is no discussion of intent, of consciousness, or of the type of freedom that admits of moral operators of praise or blame. The robotic notion of autonomy is radically minimalist, as it removes ethical evaluation by definitional *fiat*.

Yet the ethical regulation of warfare is premised on the fact that the agents doing the fighting are *moral agents*, i.e. agents to whom responsibility for actions can be attributed. Principles of *jus in bello* (justice in war) are not merely about whether a soldier *can* identify a combatant from a noncombatant (the principle of distinction) or calculate whether the destruction and suffering imposed by a particular strategy is proportional to the military goal to be achieved (principle of proportionality). Rather, these principles are normative prescriptions about how a soldier ought to fight, and how we can praise or blame (or punish) him when he fails to abide by them. If we cannot hold soldiers morally accountable because they lack the very capacity for moral agency, then just war theory is threatened with what Anthony Beavers calls "ethical nihilism." This is because even if LARs are able to perform better than human beings in warfare, their actions cannot be morally evaluated, and we must look for another locus of responsibility.[15]

3. LARs: responsibility and liability for killing in war

Granting that LARs are not moral agents because they are not autonomous in the moral sense presents us with a variety of problems. Foremost among these problems is where to place responsibility when the combatants are no longer human beings but machines. Traditional notions about responsibility for killing in war follows the logical division of *jus ad bellum* and *jus in bello*. *Jus ad bellum* stipulates the conditions for a war to be considered just (such as self-defense or defense of others), whereas *jus in bello* dictates the principles of just conduct during warfare (such as noncombatant immunity and proportionality). These principles are typically considered logically distinct because the way one prosecutes war can be evaluated separately from the decision to wage war. One can go to war for the right reasons, and still manage to violate the rights of others while doing so. Soldiers, therefore, are evaluated not on the decision to go to war, as that is beyond their purview, but on how they fight.

Customarily, soldiers are held responsible for failing to uphold the principles of *jus in bello*, either by intentionally flouting them or by obeying unlawful commands. This idea is bound up with the principle of the moral equality of soldiers (MES). MES holds that soldiers are "morally equal." That is, we cannot attribute responsibility for the war to them, as they are innocent of this decision, but only hold them responsible for their actions during war. We cannot blame soldiers for fighting for their country, even if they fight on an unjust side, as they are "forced to fight" for various considerations (like duress or ignorance). Nevertheless, while ordinary soldiers on both sides ought to be considered morally equal in their blamelessness, we still hold that they are equally open to attack by virtue of their status as an active threat. Soldiers are combatants, and are considered a "dangerous class" because they are "trained to fight, provided with weapons, [and] required to fight on command."[16] Noncombatants, such as civilians, are not considered dangerous and so cannot be targeted.[17] At work here is not the notion of "innocence" or "guilt" but active threat. Civilians can certainly be considered "guilty" for supporting an unjust war, but that fact does not make them liable to be killed.[18]

Yet what does MES have to do with LARs? Whether one holds MES conceptually true or merely true for practical purposes, the doctrine is functionally necessary.[19] Soldiers on both sides of a conflict are deemed moral agents; that is they are in some manner free enough to be held accountable for their actions. Whether we hold them accountable for the decision to fight does not simultaneously affect whether we hold them accountable for upholding principles of *jus in bello* or the current laws of armed conflict. MES posits that soldiers are capable of making decisions and reflecting on their own autonomy, and thus we can only hold them responsible for those actions they choose to undertake.

LARs, on the other hand, lack this capacity for moral autonomy, and thus responsibility. The only way that one could even begin to model the features of a moral agent would be to create an artificially intelligent machine. Artificial intelligence (AI) in this case would have to be considered "strong," where the machine could match and possibly exceed human intelligence. We might also require it to have intentions, the capacity for reflection and "consciousness." To program a machine to have such capacities, computer scientists attempt a variety of approaches.[20] The current consensus, though, on achieving a level of strong AI is for systems to "learn" either by example, by trial and error, or by combining these mechanisms and "evolving." Strong AIs in this instance tend to learn like human beings – through different patterns and experiences – and, like human beings, their actions cannot be controlled or predicted.

Andreas Matthias calls this effect the "responsibility gap."[21] The responsibility gap is basically the result of creating learning machines. Programmers start off as coders, where the programmer has the capacity to control "the machine in every single detail."[22] In AI systems, however, the use of symbolic logic, neural networks, or reinforcement learning obscures the ability for the programmer to follow or control the flow of information within the system. Thus autonomous systems, like the kind the DoD aspires to create, "deprive [the programmer] of the spatial link between him and his product," as the "agent [in this case a LAR] acts outside the observation horizon of its creator, who in the case of a fault, might be unable to intervene manually" to fix the problem.[23] This is the *expected* result of this type of system and how the machine becomes autonomous.

With the case of MES, a fully autonomous weapon that has the capacity to learn, evolve, match human intelligence and "*assess the intent* of other agents in the environment," is to create a machine that can act upon the world, but does not act as a moral agent within it. Modeling the ability for a machine to act intelligently does not make that machine a moral agent. While the machine has "learned," the underlying structure of the machine is still, in Kant's terms, "determined." And while the programmer lost the ability to control the machine, that does not change the machine's moral status.

We face, therefore, two perverse outcomes from creating a class of soldiers who are non-moral agents. First, we cannot morally evaluate actions undertaken by them during war. This outcome follows Beavers' charge of "ethical nihilism." We might be able to say that a particular LAR adequately discriminated between combatants and noncombatants, but that holds no moral weight. The LAR cannot be praised or blamed for doing so, for attaching moral operators to such an evaluation would be like blaming a robotic pool cleaner because it failed to stay underwater and instead started sweeping the backyard. Since LARs are not moral agents, then by definition there can be no moral equality between soldiers on a battlefield (unless both sides employ LARs, then we might say there is a moral equality of soldiers in that both lack moral status).[24] Second, and more importantly, if we cannot attribute moral or legal responsibility to the agents on the battlefield, then we must step back from *jus in bello* considerations and return to *jus ad bellum* ones. In other words, if we cannot hold the warfighter responsible, we must either look to the manufactures/programmers, the military, political leaders, or perhaps even the civilian population.

Such a conclusion might not seem to present us with a problem. We hold domestic populations and political and military leaders morally, and sometimes legally, responsible for wars fought all the time. Indeed, we sanction leaders (either through economic or legal means), tax populations, and try military leaders in domestic or international courts. We certainly praise or blame them for wars. However, as we will see in the next section, holding such people accountable for the actions of LARs is not so straightforward and actually poses us with the problem that holding anyone responsible may be impossible.

4. Responsibility and liability

If the combatants in war are incapable of moral responsibility, then we must decide who bears the responsibility for their actions. I will try to answer the question of who is morally as well as legally responsible by looking to just war theory and contemporary law, particularly through the legal constructs of vicarious liability.[25] Vicarious liability is when "contributory fault, or some element of it is ascribed to one party, but liability is ascribed to a different party."[26] Thus while LARs may do the acting, and thus be the "cause" of harm, some other party will bear responsibility for the act. Much of the discussion about assigning vicarious responsibility for military robots focuses on software programmers and military commanders, but if we are to truly identify responsible parties, then we must also look to *jus ad bellum* considerations such as the role that political leaders and civilians play.

4.1 Software programmers

Scholars typically note that even though LARs may achieve "autonomy" they will not be capable of anything more than a "quasi-agent" status. That is, they will "enjoy only partial rights and duties."[27] While granting LARs a "quasi-agent" status seems to assume their moral and legal standing already, many point to the first step in the process: the programmer.[28] As the programmer, or manufacturer, creates the system, responsibility for creating the machine and liability for negligence might be placed with him. Legal liability in this sense can be the result of a failure to take proper care, to avoid foreseeable risks or to warn.[29] In other words, the programmer ought to take due care while creating a lethal machine, and if he has not, then the machine's actions are attributable (in whole or in part) to him.

Yet in the case of LARs, does the argument for programmers' responsibility actually work? The answer is a resounding "no." In the case of vicarious liability, there must exist a "special relationship" between the two parties, and in the case of LARs, there is no legally (or morally) relevant fact that situates the robot and its programmer in such a relationship. First, we cannot attribute vicarious responsibility by using a parent/child analogy for two reasons. One, the programmer is not considered the "guardian" of the robot. Two, and more importantly, the notion of parental liability can only apply when wrongful actions are the result of a parent's negligent acts of control over the acts of the child. The idea is that a parent must have a sufficient degree of control over the acts of the child. Yet as Matthias has pointed out, the programming structures that enable learning for autonomous systems creates a "responsibility gap" where the programmers do not have control over the system. And as Sparrow notes, holding programmers responsible for the acts of robots they cannot control would be like "holding parents responsible for the actions of their children once they have left their care."[30]

One might counter that we can still use the doctrine of *Respondeat Superior* to hold programmers responsible because this account does not presuppose control.[31] In this relationship, an employer is held responsible for acts committed by an employee in the course of employment.[32] The employer is held liable for the employee's actions even if there is no causal contribution or any direct order from the employer. Unfortunately, this also fails as a basis of liability for LARs. The modern notion of *Respondeat Superior* is not that of a master and slave where consent plays no part, but the particular relationship where both parties consent to carry out certain roles and perform particular duties. The role of consent here is crucial. Even though the employer may not order or condone the action undertaken by the employee, or even be thought to control the acts of the employee, through a mutual agreement both parties undertook particular role responsibilities, and it is only in the case of the employee carrying out the scope of his employment that that employer is held liable. In the case of LARs, there is no mutual contract or agreement, as LARs cannot be said to "consent." Moreover, in this instance the sticky conceptual difference between tort and criminal law raises its head. Vicarious responsibility is typically a civil, not criminal matter. But in the case of LARs, violations of *jus in bello* would not be considered tortious acts but criminal ones. If we were to hold a principal liable, we would have to show that where no causal contribution to the harmful act were made, knowledge of the criminal act plus acquiescence to it would be required to attribute liability to the principal.[33] This, of course, looks less like vicarious liability due to the epistemic constraints and more like a doctrine of command responsibility.

4.2 Military commanders

Perhaps we can attribute responsibility to military commanders. Indeed, the military doctrine of command responsibility is broad enough that some might claim that officers can be held morally and legally responsible for the actions of their subordinates, where the commander *should have known* what would happen.[34] Here one could rely on a framework similar to due care, in that failing to take due care, or foresee possible outcomes, one could be held responsible.[35] Unfortunately, this is not the case. Contemporary usage and prosecutions based on this doctrine require more than the vague epistemic "should have known." Modern case law requires the "effective control" of subordinates by superiors.[36]

Command responsibility is premised on the fact that there is a superior-subordinate relationship, and the "test to determine whether a person is a superior is … one of 'effective control.'"[37] Superiors must have the "material ability to prevent and punish the commission of these offenses."[38] There need not be formal documentation, rigid formalized hierarchies or direct orders to hold "superiors" to account, merely the ability to halt, prevent and punish a subordinate's action. Since effective control is the primary criterion, it also serves to exculpate superiors from prosecution, where a "person who is formally a superior in the line of command may be excluded from criminal liability if that superior does *not* exercise actual control."[39]

Looking to the case of LARs, the effective control criterion would actually exculpate leaders from legal responsibility because of the commanders' inability to control the machines. Autonomous machines are "*impossible*" to control "by a human in real-time due to its processing speed and the multitude of operational variables involved."[40] Thus if control is an impossibility, then there is no way that a commander could "prevent or punish" a violation of *jus in bello* by machines. There can be no prevention because there can be no foresight as to what the machine will actually do, and there can be no "punishment" because punishment presupposes moral personhood and the capacity to suffer.[41] Indeed, even Lin, Abney and Bekey concede that punishing a robot makes little sense.[42] Punishment is an act done to moral agents who violate a right, and punishment is not about harm but guilt. I can harm someone without wronging him, and I can equally suffer harm without being wronged or punished.

Moral responsibility for the deployment of LARs is also a difficult issue, and if we are to take any cues from the legal discussion it appears that military commanders also might not be held morally responsible for the acts of the machines. We might want to attribute some responsibility to them, as surely they decided when and where to deploy them through their strategies and tactics, but this level of moral responsibility is rather low. Perhaps they were ordered to deploy them (thus were under some sort of command or duress), or if they had no foresight into what the machine would do or believed that the machine would really act in accordance with the laws of war, then we would claim that they have mitigated moral responsibility due to epistemic constraints. They are excused in some way.

4.3 Civilians and politicians

If we cannot hold software programmers morally or legally responsible, and we might have difficulty assigning legal liability and moral responsibility to military commanders, then perhaps we should look to those individuals who make the decisions for the development, deployment and use of these weapons. In other words, perhaps we should look to the politicians who issue commands to the military and procure such weapons, as well as to those individuals who place the politicians in their offices. Civilians, after all, vote for these leaders, and they also pay taxes whereby the government has the material means to fund wars and procure weaponry. Thus we have two avenues left for ascribing responsibility for acts committed by LARs: collective responsibility of the civilian population and individual role responsibility of political leaders.

Civilian responsibility for the acts committed by LARs, though, is a tough road to travel. Typically, in just war theory when any discussion of civilian responsibility enters the fray it is in regards to the decision to wage aggressive war, not the means used in war (just or otherwise). This is not to say we could not use this framework. In discussions about holding civilians responsible, the principle tends to follow Walzer's line of reasoning: "The greater the possibility of free action in the command sphere, the greater the degree of guilt for evil deeds done in the name of everyone."[43] But given that even in democratic societies such free action is either impossible or quite inefficacious, citizens have little to no effect on foreign policy decisions, as the recent decision by President Obama to assassinate Anwar al-Alwaki proves.

One might counter that in free democratic societies, citizens ultimately vote for political officials, and so their decision to place such officials in office makes them morally responsible for the acts committed by those officials. Yet this too is a difficult pill to swallow. Voting is not an indication of anything more than mere preference. It does not obligate one to obey the laws of the land, nor does it mean that one undertakes the moral responsibility for another party's actions.[44] One might have no indication that a political official will deploy autonomous weapons in warfare at the time of casting one's ballot, or have any indication that through the various avenues of defense spending that one's tax dollars will end up buying this weaponry.

Moreover, the time-honored excuse of non-culpable ignorance may also exculpate civilians from any sort of responsibility. They had no idea that the government was using this type of technology, or even if they did know that such weapons were used and existed, they were not informed of the consequences of such action, or perhaps they were intentionally misled by the government. In any case, holding civilians morally responsible for the actions of LARs is fraught with difficulty. We might only be able to say that select civilians are morally responsible, that is they lobby for the use of such weapons, have an effect on the policy outcomes, and publically support the policies. Yet even here there is little we could do other than express our approbation, and the degree of causal contribution is so low that we could not even hope to hold these individuals legally liable.

Politicians, however, do seem the only solid locus of responsibility for the actions of LARs. Foreign policy elites, heads of state and the like are the only ones truly making the decisions to deploy such weapons. They are the "source rather than the recipient of superior orders."[45] They are assumed to have all of the available knowledge, much more than the ordinary citizen, and issue orders to military commanders. Thus we would assume that political leaders are aware of the uncontrollability of LARs, and so a decision to field them makes them morally and legally responsible for the machine's actions.

Unfortunately, such attribution of responsibility is tenuous. We might not be able to hold them legally liable given the current legal constraints on command responsibility and the lack of any international governance structures on autonomous weapons. We can use moral operators of praise or blame, but absent a shift in the requirement for effective control of subordinates and the creation of international arms regulation for autonomous weapons, legal responsibility will remain unachievable.

5. Conclusion

The deployment of LARs in combat presents us with a challenge to just war theory never before seen. First, it divorces *jus in bello* judgments of responsibility from the behavior of combatants, as the combatants are no longer considered moral agents capable of moral standing. By doing so, it forces any evaluations of responsibility to *jus ad bellum* considerations of who decides to initiate war and to use LARs in combat. Instead of deciding whether political officials started an aggressive war, and thus can be charged with a crime of aggression, we must now discern whether those officials can be held morally and legally responsible for the conduct of autonomous machines.

Moreover, due to the fact that "effective control" is a criterion in legal responsibility to cases of command responsibility and some instances of vicarious liability, the creation and use of LARs leaves us with the perverse outcome that no one can be held legally responsible for their actions. The landscape of just war has changed, and it is no longer true that "soldiers can never be transformed into mere instruments of war," and that the "trigger is always part of the gun, not part of the man."[46] In the case of LARs this is the exact opposite: a mere instrument of war is now a soldier, and the trigger is part and parcel of it.

Notes

1 L.G. Weiss, "Autonomous Robots in the Fog of War," *IEEE Spectrum*, August, 2011, pp. 31–57.
2 Indeed, Rear Adm. Matthew Klunder notes that "autonomy" is on the docket for future naval achievements. "Navy Says Autonomy is Key to Robotic Submarines," *Los Angeles Times*, 9 February 2012. And the U.S. Air Force claims that "advances in AI [artificial intelligence] will enable systems to make combat decisions and act within legal and policy constraints without necessarily requiring human input." United States Air Force, "Unmanned Aircraft Systems Flight Plan 2009–2047," p. 41. Of course, the USAF also concedes that "authorizing a machine to make lethal combat decisions is contingent upon political and military leaders resolving legal and ethical questions" (ibid.). Academics heatedly debate whether resolving such questions is even possible. Politicians and military officials merely gesture at such problems, without really grappling with the deep issues involved. For instance, the U.S. Congress formed the "Congressional Unmanned Systems Caucus" to "seek fair and equitable solutions to challenges created by UAV [unmanned aerial vehicles] operations in the U.S. National Air Space (NAS)." Yet the Caucus seems to place more weight on "acknowledging" the value of these systems and developing and producing more of them than fully engaging with any ethical or legal problems such weapons might create. Congressional Unmanned Systems Caucus "Mission and Main Goals." Online. Available at: http://unmannedsystemscaucus.mckeon.house.gov/about/purpose-mission-goals.shtml (accessed 26 March, 2013).
3 I. Kant, *The Metaphysics of Morals*, in M. Gregor (ed.), Cambridge: Cambridge University Press, 2006, p. 19.
4 I. Kant, *The Grounding for the Metaphysics of Morals*, J. Ellington (trans.), Indianapolis: Hackett Publishing Co, 1993, p. 23.

5 The notion of acting free from any other determining force is for Kant crucial. The only ground that is allowed to move us to act is the moral law, or duty. But other considerations, such as hunger, thirst, desire, glory, fear, etc. are not sufficient for the act to be considered "free" and thus moral.

6 Autonomy of the will is the property that the will has of being a law to itself (independently of any property of the objects of volition). The principle of autonomy is this: "Always choose in such a way that in the same volition the maxims of the choice are at the same time present as universal law … [T]he above principle of autonomy is the sole principle of morals" (Kant, *The Grounding for the Metaphysics of Morals*, p. 44–45). The idea of willing a maxim universally is one formulation of Kant's categorical imperatives. To will a maxim universally means to will that all other agents in the world also will this same maxim of action. If one's action would be frustrated by everyone doing the same thing, then the act (and the maxim) is considered morally wrong.

7 Waldron attempts to understand the difference between the modern notions of "personal autonomy," that is merely choosing projects for oneself regardless of the content of said project, and "moral autonomy," or choosing personal projects in connection with a conception of "the good." His argument finds that Kant's theory of autonomy, and indeed even more contemporary liberal theories of autonomy, cannot keep both forms of autonomy separate. The discussion is rather detailed on both the Kantian and the contemporary accounts, but Waldron's conclusion is that the capacity for choice, along with capacities for self-reflection, consciousness and the recognition that acting towards some conception of "the good" is bound up in both accounts. Contemporary liberal theorists thus draw off of Kantian premises, and these theorists cannot maintain a strict logical division between both accounts. Thus for our purposes in this essay, we can rely on Kant's account without failing to acknowledge contemporary liberal accounts of those like Raz, Rawls or Dworkin. Cf. J. Waldron, "Moral Autonomy and Personal Autonomy," in J. Christman and J. Anderson (eds), *Autonomy and the Challenges to Liberalism*, Cambridge: Cambridge University Press, 2005, pp. 308–314.

8 This brief example highlights Kant's "fact of reason." I cannot enter into the debate about the coherence and use of Kant's fact of reason here, as it is outside the scope of this chapter. Cf. I. Kant, *Critique of Practical Reason*, M. Gregor (ed.), Cambridge: Cambridge University Press, 2010, pp. 28–29.

9 P. Lin, G. Bekey and K. Abney, "Autonomous Military Robotics: Risk, Ethics, and Design," *US Department of Navy, Office of Naval Research*, 2008, p. 4; R. Arkin, "The Ethical Case for Unmanned Systems," *Journal of Military Ethics*, 9:4, 2010, pp. 332–431; C. Allen, G. Varner and J. Zinser, "Prolegomena to Any Future Artificial Moral Agent," *Journal of Experimental Artificial Intelligence*, 12:3, 2000, pp. 251–261.

10 U.S. Department of Defense. "Unmanned Systems Integrated Roadmap FY 2011-2036," 2011. Online. Available at: http://www.defenseinnovationmarketplace.mil/resources/UnmannedSystems IntegratedRoadmapFY2011.pdf (accessed 26 March, 2013).

11 Ibid., p. 43.

12 For instance, there are "top-down," "bottom-up" and "mixed" approaches to software programming and learning. Top-down approaches provide a set of rules that a machine could not violate, while bottom-up approaches provide no set of such rules but allow the machine to learn through experience. A mixed approach would allow the machine to learn, but then when confronted with a particularly defined case would either permit or forbid certain actions. Cf. W. Wallach and C. Allen, *Moral Machines: Teaching Robots Right from Wrong*, Oxford: Oxford University Press, 2009, pp. 83–124.

13 Some do not hold this view, and view machine autonomy as an open question or that there might be potential precursors available to programmers to develop machines with intentionality and perhaps consciousness. James Moor, for instance, believes that in the future it might be possible to program machines to be virtuous agents, and thus evaluate their actions in moral terms. Presently, however, we can still evaluate or assess the actions of machines based on how well they perform their functions. The notion of programming a virtuous robot is also taken up by P. Lin, K. Abney and G.A. Bekey in their 2008 report. Others, like Luciano Floridi, believe that one can create artificial machine agents that can independently generate semantic content to symbols. This, one might argue, seems like a precursor to some form of intentionality and perhaps consciousness, as the ability to generate semantic content to symbols allows machines to learn and communicate. It is not my intention to enter the debate about this here; however, for our purposes we can respond to both sides rather briefly. For Moor, the ability to create or program virtuous robots appears to be a *non sequitur*. Programming a machine to "act virtuously" undermines the very notion of acting virtuously. One must choose to act a certain way – in Aristotle's notion, the right way, at the right time with the right disposition. Programming a machine to do this vitiates its moral worth. Second, in response to Floridi, while we might say that the ability

to create machines that learn and communicate by way of interacting with their environment is quite novel, that does not mean they are autonomous in the moral sense either. Other types of beings, such as animals, interact with and learn from their environment. Moreover, they create ways of communicating with each other based on evolutionary criteria, but we would not want to call them morally autonomous. Cf. J.H. Moor, "The Nature, Importance, and Difficulty of Machines Ethics," *IEEE Intelligent Systems*, 31:4, 2006, pp. 18–21 and L. Floridi *The Philosophy of Information*, Oxford: Oxford University Press, 2011.

14 A. Beavers, "Moral Machines and the Threat of Ethical Nihilism," in P. Lin, K. Abney and G.A. Bekey (eds), *Robot Ethics: The Ethical and Social Implications of Robotics*, MIT Press: 2012, pp. 333–344.

15 R. Sparrow, "Robotic Weapons and the Future of War," in Paolo Tripodi and Jessica Wolfendale (eds), *New Wars and New Soldiers: Military Ethics in the Contemporary World*, Aldershot: Ashgate Press, 2012, p. 123.

16 M. Walzer, *Just and Unjust Wars: A Moral Argument with Historical Illustrations*, 3rd edn, New York: Basic Books, 2000, p. 144.

17 There is of course the objection that the Doctrine of Double Effect (DDE) permits civilians to be killed when their deaths are foreseeable but unintended effects of targeting a legitimate military target. DDE is a conceptual mine field that I cannot enter into here.

18 Recently, MES' validity has come under close scrutiny. Jeff McMahan holds the principle as false, arguing that ordinary soldiers on the unjust side of a conflict are in fact responsible for the decision to go to war, and there can be no division between *jus ad bellum* and *jus in bello*. Ordinary soldiers make conscious decisions to sign up for military service, or they allow themselves to be conscripted, and so find themselves liable to be killed on the basis of this decision. What all of this amounts to is that if one holds MES as false, then one can target combatants and noncombatants based on some notion of their responsibility in the decision to wage or the prosecution of the war. However, soldiers, and possibly some civilians, on the unjust side are liable to be killed due to their decision to wage or support an unjust war. The result is that soldiers and civilians on the just side of a conflict are not liable to attack, as they are morally innocent (or in McMahan's terms "nonresponsible"). McMahan does argue that targeting civilians is not very effective for prosecuting war, and so civilians should typically not be liable to be killed. While I cannot offer a lengthy retort here, this argument to me seems false. Given McMahan's principles, civilian support for the war seems to me no different than an ordinary soldier's decision to support the war or allow himself to be conscripted. McMahan's conclusion that civilians are not liable is not based on the same principles of moral responsibility, but rather the observation that "unlike unjust combatants, civilians do not generally *pose* a threat of wrongful harm." J. McMahan, *Killing in War*, Oxford: Oxford University Press, 2009, p. 225. This is in sharp contradiction to McMahan's earlier statement that he has "explicitly rejected the view that posing a threat is the basis of liability to attack in war" (ibid., p. 34). Thus, McMahan seems to be playing with two different sets of rules for combatants and noncombatants to reach his conclusions. Rodin comes to the opposite conclusion in his reading of MES. Rodin finds that MES, while false, does not necessarily mean that one is entitled to target civilians and have increased war rights. Unlike McMahan, Rodin argues that what follows is further restriction on the conduct of war and that greater care must be taken to avoid targeting civilians. D. Rodin, "The Moral Inequality of Soldiers," in D. Rodin and H. Shue (eds), *Just and Unjust Warriors*, Oxford: Oxford University Press, 2008, pp. 44–68.

19 M. Walzer believes that MES is conceptually true, and Mapel has argued that both sides are equally made into "attackers." McMahan and Rodin argue that MES is a conceptual fiction, but practically necessary for the laws of war to function. Cf. Walzer, *Just and Unjust Wars*; D.R. Mapel, "Coerced Moral Agents? Individual Responsibility for Military Service," *Journal of Political Philosophy*, 6:2, 1998, pp. 171–189; J. McMahan, *Killing in War*, p. 108; J. McMahan, "The Ethics of Killing in War," *Ethics*, 114:1, 2004, p. 703; D. Rodin, "The Moral Inequality of Soldiers."

20 Krishnan identifies nine different programming attempts: top-down programming, bottom-up programming, expert systems, Cyc, neural networks, genetic algorithms, autonomous agent approach, nouvelle AI, and evolutionary robotics. Cf Armin Krishnan,. *Killer Robots*, Aldershot: Ashgate Press, 2009, pp. 46–53. Andreas Matthias focuses on five different types of AI programming: symbolic systems, connectionism and neural networks, reinforcement learning, genetic algorithms, and genetic programming. A. Matthias, "The Responsibility Gap: Ascribing Responsibility for the Actions of Learning Automata," *Ethics and Information Technology*, 6:3, 2004, 175–183.

21 A. Matthias, "The Responsibility Gap: Ascribing Responsibility for the Actions of Learning Automata", p. 177.

22 Ibid., p. 181.

23 Ibid., p. 182. Santoro, Marino and Tamburrini argue that the "responsibility gap" is not actually a problem with regard to autonomous learning systems. They claim that legal frameworks designed around liability can distribute responsibility and costs to programmers and manufacturers of these systems. Unfortunately, their argument does little to address the instances of moral responsibility for these systems. Thus Matthias' concern that effective control is necessary for the attribution of responsibility gains more ground when viewed from a moral, rather than a legal, standpoint. Cf. S. Matteo, D. Marino and G. Tamburrini, "Learning Robots Interacting with Humans: From Epistemic Risk to Responsibility," *AI & Society*, 22, 2008, pp. 309–311.

24 One result of this conclusion is that if we hold either the conceptual or practical arguments for MES to be true, then soldiers have a right of self-defense against their counterparts. However, if MES is not even possible because one side is not a moral agent, then justifications for self-defense seem to fall apart. A lethal autonomous robot is not defending a "self," and so lethal force cannot be justified on those grounds. The only apparent justification seems to be one of "collective" self-defense of a nation. However, this line of reasoning is fraught with its own problems. Cf. D. Rodin, *War and Self-Defense*, Oxford: Oxford University Press, 2002.

25 There are few authors who engage with the question of who is morally responsible for LARs (Sparrow being one); however, there are several that attempt to delineate the legal responsibility of those who deploy such weapons. For a good explanation of the differing positions and ways in which liability is traditionally attributed, as well as canvasing the most recent literature, cf.: Ugo Pagallo, "Robots of Just War: A Legal Perspective," *Philosophy and Technology*, 24:3, 2011, pp. 307–323.

26 J. Feinberg Collective Responsibility, *Journal of Philosophy*, 65:21, 1968, p. 675

27 P. Lin, G. Bekey and K. Abney, "Autonomous Military Robotics: Risk, Ethics, and Design," p. 55.

28 Only moral agents have rights and duties, even partial ones, and they have said rights against and duties towards other moral agents.

29 P. Lin, K. Abney and G.A. Bekey, "Autonomous Military Robotics: Risk, Ethics, and Design," pp. 56–58.

30 R. Sparrow, "Killer Robots," *Journal of Applied Philosophy*, 24:1, 2007, p. 70.

31 Lokhorst and van den Hoven explicitly invoke this route. G-J. Lokhorst and J. van den Hoven, "Responsibility for Military Robots," in P. Lin, K. Abney and G.A. Bekey (eds), *Robot Ethics: The Ethical and Social Implications of Robotics*, MIT Press, 2012, p. 151.

32 F. B. Sayre, "Criminal Responsibility for the Acts of Another," *Harvard Law Review*, 43:5, 1930, p. 693.

33 Ibid., p. 706.

34 *In re Yamashita*, 327 U.S. 1 (1946); Case No. 72: *German High Command Trial*: Trial of Wilhelm Von Leeb and Thirteen Others, 12 U.N. War Crimes Comm'n, Law Reports of the Trials of War Criminals 1 (1949). *Yamashita* held that, though no direct evidence linked General Yamashita affirmatively to his subordinates' crimes, he failed in his duties to control, prevent or punish his subordinates.

35 Lin, Bekey and Abney take this route. They claim that an autonomous robot, but not a "Kantian-autonomous-robot" (a machine with moral autonomy), would be programmed such that it would be incapable of choosing its own ends, and thus violating the rules of war, and so any responsibility for the robot's malfunction should be placed with the military commanders. This response is unsatisfactory though, as it appears that their argument implies the programming of unlawful orders, and not a rewriting of software by the machine itself. They seem to dismiss this possibility, though it is in fact not only possible but probable given autonomous systems. In the case of malfunction, then they claim it is a product liability issue. Cf. P. Lin, G. Bekey and K. Abney, "Autonomous Military Robotics: Risk, Ethics, and Design," p. 66.

36 International Criminal Tribunal for Rwanda Statute Article 6(3), "The fact that any of the acts referred to in articles 2 to 4 of the present Statute was committed by a subordinate does not relieve his or her superior of criminal responsibility if he or she knew or had reason to know that the subordinate was about to commit such acts or had done so and the superior failed to take the necessary and reasonable measures to prevent such acts or to punish the perpetrators thereof." Online. Available at: http://www.unictr.org/Legal/StatuteoftheTribunal/tabid/94/Default.aspx (accessed 26 March, 2013). International Criminal Tribunal for Former Yugoslavia Statute Article 7(3), "The fact that any of the acts referred to in articles 2 to 5 of the present Statute was committed by a subordinate does not relieve his superior of criminal responsibility if he knew or had reason to know that the subordinate was about to commit such acts or had done so and the superior failed to take the necessary and reasonable

measures to prevent such acts or to punish the perpetrators thereof." Online. Available at: http://www.icty.org/x/file/Legal%20Library/Statute/statute_sept09_en.pdf (accessed 26 March, 2013).

37 S. Boelaert-Suominen "Prosecuting Superiors for Crimes Committed by Subordinates: A Discussion of the First Significant Case Law Since the Second World War," *Virginia Journal of International Law*, 41: 4, 2001, p. 762.

38 Ibid., note 71.

39 Ibid., p. 765.

40 Matthias, "The Responsibility Gap: Ascribing Responsibility for the Actions of Learning Automata," p. 183.

41 R. Sparrow, "Killer Robots," pp. 71–73. Lokhorst and van den Hoven object to Sparrow's claim that punishment is necessary for responsibility. They charge that Sparrow's argument that suffering is necessary for punishment is overstated. Robots could, they think, suffer (given strong AI), and that even if they could not suffer, punishment is not the only effective means of behavior modification. Other alternatives exist, and so could be equally employed. While Lokhorst and van den Hoven's objections are noted, they miss the mark. Punishment is still about moral responsibility for a wrong imposed on another. If one is not a moral agent, then one cannot be punished – regardless of the question of suffering – otherwise any "harm" done is mere harm, and does not comport with the concept of punishment. Cf. Lokhorst and van den Hoven, "Responsibility for Military Robots," pp. 148–150.

42 P. Lin, K. Abney and G.A. Bekey, "Autonomous Military Robotics: Risk, Ethics, and Design," p. 60. Moreover, Asaro also notes that punishment of autonomous systems seems doubtful. P.M. Asaro, "A Body to Kick, but Still no Soul to Damn: Legal Perspectives on Robotics," in P. Lin, K. Abney and G.A. Bekey (eds), *Robot Ethics: The Ethical and Social Implications of Robotics*, MIT Press, 2012, p. 181.

43 M. Walzer, *Just and Unjust Wars*, p. 298.

44 Simmons notes that voting is merely a sign of preference or approval, but does not obligate a citizen to obey the laws. When one votes this is not an act of consent, as consent requires that an act be voluntary, intentional and informed, and acts of tacit or implied consent require that the situation one is presented with is clearly one where consent is appropriate, there is a definite period of time when objections or dissent might be noted, and a specified period of time when dissent is no longer acceptable. Cf. A.J. Simmons, *Moral Principles and Political Obligation*, Princeton: Princeton University Press, 1979. pp. 75–93.

45 M. Walzer, *Just and Unjust Wars*, p. 291.

46 Ibid., p. 311.

References

Allen, C., G. Varner and J. Zinser. "Prolegomena to Any Future Artificial Moral Agent," *Journal of Experimental Artificial Intelligence*, 12:3, 2000, pp. 251–261.

Arkin, R. "The Ethical Case for Unmanned Systems" *Journal of Military Ethics*, 9:4, 2010, pp. 332–431.

Asaro, P.M. "A Body to Kick, but Still No Soul to Damn: Legal Perspectives on Robotics," in P. Lin, K. Abney and G.A. Bekey (eds), *Robot Ethics: The Ethical and Social Implications of Robotics*, MIT Press, 2012, pp. 169–186.

Beavers, A. "Moral Machines and the Threat of Ethical Nihilism," in P. Lin, K. Abney and G.A. Bekey (eds), *Robot Ethics: The Ethical and Social Implications of Robotics*, MIT Press, 2012, pp. 333–344.

Boelaert-Suominen, S. "Prosecuting Superiors for Crimes Committed by Subordinates: A Discussion of the First Significant Case Law Since the Second World War," *Virginia Journal of International Law*, 41:4, 2001, pp. 747–785.

Congressional Unmanned Systems Caucus "Mission and Main Goals." Online. Available at: http://unmannedsystemscaucus.mckeon.house.gov/about/purpose-mission-goals.shtml (accessed 26 March, 2013).

Feinberg, J. "Collective Responsibility," *Journal of Philosophy*, 65:21, 1968, pp. 674–688.

Floridi, L. *The Philosophy of Information*, Oxford: Oxford University Press, 2011.

Hennigan, W.J. "Navy Says Autonomy is Key to Robotic Submarines," *Los Angeles Times* February 9, 2012. Online. Available at: http://articles.latimes.com/2012/feb/10/business/la-fi-0210-drone-submarine-20120210 (accessed 10 February, 2012).

International Criminal Tribunal for Rwanda. Online. Available at: http://www.unictr.org/Legal/StatuteoftheTribunal/tabid/94/Default.aspx (accessed 26 March, 2013).

International Criminal Tribunal for Former Yugoslavia. Online. Available at: http://www.icty.org/x/ file/Legal%20Library/Statute/statute_sept09_en.pdf (accessed 26 March, 2013).

Kant, I. *Critique of Practical Reason*, Mary Gregor (ed.), Cambridge: Cambridge University Press, 2010.

——*The Grounding for the Metaphysics of Morals*, James Ellington (trans.), Indianapolis: Hackett Publishing Co, 1993.

——*The Metaphysics of Morals*, Mary Gregor (ed.), Cambridge: Cambridge University Press, 2006.

Krishnan, A. *Killer Robots*, Aldershot: Ashgate Press, 2009.

Lin, P., G. Bekey and K. Abney. "Autonomous Military Robotics: Risk, Ethics, and Design," *US Department of Navy, Office of Naval Research*, 2008.

Lokhorst, G-J and J. van den Hoven. "Responsibility for Military Robots," in P. Lin, K. Abney and G.A. Bekey (eds), *Robot Ethics: The Ethical and Social Implications of Robotics*, MIT Press, 2012, pp. 145–156.

Mapel, D.R. "Coerced Moral Agents? Individual Responsibility for Military Service," *Journal of Political Philosophy*, 6:2, 1998, pp. 171–189.

Matteo, S., D. Marino and G. Tamburrini. "Learning Robots Interacting with Humans: From Epistemic Risk to Responsibility," *AI & Society*, 22, 2008, pp. 301–314.

Matthias, A. "The Responsibility Gap: Ascribing Responsibility for the Actions of Learning Automata," *Ethics and Information Technology*, 6:3, 2004, pp. 175–183.

McMahan, J. *Killing in War*, Oxford: Oxford University Press, 2009.

——"The Ethics of Killing in War," *Ethics*, 114:1, 2004, pp. 693–732.

Moor, J.H. "The Nature, Importance, and Difficulty of Machines Ethics," *IEEE Intelligent Systems*, 31:4, 2006, pp. 18–21.

Pagallo, U. "Robots of Just War: A Legal Perspective," *Philosophy and Technology*, 24:3, 2011, pp. 307–323.

Rodin, D. "The Moral Inequality of Soldiers," in D. Rodin and H. Shue (eds), *Just and Unjust Warriors*, Oxford: Oxford University Press, 2008, pp. 44–68

——*War and Self-Defense*, Oxford: Oxford University Press, 2002.

Sayre, F.B. "Criminal Responsibility for the Acts of Another," *Harvard Law Review*, 43:5, 1930, pp. 689–723.

Simmons, A. J. *Moral Principles and Political Obligation*, Princeton: Princeton University Press, 1979.

Sparrow, R. "Robotic Weapons and the Future of War," in P. Tripodi and J. Wolfendale (eds), *New Wars and New Soldiers: Military Ethics in the Contemporary World*, Aldershot: Ashgate Press, 2011.

——"Killer Robots," *Journal of Applied Philosophy*, 24:1, 2007, pp. 62–77.

U.S. Department of Defense. "Unmanned Systems Integrated Roadmap FY 2011-2036," 2011. Online. Available at: http://www.defenseinnovationmarketplace.mil/resources/UnmannedSystems IntegratedRoadmapFY2011.pdf (accessed 26 March, 2013).

Waldron, J. "Moral Autonomy and Personal Autonomy" in J. Christman and J. Anderson (eds), *Autonomy and the Challenges to Liberalism*, Cambridge: Cambridge University Press, 2005, pp. 308–314.

Wallach, W. and C. Allen. *Moral Machines: Teaching Robots Right from Wrong*, Oxford: Oxford University Press, 2009.

Walzer, M. *Just and Unjust Wars: A Moral Argument with Historical Illustrations*, 3rd edn, New York: Basic Books, 2000.

Weiss, L.G. "Autonomous Robots in the Fog of War," *IEEE Spectrum*, August, 2011, pp. 31–57. Online. Available at: http://ieeeexplore.ieee.org/iel5/6/5960134/05960163.pdf?tp=&arnumber=5960163& isnumberi=5960134 (accessed 26 March, 2013).

United States Air Force. "Unmanned Aircraft Systems Flight Plan 2009-2047" 2009. Online. Available at: http://www.govexec.com/pdfs/072309kp1.pdf (accessed 26 March, 2013).

Yamashita, (1946) 327 U.S. 1 Case No. 72: *German High Command Trial*: Trial of Wilhelm Von Leeb and Thirteen Others, 12 U.N. War Crimes Comm'n, Law Reports of the Trials of War Criminals 1, 1949.

Cyberwarfare

27

JUS IN SILICO

Moral restrictions on the use of cyberwarfare

George R. Lucas Jr

1. Introduction

Can there be such a thing as an "ethical" cyberwar, fought in compliance with the conventional principles of just war theory? Especially given that political leaders in the U.S., U.K., Australia, and major European NATO countries all unanimously and persistently report that they are already under relentless cyber attack,[1] one might reasonably wonder, instead, whether it even makes sense to talk about "ethics," morality or possible legal constraints on our behavior in the development and use of cyberweapons, or engaging in cyberwarfare.

How, then, can we meaningfully speak of ethics, law, and just war concepts when adversary nations, organized crime, and terrorists are relentlessly engaged in attacking us, harming us, and stealing us blind without regard for those concepts? The vulnerabilities, the threats posed, and the genuine harm already done are all very real. Would not a consideration of ethics or legal governance at this point merely serve merely to hamper us with constraints on our ability to respond to these vulnerabilities, and advantage adversaries who give such matters absolutely no credence whatsoever?

Nevertheless, I want to argue that we and our potential adversaries would derive considerable advantage by giving some thought to governance in both morality and the law, in that it encourages all concerned to reflect more cogently upon strategic goals that might be served by cyber conflict. An "ethical analysis" of cyber conflict invites all parties to it to think clearly about what we are doing, what we are willing (and perhaps unwilling) to do, and why. I think that it *is* therefore appropriate and important to talk about what we ourselves in places like the U.S., the U.K, Europe, and Australia can and should do in response to what appear to be a relentless barrage of espionage and cyber attacks directed against military, commercial, and vital infrastructure targets in our nation by persons or entities unknown. We must also consider whether there are limits (of an ethical sort) on what we are willing to do, and finally about whether, just as in conventional or counterinsurgency conflicts, it is really true that acknowledging and abiding by such limits automatically puts us at a disadvantage in our conflict with adversaries and criminals.[2]

2. Threats and vulnerabilities

Let us begin, then, with a consideration of the threats and vulnerabilities. Authors Richard A. Clark, Joel Brenner, and Mark Bowden (among many others) have all done a service by raising public awareness of the significance of cyber conflict, pointing out the extensive risks and vulnerabilities, and by inviting us to think more carefully about how to manage that risk.[3] At the same time, it is important not to move all the way from abject lack of concern (a fair description, for example, of the U.S. Naval Service's attitude toward cyber conflict barely two or three years ago) to an exaggerated or hysterical assessment of our vulnerabilities. Threat inflation is no more of use to us in thinking through these difficult questions than ignorance and avoidance.[4]

Conceptual confusion and linguistic equivocation (in which different parties to a dispute employ similar-sounding language in often divergent and misleading ways) is an enormous obstacle to the clear analysis of military technologies and threats, and nowhere is this more apparent than in the arena of cyber conflict:[5] For example, Clarke and Brenner both offer chilling scenarios of a potential cyber "Pearl Harbor on Steroids," with dams bursting and flooding, trains derailing, planes falling from the sky, poison gases escaping from chemical storage plants in large cities, and the like. But most of the subsequent discussion of actual cyber conflict documents criminal activity, vandalism, theft, and acts of espionage. There is a heated debate in the literature about whether well-publicized cyber events in Estonia and Georgia and Iran (that we will turn to momentarily) even constituted cyber "attacks" at all, since (as the critics complain) no lives were lost or permanent harm was done.[6] All these debates frame difficult, and as yet unanswered, questions such as:

- What constitutes the "use of force" in the cyber realm?
- When, if ever, does such force rise to the level of an "armed attack" of the sort envisioned in the United Nations Charter (e.g., Articles 2.4, 39, and 51), constituting a legitimate cause for war in self-defense?
- More generally, what is the nature of the "harm" or damage done through such attacks, when it is not explicitly kinetic or physical harm?
- When does the harm (on whatever account) done through relentless intrusion and invasion and theft of vital information and potential sabotage of vital infrastructure rise to a level that justifies retaliation, either in kind, or by means of kinetic reprisal?
- And finally, when formulating our strategies for cyber security and defense, what is the relation on the one hand between privacy, and any right an individual citizen may reasonably claim to such privacy, and to anonymity on the other? Are these really equivalent?

These are all questions about which we are still largely unclear, in part because the domain of cyber space appears to be so novel and unique,[7] and our history of backing into it until just a few years ago was so casual and largely unreflective.[8] Just as with earlier questions about professional ethics, law, and private military contracting, or the advent of military robotics, these problems and questions pertaining to cyberwarfare have arisen, not through judicious pursuit of carefully formulated strategic policies, but largely through the unreflective evolution of behaviors, and through the gradual emergence of new possibilities and unanticipated prospects over the course of time.

These, of course, are questions that have begun to be addressed in the emerging U.S. cyber security strategy, of which there are now two versions: the Department of Defense (DoD), and the Department of State/White House versions.[9] The rhetoric of both is quite distinct and different, but both manage in their own way (in American humorist James Thurber's phrase) "to amuse with their pretensions." The latter, the State Department document, is visionary and aspirational, acknowledging the cyber security threats and vulnerabilities, to be sure, but focusing largely on the prospects for global peace and international prosperity that an open, transparent, universally accessible global Internet promises to yield. For my part, I confess that I admire the vision, but find the underlying policy recommendations were perhaps too sanguine, and too naïve concerning the security threats. By contrast, the DoD document, released finally in the spring of 2011, displays the protective paternalism one might expect from responsible military, intelligence, and security forces: the document is chock full of threat assessment, cognizant of the bewildering array of vulnerabilities, and fairly bristling with proposals for defensive and counter-offensive measures in response—the cyber equivalent of barbed wire, steel, and land mines. One DoD official summed it up on May 30, 2011 for the *Wall Street Journal*, "if you shut down our power grid, maybe we will put a missile down one of your smokestacks!"[10]

This is the tough talk of deterrence, that might give pause to reasonable, self-interested adversaries. I'm less certain that criminals and terrorists will be dissuaded by it. In any case, it poses some hard questions: first, of course, given the difficult problem of attribution, *whose* smokestacks should we target? Perhaps just as important: *how many* missiles, down *how many* smokestacks? What cyber damage or harm would we need to sustain in order to provoke such a response? And the trick is, we would need to have an answer, to inform our policy. But, as Martin Libicki at the RAND Corporation points out,[11] we wouldn't want to advertise it, since adversaries invariably try to press the limits. In order for the desired deterrent effect to occur, better to keep them guessing and worrying: we need to remain deliberately vague about where those limits lie—just the sort of double-deception that the U.S. used to practice with the Soviets during the Cold War.

Finally, are "smoke stacks" and power grids the proper sorts of targets? Perhaps responding in kind to such an infrastructure attack would be appropriate, but would we want to make such attacks on civilian infrastructure part of our offensive strategy? Would the U.S. be willing itself, for example, to launch some sort of preemptive cyber attack that (to employ a variation of one of Richard Clarke's scenario) would damage or destroy the Three Gorges dam, and subject millions of ordinary farmers and citizens to drowning, starvation, and immiseration, merely to counter an armed confrontation or military standoff in the Straits of Taiwan or, worse, over competing claims of regional states over mineral rights in the South China Sea, in which the U.S. itself has no direct interest? Or, more realistically, would we be willing to do this, even in response to a large-scale preemptive cyber attack launched against our own resources as an effort to dissuade us from interfering in their conventional conflict in the Taiwan Straits?

3. Policies and responses

How are we to go about formulating policy in response to such questions and scenarios? My view is that such questions drive us back to foundational resources for dealing with crisis response, resources, and traditions that attempt to guide us in balancing important guiding principles and values against the lives and welfare of large numbers of people who might be affected by such events. This is never an easy balancing act, but we do have resources, and experience in applying them to questions like these. We find these resources in the cardinal principles of international law, that reflect centuries of philosophical evaluation of such moral dilemmas, known as the "just war tradition." That tradition, and the body of international law derived from it, counsel us in two respects: (1) *when* we are entitled to use force, or engage in an armed attack against adversaries who have harmed, or threaten to harm us; and (2) *how* we are to go about doing so.[12]

In answer to the first set of questions, the use of force is justified in this tradition only reluctantly, in behalf of a grave or serious matter of state, and only after all reasonable attempts by duly constituted or "legitimate" authorities to resolve the conflict have failed. When the resort to force is found necessary, moreover, the conventional responses to the second set of questions declare that force must be employed only to the degree required to achieve legitimate military objectives; should be directed only against representatives of the military forces of the adversary; and should never be directed deliberately against third-parties or noncombatants. These guiding principles of just war doctrine are likewise the cardinal principles of the international law of armed conflict, known broadly by their philosophical names (more than by their specific legal expression) as: *proportionality* (the "economy of force"), *military necessity*, the principle of *noncombatant immunity* and discrimination (or "distinction" in the law), and prohibitions against weapons or uses of force that inflict cruel and unnecessary suffering.

Those cardinal principles or strictures of LOAC reflect a grudging moral consensus over centuries of state practice between rivals and adversaries to attempt to limit the collateral damage of war (as we were reminded recently in the Kosovo air campaign a decade ago). We don't deliberately target civilians or civilian infrastructure, and we take reasonable care to limit the degree of force deployed in pursuit of a legitimate military objective in order to avoid disproportionate "collateral damage." I have attempted to show how such legal constraints emerge from the proper practice of the profession of arms, constituting its most sacred and fundamental values and professional principles.[13] They are thus not imposed externally as "handcuffs" on military personnel, placing us at a competitive disadvantage against ruthless and unprincipled adversaries. Rather, such norms and constraints on permissible action arise as a reflection of professional identity, and the underlying purpose of the military profession itself as a vital form of public service. The question we face presently is how, and perhaps even whether, such long-standing principles and traditions can offer any useful guidance in the cyber realm, or rightly constrain our efforts to respond to and resolve cyber conflict.

Consider, for example, that by far the greatest areas of vulnerability are not hardened, encrypted, and securely-firewalled military and security targets (although these are still surprisingly and disturbingly vulnerable). Rather, as in nuclear conflict, the areas of greatest vulnerability are civilian populations, civilian objects, and vital public infrastructure. Accordingly, most cyberweapons, and many scenarios for cyberwarfare, have been focused upon such targets, in apparent violation of the most fundamental principles of international humanitarian law and the just war tradition.[14] Critics of both, however, have offered these facts as demonstration that these approaches are antiquated, outmoded, and useless, and ought not to be invoked in the analysis and evaluation of cyber conflict, especially when the "harm" done appears to involve little or no loss of life or destruction of property.[15]

I dissent from that view, largely because the insights stemming from conventional or traditional just war doctrine and lying at the philosophical and judicial core of present international law constitute the only resources we have to bring to bear upon such questions. We must, at least, attempt (as human beings invariably are driven to do whenever faced with a set of novel circumstances) to extrapolate from the known to the unknown, by means of analogy, comparison, and interpretation. At least we must make the attempt, and explore the intuitive soundness of the results, before abandoning such resources altogether.

When attempting this interpretive extrapolation, moreover, we confront immediately an interesting cultural feature of cyber conflict: it is, after all, properly termed "information warfare," and so reflects the tolerated and traditional practices of the professional communities most deeply engaged in ISR (intelligence, surveillance, and reconnaissance): the clandestine services and intelligence communities, which are not coextensive with those of traditional combat forces. In international espionage, for example, the name of the game is usually thought to be dirty tricks and deception: to steal more information from them than they do from us, and in the ensuing conflict to "do unto them, before they do unto you." What has happened, inadvertently, is that cyber conflict has blurred the heretofore sharp, traditional boundaries between espionage, covert action, and ongoing low intensity inter-state conflict and competition on the one hand, and full-scale kinetic conflict on the other.[16] How have those boundaries moved? How have those rules and conventions changed, if at all? Are we speaking metaphorically, or literally, when we describe cyber attacks and cyberwarfare? We don't normally, for example, label a massive breach of security by enemy espionage agents as an "armed attack," or classify our response as constituting "warfare."

In any area of new or relatively unfamiliar terrain, the usual advice is to proceed with caution, speak and think carefully, and observe as closely as possible the sorts of behaviors that are actually taking place, and are found to test the limits of minimally acceptable conduct. In international law, this is known as the search for "emerging norms" of state behavior. Here, I have argued in my own writings and presentations on cyber conflict, that we have begun to have enough experience with this relatively new domain to know, both as individuals and as nations, what we would like to see transpire there, and what kinds of behaviors we would like to condemn and discourage.[17]

4. Attribution

That international norms have begun to crystalize in the conduct of cyber conflict may be demonstrated by considering four recent instances of such conflict with which the general public is now reasonably familiar: Russia versus Estonia (2007), Russia versus Georgia (2008), Israel versus Syria (2007), and Stuxnet (2010).[18] These four instances of cyber conflict, in particular, have been so thoroughly discussed, reported, and analyzed that I will not attempt here to offer any further description.[19] Instead, I will concentrate on what I believe are the lessons learned, and the norms we have begun to derive collectively from these four cases.

No one has officially taken "credit" for Stuxnet, although allegations have flown since its discovery in 2009–2010, and Richard Clark and other security and cyber experts seem confident in attributing it to a collaboration between the U.S. and Israel (a suspicion harbored ever since the worm was first discovered). The usual default on attribution is to credit those who, when questioned about these events, smile the most broadly, cough gently, and decline to comment for the record. Likewise the Russians and Israelis either deny, or refuse to discuss responsibility for the other altercations.

These difficulties in assessing credit or accountability lie at the heart of what is often termed "the attribution problem." I've come to believe that this so-called "attribution problem" is neither all that big nor all that unprecedented.[20] Cyber forensics has taken enormous strides in the detection of crime and the origins of state conflict, for one thing. For another, when in doubt, apply, not Asimov's laws, but Agatha Christie's principle: namely, ignore the background distractions, and focus upon who stands to benefit most from the deed in question. Nine times out of ten, you've got your perpetrator, and 90 percent certainty is probably close enough for government work. A government may respond (as Russia did in the Estonian case) that it can't be held responsible for the actions of "patriots, criminals, or outraged vigilantes" within its borders, but that defense is nonsense. It didn't work for the Taliban in disclaiming responsibility for what Al Qaeda did "beyond its control" but within its sovereign borders, and it probably shouldn't work here either.

Our response should be the same in cyber as in conventional conflict: "either you stop the illegal actors, arrest them or throw them out, and take responsibility for what goes on within your borders, or we will regard you as complicit in these acts." That declaration moves us from the realm of international criminal law alone, to that of inter-state conflict and LOAC.[21] That, coupled with effective cyber forensics and the "Agatha Christie principle" is probably enough to counter cyber subterfuge and take care of the attribution problem. Besides, denials, disclaimers of responsibility, and non-attribution are nothing new in warfare: the Italians denied their small flotilla of submarines were responsible for sinking or damaging British supply ships near Gibraltar early in WWII. However, when the British threatened to bomb the Italian peninsula into the Stone Age unless the attacks ceased, they mysteriously ceased!

5. Cyberweapons, tactics and targeting

Let us move on, then, to cyberweapons, tactics and targeting. The (alleged) Russian cyber attack against Estonia represented a wholesale and indiscriminate assault on civilians and civilian (and government non-military) infrastructure almost exclusively. There were no military targets, and more important, no reasonable military objectives served by the attacks. Moving a war memorial from one place of honor to another within one's sovereign borders may be cause for annoyance or even diplomatic protest, but hardly for war, and certainly not for an indiscriminate and disproportionate assault on noncombatants.

Stuxnet resides at the opposite extreme. This ingenious computer "worm" focused solely upon, and ultimately did harm only to, targets that were purely military. No one was killed, no civilians or civilian infrastructure were deliberately targeted.[22] The damage done and harm suffered was surely proportionate to the threat of harm posed by the target itself and, most importantly, every conceivable effort short of attack was undertaken to persuade the adversary to cease and desist. I will return to this point in conclusion. For the present, notice how what in ethics and law we call "new norms" of inter-state conduct are already emerging from these instances.

The middle ground is occupied by the Georgian and Syrian cases. Here the Russians showed both discrimination and restraint, employing cyber tactics to destroy or disrupt the adversarial governments and military's command and control preceding a conventional attack, limited in turn to forcing a resolution of the specific issue in dispute (the status of the breakaway province of Ossetia, and status of Russian citizens living there). This is a perfectly acceptable wartime tactic.[23] We may choose to side with our NATO allies in Georgia in that dispute, but it is a legitimate inter-state conflict, a difference of opinion with reasonable claims on both sides. Clausewitz might scold us that this is what wars are designed to solve. The same holds true in the case of the alleged Israeli bombing attack on the Syrian nuclear facility apparently under construction (with technical assistance from North Korea) at Dayr al Zawr. A cyber attack utterly dismantled Syrian radar defenses, permitting a conventional bombing raid on an illicit nuclear weapons facility, undertaken at night when deaths and collateral damage might be reasonably minimized, and presumably after diplomatic initiatives to cease and desist had utterly failed.

6. Justifying cyberattacks

In these cases, I am deliberately trying not to interpose my own personal judgment of the merits of each side's dispute: I seek only to describe how these adversaries came to resort to war, and how they conducted their conflict with cyberweapons and tactics. Here, I think, we can identify the following norms of acceptable behavior. A cyber attack is morally justified, and should be legally sanctioned, whenever the following conditions are met:

1   the underlying issue in conflict is sufficiently grave to serve as a *causus belli*
2   only the adversary's military assets are targeted, and the harm inflicted (kinetic or cyber) is proportionate and reasonable in light of the threat posed by the targeted assets
3   specifically civilian lives and infrastructure are not the object of attack, and every effort is made to avoid or minimize damage to same; and finally
4   every effort has been made short of war to resolve the dispute in question.

I think that is a pretty substantive set of conclusions to draw from these examples, and constitutes a good beginning for the ethics of cyberwarfare. It both sorts the examples into acceptable and unacceptable modes of conduct, and seems to explain our different responses to each, independent of which side we politically favor in the dispute, and so offers a reasonable guide for action in the future.[24] Interestingly, as the case of Stuxnet suggests, these norms seem to permit even a *preemptive or preventive* cyber strike, as well as guide our thinking about retaliation for an unacceptable strike on our own assets. That is, the guidelines seem to work for both offense and defense.[25]

In fact, something like this list of criteria emerged as a proposal, over a decade ago, in an interesting and path-breaking article on ethics and information warfare authored by Professor John Arquilla, currently the Chair of the Department of Defense Analysis at the Naval Postgraduate School (Monterey, CA), and modestly published at the time in a relatively obscure Rand Corporation report issued in the late 1990s.[26] Our team of resident Stockdale fellows at the U.S. Naval Academy inadvertently discovered this article while working on the Stuxnet case when it first came to widespread public attention in early 2010. I contacted Professor Arquilla to introduce myself and ask him to speak to a consortium of engineers, scientists, lawyers, and ethicists with whom I collaborate on military operations and national security. I pointed out the coincidence and observed: "John, it sure seems to me as if *whoever* developed this weapon not only read your article, but followed its ethical guidelines to the letter!"

He smiled broadly, coughed gently … and declined to comment for the record.

7. Conclusion: just war cyber security, and the logic of "moral exceptions"

Early on in this essay I enumerated a number of questions raised by the advent of cyber conflict. I have addressed some of these questions: e.g., regarding the use of force, and of cyber conflict that rises to the level of an armed attack, as well as the nature of the harm done, or that can be reasonably inflicted (and on whom) in pursuit of a satisfactory resolution of the conflict. I have had far less to offer on the question of when the harm (on whatever account) done through relentless intrusion and invasion and theft of vital information and potential sabotage of vital infrastructure (the so-called "death by a thousand cuts") rises to a level that justifies retaliation in kind, let alone by means of a conventional, kinetic reprisal. This, it seems to me, remains a matter of prudent political judgment, evincing considerations of morality only when such judgments are either wildly imprudent, or highly disproportionate to the degree of actual harm suffered through such gradual and surreptitious attacks. And there, in agreement with Martin Libicki (cited on page 369), I believe we must leave the matter as settled in the emerging cyber doctrines of responsible and otherwise law-abiding states. The evolution of cyber policy in the U.K. and Australia, for example, provides a reasonably sufficient summary of prudent policy in this realm. The sole remaining question regarding privacy and cyber security, owing to its complexity and sensitivity, I leave to a subsequent essay entirely.

When we pause finally to reflect once again on the relevance of classical just war doctrine to cyber security, we might marvel somewhat disbelievingly at what might seem to be a remarkable coincidence: namely, that a close examination of four recent instances of cyber conflict could yield norms similar to those derived, *a priori*, over a decade earlier. After all, the earlier set of guidelines for a justified cyber conflict were derived by Professor Arquilla by explicitly applying guidelines for conventional conflict (the afore-mentioned "just war theory" or doctrine) to this newly-emerging domain of conflict. The difficulty of relying on such a procedure, especially in a deductive mode, is that it will seem to be culturally and historically parochial, and perhaps also irrelevant. Critics or skeptics are likely to dismiss or ignore such efforts as a misguided or inappropriate attempt to try to govern a brand-new realm of potentially unrestricted conflict purely from the standpoint of what they (mistakenly) see as a culturally-specific debate among historical scholars in the Western tradition that was originally intended to govern a wholly different kind of conflict. Such complaints about the limited applicability of just war doctrine generally, but especially to contemporary forms of irregular warfare (such as cyberwar), are often voiced (as I noted earlier in this paper).

Demonstrating, as I have attempted to do, by contrast, that these norms emerge naturally and almost inevitably from a reflective consideration of variant forms of social behavior by their respective practitioners, illustrates a radically different understanding of these guiding principles and constraints: namely, that if we did not already possess such guidelines, we would naturally tend to "invent" them for ourselves, each time a new set of questions about the appropriateness of engaging in some new and potentially disruptive and precarious activity arose.

This, in turn, is because such criteria are not (normatively speaking) merely the result of some narrowly focused parochial and culturally bound conversation. Quite the contrary, they are the inevitable end result of a conversation or form of discourse among practitioners about the form and function of their practice itself. It would not matter what period of history, or what religious or cultural background such practitioners represented. Were they, from a standpoint of reasonable self-interest, to examine the function and efficacy of, say, armed conflict (regardless of whether they otherwise regarded such conflict, from their unique cultural standpoint, as inevitable, regrettable, or praiseworthy) they would, nonetheless, quickly come to differentiate between acceptable and unacceptable forms of it (as indeed, we find such practitioners doing from Sun Tzu and the Upanishads to Socrates and his young pupils in Plato's *Republic*). Such participants would wonder, for example, when engaging in armed conflict was appropriate, and under what conditions it might seem inappropriate or ill-advised (*jus ad bellum*), and they would quite naturally wonder about the canons of best practice, as distinguished from prohibited and unacceptable forms of conduct in the midst of justified conflict (*jus in bello*).

Indeed, I have long argued that we may discern conversations about a broad range of normally prohibited activities other than warfare itself (such as lying, civil disobedience, "whistle-blowing," conscientious objection, and defiance of lawful orders, for example) that yield guidelines highly similar to what we call "just war theory" or doctrine.[27] All of these various activities, including warfare, are themselves normally considered restricted or prohibited as a general rule. Pondering the important problem, in each case, of when it might nonetheless constitute a "lesser evil" to set these prohibitions or cautions aside and engage in these activities yields a similar set of considerations for the justification of each mode of action, and, importantly, for the constraints on appropriate forms of those exceptional actions.

Hence, our wondering now about the better and worse forms of cyber conflict (and the most appropriate means of its pursuit) is itself no different from our similar reflections and concerns about any other domain of activity that its practitioners normally avoid or eschew, but sometimes permit or engage in with the utmost caution, as a lesser evil. I have thus shown, in the case of cyber conflict, that whether we attempt to anticipate the better and worse forms of this new form of conflict by anticipation and application of prior guidelines for pursuing conventional conflict, or whether we seek to discern inductively from practice the acceptable versus unacceptable forms of it, we will invariably arrive at a series of considerations that closely resemble the familiar criteria of conventional just war tradition. That is to say, cyber conflict, just as any form of armed conflict or use of force, should only be prosecuted for a compelling and justifiable reason, and only after all reasonable attempts short of these normally prohibited measures have been attempted without success. We would, moreover, reasonably expect ourselves and others engaging in this form of conflict as a method of resolving otherwise intractable disputes (as opposed to those pursuing blind vengeance, or criminal ends) to do so only if the ends sought bore some reasonable relationship to the harm and destruction we might otherwise expect to inflict in an effort to resolve the given conflict in our favor (rather than yielding to the adversary).

That last consideration leads to the recommendation that, when engaging in cyber conflict, we inflict only as much harm or damage as is commensurate with attaining our otherwise justified ends. We would not only refrain from deliberately inflicting harm on those persons and objects who had otherwise done nothing to make themselves liable to such harm, we would also think ourselves obliged to take every precaution possible to *avoid* doing so, even if inadvertently. And we would avoid altogether inflicting widespread harm or damage in a manner that bore no relationship whatsoever to the conflict in which we were engaged, or to the ends or goals we thereby sought to obtain. In that respect (and contrary to claims of the irrelevance or obsolescence of just war thinking generally), such norms emerge from, and pertain to the practice of cyberwarfare and cyber conflict every bit as much as they do to other forms of conflict—or indeed, to a variety of other forms of activity we normally prohibit (or engage in only with extreme reservation), but for which we are, occasionally, driven by extreme circumstances to seek an exception.

Explaining and justifying exceptions of these sorts (war, cyber conflict, the apparent disloyalty of whistle-blowing, or civil disobedience) require us first to be prepared, at least, to answer publicly some very difficult questions, and to show that we have fulfilled certain necessary conditions for engaging in the otherwise proscribed activity. Just war doctrine itself is thus not an exclusive artifact of Roman Catholic theology, or of Western culture alone. Rather, it is nothing more or less than an example of this more universal (and culturally non-specific) procedure.

Notes

1 See, for example, D.E. Sanger and E. Schmitt "Cyber Attacks are Up, National Security Chief Says," *New York Times*, 27 July 2012. This is only a recent example of incessant claims of cyber attacks registered in the U.S. and elsewhere: e.g., S. Curtis "U.K. Businesses Face Weekly Cyber Attacks – Report," *Techworld*, 13:40, 24 April 2012. Online. Available at: http://news.techworld.com/security/3353135 (accessed 6 April 2013); R. Taylor "Australia Warns on Cyber Attacks," *Reuters News Service*, 30 May 2011. Online. Available at: http://www.reuters.com/article/2011/05/30/us-australia-cyber-idUSTRE74T0KH20110530 (accessed 6 April 2013). This is a tiny sampling of such warnings.

2 Again, such claims are often voiced. See, for example, the report by NPR correspondent Tom Gjelten "Extending the Law of War to Cyberspace," 22 September 2010. Online. Available at: http://www.npr.org/templates/story/story.php?storyId=130023318 (accessed 6 April 2013). In this report this charge is raised by former National Security Agency general counsel, Stewart Baker. The general form of this claim is that even if law-abiding nations like the U.S., U.K., or Australia comply with international law in this domain, other nations simply will not (and that will, presumably, place the law-abiding nations at a disadvantage in cyber conflict).

3 R.A. Clark and R.K. Knake, *Cyber War: the Next Threat to National Security and What to Do About It*, New York: HarperCollins, 2010; J. Brenner, *America the Vulnerable: Inside the New Threat Matrix of Digital Espionage, Crime, and Warfare*, New York: Penguin Books, 2011; and M. Bowden, *Worm: the First Digital World War*, New York: Atlantic Monthly Press, 2011.

4 See, for example, the treatments of this topic by highly respected journalists: J. Fallows, "Cyber Warriors," *The Atlantic Monthly*, March 2010, pp. 58–63 and S. M. Hersh "The Online Threat," *The New Yorker*, 1 November 2010, both of whom echo the concerns of Clarke and Knake, *Cyber War*.

5 CDR Todd C. Huntley, USN, complains of the problems of misuse of concepts and terminology as a fatal flaw in the analysis of cyber conflict and vulnerabilities: T.C. Huntley "Controlling the Use of Force in Cyber Space: The Application of the Law of Armed Conflict during a Time of Fundamental Change in the Nature of Warfare," *Naval Law Review* LX, 2010, pp. 1–40. See especially his characterizations of cyber activity on p. 4.

6 One such skeptic is Thomas Rid (University of London), who argues that all of the highly touted cyber "attacks" to date have constituted little more than conventional state and commercial espionage and criminal activity, none of which rises to the level of a military use of force or an "armed attack." T. Rid. "Cyber War will Not Take Place," *Journal of Strategic Studies*, 35:1, October 2011, pp. 5–32. See also his exchange with John Arquilla in *Foreign Policy*: "Think Again: Cyberwar," and Arquilla's rebuttal "Cyberwar is Already Upon Us," *Foreign Policy*, March/April 2012. Online. Available at: http://www.foreignpolicy.com/articles/2012/02/27/cyberwar (accessed 6 April 2013). I have argued in response that the concern for threat inflation, and confusion of true warfare with low-intensity conflict (espionage and covert action) is appropriate, but the author's definition of "harm," "use of force," and "armed attack" are simply too restrictive for this domain. See G.R. Lucas Jr "Permissible Preventive Cyber Warfare," in L. Floridi and M. Taddeo, (eds), *Philosophy of Engineering and Technology* (UNESCO Conference on Ethics and Cyber Warfare, University of Hertfordshire, July 2011), forthcoming from Springer Verlag.

7 Randall Dipert calls attention to what he terms the "unique ontology" of cyber objects, events, and weapons as posing the greatest challenge to understanding both this new domain, and the application of conventional conceptions of military ethics, just war doctrine, and the Law of Armed Conflict (LOAC) to it. See R. Dipert "The Ethics of Cyberwarfare," *Journal of Military Ethics* 9:4, December 2010, pp. 384–410. Michael Schmitt likewise calls attention to this puzzling feature of cyber events and objects as the principal source of difficulty in determining how to interpret and apply *jus in bello* and the black-letter provisions of international law to cyber conflict. See M.N. Schmitt "Cyber Operations and the *Jus in Bello*: Key Issues," *U.S. Naval War College International Law Studies*, 87, 2011, pp. 89–110.

8 As detailed, for example, in W.A. Owen, K.W. Dam and H.S. Lin (eds), *Technology, Policy, Law, and Ethics Regarding U.S. Acquisition and Use of Cyberattack Capabilities*. Washington, DC: National Research Council of The National Academies Press, 2009.

9 "International Strategy for Cyberspace: Prosperity, Security and Openness in a Networked World," Washington DC: Office of the President, May 2011. Online. Available at: http://www.whitehouse. gov/sites/default/files/rss_viewer/international_strategy_for_cyberspace.pdf (accessed 6 April 2013); Department of Defense, "Department of Defense Strategy for Operating in Cyberspace," Washington, DC, July 2011. Online. Available at: http://www.defense.gov/news/d20110714cyber.pdf (accessed 6 April 2013).

10 Military official quoted in S. Gorman and J.E. Barnes "Cyber Combat: Act of War."

11 *The Wall Street Journal*, 30 May 2011. Online. Available at: http://online.wsj.com/article/SB10001424 052702304563104576355623135782718.html (accessed 6 April 2013). See M. Libicki's essay, "Pulling Punches in Cyberspace," *Proceedings of a Workshop on Deterring Cyberattacks: Informing Strategies and Developing Options for U.S. Policy*. Washington, DC: The National Academies Press, 2010, pp. 123–147. Available at: http://www.nap.edu/openbook.php?record_id=12997&page=123. See also his earlier, path-breaking work in this field, M. Libicki, *Cyberdeterrence and Cyberwar*, Santa Monica, CA: Rand Corporation, 2009; *Conquest in Cyberspace: National Security and Information Warfare*, New York: Cambridge University Press, 2007.

12 There are numerous sources for these just war criteria, and for the distinction between so-called *jus ad bellum* and *jus in bello*. See, for example, G.R. Lucas Jr and W.R. Rubel (eds), *Ethics and the Military Profession: the Moral Foundations of Leadership*, 3rd Edn, New York: Pearson, 2010.

13 That somewhat novel approach to just war doctrine as a manifestation of professional ethics in a military context infuses the textbook presentation cited above. See also G.R. Lucas Jr, "'This is Not Your Father's War': Confronting the Moral Challenges of 'Unconventional' War," *Journal of National*

Security Law and Policy, 3: 2, 2009, pp. 331–342; G.R. Lucas Jr, "'Forgetful Warriors' – Neglected Lessons on Leadership from Plato's Republic," in G. Kassimeris and J. Buckley (eds), *The Ashgate Research Companion to Modern Warfare*, London: Ashgate Press, 2010; and the treatment of military ethics as professional ethics in G.R. Lucas Jr, *Anthropologists in Arms: the Ethics of Military Anthropology*, Lanham, MD: AltaMira Press, 2009.

14 This complaint has been lodged most forcefully by computer scientist Neil C. Rowe, "War Crimes from Cyberweapons," *Journal of Information Warfare*, 6:3, 2007, pp. 15–25; "Ethics of Cyber War Attacks," in L.J. Janczewski and A.M. Colarik (eds), *Cyber Warfare and Cyber Terrorism*, Hershey, PA: Information Science Reference, 2008, pp. 105–111; N.C. Rowe, "The Ethics of Cyberweapons in Warfare," *Journal of Techoethics*, 1:1, 2010, pp. 20–31.

15 R. Dipert, "The Ethics of Cyberwarfare"; T. Rid, "Cyber War will Not Take Place"; T. Rid, "Think Again: Cyberwar."

16 This is so, I have insisted elsewhere, even though a preponderance of the participants, from General Keith Alexander and VADM William McCollough onwards, wear (or wore) military uniforms. In espionage, covert action, and "psych ops," there is no restriction on targeting civilians, although this has begun to be questioned in the intelligence community's own discussions of professional ethics: see J. Goldman (ed.), *The Ethics of Spying: A Reader for the Intelligence Professional*, vols I & II, Lanham, MD: Scarecrow Press, 2005/2009; D. Perry, *Partly Cloudy: The Ethics of Espionage, Covert Action, and Interrogation*, Lanham, MD: Scarecrow Press, 2009.

17 See, for example, G.R. Lucas Jr, "Permissible Preventive Cyber Warfare."

18 There are a plethora of reliable sources for accounts of each. A very succinct and dramatic description of all four cyber conflicts is offered by R.A. Clark and R. K. Knake in *Cyber War*. An excellent summary of the circumstances leading up to the attack on Estonia and its consequences can be found in Episode 2, Season 1 of the PBS program "Wired Science" from shortly after the incident in 2007, entitled "Technology: World War 2.0," *Wired Science*, PBS, 2:1 2007. See also C. Clover, "Kremlin-backed Group Behind Estonia Cyber Blitz," *Financial Times*, London, 11 March 2009; and T. Espiner "Estonia's Cyberattacks: Lessons Learned a Year on," *ZD NET UK*, 1 May 2008. For an analysis of the attack against Georgia, see E. Tikk, K. Kaska, K. Rünnimeri, M. Kert, A-M. Talihärm, and L. Vihui, "Cyber Attacks Against Georgia: Legal Lessons Identified," *NATO Cooperative Cyber Defence Centre of Excellence*, Tallinn, Estonia, 2008; and the United States Cyber Consequences Unit (US-CCU) "Overview by the US-CCU of the Cyber Campaign against Georgia in August of 2008," *US-CCU Special Report*, August, 2009. Online. Available at: http://www.registan.net/wp-content/uploads/2009/08/US-CCU-Georgia-Cyber-Campaign-Overview.pdf (accessed 6 April 2013). In the Syrian case, see U. Mahnaimi and S. Baster "Israelis Seized Nuclear Material in Syrian Raid," *The Sunday Times*, London, 23 September 2007. For a summary of the cyber war elements of this strike, see D.A. Fulghum, R. Wall and A. Butler, "Israel Shows Electronic Prowess," *Aviation Week*, 25 November 2007. See also "Cyberwarfare Technology: Is Too Much Secrecy Bad?" *Airforce-technology. com*, 9 April 2008, Online. Available at: http://www.airforce-technology.com/features/feature1708 (accessed 6 April 2013). Finally, for Stuxnet, see W.J. Broad, J. Markoff and D.E. Sanger, "Israeli Test on Worm Called Crucial in Iran Nuclear Delay," *New York Times*, 15 January 2011. Online. Available at: http://www.nytimes.com/2011/01/16/world/middleeast/16stuxnet.html?_r=1 (accessed 6 April 2013). M. J. Gross, "A Declaration of Cyber-War," *Vanity Fair*. April 2011. Online. Available at: http://www.vanityfair.com/culture/features/2011/04/stuxnet-201104 (accessed 6 April 2013). For an equally thorough, but more recent, account of the entire Stuxnet affair see also K. Zetter "How Digital Detectives Deciphered Stuxnet, the most Menacing Malware in History," *Wired Magazine*, 11 July, 2011. Online. Available at: http://www.wired.com/threatlevel/2011/07/how-digital-detectives-deciphered-stuxnet (accessed 6 April 2013). This nickname for the worm was coined by Microsoft security experts, an amalgam of two files found in the virus's code. A study of the spread of Stuxnet was undertaken by a number of international computer security firms, including Symantec Corporation. Their report "W32.Stuxnet Dossier," compiled by noted computer security experts Nicholas Falliere, Liam O Murchu and Eric Chien, and released in February 2011, showed that the main countries affected during the early days of the infection were Iran, Indonesia and India. N. Falliere, L. O Murchu and E. Chien, "W32.Stuxnet Dossier." Online. Available at: http://www.symantec.com/content/en/us/enterprise/media/security_response/whitepapers/w32_stuxnet_dossier.pdf (accessed 6 April 2013). Despite its apparent success as a cyberweapon, concerns have been raised about proliferation and cloning of the design by third parties (e.g. terrorists). This concern is voiced explicitly in the online "infographic" documentary by P. Clair, "Stuxnet: Anatomy of a

Computer Virus," 2011. Online. Available at: http://vimeo.com/25118844 (accessed 6 April 2013). See also Ralph Langner's cyber security blog: R. Langner, "What Stuxnet is all about," *The Last Line of Cyber Defense*, 10 January 2011 and "A Declaration of Bankruptcy for US Critical Infrastructure Protection," *The Last Line of Cyber Defense*, 3 June 2011. Online. Available at: http://www.langner.com/en/2011/01/10/what-stuxnet-is-all-about (accessed 6 April 2013).

19 Clark and Knake offer a dramatic and reasonably thorough and accurate summary of each; R.A. Clark and R.K. Knake, *Cyber War*. These were also reported in a comprehensive CBS "Sixty Minutes" news documentary, S. Kroft "Cyberwar: Sabotaging the System," *CBS News, Sixty Minutes*, New York, 10 June 2010. Online. Available at: http://www.cbsnews.com/stories/2010/06/10/60minutes/main6568387.shtml?tag=currentVideoInfo;videoMetaInfo (accessed 6 April 2013).

20 See the considerable body of work by M.N. Schmitt on this problem, including: M.N. Schmitt "Cyber Operations in International Law: The Use of Force, Collective Security, Self Defense, and Armed Conflicts," in H.S. Lin et al., *Proceedings of a Workshop on Deterring Cyberattacks*, Washington, DC: The National Academies of Science, Engineering, and Medicine Press, 2010, pp. 151–178.

21 This is a contested point that, for the most part, exceeds the scope of this paper. Scholars and practitioners of international law are far from unanimous on this point. Although in the past, States have successfully resisted imputing to themselves collectively the responsibility for criminal activities within their borders, that customary practice appears to have changed dramatically in the past decade. The International Convention on Cybercrime explicitly charges States with the responsibility for cyber crimes that occur within their sovereign borders, and the United Nations Security Council has increasingly demanded that member States own up to this responsibility, United Nations Security Council "Convention on Cybercrime, Council of Europe "Convention on Cybercrime," Budapest: November 23, 2001. Online. Available at: http://conventions.coe.int/Treaty/EN/Treaties/html/185.htm (accessed 6 April 2013). An authoritative interpretation of the current status of international law on this topic, supporting the position I adopt in this lecture, is offered by Col. David E. Graham, U.S. Army (retired), D.E. Graham, "Cyber Threats and the Law of War," *Journal of National Security Law and Policy*, 4, 2010, pp. 87–102. For his part, Graham argues that a State's duty to prevent cyber attacks generates an indirect or attributed responsibility for such attacks that can be traced to sources or persons acting within the State's borders. He and Schmitt seem to agree (as does Dipert) that a combination of these factors is sufficient to attribute responsibility for an attack, and even to initiate a retaliation that may rise to the level of a justified "belligerent reprisal" under conventional international law.

22 Since initially drafting this essay in 2011, various news stories have reported on "confidential leaks" concerning explicit American involvement in designing Stuxnet and the "Flame" virus (that served to turn Iranian computers into espionage and surveillance devices), as part of an overall effort code-named "Olympic Games." Others have alleged that the "escape" or spread of the worm from the Iranian military computers (in which it had originally been surreptitiously planted) into the Internet at large had constituted a malfunction or "bug" in an updated version of the malware. It is likewise alleged that the spread of Stuxnet could potentially have disastrous results, making the weapon available to terrorists and anarchists who might easily reverse-engineer and re-use it. I think it important to note that there is little unambiguous evidence for such allegations, and moreover that, given the highly specific nature of cyberweapons whose design largely prevents them from being re-engineered or re-used for any meaningful purpose, that the fears regarding proliferation are wildly exaggerated. A very thorough summary and analysis of these various allegations, however, can be found in a new book by *New York Times* reporter, David E. Sanger, *Confront and Conceal: Obama's Secret Wars and Surprising Use of American Power*, New York: Crown Publishers, 2012.

23 Michael Schmitt's analysis of this conflict in M.N. Schmitt, "Cyber Operations and the *Jus in Bello*: Key Issues," *Naval War College International Law Studies*, 87, 2011, pp. 89–110. Along with a majority of the sources he cites, support this interpretation of the legality of the cyber component of this attack, and also of its general conformity to the restrictions of LOAC.

24 The opposition to formal governance measures is beginning to decrease in the U.S. as a formal cyber strategy begins to take shape. At the same time, acknowledging that cyber conflict is likely to resemble features of the nuclear era and the cold war, a decided preference is expressed for bilateral and multi-lateral forms of "soft law," such as John Arquilla's proposal for a declaration of "no first use" against civilian targets. See W.J. Lynn III, "Defending a New Domain: the Pentagon's Cyberstrategy," *Foreign Affairs*, 89:5, September/October 2010. Online. Available at: http://www.ciaonet.org/journals./fa/v89i5/08.html (restricted site, accessed 11 February 2011); VADM M. McConnell, "To Win the Cyber-war, Look to the Cold War," *The Washington Post Outlook*, Sunday 28 February 2010, B1;

E. Nakashima "NSA Chief Faces Questions about New Cyber-command," *The Washington Post*, Thursday 15 April 2010, A19.

25 See my forthcoming article from the UNESCO cyber security symposium "Permissible Preventive Cyberwarfare (see references below).

26 J. Arquilla, "Ethics and Information Warfare," in Z. Khalilzad, J. White and A. Marshall (eds), *The Changing Role of Information in Warfare*, Santa Monica, CA: RAND Corporation, 1999, pp. 379–401. Arquilla literally coined the term "cyber warfare" to currency, and is one of its leading analysists. I have cited some of his more recent work, above. See also J. Arquilla, "Conflict, Security, and Computer Ethics," in L. Floridi (ed.), *Cambridge Handbook of Information and Computer Ethics*, New York: Cambridge University Press, 2010, pp. 133–149.

27 E.g., in my February 2010 Dunbar Lecture at Millsaps College "New Rules for New Wars." Online. Available at: http://www.usna.edu/ethics/publications/documents/DunbarLectureMillsapsCollegeFe bruary2010NewRulesforNewWars%5B1%5D.pdf (accessed 6 April 2013). For published accounts, see G.R. Lucas Jr, "Methodological Anarchy: Arguing about War, and Getting it Right," *Journal of Military Ethics*, 6:3, 2007, pp. 246–252; the account of the significance of just war discourse in Chapter Two of *Anthropologists in Arms: the Ethics of Military Anthropology*, Lanham, MD: AltaMira Press, 2009; see also the concluding comments on understanding the "rival modes" of just war discourse in "Methodological Anarchy: Arguing About Preventive War," in R. Wertheimer (ed.), *Empowering our Military Conscience*, London: Ashgate Press, 2010, ch. II. I likewise advocate this approach to just war discourse, finally, in G.R. Lucas Jr, "The Case for Preventive War," in D. Chatterjee (ed.), *The Gathering Threat: Essays on Preventive War*, New York: Cambridge University Press, 2013; forthcoming.

References

Arquilla, J. "Cyberwar is Already Upon Us," *Foreign Policy*, March/April 2012. Online. Available at: http://www.foreignpolicy.com/articles/2012/02/27/cyberwar_is_already_upon_us (accessed 6 April 2013).

——"Conflict, Security, and Computer Ethics," in L. Floridi (ed.), *Cambridge Handbook of Information and Computer Ethics*, New York: Cambridge University Press, 2010, pp. 133–149.

——"Ethics and Information Warfare," in Z. Khalilzad, J. White, and A. Marshall (eds), *The Changing Role of Information in Warfare*, Santa Monica, CA: RAND Corporation, 1999, pp. 379–401.

Bowden, W. *Worm: The First Digital World War*, New York: Atlantic Monthly Press, 2011.

Brenner, J. *America the Vulnerable: Inside the New Threat Matrix of Digital Espionage, Crime, and Warfare*, New York: Penguin Books, 2011.

Broad, W.J., J. Markoff and D.E. Sanger "Israeli Test on Worm Called Crucial in Iran Nuclear Delay," *New York Times*, 15 January 2011. Online. Available at HTTP http://www.nytimes.com/2011/01/16/world/middleeast/16stuxnet.html?_r=1 (accessed 6 April 2013).

Clair, P. "Stuxnet: Anatomy of a Computer Virus," 2011. Online. Available at: http://vimeo.com/25118844 (accessed 6 April 2013).

Clark, R.A. and R.K. Knake, *Cyber War: the Next Threat to National Security and What to Do About It*, New York: Harper Collins, 2010.

Clover, C. "Kremlin-backed Group Behind Estonia Cyber Blitz," *Financial Times*, London, 11 March 2009.

Curtis, S. "U.K. faces Weekly Cyber Attacks," *Techworld*, 13:40, 24 April 2012. Online. Available at: http://news.techworld.com/security/3353135/uk-businesses-face-weekly-cyber-attacks--report (accessed 6 April 2013).

"Cyberwarfare Technology: Is too much secrecy bad?" *Airforce-technology.com*, 9 April 2008, Online. Available at: http://www.airforce-technology.com/features/feature1708 (accessed 6 April 2013).

Department of Defense, "Department of Defense Strategy for Operating in Cyberspace," Washington, DC, July 2011. Online. Available at: http://www.defense.gov/news/d20110714cyber.pdf (accessed 6 April 2013).

Dipert, R. "The Ethics of Cyberwarfare," *Journal of Military Ethics* 9:4, December 2010, pp. 384–410.

Espiner, T. "Estonia's Cyberattacks: Lessons Learned a Year on," *ZD NET UK*, 1 May 2008.

Falliere, N., L. O Murchu and E. Chien, "W32.Stuxnet Dossier." Online. Available at: http://www.symantec.com/content/en/us/enterprise/media/security_response/whitepapers/w32_stuxnet_dossier.pdf (accessed 6 April 2013).

Fallows, J. "Cyber Warriors," *The Atlantic Monthly*, March 2010, pp. 58–63.

Fulghum, D.A., R. Wall and A. Butler "Israel Shows Electronic Prowess," *Aviation Week*, 25 November 2007. Online. Available at: http://www.aviationweek.com/aw/generic/story.jsp?id=news/aw112607p2.xml&headline=Israel%20Shows%20Electronic%20Prowess&channel=defense (accessed 6 April 2013).

Gjelten, T. "Extending the Law of War to Cyberspace," 22 September, 2010. Online. Available at: http://www.npr.org/templates/story/story.php?storyId=130023318 (accessed 6 April 2013).

Goldman, J.(ed.), *The Ethics of Spying: A Reader for the Intelligence Professional*, vols I & II, Lanham, MD: Scarecrow Press, 2006/2010.

Gorman, S. and J.E. Barnes "Cyber Combat: Act of War," *The Wall Street Journal*, 30 May 2011. Online. Available at: http://online.wsj.com/article/SB10001424052702304563104576355623135782718.html (accessed 6 April 2013).

Graham, D.E. "Cyber Threats and the Law of War," *Journal of National Security Law and Policy*, 4, 2010, pp. 87–102.

Gross, M.J. "A Declaration of Cyber-War," *Vanity Fair*. April 2011. Online. Available at: http://www.vanityfair.com/culture/features/2011/04/stuxnet-201104 (accessed 6 April 2013).

Hersh, S.M. "The Online Threat," *The New Yorker*, 1 November 2010.

Huntley, T.C. "Controlling the Use of Force in Cyber Space: the Application of the Law of Armed Conflict during a Time of Fundamental Change in the Nature of Warfare," *Naval Law Review* LX, 2010, pp. 1–40.

"International Strategy for Cyberspace: Prosperity, Security and Openness in a Networked World," Washington DC: Office of the President, May 2011. Online. Available at: http://www.whitehouse.gov/sites/default/files/rss_viewer/international_strategy_for_cyberspace.pdf (accessed 6 April 2013).

Kroft, S. "Cyberwar: Sabotaging the System," *CBS News, Sixty Minutes*, New York, 10 June 2010. Online. Available at: http://www.cbsnews.com/stories/2010/06/10/60minutes/main6568387.shtml?tag=currentVideoInfo;videoMetaInfo (accessed 6 April 2013).

Langner, R. "What Stuxnet is all about," *The Last Line of Cyber Defense*, 10 January 2011.

——"A Declaration of Bankruptcy for US Critical Infrastructure Protection," *The Last Line of Cyber Defense*, 3 June 2011.

Libicki, M. "Pulling Punches in Cyberspace," *Proceedings of a Workshop on Deterring Cyberattacks: Informing Strategies and Developing Options for U.S. Policy*. Washington, DC: The National Academies Press, 2010, pp. 123–147. Available at: http://www.nap.edu/openbook.php?record_id=12997&page=123.

——*Cyberdeterrence and Cyberwar*, Santa Monica, CA: Rand Corporation, 2009

——*Conquest in Cyberspace: National Security and Information Warfare*, New York: Cambridge University Press, 2007.

Lucas Jr, G.R. "Permissible Preventive Cyber Warfare," in L. Floridi and M. Taddeo (eds), *Philosophy of Engineering and Technology* (UNESCO Conference on Ethics and Cyber Warfare, University of Hertfordshire, July 2011), forthcoming from Springer Verlag.

——"The Case for Preventive War," in D. Chatterjee (ed.), *The Gathering Threat: Essays on Preventive War*, New York: Cambridge University Press, 2013; forthcoming.

——"Methodological Anarchy: Arguing About Preventive War," in R. Wertheimer (ed.), *Empowering our Military Conscience*, London: Ashgate Press, 2010, ch. II.

——"'Forgetful Warriors' – Neglected Lessons on Leadership from Plato's Republic," in G. Kassimeris and J. Buckley (eds), *The Ashgate Research Companion to Modern Warfare*, London: Ashgate Press, 2010.

——*Anthropologists in Arms: the Ethics of Military Anthropology*, Lanham, MD: AltaMira Press, 2009.

——"'This is Not Your Father's War': Confronting the Moral Challenges of 'Unconventional' War," *Journal of National Security Law and Policy*, 3:2, 2009, pp. 331–342.

——"Methodological Anarchy: Arguing about War, and Getting it Right," *Journal of Military Ethics*, 6:3, 2007, pp. 246–252.

——"New Rules for New Wars." Online. Available at: http://www.usna.edu/ethics/publications/documents/DunbarLectureMillsapsCollegeFebruary2010NewRulesforNewWars%5B1%5D.pdf (accessed 6 April 2013).

Lucas Jr, G.R. and W.R. Rubel (eds), *Ethics and the Military Profession: the Moral Foundations of Leadership*, 3rd edn, New York: Pearson, 2010.

Lynn III, W.J. "Defending a New Domain: the Pentagon's Cyberstrategy," *Foreign Affairs*, 89:5, September/October 2010. Online. Available at: http://www.ciaonet.org/journals./fa/v89i5/08.html (restricted site, accessed 11 February 2011).

Mahnaimi, U. and S. Baster, "Israelis seized Nuclear Material in Syrian Raid," *The Sunday Times*, London, 23 September 2007. Online. Available at: http://www.timesonline.co.uk/tol/news/world/middle_east/article2512380.ece (accessed 6 April 2013).

McConnell, M. "To Win the Cyber-war, Look to the Cold War," *The Washington Post Outlook*, Sunday 28 February 2010, B1.

Nakashima, E. "NSA Chief Faces Questions about New Cyber-command," *The Washington Post*, Thursday 15 April 2010, A19.

Owen, W.A., K.W. Dam, and H.S. Lin (eds), *Technology, Policy, Law, and Ethics Regarding U.S. Acquisition and Use of Cyberattack Capabilities*. Washington, DC: National Research Council of The National Academies/American Academy of Sciences, 2009.

Perry, D. *Partly Cloudy: The Ethics of Espionage, Covert Action, and Interrogation*, Lanham, MD: Scarecrow Press, 2009.

Rid. T. "Think Again: Cyberwar," *Foreign Policy*, March–April 2012. Online. Available at: http://www.foreignpolicy.com/articles/2012/02/27/cyberwar (accessed 6 April 2013).

——"Cyber War will Not Take Place," *Journal of Strategic Studies*, 35:1, October 2011, pp. 5–32.

Rowe, N.C. "The Ethics of Cyberweapons in Warfare," *Journal of Techoethics*, 1:1, 2010, pp. 20–31.

——"War Crimes from Cyberweapons," *Journal of Information Warfare*, 6:3, 2007, pp. 15–25.

Rowe, N.C. "Ethics of Cyber War Attacks," in L.J. Janczewski and A.M. Colarik (eds), *Cyber Warfare and Cyber Terrorism*, Hershey, PA: Information Science Reference, 2008, pp. 105–111.

Sanger, D.E. *Confront and Conceal: Obama's Secret Wars and Surprising Use of American Power*, New York: Crown Publishers, 2012.

Sanger, D.E. and E. Schmitt, "Cyber Attacks are Up, National Security Chief Says," *New York Times*, 27 July 2012.

Schmitt, M.N. "Cyber Operations and the *Jus in Bello*: Key Issues," *U.S. Naval War College International Law Studies*, 87, 2011, pp. 89–110.

——"Cyber Operations and the *Jus in Bello*: Key Issues," *Naval War College International Law Studies*, March 2, 2011.

——"Cyber Operations in International Law: The Use of Force, Collective Security, Self Defense, and Armed Conflicts," in H.S. Lin et al., *Proceedings of a Workshop on Deterring Cyberattacks*, Washington, DC: The National Academies of Science, Engineering, and Medicine Press, 2010, pp. 151–178.

Taylor, R. "Australia Warns on Cyber Attacks," *Reuters News Service*, 30 May 2011. Online. Available at: http://www.reuters.com/article/2011/05/30/us-australia-cyber-idUSTRE74T0KH20110530 (accessed 6 April 2013).

"Technology: World War 2.0" *Wired Science*, PBS, 2:1 2007. Online. Available at: http://xfinitytv.comcast.net/tv/Wired-Science/95583/770190466/Technology%3A-World-War-2.0/videos?skipTo=189&cmpid=FCST_hero_tv (accessed 6 April 2013).

Tikk, E., K. Kaska, K. Rünnimeri, M. Kert, A-M. Talihärm, and L. Vihui, "Cyber Attacks Against Georgia: Legal Lessons Identified," *NATO Cooperative Cyber Defence Centre of Excellence*, Tallinn, Estonia, 2008.

United Nations Security Council "Convention on Cybercrime, Council of Europe "Convention on Cybercrime," Budapest: November 23, 2001. Online. Available at: http://conventions.coe.int/Treaty/EN/Treaties/html/185.htm (accessed 6 April 2013).

United States Cyber Consequences Unit (US-CCU), "Overview by the US-CCU of the Cyber Campaign against Georgia in August of 2008," *US-CCU Special Report*, August, 2009. Online. Available at: http://www.usccu.org (accessed 6 April 2013).

Zetter, K. "How Digital Detectives Deciphered Stuxnet, the most Menacing Malware in History," *Wired Magazine*, 11 July, 2011. Online. Available at: http://www.wired.com/threatlevel/2011/07/how-digital-detectives-deciphered-stuxnet/all/1 (accessed 6 April 2013).

28

UNDERSTANDING JUST CAUSE IN CYBERWARFARE[1]

Leonard Kahn

1. Introduction

New and speedy things frighten armies, while the customary and slow things are esteemed little by them.

(Machiavelli)[2]

With the discovery of a new instrument of warfare, the firearm, the whole internal organization of the army was necessarily altered, the relations within which individuals compose an army and can work as an army were transformed, and the relation of different armies to another was likewise changed.

(Marx)[3]

We may hope that machines will eventually compete with men in all purely intellectual fields. But which are the best ones to start with? Even this is a difficult decision … We can only see a short distance ahead, but we can see plenty there that needs to be done.

(Turing)[4]

What does this word *cyberattack* call to mind? For too many of us, it seems to evoke little more than images from popcorn thrillers. Cyberattacks, in this way of thinking, are just the stuff of summer blockbusters, filled with gratuitous action scenes and (somewhat ironically) spectacular computer-generated effects. To take just two examples, in *Independence Day*, nerdy but handsome David Levinson (Jeff Goldblum) saves the world from an alien invasion by uploading a virus to the invaders' mother ship, while in *Live Free or Die Hard* gruff but handsome John McClane (Bruce Willis) fights a group of terrorists trying to cripple vital computer systems across the United States. Cyberattacks are, to continue with this point of view, plot devices in forms of mindless entertainment but do not have any relevance for the real world. But this perspective is dangerously mistaken. Consider, for instance, a recently published report in the *New York Times*, according to which President Obama secretly ordered increasingly sophisticated attacks on the computer systems that run Iran's main nuclear enrichment facilities, significantly expanding America's first sustained use of cyberweapons.[5]

These alleged attacks – code named *Olympic Games* – began during the last few months of George W. Bush's presidency.[6] They continued through 2010 when the software used in the attack – now called *Stuxnet* – escaped Iran's Natanz nuclear power plant. But, interestingly, the release of the Stuxnet worm did not end the cyberattacks by the United States on Iran. Quite the contrary:

> In the following weeks, the Natanz plant was hit by a newer version of the computer worm, and then another after that. The last of that series of attacks, a few weeks after Stuxnet was detected around the world, temporarily took out nearly 1,000 of the 5,000 centrifuges Iran had spinning at the time to purify uranium.[7]

Whatever the ethical status of this operation (a point to which I shall return at the end of this chapter), it is hardly unique. In the past few years, high-profile cyberattacks have been directed at South Korea, Kyrgyzstan, Israel, Zimbabwe, and Myanmar, as well as, on repeated occasions, the United States.[8] If one had any doubts, they should be gone by now. Cyberattacks are real, and they are now part of the way the nation-states and many non-state groups interact.

The incident caused by the use of the Stuxnet worm and its aftermath, as well as by many similar events around the world over the last decade or so, raise many questions for traditional just war theory. In this chapter I focus on one of the more salient among them. In particular, I ask whether the rise of cyberattacks renders irrelevant, or even marginal, a long-established aspect of just war theory – namely, the doctrines of just cause. I argue that the doctrine remains germane, though it requires important modifications in order to accommodate aspects of warfare in the 21st century.

2. Coming to terms with the issues

We will need some terminological clarification. In this section, I offer a working definition of *cyberattack* and clean up some ambiguities regarding *just war theory*, *just cause*, and *aggression* as I am using the expressions.

Let me begin with *cyberattack*. Clearly, this is a term of art, so any definition of it will be, at least in large part, stipulative. Nevertheless, this fact does not mean that we can define *cyberattack* arbitrarily.[9] A satisfactory stipulative definition needs to meet several conditions. First, the definition must identify something worth discussing, something which is not readily available in our current vocabulary. For example, we do not need a definition which picks out the set consisting of my left foot and the Sistine Chapel ceiling since this set has no special importance (whatever the importance of its individual elements), and we do not need new definitions of *automobile* or *toaster* since we already have perfectly good terminology in these cases. Second, a good stipulative definition will make the subject matter under consideration clearer than it was without the definition. I do not, of course, mean that such a definition must be without any vagueness. Indeed, some degree of vagueness is a feature of almost all terms within natural languages, so it would be too much to expect that a definition of a term like *cyberattack* would not admit of at least some borderline cases.[10] Rather, I mean that a good stipulative definition will add sufficient clarity to the issue at hand. It will help to guide us both in distinguishing between the thing defined and other things under consideration and in distinguishing between at least some of the proper parts of the thing defined. For example, a good definition of *automobile* will provide some aid in seeing how automobiles differ from airplanes and boats, and will also provide some help in distinguishing station wagons from sedans. Third, a good stipulative definition should define the term in question by reference to other terms that are well defined without falling into circularity. For instance, a good definition of *toaster* will not invoke a concept like *thermocouple*, unless this concept can also be given a clear sense. Moreover, a good definition of *toaster* will not include concepts like *toast* or *toasted bread* unless these concepts can be defined without reference to the concept *toaster*.

Given these conditions, how should we define *cyberattack*? To answer this question, it will be useful to examine and criticize two recent but inadequate attempts. According to Martin Libicki, a cyberattack is "the deliberate disruption or corruption by one state of a system of interest to another state."[11] Eric Filiol has offered a rather different definition. Filiol writes that a cyberattack "is an attack on the real realm," i.e., the non-cyber world which proceeds in either of two ways: "by going directly through an information and communication system" or "by attacking" an information and communication system "where one or several components from the real realm depend on it (for instance, an attack on an electronic voting machine network)."[12]

Let us sort through some of the virtues and vices of these definitions. Libicki's definition is superior to Filiol's in at least one way. For Filiol's definition fails to take into consideration the fact that X can attack Y, while failing to cause any damage to Y. For instance, if Iceland tries to bring down Sweden's computer networks but fails to do so, it has still made a cyberattack on Sweden. The fact that it bungled this attack does not mean that it did not make an attack at all. So *cyberattack* should be defined in terms of attempts to disrupt or corrupt a system, rather than in terms of actual disruption or corruption. Libicki's definition clearly recognizes this point. However, Libicki's definition makes it difficult to distinguish clearly between cyberattacks and other similar yet distinct activities like the use of computers to gain state secrets (i.e., cyber-espionage, see Vatis)[13] or private financial information (i.e., virtual crime, see Howell).[14] Moreover, Libicki's definition limits cyberattacks to inter-state conflict. But this is implausible. If Euskadi Ta Askatasuna (ETA) were to try to bring down Spain's power grid, this would be no less of a cyberattack on Spain than if Portugal had tried to do it. Likewise, if Mexico attempted to disable the computers used by the Cártel de Juárez, this too would count as a cyberattack, even though the Cártel de Juárez is not a state. For that matter, if ETA were, for some reason, to attempt to disable the computers used by the Cártel de Juárez, this action would be no less a cyberattack. Filiol's definition avoids this problem.

In other respects, both definitions fail. Importantly, we should note that in principle one could disable a power grid or an air-traffic control system with a so-called logic bomb just as as one could with a bomb made of plastic explosives.[15] What we need is a definition of *cyberattack* that would allow us to distinguish between a cyberattack and a conventional attack which is meant to accomplish the same destructive goal. But on Libicki's account, any "deliberate disruption or corruption" of a system counts as a cyberattack. So Libicki's definition fails to satisfy this desideratum. Filiol's definition does not fail in quite the same way, but Filiol's talk of "the real realm" raises a red flag. What work is this talk meant to accomplish? The answer is unclear. If Filiol means to point out that cyberattacks often have dire implications for entities, such as power plants and transportation grids, that do not exist solely in cyber-space, then this is uncontroversial but not especially relevant to a definition of *cyberattack*. If, instead, Filiol means to suggest that something counts as a cyberattack only if it has such implications, then he is simply wrong. Email accounts and banking data do not have physical systems with which they are connected in the same way that the software which helps control, to take two examples, emergency services or financial institutions. But assaults on Google or on Goldman Sachs would count every bit as much as cyberattacks.[16]

So it is no easy task to give a definition of *cyberattack*; that much is undeniable. But what is the best we can do? Let me suggest the following: *X initiates a cyberattack against Y if and only if*

X deliberately attempts to disrupt the computer system or systems of Y by means of computer-to-computer contact. This definition of *cyberattack* combines the virtues of Libicki's attempt (it is broad enough to include merely attempted, as opposed to successful, attacks) with the virtues of Filiol's try (it is broad enough to include the actions of states and non-state actors, and it is narrow enough to allow us to distinguish between cyberattacks and other related but conceptually distinct phenomena such as virtual crime). Finally, this definition of *cyberattack* avoids the confusion about the relationship between cyberspace and the rest of the world inherent in both Libicki's and Filiol's approaches. To be sure, not every cyberattack is of equal importance, and some cyberattacks which have an affect on, say, a nation-states, command and control systems call for a measure of seriousness above and beyond certain other cyberattacks. But that fact need not be emphasized at the level of definition. Compare the term *harm*. Whatever the correct definition of *harm* is, it should not be confused with the definition of *serious harm*.[17] Some harms are quite trivial, and some are from from trivial. The same is true of cyberattacks. If this definition is not perfect, it is, at least, a step in the right direction and that will suffice for the purposes of this chapter.

It would be wise to make a related point in passing. I have spoken of cyber*attacks*, rather than of cyber*war* and will continue to do so. Why not use the more common term? While *cyberwar* is often used by those who comment on these and related areas, this usage is problematic. The reason for this is simple. That X attacks Y does not entail – or even imply – that X and Y are at war. To be sure, some attacks by one nation-state on another constitute acts of war, and it is an interesting question whether, for example, the United States' alleged cyberattack on Iran is an example of such an attack. But this is not a question that we can answer simply by calling the attack *cyberwar*. Moreover, as I have already noted, cyberattacks can be made by or against non-state actors as well as state actors, but it is not even clear that such non-state actors can be at war. So, for the sake of perspicacity, I will continue to speak of cyberattacks.[18]

What, then, are we to make of the term *just war theory*? Here is what I shall call the *core doctrine* of just war theory: With regard to war, there are at least some actions by individuals, by sub-state actors, and by state actors which are morally permissible, and some which are morally impermissible.[19] The claim that at least some actions are morally permissible distinguishes traditional just war theory from the position known as pacifism, while the claim that at least some actions are impermissible distinguishes it from what is somewhat perversely called realism. Though the definition of the term *war* is, as is well known, highly contentious, this is not a problem for the ideas I am pursuing in this chapter. Rather, I use the term *war* as a placeholder for whatever the best of account of war might be.

Just war theory is usually divided into three parts: *jus ad bellum*, *jus in bello*, and *jus post bellum*, though scholars differ about the depth and importance of this division. *Jus ad bellum* itself is usually divided into several sub-parts – in particular, the doctrines of just cause, last resort, proper authority, proportionality, right intention, and probability of success.[20] In the following three sections, I focus on the relationship between cyberattacks and the doctrine of just cause, though I also have occasion to mention the doctrines of last resort, of proper authority, and of proportionality in passing.

3. Cyberattacks and aggression

Let me now turn to the question which cyberattacks raises for the doctrine of just cause. It is usually claimed that a state actor goes to war justly only if it has a just cause, where having a just cause is usually understood as acting in response to the aggression of another state actor or agent of that state actor. Here, *aggression* is glossed not simply as hostility but as hostility which in itself unwarranted. As Michael Walzer puts it, "[a]ggression is not only a crime against the formal rules of international society; it is also, more importantly, an assault upon a people, a threat to their common life and even their physical survival."[21] The idea of aggression has been central to just war theory since its origins and remains so today. Philosophers as diverse as Aristotle, Cicero, Augustine, Aquinas, Grotius, Locke, and Kant agree that experiencing aggression is sufficient for meeting the just cause condition. Though there are, to be certain, many differences among the thinkers, when we turn to the details of their thinking about this matter, their agreement is central for our purposes in this chapter.[22]

Among Walzer's favored examples of aggression is the invasion by Iraq of Kuwait in 1991, though one could have just as easily cited the invasion of China in 1937 by the Japanese Empire or of Poland in 1939 by Nazi Germany. But all of these examples involve one nation-state physically aggressing against another. Germany did not simply act in a way toward Poland that was unwarranted and was aimed at causing damage to Poles; it did so by directing its military to kill Polish soldiers and civilians.

Yet just war theorists generally deny that other actions by nation-states constitute aggression in the relevant sense. Brian Orend provides an especially vivid statement of this point.

> [S]uppose that you are a small country, C, next to a big neighbor, N. In response to domestic lobby groups, the government of N decides to close its border to your forestry exports (trees, lumber, etc.). You are devastated, because your forestry sector is your economy's biggest and your economy is going to suffer severely (lost trade, layoffs, plant shutdowns, a recession). This is pretty tough treatment by N against C: it is not nice; it is completely undiplomatic, and it might even violate a trade treaty. But international law, and just war theory, insist that, rough as it may be, it is not treatment severe enough to merit warfare as a response. It is only when the tough treatment in question *is coupled with physical violence*, that we can begin to contemplate armed conflict.[23]

For instance, if in 1939 Nazi Germany had not used its military to cross its border with Poland with force but had instead imposed trade sanctions on its neighbor to the east, then it would not have thereby aggressed against Poland, and Poland would not, as a result, have had just cause to go to war with Germany. For this would not be a case of "physical violence," to repeat Orend's point.

So what is the problem? Well, on the one hand, just war theory appears to exclude cyberattacks from being forms of aggression and, therefore, from being sources of meeting the just cause condition of *jus ad bellum*. Yet, on the other hand, cyberattacks can – and, in the near future almost certainly, will – cause massive devastation to both military and civilian targets. (More on this briefly.) The problem, then, is that just war theory, at least in its post-Westphalian form, gives at least the appearance of excluding a powerful source of destruction from being a just cause for going to war. This looks counter-intuitive.

I'll return to the point in just a moment. But let me first address two concerns. First, the claim that cyberattacks can be catastrophic is likely to sound, at least to some, hyperbolic. "Yes," such a critic will say, "I grant that cyberattacks are more than just the stuff of science fiction. But the idea that a cyberattack could cause harm on the same scale as could a physical attack is not credible." In response, consider a scenario which Richard Clarke and Robert Knake call the "Exercise South China Sea." In this scenario, the United States and China come into conflict over resources off the coast of Vietnam and Thailand. China, the thought experiment continues, is pressing these nation-states to cede their rights to these resources, and the U.S. is supporting its allies in the Association of Southeast Asian Nations. In the resulting cyberattacks between the China and U.S., power plants and electrical grids are shut down in both countries as well as in Japan. In the U.S., banking systems are disabled, and the major stock markets are thrown offline, with calamitous results across the world. In both countries civilian aircraft are grounded; some freight trains are derailed, leaving the entire rail systems inoperative. Later the U.S. uses cyberattacks to destroy Chinese communication satellites causing further chaos.[24] Though Clarke and Knake describe the conflict between China and the U.S. in rather clinical terms, it is not hard to begin to imagine the human cost. When belligerents shut down power plants and electrical grids, hospitals and emergency services will be unable to continue working. Without power, doctors at hospitals will not be able to perform urgent – or even routine – surgery. Emergency rooms will not have the ability to treat patients. Intensive care wards will be incapable of providing the services necessary to keep their patients alive. Without access to electricity, the police will not be able to communicate with one another; fire departments will not be able to put out fires; and paramedics will not even be notified about who is in need of their services. This is only the beginning, of course. To take but a few more examples, water treatment plants will be unable to operate, resulting in a lack of potable water and possible outbreaks of bacterial infections like dysentery. Once transportation controls are taken out, it will be impossible to get food to large urban areas or to get significant groups of people out of these areas. The result will be riots, widespread violence, and worse. Without fuel, police and even the National Guard will not be able to mobilize and intervene to a sufficient degree (if at all). This is a grim story, to say the least.

Let me be clear: I am not claiming that China and the U.S. are destined to trade cyberattacks in the near future. On the contrary, I sincerely hope that they will never do such a thing, and I am horrified by the rather offhand manner in which this outcome is often assumed.[25] Rather, the point I have just argued is that if cyberattacks occur, they are likely to be ruinous and deadly. As I write this, at least a dozen nation-states can unilaterally impose this kind of calamity on other nation-states. These nation-states include not only China and the United States but also France, India, Iran, North Korea, Pakistan, and Russia. Moreover, it is a simple matter for one group or nation-state to "pile on" once a cyberattack has begun.[26]

Now, even if the critic concedes my point, she might reply much as Bruce Berkowitz has that even if nation-states could impose this level of destruction on one another, it would be irrational for them to do so. What Berkowitz calls an "electronic Pearl Harbor" makes "no sense." Why? "It is hard to imagine," Berkowitz writes, "how any of the scare scenarios describing a bolt-out-of-the-blue cyber strike would help a country, terrorist organization, or anyone else achieve a strategic objective."[27] Even if it were true, as Berkowitz thinks, that no group or nation-state were likely to launch a unilateral cyberattack on the United States, this fact would hardly resolve the questions which cyberattacks raise for the just cause condition of just war theory. It is implausible to think that Pakistan, let us concede just for the moment, would be rational to try to disrupt the computer networks responsible for civil air transportation in the U.S. It hardly follows that it might not gain from doing so in Bangladesh or India. Much the same is true, *mutatis mutandis*, for a growing number of groups and nation-states around the world. But even the idea that the United States is safe from a unilateral attack is problematic. Berkowitz contends that something like an electronic Pearl Harbor "makes no sense" because the actual attack on Pearl Harbor by the Japanese Empire has now been shown not to make sense either since it led to the Empire's destruction and the deaths of hundreds of thousands of Japanese soldiers and civilians. Yet this reasoning is naïve at several levels. To begin with, some within the decision-making hierarchy in the Japanese Empire, including Admiral Isoroku Yamamoto, realized at the time that the attack on Pearl Harbor made little sense, given Japan's aims.[28] This fact did not prevent the attack from happening. Furthermore, recent events have made appallingly clear how insensitive government leadership can be to whether their plans of attack "make no sense."[29] Finally, it is not at all clear whether a group or nation-state would – or should – take Pearl Harbor to be the relevant model. It might just as easily look to Vietnam or, more recently, Afghanistan or Iraq. These models are considerably less likely to discourage a potential belligerent.

Rousseau remarked that "Sometimes it is possible to kill a state without killing any of its members."[30] Perhaps he was right, but using a cyberattack is unlikely to bring about this state of affairs. In light of this fact, would it not be reasonable to say that cyberattacks like the one just described could meet the just cause condition of just war theory? Wouldn't a sovereign nation-state which suffered a cyberattack of this sort satisfy at least a necessary condition for responding militarily?

4. Finding a place for cyberattacks in just war theory

"Traditional military ethics would answer all these questions negatively," as Patrick Lin, Fritz Allhoff, and Neil Rowe have recently reminded us.[31] And, to be sure, some have simply given up trying to answer these questions within the framework of just war theory. François Chauvancy, for example, advocates a move away from talk of aggression and toward the identification of the "enemy" and of "risks and threats."[32] But the answer to both questions, I think, is *yes*. The real question is how this response fits into the framework of just war theory. It is to that question that I now turn.

Let me begin by suggesting that the narrow reading of the just cause condition stands in need of a reason. That is to say, if the right way to understand aggression is solely in terms of what Orend calls "physical violence," then there must be a good reason for understanding it this way. But what could this reason be? The most credible answer appears to be that limiting our understanding of aggression to physical violence is the best way to both respect and promote human rights.[33] In fact, Orend himself accepts this view and argues that it is the dominant understanding of *jus ad bellum* since the work of Locke and Kant.[34] Nevertheless, respecting and promoting are activities which require context in order to be reasonable and, for that matter, intelligible. In one social context, we show our respect for another person by shaking her hand when we meet; in another social context we do not. Likewise, in one context we promote, say, good government by encouraging people to take a direct hand in ruling; in another we promote the same end by fostering an environment in which people communicate with their representatives. I agree that there are some social contexts in which the best way to respect and promote human rights is to understand aggression solely in terms of physical violence. But it is far from self-evident that in every context this is the best way to do so.

In fact, as things now stand, failing to recognize certain forms of cyberattacks as aggression would fail to best promote and respect human rights. Let me explain. While the term *human right* is – and for the foreseeable future will remain – at least somewhat controversial, I here follow Thomas Pogge's definition:

> [T]he postulate of a human right to X entails the demand that, insofar as reasonably possible, any coercive social institution be so designed that all human beings affected have secure access to X. A human right is a moral claim *on* any coercive social institution imposed on oneself and therefore a claim *against* anyone involved in their design or imposition.[35]

It seems fairly clear on this account that the citizens of a modern nation-state have a human-right claim against their own state to provide the basic elements of life: security and safety, food and water, and the like.[36] It seems equally clear that one of the ways in which modern nation-states provide these elements is by protecting their citizens against the actions of other nation-states. In extreme circumstances, doing so means going to war. But if it is possible that a nation-state must go to war to defend its own citizens' human rights, then it must surely be the case that the nation-state does not thereby act unjustly. And if that is true, then the nation-state must meet the just cause condition of *jus ad bellum*. Since in our present situation, a nation-state might have to go to war to protect its citizens from the damage done by cyberattacks, and since we have just seen that doing so would not, thereby, fail to meet the just cause condition, it follows that cyberattacks can count as aggression on the level relevant to just war theory.

A few clarifications are in order. I am not at all suggesting that a cyberattack *per se* is sufficient to justify a war. The just cause condition is one of many conditions which must be met in order for a nation-state to go to war justly. Before a war, a number of further conditions must be met, three of which are worth mentioning here. One such condition is proportionality.[37] While a cyberattack can have horrible consequences, in many cases it will not. As it is false that just any physical attack whatsoever would warrant going to war, so too it is false that just any cyberattack would. Another such condition is last resort.[38] While I argue that cyberattacks should be seen on much the same level at which physical attacks are seen, I do not mean that even an outrageous cyberattack is itself sufficient justification for going to war. The parties in question must exhaust all reasonable alternatives before a war is justified. A final matter that is relevant here is discrimination between combatants and non-combatants.[39] Though this is a condition of *jus in bello* rather than *jus ad bellum*, its importance in a discussion of cyberwar should not be underestimated.[40] Recall that in Clarke and Knake's description of Exercise South China Sea, both China and the United States repeatedly took aim at largely civilian targets like power plants. This is no accident. As the authors envision the exercise, the "U.S. Cyber Command team receives instructions from the Control Team playing the White House and Pentagon to *avoid* attacks on the military command and control systems, and on defensive weapons like air defense."[41] Though they are initially told not to use cyberattacks against air traffic control and the banking sector, these restrictions loosen as the exercise unfolds. In others words, the U.S. is targeting civilians rather than their enemy's military. Why? In part because the civilian targets are much easier to damage but also, in part because too much disruption to China's military command and control system would make it difficult to keep the war from escalating out of control. Of course, we must keep in mind that Clarke and Knake are inventing this exercise, and we cannot conclude from this that any nation-state's government would authorize cyberattacks against civilians for these reasons. The point to keep in mind is that such attacks are violations of principles of *jus in bello* and ought to be condemned as such. The problem is not that they are cyberattacks, *per se*; it is that they are attacks against the innocent and the defenseless.

Conclusion

By way of conclusion, let me return to the U.S.'s recent alleged cyberattacks on Iran. David Sanger tells us that

> American cyberattacks are not limited to Iran, but the focus of attention, as one administration official put it, "has been overwhelmingly on one country." There is no reason to believe that will remain the case for long. Some officials question why the same techniques have not been used more aggressively against North Korea. Others see chances to disrupt Chinese military plans, forces in Syria on the way to suppress the uprising there, and Qaeda

operations around the world. "We've considered a lot more attacks than we have gone ahead with," one former intelligence official said.[42]

We would do well to think very hard about this, and just war theory is still a germane guide to doing so, as I have argued.

Notes

1 I am very grateful to Adam Henschke, Kimberly Kahn, Robert Kraus, and Bill Rhodes for extremely helpful comments on earlier drafts of this chapter. I am also much in debt to my excellent students at the U.S. Air Force Academy for pushing me to think through issues discussed in this paper. In accordance with the Freedom of Information Act 35–101, I note that the views expressed here are those of the author and do not necessarily reflect the official policy or position of the United States Air Force Academy, the Air Force, the Department of Defense or the U.S. Government.

2 N. Machiavelli, "The Art of War," in P. Constantine (ed. & trans.), *The Essential Writings of Machiavelli*, New York: Modern Library, 2007.

3 K. Marx, "Wage-Labour and Capital," in R.C. Tucker (ed.), *The Marx-Engles Reader*, 2nd edn, New York: Norton, 1978.

4 A.M. Turing, "Computing Machinery and Intelligence," *Mind* 59, 1950, pp. 433–460.

5 D. Sanger, "Obama Ordered Sped Up Wave of Cyberattacks against Iran," *New York Times*, 1 June online edition, 2012. Online. Available at: http://www.nytimes.com/2012/06/01/world/middleeast/obama-ordered-wave-of-cyberattacks-against-iran.html?_r=1&pagewanted=all (accessed 6 April 2013).

6 Here and throughout this chapter, I refer to these attacks as "alleged" since the U.S. government has never confirmed its role in them.

7 D. Sanger, "Obama Ordered Sped Up Wave of Cyberattacks against Iran."

8 J. Carr, *Inside Cyber Warfare*, Sebastopol, CA: O'Reily Media, 2010, pp 37–38.

9 H-J. Glock, *What is Analytic Philosophy?* Cambridge, UK: Cambridge University Press, 2008, p. 13.

10 T. Williamson, *Vagueness*, London: Routledge, 1994.

11 M. Libicki, *Cyberdeterrence and Cyberwar*, Santa Monica, CA: RAND, 2009, p. 23.

12 E. Filiol, "Operational Aspects of a Cyberattack: Intelligence, Planning and Conduct," in D. Ventre (ed.) *Cyberwar and Information Warfare*, Hoboken, NJ: John Wiley & Sons, 2011, p. 249.

13 M. Vatis, "Government Perspective," in Y. Alexander and M.S. Swetman (eds), *Cyber Terrorism and Informational Warfare: Threats and Responses*, Ardsley, NY: Transnational Press, 2001, p. 3.

14 B.A. Howell, "Real-World Problems of Virtual Crime," in J. M. Balkin, J. Grimmelmann, E. Katz, N. Kozlovski, S. Wagman and T. Zarsky (eds), *Cybercrime: Digital Cops in a Networked Environment*, New York: New York University Press, 2007, pp. 87–105.

15 For example, R.A. Clarke and R.K. Kane, *Cyberwar: The Next Threat to National Security and What to do about It*, New York: Harper Collins, 2010, pp. 54–62.

16 I have not attempted to weed out all of the flaws in the definitions of Libicki and Filiol. Nor have I tried to give an exhaustive survey of the definitions of *cyberattack* offered in the literature. At some point, this becomes an exercise of merely academic interest.

17 M. Hanser, "The Metaphysics of Harm," *Philosophy and Phenomenological Research* 77:2, 2008, pp. 421–450; J. J. Thomson, "More On The Metaphysics of Harm," *Philosophy and Phenomenological Research* 82:2, 2010, pp. 436–458.

18 F-B. Huyghe, "Cyberwar and Its Borders," in D. Ventre (ed.), *Cyberwar and Information Warfare*, Hoboken, NJ: John Wiley & Sons, 2011, pp. 1–30. Further, we can ask, do all incidents of cyberwar count as cyberattacks? In a narrow sense of *cyberwar*, the answer is "yes." It makes good sense to have a term that is limited to exchanges of cyberattacks. But in a broader sense of *cyberwar*, the answer is "no." Taking out a cluster of mainframe computers with a guided missile would count as an instance of cyberwar, in this looser sense of the term. Both the narrow and the broad sense of *cyberwar* have their uses, and the ambiguity should not be problematic, provided that we take due care. I am grateful to Adam Henschke for pressing me on this point.

19 B. Orend, *The Morality of War*, Calgary, Alberta: Broadview, 2006, p. 39; F. Kamm, *Ethics for Enemies: Terror, Torture, and War*, Oxford: Oxford University Press, 2011, p. 119.

20 N. Fotion, *War and Ethics: A New Just War Theory*, London: Polity, 2007, pp. 10–20; J.C. Ficarrotta, *Kantian Thinking about Military Ethics*, Surrey, UK: Ashgate, 2010, pp. 107–118. Further, I recognize

that some scholars disagree about how many sub-parts of *jus ad bellum* there are, but this point need not detain us here.

21 M. Walzer, *Arguing about War*, New Haven, CT: Yale University Press, 2004, p. 91. See also M. Walzer, *Just and Unjust Wars*, New York: Basic Books, 1978, p. 58.

22 E.g. Aristotle, *Politics* (Book II, Chapter 9), Cicero, *De Officiis* (Book III, Section 21), Augustine, *On Free Choice of the Will* (Book I, Chapter 5), Thomas Aquinas, *Summa Theologicae* (II-II, Q40), Hugo Grotius *On the Law of War and Peace* (Book II, Chapter 1), John Locke, *Second Treatise of Government* (Chapter 2), Immanuel Kant, *The Metaphysics of Morals* (Section I, 60). More recently, see Dower (2009) and McMahan (2009). To be sure, many of these authors disagree about whether, in addition of experiencing aggression, anything else is sufficient for meeting the just cause condition, but we can put that point aside here.

23 B. Orend, *The Morality of War*, Calgary, Alberta: Broadview, 2006, p. 32, emphasis original.

24 R.A. Clarke, and R.K. Knake, *Cyberwar: The Next Threat to National Security and What to Do About It*, New York: Harper Collins, 2010, pp. 180–182.

25 By, Thompson, among others, L. Thompson, "U.S. Headed for Cyberwar Showdown with China in 2012," *Forbes*, December 21, 2011.

26 C.C. Demchak, *Wars of Disruption and Resilience*, Athens, GA: University of Georgia, 2011, p. 21.

27 Berkowitz, B. *The New Face of War: How War Will Be Fought in the 21st Century*, New York: Free Press, 2003, p. 154.

28 For instance, see G.W. Prange, *At Dawn We Slept: The Untold Story of Pearl Harbor*, New York: Penguin, 1982, p. 11.

29 S. M. Hersh, *Chain of Command: The Road from 9/11 to Abu Ghraib*, New York: Harper Collins, 2004; T. Ricks, *Fiasco: The American Military Adventure in Iraq*, New York: Penguin, 2006.

30 J.-J. Rousseau, "The Social Contract," in D.A. Cress (ed. & trans.) *The Basic Political Writings*, Indiana: Indianapolis: Hackett, 1983.

31 P. Lin, F. Allhoff and N. Rowe, "Is It Possible to Wage a Just Cyber War?" *The Atlantic*, June 5, 2012. Online. Available at: http://www.theatlantic.com/technology/archive/2012/06/is-it-possible-to-wage-a-just-cyberwar/258106 (accessed 30 June 2012).

32 F. Chauvancy, "War of Meaning, Cyber War, and Democracy," in D. Ventre (ed.), *Cyberwar and Information Warfare*, Hoboken, NJ: John Wiley & Sons, 2010, p. 60.

33 D. Luban "Just War and Human Rights," *Philosophy & Public Affairs* 9:2, 1980, pp. 160–181; M. Ignatieff, "Human Rights, Sovereignty, and Intervention," in N. Owen (ed.), *Human Rights, Human Wrongs: The Oxford Amnesty Lectures 2001*, Oxford: Oxford University Press, 2001, pp. 49–88; P. Sutch, "Human Rights and the Use of Force: Assertive Liberalism and Just War," *European Journal of Political Theory* 11, 2012, pp. 172–190.

34 B. Orend, *The Morality of War*, Calgary, Alberta: Broadview, 2006, p. 19. See also B. Orend, *Human Rights*, Calgary, Alberta: Broadview, 2002.

35 T. Pogge, *World Poverty and Human Rights*, 2nd edn, London: Polity, 2008, p. 52, emphasis original.

36 A. Altman and C. Wellman *A Liberal Theory of International Justice*, Oxford: Oxford University Press, 2009, p. 7.

37 E.g. Thomas Aquinas, *Summa Theologicae* (II-II, Q40); Desiderius Erasmus, *The Education of a Christian Prince with the Panegyric for Archduke Philip of Austria*, L. Jardine (ed.), Cambridge, UK: Cambridge University Press, 1997; and Francisco Suarez, "Justice, Charity, and War," in G.M. Reichberg, H. Syse, and E. Begby (eds), *The Ethics of War: Classic and Contemporary Readings*, Oxford: Blackwell, 2006, pp. 339–370.

38 E.g. Cicero, *De Officiis* (Book I, Section 34), Francisco Suarez, *Disputation XIII: On War*, Samuel Pufendorf, *On the Duty of Man and Citizen* (Book II, Chapter 16).

39 E.g. Thomas Aquinas, *Summa Theologicae* (II-II, Q40), Francisco de Vitoria, *On the Law of War* (Question 3), Hugo Grotius *On the Law of War and Peace* (Book III, Chapter 11).

40 E.g. M. Walzer, *Just and Unjust Wars*, p. 171.

41 R.A. Clarke and R.K. Knake, *Cyberwar: The Next Threat to National Security and What to Do About It*, New York: Harper Collins, 2010, p. 186, emphasis added.

42 D. Sanger, "Obama Ordered Sped Up Wave of Cyberattacks against Iran."

References

Altman, A. and C. Wellman, *A Liberal Theory of International Justice*, Oxford: Oxford University Press, 2009.

Aquinas, T. *Summa Theologicae*, revised edition, Translated by Fathers of the Dominican Province. Christian Classics, 1947.

Aristotle *Politics*, revised edn, E. Baker (trans.), R.F. Stalley (ed.), Oxford: Oxford University Press, 2009.

Augustine, *On Free Choice of the Will*, T. Willliam (trans.), Indianapolis, Indiana: Hackett, 1993.

Berkowitz, B. *The New Face of War: How War Will Be Fought in the 21st Century*, New York: Free Press, 2003.

Carr, J. *Inside Cyber Warfare*, Sebastopol, CA: O'Reily Media, 2010.

Chauvancy, F. "War of Meaning, Cyber War, and Democracy" in D. Ventre (ed.) *Cyberwar and Information Warfare*, Hoboken, NJ: John Wiley & Sons, 2010, pp. 31–80.

Cicero, *De Officiis*, revised edn, P.G. Walse (trans.), Oxford: Oxford University Press, 2008.

Clarke, R.A. and R.K. Knake, *Cyberwar: The Next Threat to National Security and What to Do About It*, New York: HarperCollins, 2010.

Demchak, C.C. *Wars of Disruption and Resilience*, Athens, GA: University of Georgia, 2011.

De Vitoria, F. *Political Writings*, A. Pagden and J. Lawrance (eds) Cambridge, UK: Cambridge University Press, 1992.

Dower, N. *The Ethics of War and Peace: Cosmopolitan and Other Perspectives*, Cambridge, UK: Polity, 2009.

Erasmus, D. *The Education of a Christian Prince with the Panegyric for Archduke Philip of Austria*, L. Jardine (ed.), Cambridge, UK: Cambridge University Press, 1997.

Ficarrotta, J.C. *Kantian Thinking about Military Ethics*, Surrey, UK: Ashgate, 2010.

Filiol, E. "Operational Aspects of a Cyberattack: Intelligence, Planning and Conduct," in D. Ventre (ed.), *Cyberwar and Information Warfare*, Hoboken, NJ: John Wiley & Sons, 2011, pp. 245–284.

Fotion, N. *War and Ethics: A New Just War Theory*, London: Polity, 2007.

Glock, H-J. *What is Analytic Philosophy?* Cambridge, UK: Cambridge University Press, 2008.

Grotius, H. *On the Law of War and Peace*, S.C. Neff (ed.), Cambridge, UK: Cambridge University Press, 2012.

Hanser, M. "The Metaphysics of Harm," *Philosophy and Phenomenological Research* 77:2, 2008, pp. 421–450.

Hersh, S.M. *Chain of Command: The Road from 9/11 to Abu Ghraib*, New York: Harper Collins, 2004.

Howell, B.A. "Real-World Problems of Virtual Crime," in J. M. Balkin, J. Grimmelmann, E. Katz, N. Kozlovski, S. Wagman and T. Zarsky (eds), *Cybercrime: Digital Cops in a Networked Environment*, New York: New York University Press, 2007, pp. 87–105.

Huyghe, F-B. "Cyberwar and Its Borders," in D. Ventre (ed.) *Cyberwar and Information Warfare*, Hoboken, NJ: John Wiley & Sons, 2011, pp. 1–30.

Ignatieff, M. "Human Rights, Sovereignty, and Intervention," in N. Owen (ed.) *Human Rights, Human Wrongs: The Oxford Amnesty Lectures 2001*, Oxford: Oxford University Press, 2001, pp. 49–88.

Kamm, F. *Ethics for Enemies: Terror, Torture, and War*, Oxford: Oxford University Press, 2011.

Kant, I. *The Metaphysics of Morals*, revised edn, M.J. Gregor (ed.), Cambridge, UK: Cambridge University Press, 2008.

Libicki, M. *Cyberdeterrence and Cyberwar*, Santa Monica, CA: RAND, 2009.

Lin, P., F. Allhoff, and N. Rowe "Is It Possible to Wage a Just Cyber War?" *The Atlantic*, June 5, 2012. Online. Available at: http://www.theatlantic.com/technology/archive/2012/06/is-it-possible-to-wage-a-just-cyberwar/258106/ (accessed 6 April 2013).

Locke, J. *Political Writings*, Whooton D. (ed.), Indianapolis, Indiana: Hackett, 2008.

Luban D. "Just War and Human Rights," *Philosophy & Public Affairs* 9:2, 1980, pp. 160–181.

Machiavelli, N. "The Art of War," in P. Constantine (ed. & trans.), *The Essential Writings of Machiavelli*, New York: Modern Library, 2007.

McMahan, J. *Killing in War*, Oxford: Oxford University Press, 2009.

Marx, K. "Wage-Labour and Capital," in R.C. Tucker (ed.), *The Marx-Engles Reader*, 2nd edn, New York: Norton, 1978.

Orend, B. *The Morality of War*, Calgary, Alberta: Broadview, 2006.

——*Human Rights*, Calgary, Alberta: Broadview, 2002.

Pogge, T. *World Poverty and Human Rights*, 2nd edn, London: Polity, 2008.

Prange, G.W. *At Dawn We Slept: The Untold Story of Pearl Harbor*, New York: Penguin, 1982.

Ricks, T. *Fiasco: The American Military Adventure in Iraq*, New York: Penguin, 2006.

Rousseau, J.J. "The Social Contract," in D.A. Cress (ed. & trans.), *The Basic Political Writings*, Indiana: Indianapolis: Hackett, 1983.

Sanger, D. "Obama Ordered Sped Up Wave of Cyberattacks against Iran," *New York Times*, 1 June online edition, 2012. Online. Available at: http://www.nytimes.com/2012/06/01/world/middleeast/obama-ordered-wave-of-cyberattacks-against-iran.html?_r=1&pagewanted=all (accessed 6 April 2013).

Suarez, F. "Justice, Charity, and War," in G.M. Reichberg, H. Syse and E. Begby (eds), *The Ethics of War: Classic and Contemporary Readings*, Oxford: Blackwell, 2006, pp. 339–370.

Sutch, P. "Human Rights and the Use of Force: Assertive Liberalism and Just War," *European Journal of Political Theory* 11, 2012, pp. 172–190

Thompson, L. "U.S. Headed for Cyberwar Showdown with China in 2012," *Forbes*, December 21, 2011.

Thomson, J.J. "More On The Metaphysics of Harm," *Philosophy and Phenomenological Research* 82:2, 2010, pp. 436–458.

Turing, A.M. "Computing Machinery and Intelligence," *Mind* 59, 1950, pp. 433–460.

Vatis, M. (2001) "Government Perspective," in Y. Alexander and M.S. Swetman (eds), *Cyber Terrorism and Informational Warfare: Threats and Responses*, Ardsley, NY: Transnational Press, 2001.

Walzer, M. *Arguing about War*, New Haven, CT: Yale University Press, 2004.

——*Just and Unjust Wars*, New York: Basic Books, 1978.

Williamson, T. *Vagueness*, London: Routledge, 1994.

29

PERFIDY IN CYBERWARFARE[1]

Neil C. Rowe

1. Introduction

Perfidy is an important concept in the laws of warfare. The term covers a category of ruses in which a military force impersonates neutral parties such as the Red Cross to obtain a tactical or strategic advantage.[2] Ruses and impersonation are not generally outlawed by the laws of war; impersonation of an adversary can be justifiable in some situations. But impersonation of neutral parties is generally prohibited because it can hurt both sides of a conflict, causing warfare to deteriorate to chaos. This is because conflicting parties depend on neutral parties to provide food, clothing, shelter, and information. Members of civilian organizations can be especially important in providing humanitarian assistance, evacuating civilians from the area of conflict, providing communications to nonmilitary organizations, and providing connections to what exists as government. These things are not the job of military organizations and it is unreasonable to expect military organizations to provide them. So impersonation of civilians lowers the trust in people appearing to be civilians, making it more difficult for civilians to act freely, and increasing the chances of them being harmed.[3]

Article 37 of the 1977 Protocol I Additional to the Geneva Conventions provides one definition of perfidy as acting to "kill, injure, or capture an adversary" by "feigning of civilian, noncombatant status." This identifies the feigning itself as the crime. This reflects a key component of just-war theory, the discrimination of civilians from combatants. Cyber perfidy can be defined as the feigning of civilian computer software, hardware, or data as a step towards doing harm to an adversary.

A good example of cyber perfidy is the Stuxnet worm and its associated malware.[4] Its ultimate target was command-and-control of particular kinds of centrifuge control equipment from Siemens Corporation, but it used worm methods to spread primarily across many kinds of civilian computers and networks. It thus infected a wide range of objects in cyberspace, masquerading as normal versions of those objects. This infection was quite illegal in most countries because it violated end-user license agreements (EULAs) for Siemens and primarily for the Microsoft Windows operating system, even though it did no dramatic direct harm to all but a small fraction of targeted machines. However, the ideas behind Stuxnet are now being used by the criminal cyberattacker community at a net negative cost to world society.[5] Addressing the threats posed by Stuxnet has required work by security-software companies to detect its signatures and implement checking for them. Stuxnet only delayed its intended targets in the Iranian nuclear program a few months, so it appears to have been ineffective against its primary target while having harmful side effects.

Unfortunately, cyber perfidy is more central to cyberwarfare than traditional perfidy is to conventional warfare. That is because computer systems are designed to be highly reliable and resistant to attempts to subvert them for malicious purposes. In fact, computers and digital devices are far more reliable than most non-computer technology per action taken because the digital world is generally far more controllable than the physical world, though it does not always seem apparent because of the tremendous number of actions taken in the digital world. You also need authorization to do something with a computer or digital device. So direct attacks on a computer by sending it unauthorized malicious instructions will just be ignored. Similarly, direct attacks by sending it massive amounts of data will rarely work because most computers have data-rate limiters that control the amount of data they see. Public Web sites accept higher rates but most now have rate limiters too, unlike the country of Georgia for the cyberattacks on its government Web sites in 2008.[6]

That means that an attacker must almost always impersonate a legitimate user of a computer or digital device to get access to it for a cyberattack during cyberwarfare. If they impersonate a civilian, that is cyber perfidy. That means a military attack on a civilian computer or digital device must almost always be cyber perfidious. But even if attackers identify themselves as military during an attack, it is likely that cyber perfidy is necessary for the attack to work. That is because the key civilian mechanisms that run computers and digital devices, their "operating systems", have many protections to prevent people from doing bad things with them. They have protections against changing their instructions and data in other than approved ways, such as control of access and modification rights, encryption of key data, limitations on what programs can do and where, virus and worm checking, monitoring of behavior of ongoing processes, and monitoring of network connections. So nearly all cyberattacks must involve some form of deception with the goal of modifying a victim operating system.[7] Since operating systems are civilian artifacts, serving predominantly as agents of civilian needs, changing them to accomplish an attack is cyber perfidious.

2. Defining cyber perfidy

Cyber perfidy can be identified whenever malicious software or hardware pretends to be ordinary software or hardware, where its goal is to harm software or hardware as part of a military operation. Impersonation of legitimate software by malicious software occurs frequently with criminal cyberattacks today, and is essential to the most serious compromises such as rootkits (taking over the entire operating system of a computer)[8] and botnets (enslaving a set of computers).[9] Most current cyberattacks involve subversion of the Microsoft Windows operating system. Such impersonation enables cybercriminals to make money by sending spam email through compromised computers, hosting phishing scams, attacking sites they do not like, launching "denial-of-service" blockades against sites, and blackmailing sites by threatening attacks against them. Nearly all proposed offensive cyberwarfare techniques use impersonation too. But that could be cyber perfidious.

Impersonation of legitimate software and hardware is illegal in nearly every country in the world, as it is a form of tampering with a product. Nearly all EULAs for software and hardware exclude warranty after modification. Modification means the producer cannot be responsible for what it does, since even a small change in a program can create a big difference in behavior. This has not deterred criminals. But it is a different matter for a legal government to use these tactics. Guns have legitimate uses in police work and hunting, but there are few legitimate uses for cyberweapons in the civilized world, just as there are few legitimate uses for chemical, biological, and nuclear weapons. (A possible exception is "red teaming" to test the cyber-security of systems, deliberately attacking them using as many tricks as possible, but this is generally a crude and inefficient method of testing systems, and many better tools are available.)

Tampering with consumer products is a serious crime in criminal law.[10] In the United States, the Federal Anti-Tampering Law (USC Title 18 Chapter 65, "Malicious Mischief") defines several categories including "whoever, with intent to cause serious injury to the business of any persons, taints any consumer product or renders materially false or misleading the labeling of, or container for, a consumer product." This has a penalty of up three years in prison; tampering that causes bodily harm receives up to twenty years. These laws clearly apply to software as a consumer product under the classification of "device" where malicious modification renders misleading the labeling of the software.

We are starting to see international cooperation on extending the laws of war to cyber-weapons.[11] Identifying and labeling cyber perfidy is in the tradition of "just war" theory where civilians are not legitimate primary targets.[12] Or as Hugo Slim[13] puts it, it is wrong to attack those who cannot harm you. General-purpose computer software and hardware is carefully designed not to harm anyone. While military software may be installed on systems that could be legitimate targets, the general-purpose services on systems are like human civilians, and should not be legitimate targets of attacks by analogy to just-war theory. Computer programs have grown so much in sophistication and complexity in recent years that they are no longer always "mechanisms," but are approaching "artificial intelligences" that are like people in some ways. Most of these programs would qualify strictly as "noncombatants"[14] since they do not contribute to military operations.

2.1 Cyber-resources that are possible targets of perfidy

Not all cases of software and hardware impersonation should be labeled as perfidious, however. Ruses are accepted as legitimate tactics of warfare when impersonation is done of military personnel and civilian non-neutral parties such as truck drivers bringing materiel. So to qualify as cyber perfidy, the target of the impersonation should be something primarily used by civilians. Then to constitute a war crime, the perfidy must be used to launch an attack. Non-cyber perfidy need not directly damage the object of its impersonation, but some such collateral damage is inevitable with cyber perfidy since the functionality of existing software or data is changed and will not revert to normal functionality without explicit action. That is another argument why cyber perfidy is a serious matter.

An analogy in conventional warfare would be a well. Generally speaking, poisoning a well is not acceptable by the laws of warfare, although it could provide the important tactical advantage of forcing a civilian population to move on.[15] In a village where a communal well is the only source of water, poisoning it would be attacking a resource too central to the civilian community to satisfy the criterion of discriminability of civilian targets from military ones. It is even more a war crime if the poisoning is not announced and people start dying without knowing the cause.[16] Cyber perfidy is similar to the poisoning without announcement, since the effectiveness of cyberattacks generally depends on keeping them secret as long as possible.

Consider some cyber-services whose modification would fulfill this definition of cyber perfidy and which would be especially useful to a cyberattacker:

- The security kernel of an operating system. This controls what rights programs have to do things, in particular to change items in memory or secondary storage. It maintains the functionality of the operating system (its "integrity"), and without it many kinds of harm are possible. Most criminal cyberattacks want to compromise it and exploit it.
- The file management features of an operating system. Software is useless unless it can manage files. Attacks do not need to affect all files, just certain critical ones.
- The update manager. Since software is usually created without guarantees, updates are essential to quickly block new kinds of attacks. Attacks on the manager can prevent timely defenses or could install malicious ones.
- The networking software. Some important applications critically depend on access to a network. This is particularly true of small wireless devices which need networking to complete basic tasks for which they lack resources.
- Electronic mail services. People need to communicate.
- The hardware (integrated circuits) that implements the central-processing unit (CPU) of the computer. If these can be changed, then the computer can be run any way an attacker wants. However, this requires physical access to the machine and cannot be done over the Internet.

Attacks on the above cyber-services should be considered cyber perfidious if they happen on civilian computers or networks. For cyber-services on a military computer or network, it is more arguable whether the term applies. At issue is whether an attack could spread to civilians; for instance, if a virus attack on a military computer could easily spread to civilian computers, then it could be cyber perfidious. (U.S. military networks are connected to civilian networks in ways not always realized.) But tampering with a product or poisoning a well used by military personnel could be considered as violating the laws of war anyway even if it does spread to other instances.

By contrast, consider some cyber-services that could be impersonation targets[17] but for which this could not be cyber perfidy:

- Weapons systems. These are legitimate targets of cyberweapons.
- Military planning and coordination systems ("command and control"). These are legitimate targets of cyberweapons.
- Management of specifically military organizations and their contractors.
- Specific manufacturing software for weapons. That was the intended target of Stuxnet, but does not excuse its collateral damage.
- Web pages on military or government Web servers. These are an important target of military propaganda or "influence" operations.

2.2 Methods of tampering

The tampering with software or hardware in cyber perfidy can have several effects:

- The service can be modified to support an attack, such as browsers infected by malware that direct Web users to certain attacker-designed pages that help launch attacks.
- The service can be modified to malfunction so that users cannot do what they normally can, such as electronic mail services modified to malfunction during an attack and thus fail to provide warnings to other sites.

- The service can be modified to directly create harmful new effects, such as launching cyberattacks on other sites.
- The service can be modified to actually harm people, such as launching attacks against water treatment plants or hospital computer systems.

A "strict constructionist" approach might consider only the last to be cyber perfidy. But a "loose constructionist" argument can be made for all of these. There is rarely any military necessity for cyberattacks to do these things, since there are many better weapons for achieving military goals. Cheapness and simplicity are not a justification for using a weapon, as there are many horrible cheap and simple weapons like mines. David Lonsdale[18] points out that cyberwarfare, like most innovations in warfare, was initially hoped to be more precise in effects than conventional warfare. But this has not been true because of the dependence of most cyberweapons on flaws in software – and flaws can get fixed unexpectedly – and the easy ability to use deception in cyberspace by potential targets. Thus the tampering with software and data necessary to accomplish a cyberattack must often be substantial to ensure a militarily significant effect. This makes it easier for the tampering to spill into civilian software and data.

2.3 Perfidy involving human cybercombatants

Another aspect of the definition of perfidy in the laws of war is identification of combatants. Cyberwarfare risks violating this because the combatants tend to be unseen; they may be programmers or software users in a military organization who do not think of themselves as soldiers. However, if they help launch attacks, they are legitimate targets of retaliation in the form of bombs and targeted assassinations. That means that cybercombatants should announce the geographical locations of their cyberwarfare groups in advance of hostilities to avoid perfidy.

2.4 Repairing the damage of cyberattacks

Some of the damage of cyber perfidy is short-term: time delays from added malicious activity, space wasted, reduced resources to deal with concurrent criminal cyberattacks, and personnel time for investigation since most critical-infrastructure systems have humans monitoring for anomalous behavior and investigating it. But cyber perfidy also results in long-term damage and entails costs to clean up afterwards. Because careful deception is generally necessary for the perfidy, and the attack must be overwhelming to have a significant tactical effect, many things may need to be repaired. It is very hard to recognize unauthorized changes to software and data. While software may be restorable from backup, that may not be possible with data that needs to be timely. And the backup may itself be tainted, so restoration from backup may be impossible. Thus most cyberattacks are "dirty" weapons that leave a mess. Nonetheless, it is possible to design "cleaner" cyberweapons by making their effects reversible[19] and that can be encouraged.

Another serious problem is that cyberattacks of all kinds are quickly analyzed and dissected by the information-security community in an effort to prepare for similar future attacks. After some dispute in the 1990s, the consensus today is that it is better for the public interest to report new attacks and get public fixes than to conceal attacks and the vulnerabilities that led to them.[20] This analysis is done publicly on sites such as www.kb.cert.org (the US-CERT Vulnerability Notes Database), cve.mitre.org (the Common Vulnerabilities and Exposures site), web.nvd.nist.gov (the National Vulnerability Database), and www.securityfocus.com (the Bugtraq wikis for reporting vulnerabilities). The results of such analysis and reverse engineering are quickly available to criminal cyberattackers. Stuxnet is an example because many of its new propagation methods targeted the widespread Microsoft Windows operating system and had nothing to do with centrifuges. Analysis or reverse engineering of a conventional weapon is usually not help- ful for accomplishing new attacks because most conventional weapons use well-understood principles (like mines), or are expended upon attack (like missiles), or do not provide key information contributing to their effectiveness (such as bullets, which do not reveal the military intelligence and planning used to target them). On the other hand, a good part of the damage of a cyberweapon will be in its subsequent enabling of criminal cyberattacks against civilians far from the scene of the original attack.

3. Objections to the concept of cyber perfidy

Various objections have been raised to this notion of cyber perfidy. For one thing, cyber per- fidy does not seem to invoke strong emotions. Traditional perfidy can invoke strong emotions, since attacking neutral parties elicits strong moral condemnation in most legal and ethical sys- tems. Warfare that attacks human health, like poison gas, often invokes a particularly visceral fear.[21] Such visceral responses generally occur in regard to threats that have been with the human race for millions of years. Unfortunately, computers are very new in the evolution of the human race and our emotional systems are not tied to them (except maybe in tampering with computer-based children's toys). But maybe attacks on them should create equal fear and outrage too considering how important they are in our lives. So we need to evaluate objec- tively whether the damage due to cyber perfidy can be similar to the damage due to traditional perfidy, not from a gut feeling. We argue here that it is.

Some have argued that the notion of perfidy is based on the threat to human lives.[22] Thus shooting Red Cross personnel would be murder but disabling a computer would just be van- dalism. Certainly cyber perfidy could threaten human lives if it results in violence, as with Stuxnet causing uncontrollable acceleration in centrifuges. But the Geneva Convention section on perfidy includes injuring and capturing adversaries as a result of perfidy as well as killing. We argue that is because the key casualty of perfidy is trust, not lives. If we cannot trust neutral parties, we will be unwilling to use them for their intended purposes.[23] Even when Red Cross personnel are not in mortal danger, the value of the Red Cross is greatly reduced when they cannot be trusted. Damage to trust, when spread over many instances, can be equal or worse than a harm done to any one individual. Consider financial services such as banking, on which everyone depends. A cyberattack that targets banking and reduces its trust could be highly sig- nificant. This could be done by targeting online banking with malicious software that changed monetary amounts randomly so no one could tell how much money they had in their accounts. If the damage to a banking system affects many customers, the harm done to each of them could add up to the harm of several murders. Militaries often risk soldiers in order to achieve tactical and strategic goals that are considered more valuable than the individual lives of soldiers.

A further objection to the concept of cyber perfidy is that it does not involve explosives, a concern of the laws of war. However, cyber perfidy can have an analogous effect to an explo- sion in cyberspace (hence the term "logic bomb") in that it can reduce a sophisticated software device to a set of unconnected fragments. Cyber perfidy can also be like a booby trap since it must be activated primarily by normal activities of its victim to do its damage. Booby traps are outlawed by the United Nations Convention on Certain Conventional Weapons Protocol II (1996 as amended).[24] Many clever forms of booby traps were used with improvised explosive devices (IEDs) by Iraqi insurgents between 2003 and 2011, in violation of the Convention and were universally condemned. For instance, explosive devices were hidden in trash or other everyday objects, violating the prohibition against using "apparently harmless portable objects which are specifically designed and constructed to contain explosive material." Cyber perfidy tries to hide its malicious intent inside standard or "everyday" code in an analogous way.

A different concern is that cyberweapons may just seem awful because they are new, and cyberweapons may well become an accepted part of future warfare. Objections were raised to torpedoes early in the twentieth century for this reason, and some argued they violated the "civilized" nature of naval warfare.[25] Today torpedoes are well accepted in military arsenals. However, torpedoes are visible objects that use conventional munitions. They can be seen leaving the attacker who must be nearby, they have a direction, they cause clear damage all at once at a target, and the damage is generally localized with a clear cause. None of these things applies to cyberweapons, which makes them much more difficult to monitor. Thus objections to cyberweapons should not be dismissed merely because they are new.

Some may consider that cyberweapons are the natural result of the evolution of warfighting technology towards greater control of technology,[26] and we should not object to "progress." One response mentioned earlier is that countermeasures to cyberweapons like better information-security practices by defenders and deliberate deception are making it uncertain that these weapons provide commanders with greater control of conflict. Another is that "progress" has brought us chemical, biological, and nuclear weapons in the last hundred years, yet international laws and other incentives prevent countries from using them.

Following just-war theory, some might hold that cyber perfidy exploits a "dual-use" technology of information systems and such double effects are accepted in warfare provided the primary effect is military.[27] However, the most effective targets of cyberweapons as described earlier are things like operating systems that are inherently civilian in nature. Furthermore, the fraction of military traffic carried on the Internet is a small fraction of the total traffic, so attacking the Internet has little dual-use effect on military systems. However, attacking a specifically military network that is substantially unconnected to the Internet would be an exception, and could be appropriately justified by the dual-use principle.

A final objection is that cyber perfidy is generally used as a stepping stone to enable well-focused attacks on a few key targets, so it is desirable for attackers to design its perfidy so that it is mostly harmless to the stepping stones. However, an important principle in the laws of war is that neutrality of non-participants must be respected.[28] Operating systems have no stake in either side of a conflict. To co-opt them for launching an attack on another country, as the Russians did with computers in a range of countries including the United States during the Georgia attacks of 2008, is like violating the neutrality of a country as Germany did to Belgium in World War I and for which it was roundly criticized for. Attacks that use more substantial resources of a country such as setting up botnets within them could be considered similar to forced conscription or at least forced labor in munitions plants as the Germans did in France in World War II, again tactics outlawed in the laws of war.

4. International agreements on cyber perfidy

Since cyber perfidy can lead to uncontrollable consequences in warfare, it is important to seek international agreements to control it. Three useful ideas that should be included in such agreements are international cooperation in detection, policy on attribution of attacks by attackers, and policy mandating selection of nonperfidious methods for attacks.

Cyber perfidy can be detected by comparing the bit patterns of critical software before and after an attack on it. This can be done efficiently by comparing hash codes. When software is installed on a computer, hash codes using one of the standard algorithms like SHA-1 can be computed on their files, and can be recomputed periodically. If they change that means that the software has been modified. Hash codes on a broad range of software and its updates can also be obtained for free from the National Software Reference Library (NSRL) maintained by the U.S. Government organization NIST, and commercial companies like Bit9 provide supplementary hash codes. If comparison of hash codes is so simple, why is it not done routinely to protect computer systems? It would slow systems considerably since there are many files to check. Also, a rootkit that commandeers an operating system can disable checking software or make it give false results, so the hash codes are unreliable once a serious attack has succeeded against a computer system. And certainly there are legitimate cases where software must be changed to update it in response to discovered bugs.

International cooperation will aid in detecting cyberattacks and their precursors because cooperation greatly helps in controlling criminal cyberattacks today, as discussed above. Early reports of possible attack patterns suggesting nation-sponsored cyberwarfare can be identified in the far larger volume of normal attacks, and summarized and reported to international agencies.

One of the most disturbing features of cyber perfidy is the difficulty of attributing it. Attribution is possible in some cases: A country may announce responsibility for an attack, or we may be able to trace its origin across the Internet using a number of techniques, or we may be able to find source code for a distinctive cyberweapon during a police raid. But attribution is more difficult in cyberconflict than in conventional conflict. When a missile is launched at a country, there are clues to who launched it in its path and velocity vector. When software or hardware is maliciously changed, there are frequently no clues; Stuxnet has still not been attributed two years afterwards. Detecting the source of a cyberattack is difficult because cyberattacks frequently hide or falsify their origins. Detecting the true origin of an external cyberattack requires broad monitoring of the Internet, and to do it truly effectively agencies must access information not normally available. But also attacks can be planted by insiders and do not need to come in over the Internet at all, or they can originate from tainted storage media. Thus attribution is very difficult with cyberattacks involving cyber perfidy. A country may just assume it is due to a long-time adversary when it has actually been caused by a trouble-making third party.

Therefore, we have argued elsewhere that responsible countries, or just countries wishing to ensure that their attacks have a precise effect, label their cyberattacks in some way,[29] much as the Hague Convention stipulates that belligerents should have a "fixed distinctive emblem recognizable at a distance." It is hard to conduct a war fairly when it is unclear who is attacking whom. So a label or signature is needed, and must be concealed from casual inspection, so techniques of steganography must be used to hide its existence until the attacker chooses to reveal it. In addition, the signature itself needs to be encrypted with a key known to the attacker or a neutral agent so that by decrypting it the attacker can prove that they are the source of the attack. International agreements can specify standards on the form and methods of signatures.

Another possible subject of international agreements is restrictions on cyberattacks to avoid cyber perfidy. Section 2, "Defining cyber perfidy," gave a list of perfidious targets and methods that could be stipulated. While nonperfidious attacks may have harder challenges to achieve desired damage, the damage can still be severe. In fact, it is often easier to attack applications software than the operating system because most protections are designed for operating systems. That is because most criminal attackers want broad effects and will get most leverage from attacking the operating system. However, cyberwarriors do not have these goals and, if desired, can rely on more targeted methods such as modifying a small set of applications software by methods such as viruses. The situation is similar to bombing a specific building in Baghdad without damaging the neighboring civilian buildings, which was done successfully during U.S. military operations in 1991 and 2003. Computers permit more precise control than bombs and ought to offer more precise effects, particularly when their targets are not as powerful as an operating system.

What recourse does the world community have if countries persist in engaging in cyber perfidy? Sanctions that target a country's ability to do Internet commerce are appropriate. With international cooperation, sanctions could be powerful tools. In addition, since cyber perfidy generally violates product-tampering laws, those laws could be enforced by traditional criminal legal proceedings in the countries victimized.

5. Conclusions

Does defining something as cyber perfidy really matter? We believe so because there are policy implications: Perfidious actions can be considered off-limits to a civilized and decent society. Less scrupulous countries may still engage in cyber perfidy. But then we will have an additional mark against them that we can use in motivating international coalitions against them.

Most discussion of cyberweapons treats them as similar to other weapons. But cyberspace is a fundamentally different technology than that of explosives because its weapons need not be physically localized, need not be large compared to their effect, and need not have damage that can be easily recognized. For these reasons the laws of war need to address cyberweapons from a fresh perspective. Clearly certain aspects of cyberweapons could be highly dangerous. Cyber perfidy would seem a good thing to prohibit in the laws of war because of its uncontrollability and destabilizing effects. It is, however, just one of the many ethical problems raised by cyberwarfare.[30]

Notes

1 The views expressed are those of the author and do not represent those of the U.S. Government.
2 ICRC (International Committee of the Red Cross) "International humanitarian law – treaties and documents," 2007. Online. Available at: http://www.icrc.org/ihl.nsf (accessed 1 December, 2007).
3 Orend, B. *The Morality of War*, Toronto, CA: Broadview Press, 2006.
4 Gross, M. "A declaration of cyber-war," *Vanity Fair*, April 2011.
5 Kaplan, D. "New malware appears carrying Stuxnet code," *SC Magazine*, October 18, 2011. Online. Available at: http:www.scmagazine.com/new-malware-appears-carrying-stuxnet-code/article/214707 (accessed 1 August, 2012); US-CCU (United States Cyber Consequences Unit) "Overview by the US-CCU of the Cyber Campaign against Georgia in August of 2008," US-CCU Special Report, August, 2009. Online. Available at: http://www.registan.net/wp-content/uploads/2009/08/US-CCU-Georgia-Cyber-Campaign-Overview.pdf (accessed 2 November, 2009).
6 Ibid.
7 Denning, D. *Information Warfare and Security*, Boston, MA: Addison-Wesley, 1999.
8 Kühnhauser, W. "Root kits: an operating systems viewpoint," *ACM SIGOPS Operating Systems Review*, 38:1, 2004, pp. 12–23.
9 Bailey, M., E. Cooke, F. Jahanian, Y. Xu and M. Karir, "A survey of botnet technology and defenses", *Proc. Conf. for Homeland Security: Cybersecurity Applications and Technology*, March, 2009.
10 Doeg, C. "Product tampering – a constant threat," in *Crisis Management in the Food and Drinks Industry*, 2nd edn, New York: Springer Science+Business Media, 2005.
11 Hollis, D. "New tools, new rules: international law and information operations," in G. David and T. McKeldin (eds), *The Message of War: Information, Influence, and Perception in Armed Conflict*, Temple University Legal Studies Research Paper No. 2007–15, Philadelphia, PA, USA, 2007; Wingfield, T. "International law and information operations," in F. Kramer, S. Starr and L. Wentz (eds), *Cyberpower and National Security*, Washington DC: National Defense University Press, 2009, pp. 525–542.
12 Walzer, M. *Just and Unjust Wars: A Moral Argument with Historical Illustrations*, New York: Basic Books, 1977.
13 Slim, H. *Killing Civilians: Method, Madness and Morality in War*, NY: Columbia University Press, 2008.

14 Kaurin, D. "When less is more: expanding the combatant/noncombatant distinction," in M. Brough, J. Lango, and H. van der Linden (eds), *Rethinking The Just War Tradition*, New York: SUNY Press, 2007.

15 Walzer, *Just and Unjust Wars.*

16 Gutman, R. and D. Rieff, *Crimes of War: What the Public Should Know*, New York: Norton, 1999.

17 Clarke, R. and R. Knake, *Cyber War: The Next Threat to National Security and What to Do About It*, New York: HarperCollins, 2010.

18 Lonsdale, D. *The Nature of War in the Information Age*, London, UK: Frank Cass, 2004.

19 Rowe, N. "Towards reversible cyberattacks," in *Leading Issues in Information Warfare and Security Research*, Volume I, Academic Publishing, 2011, pp. 145–158.

20 TechRepublic (2005) "Flaw finders go their own way", January 26. Online. Available at: www.techrepublic.com/forum/discussions/9-167221 (accessed 1 August 2012).

21 Price, R. *The Chemical Weapons Taboo*, Ithaca, NY: Cornell University Press, 1997.

22 Slim, H. (2008) *Killing Civilians: Method, Madness, and Morality in War*, NY: Columbia University Press; TechRepublic (2005) "Flaw finders go their own way", January 26. Online. Available at: www.techrepublic.com/forum/discussions/9-167221 (accessed 1 August 2012).

23 Walzer, M. *Just and Unjust Wars.*

24 United Nations "Disarmament: The Convention on Certain Conventional Weapons," Online. Available at: www.unog.ch/80256EE600585943/%28httpPages%29/4F0DEF093B4860B4C125718 0004B1B30 (accessed 9 June, 2012).

25 Johnson, J. *Can Modern War Be Just?* New Haven, CT: Yale University Press, 1984.

26 Libicki, M. *Conquest in Cyberspace: National Security and Information Warfare*, New York: Cambridge University Press, 2007.

27 Walzer, M. *Just and Unjust Wars.*

28 Ibid.

29 Rowe, N. "Towards reversible cyberattacks," in *Leading Issues in Information Warfare and Security Research*, Volume I, Academic Publishing, 2011, pp. 145–158.

30 Rowe, N. "The ethics of cyberweapons in warfare," *International Journal of Technoethics*, 1:1, January–March 2010, pp. 20–31.

References

Bailey, M., E. Cooke, F. Jahanian, Y. Xu and M. Karir, "A survey of botnet technology and defenses," *Proc. Conf. for Homeland Security: Cybersecurity Applications and Technology*, March, 2009.

Clarke, R. and R. Knake, *Cyber War: The Next Threat to National Security and What to Do About It*, New York: HarperCollins, 2010.

Denning, D. *Information Warfare and Security*, Boston, MA: Addison-Wesley, 1999.

Doeg, C. "Product tampering – a constant threat," in *Crisis Management in the Food and Drinks Industry*, 2nd edn, New York: Springer Science+Business Media, 2005.

Gross, M. "A declaration of cyber-war," *Vanity Fair*, April 2011.

Gutman, R. and D. Rieff, *Crimes of War: What the Public Should Know*, New York: Norton, 1999.

Hollis, D. "New tools, new rules: international law and information operations," in G. David and T. McKeldin (eds), *The Message of War: Information, Influence, and Perception in Armed Conflict*, Temple University Legal Studies Research Paper No. 2007–15, Philadelphia, PA, USA, 2007.

ICRC (International Committee of the Red Cross) "International humanitarian law – treaties and documents," 2007. Online. Available at: www.icrc.org/ihl.nsf (accessed 1 December, 2007).

Johnson, J. *Can Modern War Be Just?* New Haven, CT: Yale University Press, 1984.

Kaplan, D. "New malware appears carrying Stuxnet code," *SC Magazine*, October 18, 2011. Online. Available at: http://www.scmagazine.com/new-malware-appears-carrying-stuxnet-code/article/ 214707 (accessed 1 August, 2012).

Kaurin, D. "When less is more: expanding the combatant/noncombatant distinction," in M. Brough, J. Lango and H. van der Linden (eds), *Rethinking the Just War Tradition*, New York: SUNY Press, 2007.

Kühnhauser, W. "Root kits: an operating systems viewpoint," *ACM SIGOPS Operating Systems Review*, 38:1, 2004, pp. 12–23.

Libicki, M. *Conquest in Cyberspace: National Security and Information Warfare*, New York: Cambridge University Press, 2007.

Lonsdale, D. *The Nature of War in the Information Age*, London, UK: Frank Cass, 2004.

Orend, B. *The Morality of War*, Toronto, CA: Broadview Press, 2006.

Price, R. *The Chemical Weapons Taboo*, Ithaca, NY: Cornell University Press, 1997.

Rowe, N. "The ethics of cyberweapons in warfare," *International Journal of Technoethics*, 1:1, January–March 2010, pp. 20–31.

——"Towards reversible cyberattacks", in *Leading Issues in Information Warfare and Security Research*, Volume I, Academic Publishing, 2011, pp. 145–158.

Slim, H. *Killing Civilians: Method, Madness and Morality in War*, NY: Columbia University Press, 2008.

TechRepublic (2005) "Flaw finders go their own way", January 26. Online. Available at: www. techrepublic.com/forum/ discussions/9-167221 (accessed 1 August 2012).

United Nations "Disarmament: The Convention on Certain Conventional Weapons," Online. Available at: http://www.unog.ch/80256EE600585943/%28httpPages%29/4F0DEF093B4860B4C125718000 4B1B30 (accessed 9 June, 2012).

US-CCU (United States Cyber Consequences Unit) "Overview by the US-CCU of the Cyber Campaign against Georgia in August of 2008," US-CCU Special Report, August, 2009. Online. Available at: http://www.registan.net/wp-content/uploads/2009/08/US-CCU-Georgia-Cyber-Campaign-Overview.pdf (accessed 2 November, 2009).

Walzer, M. *Just and Unjust Wars: A Moral Argument with Historical Illustrations*, New York: Basic Books, 1977.

Wingfield, T. "International law and information operations," in F. Kramer, S. Starr and L. Wentz, (eds), *Cyberpower and National Security*, Washington DC: National Defense University Press, 2009, pp. 525–542.

INDEX